Elements of LITERATURE

Ronald A. Horton, Ph.D

Donnalynn Hess, M.A.

Steven N. Skaggs

Teacher's Edition

BJU PRESS
Greenville, South Carolina

TO THE TEACHER

It is well known that in earlier times children often got their first lessons in reading from the Bible. Although other helps were used, the Bible was the foundation of their reading experience. Christian education today still gives prominence to the Bible in the child's first exposure to the world of the printed page. It is less well known that the Bible can and should be equally central in the further development of reading skills and in the expansion of reading experience.

In the English curriculum the study of literature is the primary means of developing adolescent reading skills beyond the elementary level. Analyzing literature for structure and theme helps students learn to read for ideas and get the gist of their reading more quickly and accurately. Learning how writers convey meaning indirectly by metaphor, allegory, symbol, irony, and allusion attunes students to modes and nuances beyond the awareness of most younger children. The serious study of imaginative literature opens the door to a vast new realm of reading comprehension and pleasure. All artful writing takes on greater richness and breadth of significance.

Improved Bible study will be an inevitable benefit of developing these skills. Students will be sensitive and responsive to meanings in the Scriptures—even very basic ones—that were beyond them before. Students will be aware of the beauty and power of Biblical expression and understand how artistry clarifies and reinforces meaning. For sheer variety and magnificence of artistic effects and structural finesse, the Bible is incomparable. It supernaturally excels in artistry of form as well as in truth of content. It is an artistry, however, subservient to and disciplined by its message.

If all this is true, then the Bible is a natural beginning place for improving a student's reading comprehension and enjoyment. The Bible can serve secondary students in a way correspondent to that in which it has served elementary students in years past. It can form the foundation of the second, more advanced stage of their reading experience.

We have, then, a strong professional as well as spiritual rationale for the method of the textbook served by this teacher's edition. ELEMENTS

Note:
The fact that materials produced by other publishers may be referred to in this volume does not constitute an endorsement of the content or theological position of materials produced by such publishers. Any references and ancillary materials are listed as an aid to the student or the teacher and in an attempt to maintain the accepted academic standards of the publishing industry.

Advisory Committee
from the administration, faculty, and staff of Bob Jones University

William L. Yost, Ph.D.
Chairman of the Division of Secondary Education, Bob Jones University. Educational advisor.

Gere Stratton
Faculty, Bob Jones Academy. Grade-level consultant.

ELEMENTS OF LITERATURE Teacher's Edition

Front Cover
Photodisc

Book Editors
Ronald A. Horton, Ph.D.
Donnalynn Hess, M.A.
Steven N. Skaags
Janie Caves McCauley
June Cates
Leslie Nering Malone

Project Editor
Sarah White

Cover Design
Joseph Tyrpak

Compositor
Carol Anne Ingalls

Project Manager
David Harris

"A Miserable Merry Christmas" from *The Autobiography of Lincoln Steffens* by Lincoln Steffens. Copyright 1931 by Harcourt, Inc. and renewed 1959 by Peter Steffens. Reprinted by permission of the publisher.

Illustration and photograh credits are listed on page 464.

Produced in cooperation with the Bob Jones University Division of English Language and Literature of the College of Arts and Science, the School of Religion, and Bob Jones Academy.

© 2001 BJU Press
Greenville, South Carolina 29614

ISBN 978-1-57924-636-5

15   14   13   12   11   10   9   8   7   6   5

OF LITERATURE consists of eleven units grouped into three parts: "The Marks of Literature," "The Modes of Literature," and "The Forms of Literature." Each unit focuses on a literary concept or type. An introduction defines it using examples from the Bible. Then various selections illustrate it from non-Biblical examples. These selections are literature of high quality that can appeal to the adolescent mind. Continuing the formal study of literature with the Bible is wise educationally, for it allows students to start with material with which many of them are already familiar while also taking them to the summit of the expressive possibilities of language. It is also, of course, wise spiritually. For in the process, the students are learning that they may take the Bible as their standard in every area of their experience— that it should, in fact, be the center of their entire mental and emotional world.

ELEMENTS OF LITERATURE is the second literature textbook in the BJU Press sequence with a specific cognitive function. The first was the ninth-grade text *FUNDAMENTALS OF LITERATURE.* Together these texts provide a basic literary-critical vocabulary for the technical discussion of artistic writing. They are intended as a bridge from the reader-type textbooks on the junior high level to the more analytical textbooks in the eleventh and twelfth grades. These texts give the student a complete approach to the study of literature. As books which define key literary concepts from the Bible, they are the cornerstone of the secondary literature curriculum materials of BJU Press.

While emphasizing the value of the concepts and skills it teaches for the study of Scripture, this book is careful to maintain the distinction between the Bible and other literature. The Christian teacher of literature cannot afford to leave any doubt about his belief in the uniqueness of the divinely inspired writings of Scripture. The study of Biblical metaphors, allegory, irony, allusions, and themes can otherwise be construed to imply that the Bible is only a work of man and differs from other human writings only in degree. Secular courses in "the Bible as literature" raise doubt about the supernatural nature of Scripture simply by ignoring it. If the artistry of Scripture and its divine ori-

Acknowledgments

A careful effort has been made to trace the ownership of selections included in this textbook in order to secure permission to reprint copyrighted material and to make full acknowledgment of their use. If an error or omission has occurred, it is purely inadvertent and will be corrected in subsequent editions provided written notification is made to the publisher. Furthermore, the publisher has pursued all reasonable action in order to comply with the written requests of the various copyright owners.

ROBERT BENCHLEY: "How to Get Things Done." © Copyrighted, Chicago Tribune Company. All rights reserved. Used with permission.

RAY BRADBURY: "The Drummer Boy of Shiloh." Reprinted by permission of Don Congdon Associates, Inc. Copyright © 1960 by Ray Bradbury. Renewed 1988 by Ray Bradbury.

FRAY ANGÉLICO CHÁVEZ: "Rattlesnake" by Fray Angélico Chávez from *Literature: An Introduction to Reading and Writing* © by Houghton Mifflin.

E. E. CUMMINGS: "maggie and milly and molly and may." Copyright © 1956, 1984, 1991 by the Trustees for the E. E. Cummings Trust, from *Complete Poems: 1904-1962* by E. E. Cummings, edited by George J. Firmage. Used by permission of Liveright Publishing Corporation.

WALTER DE LA MARE: "The Listeners." The Literary Trustees of Walter de la Mare and The Society of Authors as their representative.

EMILY DICKINSON: "A Bird Came Down the Walk" from *Bolts of Memory: New Poems of Emily Dickinson*, edited by Mabel Loomis Todd and Millicent Todd Bingham. Copyright 1945 by Trustees of Amherst College. Reprinted by permission of Harper & Row, Publishers, Inc. This poem appears on page 12 of our text.

"It Sifts from Leaden Sieves" from *Bolts of Memory: New Poems of Emily Dickinson*, edited by Mabel Loomis Todd and Millicent Todd Bingham. Copyright 1945 by Trustees of Amherst College. Reprinted by permission of Harper & Row, Publishers, Inc. This poem appears on page 58 of our text.

EMILY DICKINSON: "A Prompt, Executive Bird." Reprinted by permission of the publishers and the Trustees of Amherst College from *The Poems of Emily Dickinson*, Thomas H. Johnson, ed., Cambridge, Mass.: The Belknap Press of Harvard University Press, Copyright © 1951, 1955, 1979 by the President and Fellows of Harvard College.

DAVID DUBBER: "Crossing the Bar on a Fiberglas Pole." Reprinted by permission of David Dubber.

MAX EASTMAN: "At the Aquarium." Copyright Yvette Eastman (Mrs. Max Eastman) from *Poems of Five Decades* by Max Eastman 1954. All rights reserved.

PAUL ENGLE: "An Old-Fashioned Iowa Christmas." "An Old-Fashioned Iowa Christmas" by Paul Engle. From *Prairie Christmas*, by Paul Engle. Copyright © 1958, 1959, 1960 and renewed 1988 by Paul Engle. Reprinted by permission of David McKay Co., a division of Random House, Inc.

ROBERT FROST: "A Considerable Speck" from *The Poetry of Robert Frost* edited by Edward Connery Lathem. Copyright 1936, 1942, 1951 by Robert Frost. Copyright 1964, 1970 by Lesley Frost Ballantine. © 1923, 1969 by Henry Holt & Co., LLC. Reprinted by permission of Henry Holt and Company, LLC.

"Dust of Snow" from *The Poetry of Robert Frost* edited by Edward Connery Lathem. Copyright 1936, 1942, 1951 by Robert Frost, Copyright 1964, 1970 by Lesley Frost Ballantine, © 1923, 1969 by Henry Holt & Co., LLC. Reprinted by permission of Henry Holt and Company, LLC.

"The Span of Life" from *The Poetry of Robert Frost* edited by Edward Connery Lathem. Copyright 1936, 1942, 1951 by Robert Frost, Copyright 1964, 1970 by Lesley Frost Ballantine, © 1923, 1969 by Henry Holt & Co., LLC. Reprinted by permission of Henry Holt and Company, LLC.

ROBERT HILLYER: "The Wise Old Apple Tree in Spring" from "Pastorals" reprinted from *Collected Poems*, by Robert Hillyer. Copyright 1933 and renewed 1961 by Robert Hillyer. Copyright © 1961 by Robert Hillyer. Reprinted by permission of Alfred A. Knopf, Inc.

EDWIN A. HOEY: "Foul Shot" by Edwin Hoey, published by *Read Magazine*. Copyright 1962 by American Education Publishers.

LANGSTON HUGHES: "Epigram." Reprinted by permission of Harold Ober Associates, Inc. Copyright © 1957 by Ballantine Books. Copyright renewed 1985 by George Houston Bass.

---

gin are disregarded, literary analysis can promote unbelief. Just as it degrades the character of Christ to speak of Him simply as a great man (although He was that), so it degrades the nature of the Scriptures to speak of them as simply great literature (although they are that). For this reason, ELEMENTS OF LITERATURE for Christian Schools (like FUNDAMENTALS OF LITERATURE for Christian Schools) continually points out the supportiveness of Biblical artistry to the Biblical message and to its intentions concerning the reader or hearer. It also makes frequent reference to the supernatural origin and character of the Scriptures.

The book is designed for a one-semester course, although it can be modified to accommodate a full-year course if taught along with composition and grammar. **Appendix A: Suggested Teaching Schedule** (at the back of this text) follows the one-semester plan. The schedule leaves one week (week 9) for testing or extra time to adjust assignments. Also available from BJU Press are *Great Expectations, Julius Caesar, The Scarlet Letter,* and *The Pilgrim's Progress.* Student books are sold in softcover; teacher's editions (which include a copy of the work) are also available. You may wish to teach one of these in addition to the text or substitute it for *Romeo and Juliet.* In other sections, you may choose to teach fewer pieces than are offered for study. As the teacher, you know what is best for your class. We do suggest, however, that you teach some selections from every unit.

The specific teacher instructions for each literary selection are at the beginning of each selection. These include the overview, introduction, analysis of the selection, and application of the selection. The objectives, additional activities, and resources are found on the side of the selection. Answers to the student questions about works are answered on the page on which the student questions appear. For more assistance in your lesson preparation and grading, appendixes and rubrics, referenced at appropriate points throughout the teacher's edition, are located at the end of this text.

The writers of this teacher's edition have tried to design a book that will help you become an efficient and effective literature teacher. But this manual is merely a book of ideas, a useless tool until you put its ideas into practice as you deem best. You alone know the individual needs and capabilities of your students, and we hope that this manual will give you valuable assistance as you strive in God's strength to influence your students to live for Him.

FURTHER HELPS

Notes pertaining to specific passages of the student text are color-coded to match the passage to be discussed.

In order to simplify preparation for the busy teacher or home school parent, the following icons appear in the margins of this text.

Potential Problems
potentially controversial issues pertaining to a selection

Writing Assignments
suggestions for writing activities

About the Story, Essay, or Poem
answers to end-of-selection questions

Contents

THE MARKS OF LITERATURE

IMAGINATIVE COMPARISON

SOUND AND SYNTAX

THOUGHT AND THEME

THE MODES OF LITERATURE

ALLUSION

SYMBOL

IRONY

THE FORMS OF LITERATURE

BIOGRAPHY

SHORT FICTION

LYRIC POETRY

DRAMA

PERSONAL ESSAY

Introduction

ELEMENTS OF LITERATURE for Christian Schools® is divided into three major units. In "The Marks of Literature" we will learn about attributes common to all great literature: imaginative comparison (such as metaphor, personification, synecdoche); sound and syntax (rhyme, alliteration, consonance); and thought and theme (organization, symmetry, parallelism). Next we will move on to a study of the customary ways literature is expressed—through allusion, symbol, and irony—in "The Modes of Literature." Finally and most comprehensively, we will look at "The Forms of Literature," a section including biography, short fiction, lyric poetry, drama, and personal essay. You will notice, however, that regardless of the area of study, we will always stay close to Scripture and use it as our starting point. Why?

Scripture is undeniably the world's greatest literature, in both cultural influence and artistic excellence. For sheer variety and magnificence of stylistic effects as well as structural finesse, the Bible is incomparable. It supernaturally excels in artistry of form as well as in truth of content. Although the Bible is literature—extraordinary writing above all extraordinary writing—we must never speak of it merely as literature. Just as it degrades the character of Christ to speak of Him simply as a great man (though He was that), so it degrades the nature of Scripture to speak of it simply as great literature (though it is that). If the artistry of Scripture is detached from the message and authority of Scripture and its divine origin is disregarded, literary analysis can promote unbelief. The artistry of Scripture does not exist for its own sake but is subservient to and disciplined by its message. It results, mysteriously, from the fusion of human capacity with divine power.

Where human and divine meet in the double nature of the written Word is as impossible to determine as where they meet in the double nature of Christ, the incarnate Word. But because God saw fit to give supernatural character to human verbal materials, the Bible must be studied as human communication that uses the same verbal resources available to writers not supernaturally inspired. We can study its poetry as poetry, its allegory as allegory, its irony as irony, its artful structuring as artful structuring. For this reason, the study of the Bible as literature benefits and is benefited by the study of other literature. To know the Bible as a work of literature is to have taken a large step toward our goals as advanced readers and capable writers. It is also to have expanded our abilities to appropriate truth.

INTRODUCTION

The introduction to this edition emphasizes and explains the book's overall structure and discusses the Scriptural basis for this study of literature. Read and discuss it with your class on the first day to help them get "the big picture" of where the text is going and why it approaches the subject as it does.

FURTHER HELPS

Additional activities

Have the students choose a specific verse from one of the poetic passages mentioned in the Discussion section at the bottom of this page and analyze it, using what they have learned thus far.

Journal entry idea

(NOTE: Throughout this text ideas will be given for journal entries. Have students keep a journal throughout their study of literature this year. Periodically collect the journals to check that students are writing entries when assigned. If entries are graded for more than completion, grade primarily on quality of content, not on quantity nor on grammatical perfection. Remind students that a journal is not a diary—you will be reading their entries, which should contain ideas that pertain to the study of literature and writing.)

Part I

The Marks of Literature

The Bible records the beginning of poetry in its book of beginnings, Genesis. Adam is naming the creatures, perhaps as a scientist systematically gives names to living things. He realizes that the animals have been created in sexual pairs. He also realizes that he has not been given a mate. The Lord then puts Adam into a deep sleep and creates a mate for him from the flesh of his side. When the Lord brings the lovely creature to Adam, he understands instantly that "this one" is different.

> This [lit. "this one"] is now bone of my bones,
> and flesh of my flesh:
> she ["this one"] shall be called woman [lit. "From Man"],
> because she ["this one"] was taken out of [or "from"] Man.

Adam is saying, "This one is for me. She is from man, and therefore 'From Man' will be her name." Adam's response is scientific, defining and naming a new creature. But it is also imaginative and artful. Love at first sight between the first man and first woman inspired the first poem.

Adam's response is the simplest of poems, yet richly expressive. It is more than a scientific or purely logical definition of woman. We might compare it to the dictionary definition of *woman* as "an adult female human" (*The American Heritage Dictionary,* 2000). Adam's definition has a similar meaning but expresses it indirectly through metaphor. We use metaphor when we describe one thing in terms of another. Adam uses a particular type of metaphor, or imaginative comparison, in which a part of something stands for the whole. Eve is bone (of Adam) and flesh (of Adam). Obviously, she is more. But depicting her in this way helps to emphasize an important truth: the oneness

PREPARATION

The Marks of Literature Introduction

Overview

This essay defines the basic features of literature (imaginative comparison and patterned sound, syntax, and sense), using for an example the first poem recorded in Scripture. It makes crucial distinctions between (1) poetry and prose and (2) artistic and inartistic writing. These distinctions are not entirely separate categories but rather opposite ends of a spectrum between which a particular work will fall.

Potential problems

Students may need to be persuaded that (1) writing may be poetry and not use rhyme and (2) the Bible contains much poetry as well as prose.

DISCUSSION

Introduction

Ask students to distinguish poetry from prose. What makes a poem a poem? What makes writing poetic? Then, ask them what parts of the Bible are in poetry (in the original languages). The Psalms, Proverbs, Song of Solomon, and Lamentations are examples of

poetic books in the Bible. Moses' song (Exod. 15) and Jacob's blessing of his sons (Gen. 49) are also examples of Old Testament poetry. The Magnificat (Luke 1:46-55) and the Benedictus (Luke 1:68-79) are two examples of New Testament poetry.

Since God made a distinction between poetry and prose in the Scriptures, it would seem we should not read poetry in the same way we read prose. We, therefore, need to learn how to read poetry.

Analysis

Here is a good opportunity for a first lesson in aesthetics. Draw the students' attention to the characteristics of artistic writing. Artistic writing has order (the patterning of syntax, sound, "the way in which linguistic elements (as words) are put together to form . . . phrases or clauses" *(Merriam-Webster Collegiate Dictionary,* 10th ed., 1994)

Bring to class (or have the students bring to class) pictures of animals. Using the pictures as motivation, have each student write a descriptive paragraph about one of the animals he finds especially intriguing. Have students include at least one metaphor in their description.

Resources

The Oxford Book of American Verse (New York: Oxford University Press, 1950). "In a Station of the Metro" by Ezra Pound is included in this collection.

---

of man and woman in marriage. This truth is stated in terms that are not metaphorical in the next verse (Gen. 2:24).

What we call poetry is writing that is imaginative and artfully shaped. Notice that Adam's poem, besides being imaginative, has a pleasing symmetry. The sentence structure (syntax) divides the poem into halves; each half is a complete statement. These halves are divided again into pairs of lines. In the first pair of lines, the idea of "bone of my bone" is repeated in "flesh of my flesh." In the second pair the phrase "from man" is repeated. This pair is also linked logically by cause (line 4) and effect (line 3). The four lines of the poem therefore are linked by syntax, sound, and sense. The result is a unified metaphoric expression of a great truth.

This is now bone of my bones,	1
and flesh of my flesh.	2
She shall be called woman, (effect)	3
because she was taken out of man. (cause)	4

The main elements of poetry then are metaphor and patterned syntax, sound, and sense. The following three units treat these ingredients in order. They illustrate them, however, with both poems and prose, for both poems and prose can display the imagination and artistry of poetic writing. To the extent that writing has metaphor and pattern, we say that it is poetic, regardless of whether it is written in lines that rhyme. To the extent it lacks metaphor and pattern, we say that it is prosaic. Consider the poetic qualities of the prose selections included. These qualities, more generally, distinguish writing we call literature from writing that is not.

---

and sense). However, there is also something dynamic about its imagination and creativity. Also point out that aesthetic response is built into human nature and reflects God's interest in the beautiful. Adam was acting just as naturally in naming the creatures imaginatively (using the affective part of his intelligence) as in classifying them scientifically (using the cognitive part of his intelligence). Poetry generally appeals to both, but it essentially is affective.

Read the introduction to Part I, The Marks of Literature, aloud in class, taking time to analyze the example given.

To reinforce these concepts, you may want to analyze a second example. Ezra Pound's "In a Station of the Metro" would be a good choice. Like Adam's poem in Genesis, "In a Station of

the Metro" is beautiful in its simplicity, and it vividly illustrates the elements of poetry (imaginative comparison and patterned sound, syntax, and sense).

Application

Have the students choose a word. First have them define their word scientifically. Then have them write a two- to four-line poem that imaginatively defines their word. Of course, Adam's poem may serve as an example. As the students write their poems, encourage them to concentrate on the elements of poetry they have just learned.

*Imaginative Comparison
Introduction*

FURTHER HELPS

Additional activities

1. Encourage students to write down any imaginative comparisons (see boldfaced terms, page 4) they come across in their devotional reading. Have them share these examples with the class.

2. For variety you may want to have the students draw a humorous set of posters illustrating the different types of imaginative comparisons.

Journal entry idea
Give the students openings for several imaginative comparisons; have them choose one and provide a conclusion. Then have them write a few sentences explaining the metaphor they have created. Following are some examples:

Youth is like _____. (simile)
Loneliness is _____. (metaphor)
The ocean _____. (personification)

UNIT ONE

PREPARATION

Imaginative Comparison Introduction

Overview

This unit introduction is the first of three that build on and expand the definition of poetry developed in the introduction to Part I, The Marks of Literature. It focuses on metaphor, classifying it into types: simile, personification, metonymy, and synecdoche. It stresses that metaphoric language is not merely ornamental—it adds precision and richness to meaning.

Potential problems

Metaphor has both restrictive and inclusive meaning. What is given in the introduction to Part I is the inclusive meaning: expressing one thing in terms of another. This definition includes simile, metonymy, synecdoche, personification, and so on. In its more restrictive sense, a metaphor is the stated or implied equivalence of two things: "life is a race" (stated); "the race of life" (implied, cf. Heb. 12:1).

DISCUSSION

Introduction

Ask the students for examples of some common metaphors used in today's advertising, trade jargon, nicknames, and so on. Note that clichés are often worn-out metaphors, especially similes ("__ as a __"). After reading the introduction aloud (page 4), ask the students what makes the Biblical metaphors in the introduction (especially in paragraph one) more effective than the clichés or other examples they have thought of. *(The metaphors in the introduction are unusual, not stale, and therefore provoke interest.)*

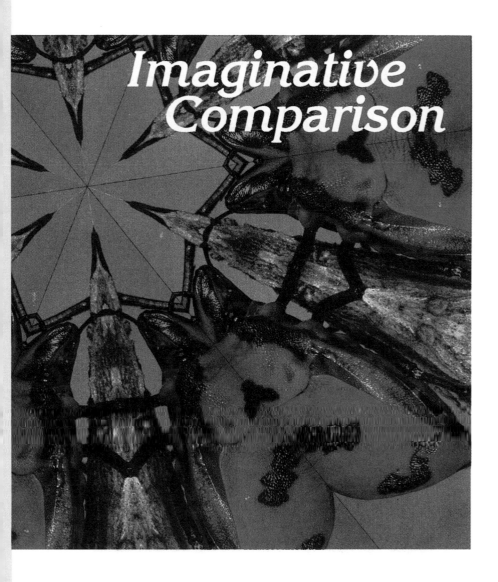
Imaginative Comparison

Resources

M. H. Abrams, *A Glossary of Literary Terms*, 7th ed. (Harcourt College Publishers, 1998). This book is a valuable tool not only for metaphor but also for all other literary terms your students will be studying throughout this course.

Benjamin Keach, *Preaching from the Types and Metaphors of the Bible* (Michigan: Kregel Publications, 1972).

Analysis

The main discussion of this material should consist of your clarifying the nature and types of metaphors for the students, using the examples mentioned and adding others of your own. You could have the students think of the following metaphoric names for Christ: the Good Shepherd, the Door, the Vine, the Bread of Life, the Way, the Bridegroom, the Lamb, the Lion of Judah, the Great Physician, and so forth. Then, using these examples, show them how imaginative comparison has the power to compress great amounts of meaning into a small, concrete embodiment and to make that meaning easy to grasp and remember. These examples also reinforce the concept that metaphor is a major resource of prose as well as of poetry.

Direct the students to complete **Appendix B: Imaginative Comparison Worksheet,** in which they are asked to identify metaphors (in a restrictive sense), similes, metonymies, synecdoches, and personifications. After identifying these imaginative comparisons, students may wish to create some of their own.

Application

As a class, have the students look up several metaphoric names for either God the Father or God the Holy Spirit. From this list have the students choose one specific imaginative comparison and analyze their choice using what they have learned. As they make their analysis, remind them to look at the metaphor in the context of the passage in which it is found. You may wish to use questions like the following to start them thinking: What divine attribute does this metaphor reinforce? What great truth(s) can be inferred from the metaphor? What makes the metaphor easy to grasp or remember?

When Joab wanted King David to forgive and restore the banished Absalom, David's handsome son, he used trickery. He got a woman, known for her wisdom, to act the part of a widow whose only son was condemned to death for having killed his brother. She pled before the king not to allow his accusers, her kinsfolk, to "quench [her] coal that is left" (II Sam. 14:7). The woman, wise in words as in thought, used an imaginative comparison or **metaphor** to add force to her persuasion. Her metaphor depicts her son as a burning coal and life as a fire, though the comparison is not explicitly stated. She needed her son's help just as all human beings need fire for warmth and for preparing food. Then she added, "For we must needs die, and are as water spilt on the ground, which cannot be gathered up again" (14:14). Here the comparison is stated: "we . . . are as water." An imaginative comparison that uses the words *like, as, as if,* or some similar expression is known as a **simile,** a type of metaphor. The wise woman's simile emphasizes the finality of death. Once life is "spilt," it "cannot be gathered up again." We die soon enough, she says, and death is irreversible.

If the wise woman had represented an object as a person rather than a person as an object ("my coal"), she would have used another type of metaphor known as personification. **Personification** gives human characteristics to objects, ideas, abstractions, or animals. Notice, for example, Isaiah 55:12: the mountains and hills "break forth . . . into singing, and all the trees of the field . . . clap their hands."

Two other types of metaphor, metonymy and synecdoche, appear commonly in the Scriptures as in literature and in our ordinary speech. When the prophet Nathan, speaking for God, rebukes David for his great sin, he declares, "The sword shall never depart from thine house" (II Sam. 12:10). In this verse the word *sword,* a physical instrument of death, stands for death. The word *house,* a physical shelter for families, stands for family and descendants. These words are examples of **metonymy,** an expression in which a related thing stands for the thing itself. In Matthew 13:16 the Lord uses a similar type of metaphor. When speaking with His disciples, Christ says, "Blessed are your eyes for they see." Here, *eyes* stands for the whole man. An expression in which a part stands for the whole is known as a synecdoche.

When Adam named the animals, he may have named them scientifically, indicating their species, or humorously, or even in both ways. In any case, he may have used imaginative comparisons, as in his naming of Eve. Poets, like all of us, use such comparisons for humor, but also for clarification. As you read the selections in this unit, notice the way in which literature of imagination differs from mere literature of information. Notice particularly that imaginative comparisons add richness and precision of meaning to the ideas they represent while making our reading more enjoyable.

We do not usually think of Mark Twain (Samuel Clemens) as a poet. But much of his prose is highly poetic. In the following selections Twain uses imaginative comparisons to make his prose vivid and appealing. What imaginative comparisons does he use in the paragraphs from chapter 14 of Tom Sawyer? In the second selection, what type of metaphor does he use to create a humorous effect?

Dawn in the Forest

Mark Twain

When Tom awoke in the morning, he wondered where he was. He sat up and rubbed his eyes and looked around. Then he comprehended. It was the cool gray dawn, and there was a delicious sense of repose and peace in the deep pervading calm and silence of the woods. Not a leaf stirred; not a sound obtruded upon great Nature's meditation. Beaded dewdrops stood upon the leaves and grasses. A white layer of ashes covered the fire, and a thin blue breath of smoke rose straight into the air. Joe and Huck still slept.

Now, far away in the woods a bird called; another answered; presently the hammering of a woodpecker was heard. Gradually the cool dim gray of the morning whitened, and as gradually sounds multiplied and life manifested itself. The marvel of Nature shaking off sleep and going to work unfolded itself to the musing boy. A little green worm came crawling over a dewy leaf, lifting two-thirds of his body into the air from time to time and "sniffing around," then proceeding again—for he was measuring, Tom said; and when the worm approached

OBJECTIVES

The students will be able to

- Identify poetic elements in prose writing.
- Define and illustrate imagery.
- Define and illustrate personification.

personification

The phrase "beaded dewdrops" exemplifies a meaning of *bead* that was originally metaphoric. *Bead,* in the archaic definition, referred to praying; small globular bodies were used as "telling beads" or for counting prayers (cf. prayer beads). In this context, the "beaded dewdrops" upon the leaves and grasses metaphorically reinforce the idea of "Nature's meditation" or "prayer."

concrete, detailed imagery

PREPARATION

"Dawn in the Forest," "What Stumped the Bluejays"

Overview

This assignment introduces students to an example of poetic prose. On a scale between pure poetry and pure prose, "Dawn in the Forest" falls on the prose side of center but not far from the midpoint. The description records the sensations of Tom Sawyer while he and the forest are waking up together. The second selection is a humorous piece that aptly illustrates personification.

Potential problems

You may wish to caution your students about indiscriminate reading of Twain's works. The selections included here are free of objectionable elements. This is not true of all his works, however. Several of Twain's works would be considered inappropriate for recreational reading.

DISCUSSION

Introduction

Ask students whether they have ever awakened in a strange place and for a moment forgotten where they were. Were they, for that moment or duration of time, especially sensitive to sights and sounds? Does the mind make strange associations when asleep or half-asleep? Who other than Tom is waking up, according to the poetic description?

FURTHER HELPS

Resources

Jerry Allen, *The Adventures of Mark Twain* (Boston: Little, Brown and Company, 1954). An entertaining general biography.

Paul Baender, ed., *The Works of Mark Twain*, Vol. 19: *What Is Man? and Other Philosophical Writings* (Berkeley: University Press, 1973).

Norton Anthology of English Literature, Volumes 1 and 2, 7th ed. (New York: W. W. Norton & Company, 1999). Good sources for other poems you may wish to use as examples.

Dixon Wector, *Sam Clemens of Hannibal* (Boston: Houghton Mifflin Company, 1952). Deals specifically with Twain's childhood.

Paul M. Zall, ed., *Mark Twain Laughing* (Knoxville: University of Tennessee Press, 1985). Gives general anecdotes.

him, of its own accord, he sat as still as a stone, with his hopes rising and falling, by turns, as the creature still came toward him or seemed inclined to go elsewhere; and when at last it considered a painful moment with its curved body in the air and then came decisively down upon Tom's leg and began a journey over him, his whole heart was glad—for that meant that he was going to have a new suit of clothes—without the shadow of a doubt a gaudy piratical uniform. Now a procession of ants appeared, from nowhere in particular, and went about their labors; one struggled manfully by with a dead spider five times as big as itself in its arms, and lugged it straight up a tree trunk. A brown spotted ladybug climbed the dizzy height of a grass blade, and Tom bent down close to it and said, "Ladybug, ladybug, fly away home, your house is on fire, your children's alone," and she took wing and went off to see about it—which did not surprise the boy, for he knew of old that this insect was credulous* about conflagrations,* and he had practised* upon its simplicity more than once. A tumblebug came next, heaving sturdily at its ball, and Tom touched the creature, to see it shut its legs against its body and pretend to be dead. The birds were fairly rioting by this time. A catbird, the Northern mocker, lit in a tree over Tom's head, and trilled out her imitations of her neighbors in a rapture of enjoyment; then a shrill jay swept down, a flash of blue flame, and stopped on a twig almost within the boy's reach, cocked his head to one side and eyed the strangers with a consuming curiosity; a gray squirrel and a big fellow of the "fox" kind came scurrying along, sitting up at intervals to inspect and chatter at the boys, for the wild things had probably never seen a human being before and scarcely knew whether to be afraid or not. All Nature was wide awake and stirring, now; long lances of sunlight pierced down through the dense foliage far and near, and a few butterflies came fluttering upon the scene.

credulous: naive
conflagrations: destructive fires
practised: played tricks

Analysis

The description in "Dawn in the Forest" is structured by time (the phases of sunrise) and is therefore a simple narrative. This time structure is emphasized by personification. The stillness of the "cool gray dawn" was "great Nature's meditation." As the "cool dim gray of the morning whitened" and "sounds multiplied," there unfolded "the marvel of Nature shaking off sleep and going to work." Then as "long lances of sunlight pierced down through the dense foliage far and near" and the forest creatures broke out in full chorus and activity, "All Nature was wide awake and stirring." The description proceeds by enumeration of sights and sounds mainly, although touch and smell are not excluded.

The first Twain selection is especially good for defining and illustrating imagery—hence the text's highlighting of various passages. An *image* is a word or phrase that appeals to one of the five senses. *Imagery* therefore is almost synonymous with *concreteness*. An image normally forms the "picture side" of a metaphor.

Using "About the Stories" question 1 (page 10), continue your discussion on images and metaphors of Twain's "Dawn in the Forest." Then using questions 2-4, turn the discussion to the second selection, "What Stumped the Bluejays."

Application

Have each student choose an animal, object, or idea and write a descriptive paragraph personifying what he has chosen. Students could choose something from the following lists or come up with their own choice. See **Writing Rubric 1-1: Personification Paragraph** in the back of this text. (Note that the grading scale given with each rubric is a suggestion; teachers should use a scale appropriate to their situation.)

two hours and a half was one of the most exciting and astonishing spectacles I ever struck. He never stopped to take a look any more—he just hove 'em in and went for more. Well, at last he could hardly flop his wings, he was so tuckered out. He comes a-drooping down, once more, sweating like an ice-pitcher, drops his acorn in and says, "*Now* I guess I've got the bulge on you by this time!" So he bent down for a look. If you'll believe me, when his head come up again he was just pale with rage. He says, "I've shoveled acorns enough in there to keep the family thirty years, and if I can see a sign of one of 'em I wish I may land in a museum with a belly full of sawdust in two minutes!"

He just had strength enough to crawl up on to the comb and lean his back agin the chimbly, and then he collected his impressions and begun to free his mind. I see in a second what I mistook for a fit o' rage in the mines was only just the rudiments, as you may say.

Another jay was going by, and heard him, and stops to inquire what was up. The sufferer told him the whole circumstance, and says, "Now yonder's the hole, and if you don't believe me, go and look for yourself." So this fellow went and looked, and comes back and says, "How many did you say you put in there?" "Not any less than two tons," says the sufferer. The other jay went and looked again. He couldn't seem to make it out, so he raised a yell, and three more jays come. They all examined the hole, they all made the sufferer tell it over again, then they all discussed it, and got off as many leather-headed opinions about it as an average crowd of humans could have done.

They called in more jays; then more and more, till pretty soon this whole region 'peared to have a blue flush about it. There must have been five thousand of them; and such another jawing and disputing, you never heard. Every jay in the whole lot put his eye to the hole and delivered a more chuck-headed opinion about the mystery than the jay that went there before him. They examined the house all over, too. The door was standing half open, and at last one old jay happened to go and light on it and look in. Of course, that knocked the mystery galley-west in a second. There lay the acorns, scattered all over the floor. He flopped his wings and raised a whoop. "Come here!" he says, "Come here, everybody; hang'd if this fool hasn't been trying to fill up a house with acorns!" They all came a-swooping down like a blue cloud, and as each fellow lit on the door and took a glance, the whole absurdity of the contract that that first jay had tackled hit him home and he fell over backward suffocating with laughter, and the next jay took his place and done the same.

Well, sir, they roosted around here on the housetop and the trees for an hour, and guffawed over that thing like human beings. It ain't any use to tell me a bluejay hasn't got a sense of humor, because I know better. And memory, too. They brought jays here from all over the United States to look down that hole, every summer for three years. Other birds, too. And they could all see the point, except an owl that come from Nova Scotia to visit the Yo Semite, and he took this thing in on his way back. He said he couldn't see anything funny in it. But then he was a good deal disappointed about Yo Semite, too.

About the Stories

1. An image is a word or phrase that appeals to one of the five senses. Twain's first selection is filled with such images. Give at least one example from "Dawn in the Forest" for each of the following sensory images:
   a. sight
   b. sound
   c. touch
   d. smell
2. What imaginative comparison does Twain use to create humor in "What Stumped the Bluejays"?
3. Obviously, the second selection is written "tongue-in-cheek." At what point in the story are you convinced of the storyteller's facetious or playful intent? (Give a specific phrase or sentence from the story.)
4. Give at least three quotations that support your answer for question 3.

About the Stories

1. In addition to the answers below, have the students find several examples of other imaginative comparisons in "Dawn in the Forest." Tom sits "still as a stone" (simile), for example, or "A catbird . . . trilled out her imitations of her neighbors in rapture of enjoyment" (personification).

   a. sight: jay as "a flash of blue flame," "long lances of sunlight"
   b. sound: a woodpecker's "hammering"
   c. touch: "when the worm approached him, of its own accord, he sat still as a stone, with his hopes rising and falling, by turns, as the creature still came toward him or seemed inclined to go elsewhere; and when at last it considered a painful moment with its curved body in the air and then came decisively down upon Tom's leg and began a journey over him, his whole heart was glad."
   d. smell: "a thin blue breath of smoke rose straight into the air"; this could also be a sight image

2. personification

3. Any one of the first three sentences would be a valid answer to this question. By the third sentence, however, it should be obvious that Twain is being facetious.

4. Answers will vary. But students should have little trouble finding appropriate quotations, since there are myriad throughout the piece that reveal the tongue-in-cheek tone.

About the Author

As a boy, Mark Twain (1835-1910) was the prototype of the central characters he created in *Huckleberry Finn* and *Tom Sawyer*. He reveled in the rugged frontier life of his boyhood home, and his childhood adventures in Hannibal, Missouri, still live on in the pages of these books. But Twain's humorous and suspenseful storytelling was also, in part, a legacy left him by "Uncle Dan'l," a kindly older slave on his uncle's farm. Uncle Dan'l's country wisdom and superstition are most evident in *Huckleberry Finn.* In this story, Twain immortalized his old friend.

Twain's tone, however, is not always good-natured. Although his cynical side is apparent in several of his fictional works, it is clearly stated in his philosophical writings. In "Three Statements of the Eighties," Twain presents God as a mere clock-winder of the universe and man as insignificant. Twain also believed that morality and the Bible were human inventions, asserting that men are shaped by environment and education. He states that "to trust the God of the Bible is to trust in an irascible, vindictive, fierce and ever fickle and changeful master."

Having denied God's revelation to man through Scripture, Twain naturally denied the individual's accountability to God. According to Twain, man is a machine incapable of making decisions independently. He cannot be blamed for the evil he commits nor praised for the good he does. He claimed that man was "most likely not even made *intentionally,*" presenting as proof the imperfect nature of people (cf. *The Characters of Man,* 1885). He once commented that he had more respect for animals than he had for people. People, he said, take pleasure in inflicting pain on others, even though they have the moral sense to know better.

Twain's outlook was both self-centered and ultimately hopeless. Denying that he was created in the image of God, Twain was able to rid himself of feeling any responsibility to his Creator. At the same time, however, he defiantly cut himself off from God's love. Twain's skepticism was clearly not the honest questioning of a seeker of truth but the deliberate defiance of a confessed rebel.

PREPARATION

"A Bird Came Down the Walk," "A Prompt, Executive Bird"

Overview

The first poem, "A Bird Came Down the Walk," is much like Twain's selection "Dawn in the Forest": both are dense with detailed imagery, both use imaginative comparison strategically, and both make an otherwise trivial incident into an event. The second selection, "A Prompt, Executive Bird," provides a good opportunity to compare an imaginative definition with a scientific or dictionary definition.

Potential problems

The syntax of the last sentence in "A Bird Came Down the Walk" may be difficult. Have students analyze it, noting the coordinate structure of the ending. The two comparisons, of ships and of butterflies, illustrate the softness of the bird's flight.

The compression of thought and unfamiliarity of diction and allusion in "A Prompt, Executive Bird" will require close attention and, probably, some use of a dictionary.

OBJECTIVES

The students will be able to

• Analyze and discuss how a poet uses imagery and imaginative comparison to make a seemingly trivial incident memorable.

• Use a dictionary and a grammar text to better understand and enjoy poetry.

• Identify the use of literary puns.

Students may repunctuate the last "sentence" in a variety of ways; discuss with them the ambiguity of the poem—it is unclear where the last sentence begins. Does "Like one in danger" describe the speaker or the bird? What about "Cautious"? Point out that the students' decisions on these issues will affect their punctuation. One possible answer would be "I offered him a crumb, and he unrolled his feathers and rowed him[self] softer home than oars divide the ocean—too silver for a seam—or butterflies, off banks of noon, leap, plashless as they swim."

A Bird Came Down the Walk

Emily Dickinson

In the poems of Emily Dickinson, the common creatures of nature—the birds, butterflies, and other inhabitants of a New England garden—appear as personalities. Obviously, Dickinson takes such "personalities" seriously. Her careful selection of detail and extraordinary imaginative comparisons help to convince us of their importance too. While scrutinizing them through the poet's eyes, we are also examining human life. In the first of the following poems, the poet is not only observing but also being observed, and both perspectives seem valid. In the second poem, the brisk, assertive manner of the blue jay suggests the busy, self-important air of some public officials. Notice that your grammar studies can help you understand the last sentence of the first poem. Repunctuate it in a more modern style. Notice that a dictionary can help you understand the references in the second poem. Your grammar handbook and your dictionary at times are your best friends in the study of poetry.

A Bird came down the Walk—
He did not know I saw—
He bit an Angleworm in halves
And ate the fellow, raw,

And then he drank a Dew   5
From a convenient Grass—
And then hopped sidewise to the Wall
To let a Beetle pass—

He glanced with rapid eyes
That hurried all around—   10
They looked like frightened Beads, I thought—
He stirred his Velvet Head

Like one in danger, Cautious,
I offered him a Crumb
And he unrolled his feathers*   15   *unrolled . . . feathers:*
And rowed him softer home—   *i.e., as mariners*
                                                                     unroll sails

DISCUSSION

Introduction

Before beginning an analysis of each poem, have the students read the poems aloud. Let them enjoy the sound of the poet's words and her terse, forthright style. Encourage them in reading to use their interpretative skills. (This should be done with every poem studied. Oral reading will help students enjoy poetry; analysis will help them understand the elements that make it enjoyable.)

Analysis

"A Bird Came Down the Walk"

In this first poem Dickinson makes vivid the encounter between a bird and an inquisitive human being by using concrete details and, in the last two stanzas, by imaginative comparisons. The speaker offers friendship. She wishes no harm to the bird. She does not mean to capture it. But perhaps, in a way, she does capture it—like a photographer "captures" his subject on film. In the poem we do have the bird very much before us.

The first line introduces and sums up the incident to follow in layman's terms. "A bird came down the walk." "So what?" most people would say. The job of the poem is to make the incident

an event—to give it momentousness, as in the mind of a child or of a blind person able to see for the first time. The second line generates interest. The poet is spying on the bird. There is something concealed worth seeing. A series of details follows, climaxing with the poet's act of friendship (line 14). She is passive up to this point. The consequence (*denouement* in the language of critical analysis) is the bird's flight (in both senses of the word). The poem makes an apparently trivial, casual occurrence an *event*.

It follows the structure of a simple narrative—rising action, climax, falling action, denouement. The poem ends strongly with two comparisons of the bird's flight: to ships (feathers/sails, wings/oars, flying/putting out to sea) and to butterflies (flying/leaving flower beds). The

Than Oars divide the Ocean,
Too silver for a seam—
Or Butterflies, off Banks of Noon*
Leap, plashless as they swim.

Banks . . . Noon: i.e.,
banks of flowers at
midday (with a pun
on riverbanks)

A Prompt, Executive Bird

Emily Dickinson

A prompt, executive bird is the Jay,
Bold as a Bailiff's hymn,*
Brittle and brief in quality—
Warrant* in every line;

Sitting a bough like a Brigadier,*   5
Confident and straight,
Much is the mien* of him in March*
As a Magistrate.

Bailiff's hymn:
summons

Warrant: (1) legal writ
of authorization, as
a summons (2)
authority, proof
(used here as a pun)
Brigadier: commander
of a military brigade
mien: manner
in March: (1) in March
(2) while marching
(used here as a pun)

About the Poems

1. Dickinson's first poem transforms a seemingly trivial incident into a memorable event. List at least three specific details she gives that capture your interest and make the event vivid.
2. How does Dickinson's imaginative definition of the blue jay compare with the scientific, dictionary definition?
3. What three specific professions does Dickinson associate with the "prompt, executive" jay?
4. What other birds might be associated with specific professions?

FURTHER HELPS
Additional activities

1. In "A Hymn to God the Father" (see **Appendix C**), John Donne uses a serious literary pun. Copy the poem onto an overhead transparency. Then read the poem aloud and help the students identify the pun on the author's name used throughout the poem ("Donne" is pronounced the same as "done") and the pun in the last stanza on *Son* (Son—the spiritual light of the world/sun—the physical light of the world).

   Reread the poem aloud once again, pausing after each stanza to discuss the significance of the play on words. (Romans 7 and 8 are good passages to use in conjunction with this poem.)

2. Have the students choose another poem by Emily Dickinson that they especially like and share it with the class. Also, have them identify and explain the significance of any sensory images they find in the poem.

3. Emily Dickinson has an interesting history. (See "About the Author," page 14.) During her lifetime she had only seven poems published. Encourage a student to read about her and then to give a brief report to the class.

two comparisons are linked visually by the pun on *banks:* flower banks and river banks. (A pun is a play on words that are either identical in sound—homonyms—or very similar in sound, but sharply diverse in meaning.) The butterflies are visualized as leaping into the water from shore.

If students need further discussion on the use of literary puns, you could use "A Hymn to God the Father" by John Donne as an additional illustration. (See Additional Activities in the margin on page 12.) (Discussion of "A Prompt, Executive Bird" continues after "About the Poems.")

About the Poems

1. *Answers may vary; accept any incidents from the poem as long as students can explain why they chose them.*

2. *Answers may vary but should include that the dictionary definition is scientific while Dickinson's description is imaginative, using similes and personification.*

3. *Bailiff, Brigadier, Magistrate*

4. *Answers may vary.*

"A Prompt, Executive Bird"

To begin your analysis of the second poem, ask the students what birds they are familiar with. Then ask them what trades or professions these birds, if they were human beings, would practice. Also ask them whether they associate birds with human personality types. Then have them compare their impressions with Dickinson's impressions of the blue jay. Finally, reverse the direction of the comparison by noting that human beings are sometimes characterized as birds. What kind of person is called a chicken? a jay bird? a loon?

This selection consists largely of a series of similes and uses both imaginative comparisons and puns to create the sharp visual and mental

Journal entry idea
Have the students write a paragraph or two discussing their reaction to the ideas expressed in Donne's poem. (See Additional Activities, #1, above.)

Journal entry idea
Instruct the students to closely observe an animal and its behavior. Then have them record their observations.

Journal entry idea
Have the students look for experimental methods Dickinson used in her poetry (e.g., capitalization of words within a line of poetry, coined word *plashless*). Let the students invent a word and then give a definition for it.

Resources

Thomas M. Davis, *14 by Emily Dickinson* (Chicago: Scott, Foresman, 1964). This source provides a representative selection of Dickinson's poetry and the critical analyses developed through differing interpretations of the chosen poems.

Robert L. Lair, *Barron's Simplified Approach to Emily Dickinson* (Woodbury, New York: Barron's Educational Series, 1971). This source provides a superb introductory guide with full comments on poetic form for 150 Dickinson poems.

About the Author

Emily Dickinson's (1830-1886) legendary reclusiveness often overshadows other details of her life and work. Critics no longer dispute her eccentricity and her decision to receive few guests. They do not, however, always give the poet credit for her solid friendships with scholarly men and women who acted as mentors, literary critics, and confidants. For example, Col. T. W. Higginson of the *Atlantic Monthly* and Dickinson enjoyed a lifelong friendship which provided valuable literary criticism and mental challenges for the lady poet.

Another notable influence in Dickinson's life was Professor Hitchcock, a teacher and unflagging lover of nature. As a young woman, Dickinson loved to take long walks and enjoy the beauty and unique charm of her home in Amherst, Massachusetts. Her best poetry synthesizes the mental images and deep emotions connected with this region, which at that time was still rural. Hitchcock encouraged this quality in the young woman. He often organized field trips for his students and friends. This innovative method of teaching brought him criticism but succeeded in giving those like Dickinson a sound scientific background which later proved useful.

The professor also influenced Dickinson's religious views. Hitchcock believed in the immortality of the soul, not because the Bible taught it, but because he saw the principle of rebirth in the cycle of seasons. Dickinson absorbed these ideas and later used them in her poems.

Dickinson's year at Mount Holyoke Female Seminary further shaped her "religious" views. During her stay at the school, she learned of Christ but wrote of her inability to make a decision for Him. She could not settle "the one thing needful." A thorough study of Dickinson's works indicates that she never did make that needful decision. Several of her poems show a presumptuous attitude concerning her eternal destiny and a veiled disrespect for authority in general. Throughout her life she viewed salvation as a gamble, not a certainty. Although she did view the Bible as a source of poetic inspiration, she never accepted it as an inerrant guide to life.

---

impression of the object described. Point out that the entire poem is based on a single metaphor: blue jay/self-important human being. The governing metaphor is elaborated into constituent metaphors: a bailiff (his summons), brigadier, magistrate. Have the students find out what they can about those figures from a dictionary. Also have them look up words they don't know or only partially know—"executive," "brittle," "straight," as well as those defined in the side notes. Have them analyze grammatically the structure of the independent clauses (one per stanza). In this way they will see how a dictionary and a grammar handbook can help them understand poetry. Then, compare the richness of meaning in the poem with that of the dictionary definition of *blue jay*.

Application
Have the students write a short poem making a trivial incident into a memorable event. Ask them to structure their poems as Dickinson did—introduction, rising action, climax, falling action, denouement. They should be sure to use specific images, metaphors, similes, and/or puns that will create vivid visual or mental impressions. They can either choose a subject from the list below or come up with their own idea.

The purpose of this exercise is to clarify concepts and to help students enjoy writing. It should be graded for effort and completion only. You may, however, wish to collect their work and comment on content, images, and so

on. This would give you an opportunity to encourage them and to alleviate some of their apprehensions about the writing process. See **Writing Rubric 1-2: Plotted Poem.**

crossing the street	saying good-bye
mending a garment	finding a penny
threading a needle	seeing a favorite
reading a book	color
eating an orange	buying a new dress
riding a bike	or suit
smelling perfume	holding a child's
touching velvet	hand
seeing a butterfly	running uphill (or
setting the table	downhill)
waxing a car	hailing a taxi
flying a kite	

The Fly

John Ruskin

Insects as well as birds can furnish human parallels for the imagination. Notice the way in which the nineteenth-century essayist John Ruskin employs metaphor and simile to describe the fly. Notice also that his description focuses on a single trait.

We can nowhere find a better type of perfectly free creature than in the common housefly. In every step of his swift mechanical march, and in every pause of his resolute observation, there is one and the same expression of perfect egotism, perfect independence and self-confidence, and conviction of the world's having been made for flies. Strike at him with your hand; and to him the aspect of the matter is what to you it would be if an acre of red clay, ten feet thick, tore itself up from the ground and came crashing down with an aim. He steps out of the way of your hand and alights on the back of it. You cannot terrify him. He has his own positive opinion on all matters—not an unwise one, usually, for his own ends—and will ask no advice of yours. He has no work to do, no tyrannical instinct to obey. The earthworm has his digging; the bee her gathering and building; the spider her cunning network; the ant her treasury and accounts. All these are comparatively slaves, or people of business. But your fly, free in the air, free in the chamber—a black incarnation of caprice—wandering, investigating, flitting, flirting, feasting at his will, with rich variety of choice in feast, from the heaped sweets in the grocer's window to those of the butcher's backyard—what freedom is like this?

OBJECTIVES

The students will be able to

- Identify the poetic in writing, whether in poetry or prose.
- Defend the idea that unrestricted freedom is not a good thing.
- Discuss a writer's sense of structure.

thesis statement

PREPARATION

"The Fly"

Overview

Ruskin's paragraph on the fly offers another example of prose with a high density of imaginative comparison and imagery. The fly is the perfect self-directed egotist, governed by no laws or rules other than his own whims. Of course, he seems rather indiscriminate in his choices.

DISCUSSION

Introduction

Freedom is the most highly valued commodity in the modern world. Political freedom—the ability to determine our own rulers—is one of the greatest freedoms we have. But few are satisfied with that. They want moral freedom as well. To those who think "doing as you please" is the noblest principle of life, observe the example of Ruskin's fly. According to Ruskin, "there is not any organic creature, but in its history and habits it shall exemplify or illustrate to us some moral excellence or deficiency or some point of God's providential government, which it is necessary for us to know" (*The Religion of Ruskin*, p. 100). With what detail does

Ruskin end his description of the fly? *(The description ends with the fly moving indiscriminately from sweets to rotting meat.)* Is there a lesson here? *(Like the fly, man is often unwise in his choices when given too much freedom.)* (Discussion of "The Fly" continues after "About the Essay.")

FURTHER HELPS

Additional activities

1. Have your students look at Proverbs 6:6-8 and 30:25. Draw their attention to the figurative language used to describe the ant. What human characteristics are ascribed to it? What did the author intend to teach the reader?

2. Have the students find out what Scripture has to say about freedom. (Possible passages are John 8:32, 36; Rom. 6:18, 22; 8:2; Gal. 5:1; and I Pet. 2:13-16). Compare Ruskin's description of the fly's "freedom" with the Scriptural view.

Resources

The following sources provide good biographical information about the author.

William Burgess, *The Religion of Ruskin* (New York: Fleming H. Revell Company, 1907).

George P. Landow, *Ruskin* (Oxford: Oxford University Press, 1985).

Reginald H. Wilenski, *John Ruskin: An Introduction to Further Study of His Life and Work* (AMS Press, 1978).

About the Essay

1. On what one trait does Ruskin focus in his description of the fly?
2. Keeping Ruskin's paragraph in mind, what word or phrase would you use to describe the fly?
3. Choose one imaginative comparison Ruskin uses that you found especially interesting or vivid.
4. Identify the imaginative comparison you chose (metaphor, simile, personification, etc.).

About the Author

John Ruskin (1819-1900), eminent spokesman of the Victorian Age, possessed a deep appreciation for the beauty of God's creation and the joy of man's imaginative thought. His attitudes eventually developed into a philosophy of understanding life through visual imagery. His descriptions of commonly overlooked aspects of nature, such as small animals, plants, and even minerals, illustrate this philosophy.

Ruskin's acute perceptions matured early in life. Since his Victorian mother disapproved of toys, small John had to amuse himself. His close examination of the flowers in the family garden fostered a love for color and pattern and encouraged a meticulous, scientific attention to detail.

Ruskin began his formal writing career as an art critic, publishing a five-volume set entitled *Modern Painters,* which expounded his theories of art and philosophy and promoted the work of his favorite artists. Among these was John Turner, a controversial landscape painter destined to become a famous Romantic artist. In addition to art, Ruskin exerted influences on the architecture of his day by encouraging a return to Gothic style.

Later, Ruskin's interests encompassed political, social, and economic issues. He felt the English people were becoming too preoccupied with the Industrial Revolution to appreciate art and beauty. He set out to provide a philosophy that encompassed the arts, religion, and the everyday working life in his work entitled *Unto This Last.* His work became a guide to the leaders of the English Socialist movement.

Ruskin's personal religion emphasized a love for beauty and goodness and a thorough knowledge of the English Bible. However, his writings also show that he espoused empiricism, a philosophy which teaches that knowledge stems directly from man's experience. According to this dangerous doctrine, we can only trust what is felt or seen. Although the study of Ruskin can help us better appreciate the visible world, we must remember that truth is not bound by man's experience.

About the Essay

1. *Ruskin focuses on the fly's independence.*

2. *Answers will vary but may include capricious, confident, egotistical, self-centered, resolute.*

3. *Answers will vary but may include "his swift mechanical march" (metaphor, personification), his "perfect egotism" (personification), the comparison of a human hand with "an acre of red clay" (metaphor).*

4. *Answers will vary; see examples given in number 3.*

Analysis

"The Fly" is an excellent example of Ruskin's imaginative, insightful view of nature. Ruskin's characteristic techniques of word painting help those of us who may wonder how anyone could find a common housefly beautiful or interesting. His artful description helps us see the fly as more than a small, irritating insect by drawing our attention to facets of the fly's existence that we have probably never considered. Such artful description expands our view of our world. According to Ruskin, "he who can take no interest in what is small, will take false interest in what is great; he who cannot make a bank sublime, will make a mountain ridiculous."

This carefully developed paragraph has a distinct beginning, middle, and end. Notice how the end links with the beginning. The opening sentence states a thesis. The thesis is supported by specifics: his impudence (when struck at), his freedom from instinct (cf. the instinct-bound earthworm, bee, spider, ant), and his freedom of choice (e.g., grocer's and butcher's delicacies). The language verges on the metaphoric in such instances as "mechanical march," "digging," "treasure and accounts," "slaves," "people of business." One conspicuous instance that demonstrates how figurative expression can intensify meaning is the simile "an acre of red clay." Here we have the comparison of two things essentially unlike (human hand / acre of red clay) on the basis of a resemblance in one aspect (the "threat" they pose). The phrase "is what to you it would be" functions as *like, as,* or *as if.*

A Noiseless Patient Spider

Walt Whitman

The organization of a poem can convey an imaginative comparison. For example, a spider looses a silk filament in the attempt to find anchorage for a new web. Similarly, a mind probes the universe to find anchorage for belief. A poet can create a metaphor by expressing the comparison in a phrase (my spider-filaments of thought). Walt Whitman, however, chose to draw out the comparison into stanza-length sections. The first section of his poem presents the image or vehicle *of comparison. The second presents the idea that the vehicle points to or carries.*

A noiseless patient spider,
I marked where on a little promontory it stood isolated,
Marked how to explore the vacant vast surrounding,
It launched forth filament, filament, filament, out of itself,
Ever unreeling them, ever tirelessly speeding them.   5

And you O my soul where you stand,
Surrounded, detached, in measureless oceans of space,
Ceaselessly musing, venturing, throwing, seeking the spheres to connect them,
Till the bridge you will need be formed, till the ductile anchor hold,
Till the gossamer thread you fling catch somewhere, O my soul.   10

OBJECTIVES

The students will be able to

- Analyze the use of metaphor in Whitman's "A Noiseless Patient Spider."
- Discuss the popular notion of an honest religious seeker remaining without answers.

FURTHER HELPS

Additional activities

1. Have a student research how a spider forms its web and share this with the class.

2. If you have students interested in art, have them use their creativity to do a visual representation of the poem. Encourage them to notice any images in the poem that can be translated into a visual statement (e.g., "isolated," "launched forth," "tirelessly speeding").

3. Have the class examine the extended metaphor in Oliver Wendell Holmes's "The Chambered Nautilus."

Resources

Gay Wilson Allen, *Walt Whitman Handbook* (Chicago: Packard and Company, 1946). See chapter III, "Whitman's Fundamental Ideas."

As time permits, continue your discussion with the "About the Essay" questions (page 16).

Application

Have the students write a rough outline of "The Fly" using the paragraph's first sentence as the thesis. Discuss similarities and differences among their outlines or create an outline together as a class. While answers may vary, a suggested outline follows.

Thesis: We can nowhere find a better type of perfectly free creature than in the common housefly.

I. He is convinced the world was made for him.
   A. He has perfect egotism.
   B. He has perfect independence.
   C. He has perfect self-confidence.

II. He is completely unconcerned with human activity.
   A. You cannot terrify him.
   B. He asks no advice of you.

III. He has no work to do.
   A. Earthworms dig.
   B. Bees gather and build.
   C. Spiders build webs.
   D. Ants keep a treasury and accounts.

Restatement: What freedom is like this?

PREPARATION

"A Noiseless Patient Spider"

Overview

In Whitman's poem a spider trying to start a web mirrors a mind looking for certainty, trying to make sense out of the universe. His poem illustrates the extended metaphor (later identified as analogy).

Potential problems

Read "About the Author," page 18, with the students to warn them of the philosophical errors that permeate Whitman's writings. (Discussion of "A Noiseless Patient Spider" continues after "About the Poem.")

Joseph Beaver, *Walt Whitman—Poet of Science* (New York: King's Crown Press, Morningside Heights, 1951). This source is especially enlightening on the selection "A Noiseless Patient Spider."

About the Poem

1. What image or vehicle of comparison does Whitman introduce in the first section of the poem?
2. Does Whitman's poem have meter or rhyme?
3. Does the actual shape of the poem seem appropriate to its thought? Why or why not?

About the Author

Walt Whitman's (1819-1892) views of man and nature have been very influential. His humanistic view of man, for example, is reflected not only in today's literature but in the very fabric of our society. According to Whitman, "the last, best dependence is to be upon humanity itself, and its own inherent, normal, full-grown qualities, without any superstitious support whatever." What a Christian would call sin, Whitman dismisses as an excusable and inevitable result of failing to progress in the struggles of evolution. To Whitman the individual's responsibility is to improve himself—until death, at which time his soul returns to a cosmic Oversoul, or source of all life.

Whitman's view of nature is no less prevalent. As a pantheist, Whitman possessed an ardent faith in nature. To him nature was both a manifestation of deity and deity itself. Whitman's purpose in writing *Leaves of Grass,* his most famous collection of poetry, was to build a bridge between his soul and nature, a bridge that would lead to ultimate truth. Although, in our selection, Whitman leaves unanswered the question of where we find ultimate meaning, his poem *Song of Prudence* leaves no doubt as to Whitman's method of determining truth. In this poem he states, "Whatever satisfies souls is true."

Although we can appreciate the literary quality of many Whitman poems, we must, of course, be careful to evaluate their message in light of Scriptural standards. Unlike Whitman, we as Christians recognize that "there is a way which seemeth right unto a man, but the end thereof are the ways of death" (Proverbs 14:12).

 About the Poem

1. *The English critic I. A. Richards introduced the terms* tenor, *the usually abstract idea that is the subject of the metaphor, and* vehicle, *the usually concrete idea that expresses it. In this poem the spider starting a web in stanza 1 is the vehicle; Whitman, as representative man, is the tenor. Tenor and vehicle each occupy a stanza. The poem depicts the fragility and perhaps futility of human speculative reasoning, summing up centuries of philosophical theorizing in a single vivid image.*

2. *The poem is written in free verse, without rhyme or meter. If students question its being a poem, refer them to the definition of poetry in the introduction to Part 1 (page 1).*

3. *Answers will vary. Some have said, however, that the poem's shape gives the visual impression of a spider weaving long, delicate strands of filament.*

DISCUSSION

Introduction

"A Noiseless Patient Spider" could have been written only by a man who carefully observed nature firsthand with a capacity for drawing parallels between natural phenomena and higher spiritual concepts. Notice, for example, Whitman's double use of the verb "to mark" in lines 2 and 3 to describe the thoughtful notice he took of the instinctive habits of a spider, behavior he compares later in the poem to the soul's search for connection and foundation.

The poem shows the human mind incessantly probing the mysteries of its environment, looking for some basis for belief. Second Timothy 3:7 speaks of unbelievers who are "ever learning, and never able to come to the knowledge of the truth" (cf. Deut. 30:11-14). Whitman's spider is like unbelieving man hopelessly searching for some truth other than God's truth. The metaphor is nonetheless effective.

The Spider and the Wasp

Alexander Petrunkevitch

The Russian-American zoologist Alexander Petrunkevitch gave most of his life to the study of spiders. His best-known essay proves that scientific writing can rise to the level of literature. Notice that as literature of information, rather than of imagination, it makes little use of imaginative comparisons. There is one prominent simile, however. Can you find it?

To hold its own struggle for existence, every species of animal must have a regular source of food, and if it happens to live on other animals, its survival may be very delicately balanced. The hunter cannot exist without the hunted; if the latter should perish from the earth, the former would, too. When the hunted also prey on some of the hunters, the matter may become complicated.

This is nowhere better illustrated than in the insect world. Think of the complexity of a situation such as the following: There is a certain wasp, *Pimpla inquisitor*, whose larvae feed on the larvae of the tussock moth. *Pimpla* larvae in turn serve as food for the larvae of a second wasp, and the latter in their turn nourish still a third wasp. What subtle balance between fertility and mortality must exist in the case of each of these four species to prevent the extinction of all of them! An excess of mortality over fertility in a single member of the group would ultimately wipe out all four.

This is not a unique case. The two great orders of insects, Hymenoptera and Diptera, are full of such examples of interrelationship. And the spiders (which are not insects but members of a separate order of arthropods) also are killers and victims of insects.

The picture is complicated by the fact that those species which are carnivorous in the larval stage have to be provided with animal food by a vegetarian mother. The survival of the young depends on the mother's correct choice of a food which she does not eat herself. In the feeding and safeguarding of their progeny the insects and spiders exhibit some interesting analogies to reasoning and some crass examples of blind instinct. The case I propose to describe here is that of the tarantula spiders and their archenemy, the digger wasps of the genus Pepsis. It is a classic example of what looks like intelligence pitted against instinct—a strange situation in which the victim, though fully able to defend itself, submits unwittingly to its destruction.

Most tarantulas live in the Tropics, but several species occur in the temperate zone and a few are common in the southern U.S. Some varieties are large and have powerful fangs with which they can inflict a deep wound. These formidable looking spiders do not, however,

OBJECTIVE

The students will be able to

• Illustrate the difference between literature of imagination and literature of information.

See highlighted sentence, page 23.

thesis statement

FURTHER HELPS

Additional activities

1. See if the students can think of other ways in which God maintains a balance in nature (e.g., eagles eat rabbits; opossums eat insects).

2. If any student has ever seen a tarantula, encourage him to tell the other class members about it.

3. Although Petrunkevitch uses little imaginative comparison in his essay, it is nonetheless very interesting reading. How does he accomplish this? Have the students identify specific words or phrases that transform what could have been dull, scientific description into exciting narrative description.

4. Have a student or students research one of the following: the relationship between protozoa and the termite; the

Analysis

"A Noiseless Patient Spider" vividly conveys the plight of the unbeliever. Lines 7 and 8, for example, describe the soul as "detached" and "surrounded" by the emptiness of the universe. These lines echo the thought expressed in lines 2 and 3 which describe the spider as "isolated" in "the vacant vast surrounding." The metaphor is a picture of the natural man. The launching forth of "filament, filament, filament, out of itself" (line 4) is Whitman's way of describing man's search for truth, for connectedness with something more secure than himself. The unbeliever who is "ceaselessly musing" (line 8) is the antithesis to the Christian who possesses a secure "anchor" (cf. line 9 of the poem). Whitman's mooring is self. Notice, however, that

this is an uncertain "anchor" at best, for although the poet flings out "gossamer threads" of "ceaseless musing," he possesses no assurance of truth.

Whitman's view of God, man, and nature can be summarized in the following quotation from *Leaves of Grass:* "I hear and behold God in every object, yet understand God not in the least, nor do I understand who there can be more wonderful than myself." (Note II Tim. 3:1-2 and Rom. 1:24, 26-27, 31 for evaluating Whitman's godless worship of self.)

Despite Whitman's philosophy, his poem is an excellent example of imaginative comparison using science and nature. Like several other authors in Unit 1, he compares an insect with a

human being, giving it human personality. This comparison determines the structure of the poem. Continue the discussion on structure using the "About the Poem" questions (page 18).

Application

As mentioned in the introduction, Whitman's poem illustrates the power of an effective metaphor. As Christians, however, we recognize that the poem's message is erroneous. Obviously, Whitman does not acknowledge the authority of God's written revelation, the Bible, which contains answers to man's questions. With these facts in mind, have the students choose one of the following historical characters: Moses, Elijah, Ahab, Saul, relationship between the yucca moth and the yucca plant (illustrated in BJU Press's *BIOLOGY for Christian Schools,* 2nd ed. [1994], page 461).

5. In this unit the students have read about animals. If time allows, have them look at other prose pieces or poetry about animals and share their favorite ones with the class. One author of animal poems is Ogden Nash.

Resources

Thomas Cooley, ed., *The Norton Sampler: Short Essays for Composition,* 2nd ed. (New York: W.W. Norton & Company, 1982).

Robert A. Schwegler, ed., *Patterns in Action,* 2nd ed. (Illinois: Scott, Foresman and Company, 1988).

---

attack man; you can hold one in your hand, if you are gentle, without being bitten. Their bite is dangerous only to insects and small mammals such as mice; for a man it is no worse than a hornet's sting.

Tarantulas customarily live in deep cylindrical burrows, from which they emerge at dusk and into which they retire at dawn. Mature males wander about after dark in search of females and occasionally stray into houses. After mating, the male dies in a few weeks, but a female lives much longer and can mate several years in succession. In a Paris museum is a tropical specimen which is said to have been in captivity for 25 years.

A fertilized female tarantula lays from 200 to 400 eggs at a time; thus it is possible for a single tarantula to produce several thousand young. She takes no care of them beyond weaving a cocoon of silk to enclose the eggs. After they hatch, the young walk away, find convenient places in which to dig their burrows and spend the rest of their lives in solitude. Tarantulas feed mostly on insects and millepedes. Once their appetite is appeased, they digest the food for several days before eating again. Their sight is poor, being limited to sensing a change in the intensity of light and to perception of moving objects. They apparently have little or no sense of hearing, for a hungry tarantula will pay no attention to a loudly chirping cricket placed in its cage unless the insect happens to touch one of its legs.

But all spiders, and especially hairy ones, have an extremely delicate sense of touch. Laboratory experiments prove that tarantulas can distinguish three types of touch: pressure against the body wall, stroking of the body hair and riffling of certain fine hairs on the legs called trichobothria. Pressure against the body by a finger or the end of a pencil, causes the tarantula to move off slowly for a short distance. The touch excites no defensive

response unless the approach is from above where the spider can see the motion, in which case it rises on its hind legs, lifts its front legs, opens its fangs and holds this threatening posture as long as the object continues to move. When the motion stops, the spider drops back to the ground, remains quiet for a few seconds and then moves slowly away.

The entire body of a tarantula, especially its legs, is thickly clothed with hair. Some of it is short and woolly, some long and stiff. Touching this body hair produces one of two distinct reactions. When the spider is hungry, it responds with an immediate and swift attack. At the touch of a cricket's antennae the tarantula seizes the insect so swiftly that a motion picture taken at the rate of 64 frames per second shows only the result and not the process of capture. But when the spider is not hungry, the stimulation merely causes it to shake the touched limb.

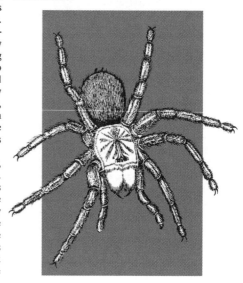

Solomon, Asaph (author of several Psalms), or Pilate. Have them use Scripture (and possibly a commentary and/or a concordance) to research these men and answer questions such as the following: What was his view of man? What was his view of God? Give at least one crisis or dilemma he faced. How did he view his dilemma? What actions, if any, did he take? What were the immediate consequences of his actions? Were there any long-term consequences? What does the study of this man reveal to you about man's control over his circumstances? List at least one other lesson you learned from your study. See **Appendix D: Bible Character Sketch** for a handout to go with this activity.

PREPARATION
"The Spider and the Wasp"
Overview

This article describes a battle between a tarantula and a wasp as an illustration of the distinction between instinct and intelligence. Barren of metaphor (almost), it is nevertheless a mode of expository prose. It shows the difference between literature of imagination and literature of information.

Potential problems

There are some intimations of evolutionism here (the struggle of the species) but no direct mention. Evolution need not be inferred from any of its statements.

DISCUSSION
Introduction

Begin by asking your students to compare Ruskin's essay on the fly with Petrunkevitch's. Both contrast instinct and "intelligence" in the insect world. The style and purpose of the two authors, however, are distinctly different.

The trichobothria, very fine hairs growing from disklike membranes on the legs, were once thought to be the spider's hearing organs, but we now know that they have nothing to do with sound. They are sensitive only to air movement. A light breeze makes them vibrate slowly without disturbing the common hair. When one blows gently on the trichobothria, the tarantula reacts with a quick jerk of its four front legs. If the front and hind legs are stimulated at the same time, the spider makes a sudden jump. This reaction is quite independent of the state of its appetite.

These three tactile responses—to pressure on the body wall, to moving of the common hair and to flexing of the trichobothria—are so different from one another that there is no possibility of confusing them. They serve the tarantula adequately for most of its needs and enable it to avoid most annoyances and dangers. But they fail the spider completely when it meets its deadly enemy, the digger wasp Pepsis.

These solitary wasps are beautiful and formidable creatures. Most species are either a deep shiny blue all over, or a deep blue with rusty wings. The largest have a wing span of about four inches. They live on nectar. When excited, they give off a pungent odor—a warning that they are ready to attack. The sting is much worse than that of a bee or common wasp, and the pain and swelling last longer.

In the adult stage the wasp lives only a few months. The female produces but a few eggs, one at a time at intervals of two or three days. For each egg the mother must provide one adult tarantula, alive but paralyzed. The tarantula must be of the correct species to nourish the larva. The mother wasp attaches the egg to the paralyzed spider's abdomen. Upon hatching from the egg, the larva is many hundreds of times smaller than its living but helpless victim. It eats no other food and drinks no water. By the time it has finished its single gargantuan meal and become ready for wasphood, nothing remains of the tarantula but its indigestible chitinous skeleton.

The mother wasp goes tarantula-hunting when the egg in her ovary is almost ready to be laid. Flying low over the ground late on a sunny afternoon, the wasp looks for its victim or for the mouth of a tarantula burrow, a round hole edged by a bit of silk. The sex of the spider makes no difference, but the mother is highly discriminating as to species. Each species of Pepsis requires a certain species of tarantula, and the wasp will not attack the wrong species. In a cage with a tarantula which is not its normal prey the wasp avoids the spider, and is usually killed by it in the night.

Yet when a wasp finds the correct species, it is the other way about. To identify the species the wasp apparently must explore the spider with her antennae. The tarantula shows an

---

Ruskin's diction is more colorful—quasi-metaphoric—and his simile is more imaginative (though no better suited to his artistic purpose). But Petrunkevitch, a scientist, is clearly seeking to inform, and his style supports his purpose.

Analysis

Although informative rather than imaginative, "The Spider and the Wasp" is a splendidly written article that should help students discern the difference between literature of imagination and literature of information. It has clear structuring (pattern) in its contrasting of the two adversaries in terms of intelligence (the wasp) and instinct (the spider), but it is almost devoid of imaginative comparison. Scientific writing,

of course, needs to be kept as plain and direct as possible, although it does use analogies sparingly for clarification. Have students identify the beginning (paragraphs 1-5), middle, and end (last four paragraphs) of the article. Have them locate the thesis (beginning of paragraph 5 and expanded in the last four paragraphs of the article). The thesis is supported by a single example: the contest of the spider and the wasp. Ask students when the wasp also seems directed by instinct. Note that Petrunkevitch is ascribing intelligence to the wasp in only a very relative sense.

As time permits, answer the "About the Essay" questions (page 23).

Application

The Eskimos have a saying that aptly illustrates one facet of the balance in nature: "The wolf and the caribou are one. The caribou feed the wolf, and the wolf keep the caribou strong [through the chase]." Have the students investigate the predator-prey relationship and choose one example that interests them. Then, have them write either an imaginative or informative paragraph that describes the relationship they have chosen. See **Writing Rubric 1-3: Predator-Prey Paragraph.**

amazing toleration to this exploration. The wasp crawls under it and walks over it without evoking any hostile response. Having satisfied itself that the victim is the right species, the wasp moves off a few inches to dig the spider's grave. Working vigorously with legs and jaws, it excavates a hole 8 to 10 inches deep with a diameter slightly larger than the spider's girth. Now and again the wasp pops out of the hole to make sure that the spider is still there.

When the grave is finished, the wasp returns to the tarantula to complete her ghastly enterprise. First she feels it all over once more with her antennae. Then her behavior becomes more aggressive. She bends her abdomen, protruding her sting, and searches for the soft membrane at the point where the spider's leg joins its body—the only spot where she can penetrate the horny skeleton. From time to time, as the exasperated spider slowly shifts ground, the wasp turns on her back and slides along with the aid of her wings, trying to get under the tarantula for a shot at the vital spot. During all this maneuvering, which can last for several minutes, the tarantula makes no move to save itself. Finally the wasp corners it against some obstruction and grasps one of its legs in her powerful jaws. Now at last the harassed spider tries a desperate but vain defense. The two contestants roll over and over on the ground. It is a terrifying sight and the outcome is always the same. The wasp finally manages to thrust her sting into the soft spot and holds it there for a few seconds while she pumps in the poison. Almost immediately the tarantula falls paralyzed on its back. Its legs stop twitching; its heart stops beating. Yet it is not dead, as is shown by the fact that if taken from the wasp it can be restored to some sensitivity by being kept in a moist chamber for several months.

After paralyzing the tarantula, the wasp cleans herself by dragging her body along the ground and rubbing her feet, sucks the drop of blood oozing from the wound in the spider's abdomen, then grabs a leg of the flabby, helpless animal in her jaws and drags it down to the bottom of the grave. She stays there for many minutes, sometimes for several hours, and what she does all that time in the dark we do not know. Eventually she lays her egg and attaches it to the side of the spider's abdomen with a sticky secretion. Then she emerges, fills the grave with soil carried bit by bit in her jaws, and finally tramples the ground all around to hide any trace of the grave from prowlers. Then she flies away, leaving her descendant safely started in life.

In all this the behavior of the wasp evidently is qualitatively different from that of the spider. The wasp acts like an intelligent animal. This is not to say that instinct plays no part or that she reasons as man does. But her actions are to the point; they are not automatic and can be modified to fit the situation. We do not know for certain how she identifies the tarantula—probably it is by some olfactory or chemo-tactile sense—but she does it purposefully and does not blindly tackle a wrong species.

On the other hand, the tarantula's behavior shows only confusion. What makes the tarantula behave as stupidly as it does? No clear, simple answer is available. Possibly the stimulation by the wasp's antennae is masked by a heavier pressure on the spider's body, so that it reacts as when prodded by a pencil. But the explanation may be much more complex. Initiative in attack is not in the nature of tarantulas; most species fight only when cornered so that escape is impossible. Their inherited patterns of behavior apparently prompt them to avoid problems rather than attack them. For example, spiders always weave their webs in three dimensions, and when a spider finds that there is insufficient space to attach certain threads in the third dimension, it leaves the place and seeks another, instead of finishing the web in a single plane. This urge to escape seems to arise under all circumstances, in all phases of life and to take the place of reasoning. For a spider to change the pattern of its web is as impossible as for an inexperienced man to build a bridge across a chasm obstructing his way.

In a way the instinctive urge to escape is not only easier but more efficient than reasoning. The tarantula does exactly what is most efficient in all cases except in an encounter with a ruthless and determined attacker dependent for the existence of her own species on killing as many tarantulas as she can lay eggs. Perhaps in this case the spider follows its usual pattern of trying to escape, instead of seizing and killing the wasp, because it is not aware of its danger. In any case, the survival of the tarantula species as a whole is protected by the fact that the spider is much more fertile than the wasp.

About the Essay

1. What is the one prominent simile in Petrunkevitch's essay? Support your answer with a quotation from the essay.
2. State one major difference between Ruskin's description of the fly and Petrunkevitch's description of the tarantula and the wasp.
3. Petrunkevitch states the thesis of his essay in paragraph five. What is this thesis?
4. What possible answer could you give to Petrunkevitch's question: "What makes the tarantula behave as stupidly as it does?"

About the Author

Alexander Petrunkevitch (1875-1967) was an expert in the study of spiders. He authored an *Index Catalogue of Spiders of North, Central and South America,* as well as other works of interest to biologists. In addition to his scientific writings, he wrote several philosophical works in German. He also translated English literature into his native Russian and Russian literature into English. This accomplished scholar held positions at Yale and at Indiana University and lectured at Harvard University.

Little information is available in English about Petrunkevitch's views or lifestyle. We are certain that he was an astute observer, capable of analyzing natural processes and explaining them with the flair of a storyteller. His famous essay "The Spider and the Wasp" bears the marks of good literature: excellent form, smooth transitions between thoughts, and suspense-building narrative techniques.

Petrunkevitch's scholarship and his ability to make scientific data readable give his works universal value. The other authors in this unit are literary people making use of natural imagery. Petrunkevitch is a scientist using literary tools to enhance his technical writing.

 About the Essay

4. *God established a hierarchical order in the natural world, a delicate balance that is maintained by the instinct and "intelligence" of His creatures.*

1. *The simile is found at the end of the next to last paragraph; a spider is compared to a man: "For a spider to change the pattern of its web is as impossible as for an inexperienced man to build a bridge across a chasm obstructing his way."*

2. *Answers will vary. The discussion under the Analysis section should prepare the students for this question.*

3. *The thesis is stated in the first sentence of the paragraph: "In the feeding and safeguarding of their progeny the insects and spiders exhibit some interesting analogies to reasoning and some crass examples of blind instinct."*

UNIT TWO

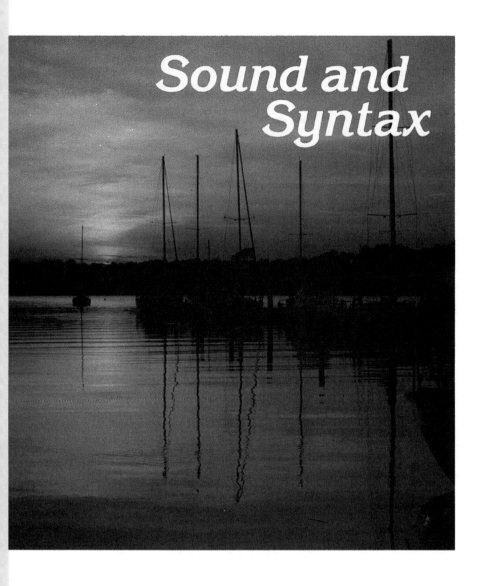

Sound and Syntax

FURTHER HELPS

Additional activities

You may wish to have students complete **Appendix F: The King James Version—A Metrical Study** for homework or in class with a partner after you have discussed the Analysis section for the Sound and Syntax Introduction.

Resources

Laurence Perrine, *Literature: Structure, Sound, and Sense* (New York: Harcourt Brace Jovanovich, 1978). The units "Musical Devices" and "Sound and Meaning" may give teachers additional ideas and examples.

Judges 4:21 tells in direct fashion the grim details of Sisera's death by the hand of a woman, Jael. "Then Jael Heber's wife took a nail of the tent, and took a hammer in her hand, and went softly unto him, and smote the nail into his temples, and fastened it into the ground: for he was fast asleep and weary." The description is simple and straightforward. It ends with the terse comment, "So he died." In the next chapter the prophetess Deborah celebrates the defeat of Sisera and the Canaanites in song. Verses 26 and 27 dwell poetically on the details.

> She put her hand to the nail,
> and her right hand to the workmen's hammer;
> and with the hammer she smote Sisera,
> she smote off his head, when she had pierced and stricken through his temples.
>
> At her feet he bowed, he fell, he lay down:
> at her feet he bowed, he fell:
> where he bowed, there he fell down dead.

Notice the repetition of phrases with variation in verse 26. The word "hand" in line 1 becomes "right hand" in line 2, where we have instead of "nail," "the workmen's hammer." In line 3 Sisera is smitten (pierced) with hammer and nail; in line 4, he is smitten (decapitated), evidently with a sword.

Verse 27 mockingly describes the death blow in battle terms. The bowing, in reality, was his kneeling to ask protection. The lying down was from exhaustion. The dying occurred in sleep. But the poem represents these actions as the motions of one struck down in combat. Sisera, as it were, bends from the force of the blow and crumples lifeless. The mockery is strengthened by repetition. Line 2 repeats line 1 with the exception of the clause "he lay down." Line 3 repeats line 2, dropping, however, the first three words and adding two at the end. Repetition with variation is a basic technique of ancient battle poetry. The three strongly accented monosyllables "fell down dead" bring the description to a thudding close. The rhythm of the poem along with the heavy repetition emphasizes the shame, for a military man, of death by a woman.

Patterned repetition of all types—of sound and syntax as well as of thought—is more common in poetry than in prose. The rhythmical units of poetry tend to be more uniformly alike than those of prose, which are looser and less predictable. When the accented syllables in poetic rhythm occur at fairly equal intervals throughout a poem, we say that the poem has **meter**. The units of meter are known as poetic **feet**. Notice, for example, the nearly regular alternation of accented and unaccented syllables in Tennyson's "The Eagle."

> He clasps the crag with crooked hands.
> Close to the sun in lonely lands,
> Ringed with the azure world, he stands.
>
> The wrinkled sea beneath him crawls,
> He watches from his mountain walls,
> And like a thunderbolt he falls.

PREPARATION

Sound and Syntax Introduction

Overview

Unit 2 expands and illustrates the second part of the definition of poetry: patterned repetition (see "Marks of Literature," pages x-1). It focuses on the effects of sound and syntax, explaining rhyme, meter (briefly), and other common kinds of sound repetition. These elements, like imaginative comparison, are found in both poems and poetic prose.

DISCUSSION

Introduction

Read the introduction (pages 26-27) aloud in class. Be sure that the students grasp the concepts illustrated in Tennyson's poem "The Eagle."

Analysis

The explanations of the concepts introduced in the opening essay should be adequate for the purposes of the course. If the students have not used the BJU Press ninth-grade literature text, *FUNDAMENTALS OF LITERATURE*, you may want to review the following:

Types of metrical feet
iambic (⌣ ⁄)
trochaic (⁄ ⌣)
anapestic (⌣ ⌣ ⁄)
dactylic (⁄ ⌣ ⌣)
spondaic (⁄ ⁄)

Terms for feet per line
monometer (one foot per line)
dimeter (two feet per line)
trimeter (three feet per line)
tetrameter (four feet per line)
pentameter (five feet per line)
hexameter (six feet per line)
heptameter (seven feet per line)
octameter (eight feet per line)

The first line contains four poetic feet, each of which consists of an unaccented syllable followed by an accented. "He *clasps* the *crag* with *crook*ed *hands*." Meter, the regular arrangement of stressed and unstressed syllables, characterizes the poetry of most European languages. However, some modern poets, following the example of Walt Whitman, have abandoned meter for the irregular rhythms of **free verse,** which uses neither meter nor rhyme.

Rhyme is the most obvious form of sound repetition in poetry. In Tennyson's poem the ends of the first three lines correspond in sound, as do those of the last three lines. Lines or parts of lines are said to rhyme when they show a similarity of sound from the vowel of the last accented syllable onward, with dissimilarity in the preceding consonants: h*ands*, l*ands*, st*ands*, cr*awls*, w*alls*, f*alls*. In the best rhymed poetry, the rhyming words are important words in the poem.

The first line of Tennyson's poem also illustrates three other forms of sound repetition common in poetry: alliteration, consonance, and assonance. **Alliteration** is the repetition of initial consonant sounds in accented syllables: *c*lasps, *c*rag, *c*rooked. **Consonance** is the repetition of terminal consonant sounds in accented syllables: clasp*s*, hand*s*. Finally, **assonance** is the repetition of vowel sounds in accented syllables: cl*a*sps, cr*a*g, h*a*nds.

As you read the following selections, be alert to the ways in which sound and syntax support meaning. Skilled writers can adapt their styles to create a wide range of effects. A good ear for the sounds of poetry and prose is to some extent a gift from birth. But you can also develop a good ear by reading with attentiveness to sound and sentence structure. For this purpose, there is no writing in English that equals the Authorized (King James) Version of the Bible.

You might also want to review the method of describing a rhyme scheme by designating the first rhyme sound *a,* the second *b,* the third *c,* and so forth. Tennyson's "The Eagle" can be described as a six-line poem in iambic tetrameter (iambic feet are dominant) rhyming *aaa bbb.*

NOTE: Do not require students to spend a great deal of time memorizing all the terms given above. Knowing that these ideas exist and having a cursory awareness of them are sufficient for the high school level. Few well-written poems follow one pattern (such as iambic pentameter) rigidly throughout or follow a prescribed rhyme scheme. Poetry by its very nature is free from much externally imposed restriction. Many students become frustrated in their study of poetry and lose their enjoy-ment of it because they are required to dissect it rather than absorb it.

Together in class do **Appendix E: Psalm 1 Scansion.** Have the students examine the psalm, noting the repetitions of sound and syntax and the rhythmical and structural parallelism (e.g., lines 2 and 3; lines 1-9 and 10-15). See Appendix E for further explanation.

Application

Have the students choose a poem or a poetic passage from Scripture that they especially like. (You might even allow them to write a short poem for this exercise.) Using the selection of their choice, have them identify the repetitions of sound, the meter, and any structural parallelism they notice. You might also encourage them to state how they think these devices of sound and syntax support the meaning of the poem.

"All Day I Hear," "Winter Ocean"

personification, alliteration

alliteration, simile, personification

assonance
Notice also consonance throughout (repeated /s/ endings).

The following two poems show the sea in quite different moods. Each depends heavily upon sound effects to create its mood. The long o rhymes of the first poem suggest the melancholy of the ocean breaking with tedious regularity on the shore. (The use of words that sound like what they mean is known as onomatopoeia.) The rhyme of the second poem, though carefully arranged, is less noticeable. The busy, blustering energy of the ocean is suggested by staccato rhythms and heavy alliteration and assonance.

All Day I Hear

James Joyce

All day I hear the noise of waters
   Making moan,
Sad as the sea-bird is, when going
   Forth alone,
He hears the winds cry to the waters'   5
   Monotone.

The grey winds, the cold winds blowing
   Where I go.
I hear the noise of many waters
   Far below.   10
All day, all night, I hear them flowing
   To and fro.

"All Day I Hear." "Chamber Music XXXV," "All day I hear the noise of . . . ," from *Collected Poems* by James Joyce. Copyright 1918 by B. W. Huebsch, Inc., 1927, 1936 by James Joyce, 1946 by Nora Joyce. Used by permission of Viking Penguin, a division of Penguin Putnam, Inc.

PREPARATION

"All Day I Hear," "Winter Ocean"

Overview

The first poem has a simple rhyme scheme: *aaa bbb,* like Tennyson's "The Eagle." The recurrence of /ō/ sounds in the rhymes and elsewhere contributes to the gloom of the poem. The second poem is less a mood piece; in this selection the use of sound conveys a vivid picture of the ocean's energy and vibrance.

Note that "All Day I Hear" is an example of what the note on the bottom of page 27 refers to. It is basically iambic hexameter; however, a rigorous and unrealistic attempt to force each line into that pattern will result in awkward-sounding lines such as "The **grey** winds, **the** cold **winds** blow**ing** / Where **I** go." Too often this is what students think poetry "sounds like": stilted and mechanical. The opposite is the case.

Potential problems

As "About the Author" indicates (page 29), Joyce's works cannot be endorsed wholesale by the Christian.

DISCUSSION

Introduction

Physical surroundings can affect disposition. The monotony of the sea, for example, can be relaxing or depressing. The sea can also be invigorating, unpredictable, or even terrifying. The two poems in this lesson show us these varied "dispositions" of the sea.

Analysis

"All Day I Hear"

The first poem uses sound and imagery (imaginative comparison) to create and sustain an atmosphere of melancholy. It hints at a dismal journey soon to be endured. Read the poem aloud. Ask the students what word or phrase they would use to describe the poem. *(See "About the Poems" question 1 for suggested answers.)* Then, draw their attention to the circular structure of the piece. Have them notice how the end links with the beginning. The first line

About the Author

James Joyce (1882-1941) relied on both the sound and the sense of words to communicate his ideas and images. A lover of clever word play, Joyce could create an effective pun or invent a word to suit every need. His facility with words, clearly evident in "All Day I Hear," is admirable.

Chamber Music, the slim volume of verse from which our selection is taken, was one of Joyce's first endeavors in poetry. It reflects his early Romantic outlook (characterized by a reverence for nature and a belief in man's innate goodness). These early poems, though at times melancholy, are not marred by the despair which marks many of Joyce's later works, a despair spawned by the world's refusal to warmly embrace his initial literary vision.

Although a comprehensive knowledge of Joyce's writing is not a necessary or even a healthy goal, a general awareness of his literary impact helps us better understand contemporary trends in literature. The influence of his novels cannot be underestimated. Still, most of these works hold little ideological value. Joyce's use of cryptic allusions and veiled obscenities as well as his inflated sense of self-importance (especially evident in his autobiographical work, *The Portrait of the Artist as a Young Man*) preview both the style and attitude of many twentieth-century writers.

Winter Ocean

John Updike

Many-maned scud-thumper,* tub
of male whales, maker of worn wood, shrub-ruster, sky-mocker, rave!
portly pusher of waves, wind-slave.

scud: wind-driven clouds and rain

About the Poems

1. "All Day I Hear" could be called a mood piece. What word or phrase would you use to describe the mood of Joyce's poem?
2. How would you describe the speaker in Joyce's poem?
3. How do the moods of the two poems differ?
4. Which of the two poems do you think makes fuller use of imaginative comparison? (Support your answer with specific examples from the poem.)

FURTHER HELPS

Additional activities

Have your students examine another poem from Joyce's early collection, *Chamber Music* (I and III are good selections). Have them point out the myriad metaphors and allusions to nature.

Resources

Herbert Gorman, *James Joyce* (n.p.: Rinehart & Company, 1948).

James Joyce, *Chamber Music* (London: Jonathon Cape, 1949).

Virginia Moseley, *Joyce and the Bible* (Dekalb, Illinois: Northern University Press, 1967).

Darcy O'Brien, *The Conscience of James Joyce* (Princeton, New Jersey: Princeton University Press, 1968).

Line 1 incorporates alliteration, assonance, metaphor ("Many-maned," "tub"), onomatopoeia ("thumper").

Line 2 incorporates assonance, alliteration, personification ("rave!").

Line 3 incorporates alliteration and personification ("portly pusher," "wind-slave").

All 3 lines incorporate synecdoche—indeed the entire poem could be seen as a list of the parts of the sea that represent the whole.

---

of stanza 1 is expanded in the last two lines of stanza 2. Point out, too, the progression from "All day" in the first line to "All day, all night" in the last. Next, ask them about the speaker or persona of the poem. Who is he? A fisherman? Small fishing boats do not go out in winter. Someone facing and dreading death? How would they describe him? *(Lines 2 and 3 of stanza 1 introduce one comparison: the poet is sad as a sea bird "going / Forth alone." The first line of stanza 2 completes the comparison: he is setting out alone where the winds are cold.)* Although the second stanza adds some details—rather odd ones—it still leaves the meaning open and unrestricted. (Discussion of "Winter Ocean" continues after "About the Poems.")

 About the Poems

1. *Answers will vary but may include dismal, melancholy.*
2. *Lines 2 and 3 of stanza 1 introduce one comparison: the poet is sad as a sea bird "going / Forth alone." The first line of stanza 2 completes the comparison: he is setting out alone where the winds are cold.*
3. *Joyce's poem is, as stated above, dismal and melancholy. Updike's, on the other hand, is blustering, tumultuous. This is conveyed primarily through the staccato rhythm and the speaker's defiant, confrontational tone.*
4. *Answers may vary, although "Winter Ocean," in*

spite of its brevity, would probably be the better choice. It includes onomatopoeia, metaphor, personification, and metonymy.

"Winter Ocean"

Updike's picture of the sea is an interesting contrast to Joyce's melancholy, enigmatic sketch. Read Updike's poem aloud. Ask the students to describe the poem, using specific examples from the poem to justify their description. How does the mood of this piece differ from the mood in Joyce's poem? *(The staccato rhythm helps convey a blustering, tumultuous atmosphere.)* Who is the speaker or persona of this poem? How do the speakers of the two poems differ? *(The speaker in Updike's poem is not melancholy but rather defiant, confrontational, hurling insults at the "Many-maned scud-thumper.")*

OBJECTIVE

The students will be able to

• Analyze and discuss the effective use of metaphoric expressions and sound devices in creating and sustaining tension.

onomatopoeia, alliteration

assonance

FURTHER HELPS

Additional activities

Journal entry idea

After completing the reading of "The Leak," have the students reread the last paragraph of the story. Although many of them have not yet faced the threat of losing someone close to them, they may have had some experience that evoked the same feelings the captain expresses. Have them write about such an experience. The entry may be based on either fact or an imaginary experience.

The Leak

Lincoln Colcord

Colcord gives us a vivid picture of the power and fury of the sea. In this intense narrative, the wind-lashed ocean emerges as the formidable antagonist of the hero, Captain Blair. Notice the way Colcord uses the repetition of onomatopoetic words and terse phrases to build and sustain the tension of the narrative.

I

Clangity-clang! Clangity-clang! Clangity-clang! The incessant sound of the pumps drummed through the gale; forward, aft, below in the cabin, it penetrated like the stroke of doom. Captain Blair hung to the weather rail, listening to the metallic beat; it had been in his ears for days, sleeping or waking, so that now he heard nothing else. Clangity-clang! Clangity-clang! Clangity-clang! How long would she last at this rate? Another week? Another day?

Overhead the wind howled in the rigging; the old bark staggered with a stiff, unwieldy motion, wallowing like a log in the wicked cross-sea of the Gulf Stream. He felt her distress under his feet. She was fighting a good fight; but she was old. The spirit of battle had gone from her, the youth, the energy, the power. This terrible cargo—nitrate from Pisagua, heavy as lead! It bore down massively within her; from her bottom and 'tween decks the bags of nitrate rose in two huge elongated pyramids, running the length of the ship, free of the sides, so that a man could walk around them. By this time the bags had consolidated; they would have to be dug apart with pickaxes; they formed two enormous rigid and rock-like lumps in the bowels of the vessel, threatening to tear her bodily open as she wrenched from crest to trough of the sea. Nitrate puts a

frightful strain upon any ship. She was old.

Captain Blair had rounded the Horn with her; he was bringing her "on the coast" in the winter time. All the passage he had dreaded this last and worst encounter with the elements, but he had hardly anticipated so much ill luck. He had hoped against hope, even, that he might slip in from Hatteras between storms. Lucky men sometimes did. There were more reasons than one, this time, behind his prayer for a favorable slant. He *had* to get in quickly; his wife lay sick in bed down below.

Clangity-clang! Clangity-clang! Clangity-clang! He left the rail, pacing the deck fiercely, buffeted by rain and spray as he faced forward, blown aft at a jog-trot as he turned his back to the wind. The gale had grown colder; it showed signs of snow. As he struggled to and fro an endless stream of thought passed like fire through his head.

A week now of unremitting northeast gale; a week of constant trouble, of deepening anxiety. Day after day he had paced his little corner of the quarter-deck, cold, wet, with raw face and chafed wrists, until he had forgotten that he owned such a thing as a body. He had scarcely slept for forty-eight hours. All this did not matter, was nothing, if they could only have got somewhere. But the bark had been hove-to on the port tack, drifting back across the Gulf Stream, steadily away from

---

Updike's poem gives us the impression that the speaker is "telling off" a bully, calling him insulting names, giving him some of his own medicine. What in this poem is the final insult? *(The final insult is "wind-slave." This "bully" is actually no more than a slave of the wind.)*

Next, have the students identify the metaphors, similes, and personifications in each poem to determine which makes fuller use of imaginative comparison. Finally, have them identify the sound devices (alliteration, assonance, etc.) in the two selections. Which of the poems relies more heavily on sound to communicate its meaning? *(Answers may vary. Joyce's poem uses moaning sounds and repeated /s/ sounds to mirror the speaker's sadness and the sound of the sea; Updike's uses brusque, short, clipped syllables that show the speaker's defiance.)*

Application

Direct the students to complete **Appendix G: Sound and Syntax—Scripture and the Sea.**

PREPARATION

"The Leak," "Storm Fury"

Overview

Both selections in this lesson use sound and imagery to portray the fury of the sea. The Colcord story, an intense narrative, relies heavily on onomatopoetic words. The short passage of dialogue from Shakespeare's *Othello* is packed with both metaphoric expression and sound repetition.

DISCUSSION

"The Leak"

Introduction

Read Colcord's story aloud in class or have the students read it aloud. Before they begin the reading, alert them to the importance of sound devices in the story. Sensitivity to the sound devices is especially effective for creating and sustaining tension throughout the narrative.

port. It was the only course. To wear her around and head inshore would have been madness, would have accomplished no end. Hatteras, a treacherous low cape* with outlying sand banks, lay in wait for those who defied the lee shore in a northeaster; that terrible lee shore stretching south from New York for hundreds of miles, a straight line of merciless sand, the graveyard of ships and men.

cape: land projecting into a body of water

On the second day of this last gale the bark had sprung a leak without warning. Her strength, holding out till the final test, had suddenly given way. Since then they had stood at the pumps night and day. They had pumped with the whole watch, six men, three on a side; they had done nothing but pump. They had barely been able to keep her free.

Clangity-clang! Clangity-clang! Clangity-clang! Captain Blair could never accustom himself to the sound; he listened to it acutely, as if it had just begun; it vibrated behind every thought, ceaseless, urgent, diabolical. It didn't belong to a ship, that sound; it was driving him mad. Why were they so hard on him? Why? Why? He stopped short, shaking his clenched hands in the face of the gale. Why wouldn't they let up a little? What had he done? He *must* get in—couldn't they see? His wife was dying!

The mate came aft, drew up beside him, shouted in his ear. "Gaining a little, sir!"

Captain Blair nodded. Words choked him; he drove his nails into the palms of his hands. "Keep on pumping!"

A squall burst upon them, bowing their heads, driving them to the rail for a hold. The mate's answer was snatched away, like water blown from the mouth of a pipe. "Men . . . pump . . . much longer!"

"Shut up and go forward!"

The mate gazed at Captain Blair in perplexity for a moment, then turned and battled down the alleyway. A terrific sea shook the old bark from stem to stern; the crest of it leaped aboard between the main and mizzen rigging, and swirled aft in a river of foam. The captain received it grimly, standing with feet braced apart, letting the water spurt to the tops of his rubber boots. He wondered if any men had been washed away from the pumps. When the lull came he listened. Clangity-clang! Clangity-clang! Clangity-clang!

What was she thinking about, down below—the wife who had gone with him bravely on so many voyages, who had made life all that it was to him by her love and sacrifice? That heavy sea must have startled her. Perhaps she had heard them shouting when the mate had come aft. Sounds had a way of carrying to the cabin. He must go down and reassure her.

He threw back the sliding door of the companion, stepped inside, and shut the cover carefully as he descended. Darkness was coming on; the steward had lighted the lamp in the after cabin. Captain Blair glanced at the chart pegged out on the table, and swore below his breath. For three days he had not seen the sun. What was the use of a chart, if they were never to know their position, if they were never to get anywhere?

A weak voice spoke from the room abaft* the cabin. "Is that you, Bert? What is it? Oh, what is it?"

abaft: toward the stern

He went in without taking off his oilskin coat. The room looked cheerless; the air was close, damp, chilly, full of the depression of sickness and the odors that came up from the hold of the leaking vessel. In the shadow of the bunk lay his wife, chocked off with pillows, so that the ship's rolling and pitching would

Resources

Rudyard Kipling, *Captains Courageous* (New York: Airmont Publishing Company, 1963).

Potential problems

Discuss with students the story's reference to luck (page 30) and its implied reference to the Fates ("Why were they so hard on him?" page 31). You may want to have students look up an article about the Fates in an encyclopedia. Lead them to understand that a fatalistic world-view based on happenstance is directly opposed to a Biblical world-view. (Note that in spite of these references, Captain Blair believes in God and asks His forgiveness.)

Analysis

Following the reading, ask the students to identify one obvious onomatopoetic device that Colcord uses to sustain tension in his story. *(The repetition of the pump's "clangity-clang" is one example. Students may find others.)* Next, have them identify at least one example of sound device (assonance, consonance, or alliteration) and imaginative comparison (metaphor, simile, or personification). *(Answers will vary. Some possibilities are the examples of alliteration in paragraph 2 and the examples of personification in paragraph 5.)* Also, have the students identify one specific phrase or passage that they think is especially effective in creating the story's tense atmosphere. *(Answers will vary.)* Be sure that they give the rationale behind their choice.

Having analyzed these specific literary devices, take some time to discuss the story's theme. Use the following to initiate discussion:

1. What is the story's central conflict? *(The central conflict is man at war with himself; man against nature is also evident, but the captain's internal conflict is more significant.)*

2. Using specific quotations from the story, show the captain's vacillation and uncertainty. *(Answers will vary.)*

3. How do the captain's and his wife's attitudes differ? How are they alike? *(Answers will vary. You may want to point out that the wife's confidence in her husband not only tends to ease her fears but also allows her to encourage him. This confidence and encouragement spurs his determination and enables him to focus on his duty despite the overwhelming circumstances.)*

4. Discuss the significance of the last paragraph in the story. Why does the captain cry out

The Leak

for forgiveness? *(He recognizes that his anger is unjustified. God in His mercy has allowed his wife to live. The hardships they have endured generally are nothing compared to the love they have shared. More specifically, the dangers they have just experienced have merely served to remind the captain how valuable that love has been and still is.)*

disturb her as little as possible. She turned her face as he entered, and attempted a smile.

"Has anything happened?" she asked again, fearfully.

"No," he answered. "Nothing." He took the hand that she stretched out over the edge of the bunk. "I just came down to see how you were."

"How cold your hands are! Give me the other."

"They only seem cold to you."

"I was frightened. I heard someone shout—and then that awful sea!"

"Down here it sounds worse than it is. That wasn't bad."

"I always think of you—of what might happen."

"Nonsense! You ought to know me well enough—nothing can happen to *me.*"

"You don't stop to think. You're so impulsive."

He laughed—he had heard it often. "As if there wasn't enough to worry about!" he said. "But I think the gale is nearly over."

"Oh, I hope so! Is she still leaking?"

"Not so badly now."

"Then everything is better?"

"Yes—everything. How are you feeling tonight, girlie?"

She pressed his cold hands. "Better, I think. It pains a little—when she pitches. Isn't it very rough?"

He choked, and suddenly bowed his head on the edge of the bunk.

"My poor boy!" She stroked his cheek, half-crying. "It's been so hard on you! You mustn't worry about me, dear. I'll be all right. You have the ship on your shoulders."

He sank beside the bunk, trying to hide the tears. The ship on his shoulders? More than that! More than that! She was helping, doing what she could. She knew.

Another sea breached the vessel, and his wife clung to him in terror until it had passed over. She had never been able to overcome her fear of these waves that made the ship tremble as if she had struck a rock; with an experience covering many years and countless gales, they always sent her heart into her mouth. She had not been cut out for the sea.

Captain Blair could feel what was going on above his head; his sailor-instinct told him that the old bark was hard pressed. He listened; and in the brief lull that came after the shock of the sea, the pumps drummed on like a heart palpitating somewhere deep in the vitals of the ship. Clangity-clang! Clangity-clang! Clangity-clang!

II

Should he put back to Bermuda? The question pursued him about the decks; it faced him in the darkness at every turn. He had left his wife sleeping; she might sleep for a few minutes, for half an hour—it never lasted long. Should he keep up the fight? Should he give in? What should he do?

He knew what it meant to put back to Bermuda. They would rob him of the bark; they lived on disabled vessels there, like vultures in the wake of an army. The cargo would be unloaded, probably reshipped; the bark would have to be repaired. All this would cost more than she was worth. He owned a quarter of her himself; it represented twenty hard years of following the sea. How could he afford to lose it? He was young no longer; where would he begin anew? And then, there was his duty to the owners; his duty as a master mariner to get the ship, his trust, to her destination.

These things would weigh nothing if his wife died. *Died!* The thought lashed him like a whip. Hidden by the night, his voice drowned by the roar of the storm, he cried out in torment and beat the rail with his fists. What to do? Were there capable doctors at Bermuda? Would it avail anything, in the end, if he put back? Might it not be a disastrous mistake?

He knew vaguely that some serious operation would be necessary to save his wife.

The week passed before him, day after day of drifting, while he had hoped for a change—all wasted time now, gone forever. He was a sailor, a man of duty; his training had been to put duty first and sentiment last. He began to think that this was all wrong. Experience, convention, the very creed of an onerous* and sometimes bitter life, were going by the board. What could it possibly matter—success, reputation, savings, life itself? His wife might die!

---

onerous: burdensome

Yet he had kept on; he wanted still to keep on. It *must* be right—he felt it strongly. It was a test, they were trying him again; it was the same old fight of truth, the fight that he had always been in, coming now in a new guise—but harder this time, with a keener stroke, with a deeper thrust. His wife! They had touched him vitally. They were unfair.

"No!" he cried aloud, out of a desperate heart. "I mustn't put back—not yet. I'll fight—like the old bark—a while longer, as long as I can!"

A little later he went below and found his wife still asleep. For a while he stood beside the bunk, watching her pallid* face—thinking. Was he being fair to her? Yes!—the highest fairness—right. He loved her. If he could be sure of help for her at Bermuda there would be no question. But they might be longer, now, in getting to Bermuda, than if they kept on to New York. And she understood.

---

pallid: extremely pale

Once more he took up the watch on deck; he felt that sleep would never touch him again. Clinging to the weather rail he peered to windward as if trying to discern the secrets of the storm. The wind screamed in his ears; a huge wave lifted its white shoulder above him, showing a weird light against the solid blackness of sky and sea. The miles upon miles of waste and angry waters surrounding him, became a vivid entity to his distracted mind. Off there, the land, a long line, not very high, just rising above the sea—a continent, teeming with life, solid ground for the feet of men. Then water, nothing but water, rising and falling, lashed to fury and destruction, black with the shadow of overhanging clouds. Here a ship, a tiny object, lost in the night, struggling alone against the power of the sea. Off there to leeward a small island—a long way off, and very small. Wind, and rain, and despair. God in Heaven! What to do? What to do?

III

In the early morning the storm broke unexpectedly. The wind jumped into the northwest, the vessel headed up, and within an hour the sea had begun to fall. As it grew calmer the seams of the old bark tightened, and they were able to ease up a little on the pumps. They made sail at once; voices rang out, a cheerful activity awoke on the storm-swept deck. The sun broke through the clouds soon after dawn; at eight o'clock Captain Blair got a clear reading for the first time in seven days.

He ran below often during the forenoon* to speak with his wife. The change of weather was like a breath of new life to her. She lay propped up in the bunk, feasting her eyes on the sunlight that streamed through the open window. With something to look forward to, something to take up her mind, the pain was easier to bear; she allowed herself to hope again. If only the ship would stay quiet! It seemed to her that she could not have lived through another day of the storm.

---

forenoon: time between sunrise and noon

At noon she heard her husband come below to work his sight. Ordinarily she had helped him at this duty, looking up logarithms, bending with him above the table while he ticked off the latitude and longitude. Then they would hold a discussion over the day's run; or, perhaps, she would measure with the dividers the remaining distance to port, and speculate as to how much longer they would be.

"Bring in the chart, and show me where we are," she called from the bunk.

He held it upright for her, and pointed out the little circle that marked their position. "Not as bad as I feared," he said. "The Gulf Stream has set us north. I thought we must be in it."

"Then we'll have to beat up, if this wind holds?"

He nodded, proud of her knowledge. It had always been a secret trouble to him that, with all their sailing together, she had not entered more fully into the spirit of the sea-life, or learned to enjoy the side of it that meant such a deep satisfaction to him.

"It *must* hold!" she cried suddenly. "Of course it will hold. A clearing-off wind, after this storm! It ought to blow for weeks."

"Yes, dear," he said. "We're going to get in now." She could not see the old expression in his eyes, the look of a hunted animal.

He bent down to kiss her. She was trying to speak again.

"What is it, dear?"

"Hurry! Oh, hurry!"

A broken cry escaped him. "I'll take the masts out of her! I'll get in some way! My poor girl——"

"I know you will," she said. "And you'll be careful, too."

As the sun went down that afternoon, Captain Blair stopped his pacing and stood by the weather rail for some time, scanning the heavens. The west glowed with a pale yellow light, the sea had grown quite smooth, the bark heeled sharply to a stiff breeze. He gazed at the placid yellow sunset in bitterness of heart. It seemed so perfect, so beautiful; and yet, according to every sign that he knew, it was false and ominous. He hated a Nature that could be guilty of such treachery.

The mate came up beside him, full of excitement at their good luck. "This is something like it, sir!" he exclaimed. "I can almost see the old Statue up the bay."

Captain Blair shook his head. "It won't last!" he said sharply.

"Why, cap'n, there isn't a cloud in the sky!"

"Never mind—I've seen this before. The wind didn't go around the right way; it backed into the nor'west. It has too much northerly in it now. I'll give us one day of clear weather; tomorrow we have a change."

The mate walked away, disappointed; Captain Blair waited alone to see the last of the sun. This was better than the storm, at any rate, and he gave thanks for it; but he had come "on the coast" too many times to build castles in the air. He had an even chance of getting in—that was all.

"I'm glad I didn't put back," he said to himself. "I'm glad I decided before the gale broke. I may get my reward."

That night a wide, brassy ring encircled the moon. Three bright stars twinkled within its circumference. On the following day the northwest wind died out gradually, and a gray film of clouds spread over the sky. A faint breeze sprang up from the eastward, a raw, cold wind, carrying a hint of snow. Still the sea remained smooth. For two days and two nights this strange state of the weather continued. They kept on, heading diagonally in for New York, making a fair course and sailing by dead-reckoning. On the morning of the third day they picked up the edge of soundings with the deep-sea lead, and knew that they were within a hundred miles of port.

IV

The weather that morning looked very threatening. Overhead the haze had grown thicker; the wind moaned in the rigging with an insistent note; the swell running in from the open Atlantic had in it a new life, a menace of latent power. A storm was close at hand.

Captain Blair paced the quarter-deck in agony, as he felt the forces of the elements gathering against him. He weighed his chances over item by item; there were many contingencies* that had to be taken into account, each offering problems and difficulties. Caught by a northeast snowstorm in the angle made by Long Island and the Jersey coast, he could hope for no mercy. A strong ship might possibly be driven to sea again out of that pocket, under a press of canvas; but he would not dare to carry sail too hard on the old bark. Dismasted! The thought made him physically weak. Helpless, drifting, cast ashore! No—if the storm came on he would be obliged, in common caution, to heave her to under shortened sail. Then, suppose she wasn't able to scratch by that snare to leeward, the dread corner of Hatteras? If she didn't weather it, the alternative was to fetch up on a leeshore—to die. He must guard against being drawn too far into the trap. No ship ever made the approaches to New York harbor in a snowstorm.

---

contingencies: possibilities

His only hope of arrival lay in picking up a tug. Often he had met them here, a hundred miles at sea. They were always cruising about, on the lookout for ships. He remembered a time when, with a fair wind and pleasant weather, he had refused a tow until he was abreast the Scotland Lightship. He had saved a few dollars then; now he would sell his soul for the same chance.

Noon passed, and still he headed inshore under shortened sail. How long could he tempt Providence? How long? Another hour would turn the scales; by that time he would *have* to get in, somehow—or lose the ship on the Jersey shore. The storm was making up minute by minute. He searched the horizon for a trail of smoke, for the sails of a cutter. Where were all the towboats? That harbor just beyond the horizon was full of them. Where were the pilot-boats? *Was he to be kept outside, after all?*

In his mind's eye he saw the coasts to leeward and across his bow; they seemed to press in upon him, narrowing their angle, closing on his tracks. Again he went over the courses, figuring the least possible margin of safety. If the gale held in the northeast, and he wore around on the port tack, he ought to slide off between southeast and south-southeast by driving the bark a little. That would open up the leak once more. It would probably open up anyway. But the wind might come on too heavy to allow him to carry even a little sail; worse than this, it might draw in from east-northeast, or from *due east,* around the end of Long Island. They were lost already if it came from due east!

He stopped short, facing the truth. He need hope for no tugboat; he felt in his bones that they would not be permitted to get in. The air thickened to leeward; a section of horizon disappeared behind a white veil. Snow was coming up the wind. Inch by inch the horizon vanished, swallowed up by the approaching terror. In ten minutes the face of the sea would be completely hidden. And still no tug in sight.

"Land ahead!" sang out a voice forward.

Captain Blair whirled, uttering a savage oath. "Fire Island! No use!" He would not look; going to the stern,* he shut his eyes and stood silent for some time.

---

stern: the rear of a ship or boat

He had made up his mind. Night and a snowstorm were upon him; and he had put the old bark into the very jaws of death. Time to finish playing and get to work—time to tear out hope from the heart—time to do what had to be done—time to forget what might have been.

"Wear ship!" His voice rang out sharply above the rising gale. "Mr. Forsyth, lower the spanker down on deck. Get your men on the weather braces. Let her run off a little, there."

Almost in. Captain Blair rested his hands on the stern-rail, and gazed dully at the low sandy coast of Fire Island, a fading line on the northern horizon. Almost in! A few flakes of snow drove past the stern; an opaque cloud crept stealthily toward them on the water. The captain's eyes fell to the wake, watching the old bark gather headway on the port tack. When he looked up, the land had been obliterated. He was not to see it again for many days.

Back into the storm, into the open Atlantic, across the Gulf Stream—back to the old fight—back to the endless exile—back to the reproach of failure, to the anguish and despair in eyes that he loved. "Hurry! Oh, hurry!" she had begged him. Hurry away! Hurry offshore! Drive—drive—drive. Pound—pound—pound. Claw to windward. Race through the gale. Strain—surge. Howl, wind. Laugh, death. Open, seams. Back to the pumps. Back to sea—and almost in.

He entered his wife's room quietly, and took her hand without speaking. For a moment they gazed at each other, a world of pain and love in their eyes.

"I heard," she said.

Something gave way suddenly in his brain; he sank to his knees beside the bunk, sobbing like a child. "I had to do it! I had to do it! I promised to get you in today!"

"Never mind. We'll get in tomorrow."

"No! No! No! Never! Never! We'll never get in!"

"You mustn't say such things."

"I can't stand it! It's too much."

"You must, dear. Be brave—for my sake."

He looked at her, speechless. A great cry tore from the depths of his soul—"Oh-h-h!" "I'm a weak wretch, dear, to break down like this. It's *you* who are suffering, it's *you* who are being brave! You make me ashamed. You are the bravest woman that ever lived. But I love you so much. Sometimes I feel absolutely lost. It's in my mind."

"Poor boy—I know. Don't think of me. I'm feeling better today. Think only of the ship."

He turned away, looking at the blank wall of the room. "I promised to get you in."

"You're doing the best you can. That is enough for me."

Hour after hour he sat in the gloomy cabin, gripping the arms of the chair with both hands, staring straight ahead. The night passed slowly. What was the use of going on deck? They were only driving through the storm—driving away. If anything happened the mate would call him. He could feel the condition of the ship by her plunges; when it got too bad he would go up and take in the reefed upper-top sails.

The mate came to the forward-cabin door, knocked, and stuck in his head. He was covered with ice and snow; two pendants of frozen tobacco juice hung from the ends of his mustache.

"She's leaking again, sir," he said. "Pretty badly. Eighteen inches——"

"Pump, then!"

The door closed; the mate stamped away through the forward-cabin. A squall struck the vessel; she careened wildly, the voices of her hull shrieking aloud under the strain. Captain Blair sat on, motionless, with unwinking eyes. He saw into the future plainly. God was indeed hard on him. Why? Why? Why? What had *he* done?

The wind lulled; and a familiar sound struck his ears, throbbing through the ship like the vibrations of distant machinery. Clangity-clang! Clangity-clang! Clangity-clang!

V

It was on a night two weeks later that the old bark crept past the lights of Atlantic City. The long northeaster had blown her far to sea; but it had cleared off properly at last, coming around to the southward with a short gale that had brought them back a good two hundred miles. The offshore wind that had followed, clear, squally, piercing cold, had yet allowed them to hold their own and keep up under the lee of the land. Now it had blown itself out to a gentle breeze; the sea was as level as a floor. A high peace brooded above the world; out of a guileless sky the serene stars looked down in surprise and curiosity. The old bark crept on, deep, ice-covered, in sore distress. Her ropes were frozen in the runners; her decks were piled with snow. In the great stillness her pumps clanged fiercely, flinging their challenge to an encroaching sea.

Captain Blair watched the line of brilliant lights along the western horizon. They were happy in there; they were laughing, dancing, carousing! They had been at it when he wore ship off Fire Island, two weeks ago. Perhaps they'd enjoyed the snowstorm, glad of any diversion. What did they care? What did they feel? What did they know? When they looked seaward from the boardwalk, admiring the handsome ships, did they suppose that God was marshalling them back and forth on the water for their amusement? The pretty ships! What of the men? Did those parasites ever look beyond their own selfish, thoughtless lives? He cursed them—he hated them.

A rare smell of the land filled his nostrils; even in winter the earth sends out a message to her sons on the sea. He breathed it deeply, letting it sink into his soul. His wife still lived—lingered somewhere between life and death. Would she live through what was yet to come?

He knew that he would get in this time. Nothing could stop him now. The elements had done their worst—he had won. There would be another day or two of calm, pleasant weather; the token of it ran in that crisp, sweet air. As he paced the deck, memories crowded upon him—visions of a certain seaport village, of the faces of men and women long since dead, of simple boyhood scenes; sights of the street there, running up a hill, of the familiar houses, of his house, where his mother now lived alone. Home! Were they to go home again? Then, in a flash, his thoughts leaped forward into the recent gale. He saw the menace of the angry Atlantic, he felt the struggle of the old bark, he heard the pumps pounding above the noise of the storm. The men had sobbed with the cold as they bent to the handles. They were still at it. Clangity-clang! Clangity-clang! Clangity-clang! That sound would haunt him to the grave. But they had weathered the gale at last, they had won—

Would his wife live—even now, even now?

The mate came stumbling aft. "Cap'n! Steamer dead ahead! I see her red and green."

Captain Blair's heart leaped in his breast. Could it be a towboat, so far outside, in the middle of the night? He waited five minutes; the lights were almost upon them, still showing both red and green. A whistle shrieked—the sweetest sound that had ever greeted his ears. It was a towboat, making directly for the bark.

"Stop those pumps!" cried the captain. "It'll never do to let him know that we're leaking."

The tug rounded-to on the bark's weather quarter, with a loud hissing of steam. A faraway hail came across the water.

"Ship ahoy? What ship is that?"

"Bark *Adelaide,* from Pisagua to New York."

"Do you want a tow?"

"How much will you take me in for?"

"One hundred and fifty dollars!"

"Hook onto us!" Captain Blair ground his teeth. "Fifty dollars too much," he said to himself. "It's worth it—I'll pay it myself."

The tug veered closer to the quarter.

"What kind of a passage have you had, Cap'n Blair?"

"Why, hello, Dan Reilly, is that you? Where were all you fellows two weeks ago?"

"Were you off here then?"

A lump of bitterness and misery rose in Captain Blair's throat. *"Was I off here then?"* he shouted furiously. "I've been twenty-five days from Hatteras to New York! My wife is sick. So get us in as quick as God will let you!"

Under the high, clear stars, across the glassy water, the old bark trailed in from sea. Amidships her pumps clanged ceaselessly; ropes lay about the deck in confusion, where they had managed to start the frozen gear and get in the canvas. Aloft a few men worked slowly and painfully, trying to furl the upper sails. In past the twin lightships, in past the winking eye of Navesink—boarded by the pilot—into the mouth of the old ship-channel, in past the Romer bug-light, in past the range-lights on Sandy Hook, in past the blaze of Coney Island—in from sea. The glow of the great city filled the northern sky; the land loomed closer in the darkness; lights multiplied, shifted, approached—the lights of port. Life touched them once more; their ears caught the faint, ghostly murmur of the awakening land. Over the waste astern, the open Atlantic, dawn broke in a cloudless sky.

They saw the city, the towering buildings, the wide sweep of Brooklyn Bridge. They saw the Statue, calm, aloof, indifferent to storms, unmoved at life or death. They saw the land to port and starboard, the hills of Staten Island, the gleaming fields of snow, the houses rising roof on roof, the spires, the forts, the broad harbor, the swift ferries, the bustling tugs. Only the sailor knows the full beauty of the land, the hidden truth. Only the sailor, in from sea.

He sat in the after-cabin, waiting to hear their fate. In the deep silence of the ship resting at anchor, the pumps clanged with a loud, monotonous sound. He gripped the arms of the chair with both hands; his soul shrank before the greatest fear that he had ever known. The door behind him opened and closed. The doctor stepped out into the cabin.

"What chance, doctor? Tell me, say something!"

"I can't tell—I can't be sure. She must be taken to a hospital at once."

"I've kept the towboat alongside. Will you see to the business, doctor? I'll go with you; but you must take entire charge. I don't know much about hospitals. I've been through a hard time, sir."

VI

Late that night Captain Blair came off aboard in a shore boat, and climbed the side ladder. The mate met him at the rail.

"What news, cap'n?" he asked hesitatingly.

"She pulled through, Mr. Forsyth."

"Thank God, sir!"

Captain Blair turned away with tears in his eyes. He could not trust himself to speak.

Down below a dim light burned above the chart-table. He stopped in the center of the cabin, and looked around like a man in a dream. The hour in the hospital stood before him, was burned into his memory for all time. She had been off somewhere, in some horrible place—unconscious, perhaps dying—and nothing for him to do. But he had seen her since, she had known him.

What was it that seemed so strange about the vessel? He found himself listening. Silence. The pumps were quiet! She had stopped leaking.

He went into his wife's room. The bed had been made up freshly; the air of sickness was gone. He wouldn't sleep there—until she came back. Unutterable thoughts besieged him, flashes of pain beyond words. Storm and disappointment and torture and fear. What a life to give a woman! What a life for a man to live! They had won this time—but the cost, the frightful cost.

He saw her face as she lay on the cot in the hospital. He recalled her whisper: "This is your reward!" Black hatred of the world surged in his heart. *Reward!* Yes—but why had it been necessary for them to do such awful penance? What had *they* done?

He looked up at her picture, hanging on the wall of the room. The brave eyes seemed to chide him. If she were here now, what would she say? "You mustn't think such things!" He knelt beside the bunk, stretching his arms full length across the empty bed. "God forgive me!" he cried from a torn heart. "She'll live! She'll live!"

"Storm Fury"

Next, turn the students' attention to the passage from Shakespeare's *Othello*. This selection may prove more difficult than the story for them to analyze. Although the passage is heavily glossed, they may benefit from additional help from a dictionary. Have them identify any words they find that are unfamiliar or used in an unfamiliar context. Then, have them look up the definition of these words and place them in context in the passage.

Once they have mastered the unfamiliar words and syntax, have them identify, one by one, the instances of metaphoric expression and sound repetition that appear in this passage. They should be able to recognize "spoke aloud" *(personification);* "ruffian'd" *(personification [notice the*

Storm Fury

William Shakespeare

One of the most memorable descriptions of the sea in literature is this passage from Shakespeare's Othello *(II.i.1-16). The Venetian outpost of Cyprus is awaiting arrival by sea of its general, Othello, and his wife, Desdemona. A fearsome storm has delayed them. The Venetians are anxious. Notice that the repetition of sound (alliteration, assonance, consonance, rhythm) joins with metaphors of vast scope and force to suggest the immensity of the storm's power.*

Montano	What from the cape can you discern at sea?
1 Gentleman	Nothing at all: it is a high-wrought flood.
	I cannot 'twixt the heaven and the main*
	Descry a sail.
Montano	Methinks* the wind hath spoke aloud at land;
	A fuller blast ne'er shook our battlements.
	If it hath ruffian'd so upon the sea,
	What ribs of oak, when mountains melt on them
	Can hold the mortise?* What shall we hear of this?
2 Gentleman	A segregation* of the Turkish fleet.
	For do but stand upon the foaming shore,
	The chidden billow seems to pelt the clouds;
	The wind-shaked surge, with high and monstrous mane,
	Seems to cast water on the burning Bear*
	And quench the Guards* of th' ever-fixed pole.
	I never did like* molestation view
	On the enchaféd flood.

main: ocean

5 *Methinks:* it seems to me

Can hold the mortise: stay joined to the ship

10 *segregation:* dispersion, scattering

Bear: constellation in Ursa Major

15 *Guards:* two stars in Ursa Minor aligned with the Pole Star

like: such

---

conversion of noun to verb]); "Seems to cast water on the burning Bear" *(extended simile);* "aloud . . . land," "blast . . . battlements," and "mountains . . . melt . . . mortise" *(alliteration);* "ribs . . . mountains . . . mortise" *(consonance);* "burning Bear" *(alliteration);* "blast . . . battlements," "hold . . . mortise," and "foaming shore" *(assonance).* Finally, have the students read the passage aloud, emphasizing the sound play. You may want to ask three students to read, assigning a "role" to each.

Application

Using the words from the following list, have the students write seven sentences, one to illustrate each of the following: metaphor, simile, personification, alliteration, assonance, consonance, and onomatopoeia.

anchor	shipmaster
plank	gun deck
captain	shipmates
reef(s)	harpoon
compass	shipwreck
sail (n. or v.)	man-of-war
dolphin(s)	waves
sailors	mutineers
dory	whale(s)
shark(s)	mutiny
fog	yardarm
ship	octopus
fleet	

Then, have them write either a short dramatic sketch or narrative incorporating one or more of their sentences to create or sustain tension throughout the piece. See **Writing Rubric 2-1: Seven Sentences and a Sketch.**

About the Story and Poem

1. What is one obvious onomatopoetic device Colcord uses to sustain tension in "The Leak"?
2. Find an example of *one* of the following in Colcord's story: assonance, consonance, alliteration.
3. Identify one specific phrase or passage from the story which you felt was especially effective in creating an atmosphere of tension. Give reasons for your choice.
4. Identify two of the metaphoric expressions used in the passage from *Othello*.
5. Identify two instances of sound repetition that appear in the passage from Shakespeare.

 About the Story and Poem

1. *The repetition of the pump's "clangity-clang" is the most obvious. Students may find others.*

2. *Answers will vary but may include assonance— "the pumps drummed"(paragraph 1), "his voice drowned by the roar of the storm, he cried out in torment"(last paragraph on page 33); consonance—"A faint breeze sprang up from the eastward, a raw, cold wind, carrying a hint of snow" (last paragraph on page 35); alliteration—"Clangity-clang! Clangity-clang!""he ought to slide off between southeast and south-southeast"(paragraph 5 on page 36).*

3. *Answers will vary; accept any passage as long as students can give the rationale behind their choice.*

4. *Answers will vary but may include "spoke aloud," "ruffian'd"(personification);"Seems to cast water on the burning Bear"(extended simile).*

5. *Answers will vary but may include "aloud . . . land,""blast . . . battlements,""mountains . . . melt . . . mortise," and "burning Bear"(alliteration);"ribs . . . mountains . . . mortise"(consonance);"blast . . . battlements,""hold . . . mortise," and "foaming shore"(assonance).*

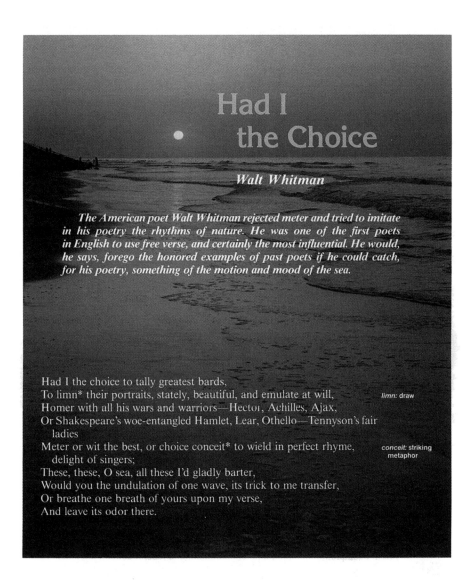

Had I the Choice

Walt Whitman

The American poet Walt Whitman rejected meter and tried to imitate in his poetry the rhythms of nature. He was one of the first poets in English to use free verse, and certainly the most influential. He would, he says, forego the honored examples of past poets if he could catch, for his poetry, something of the motion and mood of the sea.

Had I the choice to tally greatest bards,
To limn* their portraits, stately, beautiful, and emulate at will,   *limn: draw*
Homer with all his wars and warriors—Hector, Achilles, Ajax,
Or Shakespeare's woe-entangled Hamlet, Lear, Othello—Tennyson's fair
   ladies
Meter or wit the best, or choice conceit* to wield in perfect rhyme,   *conceit: striking metaphor*
   delight of singers;
These, these, O sea, all these I'd gladly barter,
Would you the undulation of one wave, its trick to me transfer,
Or breathe one breath of yours upon my verse,
And leave its odor there.

Limn (line 2) is pronounced "lim."

PREPARATION

"Had I the Choice," "The Fruits of Toil"

Overview

Whitman here illustrates in the form of the poem the qualities he is after in his poetry—the free-flowing rhythms of nature, the natural rather than the artificial. He rejects the standard subject matter and form of the dominant poetic tradition. Modern poets have followed him. Duncan, through narrative, also attempts to portray the mood and motion of the sea in the "Fruits of Toil."

DISCUSSION

"Had I the Choice"

Introduction

Read Whitman's poem aloud, noting the allusions to Homeric and Shakespearean heroes. (Such allusions anticipate Unit 4.) The poem places in opposition the artificial and the natural. Homer represents the classical tradition. Greek literature begins with Homer. Hector is the greatest warrior of Troy; Achilles and Ajax are the chief warriors of the Greek armies besieging the city. Hamlet, Lear, and Othello are heroes of three of Shakespeare's four greatest tragedies, the other being Macbeth. "Tennyson's fair ladies" refers to Tennyson's treatment of Arthurian legend in a number of

poems, mainly in his *Idylls of the King* and also *The Princess.* Whitman rejected the entire literary tradition he inherited, both classical and English, in order to write as an American and a modern.

Analysis

The poem consists of one flowing, undulating sentence arranged in free-verse style, in a form suggestive of a wave. It is almost a shaped poem, whose typographical appearance represents its subject. The poem, a prayer to the sea, is a fulfillment of itself. Whitman knew no God but nature and himself as the center of nature. Whitman's philosophy of independent self-expression is not Biblical. His poetry, ironically, would not be as good as it often is had he

Additional activities

After completing the Application section for "The Fruits of Toil" (page 46), have the students write their own hymn. You may wish to do this as a group project, having several students work on the text together. Also, if you have students interested in musical composition, encourage them to write an accompaniment for the text. If they have trouble getting started, you may want to have them use a reference tool like Strong's *Exhaustive Concordance* to look up several Scripture references to the sea. Many hymn writers use Biblical allusions in their work; your students may want to do so as well.

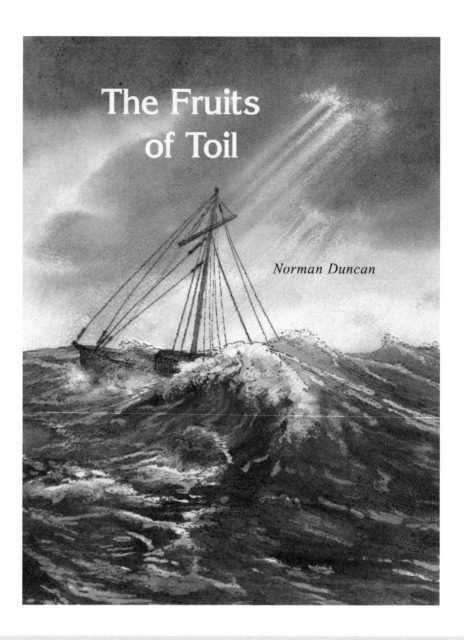

The Fruits of Toil

Norman Duncan

followed his own principles and dispensed with disciplined craftsmanship. Notice, for example, the rise and fall of the poem's lines. Ask the students what this sound pattern might suggest. *(Although the length of lines varies, the stress falls at rather even intervals, giving the impression of the rise and fall of waves upon the sea.)* Have the students state the theme of the poem in their own words. *(Answers to this question will vary. See "About the Poem and Story" question 2, page 53.)*

"The Fruits of Toil"

Like Whitman, Duncan tries to capture the motion and mood of the sea through the use of sound devices and syntax. Read the following description of Solomon and Priscilla aloud: "when he sat on the bench with Priscilla, he looked through the gloaming shadows gathered over the harbour water and hanging between the great rocks, to the golden summer approaching, and dreamed gloriously of the fish he would catch in his trap." Notice the undulating rhythm in this reference, which continues through the next two paragraphs of dialogue. Then begins a description of the sea: "Dusk and the mist touched the hills, and, in the dreamful silence, their glory faded." But notice the next phrase, "the rocks turned black"; the dreamlike mood is interrupted. The single-syllable words coupled with the color imagery produce a bleak, ominous effect. After pointing out this specific example, you may want to have the students come up with other effective uses of sound (e.g., alliteration, onomatopoeia, consonance), syntax (e.g., repetition of certain phrases or arresting rhythm), and color imagery (e.g., descriptions of the sunset, the sea, the ship that comes for Solomon). Have them read each aloud and comment on the effect Duncan creates through these devices.

Next have them reread the closing paragraph of the story, noting the Biblical allusions, and then read Luke 8:22-25. Have them compare and contrast the "might and malignance of the sea" in these two examples. (See "About the Poem and Story" question 4, page 53.)

Finally, discuss the theme of the story by asking questions such as the following: What is the central conflict of the story? *(See highlighted section, page 45.)* What are the major events? How would you describe Solomon? *(grateful, loving, religious, hard-working, indomitable)* How does he view life generally and toil specifically? *(He*

As in the foregoing poem, the author of this selection attempts to recreate for us the motion and mood of the sea. Notice that Duncan uses both sound and syntax to reveal the patience of man and the tamelessness of the sea. Compare, for example, the rhythm of the sentences that describe Solomon's perpetual dreaming with those describing the sea's stubborn refusal to yield its bounty.

Now the wilderness, savage and remote, yields to the strength of men. A generation strips it of tree and rock, a generation tames it and tills it, a generation passes into the evening shadows as into rest in a garden, and thereafter the children of that place possess it in peace and plenty, through succeeding generations, without end, and shall to the end of the world. But the sea is tameless: as it was in the beginning, it is now, and shall ever be—mighty, savage, dread, infinitely treacherous and hateful, yielding only that which is wrested* from it, snarling, raging, snatching lives, spoiling souls of their graces. The tiller of the soil sows in peace, and in a yellow, hazy peace he reaps; he passes his hand over a field, and, lo, in good season he gathers a harvest, for the earth rejoices to serve him. The deep is not thus subdued; the toiler of the sea—the Newfoundlander of the upper shore—is born to conflict, ceaseless and deadly, and, in the dawn of all the days, puts forth anew to wage it, as his father did, and his father's father, and as his children must, and his children's children, to the last of them; nor from day to day can he foresee the issue, nor from season to season foretell the worth of the spoil, which is what chance allows. Thus laboriously, precariously, he slips through life: he follows hope through the toilsome years; and past summers are a black regret and bitterness to him, but summers to come are all rosy with new promise.

---

wrested: obtained by force

Long ago, when young Luke Dart, the Boot Bay trader, was ambitious for Shore patronage, he said to Solomon Stride, of Ragged Harbour, a punt* fisherman: "Solomon, b'y, an you be willin', I'll trust you with twine for a cod-trap. An you trade with me, b'y, I'll trade with you, come good times or bad." Solomon was young and lusty, a mighty youth in bone and seasoned muscle, lunged like a blast furnace, courageous and finely sanguine. Said he: "An you trust me with twine for a trap, skipper, I'll deal fair by you, come good times or bad. I'll pay for un, skipper, with the first fish I cotches." Said Luke Dart: "When I trust, b'y, I trust. You pays for un when you can." It was a compact, so, at the end of the season, Solomon built a cottage under the Man-o'-War, Broad Cove way, and married a maid of the place. In five months of that winter he made the trap, every net of it, leader and all, with his own hands, that he might know that the work was good, to the last knot and splice. In the spring, he put up the stage and the flake, and made the skiff; which done, he waited for a sign of fish. When the tempered days came, he hung the net on the horse, where it could be seen from

views life as hard but always believes a better day is coming. He believes his hard toil will lead to financial profit but is satisfied with the minimal "luxuries" life gives him.) How would you describe Priscilla? *(patient, curious)* What are Priscilla and Solomon's goals? How do Solomon and Priscilla respond to the major events of the story? How does Luke Dart respond to Solomon? *(Luke is repeatedly referred to as honest and as a friend to Solomon. He not only forgives the debt at the story's end but supplies a little money to meet Priscilla's needs.)* What is the resolution of the story? *(See next paragraph.)* What is the significance of the "ship" Solomon sees when he is dying? *(See next paragraph.)* What is the significance of the Biblical allusion of the "seven thunders"? *(The Lord did not permit John to write what the seven thunders uttered in Rev. 10:2-4. This sup-*

ports the story's theme of God's power and man's limitation—we cannot know what the thunders uttered until we are in heaven. Note also the symbolic link between the thunders and the ship that comes for Solomon at the story's end ["seven stars they be, in all," page 51].) In answering these questions, have the students use specific quotations from the story to support their answers.

Following this discussion, ask the students to try stating the theme of the story in one or two sentences. Specific responses will, of course, vary. But in stating the theme some reference should be made to how the story shows man's weakness and God's power. The fury of the sea coupled with the Biblical allusions provides a vivid picture of man's limitations. "They be many things strong men knows nothin' about," Solomon tells Luke Dart. Solomon's response to the major events in the story reinforces the hope available to those who acknowledge the Creator. Solomon is often "defeated" by the sea, but he is never destroyed. He maintains not only an awe of the sea's power but a love for its beauty. The tone of the selection gives us the impression that Solomon understands the sea not only as a concrete entity but also as a symbol of God's omnipotence. Solomon understands that nature declares the glory of God. He sees beyond the material to the spiritual. His "spiritual eyes" are what enable him to see even the bleakest times as bearable. This concept is reinforced in his final "vision" of the ship of souls. When describing his vision to Luke, Solomon concedes, "maybe—she do be invisible t' mortal eyes. . . . maybe 'tis that my eyes

Note repeated references to Solomon's thigh and how it changes through the story. Also note that each time Solomon and Priscilla rest and talk of the future, the night begins to fall. Ask students what this might symbolize. *(Answers may vary; perhaps the relentless difficulty of their lives; perhaps the inevitability of death. At the very least it adds to the story's somber mood.)*

the threshold of the cottage. In the evenings he sat with Priscilla on the bench at the door, and dreamed great dreams, while the red sun went down in the sea, and the shadows crept out of the wilderness.

---

punt: open flat-bottomed boat with square ends, propelled with a pole and used in shallow water

---

"Woman, dear," said this young Solomon Stride, with a slap of his great thigh, " 'twill be a gran' season for fish this year."

"Sure, b'y," said Priscilla, tenderly; " 'twill be a gran' season for fish."

"Ay," Solomon sighed, " 'twill that—this year."

The gloaming shadows gathered over the harbour water, and hung, sullenly, between the great rocks, rising all roundabout.

" 'Tis hardy t' three hundred an' fifty dollars I owes Luke Dart for the twine," mused Solomon.

" 'Tis a hape o' money t' owe," said Priscilla.

"Hut!" growled Solomon, deep in his chest. " 'Tis like nothin'."

" 'Tis not much," said Priscilla, smiling, "when you has a trap."

Dusk and a clammy mist chased the glory from the hills; the rocks turned black, and a wind, black and cold, swept out of the wilderness and ran to sea.

"Us'll pay un all up this year," said Solomon. "Oh," he added, loftily, " 'twill be easy. 'Tis t' be a gran' season!"

"Sure!" said she, echoing his confidence.

Night filled the cloudy heavens overhead. It drove the flush of pink in upon the sun, and, following fast and overwhelmingly, thrust the flaring red and gold over the rim of the sea; and it was dark.

"Us'll pay un for a trap, dear," chuckled Solomon, "an' have enough left over t' buy a——"

"Oh," she cried, with an ecstatic gasp, "a sewin' machane!"

"Iss," he roared. "Sure, girl!"

But, in the beginning of that season, when the first fish ran in for the caplin and the nets were set out, the ice was still hanging off shore, drifting vagrantly with the wind; and there came a gale in the night, springing from the northeast—a great, vicious wind, which gathered the ice in a pack and drove it swiftly in upon the land. Solomon Stride put off in a punt, in a sea tossing and white, to loose the trap from its moorings. Three times, while the pack swept nearer, crunching and horribly groaning, as though lashed to cruel speed by the gale, the wind beat him back through the tickle; and, upon the fourth essay,* when his strength was breaking, the ice ran over the place where the trap was, and chased the punt into the harbour, frothing upon its flank. When, three days thereafter, a west wind carried the ice to sea, Solomon dragged the trap from the bottom. Great holes were bruised in the nets, head rope and span line were ground to pulp, the anchors were lost. Thirty-seven days and nights it took to make the nets whole again, and in that time the great spring run of cod passed by. So, in the next spring, Solomon was deeper in the debt of sympathetic Luke Dart—for the new twine and for the winter's food he had eaten; but, of an evening, when he sat on the bench with Priscilla, he looked through the gloaming shadows gathered over the harbour water and hanging between the great rocks, to the golden summer approaching, and dreamed gloriously of the fish he would catch in his trap.

---

essay: attempt

"Priscilla, dear," said Solomon Stride, slapping his iron thigh, "they be a fine sign o' fish down the coast. 'Twill be a gran' season, I'm thinkin'."

do be opened t' such sights. Maybe she've turned in—for me." Though many of Solomon's earthly crafts had been destroyed, the craft that comes to him at the end of his days is "A gran' craft!" It is one that no earthly sea can destroy.

Application

There are several hymns and poems that use the sea as a metaphor to mirror life's conflicts (e.g., "Master, the Tempest Is Raging"). Have each student choose one such hymn or poem to share with the class. Each should briefly state the message of the selection he has chosen and show a specific imaginative comparison or sound device that was used to reinforce the meaning of the piece.

For further review of Units 1 and 2, see **Appendix H: Units 1 and 2 Review Crossword.**

One quintal equals roughly 220 pounds.

Cream of tartar is a salt used in baking powder; Solomon is saying he has spent nine dollars on this "luxury" over seven years (cf. Solomon's deathbed references to baking powder and sugar, page 52).

"Sure, b'y," Priscilla agreed; " 'twill be a gran' cotch o' fish you'll have this year."

Dusk and the mist touched the hills, and, in the dreamful silence, their glory faded; the rocks turned black, and the wind from the wilderness ruffled the water beyond the flake.

"Us'll pay Luke Dart this year, I tells you," said Solomon, like a boastful boy. "Us'll pay un twice over."

" 'Twill be fine t' have the machane," said she, with shining eyes.

"An' the calico t' use un on," said he.

And so, while the night spread overhead, these two simple folk feasted upon all the sweets of life; and all that they desired they possessed, as fast as fancy could form wishes, just as though the bench were a bit of magic furniture, to bring dreams true—until the night, advancing, thrust the red and gold of the sunset clouds over the rim of the sea, and it was dark.

"Leave us goa in," said Priscilla.

"This year," said Solomon, rising, "I be goain' t' cotch three hundred quintals o' fish. Sure, I be—this year."

" 'Twill be fine," said she.

It chanced in that year that the fish failed utterly; hence, in the winter following, Ragged Harbour fell upon days of distress; and three old women and one old man starved to death—and five children, of whom one was the infant son of Solomon Stride. Neither in that season, nor in any one of the thirteen years coming after, did this man catch three hundred quintals of cod in his trap. In pure might of body—in plentitude and quality of strength—in the full, eager power of brawn—he was great as the men of any time, a towering glory to the whole race, here hidden; but he could not catch three hundred quintals of cod. In spirit—in patience, hope, courage, and the fine will for toil—he was great; but, good season or bad, he could not catch three hundred quintals of cod. He met night, cold, fog, wind, and the fury of waves, in their craft, in their swift assault, in their slow, crushing descent; but all the cod he could wrest from the sea, being given into the hands of Luke Dart, an honest man, yielded only sufficient provision for food and clothing for himself and Priscilla—only enough to keep their bodies warm and still the crying of their stomachs. Thus, while the nets of the trap rotted, and Solomon came near to middle age, the debt swung from seven hundred dollars to seven, and back to seventy-three, which it was on an evening in spring, when he sat with Priscilla on the sunken bench at the door, and dreamed great dreams, as he watched the shadows gather over the harbour water and sullenly hang between the great rocks, rising all roundabout.

"I wonder, b'y," said Priscilla, "if 'twill be a good season—this year."

"Oh, sure!" exclaimed Solomon. "Sure!"

"D'ye think it, b'y?" wistfully.

"Woman," said he, impressively, "us'll cotch a hape o' fish in the trap this year. They be millions o' fish t' the say," he went on excitedly; "millions o' fish t' the say. They be there, woman. 'Tis oan'y for us t' take un out. I be goain' t' wark hard this year."

"You be a great warker, Solomon," said she; "my, but you be!"

Priscilla smiled, and Solomon smiled; and it was as though all the labour and peril of the season were past, and the stage were full to the roof with salt cod. In the happiness of this dream they smiled again, and turned their eyes to the hills, from which the glory of purple and yellow was departing to make way for the misty dusk.

"Skipper Luke Dart says t' me," said Solomon, "that 'tis the luxuries that keeps folk poor."

Priscilla said nothing at all.

"They be nine dollars agin me in seven years for crame o' tartar," said Solomon. "Think o' that!"

"My," said she, "but 'tis a lot! But we be

Note implied passage of time (cf. first mention of the bench, page 46 top).

metaphor (capsize = upset her mind)

used to un now, Solomon, an' we can't get along without un."

"Sure," said he, " 'tis good we're not poor like some folk."

Night drove the flush of pink in upon the sun and followed the red and gold of the horizon over the rim of the sea.

" 'Tis growin' cold," said she.

"Leave us goa in," said he.

In thirty years after that time, Solomon Stride put to sea ten thousand times. Ten thousand times he passed through the tickle rocks to the free, heaving deep for salmon and cod, thereto compelled by the inland waste, which contributes nothing to the sustenance of the men of that coast. Hunger, lurking in the shadows of days to come, inexorably drove him into the chances of the conflict. Perforce he matched himself ten thousand times against the restless might of the sea, immeasurable and unrestrained, surviving the gamut of its moods because he was great in strength, fearlessness, and cunning. He weathered four hundred gales, from the grey gusts which come down between Quid Nunc and the Man-o'-War, leaping upon the fleet, to the summer tempests, swift and black, and the first blizzards of winter. He was wrecked off the Mull, off the Three Poor Sisters, on the Pancake Rock, and again off the Mull. Seven times he was swept to sea by the offshore wind. Eighteen times he was frozen to the seat of his punt; and of these, eight times his feet were frozen, and thrice his festered right hand. All this he suffered, and more, of which I may set down six separate periods of starvation, in which thirty-eight men, women, and children died—all this, with all the toil, cold, despair, loneliness, hunger, peril, and disappointment therein contained. And so he came down to old age—with a bent back, shrunken arms, and filmy eyes—old Solomon Stride, now prey for the young sea. But, of an evening in spring, he sat with Priscilla on the sunken bench at the door, and talked

hopefully of the fish he would catch from his punt.

"Priscilla, dear," said he, rubbing his hand over his weazened thigh, "I be thinkin' us punt fishermen'll have a—"

Priscilla was not attending; she was looking into the shadows above the harbour water, dreaming deeply of a mystery of the Book, which had long puzzled her; so, in silence, Solomon, too, watched the shadows rise and sullenly hang between the great rocks.

"Solomon, b'y," she whispered, "I wonder what the seven thunders uttered."

" 'Tis quare, that—what the seven thunders uttered," said Solomon. "My, woman, but 'tis!"

" 'An' he set his right foot upon the sea,' " she repeated, staring over the greying water to the clouds which flamed gloriously at the edge of the world, " 'an' his left foot on the earth—' "

" 'An' cried with a loud voice,' " said he, whispering in awe, " 'as when a lion roareth; an' when he had cried, *seven thunders uttered their voices.*' "

" 'Seven thunders uttered their voices.' " said she; " 'an' when the seven thunders had uttered their voices, I was about to write, an' I heard a voice from heaven sayin' unto me, Seal up those things which the seven thunders uttered, an' write them not' " (Revelation 10:2-4).

The wind from the wilderness, cold and black, covered the hills with mist; the dusk fell, and the glory faded from the heights.

"Oh, Solomon," she said, clasping her hands, "I wonder what the seven thunders uttered! Think you, b'y, 'twas the kind o' sins that can't be forgiven?"

" 'Tis the seven mysteries!"

"I wonder what they be," said she.

"Sh-h-h, dear," he said, patting her grey head; "thinkin' on they things'll capsize you an you don't look out."

The night had driven all the color from the sky; it had descended upon the red and

gold of the cloudy west, and covered them. It was cold and dark.

"'An' seven thunders uttered their voices,'" she said, dreamily.

"Sh-h-h, dear!" said he. "Leave us goa in."

Twenty-one years longer old Solomon Stride fished out of Ragged Harbour. He put to sea five thousand times more, weathered two hundred more gales, survived five more famines—all in the toil for salmon and cod. He was a punt fisherman again, was old Solomon; for the nets of the trap had rotted, had been renewed six times, strand by strand, and had rotted at last beyond repair. What with the weather he dared not pit his failing strength against, the return of fish to Luke Dart fell off from year to year; but, as Solomon said to Luke, "livin' expenses kep' up wonderful," notwithstanding.

"I be so used t' luxuries," he went on, running his hand through his long grey hair, "that 'twould be hard t' come down t' common livin'. Sure, 'tis sugar I wants t' me tea—not black-strap. 'Tis what I l'arned," he added, proudly, "when I were a trap fisherman."

"'Tis all right, Solomon," said Luke. "Many's the quintal o' fish you traded with me."

"Sure," Solomon chuckled; "'twould take a year t' count un."

In course of time it came to the end of Solomon's last season—those days of it when, as the folk of the coast say, the sea is hungry for lives—and the man was eighty-one years old, and the debt to Luke Dart had crept up to $320.80. The offshore wind, rising suddenly, with a blizzard in its train, caught him alone on the Grappling Hook grounds. He was old, very old—old and feeble and dull: the cold numbed him; the snow blinded him; the wind made sport of the strength of his arms. He was carried out to sea, rowing doggedly, thinking all the time that he was drawing near the harbour tickle; for it did not occur to him

then that the last of eight hundred gales could be too great for him. He was carried out from the sea, where the strength of his youth had been spent, to the Deep, which had been a mystery to him all his days. That night he passed on a pan of ice, where he burned his boat, splinter by splinter, to keep warm. At dawn he lay down to die. The snow ceased, the wind changed; the ice was carried to Ragged Harbour. Eleazar Manuel spied the body of Solomon from the lookout, and put out and brought him in—revived him and took him home to Priscilla. Through the winter the old man doddered about the harbour, dying of consumption. When the tempered days came—the days of balmy sunshine and cold evening winds—he came quickly to the pass of glittering visions, which, for such as die of the lung trouble, come at the end of life.

In the spring, when the *Lucky Star,* three days out from Boot Bay, put into Ragged Harbour to trade for the first catch, old Skipper Luke Dart was aboard, making his last voyage to the Shore; for he was very old, and longed once more to see the rocks of all that coast before he made ready to die. When he came ashore, Eleazar Manuel told him that Solomon Stride lay dying at home; so the skipper went to the cottage under the Man-o'-War to say good-bye to his old customer and friend—and there found him, propped up in bed, staring at the sea.

"Skipper Luke," Solomon quavered, in deep excitement, "be you just come in, b'y?"

"Iss—but an hour gone."

"What be the big craft hangin' off shoare? Eh—what be she, b'y?"

There had been no craft in sight when the *Lucky Star* beat in. "Were she a fore-an'-after, Solomon?" said Luke, evasively.

"Sure, noa, b'y!" cried Solomon. "She were a square-rigged craft, with all sail set—a great, gran' craft—a quare craft, b'y—like she were made o' glass, canvas an' hull an' all; an' she had shinin' ropes, an' she were shinin' all over. Sure, they be a star t' the tip o' her bowsprit, b'y, an' a star t' the peak o' her mainmast— seven stars they be, in all. Oh, she were a gran' sight!"

"Hem-m!" said Luke, stroking his beard. "She've not come in yet."

"A gran' craft!" said Solomon.

" 'Tis accordin'," said Luke, "t' whether you be sot on oak bottoms or glass ones."

"She were bound down north t' the Labrador," Solomon went on quickly, "an' when she made the Grapplin' Hook grounds she come about an' headed for the tickle, with her sails squared. Sure she ran right over the Pancake, b'y, like he weren't there at all, an'— How's the wind, b'y?"

"Dead off shore from the tickle."

Solomon stared at Luke. "She were comin' straight in against the wind," he said, hoarsely. "Maybe, skipper," he went on, with a little laugh, "she do be the ship for souls. They be many things strong men knows nothin' about. What think you?"

"Ay—maybe; maybe she be."

"Maybe—maybe—she do be invisible t' mortal eyes. Maybe, skipper, you hasn't seed her; maybe 'tis that my eyes do be opened t' such sights. Maybe she've turned in—for me."

The men turned their faces to the window again, and gazed long and intently at the sea, which a storm cloud had turned black. Solomon dozed for a moment, and when he awoke, Luke Dart was still staring dreamily out to sea.

"Skipper Luke," said Solomon, with a smile as of one in an enviable situation, " 'tis fine t' have nothin' agin you on the books when you comes t' die."

"Sure, b'y," said Luke, hesitating not at all, though he knew to a cent what was on the books against Solomon's name, " 'tis fine t' be free o' debt."

"Ah," said Solomon, the smile broadening

gloriously, " 'tis fine, I tells you! 'Twas the three hundred quintal I cotched last season that paid un all up. 'Twas a gran' cotch—last year. Ah," he sighed, " 'twas a gran' cotch o' fish."

"Iss—you be free o' debt now, b'y."

"What be the balance t' my credit, skipper? Sure I forget."

"Hem-m," the skipper coughed, pausing to form a guess which might be within Solomon's dream; then he ventured: "Fifty dollars?"

"Iss," said Solomon, "fifty an' moare, skipper. Sure, you has forgot the eighty cents."

"Fifty-eighty," said the skipper, positively. " 'Tis that. I call un t' mind now. 'Tis fifty-eighty—iss, sure. Did you get a receipt for un, Solomon?"

"I doan't mind me now."

"Um-m-m—well," said the skipper, "I'll send un t' the woman the night—an order on the *Lucky Star*."

"Fifty-eighty for the woman!" said Solomon.

" 'Twill kape her off the Gov'ment for three years, an she be savin.' 'Tis fine—that!"

When the skipper had gone, Priscilla crept in, and sat at the head of the bed, holding Solomon's hand; and they were silent for a long time, while the evening approached.

"I be goain' t' die the night, dear," said Solomon at last.

"Iss, b'y," she answered; "you be goain' t' die."

Solomon was feverish now; and, thereafter, when he talked, his utterance was thick and fast.

" 'Tis not hard," said Solomon. "Sh-h-h," he whispered, as though about to impart a secret. "The ship that's hangin' off shoare, waitin' for me soul, do be a fine craft—with shinin' canvas an' ropes. Sh-h! She do be 'tother side o' Mad Mull now—waitin'."

Priscilla trembled, for Solomon had come to the time of visions—when the words of the dying are the words of prophets, and contain

Solomon's words here may have a double meaning—not only physical but also spiritual. Ask students whether they think Solomon is lying to Luke here or is confused because his mind is failing. *(Based on Solomon's character throughout the rest of the story, it is doubtful that he is lying here—he believes he is a creditor to Luke, not a debtor.)* Discuss with students the possibility that Solomon's name is an allusion (see Unit 4, page 92, for definition) to King Solomon. How does he display wisdom in the story?

Note how Solomon wisely makes provision for Priscilla after his death. ("'Twill kape her off the Gov'ment" is a reference to Priscilla's having to receive government monies to make ends meet.)

Note the way in which Solomon's body is compared metaphorically to a ship. Note how Death and the sea are personified. Also note the fine simile comparing the sea to "a lusty youth" in contrast to Solomon. See highlighted section on page 53, where this image of the ocean's remaining a strong youth while men age and die is continued.

revelations. What of the utterings of the seven thunders?

"Sure the Lard he've blessed us, Priscilla," said Solomon, rational again. "Goodness an' marcy has followed us all the days o' our lives. Our cup runneth over."

"Praise the Lard," said Priscilla.

"Sure," Solomon went on, smiling like a little child, "we've had but eleven famines, an' we've had the means o' grace pretty reg'lar, which is what they hasn't t' Round 'Arbour. We've had one little baby for a little while. Iss—one de-ear little baby, Priscilla; an' there's them that's had none o' their own, at all. Sure we've had enough t' eat when they wasn't a famine—an' bakin' powder, an' raisins, an' all they things, an' sugar, an' rale good tea. An' you had a merino dress, an' I had a suit o' rale tweed—come straight from England. We hasn't seed a railroad train, dear, but we've seed a steamer, an' we've heard tell o' the quare things they be t' St. Johns. Ah, the Lard he've favored us above our deserts. He've been good t' us, Priscilla. But, oh, you hasn't had the sewin' machane, an' you hasn't had the peach-stone t' plant in the garden. 'Tis my fault, dear—'tis not the Lard's. I should 'a' got you the peach-stone from St. Johns, you did want un so much—oh, so much! 'Tis that I be sorry for, now, dear; but 'tis all over, an' I can't help it. It wouldn't 'a' growed anyway, I know it wouldn't; but you thought it would, an' I wisht I'd got un for you."

" 'Tis nothin', Solomon," she sobbed. "Sure, I was joakin' all the time. 'Twouldn't 'a' growed."

"Ah," he cried, radiant, "was you joakin'?"

"Sure," she said.

"We've not been poor, Priscilla," said he, continuing, "an' they be many folk that's poor. I be past me labor now," he went on, talking with rising effort, for it was at the sinking of the sun, "an' 'tis time for me t' die. 'Tis time—for I be past me labor."

Priscilla held his hand a long time after that—a long, silent time, in which the soul of the man struggled to release itself, until it was held but by a thread.

"Solomon!"

The old man seemed not to hear.

"Solomon, b'y!" she cried.

"Iss?" faintly.

She leaned over him to whisper in his ear, "Does you see the gates o' heaven?" she said. "Oh, does you?"

"Sure, dear; heaven do be—"

Solomon had not strength enough to complete the sentence.

"B'y! B'y!"

He opened his eyes and turned them to her face. There was the gleam of a tender smile in them.

"The seven thunders," she said. "The utterin's of the seven thunders—what was they, b'y?"

" 'An' the seven thunders uttered their voices,' " he mumbled, " 'an'—' "

She waited, rigid, listening, to hear the rest; but no words came to her ears.

"Does you hear me, b'y?" she said.

" 'An' seven—thunders—uttered their voices,' " he gasped, " 'an' the seven thunders—said—said—' "

The light failed; all the light and golden glory went out of the sky, for the first cloud of a tempest had curtained the sun.

" 'An' said—' " she prompted.

" 'An' uttered—an' said—an' said—' "

"Oh, what?" she moaned.

Now, in that night, when the body of old Solomon Stride, a worn-out hulk, aged and wrecked in the toil of the deep, fell into the hands of Death, the sea, like a lusty youth, raged furiously in those parts. The ribs of many schooners, slimy and rotten, and the white bones of men in the offshore depths, know of its strength in that hour—of its black, hard wrath, in gust and wave and breaker. Eternal in might and malignance is the sea! It groweth not old with the men who toil from its coasts. Generation upon the heels of generation, infinitely arising, go forth in hope against it, continuing for a space, and returning spent to the dust. They age and crumble and vanish, each in its turn, and the wretchedness of the first is the wretchedness of the last. Ay, the sea has measured the strength of the dust in old graves, and, in this day, contends with the sons of dust, whose sons will follow to the fight for an hundred generations, and thereafter, until harvests may be gathered from rocks. As it is written, the life of a man is a shadow, swiftly passing, and the days of his strength are less; but the sea shall endure in the might of youth to the wreck of the world.

About the Poem and Story

1. What does the rise and fall of the poem's lines suggest?
2. State the theme of the poem in your own words.
3. Give at least two examples of Duncan's use of alliteration.
4. Reread the closing paragraph of the story; next, read Luke 8:22-25. Compare and contrast the "might and malignance of the sea" in these two examples.
5. State the theme of the story in your own words.

Note the Bible allusions with which the story concludes: The life of man is like a shadow—Ps. 102:11; 144:4; Eccles. 6:12. The sea's enduring "to the wreck of the world"—Rev. 21:1 ("the first heaven and the first earth were passed away; and there was no more sea"). How is the story's ending with a reference to Revelation appropriate? *(Priscilla's curiosity about the seven thunders is based on the Book of Revelation. The seven stars Solomon sees on the ship could be a reference to Revelation 1:16.)*

About the Author

Norman Duncan (1871-1916) was born in Canada and attended the University of Toronto. After two years with the New York *Bulletin,* he wrote for the New York *Evening Post* and published his first fiction piece. Duncan spent his summers as a traveling correspondent for such prestigious magazines as *McClure's* and *Harper's* but returned to the States during the school year to fulfill his duties as an English professor.

While serving as correspondent, Duncan visited many picturesque places, among them the Grand Banks region, scene of Kipling's *Captains Courageous.* The rugged life of the people of Newfoundland inspired many of Duncan's popular sea stories. His adventure-filled novels often take the Labrador coast for their setting. One of the best of these books, *Dr. Luke of the Labrador,* recounts the unselfish work of a doctor who tirelessly overcomes various obstacles to care for his patients. Most of Duncan's works, including his exciting *Billy Topsail* stories for boys, teach strong moral values such as bravery, hard work, and generosity of heart.

About the Poem and Story

1. *The poem is one flowing, undulating sentence arranged in free verse, suggesting the motion of a wave.*

2. *Answers may vary but should include that the speaker would forgo the honored examples of past poets if he could catch, for his poetry, something of the motion and mood of the sea.*

3. *Answers may vary; one example from near the end of page 46 would be "he looked through the gloaming shadows gathered over the harbour water and hanging between the great rocks, to the golden summer approaching, and dreamed gloriously of the fish he would catch in his trap."*

4. *Duncan's closing paragraph is a gripping account of the apparently eternal "might and malignance" of the sea. The account in Luke, of Christ's calming of the stormy sea, reminds the Christian that the Lord is in control of everything, even the seemingly untamable sea.*

5. *Answers may vary but should include some reference to the story's showing man's weakness and God's power. The fury of the sea coupled with the Biblical allusions provides a vivid picture of man's limitations.*

UNIT THREE

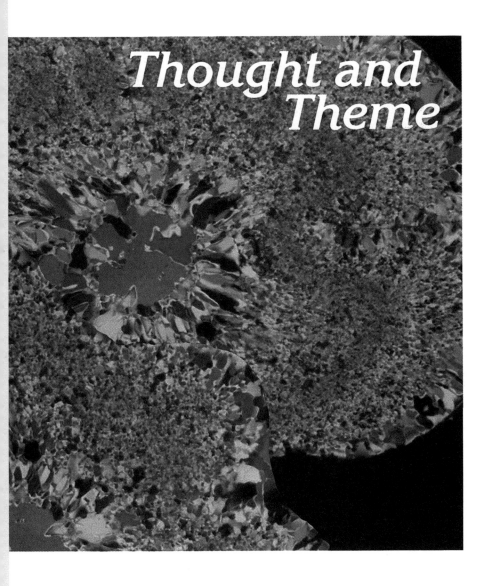

Thought and
Theme

FURTHER HELPS

Additional activities

Journal entry idea

Have the students recount an experience from which they learned a valuable lesson. This lesson would be the theme or central idea they wish to convey. Encourage them to use contrast, repetition, and parallels that reinforce the point they are trying to make. Perhaps their intended audience could be elementary-age children. Stories told on that level often incorporate easily recognizable contrast, repetition, and parallelism.

We usually do not think of preaching as poetic or of poetry as very important in preaching. But the great preachers of the Old Testament—the prophets—often spoke to the people in poetry. Their poetry, like the Psalms, uses imaginative comparison, grammatical repetition, and artful patterns of thought. All of these occur in Jeremiah's message on the sign of the unmarried prophet (Jer. 16—17:18). Verses 5-6 of chapter 17, for example, compare the misery of the man who trusts in himself and in other men to the desolation of the desert shrub. Verses 7-8 compare the blessedness of the man who trusts in God to the prosperity of a tree planted by a stream that never fails in drought.

> Thus saith the Lord:
> Cursed be the man that trusteth in man,
> and maketh flesh his arm,
> and whose heart departeth from the Lord. (v. 5)
>
> For he shall be like the heath in the desert,
> and shall not see when good cometh;
> but shall inhabit the parched places in the
>   wilderness,
> in a salt land and not inhabited. (v. 6)
>
> Blessed is the man that trusteth in the Lord,
> and whose hope the Lord is. (v. 7)
>
> For he shall be as a tree planted by the
>   waters,
> and that spreadeth out her roots by the
>   river,
> and shall not see when heat cometh,
> but her leaf shall be green;
> and shall not be careful in the year of
>   drought,
> neither shall cease from yielding fruit. (v. 8)

Each pair of verses begins with a proclamation (verses 5 and 7) and ends with an explanation (verses 6 and 8). The proclamations contrast: the first is a curse, the second a blessing. The explanations also contrast: the ungodly man will not know when good comes; the godly man will not know when evil comes.

The verses themselves also show strict organization. Verse 8, for example, divides into three pairs of ideas. In the first pair, the godly man is like a tree that (a) has been planted by a river (the action of another), and (b) spreads out its roots by the river (its own action). The second and third pairs give the consequence. In the second pair it is said that the tree (a) will not suffer from heat but (b) will remain green. In the third pair, the thought parallels but also intensifies that of the second: the tree (a) will not need to conserve moisture anxiously during drought but (b) will continue bearing fruit. A season of heat is less specific than a year of drought, and leaf-bearing is less significant than fruit-bearing.

PREPARATION

Thought and Theme Introduction

Overview

This essay completes the discussion of the fundamental elements of poetic writing presented in Part I and expanded in Units 1 and 2. We here consider the patterning of thought units in a work and the repetition of an idea as a theme. This is one of the most important units in the book for improving a student's reading and writing skills.

Potential problems

The discussion of Jeremiah 17:5-8 and Jonah includes detailed analysis. Be sure to go through it in class with the students so that they will not get bogged down.

DISCUSSION

Introduction

Point out to the students that parallelism, whether of syntax or of larger organizational units, is useful for emphasizing contrasts. Draw their attention, for example, to Matthew 6:19-20.

Analysis

Read the introduction aloud in class. Explain to the students that sameness with significant difference, repetition with meaningful variation, is also an important aesthetic principle. The passages from Jeremiah and Jonah both exhibit this feature, known as antithetical parallelism. It is functional for contrasting the results of obedience and disobedience, wisdom and folly. It also gives these sections of the Bible a pleasing aesthetic shape.

Parallelism with variation is also a common way to link the end of a work with its beginning. Notice, for example, how some elements of Genesis 1-3 reappear in Revelation 20—22 (see *Christian Education: Its Mandate and Mission*, Greenville, S.C.: Bob Jones University Press, 1992). After discussing Jeremiah 17:5-8, have the students analyze the organization and imagery of Psalm 1.

Resource

Ronald A. Horton, *Christian Education: Its Mandate and Mission* (Greenville, S.C.: Bob Jones University Press, 1992).

Symmetry also appears in Biblical prose narrative. The story of the prophet Jonah divides into halves, introduced by parallel passages.

> Now the word of the Lord came unto Jonah the son of Amittai, saying, Arise, go to Nineveh, that great city, and cry against it; for their wickedness is come up before me.
> But Jonah rose up to flee unto Tarshish from the presence of the Lord. . . . (1:1-3)

> And the word of the Lord came unto Jonah the second time, saying, Arise, go unto Nineveh, that great city, and preach unto it the preaching that I bid thee.
> So Jonah arose, and went unto Nineveh, according to the word of the Lord. (3:1-3)

The similar wording of God's two commands to Jonah points up the difference in what follows. Jonah disobeys the voice of God the first time, but obeys the second time. And the consequences of his disobedience are different from the consequences of his obedience.

The parallelism just noted between the beginnings of the first half (chapters 1-2) and the second (chapters 3-4) is fairly obvious. The parallelism of what follows is less noticeable. We can visualize it in this way.

	Part I	Part II
The call of God	warning of Nineveh	warning of Nineveh
Jonah's response (1)	flight to Tarshish	journey to Nineveh
God's response (1)	judgment of Jonah	salvation (spiritual and physical) of Nineveh
Jonah's response (2)	repentance	indignation
God's response (2)	salvation (physical) of Jonah	persuasion of Jonah

Biblical symmetry exists therefore in both large and small units—in books and chapters and in verses and parts of verses. Is this symmetry useful or is it simply for the sake of beauty? Notice that the parallelism in both the passage from Jeremiah and the book of Jonah sharpens the contrast between God's way and man's way. Obedience to God brings blessing, to the individual and to others served by him. Disobedience to God brings blight to an individual, to a city, and even to a great nation.

What we have found in these Biblical examples is characteristic of all artful writing: an arrangement of the thought units into a system. Seeing the structural units of a work is often necessary to discovering its main point, or **theme.** In the hymn "Come, Thou Almighty King," both plan and theme are obvious. Three stanzas are devoted to the three Persons of the Trinity and then a concluding stanza to "the great One in Three." The theme is the goodness and greatness of God. Most of the following selections are organized less obviously. As you read, look for their structure and theme.

Application

Have the students choose one of the stories from Units 1 or 2 or some other short story they have especially enjoyed. (This activity can be done as either an individual or a group project.) Have them jot down how the story was organized. For example, was it organized chronologically or perhaps spatially (what happened in the house versus what happened in the barn)? Then have them tell why they think the author chose that organization. You may also wish to discuss with them other ways the author could have organized the piece. Have them evaluate whether another organization would have been more or less effective in conveying the story's theme. Be sure that they give a rationale for their response.

OBJECTIVES

The students will be able to

- Analyze and discuss the design and arrangement in a work.
- Discuss the precedence of work and duty over rest and pleasure.
- Write an essay demonstrating that inward character, rather than outward environment, is responsible for the quality of human life.

i.e., gray snow-clouds

cosmetics imagery

FURTHER HELPS

Additional activities

Choose from the activities below after your students have read all three poems ("It Sifts from Leaden Sieves," "Snow-Bound," and "Winter").

1. Whittier alludes to Aladdin's wondrous cave (lines 76-79). Have a student look up this tale from *The Arabian Nights* and tell the class about Aladdin's cave.

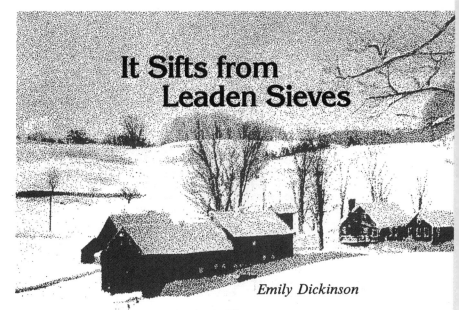

It Sifts from Leaden Sieves

Emily Dickinson

To see thought units of a poem, especially a short one, we should pay close attention to the sentence structure. The following poem uses a series of statements with the same grammatical subject. "It" powders, fills in, smoothes, wraps, veils, and makes ruffles. The descriptive details do not follow a spatial order natural to the scene description. That is, they do not follow the order of far to near, up to down, left to right, inside to outside, or vice versa. The order of details is determined by a metaphor that extends throughout the poem. The poem personifies "It" as a skilled cosmetician and seamstress beautifying an aging woman.

It sifts from leaden sieves,
It powders all the wood.
It fills with alabaster wool
The wrinkles of the road.

It makes an even face   5
Of mountain and of plain—
Unbroken forehead from the east
Unto the east again.

PREPARATION

"It Sifts from Leaden Sieves,"
"Snow-Bound," "Winter"

Overview

The first poem is a good place for students to begin in their study of organization. The structure is not logical but chronological. The snow is a skilled cosmetician-dressmaker, preparing a challenging specimen to be admired by the public. The specimen is the landscape, the world before the poet's eyes.

Whittier's well-loved autobiographical poem "Snow-Bound" exhibits an organization based on contrasts—alternating repetitions. Also its progression from work to rest is an important principle of life (cf. John 9:4).

The last poem is a song written for a play. It was not intended to be a profound statement on human life or a subtle and intricately designed vehicle of meaning. It can therefore be overanalyzed. There are some simple patterns in it, however. Also, it raises some interesting questions about the effect of environment on life.

DISCUSSION

"It Sifts from Leaden Sieves"

Introduction

Read Dickinson's poem aloud. Then ask the students to identify "It" *(snow)* and the aging woman *(the landscape)*. Have them explain the metaphors in light of this basic imaginative

comparison. What other elements of nature are commonly personified? You may wish to review with the students the references to personifications of nature in the following works from this text: "Dawn in the Forest," "A Prompt, Executive Bird," "All Day I Hear," "Winter Ocean," "The Leak," "Storm Fury," and "The Fruits of Toil."

Analysis

In this riddle poem a number of separate metaphors combine to support the basic imaginative comparison. "It," "alabaster wool," "fleeces," and "celestial veil" represent the snow; "leaden sieves," the clouds (you may need to define "sieves" for some students); "wrinkles," ruts; "even face" and "unbroken forehead," snow-smoothed terrain; "summer's empty

It reaches to the fence,
It wraps it rail by rail   10
Till it is lost in fleeces;
It deals celestial veil

To stump and stack and stem—
A summer's empty room—
Acres of joints where harvests were,   15
Recordless,* but for them.

Recordless:
unrecorded

It ruffles wrists of posts
As ankles of a queen,
Then stills its artisans* like ghosts
Denying they have been.   20

artisans: workers

Discuss with students the significance of the last two lines on both a literal level (once the snow has fallen, the way in which it got there seems a mystery) and the symbolic (perhaps a reference to the vanity of an old woman who denies she is wearing makeup).

2. Share other poems about snow with your class. One such example is "The Snow-Storm" by Emerson. Have them bring any of their favorites to class.

Announced by all the trumpets of the sky,
Arrives the snow; and, driving o'er the
    fields,
Seems nowhere to alight; the whited air
Hides hills and woods, the river and the
    heaven,
And veils the farm-house at the garden's
    end.
The sled and traveller stopped, the
    courier's feet
Delayed, all friends shut out, the house-
    mates sit
Around the radiant fireplace, enclosed
In a tumultuous privacy of storm.

3. Whittier called his poem "Snow-Bound" an *idyll* (pronounced like "idle"). Have a student look up the dictionary definition of *idyll* and tell the class whether Whittier's poem fits the definition. Why or why not? *(Merriam-Webster's Collegiate Dictionary, 10th ed., defines* idyll *as "a simple descriptive work in poetry or prose that deals with rustic life or pastoral scenes or suggests a mood of peace and contentment." "Snow-Bound" fits the description well.)*

room," the harvested fields; "wrists," indentations on a lathe-turned post; and "artisans" (helpers), wind, cold, and other climatic forces. Notice too that verbs as well as nouns can be metaphoric: "sifts," "powders," "wraps," and "ruffles."

The thought units of the poem are the actions of the snow on the landscape, the aging woman. The order of the snow's activities is that which a beautician-seamstress would follow: first the makeup, then the clothes. The order is one of time sequence. It is determined by the imaginative side of the metaphor (the work of a beautician-seamstress) rather than the subject side (the actual process of the snowfall).

After reading the poem, elicit from the students that yes, this is a major theme of the poem. They may note others.

Discuss with students—what do these lines mean? *(The speaker and his family are able to recognize in the weather signs [a circle around the sun, its faint light] an "ominous prophecy" of the coming storm.)*

metaphors

4. Have one or more students make a collage or bulletin board of all the different images depicted in the poem "Snow-Bound" (e.g., farm life, farm animals, snowscape, indoor and outdoor situations).

Journal entry idea
Have the students write a seasonal poem, taking special care to effectively organize the poem (according to time, place, or logic).

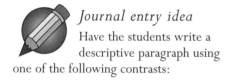

Journal entry idea
Have the students write a descriptive paragraph using one of the following contrasts:

Snow-Bound

John Greenleaf Whittier

Whittier's famous description of a New England snowstorm follows chronological order—by days and nights. It shows the effects of the storm on the landscape and on human activity. The chores are first preparatory, then remedial. Both before and after the storm everyone works. When the work is done, all enjoy the security and comfort resulting from their labors. Even the animals—those in the barn and those around the hearth—seem pleased. Outdoor scenes contrast with indoor. Nature's activity prompts man's. Work precedes pleasure. Could this be the theme?

The sun that brief December day
Rose cheerless over hills of gray,
And, darkly circled, gave at noon
A sadder light than waning moon.
Slow tracing down the thickening sky   5
Its mute and ominous prophecy,
A portent seeming less than threat,
It sank from sight before it set.
A chill no coat, however stout,
Of homespun stuff could quite shut out,   10
A hard, dull bitterness of cold,
That checked, mid-vein, the circling race
Of life-blood in the sharpened face,
The coming of the snowstorm told.
The wind blew east; we heard the roar   15
Of Ocean on his wintry shore,
And felt the strong pulse throbbing there
Beat with low rhythm our inland air.
Meanwhile we did our nightly chores,
Brought in the wood from out of doors,   20
Littered the stalls, and from the mows,*
Raked down the herd's-grass* for the cows:
Heard the horse whinnying for his corn;
And, sharply clashing horn on horn,
Impatient down the stanchion rows*   25
The cattle shake their walnut bows,*
While, peering from his early perch
Upon the scaffold's pole of birch
The cock his crested helmet bent
And down his querulous* challenge sent.   30

mows: storage places for hay or grain
herd's-grass: timothy hay or redtop

rows: posts used for controlling cattle
bows: collars attached to the stanchions

querulous: irritable, complaining

"Snow-Bound"

Draw the students' attention to the title of the poem. What meanings does it have in the light of the poem? Point out that the narrative seems to stress what the storm has been unable to do to the human spirit. These industrious, resourceful folk do not seem altogether "bound" in by the storm.

Several long, inverted or convoluted sentences may be difficult for the students (e.g., in line 14 "The coming of the snowstorm" is the direct object of the verb "told"). If possible, have the students listen to a recording of the poem before starting the discussion. If you cannot procure a recording, read the poem aloud.

As the headnote indicates, "Snow-Bound" is a clearly structured poetic narrative. Like Dickinson's "It Sifts from Leaden Sieves," it is organized by time sequence. But here, the chronology pertains to the storm activity, not to an imaginative vehicle portraying it (the actions of Dickinson's cosmetician-seamstress). The excerpt includes the activities of two days, the storm's action producing man's. The narrative takes us from daytime scenes (the approach of the storm) to evening (the nightly chores—gathering firewood, provisioning the animals in the barn) to daytime (the splendor of the next morning, the digging of a path to the barn and tending of the animals) to evening (the pleasures of a blazing hearth). The description alternates between natural and domestic, outdoor and indoor (if we may consider the barn do-

mestic and indoor). Notice that work precedes rest; strenuous effort precedes pleasure. This is a theme.

Call attention to the frequent metaphoric expressions—e.g., "blue walls of the firmament," "the clothes-line posts / Looked in like tall and sheeted ghosts," "The bridle-post an old man sat," "horned patriarch," "The sun, a snow-blown traveller," "The great throat of the chimney laughed." Point out the parallelism (repetition of sound and syntax) in the last four lines, as well as elsewhere.

Unwarmed by any sunset light
The gray day darkened into night,
A night made hoary with the swarm
And whirl-dance of the blinding storm,
As zigzag, wavering to and fro   35
Crossed and recrossed the winged snow:
And ere the early bedtime came
The white drift piled the window-frame,
And through the glass the clothes-line posts
Looked in like tall and sheeted ghosts.   40

So all night long the storm roared on:
The morning broke without a sun;
In tiny spherule* traced with lines   *spherule:* miniature
Of Nature's geometric signs,   sphere
In starry flake, and pellicle,*   45   *pellicle:* small pellet
All day the hoary meteor fell;
And, when the second morning shone,
We looked upon a world unknown,
On nothing we could call our own.
Around the glistening wonder bent   50
The blue walls of the firmament,
No cloud above, no earth below,—
A universe of sky and snow!
The old familiar sights of ours
Took marvellous shapes; strange domes and towers 55
Rose up where sty or corncrib stood,
Or garden-wall, or belt of wood;
A smooth white mound the brush-pile showed,
A fenceless drift that once was road;
The bridle-post an old man sat*   60   *an old man sat:* sat
With loose-flung coat and high cocked hat;   like an old man
The well-curb had a Chinese roof;
And even the long sweep,* high aloof,   *long sweep:* pole on a
In its slant splendor, seemed to tell   pivot with a bucket
Of Pisa's leaning miracle.*   65   at one end to raise
A prompt, decisive man, no breath   water from a well
Our father wasted: "Boys, a path!"   *Pisa's leaning miracle:*
Well pleased, (for when did farmer boy   Italy's famed leaning
Count such a summons less than joy?)   tower; the baptistry
Our buskins* on our feet we drew;   70   of the cathedral of
With mittened hands, and caps drawn low,   Pisa
To guard our necks and ears from snow,   *buskins:* leather boots
We cut the solid whiteness through.

first night

personification

simile

second day

metaphors

metaphor, allusion (See Unit 4.)

the beauty/danger of a snowstorm
the merry/melancholy mood of the rain
the frightening/soothing effect of the
    wind
the weariness/warmth of the sun

Resources

Whitman Bennett, *Whittier, Bard of Freedom* (New York: Kennikat Press, 1972).

Chauncey J. Hawkins, *The Mind of Whittier: A Study of Whittier's Fundamental Religious Ideas* (New York: Haskell House Publishers, 1973).

John B. Pickard, *John Greenleaf Whittier: An Introduction and Interpretation* (New York: Barnes & Noble, 1961).

Edward Wagenknecht, *John Greenleaf Whittier: A Portrait in Paradox* (New York: Oxford University Press, 1967).

allusion (See Unit 4.)

metaphors

simile, allusion

personification

And, where the drift was deepest, made
A tunnel walled and overlaid   75
With dazzling crystal: we had read
Of rare Aladdin's wondrous cave,*
And to our own his name we gave,
With many a wish the luck were ours
To test his lamp's supernal* powers.   80
We reached the barn with merry din,
And roused the prisoned brutes within.
The old horse thrust his long head out,
And grave with wonder gazed about;
The cock his lusty* greeting said,   85
And forth his speckled harem led;
The oxen lashed their tails, and hooked,*
And mild reproach of hunger looked;
The horned patriarch of the sheep,
Like Egypt's Amun* roused from sleep,   90
Shook his sage head with gesture mute,
And emphasized with stamp of foot.
All day the gusty north wind bore
The loosening drift its breath before;
Low circling round its southern zone,   95
The sun through dazzling snow-mist shone.
No church bell lent its Christian tone
To the savage air, no social smoke
Curled over woods of snow-hung oak.
A solitude made more intense   100
By dreary-voicéd elements,
The shrieking of the mindless wind,
The moaning tree-boughs swaying blind,
And on the glass the unmeaning beat
Of ghostly finger tips of sleet.   105
Beyond the circle of our hearth
No welcome sound of toil or mirth
Unbound the spell, and testified
Of human life and thought outside.
We minded* that the sharpest ear   110
The buried brooklet could not hear,
The music of whose liquid lip
Had been to us companionship,
And, in our lonely life, had grown
To have an almost human tone.   115

Aladdin's wondrous cave: from *Arabian Nights;* a secret cave wherein was hidden vast treasure

supernal: heavenly

lusty: cheerful, vigorous

hooked: moved their heads in a hooking motion

Egypt's Amun: Egyptian deity revered as king of the gods; also spelled Amana or Amon

minded: took notice

As night drew on, and, from the crest
Of wooded knolls that ridged the west,
The sun, a snow-blown traveller, sank
From sight beneath the smothering bank,
We piled, with care, our nightly stack   120
Of wood against the chimney-back,—
The oaken log, green, huge, and thick,
And on its top the stout back-stick;
The knotty forestick laid apart,
And filled between with curious art   125
The ragged brush; then, hovering near,
We watched the first red blaze appear,
Heard the sharp crackle, caught the gleam
On whitewashed wall and sagging beam,
Until the old, rude-furnished room   130
Burst, flower-like, into rosy bloom;
While radiant with a mimic flame
Outside the sparkling drift became,
And through the bare-boughed lilac-tree
Our own warm hearth seemed blazing free.   135
The crane and pendent trammels* showed,
The Turks' heads* on the andirons glowed;
While childish fancy, prompt to tell
The meaning of the miracle,
Whispered the old rhyme: *"Under the tree,*   140
When fire outdoors burns merrily,
There the witches are making tea."

The moon above the eastern wood
Shone at its full; the hill-range stood
Transfigured in the silver flood,   145
Its blown snows flashing cold and keen,
Dead white, save where some sharp ravine
Took shadow, or the sombre green
Of hemlocks turned to pitchy black
Against the whiteness at their back.   150
For such a world and such a night
Most fitting that unwarming light,
Which only seemed where'er it fell
To make the coldness visible.

trammels: hanging pothooks
Turks' heads: turban-like ornaments

second night

personification

simile, metaphor

Discuss this section with the students. What is happening here? *(The indoor fire is being reflected on a snowdrift outside, causing the children to remind each other of an old fable.)*

From here to the end of the poem note the precise skill with which Whittier contrasts the "cold," "keen," "dead white," and "pitchy black" moonlit night with the warm, "red," merry indoor scene with its food, drink, pets, and family.

Shut in from all the world without,   155
We sat the clean-winged hearth about,
Content to let the north wind roar
In baffled* rage at pane and door,   *baffled*: frustrated, stymied
While the red logs before us beat
The frost-line back with tropic heat;   160
And ever, when a louder blast
Shook beam and rafter as it passed,
The merrier up its roaring draught
The great throat of the chimney laughed;
The house dog on his paws outspread   165
Laid to the fire his drowsy head,
The cat's dark silhouette on the wall
A couchant* tiger's seemed to fall;   *couchant*: reclining
And, for the winter fireside meet,*   *meet*: appropriate
Between the andirons' straddling feet,   170
The mug of cider simmered slow,
The apples sputtered in a row,
And, close at hand, the basket stood
With nuts from brown October's wood.

What matter how the night behaved?   175
What matter how the north wind raved?
Blow high, blow low, not all its snow
Could quench our hearth fire's ruddy glow.

About the Author

John Greenleaf Whittier (1807-1892) was born into a close-knit New England family known for its simple Quaker values. Although Whittier received little formal education, he completed nearly 150 poems and became a recognized poet by the time he was twenty-one.

Although Whittier enjoyed great popularity as a reformist author, the writing of the timeless masterpiece "Snow-Bound" marks the beginning of his fame as a great literary figure. Not until Whittier was almost sixty did he attempt writing verse of high literary quality. "Snow-Bound," written in the poet's quiet old age, reflects the home-centered values he had always cherished. The style of the poem is simple but deeply moving; it displays much local color but is universal in its appeal to the imagination. The nostalgic themes in "Snow-Bound" proved a welcome balm for weary Americans recovering from the Civil War. The poem was an immediate literary and financial success.

In later life, Whittier became something of an American institution, reflecting the idealistic side of the American heart and mind. In the approximately one

"Winter"

As the theme of this poem seems to imply, the winter is not what it is sometimes praised to be—in Christmas card illustrations, for example. Life is more difficult for both animals and man. But there can be "A merry note," both indoors (the sound of cooking) and outdoors (the cry of the owl). Ask the students whether they think indoor life improves during the winter. Discuss with them ways in which they think it does or does not.

Shakespeare's poem divides evenly into two identical stanzas. The severity of winter is a backdrop for both human and animal activity. Life goes on, indoors and outdoors, and for that there is much to give thanks. There is also, or can be, that "merry note" ending the day as

it ends the stanzas: the kitchen sounds and the cry of the owl.

Each stanza takes us from morning to evening. Winter complicates daytime activities but enhances nighttime activities, even the most tedious and mundane, with a special pleasure. In northern agricultural communities, at least, the household economy changes seasonally; and families are likely to have more time together during the long nights of winter. Social life, then, centers more in the home. In stanza 1 the first two lines take us outside; the next two, inside (or partially so). In stanza 2 the first four lines alternate between outside and inside. The fifth line of stanza 1 is outside; the fifth of stanza 2, inside. The refrain ("Then . . .") combines outside (the owl) and inside (greasy Joan)

scenes. The stanzas also move from the disagreeable to the agreeable, though "greasy Joan" may not elicit entirely positive associations. Shakespeare does not romanticize nature, here or elsewhere. What makes nature enjoyable or merely endurable is the goodness and strength of human character and relationships. Notice the contrast in the poem between what nature is doing to man (and the animals) and what man is doing to nature in order to survive. The positive values are linked with the latter. (Discussion of the poems continues after "About the Poems.")

hundred hymn texts written toward the end of his life, Whittier showed his religious devotion and gift for didactic writing. His enduring reputation as the voice of rural New England is well merited.

Winter

William Shakespeare

The organization of a literary work is often signaled by contrasts. In the excerpt from "Snow-Bound" we may see the importance of indoors and outdoors, day and night, work and rest, cold and warmth, in the structure of the poem. Which of these contrasts are important in the following song from Shakespeare's Love's Labour's Lost?

When icicles hang by the wall,
   And Dick the shepherd blows his nail,*
And Tom bears logs into the hall,*
   And milk comes frozen home in pail,
When blood is nipped and ways be foul,   5
Then nightly sings the staring owl,
     "Tu-whit, tu-who!"
A merry note,
While greasy Joan doth keel* the pot.

When all aloud the wind doth blow,   10
   And coughing drowns the parson's saw,*
And birds sit brooding in the snow,
   And Marian's nose looks red and raw,
When roasted crabs* hiss in the bowl,
Then nightly sings the staring owl,   15
     "Tu-whit, tu-who!"
A merry note,
While greasy Joan doth keel the pot.

blows his nail: that is, to warm his hand
hall: the great hall of a large, rural house

keel: stir (to keep it from boiling over)

saw: wise saying

crabs: crab apples (British: wild apples, somewhat smaller and sourer than domesticated ones)

About the Poems

1. In the poem, "It Sifts from Leaden Sieves," what is "It"?
2. What is the "aging woman"?
3. Why do you think Whittier titled his poem "Snow-Bound"?
4. Shakespeare, like Whittier, makes use of contrasts in his poem. What are some of these contrasts?

About the Poems

1. *snow*

2. *the landscape*

3. *The title summarizes what happens to the people in the poem physically; however, it is ironic in that these industrious, resourceful folk do not seem altogether "bound" in by the storm.*

4. *The primary contrast is between the struggles caused by the winter and the "merry note" sung by the owl and the warmth of home and hearth implied by the last line of each stanza.*

Application

The themes expressed in these poems reinforce two important Biblical principles: (1) the precedence of work and duty over rest and pleasure and (2) the importance of inward character rather than external circumstances in determining the quality of life. Discuss these principles with the students, pointing out how the rejection of these principles hinders growth. There is, for example, a popular belief that a difficult or unstable home environment will handicap or destroy a person. Turn the students' attention to Ezekiel 18. In this passage, God makes clear that a father's sin need not affect his children. The principles of individual accountability and the availability of God's grace are reinforced.

In connection with these principles, you might discuss the life of Joseph. Despite his being rejected by his brethren, sold into slavery, and imprisoned unjustly, Joseph was untainted by bitterness. His inner man was unmoved by his external circumstances. God richly blessed him, making him a great spiritual and temporal leader. There are many other examples in both the Old and New Testaments. As time permits, have your students discuss other examples.

You may also wish to have them do the following writing assignment: Choose a character from the Bible who underwent great hardships but served the Lord nonetheless. Potential choices are myriad: Moses, Jacob, Joseph, Esther, Ruth, David, Abigail, Mary, Paul, Peter, and so on. See **Writing Rubric 3-1: A Faithful Follower.**

sound imagery

touch imagery

FURTHER HELPS

Additional activities

1. Find different words Engle uses to appeal to the senses. List these in columns.

2. Engle arranges his essay in chronological order. Have the students notice the events beginning with the departure from the farm.

3. After reading "Snow in the Suburbs," discuss with the students what it might be like to be homeless in a large city on Christmas. What difficulties and feelings would accompany such circumstances? Remind them that Joseph, Mary, and

An Old-Fashioned Iowa Christmas

Paul Engle

Unlike William Shakespeare's "Winter," Paul Engle's account of his family Christmas includes only the pleasant aspects of the season. The central contrast is temporal (one of time): Christmas years ago and Christmas now. Obviously Engle prefers what he considers the "good old days." He makes his preference clear in a statement repeated several times with slight modification. This statement introduces the main units of the description. Within these units the organization is either spatial (city streets and country roads, barn and house) or temporal (before, during, and after dinner).

Every Christmas should begin with the sound of bells, and when I was a child mine always did. But they were sleigh bells, not church bells, for we lived in a part of Cedar Rapids, Iowa, where there were no churches. My bells were on my father's team of horses as he drove up to our horseheaded hitching post with the bobsled that would take us to celebrate Christmas on the family farm ten miles out in the country. My father would bring the team down Fifth Avenue at a smart trot, flicking his whip over the horses' rumps and making the bells double their light, thin jangling over the snow.

There are no such departures any more: the whole family piling into the bobsled with a foot of golden oat straw to lie in and heavy buffalo robes to lie under, the horses stamping the soft snow, and at every motion of their hoofs the bells jingling, jingling.

There are no streets like those any more: the snow sensibly left on the road for the sake of sleighs and easy travel. We could hop off and ride the heavy runners as they made their

---

PREPARATION

"An Old-Fashioned Iowa Christmas," "Snow in the Suburbs"

Overview

This first selection, like the two preceding, has to do with winter and is built on contrasts: the present versus the past, city versus country. The headnote calls attention to the main structural units. Engle's account of his boyhood Christmas is beautifully shaped and styled and is also powerfully persuasive.

From the country (in Engle's essay) we pass to the city in Thomas Hardy's splendid little poem. The headnote describes the organization. The thought units show both symmetry and

progression. The last line shows the intensity able to be generated by understatement.

DISCUSSION

Introduction

Spend a brief time discussing with the students the contrasts between a "city" and a "country" Christmas. Which do they think would be more appealing? Engle's description is nostalgic and appealing, Hardy's rather bleak. Do the writers' varying descriptions influence your answer to the first question?

Analysis

"An Old-Fashioned Iowa Christmas"

Have the students find the main structural units in the essay. The headnote indicates these. The narrative is framed by the sounds of harness bells. Its main units are introduced by the statement "There are no such . . . any more." It gains its effect largely by multiplying details in parallel structures. Notice, for example, paragraph 5 and the second sentence of paragraph 6, which are highlighted.

Have the students find other examples of parallelism within or between sentences. Also have them find and identify the imaginative comparisons (e.g., the simile "hissing and darting out hissing, tearing sound over the packed snow. And along the streets we met other horses, so that we moved from one set of bells to another. There would be an occasional brass-mounted automobile laboring on its narrow tires and as often as not pulled up the slippery hills by a horse, and we would pass it with a triumphant shout for an awkward nuisance which was obviously not here to stay.

The country road ran through a landscape of little hills and shallow valleys and heavy groves of timber. The great moment was when we left the road and turned up the long lane on the farm. Near the low house on the hill, with oaks on one side and apple trees on the other, my father would stand up, flourish his whip, and bring the bobsled right up to the door of the house with a burst of speed.

There are no such arrivals any more: the harness bells ringing and clashing like faraway steeples, the horses whinnying at the horse in the barn and receiving a great, trumpeting whinny in reply, the dogs leaping into the bobsled and burrowing under the buffalo robes, a squawking from the hen house, a yelling of "Whoa, whoa," at the excited horses, boy and girl cousins howling around the bobsled, and the descent into the snow with the Christmas basket carried by my mother.

While my mother and sisters went into the house, the team was unhitched and taken to the barn to be covered with blankets and given a little grain. That winter odor of a barn is a wonderfully complex one, rich and warm and utterly unlike the smell of the same barn in summer: the body heat of many animals weighing a thousand pounds and more; pigs in one corner making their dark, brown-sounding grunts; milk cattle still nuzzling the manger for wisps of hay; horses eying the newcomers; oats, hay, and straw, tangy still with the live August sunlight; the sharp odor of leather harness rubbed with neat's-foot oil to keep it supple; the molasses-sweet odor of ensilage* in the silo where the fodder was almost fermenting. It is a smell from strong and living things, and my father always said it was the secret of health, that it scoured out a man's lungs. He would stand there, breathing deeply, one hand on a horse's rump, watching the steam come out from under the blankets as the team cooled down from their rapid trot up the lane. It gave him a better appetite, he argued, than plain fresh air, which was thin and had no body to it.

---

ensilage: fodder kept in a silo

A barn with the cattle and horses is the place to begin Christmas; after all, that's where the original event happened, and that same smell was the first air that the Christ Child breathed.

By the time we reached the house, my mother and sisters were wearing aprons and busying themselves in the kitchen, as red-faced as the women who had been there all morning. The kitchen was the biggest room in the house, and all family life save sleeping went on there. My uncle even had a couch along one wall where he napped and where the children lay when they were ill. The kitchen range was a tremendous black and gleaming one called a Smoke Eater, with pans bubbling over the holes above the fire box and a reservoir of hot water at the side, lined with dull copper, from which my uncle would dip a basin of water and shave above the sink, turning his lathered face now and then to drop a remark into the women's talk, waving his straight-edged razor, as if it were a threat, to make them believe him. My job was to go to the woodpile out back to split the chunks of oak and hickory and keep the fire burning.

It was a handmade Christmas. The tree came from down in the grove, and on it were many paper ornaments made by my cousins, as well as beautiful ones brought from the

sight imagery

Note structural parallelism; sound imagery; smell imagery. Note also the assonance in the phrase "brown-sounding" in the next paragraph. You may wish to point out to students that this is an example of a literary device known as *synesthesia,* expressing one sense (in this case, sound) in terms of another (color).

reference to Christ

the Christ Child experienced such circumstances on that first Christmas. Nor was this the last time that Christ would be "homeless." As He later told His disciples, "Foxes have holes, and birds of the air have nests, but the Son of man hath not where to lay his head." It is ironic that the Creator of all things should have experienced such circumstances. Yet the irony takes on deeper significance when we recognize that He willingly endured such circumstances for a sin-cursed world. Discuss with your students what they might do for those who have such burdens. They might, for example, collect money to buy toys and deliver them to the children in a nearby children's home. Or they could, as a class, volunteer to help the local rescue mission.

4. Have the students take the information in the poem "Snow in the Suburbs" and

its bill at the end of its curving neck like a feathered snake").

Notice, too, that the description runs the gamut of the senses. Have the students locate examples of imagery of sight, sound, taste, smell, and touch. You may wish to define *image* for the students as "a word or phrase that appeals to one of the senses." Then ask which one of the senses is especially emphasized. *(smell)* Point out the symbolism of the last two sentences and allow the students to explain it. *(It is a reference to the Christian faith that made all these activities, as blessings, meaningful.)* What other references to Christ appear in the essay? *(See highlighted portions in paragraphs 7, 16, 17, and 21.)*

put it into a prose paragraph. Encourage them not to lose all the poetic literary devices—as we have seen, prose can contain metaphor, simile, personification, and so on.

5. Have students bring in pictures depicting Christmas in the country and Christmas in the city. Together note the differences in the scenes.

Journal entry idea

Notice how Engle uses a myriad of details in his descriptive paragraphs (e.g., paragraphs 6, 9, 10). Allow the students to try writing a similar descriptive paragraph.

Resources

Paul Engle, *A Prairie Christmas* (New York: Longman, 1960).

Paul Engle, *An Old-Fashioned Christmas* (New York: Dial Press, 1964).

Black Forest* where the family originally lived. There were popcorn balls, paper horns with homemade candy, and apples from the orchard. The gifts tended to be hand-knit socks or wool ties or fancy crocheted "yokes" for nightgowns, tatted collars for blouses, doilies with fancy flower patterns for tables, and tidies* for chairs. Once I received a brilliantly polished cow horn with a cavalryman crudely but bravely carved on it. And there would usually be a cornhusk doll, perhaps with a prune or walnut for a face, and a gay dress of an old corset-cover scrap with its ribbons still bright. And there were real candles burning with real flames, every guest sniffing the air for the smell of scorching pine needles.

Black Forest: mountainous region in southwestern West Germany
tidies: decorative protective coverings for the armrest or headrest of a chair

There are no dinners like that any more: every item from the farm itself, with no deep freezer, no car for driving into town for packaged food. The pies had been baked the day before, pumpkin, apple, and mince; as we ate them, we could look out the window and see the cornfield where the pumpkins grew, the trees from which the apples were picked. The bread had been baked that morning, heating up the oven for the meat, and as my aunt hurried by I could smell in her apron that freshest of all odors with which the human nose is honored—bread straight from the oven. There would be a huge brown crock of beans with smoked pork from the hog butchered every November.

There would be every form of preserve: wild grape from the vines in the grove, crab-apple jelly, wild blackberry and tame raspberry, strawberry from the bed in the garden, sweet and sour pickles with dill from the edge of the lane where it grew wild, pickles from the rind of the same watermelon we had cooled in the tank at the milk house and eaten on a hot September afternoon.

Cut into the slope of the hill behind the house, with a little door of its own, was the vegetable cellar, from which came carrots, turnips, cabbages, potatoes, squash. And of course there was the traditional sauerkraut, with flecks of caraway seed. I remember one Christmas Day when a ten-gallon crock of it in the basement, with a stone weighing down the lid, had blown up, driving the stone against the floor of the parlor.

All the meat was from the home place, too. Most useful of all was the goose—the very one which had chased me the summer before, hissing and darting out its bill at the end of its curving neck like a feathered snake. Here was the universal bird of an older Christmas: its down was plucked, washed, and hung in bags in the barn to be put into pillows; its awkward body was roasted until the skin was crisp as a fine paper; and the grease from its carcass was melted down, a little camphor added, and rubbed on the chests of coughing children. We ate, slept on, and wore that goose.

And of course the trimmings were from the farm, too: the hickory-nut cake made with nuts gathered in the grove after the first frost and hulled out by my cousins with yellowed hands; the black-walnut cookies, sweeter than any taste; the fudge with butternuts crowding it. In the mornings we would be given a hammer, a flatiron, and a bowl of nuts to crack and pick out for the homemade ice cream.

All families had their special Christmas food. Ours was called Dutch bread, made from a dough halfway between bread and cake, stuffed with citron and every sort of nut from the farm—hazel, black walnut, hickory, butternut. A little round one was always baked for me in a baking-soda can, and my last act on Christmas Eve was to put it by the tree so that Santa Claus would find it and have a snack—after all, he'd come a long, cold way

Engle claims the goose was the "universal bird" of his childhood Christmases. Ask students what the "universal bird" of today's Christmas is. *(turkey)*

Discuss this statement with the students. How is this true in light of the preceding paragraph? Discuss also how different the family's conserving and use of every part of their resources differs from today's "disposable" society.

taste imagery

to our house. And every Christmas morning, he would have eaten it. My aunt made the same Dutch bread and we smeared over it the same butter she had been churning from their own Jersey milk that same morning.

To eat in the same room where food is cooked—that is the way to thank the Lord for His abundance. The long table, with its different levels where additions had been made for the small fry, ran the length of the kitchen. The air was heavy with odors, not only of food on plates but of the act of cooking itself along with the metallic smell of heated iron from the hard-working Smoke Eater, and the whole stove offered us its yet uneaten prospects of more goose and untouched pies. To see the giblet gravy made and poured into a gravy boat is the surest way to overeat its swimming richness.

The warning for Christmas dinner was always an order to go to the milk house for cream, where we skimmed from the cooling pans of fresh milk the cream which had the same golden color as the flanks of the Jersey cows which had given it. The last deed before eating was grinding the coffee beans in the little mill, adding that exotic odor to the more native ones of goose and spiced pumpkin pie. Then all would sit at the table and my uncle would ask the grace, sometimes in German, but later, for the benefit of us ignorant children, in English:

Come, Lord Jesus, be our guest,
Share this food that you have blessed.

My aunt kept a turmoil of food circulating, and to refuse any of it was somehow to violate the elevated nature of the day. To consume the length and breadth of that meal was to suffer! But we all faced the ordeal with courage. Uncle Ben would let out his belt—a fancy Western belt with steer heads and silver buckle—with a snap and a sigh. The women managed better by always getting up from the table and trotting to the kitchen sink or the Smoke Eater or outdoors for some item left in the cold. The men sat there, grimly enduring the glory of their appetites.

After dinner, late in the afternoon, the women would make despairing gestures toward the dirty dishes and scoop up hot water from the reservoir at the side of the range. The men would go to the barn and look after the livestock. My older cousin would take his new .22 rifle and stalk out across the pasture with the remark, "I saw that fox just now, looking for his Christmas goose." Or sleds would be dragged out and we would slide in a long snake, feet hooked into the sled behind, down the hill and across the westward sloping fields into the sunset. Bones would be thrown to the dogs, suet* tied in the oak trees for the juncos* and winter-defying chickadees, a saucer of skimmed milk set out for the cats, daintily and disgustedly picking their padded feet through the snow, and crumbs scattered on a bird feeder where already the crimson cardinals would be dropping out of the sky like blood. Then back to the house for a final warming up before leaving.

---

suet: fatty tissue from the kidneys of cattle and sheep, used in cooking and making candles
juncos: North American birds of the genus *Junco,* having predominantly gray plumage

---

There was usually a song around the tree before we were all bundled up, many thanks all around for gifts, the basket loaded as when it came, more so, for leftover food had been piled in it. My father and uncle would have brought up the team from the barn and hooked them into the double shafts of the bobsled, and we would all go out into the freezing air of early evening.

And now those bells again as the horses, impatient from their long standing in the barn, stamped and shook their harness, my father holding them back with a soft clucking in his throat and a hard pull on the reins. The smell of wood smoke flavoring the air in our noses, the cousins shivering with cold, "Good-bye, good-bye," called out by everyone, and the bobsled would move off, creaking over the frost-brittle snow. All of us, my mother included, would dig down in the straw and pull the buffalo robes up to our chins. As the horses settled into a steady trot, the bells gently chiming in their rhythmical beat, we would fall half asleep, the hiss of the runners comforting. As we looked up at the night sky through half-closed eyelids, the constant bounce and swerve of the runners would seem to shake the little stars as if they would fall into our laps. But the one great star in the East never wavered. Nothing could shake it from the sky as we drifted home on Christmas.

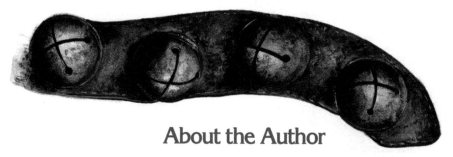

About the Author

Paul Engle (1908-1991), the author of the nostalgic narrative "An Old-Fashioned Iowa Christmas," earned the reputation as successor of Walt Whitman's optimistic style. In over a dozen volumes of poetry, Engle expressed his deeply felt reactions to American life. The longer Engle wrote, the closer he came to the concentrated, powerful form he desired.

In addition to prose, Engle wrote poetry and drama. He also edited a variety of books and literary periodicals. His best work, however, drew inspiration from his memories of life in Iowa and his belief in the values of the "American Dream" (prosperity through energetic effort). His sense of American idealism suffered attack from critics accustomed to the cynicism and defeatism of contemporary American writing. Despite such criticism, however, Engle's straightforward style of writing and teaching yielded important awards, and his influence on aspiring writers continued late in his life through his position as professor and director of creative writing at the University of Iowa.

beautiful imagery based on careful re-creation of details of a childhood memory

reference to Christ

Snow in the Suburbs

Thomas Hardy

The plan and theme of a work sometimes become apparent to the reader only after a number of careful readings. The organization of the following poem is quite intricate. It takes us from general description of inanimate objects (stanza 1) to specific description of animate objects (stanzas 2-3). Stanza 1 moves from universal assertions ("Every branch . . . twig . . . fork . . . street and pavement") to particular assertions ("Some flakes. . . . The palings"). Stanza 2 shows the effects of the snow (humorous) on a sparrow; stanza 3, the effects of the snow (serious) on a cat. The last line, "And we take him in," ends the movement from inanimate to animate, impersonal to personal, humorous to serious description. It also suggests man's duty to the helpless, the poem's theme.

> Every branch big with it,
>   Bent every twig with it;
> Every fork like a white web-foot;
> Every street and pavement mute:
> Some flakes have lost their way, and grope back upward, when   5
> Meeting those meandering down they turn and descend again.
>   The palings are glued together like a wall,
>   And there is no waft of wind with the fleecy fall.
>
> A sparrow enters the tree,
>   Whereon immediately   10
> A snow-lump thrice his own slight size
> Descends on him and showers his head and eyes,
>   And overturns him,
>   And near inurns* him,   *inurns: burie
> And lights on a nether twig, when its brush   15
> Starts off a volley of other lodging lumps with a rush.
>
> The steps are a blanched slope,
>   Up which, with feeble hope,
> A black cat comes, wide-eyed and thin;
>   And we take him in.   20

"Snow in the Suburbs"

A snow scene can mean many things to many people—hard work to a highway department crew, thrilling recreation to children released from school, suffering to the impoverished aged who dread a winter without heat. Some of these perspectives appear in the selections in this unit. More than one perspective appears in this poem by Hardy.

The headnote for Hardy's poem is unusually detailed. Point out that the description chronicles a growth in concern in the observer-poet. It first focuses on inanimate nature, which it describes objectively, showing the beauty of the scene. Then, the focus shifts to animal life (the sparrow) with a tone of mild amusement. Finally, the focus shifts to the human dwelling from which the scene has been observed, resting on the steps, which (covered by snow) seem to deny access. The tone now is serious ("with feeble hope"). The last action of the poem is by the observer rather than by the observed. It is the response to what has been observed and the result of the emotional progression implied in the poem.

Hardy exercised great care in the development of this poem to get the maximum emotional effect from the cat's predicament. The opening scene of wintry isolation and loneliness in the "mute" streets leads into the lengthened fifth and sixth lines, where snowflakes wander aimlessly. The stillness and sense of paralysis is heightened by the lack of wind and by images such as the snow's gluing together the fence palings.

The introduction of the sparrow into the poem brings movement with direction, a contrast to the "meandering" snowflakes. The bird's purpose is to enter the tree, his rightful home and place of refuge. Yet even here his aims are thwarted. The "snow-lump" overwhelms his "slight size" and moves on, heedless of the damage it does. This stanza offers an example of Hardy's use of internal rhyme, in lines 13 and 14. Also, notice that these lines are very short, emphasizing the bird's situation and the rapid motion of the overpowering snow-lump.

Continuing to the end of the stanza, the reader notices Hardy's use of learned words such as "inurns" and "nether." Hardy made a practice of using any word that precisely conveyed the meaning and rhythm he desired. If an archaic or regional word suited his need, Hardy em-

About the Author

Thomas Hardy (1840-1928) was an enthusiastic walker, cyclist, and outdoorsman. This keen appreciation of nature is evident in his writing. In many of Hardy's stories, for example, weather and environment not only reflect the moods of the main characters, but also seem to control these characters' destinies. In the lighthearted selection "Tony Kytes, the Arch-Deceiver" (pp. 283-89), environment is significant in shaping both the plot and the characters.

Although the role of environment is typical of Hardy, the lighthearted tone of the Tony Kytes selection is not. Hardy's outlook was generally gloomy. Often he portrayed both God and nature as unsympathetic forces. Although Hardy liked to present the harsher side of nature, he did have a tender heart toward animals and promoted efforts to prevent cruelty to them. His pets appear in his poetry, and sometimes, as in "Snow in the Suburbs," they are the basis for memorable imagery.

This dark view does not erase the fact that Hardy was a writer of great technical skill and emotional power. As readers of literature, we can appreciate the style and design of his work, especially his poetic works, without embracing his despair.

About the Essay and Poem

1. What distinctive sound begins and ends the experience Engle describes in his narrative?
2. Engle's preference for "the good old days" is made clear in a statement repeated several times with slight modification. What is that statement?
3. Engle uses several imaginative comparisons to make his essay vivid and appealing. List two imaginative comparisons that you found especially effective.
4. From the country in Engle's essay we pass to the city in Hardy's poem. Like Engle, Hardy uses imaginative comparisons to create a specific mood. Having read these two selections, would you prefer a "country" or a "city" Christmas? Explain your answer.
5. Using an imaginative comparison, describe some incident or mood from a past Christmas of your own.

ployed it, and part of the literary value and charm of his poetry results from this.

Even by the time the reader finishes the poem, he may not have noticed the alliteration Hardy employs. Alliteration occurs as "fleecy fall" and "waft of wind" in line 8. Also apparent is some assonance. One example occurs in line 11 with the words "slight size." Although subtle, these stylistic effects powerfully unite the poem's imagery. Identify as many examples of alliteration and assonance as possible in class.

Hardy's use of color is also significant. Although gray tones appear most frequently, our poem presents stark contrasts between white and black. Throughout "Snow in the Suburbs," Hardy gives the reader a sense of a wet, sticky snowfall and a desolate landscape. The sharp contrast of the black cat with his bleak white background helps us to better appreciate the speaker's act of hospitality in the last line. (Discussion of "An Old-Fashioned Iowa Christmas" and "Snow in the Suburbs" continues after "About the Essay and Poem.")

 About the Essay and Poem

1. *harness bells*

2. *"There are no such . . . any more."*

3. *Answers may vary but might include "the harness bells ringing and clashing like faraway steeples" (page 67); "pigs in one corner making their dark, brown-sounding grunts" (page 67); "the goose— the very one which had chased me the summer before, hissing and darting out its bill at the end of its curving neck like a feathered snake" (page 69).*

4. *Answers may vary. Accept any answer that students can defend based on the poems.*

5. *Answers may vary but should include some form of imaginative comparison (simile, metaphor, personification, etc.).*

 Application

Have the students write a short essay on one of their own past Christmases, telling about some unique family tradition or an unusual incident. They may wish to use their answer to "About the Essay and Poem" question 5 as a springboard for their essay. Or, if they choose, have them write a fictional piece rather than an essay. In either case,

The Return of the Rangers

Kenneth Roberts

Kenneth Roberts, a well-known staff correspondent for the Saturday Evening Post, also wrote novels and travel books. The following selection, taken from his novel Northwest Passage, conveys the peril and captures the flavor of the early Northwest. Captain Rogers and his Rangers had recently completed an arduous military mission and were scheduled to rendezvous with military personnel who could provide them with essential provisions. Only a few of the men were strong enough to make the trip; the rest had to stay behind and wait for rescue. When Rogers and his pitiful band finally arrived at the rendezvous point, they discovered that the military officers had fled—taking the necessary provisions with them. Despite overwhelming odds, Rogers determined three things: to get himself and his men to the military fort safely, to return with provisions for the men he left behind, and finally to discover the names of those who fled and left them to die.

encourage them to make the setting and characters appealing. Their purpose should be, like Engle's, to make us feel we have "missed" having such a Christmas. If time permits, have the students exchange their stories with each other and make positive comments on the story's effect. You may wish to have the students read their stories aloud. See **Writing Rubric 3-2: A Classic Christmas.**

PREPARATION

"The Return of the Rangers," "I Will Praise the Lord at All Times"

Overview

The excerpt from *Northwest Passage* provides a good opportunity for students to discern theme by focusing on a story's literary details: conflict, character, plot, and resolution. Cowper's poem clinches the unit's topical emphasis: organization and theme.

Potential problems

Although the excerpt from *Northwest Passage* included here is free of objectionable elements, other sections of the novel may pose problems. The novel's circumstances cause Rogers's moral character to degenerate. By the end of the story, we pity rather than admire the captain. The book does, however, have a positive moral tone: the narrator's viewpoint helps us understand that the captain's wrong behavior is both evil and destructive. Still, the entire book should not be suggested for recreational reading. If read, it should be in a setting where the negative elements of the work can be discussed and used to make a positive point.

I

Somewhere I have heard that after the first three days of fasting a man has no further desire for food, and that after thirty days he feels no discomfort whatever: that his brain is clear, his body pure, and his endurance almost unlimited. I suspect that statement in toto. I don't believe in the benefits of fasting, and ever since I tried it in the company of Major Robert Rogers on the St. Francis Expedition, I have been strongly opposed to it.

After we had seen the logs of our raft plunge over the edge of the falls, we dragged ourselves higher up the bank, dropped to the ground and lay there. Even Rogers was supine* for a time—though not for long. He got to his knees. "This is no place to stay," he said. "We can't stay anywhere without a fire. We'd freeze. There'll be wood on the bank below the falls." He stood up, swaying. "That's where we go next," he said. "Come on."

supine: lying on one's back

We crawled after him; and it was as he said. There was wood in plenty along the shore and beyond the falls, though not such wood as would build a raft. There were whole trees, hard wood for the most part, and waterlogged; windrows* of twigs and branches; untold quantities of splintered pines of varying sizes, shattered by the ice-jams of previous springs.

windrows: rows made of twigs, branches, or leaves that have been heaped up by the wind

Rogers shook his head when we had crawled over the largest of those woodheaps. "The only thing we can do today," he told us, "is try to get warm. Maybe tomorrow we can figure out something better."

We built ourselves another fence and a roaring fire of driftwood: then stripped ourselves and dried our shredded blankets and our sorry remnants of garments. So tattered and so rotted were those wretched rags that they were next to worthless as covering, and worse than worthless as protection against cold.

Our persons, in a way, were as bad as our clothes. I was ashamed, almost, to look at Rogers and Ogden. Their scrawny bodies seemed caricatures of what they ought to be—like bodies formed by a sculptor with no knowledge of anatomy. Their muscles were stringy as those of a skun wildcat: their knees and elbows strangely knobby: their stomachs hollowed and their ribs protuberant* like those of a hake* that has lain for days upon the beach.

protuberant: bulging
hake: a marine fish related to and resembling cod

Rogers was covered with scars—red scars, blue scars, white scars. Some were bullet wounds, while others looked as though made by the claws or teeth of animals. Ogden's two bullet-holes, so recently healed, were flaming purple, rimmed with crimson.

When the strips we called our clothes were dry, we huddled close to the fire, listening to the everlasting roar of White River Falls. The fire warmed me, and drugged by that warmth and the thunder in my ears, I neither knew how we could move from where we were, nor did I care.

II

It was a good thing for us, in a way, that we were wrecked at White River Falls. If the falls had not been there to provide us with the windrows of firewood: if we had spent the night in a spot where we would have had only the fuel that we cut, we would probably have died of exhaustion and cold. Our exertions on the raft had drained us of our last reserves of strength, and it was beyond our power to

DISCUSSION

Introduction

Both of the selections in this lesson reflect the seasonal motif. The theme of each also provides opportunity for discussing two attributes of God: His greatness and His goodness. Draw the students' attention to the fact that "The Return of the Rangers," like "The Fruits of Toil," reminds us that nature can be austere as well as beautiful. Although God has allowed man "to have dominion over the works of His hands," there are times when man must muster all of his resources if he is to overcome the austerity of the natural world.

Analysis

"The Return of the Rangers"

Assign the students to read the entire excerpt before class. Ask them to jot down several images that Roberts uses to convey the austerity of nature as they read.

Following your reading, discuss these images and then examine the literary details of the story, using the following questions. What is the story's central conflict? *(There are really two conflicts your students could identify: man against nature—the fight of Rogers and his men to survive; man against man—the conflict between Lieutenant Stephens and Rogers over the lieutenant's desertion of the Rangers. Both conflicts are significant.)* What is the climax of the excerpt? *(For this specific excerpt your students could identify one of two incidents as climactic: the struggle of getting the raft down the second falls or Rogers's discovery of who deserted him and his men.)* What are the causes and results of each event? How does each character respond to the events and to the other characters? How is the conflict resolved? As the students answer the questions, jot down their responses on the chalkboard.

Once you have this information on the chalkboard, have the students determine what one idea is supported most by the story's details. Then have them state this idea (the theme) in a sentence or two. *(Students should convey the idea that there are times when man must muster all of his resources if he is to overcome the austerity of the natural world.)*

drive a hatchet into a tree. As for the cold, it was so bitter that in the morning the mist from the falls had cased every branch and rock and dead leaf in a glittering envelope of ice.

We lay beside the fire until the sun had come up to take off the knife-like bite of the air.

"We'll have to eat," Rogers said. "If we don't get something in us we can't stick on the raft."

"What raft?" Ogden asked.

"We'll get a raft," Rogers said.

"I don't know how," Ogden said. "If I try to swing a hatchet, I'll cut off my legs."

"Don't worry about that," Rogers said. "I'll get the raft if you'll find the food. Listen!"

Behind us, on the dark slope of the valley, a red squirrel chirred. Far away another answered. We could hear them chipping and chapping at each other: I knew just how they looked, jerking their tails and sliding spasmodically around tree-trunks with outspread legs.

"There's the food," Rogers said. "There's only one good mouthful to a roasted red squirrel, even if he's hit in the head, but all we need is a few good mouthfuls."

"I guess we can knock down a few," Ogden said. "I don't know about getting 'em back here, if I shoot more than one. One's about all I can carry." He reached for his musket. "We better draw our loads and reload," he told me. "We can't afford to miss."

"Before you go," Rogers told us, "help me with the wood. There's only one way to get trees for a raft, and that's to burn 'em down."

We stacked piles of firewood at the base of six spruces near the water's edge: then dragged ourselves up the bank, leaving Rogers and Billy crawling from pile to pile, kindling the fires that were to fell the trees we no longer had the strength to hack down ourselves.

Ogden and I shot five squirrels during the morning, and found it difficult—not only because we couldn't hurry to a squirrel when we heard one, but because we had to wait for the squirrels to sit still: then shoot from a rest because of being unable to hold the sights steady unless we did so. Hunger cramps caught us with increasing frequency, and if a hunger cramp took hold while we were drawing a bead on a squirrel, there was nothing to do but double up and wait until it went away.

We came back, late in the morning, dividing the fifth one equally; and while we picked the meat from their mouse-like bodies, one of the trees came down with a crash.

Rogers drove us out again as soon as we had eaten. "Keep on hunting," he told us. "Shoot anything you find. I'll have these trees burned into lengths by the time you get back."

It seemed to me I couldn't drag my legs up the slope of that valley again, but somehow we did it, using our muskets as walking sticks and leaning frequently against trees. So far as I could feel, my roast squirrel had done me no good: I needed a side of mutton or a cow's hind-quarter to quiet the aching void within me. I thought bitterly of Cap Huff's idle remark about a goose being a little more than one man could eat alone, but not quite enough for two. How little Cap had known of hunger! A whole goose would not more than take the edge off my appetite.

Not far from us a partridge went out of a thicket with a thunderous roar. From the blundering sound he made among the branches, I was sure he had lit at no greater distance.

"He's in the tree," I whispered to Ogden. Ordinarily, the breast of a partridge makes a toothsome preliminary to a simple meal; but as a meal itself it's not worth considering. Just now, however, this partridge seemed more desirable than anything on earth.

"Can you see him?" Ogden asked faintly.

I said I couldn't, but knew about where he was.

"Go ahead and get him," Ogden said. "I'll move off to the left and make a noise doing it, so he'll watch me. You sneak around and take him in the rear."

He lowered himself among the dead leaves and threw his arms and legs about, making feeble moaning sounds. I hoped the partridge would find such a noise impressive as I crept around the thicket and stood watching breathlessly. The trees were naked: leafless. In none of them could I see anything that looked like a bird, and I was about to call to Ogden when I saw a movement at one end of a swelling on the branch of an oak. It was the partridge, cocking an eye at Ogden's strange behavior.

I found a good rest, took careful aim and let him have it. When he scaled away from the limb on a long slant, Ogden and I stumbled as fast as we could to where he came down. It was rocky ground, clear of heavy undergrowth, and dotted with an occasional juniper bush and a thin covering of leaves; but the partridge was nowhere in sight.

"You sure he came down here?" Ogden asked.

I said I was; that he was hit hard.

"Yes, I saw him. I guess he was hit all right," Ogden agreed, "but I don't believe he came down here. We'd see him if he had. He must have gone beyond those rocks."

We went there and searched; we walked in circles, sought beneath every juniper: almost looked under every fallen leaf; but we found nothing.

"You're sure he came down at all?" Ogden asked finally.

I just nodded. The thought of losing that partridge shut off my voice completely; I was afraid that if I tried to speak, I'd sob instead.

Ogden, hollow-eyed, stared at the ground. "Guess you—guess you missed him," he said in a whisper. And then his wretched staring eyes seemed to enlarge. "Well, if that don't beat all!"

He was staring at a flat juniper that had a few brown oak leaves on it. Before my eyes the oak leaves magically altered and became a partridge—an enormous cock partridge, with ruff-feathers four inches long and a tail the size of a fan. We must have walked across him and around him twenty times.

I went down on my knees and picked him up. He was still warm—the fattest, most beautiful, angelic partridge I had ever seen. The musket ball had broken his back and left his breast untouched.

I looked up at Ogden. "I'm mighty glad you found him, Captain. Mighty glad."

"I *knew* you hit him," Ogden said. "That was a mighty pretty shot, Langdon—the best shot I ever hope to see."

III

When we returned to the falls, all six trees were down, and under each burned two fires, so to separate them into proper lengths for a raft. Rogers sat at the edge of the stream, his forehead resting on his drawn-up knees, and beside him lay Billy, asleep.

The Major looked up. He was a sight. His face and hands were black with soot: as black as Pomp Whipple's; and his eyes glared at us whitely, looking to see whether we had shot anything. I slipped the partridge's head from under my belt in back and held it up for him to see.

"Let's eat it before our luck changes!" he said.

We ate the intestines first, washed and placed on a hot stone to roast. Then we had half a squirrel apiece, cut along the backbone. The partridge was more difficult to divide evenly. Having agreed that a newly-shot partridge is better raw than cooked, we seared him no more than enough to hold the meat together. Then we took off the breast and, after considerable discussion and measuring, split

Allusion; also note emphasis on seemingly endless suffering through Roberts's use of words such as "endlessness," "eternal," and "everlasting."

them in what we agreed were equal parts. The carcass, mattering less, was quartered without argument.

Before we slept that night the twelve fires had done their work, and twelve logs lay on the bank, with nothing more to be done except get them into the water and fasten them together into a raft. To me, that night, the task appeared about as easy as pushing a porcupine through a musket barrel.

IV

Nowadays whenever I dream of the building of that second raft, I wake myself up by whimpering aloud, because I've been straining to move a vast log that will not budge, yet must, or death awaits me.

We drove stakes in shallow water where the bottom was soft. Then we inched a log to the bank, tumbled it to the shingle, and worried it into the stream. We couldn't roll it, because we had to leave protruding branches for binding the raft together.

In moving a log, we worked however we could: leavering it with stakes: sliding it over driftwood: lying on our backs to ease our hunger cramps, and pushing with heels or shoulders, so that from head to foot we were black with soot.

When we had a log in the water, we drew it to the fixed stakes, which held it in place while we went for another log. To each one we fastened a hazel switch, so there might be something by which to seize and guide it if it broke loose; and Billy stood guard at the stakes to do what he could in case they gave way.

It was noon before we had finished our labors, lashed our muskets and other wretched belongings to the uprights, cut new paddles and woven a long rope of hazel shoots.

Rogers insisted on the rope. "We don't want this one to get away from us," he muttered

over and over. "We really got to keep hold of *this* one." We thought he was right about that. We couldn't have made a third raft.

Whether it was because of the steadily increasing cold—a cold that threatened snow— or the long struggle with the logs, I cannot say; but whatever advantage we had gained from our mouthful of partridge and two mouthfuls of squirrel had now been lost. We were finished; if our lives depended on our marching a mile, we couldn't have done it.

By the time we started, poor young Billy had bad cramps and couldn't even sit upright, so we laid him on some spruce tips in the middle of the raft. With his sharp nose, his closed eyes, his mouth stretched tight over his teeth, and his dusky color, he looked tragically like a mummy without its wrappings.

We worked free of the stakes, poled ourselves slowly into midstream and sank breathless on the raft, regardless of the icy water that welled up between the logs to soak our trembling bodies. Some day, I thought, I must paint a picture of this and call it Purgatory; and then I realized such a picture would have little meaning: it couldn't show the endlessness of these journeyings—the eternal wetness and shiverings, the aching bruises to the soul and body, the everlasting hunger, everlasting toil, and everlasting exhaustion.

Rogers got to his knees, and I heard him say something about falls. The word shocked me into full consciousness. "Falls?" I asked. "More falls?"

"Not bad ones," he said thickly. "Just little falls. Wattoquitchey Falls, seven miles from here. Fifty yards long. Maybe we can ride 'em."

Ogden and I struggled painfully to our feet.

"Well, why didn't we go there to build the raft?" Ogden asked.

"I said 'seven miles,'" Rogers reminded him. "You couldn't march seven miles. And what about him?" he pointed to Billy. "Why, maybe I couldn't even hardly do it myself."

"Can we see these falls before we're on top of 'em?" I asked.

"See 'em?" Rogers said. "We've *got* to see 'em, haven't we?"

We strained our eyes downstream. A few snowflakes drifted out of the heavy sky, and from the surface of the eddying brown water rose a vapor like a faint ghost of the mist that had billowed up from White River Falls. The thought of more falls was sheerly nauseating, and I knew that if the snow came down too thickly, we might not see them until too late. . . .

Rogers broke the silence at the end of three miles. "Maybe we can ride 'em," he said again. He repeated the words in another quarter-hour. Those falls, I realized, hadn't been out of his mind all day. That was why he had insisted on making the rope of hazel switches. I wondered what would happen if we couldn't ride them; but I didn't dare ask.

V

We sighted the falls through thickening snowflakes at three o'clock, and paddled the raft over toward the left bank, so we might have opportunity to see how they looked.

At first I thought we might indeed possibly ride them, for their total drop was only about ten feet; and the quick water wasn't over fifty yards long. The closer we came, however, the more apparent it was that the raft would never get down safely unless every possible ounce of weight was removed from it. Gouts of foam shot up from the middle of the rapids, proving that the ledges beneath were sharp and dangerous; we could hardly hope to live if the raft broke up or spilled us in that turmoil.

We let the raft drop down to within a few yards of the quick water, laid one end of it against the bank and held it there with our paddles. We could see the pool at the bottom— a brown, deep pool, streaked with streamers of foam.

"I don't believe we'd better try it," Rogers said.

"Somebody's got to," Ogden said wearily. "It's the only chance we've got."

"No it isn't," Rogers said. "The best chance is for me to go down to that pool and try to catch her when she comes down."

Ogden, seized with a cramp, clutched his middle. "You can't!"

Rogers seemed not to hear him. "That's what we'll do. Take Billy ashore. Take the muskets and the rest of the stuff. I'll hold her while you do it."

Ogden hesitated.

"Captain Ogden!" Rogers said sharply. "You heard me!"

Ogden moved quickly to obey. We hurriedly collected our rusty muskets, our soaked and tattered rags of blankets, and all our other accouterments that now were rubbish; then, taking Billy by his pipestem arms, we dragged him to the bank, where he lay all asprawl, no better than a shrivelled little red corpse. At Rogers' orders we made fast the rope of hazel shoots to the stoutest of the uprights; and Ogden tested the rope while I fastened our paddles to the raft's protruding branches. The rope was firm as a cable.

"Now, whatever you do," Rogers said, "don't let go that rope till I give the signal. It'll take some time to reach the pool, and I got to undress. When I hold up my arm, turn her loose. Let the rope trail. If I miss the raft, maybe I can catch the rope." He fastened his own paddle beside ours and went ashore.

I joined Ogden, and together we clung to the rope. The raft plucked insistently at it, as if eager to be gone from us.

Picking up his musket, powder-horn and other belongings, Rogers went slowly from our sight into the dark woods, walking crouched over. The snowflakes had thickened, helping

Note powerful imagery here achieved by multiplying figures of speech. Rogers is "an atom" (metaphor) in the midst of the powerful water, snow, "screaking forest" (onomatopoeia), and "towering . . . hills" (metaphor).

Note alliteration throughout.

to hide him from us; and I thought it likely that I'd heard his voice for the last time.

The raft seemed more and more determined to swing out into the stream and go down the falls. For fear it might pull us off our feet and drag us into the rapids, we sat in the shallows, water up to our waists, our feet wedged against rocks.

"I'll bet my way was best," Ogden muttered. "One of us ought to have *tried* to ride down on it. If the Major gets a stomach cramp when he's swimming to it—" He was silent. There wasn't much more to say.

At the edge of the pool the bushes moved apart, and Rogers, a dim figure through the steadily-falling snow, could be seen peering along the shore to the left and right, seeking, evidently, for a suitable position. Then he went back into the bushes, and reappeared nearer us, crawling out on a flat rock. With agonizing slowness he put down his musket, blanket, knapsack and powderhorn, and painfully undressed.

He crouched at the edge of the rock, staring up at the falls—a lonely, naked, helpless atom in that immensity of roaring white water, drifting snowflakes, screaking forest and towering dark hills. Then he held up his arm and waved.

We let go the rope and floundered to our feet. The raft swung slowly broadside to the current and moved downstream. When it reached the quick water, it bobbed on the white riffles; flung itself forward.

It rolled and rocked. Halfway down it nosed completely under: a surge of white foam swept it from end to end. It rose again, reeling and sliding in the surges, and seemed to fling itself breathlessly to the bottom of the long slope. It plunged heavily into the swirling pool, and hung there, tilted forward, half under water. We looked to see it fall apart; but with labored slowness it came to the surface, turning gently among the clots and streaks of froth.

Rogers lowered himself from the rock. He swam arduously, with awkward jerks, as if his rump strove to rise and force his head under. He stopped once, freed his face from gouts of foam,* and rolled on his side to look for the raft, which, again in the grip of a current, moved more rapidly.

---

gouts of foam: large, shapeless waves of foam

He altered his course and swam spasmodically on. He found himself so close to it that he clutched for a log—clutched and missed. He kicked again; got a hand on the raft: another hand. He hung there for a time, his chin on the edge, his legs and body carried beneath the logs by the current; and I, watching him, felt my muscles quake; for I knew that no mere human, with an icy torrent plucking at his starved and weakened limbs, could cling for long to those charred tree-trunks. As if in answer to my fears, he struggled sluggishly, hitched himself along with fumbling hands, gripped one of the branches we had left as uprights on the logs, and drew himself partly from the water, so that his upper body lay upon the raft—lay so long motionless, that I thought he was spent. Then we saw that he was making futile upward movements with his knee. It caught the edge eventually, and he squirmed aboard to lie flat.

"I never thought he'd make it!" Ogden whispered; and I, shaking all over, found that my tongue and throat were dry as chips.

Now Rogers had got to his knees, and we saw him unlash a paddle from the uprights, and begin to work slowly toward shore.

VI

Driftwood from Wattoquitchey Falls warmed us and kept us alive that night; and with the first faint grayness of that miserable last day of October—miserable and yet ever-memorable—we put Billy in the middle of the

simile

personification

simile, allusion

raft, with our blankets under and over him, and pushed out into midstream. The snow had ceased, and had been followed by a wind so bitter that it cut and slashed us like frigid knife-blades.

There were no more falls between Wattoquitchey and Number Four: no more quick water, Rogers said—no, there was nothing but the malignant cold, which seemed determined to finish what the French and the Indians had tried so hard to do to us.

But on both sides the intervals grew broader: the hills retreated; and though the glacial wind could thus howl at us unrestrained, we thought it had the voice of a raging demon of the wilderness, frantic to see us at last slipping from his grasp.

Out of his streaming eyes, Rogers stared at the widening intervals. "We're going to make it," he said. "We're going to make it!"

It was mid-afternoon when he seized Ogden by the arm. "Look!" he cried. "Look!" He doubled over with a cramp; but thus bent he pointed awkwardly, like an actor playing the part of a hunchback. On the river bank, a hundred yards ahead, two men with axes suddenly stood.

"Why," Ogden said incredulously, "it's people again!" But I don't think Rogers could speak at all, and I know I couldn't.

The two strange, strange figures, men that weren't skeletons, men that were clothed, men that swung axes easily in ruddy strength and health—those two unbelievable men saw us, and came back along the bank, hurrying toward us.

"Don't tell 'em anything," Rogers warned us huskily as we swung the raft in toward the shore. "I'll do the talking. Don't tell anyone a thing till we find out all about the dirty skunk that ran off with our food!"

One of the men splashed toward us, caught our rope of hazel switches and drew us to land. "Where's Number Four?" Rogers asked.

They just stared.

"I'm Rogers," Rogers said. "Where's Number Four?"

"Rogers!" one of the men said, and a kind of horror was in his face. "You say you're Rogers?"

"I do!"

"I've often seen you," the man said, swallowing. "It's hard to believe!" He shook his head. "We heard you was dead, Major; and I guess it's true! You was! But anyhow, you're at Number Four, Major. It's right here, and we'll help you to the fort!"

With that, slipping and splashing in excitement, they gave us the unfamiliar help of muscular arms and got us off the raft, lifted Billy to the bank, put our belongings in a heap, and made the raft fast to the stake. They gawked at the burned ends of the logs and at the alder and hazel withes* that held them together, and kept staring at Rogers as if he'd been a hippogriff.*

---

withes: tough twigs used for binding things together
hippogriff: mythological figure with the wings, claws, and head of a griffin and the body and hindquarters of a horse

We sat down just beyond the water's edge and watched them as they made the raft fast.

"Happen to have anything to eat?" Rogers asked them whereupon, after another look at him, they sprang up the bank and departed, running. They were back in five minutes, bringing with them a bottle a third full of rum and a piece of bread the size of my fist. "That's all we got, Major," one said. "We're out chopping wood and et the rest, but there's plenty supplies at the fort. There's turnips and fresh pork."

Rogers broke the bread in four pieces. "Why, it's bread!" he said. He gave us our portions, took a mouthful of rum, then went over and looked at Billy. He poured a little rum between his lips. When Billy opened his eyes and coughed, he gave him the bread and passed us the bottle.

That mouthful of bread moistened by rum had incredible sweetness and savor. I could feel it moving warmly inside me, as though hastening to assure my cramped and aching stomach, my thumping heart, my laboring lungs and my shivering body that their long agony was over.

"Now we'll go up to the fort," Rogers told the staring woodcutters. "Guess maybe you'd better help us a little. Leave our stuff here: then come back for it. One of you can carry this Indian boy. Then we'll just lean on the two of you."

One of the men picked up Billy and carried him. The other gave Ogden and me each a shoulder, and Rogers staggered along, now and then bumping into the man who carried the Indian boy; thus we set off for the fort, which we could see, low and square, in the middle of its dismal, snowcovered clearing—that same peaceful clearing I had idly sketched on a warm September evening less than two months ago.

There was no sentry at the gate of the fort; no one on the small parade ground on which the snow had been trodden to dirty, frozen slush. Our helpers took us across the parade to the log barrack in the center. A squat tower of hewn plank rose from its northern end. The man on whom Ogden and I leaned pulled the latch-string of the door and kicked it open. In a broad stone fireplace opposite the door a fire burned, and at either end of the room were rows of bunks. In front of the fire a blanket was spread on the floor, and around it were a dozen Provincials, rolling dice.

They looked up. One said angrily, "Keep the door shut!"

"This here's Major Rogers," one of the woodcutters said in a voice that choked with excitement.

The Provincials got slowly to their feet and faced us, stared at us and frowned with unbelief, then seemed to see something terrifying.

"Who's in command of this fort?" Rogers said.

"We don't know his name, Major," a soldier said huskily. "We're strangers here."

"Go get him," Rogers ordered.

Three Provincials jumped together for the door at the end of the room, jostling and tripping in their haste.

Rogers walked drunkenly to a bench, and the staring soldiers fell away before him.

"Put Billy on the blanket and go back and get our muskets," Rogers told the woodcutters.

Ogden and I got to the bench with difficulty. The feel of a roof over my head and of a closed room, warmed by a fire, almost suffocated me.

The door at the end of the room burst open. A stolid-looking man in a wrinkled blue uniform peered at us, blinking. "Which?" he asked. "Which one?" he came to us. "They said Major Rogers! None of *you* are Major Rogers!"

"I'm Rogers," the Major said. "Now here: write down what I say. I can't repeat. What's your name?"

"Bellows," the officer said, "in charge of the King's stores." He clapped his hands to his pockets, looked confused, then hurried from the room. When he returned he had a pencil and paper. "We didn't know—" he stammered. "We heard—where did you—"

"Get canoes," Rogers said. "Load 'em with food. Send 'em up river. Mouth of the Ammonoosuc."

"These men are Provincials," Bellows said apologetically. "They're bound home. There's only—"

"Get settlers," Rogers said. "Good canoemen. Hire 'em!"

"It's pretty bad weather," Bellows said doubtfully. "Maybe when it clears off—"

Rogers rose wavering to his feet, then straightened himself to his full height and seemed to fill the room. In a strained, hoarse voice he said: "Today! Today! Now! Can't you realize there's a hundred Rangers at the mouth of the Ammonoosuc, starving! Get men and pay 'em! Get all the settlers into the fort! Call 'em in! Drum 'em up! I'll talk to 'em! Get started!"

Bellows stared at him wildly: rushed back to the door and shouted a name, adding, at the top of his lungs, "Assembly! Assembly!"

Three private soldiers tumbled into the room, one a drummer. At a gesture from Bellows he ran out on the parade ground, fumbling with his drum braces. His drum rolled and rumbled, sending chills down my spine.

To one of the other soldiers Bellows shouted, "Run to Mrs. Bellows. Get a pail of milk and a bottle of my rum."

"And some bread," Ogden said.

"All the bread she's got!" Bellows shouted.

Rogers sank down on the bench, rubbed his gaunt face with huge skeleton hands, ran his fingers through his hair. "Write an order for the food to go up river. What you got in this place?"

"Pork," Bellows said. "Fresh beef. Turnips."

"How much bread you got?"

"Not much," Bellows said. "These Provincials—"

"Let 'em go without! Put all the food you can find in those canoes, and send out for more. Send out for everything there is! Those men of mine are going to be fed, or I'll raid every house in the settlement!"

The drum rattled and rolled, rumbled and banged.

Bellows scribbled hastily on a sheet of paper and sent the third soldier flying from the barrack with it. There were people crowding in at the door, goggling at us.

Rogers raised his voice to be heard over the continuous rolling of the drum. "Tell me something," he said to Bellows. "Supplies of food were to meet us at the mouth of the Ammonoosuc. They were sent, weren't they?"

"Oh, yes," Bellows replied, and he looked frightened. "They were in charge of Lieutenant Stephens."

"So? What did he do with 'em?"

"He brought 'em back," Bellows said. "He waited several days; then he thought you and your command must have been wiped out— and he heard firing one morning and thought it might be French and Indians, so he decided he'd better start for home."

"Listen," Rogers said, and he spoke as much to the settlers and Provincials who had crowded in through the doorway as he did to Bellows. "We finished St. Francis for you. There isn't any more St. Francis, and you can begin to move up that way and clear the land and live in peace whenever you've a mind to. But this Lieutenant Stephens who got frightened and took our food away when we were firing muskets to show him we were coming— we'll have to have a settlement with him. He isn't here, is he?"

"No," Bellows said tremulously. "He's gone back to Crown Point. You'll be going that way, too, Major, I take it?"

"No, not till afterwards," Rogers answered in a choking voice.

The crowding people stared stupidly at him as he stood before them in the firelight, unbelievably gaunt, barefoot, covered with bruises, tattered strips of strouding* sagging around his legs. The shredded buckskin leggins hung loosely on his emaciated flanks; singular torn bits of garments concealed little of his ribs and bony chest: his hands were scarred, burned, sooty and pitch-stained from his labors with the raft.

strouding: coarse woolen cloth

"No, we'll see Lieutenant Stephens at Crown Point afterwards," Rogers said. "Now get me some beef—fat beef. I'm going back to Ammonoosuc myself."

About the Author

Kenneth Roberts (1885-1957) was born in Maine and maintained a lifelong interest in that state. A skilled historian, Roberts collected information about New England's fierce battles, important political decisions, and minutiae of daily life. Unlike most historians, he did not present his findings in textbooks or treatises. He chose instead to transform the historical facts gleaned from his research into fascinating stories.

Roberts had a compelling style that was cultivated during his years of work as a newspaperman. As a journalist, Roberts wrote for such well-known periodicals as the *Saturday Evening Post* and *Life*. This journalistic background, coupled with his painstaking research, made him one of America's most talented historical novelists.

"I Will Praise the Lord at All Times"

Roberts's story reinforces God's power mirrored in nature. By contrast, Cowper's poem uses nature to mirror the goodness of God as unmistakable. The poem illustrates the kind of continual communion with God spoken of in Psalm 1:2 and I Thessalonians 5:17.

Before reading the poem aloud, draw the students' attention to the fact that the title expresses the theme, a theme that is especially meaningful when we realize that Cowper (pronounced *Cooper*) waged a lifelong battle with despondency and doubt.

The poem is neatly structured into stanza-length units by the seasonal and diurnal cycles spoken of in Genesis 8:22. Notice that the poem begins in the dark of the year and ends in the dark of the day. The climax of the light imagery is in stanza 3, summer. The last two stanzas describe the times before and after the full appearance of the sun. The result is a rising and falling of intensity and a sense of finality as the dying of the day is associated with "an eternal rest."

"I Will Praise the Lord at All Times" reflects Cowper's opinion that to truly appreciate an outdoor scene, one must view it during each season of the year. The successive changes all hold special significance as they bring to the poet's mind aspects of God's character. Notice that while Cowper paints these natural beauties vividly, he does not praise them but reserves praise for the actual person of God. This is a vital aspect of true worship and praise. At a time when writers were beginning to glorify nature itself, Cowper refused to join the humanistic trend. He looked to creation not to fully reveal God but to reflect His creative genius and goodness, thereby enabling men to study the written revelation of Scripture to find out more about this wonderful Designer.

Cowper's figure of speech in line nineteen, "His bleeding beauties," deserves special consideration as a demonstration of one of the best uses of alliteration and oxymoron, the combination of seemingly contradictory ideas. The agonies of Christ's self-sacrifice blend with the beauties of the work of redemption. Cowper places this imagery in the stanza dealing with morning and links the sun's rising to the

Stanzas 1-4: The speaker will praise the Lord regardless of the season. Stanzas 5-6: The speaker will praise the Lord both day and night.

I Will Praise the Lord at All Times

William Cowper

The stanzas of a poem, like the chapters of a book, are often a guide to organization. The organization of this fine poem by Cowper is beautifully simple and clear. The Christian sees God in all seasons and in all circumstances.

Winter has a joy for me,
While the Saviour's charms I read,
Lowly, meek, from blemish free,
In the snowdrop's pensive head.

Spring returns, and brings along   5
Life-invigorating suns:
Hark! the turtle's* plaintive song   *turtle's:* turtle dove's
Seems to speak His dying groans!

Summer has a thousand charms,
All expressive of His worth,   10
'Tis His sun that lights and warms,
His the air that cools the earth.

What! has autumn left to say
Nothing of a Saviour's grace?
Yes, the beams of milder day   15
Tell me of His smiling face.

Light appears with early dawn;
While the sun makes haste to rise,
See His bleeding beauties, drawn
On the blushes of the skies.   20

Evening, with a silent pace,
Slowly moving in the west,
Shows an emblem of His grace,
Points to an eternal rest.

coming of light, just as the Resurrection of the Son of God brought the light of truth to the world. Point out to the students that they can trace Christ's life through the progression of images in the poem, beginning with the pure snow reflective of the sinless Saviour, through the turtledove's "plaintive song" echoing Christ's "dying groans," to the Resurrection, and ending with the evening's "emblem of His grace" and assurance of peace and victory. An excellent way to follow this progression is to link instances of Cowper's use of light as a motif to represent revealed truth in almost every stanza.

Continue your study of the poem by discussing "About the Story and Poem" questions 4 and 5. Answers will vary for these questions. But as each student responds, have him specify the line or lines of the poem that prompted his answer.

Application

Read the following two stanzas from another of Cowper's works, *The Task.*

God never meant that man should scale the
  heav'ns
By strides of human wisdom. In His works
Though wondrous, He commands us in His
  word
To seek Him rather, where His mercy shines.
(bk. iii, lines 221-24)

A ray of heav'nly light, gilding all forms
Terrestrial in the vast and the minute;
The unambiguous footsteps of the God
Who gives its lustre to an insect's wing,

And wheels His throne upon the rolling
  worlds.
(bk. v, lines 810-14)

Discuss briefly with the students how Cowper drew from his own experiences, observations, and feelings to express profound truths. Unlike other poets, he refused to use his gift merely for the purpose of "self-expression." He chose rather to reveal his God.

 Have the students keep Cowper's purpose for writing in mind when they draw upon a personal experience, observation, or emotion to write a descriptive paragraph or poem which will reveal their concept of their Lord.

About the Author

"God made the country, and man made the town." This famous quotation by English poet William Cowper (1731-1800) expresses his attitude toward nature and happiness. Like many other evangelical Christians of his day, Cowper asserted that country living was conducive to a virtuous life, for it provided a firsthand view of God's handiwork. Unlike Thomas Hardy, Cowper tends to paint the peaceful, benevolent side of nature. The nature imagery in Cowper's poem pictures the power and love of the Creator, while in Hardy's poem winter is bleak and overpowering.

Cowper aimed for a simple style in his writings. Although he did not always succeed, he came closest to his goal in *The Task,* his longest and most important work. The consistency with which Cowper read and studied the Bible affected not only the tone but also the diction of his best poetry. Like Scripture, these poems display great power clothed in simple language.

About the Story and Poem

1. The narrator tells his story chronologically, dividing his narrative into units that reveal the increasingly desperate situation of Captain Rogers and his Rangers. What incident serves as the climax for the narrative?
2. Unlike most of the preceding selections, Roberts's selection presents the harsher side of winter. What are some images Roberts uses to convey the austerity of the season?
3. As is evident in Cowper's poem, all of the seasons reflect some aspect of God's nature. What aspect of His nature do you think Roberts's selection reflects?
4. List for each season one specific thing which motivates Cowper to praise his God.
5. List for each season one specific thing that might motivate you to praise your God.

You may wish to have students complete **Appendix I: Unit 3 Review** before testing them on this unit.

 About the Story and Poem

1. *Students may identify one of two incidents as climactic: the struggle of getting the raft down the second falls or Rogers's discovery of who deserted him and his men.*

2. *Answers will vary but may include "So tattered and so rotted were those wretched rags that they were next to worthless as covering, and worse than worthless as protection against cold" (page 75); "if we had spent the night in a spot where we would have had only the fuel that we cut, we would* probably have died of exhaustion and cold" (page 75); "As for the cold, it was so bitter that in the morning the mist from the falls had cased every branch and rock and dead leaf in a glittering envelope of ice" (page 76).

3. *God's beauty and certainly His power.*

4. *Answers will vary. Winter—a reminder of Christ's purity; spring—a reminder of Christ's death; summer—a reminder of Christ's role in Creation; autumn—a reminder of Christ's "smiling face."*

5. *Answers will vary.*

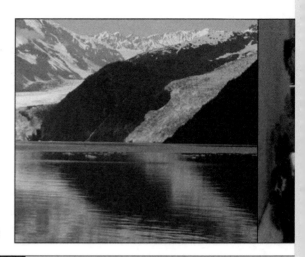

Part II
The Modes of Literature

When the prophet Nathan came to David to rebuke him for his adultery with Bathsheba and murder of Uriah, he chose an indirect approach. One must be careful, of course, how one accuses a king. The best way is to let the king condemn himself. So Nathan invented a story. He told of a rich man who, in order to entertain a traveler, killed a poor man's lamb for supper, sparing his own vast flocks. David's reaction was the expected one. "As the Lord liveth, the man that hath done this thing shall surely die. And he shall restore the lamb fourfold, because he did this thing, and because he had no pity" (II Samuel 12:5-6). "Thou art the man," said the prophet. Then David understood that the parable referred to his own sin.

Nathan's parable and David's reaction to it illustrate three modes of expression especially common in serious writing. These modes—the **symbolic,** the **ironic,** and the **allusive**—express or reinforce meaning indirectly. A parable is a kind of symbolic expression. The reference to David's sin, implied in the parable and then stated directly by Nathan, is allusion, a reference within a work of literature to something outside it. David's wrathful response to the parable is ironic in that the king is unknowingly condemning himself. David presumably would not have reacted this way had he known what Nathan knew and the reader knows. Our prior knowledge puts David's reaction in an absurd light.

PREPARATION
The Modes of Literature
Introduction

Overview

The introduction uses Nathan's rebuke of David to illustrate allusion, symbol, and irony. These indirect modes of expression may seem remote to the students until you show how prevalent they are in everyday speech.

DISCUSSION

Introduction

Explain to the students that indirect expression is not necessarily insincere or affected. It may be the most effective way to emphasize a point. The longest way around, in language as in other things, may be the shortest way home—to the conscience and the will. Point out that allusion, symbol, and irony are basic tools of advertising. They are also fundamental in high-level persuasion that aims at the deep emotional sources of our decisions and actions.

Analysis

This introductory essay is short and simple, but the section of the book it introduces ("The Modes of Literature") may be the most difficult of the three. Indirect expression, though almost universally used, is sometimes difficult to analyze. For this reason it may be best to have the students read the introduction aloud in class, taking the time while reading to carefully go over the examples provided.

Application

Have the students write advertisements using a symbol, an allusion, or irony. You may want to divide the class into groups and have each group write an ad that illustrates one of the above literary modes (symbolism, allusion, or irony).

Encourage students to be as creative as possible. They may want to create a paper ad (for a

These three special modes of expression are ways of speaking in which more is intended than may appear at first glance. All three occur frequently in everyday speech. Artfully controlled and directed, they enrich the imaginative writing we call literature.

newspaper or magazine), a video, a website banner, or something else. Give each person or group a copy of **Writing Rubric 4-1: A Persuasive Pitch** before they begin the project. When they complete their ad, they should turn the rubrics back in. Be sure they have filled out the portion that requires that they explain their use of symbol, allusion, or irony.

4

UNIT FOUR

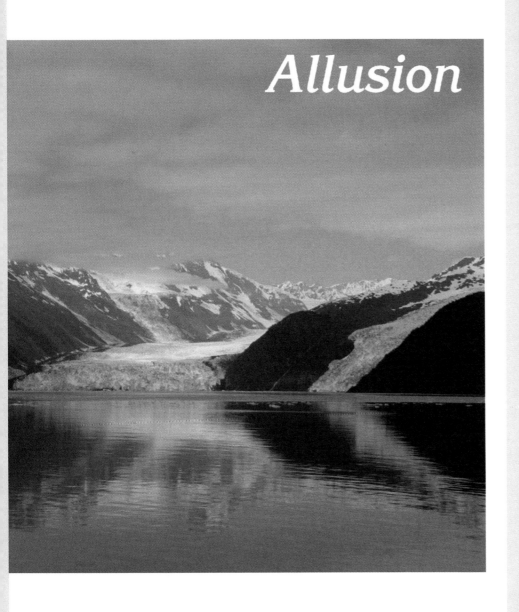

Allusion

OBJECTIVES

The students will be able to

- Define *allusion*.
- Give examples of the use of allusion in Scripture.

FURTHER HELPS

1. Look back at the following works. Allow students to find allusions in each.

   "Had I the Choice" (p. 43)

   "The Fruits of Toil" (cf. pp. 48-52 ["seven thunders," Psalm 23], 53)

   "Snow-Bound" (cf. pp. 61-62)

   "An Old-Fashioned Iowa Christmas" (cf. references to Christ on pp. 67, 70-71)

   "The Return of the Rangers" (cf. p. 78)

   These examples should help clarify for students exactly what an allusion is.

2. Have the students look for examples of allusions in news reports, newspaper articles, advertisements, and so on. Encourage them to bring examples in to share with the class. (You may want to check the examples ahead of time for appropriateness.) You might want to make this a contest or an extra-credit activity.

The divinely inspired letters of the New Testament are especially rich in literary qualities. In II Corinthians 4 and 5, for example, Paul uses allusion to encourage believers not to fear the cost of living for Christ. Paul had known physical suffering. He had been beaten, stoned, attacked by mobs, and exhausted by difficult journeys. He knew how physical hardships can scar and prematurely age the body. But he also knew that they cannot injure the soul. "Though our outward man perish, yet the inward man is renewed day by day" (4:16). Even the outward man will be renewed some day. "We know that if our earthly house of this tabernacle were dissolved, we have a building of God, an house not made with hands, eternal in the heavens" (5:1).

In metaphorically picturing the body as a tabernacle, or tent house, Paul uses an allusion. His readers would think of Abraham, a tent dweller, a pilgrim in a land he possessed only by promise. Centuries later, Abraham's descendants returned to the promised land from Egypt and built permanent houses and cities. The tent life of Abraham is to the settled life of his descendants what the present earthly life of the Christian is to his future life with God.

The tent-house allusion refers even more directly to the descendants of Abraham who lived in tents while they journeyed from Egypt to the land of promise. During this time they worshiped in a tabernacle built under the direction of Moses, a portable tent sanctuary pitched for God among the tents of His people. Later, when Israel was settled in the land, this tabernacle, threadbare and tattered, was replaced by a temple Solomon erected in Jerusalem. The tabernacle in the wilderness is to Solomon's temple what the present earthly body of the Christian is to his future heavenly body. Both bodies are meant to be habitations of God. But only the second is permanent. It is encouraging to know that though the first body (the present one) decays, the second one awaits in all its enduring perfection.

An **allusion** is a reference within a written work to something outside it. Literary allusions refer to other works of literature. Historical allusions refer to past events. The Lord Himself made constant use of allusion. His sermons and conversations repeatedly refer to what His hearers know best—Israel's history and Scriptures. He told Nicodemus, "As Moses lifted up the serpent in the wilderness, even so must the Son of man be lifted up: that whosoever believeth in him should not perish, but have eternal life" (John 3:14-15; see Numbers 21:4-9). The language of His dedicated disciples of all ages—of the hymn writers especially—has been rich in allusion to the Word and ways of God.

A writer using allusion takes for granted that he has a reader with knowledge and experience similar to his own. Older literature abounds with Biblical and classical allusions. Most of these escape the modern reader, whose education usually has not included the Bible or the Greek and Roman classics. Even today's literature is often made difficult by allusion. In fact, it can be more difficult in its way than the earlier literature. The allusions in much modern

PREPARATION

Allusion Introduction

Overview

This introductory essay defines and illustrates allusion from II Corinthians 4 and 5. It shows the value of allusion for clarifying and emphasizing truth. It also shows how a sensitivity to allusion can enrich our study of the Scripture.

DISCUSSION

Introduction

Point out to the students that the wider our knowledge of literature and history is, the greater our reading comprehension will be. The greater our mastery of the Old Testament, the fuller our understanding of the New. The better we know the Gospels, the richer will be our reading of the Epistles. Later writers, both secular and sacred, constantly echo and build on earlier writings.

Analysis

Recognizing allusion is fundamental to accurate interpretation of the inspired writings of the Scripture and all literature. Much erroneous, fanciful interpretation has resulted from ignorance of allusion or failure even to notice the existence of allusion in a work or passage of a work of literature. We can hardly understand Hebrews without some knowledge of the Pentateuch, especially Leviticus. We are likely to

interpret John Milton incorrectly unless we know the Bible and to misinterpret Wordsworth unless we know both Milton and the Bible.

Following this explanation of the importance of allusion, go over the examples in the introduction carefully, showing how tracing allusions in the Bible can illuminate meaning. Point out that one of the most important reasons for learning how to analyze literature is that it will enable us to better understand God's Word.

Application

Appendix J: Allusions to the Bard can be done either in class or for homework.

poetry are private rather than public. That is, they refer to the author's personal experiences rather than to the common experiences of mankind or even to the general reading experience of educated people. Unidentifiable personal allusions in poetry or fiction indicate that the writer does not care to communicate clearly with his reader or that he egotistically thinks himself the center of everybody's world. Sensible readers are impatient with such vagueness. But they see the value of getting the background necessary for understanding allusions to the most influential writings of the past. Because the Scriptures are so widely used as an allusive reference, to know the Bible is to be already halfway to the goal.

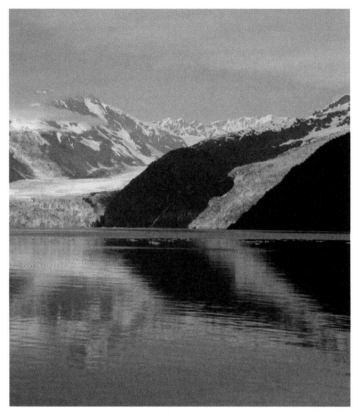

"The Donkey"

OBJECTIVES

The students will be able to

- Identify Biblical allusion.
- Defend the importance of Biblical knowledge in understanding literature.

alliteration

simile, metaphors

Ask students to think of possible Biblical allusions implied in the donkey's statement "I am dumb [i.e., silent]." *(This could be an oblique reference to Balaam's donkey [cf. Num. 22:20-35] and/or to Christ [cf. Isa. 53:7].)*

FURTHER HELPS

Additional activities

1. Direct the students to research a myth and write a short essay summarizing the story and explaining why it has continuing significance.

2. In Acts 17:28 Paul alludes to the poets Aratus and Epimenides of Crete. Paul's audience would have understood his reference. Direct the students to find additional information on these poets; discuss why Paul chose to refer to them.

The Donkey

G. K. Chesterton

Of all the ridiculous creatures of the earth, the donkey may seem the chief. But he is not, for that reason, to be despised, according to this poet.

> When fishes flew and forests walked
> And figs grew upon thorn,
> Some moment when the moon was blood
> Then surely I was born;
>
> With monstrous head and sickening cry   5
> And ears like errant wings,
> The devil's walking parody
> Of all four-footed things.
>
> The tattered outlaw of the earth,
> Of ancient crooked will;   10
> Starve, scourge, deride me: I am dumb,*   *dumb:* silent
> I keep my secret still.
>
> Fools! For I also had my hour;
> One far fierce hour and sweet:
> There was a shout about my ears,   15
> And palms before my feet.

About the Poem

1. Who is the speaker of the poem?
2. What was the donkey's one great "hour"?
3. Of what did his honor consist?
4. What lesson does this poem, based on an allusion, have for us?

About the Author

    G. K. Chesterton's (1874-1936) childhood was centered in a family that was warm and happy. As a result, Chesterton not only valued the family unit, he also believed it to be the foundation of society. In his essay "On

PREPARATION

"The Donkey"

Overview

This first selection of the unit gives students a chance to exercise their own knowledge in identifying allusion. Those with any Biblical knowledge at all should recognize the incident referred to: Jesus' entrance into Jerusalem on a donkey. The poem, like a good riddle, saves its best clue until the end.

DISCUSSION

Introduction

G. K. Chesterton was known as a master of paradox (explained in the introduction to Unit 6). The language of the first two stanzas speaks of grotesque improbabilities—incongruous combinations of features. Not only the nature but also the experience of the donkey has been contradictory. The most ridiculous and stubborn of creatures was chosen as the royal mount for the meek Son of God. (Discussion of "The Donkey" continues after "About the Poem.")

 About the Poem

1. *the donkey*
2. *Palm Sunday, when he carried Christ through the streets of Jerusalem*
3. *his association with the Son of God*
4. *We are not to glory in things the world prizes;*

rather, we should glory in knowing God (cf. Jer. 9:23-24). (The allusion referred to in the question is the poem's allusion to Palm Sunday.)

Analysis

Initiate discussion using the "About the Poem" questions.

Draw the students' attention to the first stanza, which reflects the old notion that creatures take their personal characteristics from conditions (especially astrological) prevailing at their birth. Here the reference is to the birth of the species. The poet is being facetious, of course—implying that if, indeed, conditions prevailing at one's birth affect personal characteristics, then conditions at the donkey's birth must have been extremely unusual.

the Pleasures of No Longer Being Very Young" (pp. 102-3) Chesterton expresses these values by encouraging an appreciation for older people who have coped with life's different stages. Echoing the wisdom of Proverbs, he exhorts the young to heed the wisdom of age and experience.

"The Donkey," one of Chesterton's best known poems, appeared in his early work *The Wild Knight and Other Poems*. This volume helped establish Chesterton's reputation. The poem's purpose was to mirror the value and grandeur of all life. The tone of this poem mirrors an outlook present in many of Chesterton's works. Such an outlook sometimes causes critics to label Chesterton as overly optimistic. Chesterton did choose to present the positive aspects of most situations. That he possessed a healthy optimism did not mean, however, that he was blind to the presence of evil in the world. Chesterton not only recognized the existence of evil but believed that the resulting prickings of conscience highlighted rather than detracted from the ideal of goodness. Thus convinced, he continued to use his literary gifts for humor and paradox to develop uplifting themes and teach absolute values.

Cupid's Arrows

Rudyard Kipling

Many of the stories of Rudyard Kipling show a generation gap between the young and the old. This story is sympathetic toward the young. It begins in fairy-tale fashion and ends in the same way, with the lady being carried away by her true lover. A final phrase adds a wry comment on marriage, which from a journalist's viewpoint is not as interesting as the events leading up to it. (Most of Kipling's early stories set in India were first published in a newspaper.)

Once upon a time there lived at Simla a very pretty girl, the daughter of a poor but honest District and Sessions Judge. She was a good girl but could not help knowing her power and using it. Her Mamma was very anxious about her daughter's future, as all good Mammas should be.

When a man is a Commissioner and a bachelor and has the right of wearing open-work jam-tart jewels in gold and enamel on his clothes, and of going through a door before every one except a Member of Council, a Lieutenant-Governor, or a Viceroy, he is worth marrying. At least, that is what ladies say.

The second stanza reflects the old idea of the Devil as a mocking imitator of what God has created. Again the poet is facetious. The third stanza introduces some features that begin to associate the donkey with the One who gave him special honor on a memorable day: "Scourge, deride me: I am dumb." These culminate in the last stanza with references to his "hour," the "shouts" about his enormous ears (made large for the occasion?), and the "palms" before his feet. The experience, as paradoxical as the donkey's appearance and nature, was both fierce and sweet. See Matthew 21:1-11.

Application

Draw the students' attention to Jeremiah 9:23-24. Following the reading of these verses, dis-

cuss their significance as they relate to the last "About the Poem" question: Does this poem, based on an allusion, have a lesson for us? (See "About the Poem" question 4, above.)

Finally, discuss with the students how the lesson of Chesterton's poem and the Biblical principles in Jeremiah 9:23-24 apply to today. Questions such as the following may help in getting discussion underway: What do men typically "glory in" today? Does our society tend to despise those whom they consider "ridiculous"? Do some Christians display such attitudes? Whom should we respect? What should we value?

OBJECTIVE

The students will be able to

- Identify classical allusion, a subclass of literary allusion.

Before reading "Cupid's Arrows," discuss with the students what they think of when they see this title. *(Romantic love; see "About the Story" question 1 [page 98].)* Tell the students that the title has a double meaning: it is a story about love, but it is also a story about an archery contest.

Discuss these two sentences with the students. Ask them what Kipling is implying through his tongue-in-cheek tone. *(He is mocking women who think a man is worth marrying if he has money, power, and prestige; such thinking is based on improper values.)*

Resources

Edith Hamilton, *Mythology: Timeless Tales of Gods and Heroes* (Penguin USA, 1989).

Shamsul Islam, *Kipling's "Law": A Study of His Philosophy of Life* (New York: St. Martin's Press, 1975).

Philip Mason, *Kipling: The Glass, the Shadow, and the Fire* (New York: Harper and Row, 1975).

J. E. Zimmerman, Dictionary of Classical Mythology (New York: Bantam Books, 1966).

PREPARATION

"Cupid's Arrows"

Overview

Whereas the preceding selection introduced Biblical allusion, this one introduces classical allusion. These kinds of allusion are subclasses of literary allusion. Every student acquainted with the lore of Valentine's Day should be able to identify the allusion in the story's title.

Potential problems

Kitty's rebelliousness is not commendable, though her mother is wrong in pushing the match. Make clear that a reference to college degrees or other honors received

simile

See notes below and "About the Story" question 2, page 98, for an explanation of this allusion.

Discuss what this reveals about the shallowness of Kitty's character.

metaphor

Note what Mrs. Beighton's statement reveals of her character and where her priorities are—she says, in other words, "Barr-Saggott cannot help being ugly; what's more important is that someday you'll have more social influence than even I do!"

There was a Commissioner in Simla, in those days, who was, and wore, and did all I have said. He was a plain man—an ugly man—the ugliest man in Asia, with two exceptions. His was a face to dream about and try to carve on a pipe-head afterward. His name was Saggott—Barr-Saggott—Anthony Barr-Saggott and six letters to follow. Departmentally, he was one of the best men the government of India owned. Socially, he was like unto a blandishing* gorilla.

blandishing: coaxing with flattery

When he turned his attentions to Miss Beighton, I believe that Mrs. Beighton wept with delight at the reward Providence had sent her in her old age.

Mr. Beighton held his tongue. He was an easy-going man.

A Commissioner is very rich. His pay is beyond the dreams of avarice—is so enormous that he can afford to save and scrape in a way that would almost discredit a Member of Council. Most Commissioners are mean;* but Barr-Saggott was an exception. He entertained royally; he horsed himself well; he gave dances; he was a power in the land; and he behaved as such.

mean: stingy

Consider that everything I am writing of took place in an almost prehistoric era in the history of British India. Some folk may remember years before lawn tennis was born when we all played croquet. There were seasons before that, if you will believe me, when even croquet had not been invented, and archery—which was revived in England in 1844—was as great a pest as lawn tennis is now. People talked learnedly about "holding" and "loosing," "steles," "reflexed bows," "56-pound bows," "backed" or "self-yew bows," as we talk about

"rallies," "volleys," "smashes," "returns," and "16-ounce rackets."

Miss Beighton shot exquisitely over ladies' distance—sixty yards, that is—and was acknowledged the best lady archer in Simla. Men called her "Diana* of Tara-Devi."

Diana: Roman mythological goddess of the forest

Barr-Saggott paid her great attention; and, as I have said, the heart of her mother was uplifted in consequence. Kitty Beighton took matters more calmly. It was pleasant to be singled out by a Commissioner with letters after his name, and to fill the hearts of other girls with bad feelings. But there was no denying the fact that Barr-Saggott was phenomenally ugly; and all his attempts to adorn himself only made him more grotesque. He was not christened "The Langur"—which means grey ape—for nothing. It was pleasant, Kitty thought, to have him at her feet, but it was better to escape from him and ride with the graceless Cubbon—the man in a Dragoon Regiment at Umballa—the boy with a handsome face, and no prospects.* Kitty liked Cubbon more than a little. He never pretended for a moment that he was anything less than head over heels in love with her; for he was an honest boy. So Kitty fled, now and again, from the stately wooings of Barr-Saggott to the company of young Cubbon, and was scolded by her Mamma in consequence. "But, Mother," she said, "Mr. Saggott is such—such a—is so *fearfully* ugly, you know!"

prospects: hopes for advancement

"My dear," said Mrs. Beighton, piously, "we cannot be other than an all-ruling Providence has made us. Besides, you will take precedence of your own Mother, you know! Think of that and be reasonable."

Then Kitty put up her little chin and said irreverent things about precedence, and

marriages made in disregard of parents' wishes are rarely successful.

DISCUSSION

Introduction

The classical allusions of this story are mainly ornamental, not integral to its meaning. But they do highlight the action and give it a kind of universality. Before beginning a discussion of the story, you may want to provide the following additional information about the British rule of India.

British rule in India dates from 1757 with Robert Clive's victory at Plassey, after which the territory of British India was gradually ex-

tended north to the Punjab province, bordering Afghanistan, now mostly incorporated into Pakistan. Most of British India was ruled originally by the Governor-General and Supreme Council of the British East India Company, overseen by the commissioner of the British government's India Office. After the Indian mutiny, or the Sepoy Mutiny, of 1857, the Governor-General became the viceroy, responsible to the crown, and the East India Company lost much of its control. Kipling's view of British rule is ambivalent. He applauds its efficiency and conscientiousness while ridiculing its self-satisfaction and naiveté about Indian culture.

Analysis

The plot of the story is based on one of the oldest situations in literature and life: the love triangle. Kitty has two suitors: one she tolerates and one she loves. The theme is old also: the precedence of love over position and material considerations in the choice of a mate. The mother embodies these false values and, as an authority figure, symbolizes their "precedence." The classical allusions are somewhat functional. Have the students look them up and explain their relevance.

Cupid, the boy god, son of Venus, wreaks havoc among both men and gods with his archery. He shoots two kinds of arrows: the golden-headed ones of requited love (e.g., Cubbon's) and the leaden-headed ones of unrequited love (e.g.,

Commissioners, and matrimony. Mr. Beighton rubbed the top of his head; for he was an easy-going man.

Late in the season, when he judged that the time was ripe, Barr-Saggott developed a plan which did great credit to his administrative powers. He arranged an archery tournament for ladies, with a most sumptuous diamond-studded bracelet as prize. He drew up his terms skillfully, and every one saw that the bracelet was a gift to Miss Beighton, the acceptance carrying with it the hand and the heart of Commissioner Barr-Saggott. The terms were a St. Leonard's Round—thirty-six shots at sixty yards—under the rules of the Simla Toxophilite* Society.

Toxophilite: one who loves archery

All Simla was invited. There were beautifully arranged tea tables under the deodars* at Annandale, where the Grand Stand is now; and, alone in its glory, winking in the sun, sat the diamond bracelet in a blue velvet case. Miss Beighton was anxious—almost too anxious—to compete. On the appointed afternoon all Simla rode down to Annandale to witness the Judgment of Paris turned upside down. Kitty rode with young Cubbon, and it was easy to see that the boy was troubled in his mind. He must be held innocent of everything that followed. Kitty was pale and nervous, and looked long at the bracelet. Barr-Saggott was gorgeously dressed, even more nervous than Kitty, and more hideous than ever.

deodars: cedars native to the Himalayas

Mrs. Beighton smiled condescendingly, as befitted the mother of a potential Commissioneress, and the shooting began, all the world standing in a semicircle as the ladies came out one after the other.

Nothing is so tedious as an archery competition. They shot, and they shot, and they

This is the second time Kipling has referred to Kitty's father this way. (See page 96: "Mr. Beighton held his tongue. He was an easy-going man.") Discuss with the students what Kipling is saying about Mr. Beighton's character. *(He doesn't want to cross his wife or daughter, even when he disagrees with them. He lets them—no doubt unwisely—have their way.)*

See notes below and "About the Story" question 3 on page 98 for explanation of this allusion.

This is a type of metaphor known as hyperbole (hie-PUR-buh-lee)—intentional exaggeration in order to make a point.

Barr-Saggott's). Kitty's nickname, Diana of Tara-Devi, associates her with the virgin huntress Diana, cousin of Venus, known for her skill in archery.

The Judgment of Paris was the incident that caused the abduction of Helen, which precipitated the Trojan War. Paris, a Trojan prince, was asked by the gods to judge a beauty contest between Hera (Juno), Athena, and Aphrodite (Venus). He awarded the prize, a golden apple, to Aphrodite after she had promised him the most beautiful woman in the world for a wife.

Kipling may be implying that the spectators see Paris's judgment as misguided—placing love and pleasure, represented by Aphrodite, above the domestic virtues represented by Hera or the wisdom represented by Athena. The spectators expect Kitty's judgment to place position and material considerations over love.

On the other hand, Kipling may be implying that the ugly Barr-Saggott represents the handsome Paris, and the contest is supposed to end with Barr-Saggott, like Paris, winning a beautiful wife. Kitty turns things upside-down, however, by arranging an outcome far different from what Barr-Saggott expects.

 Application

Have the students try their hand at writing a slice-of-life sketch, using one of the classical allusions from Kipling's story (or another classical allusion they have found intriguing). It may be helpful for you to bring to class one of the two works referring to mythology listed under the Resources section (p. 95). You should be able to find either work at your public library. If time permits, you may even want to read aloud one or two of the selections from Edith Hamilton's work to give the students additional ideas as well as additional exposure to classical myths. Hamilton's style is not only artistic but also very readable. Use **Writing Rubric 4-2: Alluring Allusions** for grading this writing assignment. Encourage students to be creative in the way they incorporate their allusions.

Note the symbolism of the location of the two suitors.

Note Kipling's ironic use of religious terms throughout the story ("Providence," "piously," "irreverent," "glory," "sacred"), intentionally underscoring the characters' misplaced values.

kept on shooting, till the sun left the valley, and little breezes got up in the deodars, and people waited for Miss Beighton to shoot and win. Cubbon was at one horn of the semicircle round the shooters, and Barr-Saggott at the other. Miss Beighton was last on the list. The scoring had been weak, and the bracelet, with Commissioner Barr-Saggott, was hers to a certainty.

The Commissioner strung her bow with his own sacred hands. She stepped forward, looked at the bracelet, and her first arrow went true to a hair—full into the heart of the "gold"—counting nine points.

Young Cubbon on the left turned white, and Barr-Saggott smiled. Now horses used to shy when Barr-Saggott smiled. Kitty saw that smile. She looked to her left-front, gave an almost imperceptible nod to Cubbon, and went on shooting.

I wish I could describe the scene that followed. It was out of the ordinary and most improper. Miss Kitty fitted her arrows with immense deliberation, so that every one might see what she was doing. She was a perfect shot; and her forty-six pound bow suited her to a nicety. She pinned the wooden legs of the target with great care four successive times. She pinned the wooden top of the target once, and all the ladies looked at each other. Then she began some fancy shooting at the white, which if you hit it, counts exactly one point. She put five arrows into the white. It was wonderful archery; but, seeing that her business was to make "golds" and win the bracelet, Barr-

Saggott turned a delicate green like young water-grass. Next, she shot over the target twice, then wide to the left twice—always with the same deliberation—while a chilly hush fell over the company, and Mrs. Beighton took out her handkerchief. Then Kitty shot at the ground in front of the target, and split several arrows. Then she made a red—or seven points—just to show what she could do if she liked, and she finished up her amazing performance with some more fancy shooting at the target supports. Here is her score as it was pricked off:

	Gold.	Red.	Blue.	Black.	White.	Total Hits.	Total Score.
Miss Beighton	1	1	0	0	5	7	21

Barr-Saggott looked as if the last few arrowheads had been driven into his legs instead of the target's, and the deep stillness was broken by a little snubby, mottled, half-grown girl saying in a shrill voice of triumph, "Then *I've* won!"

Mrs. Beighton did her best to bear up; but she wept in the presence of the people. No training could help her through such disappointment. Kitty unstrung her bow with a vicious jerk, and went back to her place, while Barr-Saggott was trying to pretend that he enjoyed snapping the bracelet on the snubby girl's raw, red wrist. It was an awkward scene—most awkward. Every one tried to depart in a body and leave Kitty to the mercy of her Mamma.

But Cubbon took her away instead, and—the rest isn't worth printing.

About the Story

1. Explain the classical allusion in the title.
2. Explain Kitty's nickname.
3. What is the significance of the reference to the judgment of Paris?
4. In a situation like Kitty's, what do you think a young girl should do?

About the Story

1. *The title is an allusion to Cupid, Roman god of love. See Analysis section for further explanation.*

2. *Kitty's nickname, Diana of Tara-Devi, associates her with the virgin huntress Diana, known for her skill in archery.*

3. *Paris, a Trojan prince, was asked by the gods to judge a beauty contest between Hera (Juno), Athena, and Aphrodite (Venus). The reference in "Cupid's Arrows" may imply that the ugly Barr-Saggott represents the handsome Paris, and the contest is supposed to end with Barr-Saggott, like Paris, winning a beautiful wife. Kitty turns things upside-down, however, by arranging an outcome*

far different from what Barr-Saggott expects. Or it may imply that the spectators expect to see Kitty (unlike Paris, who ranked love highest) make her choice based on the ambition and materialism of her mother's worldly wisdom.

4. *Answers may vary, but encourage students to base their answers on Biblical principles. (See "Potential problems" section, pp. 95-96.)*

PREPARATION
"Eldorado," "The Progress of Poesy"
Overview

Poe's "Eldorado" alludes to the city sought by the conquistadors of Spain and Portugal. It also can refer obliquely to heaven. In either case or both cases, it stands for a life goal, a self-conceived notion of an ideal state toward which the individual bends his efforts or for which the idealist crusades. As in the case of Waller's "dark cottages" (see page 104), an allusion is used symbolically. This poem illustrates the topic of Unit 4 but also anticipates Unit 5 on symbol.

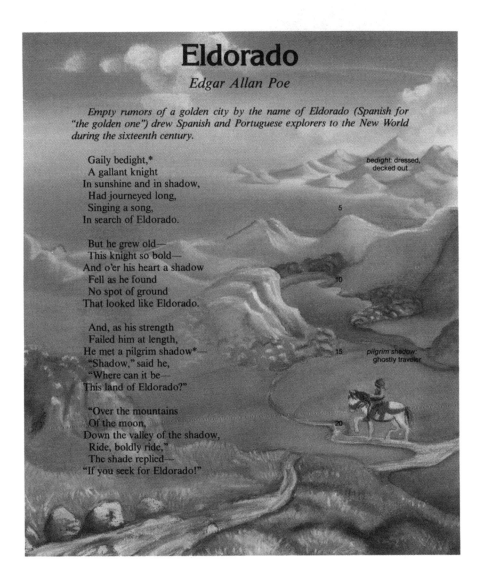

Eldorado

Edgar Allan Poe

*Empty rumors of a golden city by the name of Eldorado (Spanish for
"the golden one") drew Spanish and Portuguese explorers to the New World
during the sixteenth century.*

Gaily bedight,*
A gallant knight
In sunshine and in shadow,
Had journeyed long,
Singing a song,   5
In search of Eldorado.

But he grew old—
This knight so bold—
And o'er his heart a shadow
Fell as he found   10
No spot of ground
That looked like Eldorado.

And, as his strength
Failed him at length,
He met a pilgrim shadow*—   15
"Shadow," said he,
"Where can it be—
This land of Eldorado?"

"Over the mountains
Of the moon,   20
Down the valley of the shadow,
Ride, boldly ride,"
The shade replied—
"If you seek for Eldorado!"

bedight: dressed,
decked out

pilgrim shadow:
ghostly traveler

OBJECTIVES

The students will be able to

- Discuss man's search for immortality as a universal theme in literature.
- Give and analyze reasons that despair can overtake those who grow old without knowing Christ.

Note the change in meaning of the word *shadow* throughout the poem:

Stanza one: External shadows, perhaps symbolic of difficulties in life.

Stanza two: An internal shadow "o'er his heart"; a reference to discouragement, defeat.

Stanza three: A ghostly traveler; refers to one who has gone before the knight into death.

Stanza four: "The valley of the shadow"; an allusion to death (cf. Ps. 23:4).

FURTHER HELPS

Additional activities

1. Have the students analyze Ecclesiastes 12. Here Solomon begins with a message to young men and women on the importance of remembering their Creator "now" in the bloom of youth. This

---

"The Progress of Poesy" allegorizes the decline of the creative imagination in old age. It carries on the motif of youth versus age that runs through the end of this unit. As allegory, it anticipates Unit 5. The allegory is based on a Biblical allusion: Moses' bringing water from the rock (Exod. 17, Num. 20).

Potential problems

The title "The Progress of Poesy" will need explaining. *Poesy* here denotes the creative imagination in general and poetry in particular. *Progress* denotes (1) a royal journey or (2) an advance. In either meaning it is ironic. What is described is a dwindling or retroversion rather than a triumphant procession or advance.

DISCUSSION

"Eldorado"

Introduction

The preamble to the Constitution speaks of "the pursuit of happiness"—happiness in the sense of being fortunate or blessed. Everyone has an idea of what the old philosophers called "the highest good." To some it is an internal condition of peace; to others, material prosperity or a certain lifestyle; to still others, it is success in some endeavor—for themselves or for mankind. It is the pursuit of happiness that sends the knight on his mysterious quest in Poe's "Eldorado." Note that the title itself gives the allusion carried throughout the poem (see headnote).

Analysis

Most people—especially young people—have dreams toward which they strive. As the conquistadors failed in their quests, the poem implies that Eldorado, in the general, symbolic sense, is not to be found in this world. The "pilgrim shadow" is one who has carried his quest into the next world. His directions seem vague. Do they imply futility? Do they recommend suicide? ("Down the valley of the shadow, / Ride, boldly ride.") Is the "shadow" a successful or unsuccessful "pilgrim"? Is he still questing or now returning? If returning, did he find what he sought, or does he mean "be prepared for disappointment"? Does the poem subtly question the Christian's hope of heaven in the next life as well as the worldling's hope of finding

Note alliteration ("finds . . . fount . . . fount . . . flow," stanza one; "the mount is mute," stanza three). Also note Arnold's careful use of verbs in each stanza. The young man "rambles," "strikes," "finds," and "brings." The mature man "chops" and "sees not." The old man "totters," "feebly rakes," and "lays [down] his weary bones."

warning is made vivid by a series of images—visual, auditory, and tactile— that represent bodily decay as the decline of a great household. Like Arnold, Solomon acknowledges the decay of the body; unlike Arnold, however, he puts the decay in perspective (verses 8-14). For detailed analysis see *Companion to College English,* second edition, by Ronald Horton, pages 285-87 (Greenville, South Carolina: Bob Jones University Press, 2000).

2. As a tie to history, have the students research and write a short essay on the conquistadors. Their essays should discuss how the lives of such men may have motivated Poe to write his poem. Artistic students might do artwork showing the costumes and ships of the period. See **Writing Rubric 4-3: Conquistadors—Their Conquests and Character.**

The Progress of Poesy

Matthew Arnold

Nineteenth-century poets such as Matthew Arnold worried about the decline of their imaginative powers because of old age. This poem pictures the life of a poet (or of anyone else whose work depends on creative genius) as a searching for water.

Youth rambles on life's arid mount,
And strikes the rock, and finds the vein,
And brings the water from the fount,
The fount which shall not flow again.

The man mature with labor chops   5
For the bright stream a channel grand,
And sees not that the sacred drops
Ran off and vanished out of hand.

And then the old man totters nigh,
And feebly rakes among the stones.   10
The mount is mute, the channel dry;
And down he lays his weary bones.

---

heaven in this world? These are interesting questions, but the poem is intentionally vague and inconclusive. Certainly it offers a picture of life in which strength fails before the goal—an illusory one—is reached. Notice how the word *shadow* takes on slightly different meanings in each stanza. The last instance is, of course, an allusion to Psalm 23:4.

"The Progress of Poesy"
The "arid mount" recalls the range of Horeb and the rocky outcropping of Sinai, the mount of God. Through allusion, Arnold is associating poetic inspiration with the divine inspiration of the Law delivered by God to Moses on Mt. Sinai. Lines 2-3 add an allusion to Moses' smiting the rock to bring forth water for thirsting Israel. Poetic creativity, the poem suggests, is

mysterious and divine. (Arnold was an agnostic humanist whose only god was man.) Allusion thus carries the main weight of the meaning and also unites the poem artistically. The creative life is described in terms of the search for water. Imaginative creativity flows only in youth. In middle years it is channeled and disciplined even as it is drying up. In old age both source and channel provide nothing. The mount (now referred to as a speaking mount, like Sinai, where Israel heard the voice of God) is "mute." The last line may refer to Moses' being buried in the mountains of Edom, having failed (because of his disobedience in striking the rock) to enter the Promised Land (Exod. 17).

At least two and possibly three allusions converge in the poem (Mt. Sinai, the Law, Moses'

striking of the rock). Notice that it is organized by stanzas according to the stages of life. It almost deifies one of the powers of man: the creative imagination. Point out that in spite of what this poem claims, many of the greatest achievements of human creative genius were accomplished in old age.

Application
Arnold's pessimism is revealed in another of his poems, entitled "Growing Old." Read the poem aloud to the class. This poem can be found in **Appendix K.**

About the Author

As a national inspector of schools, Matthew Arnold (1822-1888) met hundreds of principals, teachers, and students. These conferences convinced him that English education was culturally barren. He concluded that literature, especially poetry, was the best way to incorporate spiritual concepts. As Christians we can agree with Arnold on this point, for we recognize that Scripture is replete with poetic language that helps express and clarify complex truths. Unlike Arnold, however, we believe that the form of Scripture is subservient to the absolute truth of Scripture. Arnold held no such belief. Although he emphasized the value of poetic form, he was convinced that truth is relative—that it should change and develop as society changes and develops. Churchmen, therefore, who sought to stand for the absolute values of Scripture were subject to the poet's scorn.

Besides being a school inspector and poet, Arnold was also considered a successful professor and a social critic. Despite his achievements, Arnold became dissatisfied toward the middle of his life. His thirtieth birthday brought him the sensation of being "three parts iced over." This despair toward aging is evident in "The Progress of Poesy" and provides an interesting contrast to Chesterton's essay on the same topic. Knowing each writer's philosophy helps us understand their differing responses to growing old.

About the Poems

1. What does Eldorado stand for in Poe's poem?
2. What does it suggest about the dreams of youth?
3. What Biblical allusion, basic to the poem, appears in the first stanza of Matthew Arnold's poem?
4. Does the Bible support the pessimism of Arnold's poem?

About the Poems

they are to be honored (cf. Lev. 19:32; Job 32:6; Prov. 23:22; 1 Tim. 5:1-2).

1. *Answers may vary, but possible answers include the city sought by the conquistadors; heaven; or (primarily) a life goal, a self-conceived notion of an ideal state toward which the individual bends his efforts or for which the idealist crusades.*

2. *The poem implies that Eldorado, in the general, symbolic sense, is not to be found in this world.*

3. *Moses' striking of the rock in Exodus 17:1-7 (cf. Num. 20:7-13).*

4. *Answers may vary. Students may note passages from Ecclesiastes (cf. 12:1-7) or elsewhere that might tend to support Arnold's pessimism. However, the Bible's primary view of the aged is that*

"On the Pleasures of No Longer Being Very Young," "The Soul's Dark Cottage"

allusions

FURTHER HELPS

Additional activities

1. Assign students to do brief oral reports on the historical allusions to Cardinal Wolsey (appearing as a character in Shakespeare's *Henry VIII*); Napoleon I and his battle of Marengo (a victory) and his Russian campaign (a defeat); Charles V, Holy Roman Emperor (1519-58) who retired to a monastery; and Charles I of England (1625-49), overthrown and executed by the Puritan revolutionary army. Then discuss as a class why Chesterton chose these people to allude to. (See "About the Essay and Poem" questions 3 and 4, page 105.)

2. In "The Soul's Dark Cottage" Waller employs his trademark literary pattern of antithesis by filling his poem with contrasting pairs of images.

On the Pleasures of No Longer Being Very Young

G. K. Chesterton

The next selection contrasts with the two preceding in emphasizing the advantages of age over youth. The first, by G. K. Chesterton, uses many of the devices we have already encountered—imaginative comparison, parallelism, and so forth. It is also heavily allusive. Consult an encyclopedia to identify Chesterton's historical allusions in paragraph 3.

There are advantages in the advance through middle age into later life which are very seldom stated in a sensible way. Generally, they are stated in a sentimental way; in a general suggestion that all old men are equipped with beautiful snowy beards like Father Christmas and rejoice in unfathomable wisdom like Nestor.* All this has caused the young people to be skeptical about the real advantages of the old people, and the true statement of those advantages sounds like a paradox. I would not say that old men grow wise, for men never grow wise; and many old men retain a very attractive childishness and cheerful innocence. Elderly people are often much more romantic than young people, and sometimes even more adventurous, having begun to realize how many things they do not know. It is a true proverb, no doubt, which says "There is no fool like an old fool." Perhaps there is no fool who is half so happy in his own fool's paradise. But, however this may be, it is true that the advantages of maturity are not those which are generally urged even in praise of it, and when they are truly urged they sound like an almost comic contradiction.

Nestor: Greek chieftain famous for his wisdom, consulted by King Agamemnon in the *Iliad* by Homer

For instance, one pleasure attached to growing older is that many things seem to be growing younger, growing fresher and more lively than we once supposed them to be. We begin to see significance, or (in other words) to see life, in a large number of traditions, institutions, maxims, and codes of manners that seem in our first days to be dead. A young man grows up in a world that often seems to him intolerably old. He grows up among

---

PREPARATION

"On the Pleasures of No Longer Being Very Young," "The Soul's Dark Cottage"

Overview

Chesterton's essay is a valuable reply to the pessimism of the two preceding selections concerning growing old. It also exemplifies closely textured prose with a high density of allusion. It contains examples of all the types of allusions discussed in the introduction.

The six lines from Waller's "On the Last Verses in His Book" contain two Biblical allusions. Students should be able to identify the first from their reading of the introduction to this unit. The passage also wonderfully articulates a Christian view of old age.

Potential problems

The essay expresses a perspective on life foreign to the teenager's experience and contains references to knowledge with which he is unacquainted. The insights are valuable, however, and the references are allusions, the topic of this unit.

DISCUSSION

Introduction

Young people often believe they understand life better than do those whom God has put in authority over them. But to trust the wisdom of youth over that of age is to defy the teaching and values of Scripture, especially Proverbs, which continually commands the young person to take instruction from his elders.

Analysis

"On the Pleasures of No Longer Being Very Young"

In direct contrast to Arnold, Chesterton "celebrates" growing old, specifying several advanproverbs and precepts that appear to be quite stiff and senseless. He seems to be stuffed with stale things; to be given the stones of death instead of the bread of life; to be fed on the dust of the dead past; to live in a town of tombs. It is a very natural mistake, but it is a mistake. The advantage of advancing years lies in discovering that traditions are true, and therefore alive; indeed, a tradition is not even traditional except when it is alive. It is great fun to find out that the world has not repeated proverbs because they are proverbial, but because they are practical. Until I owned a dog, I never knew what is meant by the proverb about letting a sleeping dog lie, or the fable about the dog in the manger.* Now those dead phrases are quite alive to me, for they are parts of a perfectly practical psychology. Until I went to live in the country, I had no notion of the meaning of the maxim, "It's an ill wind that blows nobody good." Now it seems to me as pertinent and even pungent as if it were a new remark just made to me by a neighbor at the garden gate.

---

the fable about the dog in the manger: One of Aesop's fables about a dog lying in a manger of hay. When the horses come in to rest, the dog barks and growls to keep them away from the hay. The moral is to not begrudge others something you cannot enjoy yourself.

Again and again, with monotonous reiteration, both my young friends and myself had been told from childhood that fortune is fickle, that riches take to themselves wings and fly, that power can depart suddenly from the powerful, that pride goes before a fall, and insolence attracts the thunderbolt of the gods. But it was all unmeaning to us, and all the proverbs seemed stiff and stale, like dusty labels on neglected antiques. We had heard of the fall of Wolsey, which was like the crash of a huge palace, still faintly rumbling through

the ages; we had read of it in the words of Shakespeare, which possibly were not written by Shakespeare; we had learned them and learned nothing from them. We had read ten thousand times, to the point of tedium, of the difference between the Napoleon of Marengo and the Napoleon of Moscow; but we should never have expected Moscow if we had been looking at Marengo. We knew that Charles the Fifth resigned his crown, or that Charles the First lost his head; and we should have duly remarked *"Sic transit gloria mundi,"** after the incident, but not before it. We had been told that the Roman Empire declined, or that the Spanish Empire disintegrated; but no German ever really applied it to the German Empire, and no Briton to the British Empire. The very repetition of these truths will sound like the old interminable repetition of truisms. And yet they are to me, at this moment, like amazing and startling discoveries, for I have lived to see the dead proverbs come alive.

Sic transit gloria mundi: so passes the glory of the world

This, like so many of the realizations of later life, is quite impossible to convey in words to anybody who has not reached it in this way. It is like a difference of dimension or plane, in which something which the young have long looked at, rather wearily, as a diagram has suddenly become a solid. It is like the indescribable transition from the inorganic to the organic;* as if the stone snakes and birds of some ancient Egyptian inscription began to leap about like living things. The thing was a dead maxim when we were alive with youth. It becomes a living maxim when we are nearer to death. Even as we are dying, the whole world is coming to life.

---

inorganic to the organic: from minerals to living tissue

Line 1: the dark ignorance of youth

Line 2: the light of discernment and experience in age

Line 3: the brute strength of youth

Line 4: the inner substance of age

Line 5: the clouded, temporal perspective of youth

Line 6: the clear, eternal view of age

Have the students write a poem on a topic important to them using this same pattern of contrasting images. See **Writing Rubric 4-4: Poetic Parallels.**

3. Have an elderly person whom you respect come to class and talk about the joys of growing old and lessons he or she has learned along the way.

Journal entry idea
Ask the students to write an essay entitled "On the Pleasures of Being Young."

Journal entry idea
Have the students interview an older person, a grandparent or other relative or perhaps an older Christian, and write about some interesting fact or lesson they learn from their discussion. They should note especially whether that person's attitude toward aging is more akin to Arnold's or Chesterton's.

---

tages in his essay. Read the essay aloud in class. Following your reading, ask the students to list some trite platitudes such as those Chesterton mentions ("fortune is fickle," "let a sleeping dog lie," etc.). Then have them explain them. Ask them whether any have had experiences that seem to illustrate the truth and value of these proverbs.

In defending the beliefs and customs passed along from parent to child that young people often reject, Chesterton is in agreement generally with Scripture (Prov. 1:8-9; Jer. 35), though Chesterton, a Catholic, places a higher value on tradition than Fundamentalists would. Nonetheless, Chesterton's view is conservative. An idea encapsulated in a memorable statement (a proverb) is likely to have been preserved be-

cause it contains truth. A custom perpetuated from generation to generation is likely to be rooted in some deep human need or sense of obligation. These meanings appear only after some years of thoughtful experience in the world. Time brings reevaluation. It also, says Chesterton, calls dead things to life.

"The Soul's Dark Cottage"

Waller reinforces Chesterton's view by contradicting the prevalent idea that intellectual and creative powers fail after midlife so that a poet is finished before he reaches old age. If we did not have the works of Milton's old age as examples of the contrary, this near-perfect little poem by Waller would demonstrate otherwise. It was one of the two most highly admired poetic passages in the eighteenth century. A poet's

well of inspiration need not run dry if it taps into the timeless truths of God's Word. Waller was an elderly man when he wrote these lines.

Lines 1-2 and 5-6 give metaphoric support to the idea stated directly in lines 3-4. The metaphors are also Biblical allusions: the first to II Corinthians 5:1-4 (which itself alludes to Israel's or the patriarchs' wanderings in tents) and the second to Moses' viewing the Promised Land from Mount Pisgah (Deut. 34:1-4). The two allusions come together when the journeys of Israel under Moses and Joshua are taken allegorically as a picture of the Christian's passage from this world to the next—the Jordan River serving as an emblem of death. This allegorizing of this segment of Israel's history is not strictly Biblical in origin but classical—an

Note Waller's use of paradox in line 3: "Stronger by weakness." See Unit 6 (page 148) for a discussion of this literary device.

The Soul's Dark Cottage

Edmund Waller

The following lines preface a volume of poetry written by a man in his eighties. They answer the objection that no one so old can write anything very much worth reading, especially anything poetic. Waller replies with two Biblical allusions, both metaphoric.

The soul's dark cottage, battered and decayed,
Lets in new light through chinks that time has made;
Stronger by weakness, wiser men become,
As they draw near to their eternal home.
Leaving the old, both worlds at once they view,   5
That stand upon the threshold of the new.

About the Author

Politics and poetry were the two great passions of Edmund Waller's (1606-1687) life. Born into a wealthy family, Waller inherited a fortune when he was only ten years old. He entered the English parliament while still a teenager and spent most of his life involved with court society and party politics. Although his involvement in a political conspiracy led to fines and banishment, Waller eventually returned to court and resumed his role as a political moderate and peacemaker.

The poetry for which Waller was most famous in his day was *panegyric,* poetry written to praise someone, often a king or patron. For Waller, the writing of panegyric served not only as a suitable hobby for a courtly gentleman but also as a political tool for the promotion of ideas and opinions. Although Waller gained a reputation for supporting with panegyric anyone who happened to be in power, he also possessed great diplomatic skills and a strong desire to promote peace and harmony in a nation torn by petty strifes and political factions. His poetry displays this lifelong desire for reconciliation of extremes. Our selection comes from his *Divine Poems,* a collection of verse written in his later years.

adaptation of the pagan mythological view of death as passage over a river. Nevertheless, it appears in many hymns and gospel songs. The metaphor of the body as a dilapidated cottage is also not precisely the same as that of the body as a tent house. But the truth is nonetheless Biblical and the effect powerful. Old age brings greater illumination ("new light") and greater breadth of vision (of "both worlds," the earthly and the heavenly). Paradoxically with the fading of physical and intellectual vitality comes increased spiritual vigor and perceptivity.

The poem is also a fine example of iambic pentameter (heroic) couplets, popular in the eighteenth century. The other two (preceding) stanzas appear below.

When we for age could neither read nor write,
The subject made us able to indite;
The soul, with nobler resolutions decked,
The body stooping, does herself erect.
No mortal parts are requisite to raise
Her that, unbodied, can her Maker praise.

The seas are quiet when the winds give o'er;
So calm are we when passions are no more!
For then we know how vain it was to boast
Of fleeting things, so certain to be lost.
Clouds of affection from our younger eyes
Conceal that emptiness which age descries.

About the Essay and Poem

1. What are some advantages of age that Chesterton identifies?
2. How does Chesterton's view of age differ from Matthew Arnold's?
3. Using an encyclopedia, identify the three historical allusions Chesterton uses in paragraph 3.
4. Why do you think Chesterton chose these allusions?
5. Like Chesterton, Waller believes that age enriches rather than diminishes creative powers. What two Biblical allusions does Waller use to support his view?

Pigeon Feathers

John Updike

In twentieth-century literature it is rare to find a short story like the following. Although we would not label Updike's story "Christian," Christians can appreciate its strong, positive statement of God's existence and man's immortality. "Pigeon Feathers" is about a young boy's search for truth. The characters who endeavor to "help" him in this quest starkly illustrate modern man's pitiable condition: "professing themselves to be wise, they became fools." The mother, for example, offers him the Romantic view of nature as god; the father presents the modernist view of science as god; and the preacher proffers the humanistic view of man as god. The grandparents, especially the grandfather, are the only characters who seem to have grasped the truth. But the boy cannot directly obtain answers from these two, for his grandfather has died, and his grandmother, now fighting disease and the insensitivity of her children, seems too disoriented to offer help. The boy, however, does find a copy of his grandfather's well-worn Bible. This discovery, coupled with the discovery of God's magnificent design in nature, supplies him with the proof he needs to affirm—like his grandfather before him—the existence of God and the immortality of man.

OBJECTIVES

The students will be able to

- Scripturally analyze answers to three basic philosophical questions: Where did I come from? Why am I here? Where am I going?

- Analyze and discuss ways in which Biblical and literary allusions do more than reinforce the theme of "Pigeon Feathers"; they are an integral part of the story's action.

You may wish to point out to the students that this is an allusion to Romans 1:22.

FURTHER HELPS

Additional activities

1. Have a group of students dramatize a scene from the short story.

2. Cover a shoebox with paper and label the box "Dear Pastor." Instruct each student to write a letter about a problem in the story, writing it as though he were David, the protagonist. Then have him put the letter in an envelope and place it in the box. Next, distribute these envelopes to different students and ask them to give good Biblical

About the Essay and Poem

1. *Answers will vary but may include "many things seem to be growing younger, growing fresher and more lively than we once supposed them to be" (page 102); "traditions are true, and therefore alive" (page 103); "I have lived to see the dead proverbs come alive" (page 103).*

2. *Chesterton's essay, specifying advantages of growing old, stands in direct contrast to Arnold's poem.*

3. *Wolsey; Shakespeare; Napoleon; Charles V; Charles I; the Roman, Spanish, German, and British Empires (any three).*

4. *Each of the allusions refers to the fall of a great person or institution. Exactly how each "fell" can be found in an encyclopedia. (Note that the "fall" of*

Shakespeare is an allusion to the myth that he did not write the plays attributed to him.) These allusions strengthen the point of the paragraph—that proverbs such as "fortune is fickle, that riches take to themselves wings and fly, that power can depart suddenly from the powerful," and so on make profound statements about life despite their familiarity.

5. *Second Corinthians 5:1-4 and Deuteronomy 34:1-4. Students may find other Scripture passages that could be allusions as well.*

PREPARATION

"Pigeon Feathers"

Overview

As mentioned in the headnote, finding a story like "Pigeon Feathers" is unusual. Although we

would not label Updike's story "Christian," Christians can appreciate the strong positive statements about God's existence and man's immortality. The story also provides an excellent opportunity for showing the fallacies of such erroneous philosophies as Romanticism, materialism, and humanism.

Potential problems

In "Pigeon Feathers" Updike directs our attention to Christ as the ultimate answer to man's search but stops short of showing the necessity of a personal relationship with Him. In his other stories, Updike places the stress on man's helplessness and isolation; rarely does he hint at hopefulness as he does in "Pigeon Feathers." It is important,

Allusions: The allusions to these specific books are not superfluous. See the first marginal note on page 119 for further details.

Allusions/Irony: The allusion to Wells (1866-1946) is particularly significant. Wells was an English author known for satirical novels and popular historical and political writings. He was also an atheist who strongly advocated socialism, feminism, and evolution. It is ironic, therefore, that Updike would choose a passage from Wells to serve as the catalyst that starts David on his journey of faith.

Thought/Theme: The reference to the mother's "unfamiliar handwriting" reflects the emotional distance already existing between David and his mother, a distance that will increase as his struggle intensifies.

Note careful, detailed use of metaphor that leads us to David's spiritual crisis—the pages become "dusty glass through which he [sees] . . . unreal and irrelevant worlds." Note also the physical response ("an unpleasant fullness came into his throat") that precedes his spiritual response.

When they moved to Firetown, things were set, displaced, rearranged. A red cane-back sofa that had been the chief piece in the living room at Olinger was here banished, too big for the narrow country parlor, to the barn, and shrouded under a tarpaulin. Never again would David lie on its length all afternoon eating raisins and reading mystery novels and science fiction and P. G. Wodehouse.* The blue wing chair that had stood for years in the ghostly, immaculate guest bedroom, gazing through the windows curtained with dotted swiss toward the telephone wires and horse-chestnut trees and opposite houses, was here established importantly in front of the smutty little fire place that supplied, in those first cold April days, their only heat. As a child, David had been afraid of the guest bedroom—it was there that he, lying sick with the measles, had seen a black rod the size of a yardstick jog along at a slight slant beside the edge of the bed and vanish when he screamed—and it was disquieting to have one of the elements of its haunted atmosphere basking by the fire, in the center of the family, growing sooty with use. The books that at home had gathered dust in the case beside the piano were here hastily stacked, all out of order, in the shelves that carpenters had built along one wall below the deep-silled windows. David, at fourteen, had been more moved than a mover; like the furniture, he had to find a new place, and on the Saturday of the second week he tried to work off some of his disorientation by arranging the books.

P. G. Wodehouse: Sir Pelham Grenville Wodehouse was an English novelist and humorist (1881-1975).

It was a collection obscurely depressing to him, mostly books his mother had acquired when she was young: college anthologies of Greek plays and Romantic poetry, Will Durant's* *Story of Philosophy,* a soft-leather set of Shakespeare with string bookmarks sewed to the bindings, *Green Mansions* boxed and illustrated with woodcuts, *I, the Tiger,* by Manuel Komroff, novels by names like Galsworthy* and Ellen Glasgow* and Irvin S. Cobb* and Sinclair Lewis* and "Elizabeth." The odor of faded taste made him feel the ominous gap between himself and his parents, the insulting gulf of time that existed before he was born. Suddenly he was tempted to dip into this time. From the heaps of books piled around him on the worn old floorboards, he picked up Volume II of a four-volume set of *The Outline of History,* by H. G. Wells.* Once David had read *The Time Machine* in an anthology; this gave him a small grip on the author. The book's red binding had faded to orange-pink on the spine. When he lifted the cover, there was a sweetish, attic-like smell, and his mother's maiden name written in unfamiliar handwriting on the flyleaf—an upright, bold, yet careful signature, bearing a faint relation to the quick scrunched blackslant that flowed with marvelous consistency across her shopping lists and budget accounts and Christmas cards to college friends from this same vaguely menacing long ago.

Will Durant: American historian (1885-1981)
Galsworthy: English author (1867-1933)
Ellen Glasgow: American novelist (1873-1945)
Irvin S. Cobb: American author (1876-1944)
Sinclair Lewis: American novelist (1885-1951)
H. G. Wells: Herbert George Wells, English author(1866-1946)

He leafed through, pausing at drawings, done in an old-fashioned stippled style, of bas-reliefs, masks, Romans without pupils in their eyes, articles of ancient costume, fragments of pottery found in unearthed homes. He knew it would be interesting in a magazine, sandwiched between ads and jokes, but in this undiluted form history was somehow sour. The print was determinedly legible, and smug, like a lesson book. As he bent over the pages, yellow at the edges, they seemed rectangles of dusty glass through which he looked down into

guidance (unlike Reverend Dobson's) for the problem in the original letter. For example, a letter might read as follows.

Dear Pastor,

I'm a fourteen-year-old boy who has just moved to a new town. I find it very difficult to make new friends. Could you give me some advice?

David

Discuss the students' replies as a class. Those that do the best job of giving Scriptural guidance might be posted on a bulletin board.

therefore, to warn students against indiscriminate reading of Updike.

DISCUSSION

Introduction

Read the headnote aloud in class. Point out to the students that in his story Updike shows us the encroachment of erroneous philosophies on faith. Pressures from godless preachers, from well-meaning but unregenerate family members, and from secular authors such as H. G. Wells and Plato cause a breakdown of faith in a God who personally created man, cares for him, and gives him an immortal soul.

Ask the students if they have ever known another young person who has faced or is facing the problems David Kern faces in the story. Take some time to discuss the needs of unsaved young people and the necessity of developing compassion for those who may not have had the advantages many Christian young people have (i.e., ready access to the Scripture and to sound Bible teaching, supportive family members). Perhaps one or two students could give a testimony in class of their search for Christ, for the real meaning of Christianity, and how the Lord saved them. This would be an excellent opportunity for a witness to fellow students who are unsaved.

Journal entry idea

Using Scripture as a basis, have each student write an entry discussing the following questions: Where did I come from? Why am I here? Where am I going?

Resources

Robert Detweiler, *John Updike,* revised edition (Macmillan Publishing Co., 1984).

Margaret Drabble, ed. *The Oxford Companion to English Literature,* 6th ed. (Oxford: Oxford University Press, 2000).

Alice and Kenneth Hamilton, *The Elements of John Updike* (Michigan: William B. Eerdmans Publishing Company, 1970).

Analysis

In "Pigeon Feathers" Updike uses his skill with patterns to solve David's dilemma. David eventually recognizes that man is made in the likeness of God, the Great Designer, who instilled in man a love of patterns and provided patterns as a mode of communication and a channel for delight and pleasure. Young David is reaching out for the assurance of that personal Jesus who is God's reliable representative.

David needs to know for certain that the historical, Biblical Jesus is not only the Way and the Truth but also the Life. The allusions to John's Gospel found in this story are significant, for John stresses the divinity of Christ. The pigeons function as messengers for the heavenly Saviour's affirmation of love and design to those on earth. The seemingly "worthless" birds echo the comforting words of Jesus in Matthew 10:29 and 31: "one of them shall not fall on the ground without your Father. . . . Fear ye not therefore, ye are of more value than many sparrows."

It may be best to read the story aloud in class, taking time to stop and discuss the thematic clues and specific examples of allusion, symbol, and irony. These references have been placed as marginal notes in the teacher's edition to discuss as you read.

Application

The erroneous philosophies represented in Updike's story are prevalent today. Men are still worshiping nature (e.g., pantheism, the New Age movement), worshiping men (humanism), and worshiping the work of men's hands (e.g., science, technology). Divide the class into three groups. Have each group list several specific ways in which each philosophy infiltrates society. Next, have the students look at several passages of Scripture that reveal the cause and provide answers for these current trends. Psalm 19, for example, makes clear that nature declares the glory of God; pantheists, however, would have us believe that nature is God. Such men have begun worshiping the symbol and have ceased worshiping the God that the symbol represents. (See Romans 2 for worship of man and Jeremiah 1:16 for worship of the works of men's hands.) Finally, have each group tell the class what they have learned. As time permits, discuss the "About the Story" questions.

Discuss this paragraph with the students. Is it an honest portrayal of the true historical facts of Christ's life? *(no)* What errors do students see in it? What rebuttals, from Scripture and other reputable sources, could they give to Wells's account?

Note how this simile ties poetically with Updike's description of the pages as "dusty glass" above.

Thought/Theme: Discuss with the students David's immediate response to Wells's blasphemy. While he is to be commended for realizing the error he has read, does the existence of churches and the nation's being "founded 'under God'" prove that Christianity is true? *(no)* Notice that David is appalled by what he reads, wondering why "the universe had not spit out this ball of tar but allowed it to continue in its blasphemy." His limited knowledge of the truth prevents him from understanding that such "challenges" are ludicrous to the true God (cf. Ps. 2). Notice as the story progresses, however, that those characters who represent false religion and erroneous philosophies become defensive—even irate—when their beliefs are challenged; often falsehood cannot endure such threatenings.

David immediately recognizes the weakness of his religious training. Though he has always thought of himself as a Christian, he is unequipped to refute these statements even though he intuitively recognizes that they are wrong.

allusions

---

unreal and irrelevant worlds. He could see things sluggishly move, and an unpleasant fullness came into his throat. His mother and grandmother fussed in the kitchen; the puppy, which they had just acquired for "protection in the country," was cowering, with a sporadic panicked scrabble of claws, under the dining table that in their old home had been reserved for special days but that here was used for every meal.

Then, before he could halt his eyes, David slipped into Wells's account of Jesus. He had been an obscure political agitator, a kind of hobo, in a minor colony of the Roman Empire. By an accident impossible to reconstruct, he (the small *h* horrified David) survived his own crucifixion and presumably died a few weeks later. A religion was founded on the freakish incident. The credulous imagination of the times retrospectively assigned miracles and supernatural pretensions to Jesus; a myth grew, and then a church, whose theology at most points was in direct contradiction to the simple, rather communistic teachings of the Galilean.

It was as if a stone that for weeks and even years had been gathering weight in the web of David's nerves snapped them and plunged through the page and a hundred layers of paper underneath. These fantastic falsehoods—plainly untrue; churches stood everywhere, the entire nation was founded "under God"—did not at first frighten him; it was the fact that they had been permitted to exist in an actual human brain. This was the initial impact—that at a definite spot in time and space a brain black with the denial of Christ's divinity had been suffered to exist; that the universe had not spit out this ball of tar but allowed it to continue in its blasphemy, to grow old, win honors, wear a hat, write books that, if true, collapsed everything into a jumble of horror. The world outside the deep-silled windows—a rutted lawn, a whitewashed barn, a walnut tree frothy

with fresh green—seemed a haven from which he was forever sealed off. Hot washrags seemed pressed against his cheeks.

He read the account again. He tried to supply out of his ignorance objections that would defeat the complacent march of these black words, and found none. Survivals and misunderstandings more farfetched were reported daily in the papers. But none of them caused churches to be built in every town. He tried to work backwards through the churches, from their brave high fronts through their shabby, ill-attended interiors back into the events at Jerusalem, and felt himself surrounded by shifting gray shadows, centuries of history, where he knew nothing. The thread dissolved in his hands. Had Christ ever come to him, David Kern, and said, "Here. Feel the wound in My side?" No; but prayers had been answered. What prayers? He had prayed that Rudy Mohn, whom he had purposely tripped so he cracked his head on their radiator, not die, and he had not died. But for all the blood, it was just a cut; Rudy came back the same day, wearing a bandage and repeating the same teasing words. He could never have died. Again, David had prayed for two separate war-effort posters he had sent away for to arrive tomorrow, and though they did not, they did arrive, some days later, together, popping through the clacking letter slot like a rebuke from God's mouth: *I answer your prayers in My way, in My time.* After that, he had made his prayers less definite, less susceptible of being twisted into a scolding. But what a tiny, ridiculous coincidence this was, after all, to throw into battle against H. G. Wells's engines of knowledge! Indeed, it proved the enemy's point: Hope bases vast premises on foolish accidents, and reads a word where in fact only a scribble exists.

His father came home. Though Saturday was a free day for him, he had been working. He taught school in Olinger and spent all his

---

The answers to each of these questions will vary and will provide an excellent springboard for further application of the story to daily life.

days performing, with a curious air of panic, needless errands. Also, a city boy by birth, he was frightened of the farm and seized any excuse to get away. The farm had been David's mother's birthplace; it had been her idea to buy it back. With an ingenuity and persistence unparalleled in her life, she had gained that end, and moved them all here—her son, her husband, her mother. Granmom, in her prime, had worked these fields alongside her husband, but now she dabbled around the kitchen futilely, her hands waggling with Parkinson's disease. She was always in the way. Strange, out in the country, amid eighty acres, they were crowded together. His father expressed his feelings of discomfort by conducting with Mother an endless argument about organic farming. All through dusk, all through supper, it rattled on.

"Elsie, I *know,* I know from my education, the earth is nothing but chemicals. It's the only thing I got out of four years of college, so don't tell me it's not true."

"George, if you'd just walk out on the farm you'd know it's not true. The land has a *soul."*

"Soil, has, no, soul," he said, enunciating stiffly, as if to a very stupid class. To David he said, "You can't argue with a femme. Your mother's a real femme. That's why I married her, and now I'm suffering for it."

"*This* soil has no soul," she said, "because it's been killed with superphosphate. It's been burned bare by Boyer's tenant farmers." Boyer was the rich man they had bought the farm from. "It used to have a soul, didn't it, Mother? When you and Pop farmed it?"

"Ach, yes; I guess." Granmom was trying to bring a forkful of food to her mouth with her less severely afflicted hand. In her anxiety she brought the other hand up from her lap. The crippled fingers, dull red in the orange light of the kerosene lamp in the center of the table, were welded by paralysis into one knobbed hook.

"Only human indi-vidu-als have souls," his father went on, in the same mincing, lifeless voice. "Because the Bible tells us so." Done eating, he crossed his legs and dug into his ear with a match miserably; to get at the thing inside his head he tucked in his chin, and his voice came out low-pitched at David. "When God made your mother, He made a real femme."

"George, don't you read the papers? Don't you know that between chemical fertilizers and the bug sprays we'll all be dead in ten years? Heart attacks are killing every man in the country over forty-five."

He sighed wearily; the yellow skin of his eyelids wrinkled as he hurt himself with the match. "There's no connection," he stated, spacing his words with pained patience, "between the heart - and chemical fertilizers. It's alcohol that's doing it. Alcohol and milk. There is too much - cholesterol - in the tissues of the American heart. Don't tell me about chemistry, Elsie; I majored in the stuff for four years."

"Yes, and I majored in Greek and I'm not a penny wiser. Mother, put your waggler *away!"* The old woman started, and the food dropped from her fork. For some reason, the sight of her bad hand at the table cruelly irritated her daughter. Granmom's eyes, worn bits of crazed crystal embedded in watery milk, widened behind her cockeyed spectacles. Circles of silver as fine as thread, they clung to the red notches they had carved over the years into her little white beak. In the orange flicker of the kerosene lamp her dazed misery seemed infernal. David's mother began, without noise, to cry. His father did not seem to have eyes at all; just jaundiced sockets of wrinkled skin. The steam of food clouded the scene. It was horrible but the horror was particular and familiar, and distracted David from the formless dread that worked, sticky and sore, within him, like a too large wound trying to heal.

Analyze with the students the family's characters, sketched out for us in this paragraph. Note the meaninglessness of the father's ways of filling his time and his childish fears; the mother's drive behind family decisions and her romantic desire to regain her childhood; and the sad state of Granmom, who should be held in esteem in the family (see Discussion sections for "The Progress of Poesy," "On the Pleasures," and "The Soul's Dark Cottage") yet is "always in the way." To use a phrase common today, David's is a dysfunctional family.

Symbols: The following argument between the mother and father is about philosophy, not fertilizer. The mother symbolizes the Romantic view of nature as god. The father symbolizes the materialistic view of science as god. Notice that neither character argues logically nor gives any proof to the validity of his belief system. The father merely points to his education as definitive proof, and the mother uses her "experience" to bolster her argument. Job's friends often used the same faulty basis for their arguments.

Note the father's mockery of Bible truth—reminiscent of H. G. Wells.

Thought/Theme: Notice the mother's strong reaction to the grandmother's crippled hand. This response shows the mother's inability to accept anything that contradicts her Romantic ideals. Old age and disease expose the flaws in nature (her god). Rather than accepting the truth that a fallen world is beset with such flaws, she lashes out. Ironically, her false religion makes her cruel, revealing that the "heartfelt emotion" theoretically associated with Romanticism is essentially a superficial sentimentality.

Note how David's view of death has changed—no longer does he think of heaven; instead he thinks only of the gruesome physical aspects of death—the person forgotten, the body decayed and a part of the ground.

Note Updike's use of *physical* imagery (through metaphor and simile) to describe the impact of David's *spiritual* crisis.

allusion

Thought/Theme: Contrast the mother's concern for earthworms with her reaction to her mother. A modern-day analogy to such "schizophrenic reasoning" is seen in the fact that many of those who believe in animal rights also support abortion.

Note the acceptance of evolution inherent in the father's statement.

He had to go to the bathroom, and took a flashlight down through the wet grass to the outhouse. For once, his fear of spiders there felt trivial. He set the flashlight, burning, beside him, and an insect alighted on its lens, a tiny insect, a mosquito or flea, made so fine that the weak light projected its X-ray onto the wall boards; the faint rim of its wings, the blurred strokes, magnified, of its long hinged legs, the dark cone at the heart of its anatomy. The tremor must be its heart beating. Without warning, David was visited by an exact vision of death; a long hole in the ground, no wider than your body, down which you are drawn while the white faces above recede. You try to reach them but your arms are pinned. Shovels pour dirt into your face. There you will be forever, in an upright position, blind and silent, and in time no one will remember you, and you will never be called. As strata of rock shift, your fingers elongate, and your teeth are distended sideways in a great underground grimace indistinguishable from a strip of chalk. And the earth tumbles on, and the sun expires, and unaltering darkness reigns where once there were stars.

Sweat broke out on his back. His mind seemed to rebound off a solidness. Such extinction was not another threat, a graver sort of danger, a kind of pain; it was qualitatively different. It was not even a conception that could be voluntarily pictured; it entered him from outside. His protesting nerves swarmed on its surface like lichen on a meteor. The skin of his chest was soaked with the effort of rejection. At the same time that the fear was dense and internal, it was dense and all around him; a tide of clay had swept up to the stars; space was crushed into a mass. When he stood up, automatically hunching his shoulders to keep his head away from the spider webs, it was with a numb sense of being cramped between two huge volumes of rigidity. That he had even this small freedom to move surprised him. In the narrow shelter of that rank shack he felt—his first spark of comfort—too small to be crushed.

But in the open, as the beam of the flashlight skidded with frightened quickness across the remote surfaces of the barn and the grape arbor and the giant pine that stood by the path to the woods, the terror descended. He raced up through the clinging grass pursued, not by one of the wild animals the woods might hold, or one of the goblins his superstitious grandmother had communicated to his childhood, but by the specters out of science fiction, where gigantic cinder moons fill half the turquoise sky. As David ran, a gray planet rolled inches behind his neck. If he looked back, he would be buried. And in the momentum of his terror, hideous possibilities—the dilation of the sun, the triumph of the insects, the crabs on the shore in *The Time Machine*—wheeled out of the vacuum of make-believe and added their weight to his impending oblivion.

He wrenched the door open; the lamps within the house flared. The wicks burning here and there seemed to mirror one another. His mother was washing the dishes in a little pan of heated pump-water; Granmom fluttered near her elbow apprehensive. In the living room—the downstairs of the little square house was two long rooms—his father sat in front of the black fireplace restlessly folding and unfolding a newspaper as he sustained his half of the argument. "Nitrogen, phosphorus, potash: these are the three replaceable constituents of the soil. One crop of corn carries away hundreds of pounds of"—he dropped the paper into his lap and ticked them off on three fingers—"nitrogen, phosphorus, potash."

"Boyer didn't grow corn."

"*Any* crop, Elsie, the human animal—"

"You're killing the *earth*worms, George!"

"The human animal, after thousands and *thous*ands of years, learned methods whereby the chemical balance of the soil may be maintained. Don't carry me back to the Dark Ages."

"When we moved to Olinger the ground in the garden was like slate. Just one summer of my cousin's chicken dung and the earthworms came back."

"I'm sure the Dark Ages were a fine place to the poor devils born in them, but I don't want to go there. They give me the creeps." Daddy stared into the cold pit of the fireplace and clung to the rolled newspaper in his lap as if it alone were keeping him from slipping backwards and down, down.

Mother came into the doorway brandishing a fistful of wet forks. "And thanks to your DDT there soon won't be a bee left in the country. When I was a girl here you could eat a peach without washing it."

"It's primitive, Elsie. It's Dark Age stuff."

"Oh, what do *you* know about the Dark Ages?"

"I know I don't want to go back to them."

David took from the shelf, where he had placed it this afternoon, the great unabridged Webster's Dictionary that his grandfather had owned. He turned the big thin pages, floppy as cloth, to the entry he wanted, and read

soul . . . I. An entity conceived as the essence, substance, animating principle, or actuating cause of life, or of the individual life, esp. of life manifested in psychical activities; the vehicle of individual existence, separate in nature from the body and usually held to be separable in existence.

The definition went on, into Greek and Egyptian conceptions, but David stopped short on the treacherous edge of antiquity. He needed to read no further. The careful overlapping words shingled a temporary shelter for him. "Usually held to be separable in existence"—what could be fairer, more judicious, surer?

His father was saying, "The modern farmer can't go around sweeping up after his cows. The poor devil has thousands and *thous*ands of acres on his hands. Your modern farmer uses a scientifically-arrived-at mixture, like five-ten-five, or six-twelve-six, or *three*-twelve-six, and spreads it on with this wonderful modern machinery which of course we can't afford. Your modern farmer can't *afford* medieval methods."

Mother was quiet in the kitchen; her silence radiated waves of anger.

"No now Elsie; don't play the femme with me. Let's discuss this calmly like two rational twentieth-century people. Your organic

Thought/Theme: David first seeks an intellectual resolution to his conflict. Turning to the dictionary, he is reassured to find that the definition of *soul* affirms the "separateness" of soul and body. From this definition, David infers not only that he has a soul but also that his soul is immortal.

Thought/Theme: Notice that the father consistently tries to win his arguments by intimidation. When he cannot logically prove his point, he reverts to scorn.

farming nuts aren't attacking five-ten-five; they're attacking the chemical fertilizer crooks. The monster firms."

A cup clinked in the kitchen. Mother's anger touched David's face; his cheeks burned guiltily. Just by being in the living room he was associated with his father. She appeared in the doorway with red hands and tears in her eyes, and said to the two of them, "I knew you didn't want to come here but I didn't know you'd torment me like this. You talked Pop into his grave and now you'll kill me. Go ahead, George, more power to you; at least I'll be buried in good ground." She tried to turn and met an obstacle and screamed, "Mother, stop hanging on my *back!* Why don't you go to *bed?*"

"Let's all go to bed," David's father said, rising from the blue wing chair and slapping his thigh with a newspaper. "This reminds me of death." It was a phrase of his that David had heard so often he never considered its sense.

Upstairs, he seemed to be lifted above his fears. The sheets on his bed were clean. Granmom had ironed them with a pair of flatirons saved from the Olinger attic; she plucked them hot off the stove alternately, with a wooden handle called a goose. It was a wonder, to see how she managed. In the next room, his parents grunted peaceably; they seemed to take their quarrels less seriously than he did. They made comfortable scratching noises as they carried a little lamp back and forth. Their door was open a crack, so he saw the light shift and swing. Surely there would be, in the last five minutes, in the last second, a crack of light, showing the door from the dark room to another, full of light. Thinking of it this vividly frightened him. His own dying, in a specific bed in a specific room, specific walls mottled with wallpaper, the dry whistle of his breathing, the murmuring doctors, the nervous relatives going in and out, but for him no way out but down into the funnel. *Never touch a doorknob again.* A whisper, and his parents' light was blown out. David prayed to be reassured. Though the experiment frightened him, he lifted his hands into the darkness above his face and begged Christ to touch them. Not hard or long: the faintest, quickest grip would be final for a lifetime. His hands waited in the air, itself a substance, which seemed to move through his fingers; or was it the pressure of his pulse? He returned his hands to beneath the covers uncertain if they had been touched or not. For would not Christ's touch *be* infinitely gentle?

Through all the eddies* of its aftermath, David clung to this thought about his revelation of extinction: that there, in the outhouse, he had struck a solidness qualitatively different, a rock of horror firm enough to support any height of construction. All he needed was a little help; a word, a gesture, a nod of certainty, and he would be sealed in, safe. The assurance from the dictionary had melted in the night. Today was Sunday, a hot fair day. Across a mile of clear air the church bells called, *Celebrate, celebrate.* Only Daddy went. He put on a coat over his rolled-up shirtsleeves and got into the little old black Plymouth parked by the barn and went off, with the same pained hurried grimness of all his actions. His churning wheels, as he shifted too hastily into second, raised plumes of red dust on the dirt road. Mother walked to the far field, to see what bushes needed cutting. David, though he usually preferred to stay in the house, went with her. The puppy followed at a distance, whining as it picked its way through the stubble but floundering off timidly if one of them went back to pick it up and carry it. When they reached the crest of the far field, his mother asked, "David, what's troubling you?"

---

eddies: currents running contrary to the main current or tradition

"Nothing. Why?"

She looked at him sharply. The greening woods cross-hatched* the space beyond her half-gray hair. Then she showed him her profile, and gestured toward the house, which they had left a half-mile behind them. "See how it sits in the land? They don't know how to build with the land any more. Pop always said the foundations were set with the compass. We must try to get a compass and see. It's supposed to face due south; but south feels a little more *that* way to me." From the side, as she said these things, she seemed handsome and young. The smooth sweep of her hair over her ear seemed white with a purity and calm that made her feel foreign to him. He had never regarded his parents as consolers of his troubles; from the beginning they had seemed to have more troubles than he. Their confusion had flattered him into an illusion of strength; so now on this high clear ridge he jealously guarded the menace all around them, blowing like a breeze on his fingertips, the possibility of all this wide scenery sinking into darkness. The strange fact that though she came to look at the brush she carried no clippers, for she had a fixed prejudice against working on Sundays, was the only consolation he allowed her to offer.

---
cross-hatched: marked with two or more sets of parallel lines
---

As they walked back, the puppy whimpering after them, the rising dust behind a distant line of trees announced that Daddy was speeding home from church. When they reached the house he was there. He had brought back the Sunday paper and the vehement remark, "Dobson's too intelligent for these farmers. They just sit there with their mouths open and don't hear a thing the poor devil's saying."

"What makes you think farmers are unintelligent? This country was made by farmers. George Washington was a farmer."

"They are, Elsie. They are unintelligent. George Washington's dead. In this day and age only the misfits stay on the farm. The lame, the halt, the blind. The morons with one arm. Human garbage. They remind me of death, sitting there with their mouths open."

"My *father* was a farmer."

"He was a frustrated man, Elsie. He never knew what hit him. The poor devil meant so well, and he never knew which end was up. Your mother'll bear me out. Isn't that right, Mom? Pop never knew what hit him?"

"Ach, I guess not," the old woman quavered, and the ambiguity for the moment silenced both sides.

David hid in the funny papers and sports section until one-thirty. At two, the catechetical* class met at the Firetown church. He had transferred from the catechetical class of the Lutheran church in Olinger, a humiliating comedown. In Olinger they met on Wednesday nights, spiffy and spruce, in the atmosphere of a dance. Afterwards, blessed by the brick-faced minister from whose lips the word "Christ" fell like a burning stone, the more daring of them went with their Bibles to a luncheonette and smoked. Here in Firetown, the girls were dull white cows and the boys narrow-faced brown goats in old men's suits, herded on Sunday afternoons into a threadbare church basement that smelled of stale hay. Because his father had taken the car on one of his endless errands to Olinger, David walked, grateful for the open air and the silence. The catechetical class embarrassed him, but today he placed hope in it, as the source of the nod, the gesture, that was all he needed.

---
catechetical: pertaining to catechism, a brief summary of basic religious principles in question and answer form
---

Reverend Dobson was a delicate young man with great dark eyes and small white shapely hands that flickered like protesting

It is unlikely that Mother will ever "get a compass and see." She is far more likely to trust her own feelings than a scientific instrument.

Irony: As with the father (see note on page 112), it is ironic that the mother, who does not believe in the true God, still keeps the Sabbath. To David this serves as one more assurance that there must be "something to Christianity." This unwitting gesture is the only positive contribution the mother makes during David's turmoil, the only consolation he receives from her.

allusions

Note the bitterness and lack of compassion in the father's heart—similar to Mother's contempt for Granmom.

Note metaphors and similes used here to support the theme of empty religion.

Symbol: Reverend Dobson's character represents the humanistic view of man as god. Notice how Updike uses the description of him to reinforce the worthlessness of Dobson's ideas and their inability to provide spiritual light. Dobson has "dark eyes," and his small hands flicker like "protesting doves" (symbol of the Holy Spirit).

Thought/Theme: Notice the verses Updike uses throughout the story. These passages from Scripture shine as the only light in David's dark world. Notice, too, that his grandfather is the only character who, through his well-worn Bible, "speaks" the truth. Although David cannot completely understand either the light or the voice, they give him the hope he needs to continue his search until he is "sealed up, safe."

This idea comes back to David's mind on page 116; see the first highlighted section on that page.

allusion

Discuss with students why Dobson's response is so shocking to David. *(He has denied the reality of heaven, a basic Christian tenet.)*

doves when he preached; he seemed a bit misplaced in the Lutheran ministry. This was his first call. It was a split parish; he served another rural church twelve miles away. His iridescent* green Ford, new six months ago, was spattered to the windows with red mud and rattled from bouncing on rude back roads, where he frequently got lost, to the malicious* satisfaction of many. But David's mother liked him, and, more pertinent to his success, the Haiers, the sleek family of feed merchants and innkeepers and tractor salesmen who dominated the Firetown church, liked him. David liked him, and felt liked in turn; sometimes in class, after some special stupidity, Dobson directed toward him out of those wide black eyes a mild look of disbelief, a look that, though flattering, was also delicately disquieting.

---

iridescent: lustrous in appearance
malicious: having a desire to harm others or see others suffer

---

Catechetical instruction consisted of reading aloud from a work booklet answers to problems prepared during the week, problems like, "I am the ____, the ____, and the ____, saith the Lord." Then there was a question period in which no one ever asked any questions. Today's theme was the last third of the Apostles' Creed. When the time came for questions, David blushed and asked, "About the Resurrection of the Body—are we conscious between the time when we die and the Day of Judgment?"

Dobson blinked, and his fine little mouth pursed, suggesting that David was making difficult things more difficult. The faces of the other students went blank, as if an indiscretion* had been committed.

---

indiscretion: lack of judiciousness in one's speech or behavior

---

"No, I suppose not," Reverend Dobson said.

"Well, where is our soul, then, in this gap?"

The sense grew, in the class, of a naughtiness occurring. Dobson's shy eyes watered, as if he were straining to keep up the formality of attention, and one of the girls, the fattest, simpered toward her twin, who was a little less fat. Their chairs were arranged in a rough circle. The current running around the circle panicked David. Did everybody know something he didn't know?

"I suppose you could say our souls are asleep," Dobson said.

"And then they wake up, and there is the earth like it always is, and all the people who have ever lived? Where will Heaven be?"

Anita Haier giggled. Dobson gazed at David intently, but with an awkward, puzzled flicker of forgiveness, as if there existed a secret between them that David was violating. But David knew of no secret. All he wanted was to hear Dobson repeat the words he said every Sunday morning. This he would not do. As if these words were unworthy of the conversational voice.

"David, you might think of Heaven this way: as the way the goodness Abraham Lincoln did lives after him."

"But is Lincoln conscious of it living on?" He blushed no longer with embarrassment but in anger; he had walked here in good faith and was being made a fool.

"Is he conscious now? I would have to say no; but I don't think it matters." His voice had a coward's firmness; he was hostile now.

"You don't."

"Not in the eyes of God, no." The unction,* the stunning impudence, of this reply sprang tears of outrage in David's eyes. He bowed them to his book, where short words like Duty, Love, Obey, Honor, were stacked in the form of a cross.

---

unction: an exaggerated earnestness particularly in language

"Were there any other questions, David?" Dobson asked with renewed gentleness. The others were rustling, collecting their books.

"No." He made his voice firm, though he could not bring up his eyes.

"Did I answer your question fully enough?"

"Yes."

In the minister's silence the shame that should have been his crept over David: the burden and fever of being a fraud were placed upon *him*, who was innocent, and it seemed, he knew, a confession of this guilt that on the way out he was unable to face Dobson's stirred gaze, though he felt it probing the side of his head.

Anita Haier's father gave him a ride down the highway as far as the dirt road. David said he wanted to walk the rest, and figured that his offer was accepted because Mr. Haier did not want to dirty his bright blue Buick with dust. This was all right; everything was all right, as long as it was clear. His indignation at being betrayed, at seeing Christianity betrayed, had hardened him. The straight dirt road reflected his hardness. Pink stones thrust up through its packed surface. The April sun beat down from the center of the afternoon half of the sky; already it had some of summer's heat. Already the fringes of weeds at the edges of the road were bedraggled with dust. From the reviving grass and scuff of the fields he walked between, insects were sending up a monotonous, automatic chant. In the distance a tiny figure in his father's coat was walking along the edge of the woods. His mother. He wondered what joy she found in such walks; to him the brown stretches of slowly rising and falling land expressed only a huge exhaustion.

Flushed with fresh air and happiness, she returned from her walk earlier than he had expected, and surprised him at his grandfather's Bible. It was a stumpy black book, the boards worn thin where the old man's fingers had held them; the spine hung by one weak hinge of fabric. David had been looking for the passage where Jesus says to one thief on the cross, "Today shalt thou be with me in paradise." He had never tried reading the Bible for himself before. What was so embarrassing about being caught at it, was that he detested the apparatus of piety. Fusty* churches, creaking hymns, ugly Sunday-school teachers and their stupid leaflets—he hated everything about them but the promise they held out, a promise that in the most perverse way, as if the homeliest crone* in the kingdom were given the Prince's hand, made every good and real thing possible. He couldn't explain this to his mother. There was no time. Her solicitude* was upon him.

fusty: having an odor of mildew or decay
crone: a withered, witchlike old woman
solicitude: the quality of being concerned or attentive

"David, what are you doing?"

"Nothing."

"What are you doing at Grandpop's Bible?"

"Trying to read it. This is supposed to be a Christian country, isn't it?"

She sat down on the green sofa, which used to be in the sun parlor at Olinger, under the fancy mirror. A little smile still lingered on her face from the walk. "David, I wish you'd talk to me."

"What about?"

"About whatever it is that's troubling you. Your father and I have both noticed it."

"I asked Reverend Dobson about Heaven and he said it was like Abraham Lincoln's goodness living after him."

He waited for the shock to strike her. "Yes?" she said, expecting more.

"That's all."

"And why didn't you like it?"

"Well; don't you see? It amounts to saying there isn't any Heaven at all."

Thought/Theme: Notice that Dobson, like the mother and father, grows defensive when his belief system is challenged. As the discussion continues, notice that Dobson's inability to answer David's questions motivates the preacher to use the boy as a scapegoat for his own shame.

allusion

Thought/Theme, Irony: Having just come from her own form of worship (a walk in the fields), the mother is disturbed by her son's reading the Bible. (See Unit 6, Irony.)

"I don't see that it amounts to that. What do you want Heaven to be?"

"Well, I don't know. I want it to be *something*. I thought he'd tell me what it was. I thought that was his job." He was becoming angry, sensing her surprise at him. She had assumed that Heaven had faded from his head years ago. She had imagined that he had already entered, in the secrecy of silence, the conspiracy that he now knew to be all around him.

"David," she asked gently, "don't you ever want to rest?"

"No. Not forever."

"David, you're so young. When you get older, you'll feel differently."

"Grandpa didn't. Look how tattered this book is."

"I never understood your grandfather."

"Well I don't understand ministers who say it's like Lincoln's goodness going on and on. Suppose you're not Lincoln?"

"I think Reverend Dobson made a mistake. You must try to forgive him."

"It's not a *question* of his making a mistake! It's a question of dying and never moving or seeing or hearing anything ever again."

"But"—in exasperation—"darling, it's so *greedy* of you to want more. When God has given us this wonderful April day, and given us this farm, and you have your whole life ahead of you—"

"You think, then, that there is God?"

"Of course I do"—with deep relief, that smoothed her features into a reposeful oval. He had risen and was standing too near her for his comfort. He was afraid she would reach out and touch him.

"He made everything? You feel that?"

"Yes."

"Then who made Him?"

"Why, Man. Man." The happiness of this answer lit up her face radiantly, until she saw his gesture of disgust. She was so simple, so illogical; such a femme.

"Well that amounts to saying there is none."

Her hand reached for his wrist but he backed away. "David, it's a mystery. A miracle. It's a miracle more beautiful than any Reverend Dobson could have told you about. You don't say houses don't exist because Man made them."

"No. God has to be different."

"But, David, you have the *evidence*. Look out the window at the sun; at the fields."

"Mother, good grief. Don't you see—" he rasped away the roughness in his throat—"if when we die there's nothing, all your sun and fields and what not are all, ah, *horror?* It's just an ocean of horror."

"But David, it's not. It's so clearly not that." And she made an urgent opening gesture with her hands that expressed, with its suggestion of a willingness to receive his helplessness, all her grace, her gentleness, her love of beauty, gathered into a passive intensity that made him intensely hate her. He would not be wooed away from the truth. *I am the Way, the Truth . . .*

"No," he told her. "Just let me alone."

He found his tennis ball behind the piano and went outside to throw it against the side of the house. There was a patch high up where the brown stucco that had been laid over the sandstone masonry was crumbling away; he kept trying with the tennis ball to chip more pieces off. Superimposed upon his deep ache was a smaller but more immediate worry; that he had hurt his mother. He heard his father's car rattling on the straightaway, and went into the house, to make peace before he arrived. To his relief, she was not giving off the stifling damp heat of her anger, but instead was cool, decisive, maternal. She handed him an old green book, her college text of Plato.*

Plato: Greek philosopher, 427?-347 B.C.

"I want you to read the Parable of the Cave,"* she said.

Parable of the Cave: An allegory in which Plato explains that man is chained and captive in a cave in which he observes reality only through shadows. Some Prisoners are unbound by a Philosopher who leads them to the Visible Sun and true knowledge.

"All right," he said, though he knew it would do no good. Some story by a dead Greek just vague enough to please her. "Don't worry about it, Mother."

"I *am* worried. Honestly, David, I'm sure there will be something for us. As you get older, these things seem to matter a great deal less."

"That may be. It's a dismal thought, though."

His father bumped at the door. The locks and jambs stuck hère. But before Granmom could totter to the latch and let him in, he had knocked it open. He had been in Olinger dithering with track meet tickets. Although Mother usually kept her talks with David a confidence, a treasure between them, she called instantly, "George, David is worried about death!"

He came to the doorway of the living room, his shirt pocket bristling with pencils, holding in one hand a pint box of melting ice cream and in the other the knife with which he was about to divide it into four sections, their Sunday treat. "Is the kid worried about death? Don't give it a thought, David. I'll be lucky if I live till tomorrow, and I'm not worried. If they'd taken a buckshot gun and shot me in the cradle I'd be better off. The *world*'d be better off. I think death is a wonderful thing. I look forward to it. Get the garbage out of the way. If I had the man here who invented death, I'd pin a medal on him."

"Hush, George. You'll frighten the child worse than he is."

This was not true; he never frightened David. There was no harm in his father, no harm at all. Indeed, in the man's steep self-disgust the boy felt a kind of ally. A distant ally. He saw his position with a certain strategic coldness. Nowhere in the world of other people would he find the hint, the nod, he needed to begin to build his fortress against death. They none of them believed. He was alone. In that deep hole.

In the months that followed, his position changed little. School was some comfort. All those people, wisecracking, chewing gum, all of them doomed to die, and none of them noticing. In their company David felt that they would carry him along into the bright, cheap paradise reserved for them. In any crowd, the fear ebbed a little; he had reasoned that somewhere in the world there must exist a few people who believed what was necessary, and the larger the crowd, the greater the chance that he was near such a soul, within calling distance, if only he was not too ignorant, too ill-equipped, to spot him. The sight of clergymen cheered him; whatever they themselves thought, their collars were still a sign that somewhere, at sometime, someone had recognized that we cannot, *cannot,* submit to death. The sermon topics posted outside churches, the flip, hurried pieties of disc jockeys, the cartoons in magazines showing

Thought/Theme: For a man who is not "worried" about dying, David's father talks a great deal about death. Notice throughout the story how often he refers to death.

You may wish to use this as an opportunity to challenge students in two areas. (1) Life is brief, even though young people do not view it that way. Challenge them by asking, "Are you born again? And if so, what are you doing for the Lord *today?*" (2) Christians are surrounded by people like David's classmates—people who are doomed to die. Are Christians attempting to reach them for Christ, to give them an eternal hope? You may also challenge the students in your class who are born again not to assume that all of their classmates have received Christ.

Note that David does not share his mother's view that the land has a soul; his father's cynical influence over him has grown. David sees nature as "mechanical" now.

Thought/Theme: This is the third step in David's journey of faith. Hope is again renewed when he awakens to the masterful design evident in the natural world.

angels or devils—on such scraps he kept alive the possibility of hope.

For the rest, he tried to drown his hopelessness in clatter and jostle. The pinball machine at the luncheonette was a merciful distraction; as he bent over its buzzing, flashing board of flippers and cushions, the weight and constriction in his chest lightened and loosened. He was grateful for all the time his father wasted in Olinger. Every delay postponed the moment when they must ride together down the dirt road into the heart of the dark farmland, where the only light was the kerosene lamp waiting on the dining-room table, a light that drowned their food in shadow and made it sinister.

He lost his appetite for reading. He was afraid of being ambushed again. In mystery novels people died like dolls being discarded; in science fiction enormities of space and time conspired to crush the humans; and even in P. G. Wodehouse he felt a hollowness, a turning away from reality that was implicitly bitter, and became explicit in the comic figures of futile clergymen. All gaiety seemed minced out on the skin of a void. All quiet hours seemed invitations to dread.

Even on weekends, he and his father contrived to escape the farm; and when, some Saturdays, they did stay home, it was to do something destructive—tear down an old henhouse or set huge brush fires that threatened, while Mother shouted and flapped her arms, to spread to the woods. Whenever his father worked, it was with rapt* violence; when he chopped kindling, fragments of the old henhouse boards flew like shrapnel and the ax-head was always within a quarter of an inch of flying off the handle. He was exhilarating to watch, sweating and swearing and sucking bits of saliva back into his lips.

rapt: deeply absorbed

School stopped. His father took the car in the opposite direction, to a highway construction job where he had been hired for the summer as a timekeeper, and David was stranded in the middle of acres of heat and greenery and blowing pollen and the strange, mechanical humming that lay invisibly in the weeds and alfalfa and dry orchard grass.

For his fifteenth birthday his parents gave him, with jokes about him being a hillbilly now, a Remington .22. It was somewhat like a pinball machine to take it out to the old kiln in the woods where they dumped their trash, and set up tin cans on the kiln's sandstone shoulder and shoot them off one by one. He'd take the puppy, who had grown long legs and a rich coat of reddish fur—he was part chow. Copper hated the gun but loved the boy enough to accompany him. When the flat acrid crack rang out, he would race in terrified circles that would tighten and tighten until they brought him, shivering, against David's legs. Depending upon his mood, David would shoot again or drop to his knees and comfort the dog. Giving this comfort to a degree returned comfort to him. The dog's ears, laid flat against his skull in fear, were folded so intricately, so—he groped for the concept—*surely*. Where the dull-studded collar made the fur stand up, each hair showed a root of soft white under the length, black-tipped, of the metal-color that had lent the dog its name. In his agitation Copper panted through nostrils that were elegant slits, like two healed cuts, or like the keyholes of a dainty lock of black, grained wood. His whole whorling, knotted, jointed body was a wealth of such embellishments.* And in the smell of the dog's hair David seemed to descend through many finely differentiated layers of earth: mulch, soil, sand, clay, and the glittering mineral base.

embellishments: acts of adorning or making beautiful

But when he returned to the house, and saw the books arranged on the low shelves, fear returned. The four adamant volumes of Wells like four thin bricks, the green Plato that had puzzled him with its queer softness and tangled purity, the dead Galsworthy and "Elizabeth," Grandpa's mammoth dictionary, Grandpa's Bible, the Bible that he himself had received on becoming a member of the Firetown Lutheran Church—at the sight of these, the memory of his fear reawakened and came around him. He had grown stiff and stupid in its embrace. His parents tried to think of ways to entertain him.

"David, I have a job for you to do," his mother said one evening at the table.

"What?"

"If you're going to take that tone perhaps we'd better not talk."

"What tone? I didn't take any tone."

"Your grandmother thinks there are too many pigeons in the barn."

"Why?" David turned to look at his grandmother, but she sat there staring at the burning lamp with her usual expression of bewilderment.

Mother shouted, "Mom, he wants to know why!"

Granmom made a jerky, irritable motion with her bad hand, as if generating the force for utterance, and said, "They foul the furniture."

"That's right," Mother said. "She's afraid for that old Olinger furniture that we'll never use. David, she's been after me for a month about those poor pigeons. She wants you to shoot them."

"I don't want to kill anything especially," David said.

Daddy said, "The kid's like you are, Elsie. He's too good for this world. Kill or be killed, that's my motto."

His mother said loudly, "Mother, he doesn't want to do it."

"Not?" The old lady's eyes distended as if in horror, and her claw descended slowly to her lap.

"Oh, I'll do it, I'll do it tomorrow," David snapped, and a pleasant crisp taste entered his mouth with the decision.

"And I had thought, when Boyer's men made the hay, it would be better if the barn doesn't look like a rookery,*" his mother added needlessly.

---

rookery: a breeding place for certain birds and animals

A barn, in day, is a small night. The splinters of light between the dry shingles pierce the high roof like stars, and the rafters and crossbeams and built-in ladders seem, until your eyes adjust, as mysterious as the branches of a haunted forest. David entered silently, the gun in one hand. Copper whined desperately at the door, too frightened to come in with the gun yet unwilling to leave the boy. David stealthily turned, said "Go away," shut the door on the dog, and slipped the bolt across. It was a door within a door; the double door for wagons and tractors was as high and wide as the face of a house.

The smell of old straw scratched his sinuses. The red sofa, half-hidden under its white-splotched tarpaulin, seemed assimilated into this smell, sunk in it, buried. The mouths of empty bins gaped like caves. Rusty oddments of farming—coils of baling wire, some spare tines for a harrow, a handleless shovel—hung on nails driven here and there in the thick wood. He stood stock-still a minute; it took a while to separate the cooing of the pigeons from the rustling in his ears. When he had focused on the cooing, it flooded the vast interior with its throaty, bubbling outpour: there seemed no other sound. They were up behind the beams. What light there was leaked through the shingles and the dirty glass windows at the far end and the small round

Symbols: The books rekindle David's fears, for they symbolize his conflict. Wells, like David's father, represents scientific materialism; Plato, like Dobson, represents classical humanism; and Galsworthy, like David's mother, represents sentimental Romanticism. However, Grandpa's Bible also stands on the shelf, a symbol of truth in the midst of error.

Imaginative Comparison: This paragraph and those following that describe the scene in the barn are especially good for showing Updike to be a master stylist. The metaphors are superb. The barn, for example ("in day, a small night"), is a metaphor for David's conflict; the minute description reinforces this imaginative comparison. Note also Updike's use of onomatopoeia and assonance to support the mood.

holes, about as big as basketballs, high on the opposite stone side walls, under the ridge of the roof.

A pigeon appeared in one of these holes, on the side toward the house. It flew in, with a battering of wings, from the outside, and waited there, silhouetted against its pinched bit of sky, preening* and cooing in a throbbing, thrilled, tentative way. David tiptoed four steps to the side, rested his gun against the lowest rung of a ladder pegged between two upright beams, and lowered the gunsight into the bird's tiny, jauntily cocked head. The slap of the report seemed to come off the stone wall behind him, and the pigeon did not fall. Neither did it fly. Instead it stuck in the round hole, pirouetting rapidly and nodding its head as if in frantic agreement. David shot the bolt back and forth and had aimed again before the spent cartridge had stopped jingling on the boards by his feet. He eased the tip of the sight a little lower, into the bird's breast, and took care to squeeze the trigger with perfect evenness. The slow contraction of his hand abruptly sprang the bullet; for a half-second there was doubt, and then the pigeon fell like a handful of rags, skimming down the barn wall into the layer of straw that coated the floor of the mow on this side.

---

preening: smoothing feathers with a beak or bill

Now others shook loose from the rafters, and whirled in the dim air with a great blurred hurtle of feathers and noise. They would go for the hole; he fixed his sight on the little moon of blue, and when a pigeon came to it, shot him as he was walking the ten inches of stone that would have carried him into the open air. This pigeon lay down in that tunnel of stone, unable to fall either one way or the other, although he was alive enough to lift one wing and cloud the light. It would sink back, and he would suddenly lift it again, the feathers flaring. His body blocked that exit. David raced to the other side of the barn's main aisle, where a similar ladder was symmetrically placed, and rested his gun on the same rung. Three birds came together to this hole; he got one, and two got through. The rest resettled in the rafters.

There was a shallow triangular space behind the cross beams supporting the roof. It was here they roosted and hid. But either the space was too small, or they were curious, for now that his eyes were at home in the dusty gloom David could see little dabs of gray popping in and out. The cooing was shriller now; its apprehensive tremolo made the whole volume of air seem liquid. He noticed one little smudge of a head that was especially persistent in peeking out; he marked the place, and fixed his gun on it, and when the head appeared again, had his finger tightened in advance on the trigger. A parcel of fluff slipped off the beam and fell the barn's height onto a canvas covering some Olinger furniture, and where its head had peeked out there was a fresh prick of light in the shingles.

Standing in the center of the floor, fully master now, disdaining to steady the barrel with anything but his arm, he killed two more that way. He felt like a beautiful avenger. Out of the shadowy ragged infinity of the vast barn roof these impudent things dared to thrust their heads, presumed to dirty its starred silence with their filthy timorous life, and he cut them off, tucked them back neatly into the silence. He had the sensation of a creator; these little smudges and flickers that he was clever to see and even cleverer to hit in the dim recesses of the rafters—out of each of them he was making a full bird. A tiny peek, probe, dab of life, when he hit it, blossomed into a dead enemy, falling with good, final weight.

The imperfection of the second pigeon he had shot, who was still lifting his wing now and then up in the round hole, nagged him.

He put a new clip into the stock. Hugging the gun against his body, he climbed the ladder. The barrel sight scratched his ear; he had a sharp, garish vision, like a color slide, of shooting himself and being found tumbled on the barn floor among his prey. He locked his arm around the top rung—a fragile, gnawed rod braced between uprights—and shot into the bird's body from a flat angle. The wing folded, but the impact did not, as he had hoped, push the bird out of the hole. He fired again, and again, and still the little body, lighter than air when alive, was too heavy to budge from its high grave. From up here he could see green trees and a brown corner of the house through the hole. Clammy with the cobwebs that gathered between the rungs, he pumped a full clip of eight bullets into the stubborn shadow, with no success. He climbed down, and was struck by the silence in the barn. The remaining pigeons must have escaped out the other hole. That was all right; he was tired of it.

He stepped with his rifle into the light. His mother was coming to meet him, and it tickled him to see her shy away from the carelessly held gun. "You took a chip out of the house," she said. "What were those last shots about?"

"One of them died up in that little round hole and I was trying to shoot it down."

"Copper's hiding behind the piano and won't come out. I had to leave him."

"Well don't blame me. *I* didn't want to shoot the poor devils."

"Don't smirk. You look like your father. How many did you get?"

"Six."

She went into the barn and he followed. She listened to the silence. Her hair was scraggly, perhaps from tussling with the dog. "I don't suppose the others will be back," she said wearily. "Indeed, I don't know why I let Mother talk me into it. Their cooing was such a comforting noise." She began to gather up the dead pigeons. Though he didn't want to touch them, David went into the mow and picked up by its tepid, horny, coral-colored feet the first bird he had killed. Its wings unfolded disconcertingly, as if the creature had been held together by threads that now were slit. It did not weigh much. He retrieved the one on the other side of the barn; his mother got the three in the middle and led the way across the road to the little southern slope of land that went down toward the foundations of the vanished tobacco shed. The ground was too steep to plant and mow; wild strawberries grew in the tangled grass. She put her burden down and said, "We'll have to bury them. The dog will go wild."

He put his two down on her three; the slick feathers let the bodies slide liquidly on one another. He asked, "Shall I get you the shovel?"

"Get it for yourself; *you* bury them. They're your kill. And be sure to make the hole deep enough so he won't dig them up." While he went to the tool shed for the shovel, she went into the house. Unlike her, she did not look up, either at the orchard to the right of her or at the meadow on her left, but instead held her head rigidly, tilted a little, as if listening to the ground.

He dug the hole, in a spot where there were no strawberry plants, before he studied the pigeons. He had never seen a bird this close before. The feathers were more wonderful than dog's hair, for each filament was shaped within the shape of the feather, and the feathers in turn were trimmed to fit a pattern that flowed without error across the bird's body. He lost himself in the geometrical tides as the feathers now broadened and stiffened to make an edge for flight, now softened and constricted to cup warmth around the mute flesh. And across the surface of the infinitely adjusted yet somehow effortless mechanics of the feathers played idle designs of color, no two alike, designs executed, it seemed, in a controlled rapture, with a joy that hung level in the air above and behind him. Yet these birds bred in the millions and were exterminated as pests. Into the fragrant open earth he dropped one broadly banded in slate shades of blue, and on top of it another, mottled all over in rhythms of lilac and gray. The next was almost wholly white, but for a salmon glaze at its throat. As he fitted the last two, still pliant, on the top, and stood up, crusty coverings were lifted from him, and with a feminine, slipping sensation along his nerves that seemed to give the air hands, he was robed in this certainty: that the God who had lavished such craft upon these worthless birds would not destroy His whole Creation by refusing to let David live forever.

About the Story

1. Identify one of the many literary allusions used in Updike's story.
2. What is the significance of the allusion you chose?
3. Identify one of the historical allusions in the story.
4. What is the significance of this allusion?
5. How has this story specifically helped you in understanding young people like David who may be seeking answers to basic philosophical questions such as the following: Where did I come from? Why am I here? Where am I going?

About the Author

In writing "Pigeon Feathers," John Updike (1932-) drew from his own experience. Like David Kern, he had moved from town to country at the age of fourteen, experienced the same painful isolation, and suffered from a similar set of family circumstances. Updike frequently writes about the breakdown of the family, forcefully presenting the consequences of America's current lack of faith and fidelity. While many of Updike's works display a grim realism and an insensibility to the provision of grace for the individual, his observations of man's unregenerate condition are astute.

Updike is not, however, entirely insensible to the concept of man's immortality and nature's cosmic design. He presents them as an unexpected gift of insight into life's true meaning. This is what David Kern, the protagonist of "Pigeon Feathers," experiences. David's eventual awareness of the existence of God and the immortality of the soul touches on a recurring theme in Updike's writing, a theme which concedes that man must possess the hope of immortality and a cosmic design. Unfortunately, his observations—though poignant—fail to acknowledge God's provision of salvation through Christ and man's individual responsibility to accept what God has graciously provided through His Son.

Thought/Theme: The hopes stirred by the dictionary's definition, the hesitant prayers, and the beauty of a dog's fur at last come together. As David gazes at the exquisite design of the pigeons' feathers, he receives "the word, the gesture, the nod of certainty." At last he is "sealed in"; mind, heart, and senses all reinforce the truth: David Kern has a soul, a soul that God has destined to live forever.

Elicit from students, however, that we must not take this to mean that David has been born again. He is headed in the right direction spiritually, but the story in no way indicates that he has placed the safety of his eternal soul in the Saviour's keeping.

About the Story

1. *Answers will vary but may include "Greek plays and Romantic poetry, Will Durant's* Story of Philosophy," *Shakespeare, H. G. Wells, P. G. Wodehouse, Plato, the Bible.*

2. *Answers may vary. Students' responses should focus on how that allusion touches on David's search for truth.*

3. *Answers may vary but might include Wells's blasphemous account of the life of Christ (page 108); the mother's Romantic perspective on life (page 109); the father's references to the Dark Ages (page 111) and George Washington (page 113); Dobson's reference to Abraham Lincoln (page 114).*

4. *Answers will vary but should focus on the way that allusion impinges on David's dilemma.*

5. *Answers may vary; see Discussion section (pp. 106-7).*

5
UNIT FIVE

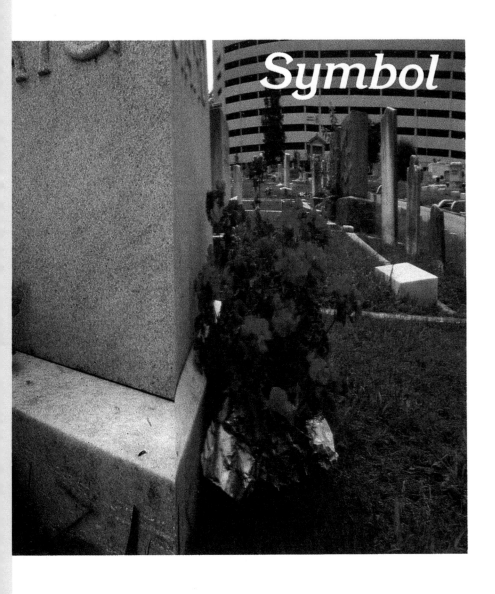

Symbol

Symbol Introduction

OBJECTIVES

The students will be able to

- Identify the main kinds of symbolic expression.
- Refute the negative views of fables derived from a misunderstanding of certain New Testament passages.

FURTHER HELPS

Additional activities

1. For further discussion: Jehoash's tale is probably the best example of a fable to be found in Scripture. It is not pure fable, however, for it has some points of at least potential correlation between the two levels of meaning. Clearer examples follow in the unit selections. Whereas parables predominate in the Bible, fables predominate in other literature.

2. For further discussion: Analogy may be used to illustrate the paradox "whosoever shall keep the whole law, and yet offend in one point, he is guilty of all" (James 2:10). One preacher has compared God's law (the Ten Commandments) to a ten-piece set of antique china—the breaking of one piece breaks the set. The value of the entire set is diminished disproportionately to the worth of a single broken piece.

In ordinary use sign and symbol have almost the same meaning. A sign is a symbolic mark, picture, object, or gesture—something that stands for something else. A symbol is an especially technical or complex sign: proofreaders' symbols, for example, or a cultural emblem such as a national flag. In the study of literature, sign and symbol are usually kept separate. A **sign** is said to mean something *other than* itself. The plus mark, for instance, means only what it represents: an arithmetical function. A literary **symbol,** on the other hand, is said to mean something *in addition to* itself. When we extend the vertical line of the plus sign downward, we produce the richest symbol known to man. The cross means itself—the wooden instrument of Christ's death—but also has come to mean much more. When Paul wrote that "the preaching of the cross is to them that perish foolishness" (I Cor. 1:18), he was referring to the whole scheme of man's redemption planned by God, of which the cross historically was the focal point. Today a reference to the cross carries two thousand years of additional religious associations as well.

Similarly, when we speak of "the empty tomb," we mean not only the physical event of Christ's resurrection but also the assurance it gives of Christ's victory over death on behalf of mankind—His power to give eternal life to all believers. It is the keystone of the believer's confidence in the gospel.

Signs as well as symbols belong to what we may call the symbolic mode in literature. The picture side of a metaphor is a kind of sign, pointing to a meaning other than itself. When the dying Jacob blessed his sons, he said, "Joseph is a fruitful bough, even a fruitful bough by a well, whose branches run over the wall" (Gen. 49:22). The branch, heavy with fruit, pictures Joseph, whose descendants will multiply greatly and bring great blessing to others. As a sign the fruitful bough is not an actual object in the narrative but a representation of something else. It exists solely for the sake of what it represents. We may visualize its difference from a symbol as follows.

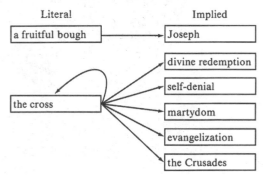

DISCUSSION

Symbol Introduction

Overview

The discussion of the symbolic mode maps the whole territory of the symbolic, from metaphor, allegory, and analogy to symbol and loosely symbolic narrative. Concepts are explained, related, and illustrated with Biblical examples and references to earlier selections.

Potential problems

The difficulty of the concepts and their interconnections may initially pose a problem. The concepts should become clearer, however, with the discussion of the selections that follow.

PREPARATION

Introduction

Before beginning the lesson, point out to the students the derivation of the word *symbol*. Its Greek ancestor is *symballein: syn* meaning "together" and *ballein* meaning "to throw." Symbolism, then, is the "throwing together" of two things and/or ideas, one represented in terms of the other. Next, discuss with the students the prevalence of symbolism in daily life. Point out that they recognize and use symbols more than they realize. Political cartoons, comic cartoons, cheers at pep rallies, road signs, and printed and nonprinted advertisements rely on symbols to convey meaning. Have the students think of names of products (e.g., cars) that are metaphoric. Mercury and Cougar are two ex-

amples. The names of sports teams also provide examples (Seahawks and Broncos).

Analysis

Before reading the introduction aloud, illustrate the difference between sign and symbol using the example in the opening two paragraphs of the essay. Draw a plus sign on the chalkboard, pointing out to the students that this sign stands for something other than itself: an arithmetical function. A literary symbol, on the other hand, means something in addition to itself. Extend the vertical line of the plus mark downward. Point out to the students that by extending this line we turn the sign into a symbol, the richest symbol known to man—the cross. Briefly discuss what the cross symbolizes. *(redemption, forgiveness, the way to heaven, etc.)* Fol-

The metaphor, a kind of sign, imaginative and momentary, means something other than itself. The symbol, with its richness of implication, means something in addition to itself.

Now if we let plants continue to stand for persons (cf. Gen. 49) and set them in motion in a story, we enter the realm of allegory. An allegorical story is an extended metaphor, in which the characters, incidents, and situations have a meaning beyond the literal level of the narrative. They stand for something else. The Old Testament offers an interesting example in the story of Jotham. After the death of Gideon, Abimelech, his son by a concubine of Shechem, plotted to become king. With the help of the men of Shechem, he killed seventy of his brothers, legitimate sons living at the family house in Ophrah. Only Jotham, the youngest, escaped. Standing on a nearby hill, Jotham interrupted the coronation festivities with a prophetic tale. In this tale, plants speak and act as persons.

> The trees went forth on a time to anoint a king over them; and they said unto the olive tree, Reign thou over us. But the olive tree said unto them, Should I leave my fatness, wherewith by me they honour God and man, and go to be promoted over the trees? And the trees said to the fig tree, Come thou, and reign over us. But the fig tree said unto them, Should I forsake my sweetness, and my good fruit, and go to be promoted over the trees? Then said the trees unto the vine, Come thou, and reign over us. And the vine said unto them, Should I leave my wine, which cheereth God and man, and go to be promoted over the trees? Then said all the trees unto the bramble, Come thou, and reign over us. And the bramble said unto the trees, If in truth ye anoint me king over you, then come and put your trust in my shadow: and if not, let fire come out of the bramble, and devour the cedars of Lebanon (Judges 9:8-15).

Jotham then went on to make the application.

> If ye then have dealt truly and sincerely with Jerubbaal [Gideon] and with his house this day, then rejoice ye in Abimelech, and let him also rejoice in you: But if not, let fire come out from Abimelech, and devour the men of Shechem, and the house of Millo; and let fire come out from the men of Shechem, and from the house of Millo, and devour Abimelech (9:19-20).

Jotham's tale has two levels of meaning, the literal level of the story itself and the implied level summarized in his explanation. The tale may be diagrammed as follows:

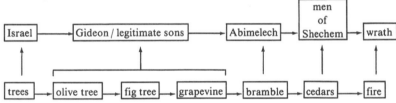

3. Read an excerpt from John Bunyan's *The Pilgrim's Progress* aloud. Have the students choose a scene from *The Pilgrim's Progress* to dramatize. See *The Pilgrim's Progress* Teacher's Edition, BJU Press.)

4. Have the students choose another of Aesop's fables they like and adapt the fable into a poem.

5. Have a student do a study on one of the parables and share with the class what he has learned from his study (e.g., the levels of meaning and the application of the parable to the student's life).

6. Read the following Stephen Crane poem aloud to the class:

I saw a man pursuing the horizon;
Round and round they sped.
I was disturbed at this;
I accosted the man.
"It is futile," I said,
"You can never—"
"You lie," he cried,
And ran on.

Guide the students in understanding that the horizon is a symbol for ideals. Then discuss the validity of the concept presented in the poem.

7. Ask the students to think of other symbols with which they are familiar. The following list may help get a discussion started.

American flag for USA
stars in the flag for states in USA
stripes in the flag for thirteen original colonies

lowing this illustration, read the introduction aloud, taking time to discuss the Biblical examples provided.

Following this discussion, it may be helpful to show the students how the terms in the essay fit together. See **Appendix L: Symbolism Defined and Illustrated.** You may wish to fill it out together in class as you work through the unit, starting today with the first part.

Application

One common analogy used against Christian education is the notion that a sheltered "hothouse" education will not prepare young people to live in the "real world." Have the students discuss this analogy. Guide them in understanding that the analogy can in fact be used as a valid support for Christian education. For example, every home gardener wants hothouse plants to set out in the spring. They prove to be the hardiest (most resistant to disease, adverse climate, etc.) and the most productive. Have the students discuss the implications of these facts on the analogy.

As time permits, see whether the students can come up with other analogies that may be viewed from another perspective.

bald eagle for strength and freedom

statue of woman blindfolded, balancing
  a set of scales with one hand and
  holding a sword in the other, for
  justice

president (outside of the USA) for the
  American people

wedding band for eternal love

dove for peace

Journal entry idea

Have the students choose a
Biblical symbol and write a
paragraph or two about the significance of

the family	water
Babylon	the lamb
bread	Aaron's rod
Egypt	the lion

the symbol. The following list of suggested topics may help get them started:

Resources

Grace Collins Hargis, *The Pilgrim's Progress
Teacher's Guide* (Greenville, S.C.: BJU
Press, 2002).

R. C. Trench, *Notes on the Parables of Our
Lord* (Michigan: Baker Book House,
1948).

Notice that the two levels connect at a number of specific points. The correlation is continuous and systematic. The tale is a *parable,* an allegorical story with two or more strictly correlated levels of meaning.

Another allegory using plants as characters appears in II Kings 14:9. King Amaziah of Judah, having subdued Edom to the south, challenged Jehoash, king of northern Israel, to meet him in battle. Jehoash replied,

> The thistle that was in Lebanon sent to the cedar that was in Lebanon, saying, Give thy daughter to my son to wife: and there passed by a wild beast that was in Lebanon, and trode down the thistle.

An explanation followed.

> Thou hast indeed smitten Edom, and thine heart hath lifted thee up: glory of this, and tarry at home: for why shouldest thou meddle to thy hurt, that thou shouldest fall, even thou, and Judah with thee?

Notice that in Jehoash's explanation the literal and implied levels of the story are not so strictly correlated as in Jotham's. Though there is a potential association of the thistle with Amaziah, the cedar with Jehoash, the marriage proposal with the battle challenge, and the trampling of the thistle with the defeat of Amaziah, the correlation is unstated and uncertain. It is also less direct and systematic. An offer of marriage is not related to a battle challenge except, in this case, as an act of presumption. The wild beast may or may not refer to the same person as does the cedar. What we have instead is a story that illustrates a moral: the danger of prideful meddling. It may be diagrammed as follows:

Jehoash's tale is more a *fable* than a parable. In a fable the details support the meaning collectively, whereas in a parable the details support the meaning individually. Allegorical stories are either parables or fables or a blend of these.

A close relative of allegory is *analogy,* an extended comparison used to explain or persuade. Examples, such as this one from Robert Law, are common in preaching. "Individual sins are like islets, which appear as separate and casual specks on the surface of the ocean, but are, in reality, the mountain peaks of a submerged continent" (*The Test of Life,* p. 133). In analogy the comparison (1) is stated ("are like"), (2) is of some length (usually a sentence or more), and (3) appeals to common knowledge or experience. Analogy's purpose is instructive. It uses a familiar thing to explain something difficult to understand. Luke 14 concludes with two analogies.

> For which of you, intending to build a tower, sitteth not down first, and counteth the cost, whether he have sufficient to finish it? Lest haply, after he hath laid the foundation, and is not able to finish it, all that behold it begin to mock him, saying, This man began to build, and was not able to finish.

> Or what king, going to make war against another king, sitteth not down first, and consulteth whether he be able with ten thousand to meet him that cometh against him with twenty thousand? Or else, while the other is yet a great way off, he sendeth an ambassage, and desireth conditions of peace.
> So likewise, whosoever he be of you that forsaketh not all that he hath, he cannot be my disciple.

The analogies teach the importance, to a prospective disciple, of calculating beforehand the cost of following Christ. The cost is "all that he hath." The Christian life is said to be like a building or a battle. These analogies also appear later in the epistles of Paul. In Luke 15 the Lord uses two other analogies (the lost sheep and the lost coin) and a parable (the lost son) to defend God's right to welcome sinners. Whereas parables, like all allegory, may be regarded as extended metaphors, analogies are extended similes.

On the frontier of allegory, nearest fable, is non-allegorical *symbolic narrative.* The story of Joseph in Genesis is nowhere allegorized in the New Testament in the manner of the story of Abraham, Isaac, and Ishmael in Galatians 4. But the symbolic aspects of Joseph's experience are so striking as to be unmistakable. In the rejection of Joseph by his brothers and his humiliation and eventual exaltation in Egypt, we can hardly fail to notice a partial parallel with the descent and ascent of the Saviour. In Joseph's treatment of his brothers, afflicting them to awaken their consciences in order to prepare them for reconciliation, we can recognize something of the "goodness and severity of God" (Rom. 11:22).

Most good imaginative literature is to some degree symbolic. That is, it has some implied breadth of meaning. Allusions, in particular, are often symbolic. Eldorado, in Poe's poem, is not only a historical allusion but also a symbol of unattainable goals and ideals. The water drawn from the rock, in Arnold's poem, is a symbol of the creative imagination, arising on demand in youth, dwindling and disappearing in adulthood. Beyond question, to get the most out of our reading, especially of artistic writing and of the Scriptures themselves, we must be aware of the symbolic mode. Some varieties of this mode appear in the selections that follow.

OBJECTIVES

The students will be able to

- Define *epigram* and *fable*.
- Defend the legitimate use of fable to teach Biblical principles.
- Discuss the issue that Scripture does not condemn the use of the allegorical mode; it condemns only those fables that masquerade as literal truth.

"Epigram": Line 1—Allusions to Gen. 2:7; 9:9-17.

Line 2—Symbolic meaning: Just as without dust in the air, rainbows could not exist (see bottom of page 131), so without difficult times in life, we could not enjoy life's good times.

Epigram

Langston Hughes

A short, simple poem can be rich in meaning. This one, a prayer, uses allusion and symbol. Explain the allusions in the first line. Then explain their symbolic meanings in the second line. Is there a scientific basis for linking the rainbow with dust?

Oh, God of dust and rainbows, help us see
That without dust the rainbow would not be.

About the Author

Despite an unsettled upbringing, Langston Hughes (1902-1967) possessed a positive outlook and a zest for living. Unlike others of his time, Hughes chose not to allow his minority status in a turbulent era to overwhelm or discourage him. Hughes possessed not only a deep sense of loyalty to his people but also a great love for America. He condemned the existence of class and racial hatred when he could, using his literary talent, for example, to fight such movements as Nazism and fascism. He spent most of his time, however, rejoicing in his heritage as a black poet, becoming a leader in the literary renaissance in Harlem during the 1920s.

In addition to the universal themes of man's desire for freedom and his endurance in suffering, Hughes's poems reveal personal joys and yearnings. He was well read and traveled widely. In Mexico he worked as a ranch hand and an English teacher. He also became a ship's steward and sailed to Africa and Holland. He was a bus boy in Paris, a journalist in Spain, and a lecturer all across America. Yet through it all, he wrote. Hughes's diversity of occupations gave him a breadth and sensitivity that proved invaluable. In his writing he honestly looked at the human condition, but he never lost his sense of humor or his enthusiasm for life. His purpose was to motivate others to better their lives and fulfill their dreams. "Words," he stated, "should be used to make people *believe* and *do*." It was this outlook as well as his literary gifts that won him worldwide recognition.

PREPARATION

"Epigram," "The Ant and the Grasshopper," "The Grasshopper and the Cricket," "The Nightingale and the Glowworm"

Overview

The familiar Biblical allusions to Genesis in "Epigram" take the student from what he knows to what he is beginning to learn: the symbolic mode. This poem also exemplifies the precision and compression of meaning we find in the best poetry. Keats's "The Grasshopper and the Cricket" is poetic description with symbolic implication. These implications appear in a comparison of Keats's view of the grasshopper with Aesop's. Finally, Cowper's poem supplies another example of a fable, this one without a stated moral.

Potential problems

The students may question the propriety of fables, with passages such as I Timothy 1:4; 4:7; II Timothy 4:4; Titus 1:14; and II Peter 1:16 in mind. Remind students that these passages do not condemn the allegorical mode, for Christ used it constantly. Remind them of Jehoash's fable (II Kings 14:9-10; II Chron. 25:18-19). The New Testament condemns certain fables that masquerade as literal truth (cf. any religious dogma that adds to or takes away from the truth of Scripture).

DISCUSSION

"Epigram"

Introduction

Take a few moments to discuss the definition of *epigram*. An epigram may be defined as "a short, highly compressed poem making a wise or humorous observation and ending with a witty twist." Originally an epitaph, it was used in classical times to give permanent, memorable form to general truths.

The Ant and the Grasshopper

Aesop

The Greek slave Aesop wrote a number of short moral tales. In these tales, Aesop's animals talk, show human intelligence and stupidity, and enjoy or suffer the consequences of their wise or unwise conduct. One of his most famous is the story of the ant and the grasshopper. Notice that all the details of the narrative support the meaning collectively, guiding us to a single moral or thesis.

One frosty autumn day an ant was busily storing away some of the kernels of wheat which he had gathered during the summer to tide him over the coming winter.

A grasshopper, half perishing from hunger, came limping by. Perceiving what the industrious ant was doing, he asked for a morsel from the ant's store to save his life.

"What were you doing all during the summer while I was busy harvesting?" inquired the ant.

"Oh," replied the grasshopper, "I was not idle. I was singing and chirping all day long."

"Well," said the ant, smiling grimly as he locked his granary door, "since you sang all summer, it looks as though you would have to dance all winter."

Moral: It is thrifty to prepare today for the wants of tomorrow.

About the Author

A fable is a pithy, traditional story that highlights an implied or explicitly stated moral. Animals often display human virtues and vices; for example, initiative and sloth are characterized in "The Ant and the Grasshopper."

The historical Aesop, a sixth-century Greek slave, was noted for his storytelling abilities. Although we can be fairly certain that he indeed authored several moral tales such as "The Ant and the Grasshopper," his reputation as the originator of the fable form lacks proof. It has been noted that this form appears in Egyptian manuscripts as early as the sixteenth century B.C. and that several others have been found which date back to the first century A.D. It was the Greeks and Italians that liberally linked Aesop's name to moral tales of various origins. These facts, however, in no way diminish the lessons we can learn from the legendary "Aesopian" fables.

Read the first poem, "Epigram," aloud. Then draw the students' attention to the first "About the Poems" question (page 136). Have them decide whether Hughes's epigram is a usual or unusual example of this genre. *(It is a good example, typical of this genre.)*

Analysis

Hughes's poem is brief, compressed, and ingenious. The first line contains two Biblical allusions in "dust and rainbows"—the first, to God's forming man from the dust of the ground; the second, to God's covenant with man that the world would never again be destroyed by flood. The second line implies another level of meaning in which "dust" stands for the tedious, troublesome part of life, and

"rainbow" for the hopeful, joyous part. The association of rainbows with dust (a scientific allusion) implies that the two can coexist and, indeed, that the one could not exist without the other. A small particle of dust is necessary to form the nucleus of a raindrop, and raindrops refract sunlight into a prismatic spectrum. Similarly, troubles and tedium are necessary to the existence of hope and to the joy of hope fulfilled. There is much symbolic meaning packed into this short, seemingly simple poem.

"The Ant and the Grasshopper"

Aesop's fable is useful for introducing the allegorical story. Though there is not enough specific point-to-point correspondence between levels of meaning to call it a parable, some

symbolic references are obvious. Have the students identify the human types corresponding to the ant and the grasshopper and also the seasonal metaphor.

The ant represents, of course, the thrifty; the grasshopper, the unthrifty. The seasons may correspond to stages of life. More specifically, they suggest times of prosperity and adversity. One should provide in good times for the bad times, the moral advises.

In most of the other allegorical stories in this unit, the interpretation will not be as conveniently stated as it is in Aesop's fable. The reader will have to formulate the meaning himself. Draw the students' attention to "About the Poems" question 2 (page 136). Have them look

Note structural parallelism: immortality of poetry/summer/grasshopper's song.

immortality of poetry/winter/cricket's song

conflating of the two creatures' songs and their blessings

about what the moral would be; then have the actors reveal the intended moral. Discuss whether their intended moral came through clearly, and if not, why not.

6. Read a humorous takeoff of a fable in *Fables for Our Time* or *Further Fables for Our Time* by James Thurber. You may wish to discuss the idea of parody and satire as you read these. (See pages 151-52 for a discussion of satire.) Be sure to read the story yourself before reading it aloud in class so that you may check for appropriateness.

7. Ask the students to find out what a fable writer is called. *(fabulist)*

8. Display an ant farm in your classroom. Note as a class the activities of the ants.

9. In "The Ant and the Grasshopper," the two animals symbolize different ideas. See if the students can think of other insects and what they might symbolize. The students could even write a fable about one of these insects.

The Grasshopper and the Cricket

John Keats

The British poet John Keats turned the tables, so to speak, on Aesop. In Keats's view, the grasshopper should not be despised. It ministers to others rather than just to itself. What practical people call idling—writing poetry, for example—may be important work. How bleak the world would be without the music of nature's poets. Human song, like nature's, is possible at every season—of the year and of the life.

The poetry of earth is never dead:
  When all the birds are faint with the hot sun,
  And hide in cooling trees, a voice will run
From hedge to hedge about the new-mown mead;
That is the Grasshopper's—he takes the lead   5
  In summer luxury,—he has never done
  With his delights; for when tired out with fun
He rests at ease beneath some pleasant weed.
The poetry of earth is ceasing never:
  On a lone winter evening, when the frost   10
  Has wrought a silence, from the stove there shrills
The Cricket's song, in warmth increasing ever,
  And seems to one in drowsiness half lost,
  The Grasshopper's among some grassy hills.

up a proverb that might be used to summarize Aesop's fable.

"The Grasshopper and the Cricket"
Ask the students what Aesop's view of the grasshopper is. *(The grasshopper, in Aesop's fable, is an idler, a worthless fellow.)* Then ask them how the grasshopper (locust) is regarded in history generally. *(Historically he is a pest, a danger to society.)* Ask them how practical people have regarded poets in the past. *(In the common view, the poet is often viewed as worthless [a waster of his own time and that of others], and sometimes as a threat to the peace of the community.)* John Keats was himself regarded negatively. Like the grasshopper, he died young—before the winter of life, at the first frost, so to speak. The cricket's song suggests the possibility of poetry in the win-

ter—of life, of circumstances. Keats never was able to prove the possibility of poetry in old age, though he desperately wished to live long enough for his poetic gift to mature. The poem thus uses the songs of insects as symbols of the poetry of man. It challenges the common view of poetry by reversing the traditional perspectives on the grasshopper. (Following this discussion, the students should be able to answer "About the Poems" question 3, page 136).

Notice how Keats introduces the images of drowsiness, sultry warmth, and the song of a chirping insect into the first eight lines, or octave, of this sonnet. Have the students identify the parallel imagery in the sestet, or last six lines. See **Appendix M: "The Grasshopper and the Cricket"—Structural Parallels.**

Note that poetry is very important to God. Notice the proportion of Scripture allocated to poetry. Students would do well to remember this when they complain about the study of poetry.

"The Nightingale and the Glowworm"
(You may wish to remind students that they have already studied a poem by Cowper [see page 86].) The headnote contains the basic materials for analysis. The poem shows the importance of both the aesthetic (represented in the nightingale) and the didactic (represented in the glowworm) functions of poetry. The nightingale accordingly "began to feel," the glowworm to deliver a "short oration." The poem thus associates song with feeling, light with reason. Both have their place in poetry.

About the Author

By the time he died at the age of twenty-six, John Keats (1795-1821) had produced an enormous amount of work which would later establish him among the most important of the English Romantic poets. Though productive, Keats's short life was full of troubles, but Keats's friends asserted that he was always cheerful and enthusiastic when discussing literature. "The Grasshopper and the Cricket" resulted from a lively evening of such literary talk with his old schoolmaster Cowden Clarke and the controversial essayist Leigh Hunt. The poem was written during a contest between Keats and Hunt which was motivated by the poets' observations concerning the grasshopper.

Keats's "contest" poem was, like many other Romantic poems, a poem of association, that is, a poem in which one association evokes another. This well-crafted piece also displays a consistent rhythm. Throughout the continuous cycle of seasons, God has infused a rhythm and beauty which Keats called "the poetry of earth." "The Grasshopper and the Cricket" is only one of many poems that reflect Keats's awareness of this order and rhythm in creation.

The Nightingale and the Glowworm

William Cowper

This meeting of a nightingale with a glowworm is probably intended as a beast fable in the manner of Aesop. The moral is not supplied, however. Notice that both the nightingale and the glowworm are creatures that "beautify and cheer the night." The one does so by song, the other by light. Probably they are meant to suggest the two traditional functions of poetry: joyous sound and wise illumination. The old poets believed that their work should not only delight but also teach. It should give both pleasure and wisdom. You may recognize the poet, William Cowper, as one of our great hymnodists. He was also the foremost English poet of his time.

Journal entry idea

Have the students suggest at least two ways that the moral of "The Ant and the Grasshopper" would be applicable to their own lives.

Journal entry idea

Have the students write a different ending to the fable by Aesop. Be sure to have them tell what new moral would fit the fable after it is rewritten.

Resources

James Ralston Caldwell, *John Keats' Fancy* (New York: Octagon Books, 1965).

Timothy Hilton, *Keats and His World* (New York: Viking Press, 1971).

Robin Mayhead, *John Keats* (London: Cambridge University Press, 1967).

Milton Meltzer, *Langston Hughes: A Biography* (Millbrook Press, 1997).

Both combine to relieve the long "night" of mortal life. Have the students answer the last "About the Poems" question (page 136). Answers to the question will vary.

Application

Have the students write the moral of this poem as Aesop might have stated it, were he the author. Discuss their responses and allow the class to vote on the best one. You might wish to use the winner on a bulletin board about the poem.

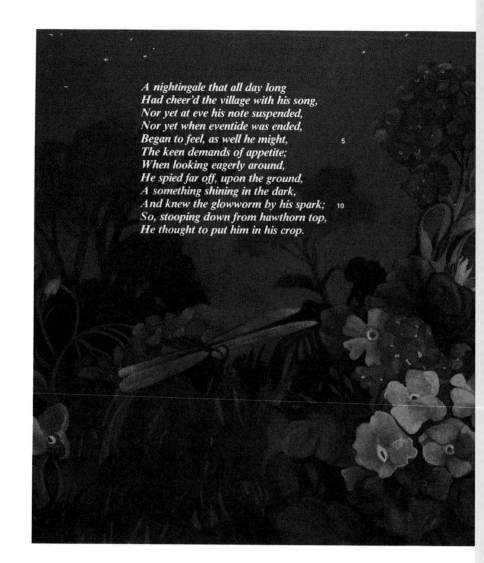

A nightingale that all day long
Had cheer'd the village with his song,
Nor yet at eve his note suspended,
Nor yet when eventide was ended,
Began to feel, as well he might,   5
The keen demands of appetite;
When looking eagerly around,
He spied far off, upon the ground,
A something shining in the dark,
And knew the glowworm by his spark;   10
So, stooping down from hawthorn top,
He thought to put him in his crop.

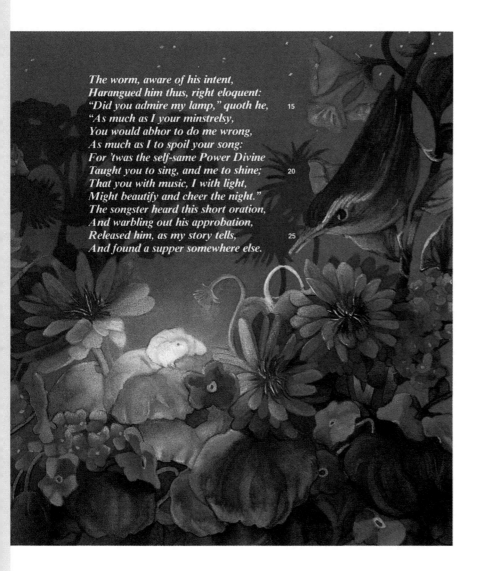

The worm, aware of his intent,
Harangued him thus, right eloquent:
"Did you admire my lamp," quoth he, 15
"As much as I your minstrelsy,
You would abhor to do me wrong,
As much as I to spoil your song:
For 'twas the self-same Power Divine
Taught you to sing, and me to shine; 20
That you with music, I with light,
Might beautify and cheer the night."
The songster heard this short oration,
And warbling out his approbation,
Released him, as my story tells, 25
And found a supper somewhere else.

OBJECTIVES

The students will be able to

- Identify alliteration.
- Discuss the effect of style on the theme of a work.
- Analyze and discuss symbolic elements in "Fable" and "maggie and milly and molly and may."

If students endeavor to scan this poem to discover a regular rhythm or rhyme, they may be frustrated. Emerson, like other transcendentalists (see page 137), was seeking to break away from established norms of poetry.

About the Poems

1. Look up the meaning of *epigram.* Is Langston Hughes's epigram a usual or unusual example of this genre?
2. The thought or thesis of Aesop's moral fable "The Ant and the Grasshopper" can be summarized by some of Solomon's proverbs. Identify a proverb that does so.
3. Keats's view of the grasshopper differs from that of Aesop's. Use one quotation from each selection to illustrate these differing viewpoints.
4. Why do you think Cowper chose to portray the nightingale as the one that feels (the pangs of hunger) and the glowworm as the one that reasons (in defense of his right to exist)?

Fable

Ralph Waldo Emerson

This fictional encounter, like Cowper's between a nightingale and a glowworm, is a fable, as the title indicates.

The mountain and the squirrel
Had a quarrel;
And the former called the latter "Little Prig."*
Bun* replied,
"You are doubtless very big;   5
But all sorts of things and weather
Must be taken in together,
To make up a year
And a sphere.
And I think it no disgrace   10
To occupy my place.
If I'm not so large as you,
You are not so small as I,
And not half so spry.
I'll not deny you make   15
A very pretty squirrel track;*
Talents differ; all is well and wisely put;
If I cannot carry forests on my back,
Neither can you crack a nut."

Prig: stuffy moralist
Bun: name for a squirrel

squirrel track: path for squirrels

About the Poems

1. *An epigram may be defined as "a short, highly compressed poem making a wise or humorous observation and ending with a witty twist." Yes, Hughes's poem is typical—it is brief, compressed, and ingenious.*

2. *"Go to the ant, thou sluggard; consider her ways, and be wise" (Prov. 6:6-8). Students may list other examples as well.*

3. *Answers may vary. Aesop portrays the grasshopper as an idler wasting his time: "since you sang all summer, it looks as though you would have to dance all winter." Keats, on the other hand, sees the grasshopper in a nobler light: "a voice will run / From hedge to hedge about the new-mown mead;*

/ That is the Grasshopper's—he takes the lead / In summer luxury,—he has never done / With his delights."

4. *Answers may vary. While both animals can be appreciated for giving beauty to the night, the glowworm, being less physically attractive than the nightingale, might need to defend the importance of his role.*

PREPARATION

"Fable," "maggie and milly and molly and may"

Overview

Emerson's "Fable" personifies a mountain and a squirrel. The moral should be fairly easy for the

students to discover. Cummings's poem continues the examples of the fable, introducing the motif of symbolic choice. It also offers an opportunity to review alliteration.

Potential problems

Ralph Waldo Emerson was a radical transcendentalist whose teaching (though it contained some truth) undermined Christian beliefs. Students should not be encouraged to read his works indiscriminately.

Note also Cummings's use of assonance: *may, play, day* (lines 1-2); *chased,
raced, sideways* (lines 7-8).

About the Author

Ralph Waldo Emerson (1803-1882) spent time almost daily in the woods
of New England walking, thinking, and jotting down his thoughts. Like his
fellow Transcendentalists, Emerson believed that universal truths could be
discovered by communing with nature. Thus, nature became a rich source
of imagery to embody his ideas. As Christians we agree with Emerson that
universal truths can be inferred from observing nature. Unlike Emerson,
however, Christians recognize that such observations are not ends in themselves.
What we see in creation should turn our focus toward the Creator—the author
of all truth. Those, like Emerson, who fail to understand this truth tend to
deify the symbol (nature) rather than acknowledge Whom the symbol represents.

maggie and milly and molly and may

e.e. cummings

*What we are is evident by what attracts us. What can we learn about
each girl from her response to the seashore?*

maggie and milly and molly and may
went down to the beach(to play one day)

and maggie discovered a shell that sang
so sweetly she couldn't remember her troubles,and

milly befriended a stranded star
whose rays five languid fingers were;   5

and molly was chased by a horrible thing
which raced sideways while blowing bubbles:and

may came home with a smooth round stone
as small as a world and as large as alone.   10

For whatever we lose(like a you or a me)
it's always ourselves we find in the sea

DISCUSSION

Introduction

These two poems, though very different in
style, have been grouped together because of a
similar theme. Ask students to read both poems
silently and then discuss what they think that
theme might be. *(Each person has strengths and
weaknesses that color his view of the world.)*

Analysis

"Fable"

"Fable" expresses one of Emerson's central
themes: human brotherhood.

The first two lines of this poem give essential
facts of its background. The quarrel seems
entirely to the squirrel's disadvantage. The

mountain is conscious of its advantage in its
contemptuous language toward the squirrel.
The squirrel, like Emerson, is a moral philosopher that some would consider boring and self-
righteous. The rest of the poem is the squirrel's
reply. The squirrel enumerates some advantages
of his own. Though he does not have intimidat-
ing size and strength, he can move—with
quickness and grace. The mountain may symbolize the massive, inert, conventional public
opinion that Emerson was trying to affect and
that viewed man with hostility and scorn. But
he could "crack a nut"—that is, in a metaphorical sense of the phrase, solve difficult philosophical problems.

The moral appears embryonically in line 17:
"Talents differ."

"maggie and milly and molly and may"

Discuss briefly Cummings's deliberately odd
style—no capital letters, forced rhyme, omission of terminal punctuation, no spacing
around internal punctuation. It seems an affec-
tation, and to an extent it is. But it does
prompt the reader to look closely and freshly at
the subjects described and to see language itself
in a more vital way.

Ask the students whether they think they know
themselves as well as others do. No doubt in
some ways each of us knows himself better
than others do; however, there are aspects to
each person's personality that others see but to
which he is blind. How do others come to
know us? They come to know us by our
choices, decisions, and responses to situations.

About the Author

E. E. Cummings (1894-1962), one of this century's most controversial poets, grew up in a happy home where reading and culture were highly valued. His education at Harvard in Greek and the classics familiarized him with the elements of the best in literature. The effectiveness of Cummings's style stems from this awareness of the traditional expectations his readers bring to poetry. At first glance, many of his poems appear to be simply letters or words scattered on the page. Shaped poetry and unusual verse arrangements, however, are not new in literature (cf. George Herbert, pp. 304-5). Unconventional format need not be a distraction. If the poem is well written, the format will either reinforce or clarify the theme.

Our selection, "maggie and milly and molly and may," is one of Cummings's most understandable works. Many of his other poems, however, are not only less accessible technically, but are also less acceptable philosophically. Some of Cummings's writings reflect a belief held by many modern authors: the belief that espousing any code of absolutes is damaging to individual creativity. Such an idea is grounded in pride, for it assumes that the God who created the desire for artistic expression in man failed to provide an acceptable outlet for such creativity. Poets such as John Milton, George Herbert, and John Donne prove the foolishness of such fears. As readers of literature we can, of course, recognize and appreciate the literary genius of Cummings and other modern poets. We should, however, reject the erroneous views presented in many of their poems.

About the Poems

1. Is the moral of Emerson's fable stated?
2. Give Emerson's poem a more revealing title.
3. Does the last line of Cummings's poem state a moral? If so, what?
4. Is Cummings's poem a parable or a fable?

Contact with the sea is one situation that elicits a variety of revealing responses.

This fable in verse ends with a stated moral (line 12). Choices (or responses to surroundings) reveal personality and character. Sometimes choices reveal us to ourselves as well as to others. Cummings's poem brings us (almost) to a common plot motif in fairytale literature—the symbolic choice. This choice tends to classify those choosing according to their values. Here it is more traits of personality, perhaps, than traits of character that are revealed. Have the students identify these traits.

Maggie finds music in nature, and her poetic soul responds.

Milly is tenderhearted toward all living things and feels toward them as toward herself, reaching out to the helpless "fingers" of the star.

Molly is terrified; she is excitable and fearful and focuses on what seems threatening and ugly.

May is a sentimentalist who invests what she finds with a world of value. Her choice is the most mysterious and perhaps the most typically human choice of all.

 Application

Have the students write a short poem or paragraph describing some recreational experience. Remind them that in a poem, words not only have literal meaning (denotative meaning), but they also serve to arouse certain images or emotions (connotative meaning). Tell the students to try to include some words and phrases that have connotative as well as denotative meaning, words and phrases that can evoke vivid images. You may wish to draw their attention to some examples from the poems they have just read: "a very pretty squirrel track," "a shell that sang," or "a horrible thing that raced sideways." See **Writing Rubric 5-2: A Recollection of Recreation.**

 About the Poems

1. *"Talents differ" (line 17). Each person or thing has a specific role to fulfill in the world; it is not right to criticize someone else because he differs from you.*

2. *Answers will vary. Any title that is more specific to the poem's text than "Fable" should be accepted.*

The Masque of the Red Death

Edgar Allan Poe

This tale comes close to being an allegory of man's proud and naive attempts to defeat the power of nature. It illustrates well Poe's creation of effect in his fiction. All the details are designed to reinforce the terror Poe desired the tale to communicate.

The Red Death had long devastated the country. No pestilence had ever been so fatal, or so hideous. Blood was its Avatar* and its seal—the redness and the horror of blood. There were sharp pains, and sudden dizziness, and then profuse bleeding at the pores, with dissolution.* The scarlet stains upon the body and especially upon the face of the victim, were the pest ban which shut him out from the aid and from the sympathy of his fellowmen. And the whole seizure, progress and termination of the disease, were the incidents of half an hour.

Avatar: incarnation, manifestation
dissolution: death

But Prince Prospero was happy and dauntless* and sagacious.* When his dominions were half depopulated, he summoned to his presence a thousand hale and light-hearted friends from among the knights and dames of his court, and with these retired to the deep seclusion of one of his castellated* abbeys. This was an extensive and magnificent structure, the creation of the prince's own eccentric yet august* taste. A strong and lofty wall girdled it in. This wall had gates of iron. The courtiers, having entered, brought furnaces and massy hammers and welded the bolts. They resolved to leave means neither of ingress or egress to the sudden impulses of despair or of frenzy from within. The abbey was amply provisioned. With such precautions the courtiers might bid defiance to contagion. The external world could take care of itself. In the meantime it was folly to grieve, or to think. The prince had provided all the appliances of pleasure. There were buffoons,* there were improvisatori,* there were ballet dancers, there were musicians, there was Beauty, there was wine. All these and security were within. Without was the Red Death.

OBJECTIVES

The students will be able to

- Define *allegory.*
- Analyze a story's conflict, character, plot, symbol, allusion, and irony and show how they reveal its theme.

You may wish to point out to students that the word *masque* in the title is spelled differently from *mask* later on in the story because in the title it refers to Prospero's ball itself, not an item of clothing.

There is an element of irony in Prospero's name (cf. *prosperous*).

The abbey is symbolic of the Prince's futile efforts to "wall out" death.

The last great plague was in the early 1600s. Since the masqueraders' costumes are of this period, it is possible that Poe was basing his "Red Death" on this historic epidemic.

FURTHER HELPS

Additional activity

Have any students interested in art do a colorful floor plan of the abbey's interior design, carefully noting Poe's description of each room.

---

3. *Yes; answers to the second question may vary but should include that our choices and/or responses to surroundings reveal our personality and character.*

4. *Answers may vary. The definitions on page 128 ("In a fable the details support the meaning collectively, whereas in a parable the details support the meaning individually") would tend to support the idea of its being a parable. However, it also could be called a fable if we define a fable as a story with a moral stated at the end.*

PREPARATION

"The Masque of the Red Death"

Overview

This story illustrates well Poe's creation of effect in his fiction. All the details are designed to reinforce the terror Poe desired his story to communicate. Notice that Poe carefully creates a stage on which the action of the story can take place.

Potential problems

The melancholy and even gruesome atmosphere of much of Poe's work may disturb some students. Explain that Poe used such atmosphere and plotting details because of his preoccupation with psychological disintegration. His narrowness of literary theory also accounts for the preoccupation with such effects. The theme of this specific selection is noteworthy: man cannot escape death. Christians, of course, not only recognize this truth but also have the answer for facing it. The problem with much of Poe's work is that, in his emphasis on degeneration, he ignores the possibility of regeneration.

DISCUSSION

Introduction

You may wish to discuss briefly with the students the Black Death. The last great plague came in the early seventeenth century. The disease was transmitted to men by fleas from infected rats and other rodents. Ignorance of the cause of the infection was a major factor in its spread. The characteristics of the illness were high fever, chills, delirium, and enlarged lymph nodes. Hemorrhages under the skin caused it to turn "black," hence the terms Black or Red Death. Understanding some of these symptoms

Prince Prospero's entertainment of "his thousand friends" is a Biblical allusion to Daniel 5 (Belshazzar's feast).

The rooms in the story symbolize life. The fact that revelers could see only one room at a time reinforces the idea that we cannot see ahead in life. The colors also symbolize the different stages of life.

blue: birth, innocence, spring

purple: deepening of blue, experience

green: youth, growth, summer

orange: maturity, ripening, autumn

white: old age, winter

violet: darker experience (cf. purple)

black with red panes: the "Red Death"

The gigantic ebony clock is a reminder of the inevitable passing of time.

---

dauntless; fearless
sagacious: shrewd, wise
castellated: built like a castle
august: admirable
buffoons: clowns
improvisatori: musical improvisers

It was toward the close of the fifth or sixth month of his seclusion, and while the pestilence raged most furiously abroad, that Prince Prospero entertained his thousand friends at a masked ball of the most unusual magnificence.

It was a voluptuous* scene, that masquerade. But first let me tell of the rooms in which it was held. There were seven—an imperial suite. In many palaces, however, such suites form a long and straight vista,* while the folding doors slide back nearly to the walls on either hand, so that the view of the whole extent is scarcely impeded. Here the case was very different; as might have been expected from the duke's love of the *bizarre.** The apartments were so irregularly disposed that the vision embraced but little more than one at a time. There was a sharp turn at every twenty or thirty yards, and at each turn a novel effect. To the right and left, in the middle of each wall, a tall and narrow Gothic window looked out upon a closed corridor which pursued the windings of the suite. These windows were of stained glass whose color varied in accordance with the prevailing hue of the decorations of the chamber into which it opened. That at the eastern extremity was hung, for example, in blue—and vividly blue were its windows. The second chamber was purple in its ornaments and tapestries, and here the panes were purple. The third was green throughout, and so were the casements. The fourth was furnished and lighted with orange—the fifth with white—the sixth with violet. The seventh apartment was closely shrouded in black velvet tapestries that hung all over the ceiling and down the walls, falling in heavy folds upon a carpet of the same material and

hue. But in this chamber only, the color of the windows failed to correspond with the decorations. The panes here were scarlet—a deep blood color. Now in no one of the seven apartments was there any lamp or candelabrum* amid the profusion of golden ornaments that lay scattered to and fro or depended from the roof. There was no light of any kind emanating* from lamp or candle within the suite of chambers. But in the corridors that followed the suite, there stood, opposite to each window, a heavy tripod, bearing a brazier of fire that projected its rays through the tinted glass and so glaringly illumined the room. And thus was produced a multitude of gaudy and fantastic appearances. But in the western or black chamber the effect of the firelight that streamed upon the dark hangings through the blood-tinted panes, was ghastly in the extreme, and produced so wild a look upon the countenances of those who entered, that there were few of the company bold enough to set foot within its precincts at all.

---

voluptuous: luxurious
vista: passage, scene
bizarre: odd, fantastic
candelabrum: a large, branched candlestick
emanating: issuing from

It was in this apartment, also, that there stood against the western wall, a gigantic clock of ebony. Its pendulum swung to and fro with a dull, heavy, monotonous clang; and when the minute hand made the circuit of the face, and the hour was to be stricken, there came from the brazen lungs of the clock a sound which was clear and loud and deep and exceedingly musical, but of so peculiar a note and emphasis that, at each lapse of an hour, the musicians of the orchestra were constrained to pause, momentarily, in their performance, to hearken to the sound; and thus the waltzers perforce ceased their evolutions; and there was a brief disconcert of the whole company; and,

---

helps us see that Poe's description—though vivid—was almost scientific.

Analysis

Although the atmosphere and plot are clear, the tone of the tale is confusing. Interpretations are many and varied. Some critics contend that the story presents a confrontation between reality and the world of imagination. Others believe that the tale has a moral. Although this second view is a departure from the fictional principles by which Poe claimed to be guided, the details of the story tend to affirm this suggestion. The conflict, characters, and plot seem to point to the futility of man's attempt to escape the clutches of death.

You may wish to read or reread the story aloud in class, taking time to stop and discuss the marginal notes provided in the teacher's copy. These notes will provide the information needed to enable the students to answer the "About the Story" questions.

Application

To help the students see the universality of Poe's theme, have them compare and contrast this story with Updike's "Pigeon Feathers." Both stories confront the problem of death. Both also rely heavily on allusion and symbol to convey their theme. The greatest contrast between the two stories is the resolution of each. Poe leaves us with the depressing realization of man's inevitable demise; Updike, on the other

hand, draws our attention to man's immortality. Neither story, however, goes far enough. Following your discussion of the stories, draw the students' attention to Philippians 1:12-28. What is Paul's attitude toward life and death? How do his attitudes differ from most people's? What should be our attitude toward life (cf. verses 20, 21, 25, 26)? What should be our attitude toward death (cf. verse 23)?

while the chimes of the clock yet rang, it was observed that the giddiest grew pale, and the more aged and sedate passed their hands over their brows as if in confused reverie or meditation. But when the echoes had fully ceased, a light laughter at once pervaded the assembly; the musicians looked at each other and smiled as if at their own nervousness and folly, and made whispering vows, each to the other, that the next chiming of the clock should produce in them no similar emotion; and then, after the lapse of sixty minutes (which embrace three thousand and six hundred seconds of the Time that flies), there came yet another chiming of the clock, and then were the same disconcert and tremulousness and meditation as before.

But, in spite of these things, it was a gay and magnificent revel. The tastes of the duke were peculiar. He had a fine eye for colors and effects. He disregarded the *decora** of mere fashion. His plans were bold and fiery, and his conceptions glowed with barbaric lustre. There are some who would have thought him mad. His followers felt that he was not. It was necessary to hear and see and touch him to be *sure* that he was not.

---

decora: Latin: dictates

He had directed, in great part, the movable embellishments* of the seven chambers, upon occasion of this great *fete;** and it was his own guiding taste which had given character to the masqueraders. Be sure they were grotesque. There were much glare and glitter and piquancy* and phantasm*—much of what has been since seen in *Hernani** There were arabesque* figures with unsuited limbs and appointments.* There were delirious fancies such as the madman fashions. There was much of the beautiful, much of the wanton,* much of the bizarre, something of the terrible, and not a little of that which might have excited

disgust. To and fro in the seven chambers there stalked, in fact, a multitude of dreams. And these—the dreams—writhed in and about, taking hue from the rooms and causing the wild music of the orchestra to seem as the echo of their steps. And, anon,* there strikes the ebony clock which stands in the hall of the velvet. And then, for a moment, all is still, and all is silent save the voice of the clock. The dreams are stiff-frozen as they stand. But the echoes of the chime die away—they have endured but an instant—and a light, half-subdued laughter floats after them as they depart. And now again the music swells, and the dreams live, and writhe to and fro more merrily than ever, taking hue from the many-tinted windows through which stream the rays from the tripods. But to the chamber which lies most westwardly of the seven, there are now none of the maskers who venture; for the night is waning away; and there flows a ruddier light through the blood-colored panes; and the blackness of the sable* drapery appals,* and to him whose foot falls upon the sable carpet, there comes from the near clock of ebony a muffled peal more solemnly emphatic than any which reaches their ears who indulge in the more remote gaieties of the other apartments.

---

embellishments: decorations
fete: festival
piquancy: liveliness, charm
phantasm: a phantom or an illusion
Hernani: a romantic play by Victor Hugo (1802-85), presented in 1830.
arabesque: fanciful (in ballet a position in which the dancer extends one leg straight backward, one arm forward, and the other arm backward)
appointments: adornments
wanton: extravagant, unrestrained
anon: again
sable: black
appals: makes pale with fear, dismay

But these other apartments were densely crowded, and in them beat feverishly the heart of life. And the revel went whirlingly on, until at length there commenced the sounding of

The masqueraders' revelry is indicative of the futile efforts of those who fear death to lose their fears in self-indulgence.

Note the Biblical allusion to Herod's unbridled extravagances (cf. Mark 6:14-29).

allusion to Revelation 19:13

Notice that death is present throughout life, appearing first in the blue room and then passing through each room before vanquishing the Prince and his guests in the black room.

midnight upon the clock. And then the music ceased, as I have told; and the evolutions of the waltzers were quieted; and there was an uneasy cessation of all things as before. But now there were twelve strokes to be sounded by the bell of the clock; and thus it happened, perhaps, that more of thought crept, with more of time, into the meditations of the thoughtful among those who revelled. And thus, too, it happened, perhaps, that before the last echoes of the last chimes had utterly sunk into silence, there were many individuals in the crowd who had found leisure to become aware of the presence of a masked figure which had arrested the attention of no single individual before. And the rumor of this new presence having spread itself whisperingly around, there arose at length from the whole company a buzz, or murmur, expressive of disapprobation* and surprise—then, finally, of terror, of horror, and of disgust.

disapprobation: disapproval, condemnation

In an assembly of phantasms such as I have painted, it may well be supposed that no ordinary appearance could have excited such sensation. In truth the masquerade license of the night was nearly unlimited; but the figure in question had out-Heroded Herod, and gone beyond the bounds of even the prince's indefinite decorum. There are chords in the hearts of the most reckless which cannot be touched without emotion. Even with the utterly lost, to whom life and death are equally jests, there are matters of which no jest can be made. The whole company, indeed, seemed now deeply to feel that in the costume and bearing of the stranger neither wit nor propriety existed. The figure was tall and gaunt, and shrouded from head to foot in the habiliments* of the grave. The mask which concealed the visage was made so nearly to resemble the countenance of a stiffened corpse that the closest scrutiny must have had difficulty in detecting

the cheat. And yet all this might have been endured, if not approved, by the mad revellers around. But the mummer* had gone so far as to assume the type of the Red Death. His vesture was dabbled in blood—and his broad brow, with all the features of the face, was besprinkled with the scarlet horror.

habiliments: clothing, attire
mummer: one who acts or plays in a mask or costume

When the eyes of Prince Prospero fell upon this spectral image (which with a slow and solemn movement, as if more fully to sustain its role, stalked to and fro among the waltzers) he was seen to be convulsed, in the first moment with a strong shudder either of terror or distaste; but, in the next, his brow reddened with rage.

"Who dares?" he demanded hoarsely of the courtiers who stood near him—"who dares insult us with this blasphemous mockery? Seize him and unmask him—that we may know whom we have to hang at sunrise, from the battlements!"

It was in the eastern or blue chamber in which stood Prince Prospero as he uttered these words. They rang throughout the seven rooms loudly and clearly—for the prince was a bold and robust man, and the music had become hushed at the waving of his hand.

It was in the blue room where stood the prince, with a group of pale courtiers by his side. At first, as he spoke, there was a slight rushing movement of this group in the direction of the intruder, who at the moment was also near at hand, and now, with deliberate and stately step, made close approach to the speaker. But from a certain nameless awe with which the mad assumptions of the mummer had inspired the whole party, there were found none who put forth hand to seize him; so that, unimpeded, he passed within a yard of the prince's person; and, while the vast assembly, as if with one impulse, shrank from the centres

of the rooms to the walls, he made his way uninterruptedly, but with the same solemn and measured step which had distinguished him from the first, through the blue chamber to the purple—through the purple to the green—through the green to the orange—through this again to the white—and even thence to the violet, ere a decided movement had been made to arrest him. It was then, however, that Prince Prospero, maddening with rage and the shame of his own momentary cowardice, rushed hurriedly through the six chambers, while none followed him on account of a deadly terror that had seized upon all. He bore aloft a drawn dagger, and had approached, in rapid impetuosity,* to within three or four feet of the retreating figure, when the latter, having attained the extremity of the velvet apartment, turned suddenly and confronted his pursuer. There was a sharp cry—and the dagger dropped gleaming upon the sable carpet, upon which, instantly afterwards, fell prostrate in death Prince Prospero. Then, summoning the wild courage of despair, a throng of the revellers at once threw themselves into the black apartment, and, seizing the mummer, whose tall figure stood erect and motionless within the shadow of the ebony clock, gasped in unutterable horror at finding the grave cerements* and corpse-like mask which they handled with so violent a rudeness, untenanted by any tangible form.

impetuosity: violent force
cerements: the winding sheet for a corpse

And now was acknowledged the presence of the Red Death. He had come like a thief in the night. And one by one dropped the revellers in the blood-bedewed halls of their revel, and died each in the despairing posture of his fall. And the life of the ebony clock went out with that of the last of the gay. And the flames of the tripods expired. And Darkness and Decay and the Red Death held illimitable* dominion over all.

illimitable: boundless

About the Story

1. What causes Prospero and his friends to take refuge in the abbey?
2. Describe the interior of the abbey (the number of rooms, the colors of each room, etc.).
3. How would you describe Prospero and his friends?
4. Would you say Poe is condoning or condemning Prospero and his revellers?
5. Identify at least one possible symbol in the story and tell what that symbol represents.

About the Story

1. *On a literal level, their desire to escape the Red Death causes them to take refuge. Symbolically, their taking refuge represents mankind's futile desire to escape death—or at least to ignore it.*

2. *There are seven rooms, arranged so that only one room is visible at a time. Each room is decorated in one color with matching stained glass windows (except the last room): blue, purple, green, orange, white, violet, and black (with scarlet windows).*

3. *Answers may vary. Prospero and his friends are primarily characterized by their love of the "gay and magnificent"—an attitude that foolishly attempts to deny the inevitability of death.*

4. *Poe's tone is clearly one of condemnation.*

5. *Answers may vary but might include Prospero's name; the abbey itself; the colors of the rooms; the "gigantic clock of ebony"; and the shrouded figure. See side margin notes throughout the story for additional explanations.*

PREPARATION

"My Star"

Overview

With this selection we move from the outer world of scientific observation to the inner world of the mind. Its spaces, some would say, are no less vast than those of the stellar heavens or those revealed by electron microscopes, though experienced only by the individual himself. Here the star is a symbol of whatever one follows (like the Wise Men of old) or particularly esteems that determines the course of his life.

DISCUSSION

Introduction

As background for this poem, read Shakespeare's Sonnet 116, especially lines 5-8. (See BJU Press's *BRITISH LITERATURE for Christian Schools*, pages 197-98.)

Analysis

This star, like Shakespeare's lover's, is a star "Whose worth's unknown." It is also "an ever-fixed mark / That looks on tempests and is never shaken"—a firm, lifelong obsession.

My Star

Robert Browning

Scholars have tried to identify Browning's "star." Was it Elizabeth Barrett, whom he married in middle age and to whom he remained passionately devoted until her early death? Was it his religious faith during a time of unbelief? Perhaps Browning deliberately left the meaning vague. Almost everyone is captivated by something whose value or even existence baffles others.

All that I know
    Of a certain star
Is, it can throw
    (Like the angled spar)*
Now a dart of red,   5
    Now a dart of blue;
Till my friends have said
    They would fain see, too,
My star that dartles the red and the blue!
Then it stops like a bird; like a flower, hangs furled: 10
    They must solace themselves with the Saturn above it.
What matter to me if their star is a world?
    Mine has opened its soul to me; therefore I love it.

> *angled spar:* Iceland spar, a translucent prismatic mineral used in optical instruments

About the Poem

1. Look up the mythological figure of Saturn in an encyclopedia. What can you learn about the god Saturn that would influence Browning's choice of the planet Saturn as an object that, in contrast to the star, anyone can see?
2. Do you, like Browning, have such a star?

OBJECTIVE

The students will be able to
- Identify symbol.

Note assonance (/är/ and /er/) and alliteration (/s/) used throughout the poem.

FURTHER HELPS
"My Star"

Additional activities

Read aloud an excerpt from Homer's *Odyssey*—Odysseus's adventure with the Cyclops, the trial of the bow, or Penelope's testing of Odysseus. All of these incidents provide material for allusions in literature. Discuss with the students why these incidents seem to provide such apt applications even today. Point out the universality of the conflicts.

Journal entry idea

Have the students write about a time when the influence or attitudes of their friends seemed unimportant in comparison to the power of an idea they believed in or an action they felt they must perform. Have them also evaluate their response. Were they right in feeling as they did? What was the outcome of their actions?

Resource

Homer, *The Odyssey.*

"Then" in line 10 refers to lines 7-8—the friends' request to see it too. The star will not show its glories to others but stops (like a bird) its flight and folds (like a flower) its beauties.

The allusion to Saturn can have any one or all of several meanings. Those born under the astrological influence of the planet Saturn were supposed to be sluggish, sullen, gloomy, cynical, scornful ironists. This may refer to Browning's liberal, skeptical friends who were unsympathetic with his religious faith or any kind of idealism. Also, the seven-day Roman festival of Saturn, known as the Saturnalia, has given its name to any unrestrained sensual orgy, especially involving drink. This festival, beginning on December 17, is immediately "above" (in the calendar) the celebration of Christmas, which commemorates both the birth of Christ and Epiphany: the following of the Star of Bethlehem by the Wise Men. The traditional twelve days of Christmas begin on December 25 and end on the day of Epiphany, January 6. This calendrical context is probably the explanation for the otherwise cryptic line 11. Line 12 associates his friends' values with the world. Line 13 shows his willingness—even joy—in being different. Every genuine Christian should be able to find personal meaning in this poem (whether or not Browning intended its message to be religious).

Application

Most young people are interested in stars of one sort or another. Ask students whether they have a "star" such as Browning's—something that continuously fascinates them, whose value others cannot understand. Discuss with them whether such an obsession is good or bad (it can, of course, be either).

About the Poem

1. *Answers may vary but might include the negative personality traits of those "born under" Saturn's supposed astrological influence or references to Saturnalia, a hedonistic Roman festival. Browning is contrasting the beauty and purity of his "star" with the base and corrupt. See Analysis Section for further information.*

2. *Answers may vary. Encourage students, however, not to think of their personal "star" as a person necessarily. It might be a life goal, a spiritual standard, or God's calling on an individual's life.*

UNIT SIX

Irony

OBJECTIVES

The students will be able to

- Define various forms of irony.
- Discuss the power of irony for good or for evil.

FURTHER HELPS

Additional activities

Read aloud the following poem by George Herbert and discuss how Herbert used irony—especially paradox—"for good."

Bitter Sweet

Ah, my dear angry Lord!
  Since Thou dost love, yet strike,
Cast down, yet help afford:
  Sure I will do the like.
I will complain, yet praise,
  I will bewail, approve:
And all my sour-sweet days
  I will lament, and love.

Journal entry idea

Ask the students if they have ever known of a case when verbal irony was misused. Have them write about the experience. Ask them also to comment on what they learned from the situation.

"The longest way round is the shortest way home," we sometimes hear. How can that be true when we learn in geometry that the shortest distance between two points is a straight line? The saying makes better sense when we remember that length can refer to time as well as distance. Any mountain traveler knows that the most direct way may not be the quickest. The statement is a seeming contradiction, a **paradox.** Why should a truth be put into so illogical a form? By surprising us and awakening our curiosity, it opens our minds to an unwelcome fact: the importance of patience. It reminds us that there are no shortcuts to success.

Christ often used such seemingly contradictory statements: "He that findeth his life shall lose it: and he that loseth his life for my sake shall find it" (Matt. 19:30). "The last shall be first, and the first last" (Matt. 20:16). These sayings must have startled the disciples and other hearers of Christ's teaching. But having been explained, they would not soon be forgotten. They state the disadvantages of self-seeking, of looking out for "number one." Perhaps the most striking paradoxes in the Bible and in all literature are the Beatitudes of Matthew 5. To consider the poor in spirit, the sorrowing, the meek, the hungering and thirsting, and so forth as fortunate seems in conflict with human experience and good sense. The Beatitudes equate happiness with conditions that most people try to avoid. But they underscore a great truth. Only those who suffer with God in this world know real joy now and will enjoy heaven hereafter.

Paradoxical statements are frequent in the Scriptures because God's truth often goes against the grain of the way people think. God's ways are not man's ways (Isa. 55:8). He "seeth not as man seeth" (I Sam. 16:7). In redemption God humbled Himself in order to be exalted (Phil. 2:5-11). In salvation man must do the same (Luke 14:11). It was the youngest rather than the eldest of the sons of Jesse that Samuel was to anoint to be ruler of Israel. It was Bethlehem rather than Jerusalem that God chose for the birthplace of Messiah, and Nazareth rather than a Judean town for His upbringing. God has purposes that He has not revealed to man and that are far beyond human understanding. There is no guarantee that "the race" will be "to the swift" or "the battle to the strong" (Eccles. 9:11). The term *paradox* can refer not only to a self-contradictory statement but also to the truth it expresses. It is a paradox that salvation has nothing to do with human merit. It is a paradox that God could suffer and die. The paradoxes of Scripture include some of the deepest of all spiritual truths.

A writer may describe a situation in such a way as to point up its paradoxical nature. In Acts 12, after Peter had been miraculously released from prison, he went to the house of John Mark's mother, Mary. Behind locked doors "many were gathered together praying." When a girl, Rhoda, heard the knocking, came to the door, and recognized Peter's voice, "she opened not the gate for gladness, but ran in, and told how Peter stood before the gate. And they said unto her, Thou art mad. But she constantly affirmed that it

---

PREPARATION

Irony Introduction

Overview

This discussion of the ironic mode surveys the full range of the ironic, beginning with the basic concept of paradox and proceeding to varieties of the paradoxical (or ironic), illustrating them from the Bible.

Potential problems

Warn students that verbal irony is a powerful weapon in the hands of a skilled practitioner—for good or for evil. Sarcasm—oral as well as written—can be devastating, and its wounds can last a lifetime. Verbal irony should not be personally motivated. It should be used constructively, if at all.

DISCUSSION

Introduction

Point out that students already use irony and understand it very well. Teenagers are unusually adept with it. Humorous exaggeration, teasing, compliments, and mock-serious clowning are the hallmarks of the conversation of this age group. It is sometimes used cruelly as well.

Analysis

Before reading the introduction aloud, show the students an outline of the essay. The analysis of irony can be organized as shown in **Appendix N: Types of Irony.** As you read through the introductory essay together, fill in the outline.

Application

Following is an example of irony found in a news magazine, *The Review of the NEWS,* June 18, 1980.

The section on plagiarism in the handbook prepared by a teaching assistant at Stanford University has been badly plagiarized by the University of Oregon. Administrators of the Oregon school concede that the plagiarism sec-was even so. Then said they, It is his angel. But Peter continued knocking: and when they had opened the door, and saw him, they were astonished. But he, beckoning unto them with the hand to hold their peace, declared unto them how the Lord had brought him out of the prison" (12:14-17). The Christians' unbelief is surprising and would be even laughable were it not so common. One would expect Christians would pray believing that their prayers would, or at least could, be answered. This contrast between what is reasonable to expect and what actually happens is known as irony of situation, or **situational irony.**

A special form of situational irony appears in the sixth chapter of the book of Esther. Haman, the king's favorite, has built a gallows on which to hang the Jew Mordecai. Mordecai will not bow to him and give him the desired respect. Haman comes to the palace expecting the king to agree with his plan. He does not know what has happened the night before. The narrative gives us this information before Haman finds it out.

> On that night could not the king sleep, and he commanded to bring the book of records of the chronicles; and they were read before the king. And it was found written, that Mordecai had told of Bigthana and Teresh, two of the king's chamberlains, the keepers of the door, who sought to lay hand on the king Ahasuerus. And the king said, What honour and dignity hath been done to Mordecai for this? Then said the king's servants that ministered to him, There is nothing done for him. And the king said, Who is in the court? Now Haman was come into the outward court of the king's house, to speak unto the king to hang Mordecai on the gallows that he had prepared for him. And the king's servants said unto him, Behold, Haman standeth in the court. And the king said, Let him come in. So Haman came in. And the king said unto him, What shall be done unto the man whom the king delighteth to honour? Now Haman thought in his heart, To whom would the king delight to do honour more than to myself? And Haman answered the king, For the man whom the king delighteth to honour, Let the royal apparel be brought which the king useth to wear, and the horse that the king rideth upon and the crown royal which is set upon his head: And let this apparel and horse be delivered to the hand of one of the king's most noble princes that they may array the man withal whom the king delighteth to honour, and bring him on horseback through the street of the city, and proclaim before him, Thus shall it be done to the man whom the king delighteth to honour. Then the king said to Haman, Make haste, and take the apparel and the horse, as thou hast said, and do even so to Mordecai the Jew, that sitteth at the king's gate: let nothing fail of all that thou hast spoken (Esther 6:1-10).

The contrast between what Haman expects and what actually happens is situational irony. But there is more. The reader has been informed before Haman so that there is also a contrast between our knowledge and his ignorance. Our prior knowledge lets us focus our attention on how Haman is thinking and behaving rather than on the unfolding events. With his ignorant boasting he seems almost a comic actor in a play. This kind of situational irony is known as **dramatic irony**. It climaxes with the hanging of Haman on the very gallows he has built for Mordecai.

tion and other parts of their handbook are identical to the Stanford version. Stanford officials noted on June 5th that the officials at Oregon have apologized and promise to revise their guidebook. —M.P.W.

Have the students identify what type of irony this excerpt illustrates. *(irony of situation)* Have them explain why the example fits into this category and what makes it so effective. *(It fits this category because one would not expect a handbook section dealing with plagiarism to have been itself plagiarized.)* You might also discuss their reactions to the piece. Did they find it humorous? Or did they react more to the injustice of the act of plagiarism itself?

Ironic overstatement is also called hyperbole.

Irony is a broad concept that refers to the paradoxical in language and in life. It refers to situations and expressions in which appearance is different from reality, or expectation differs from outcome. In the ironic there is usually an element of contradiction and often of surprise. **Verbal irony** is used of language that means something other than what it actually states. Obviously Elijah does not really mean what he literally says concerning Baal when he prods Baal's prophets: "Cry aloud: for he is a god; either he is talking, or he is pursuing, or he is in a journey, or peradventure he sleepeth, and must be awaked" (I Kings 18:27). Elijah is taunting the false prophets, ridiculing them before the people. The prophet Micaiah does not mean his words to be taken at face value when he speaks to the wicked king Ahab concerning the Syrian army: "Go ye up, and prosper, and they shall be delivered into your hand" (II Chron. 18:14). He is mocking Ahab's paid prophets, who tell the king what he wishes to hear. When verbal irony takes the form of mock praise, we call it *sarcasm*. Paul reproaches the worldly Corinthians with pretended praise: "We are fools for Christ's sake, but ye are wise in Christ; we are weak, but ye are strong; ye are honourable but we are despised" (I Cor. 4:10). Job pretends to flatter his proud friends: "No doubt but ye are the people, and wisdom shall die with you" (Job 12:2). The Corinthians are not wise, strong, or honorable except in their own estimation. Job's friends are not the authorities on God's ways that they think they are.

In some types of verbal irony the pretended meaning differs from the real meaning only in degree. David overstated his meaning when he said of his enemies, "Then did I beat them small as the dust before the wind" (Psalm 18:42). In the Bible this verbal irony occurs in poetic comparison. God, speaking through the prophet Amos, overstated His meaning in reminding the Israelites of His mighty deliverance of their fathers. "Yet destroyed I the Amorite before them, whose height was like the height of the cedars, and he was strong as the oaks, yet I destroyed his fruit from above, and his roots from beneath" (Amos 2:9).

On the other hand, the Lord understated His meaning when He said of His disciples, "Ye are of more value than many sparrows" (Matt. 10:31). We know from Mark 8:36 that God values the human soul above "the whole world." A common form of *understatement* is that in which a statement asserts something by denying its contrary. "The disciple is not above his master, nor the servant above his lord" implies that the disciple is actually below—far below—his master and should not expect better treatment (Matt. 10:24). The preaching of Paul at Ephesus created "no small stir" in the city (Acts 19:23). David, pleading for forgiveness, takes courage in the belief that "A broken and a contrite heart, O God, thou wilt not despise" (Psalm 51:17). The implication is that Paul's preaching created an uproar and that God greatly values a repentant heart.

Most irony, situational or verbal, is based on contrasting statements that do not seem to belong together. Some irony, however, is based on uncertain statements that appear to have several possible meanings. A person may do or say something that has a wider significance than he or his observer realizes. If this significance is prophetic, the irony is known as *foreshadowing*. When Abraham took Isaac to Mount Moriah to offer him as a sacrifice, Isaac asked, "Where is the lamb for a burnt offering?" Abraham replied, "My son, God will provide himself a lamb for the burnt offering" (Gen. 22:7-8). When the Lord rejected Saul as ruler of Israel, He sent Samuel to Jesse the Bethlehemite, saying "I have provided me a king among his sons" (I Sam. 16:1). These parallel statements are true in their literal senses. Abraham found a ram to sacrifice instead of his son. Samuel identified and anointed David, one of the sons of Jesse. But the statements have an additional reference to Christ, the coming Lamb of God (John 1:29) and divine Son of David (Luke 18:38-39). They foreshadow the redemption and rule of the Messiah.

Another form of verbal irony based on ambiguity is the *pun*. We usually associate the pun with humor. But the pun may be used seriously also. Joseph speaks metaphorically in explaining the dream of Pharaoh's butler. "Yet within three days shall Pharaoh lift up thy head, and restore thee to thy place" (Gen. 40:13). The phrase "lift up thy head" means exalt, raise to honor. Joseph uses the phrase literally in explaining the dream of Pharaoh's baker. "Yet within three days shall Pharaoh lift up thine head from off thee and shall hang thee on a tree" (40:19). The narrative then brings these meanings together in a pun. "And it came to pass the third day, which was Pharaoh's birthday, that he made a feast unto all his servants: and he lifted up the head of the chief butler and of the chief baker among his servants" (40:20). The phrase carries both meanings at once. When David desires to build God a house, he inquires of Him through the prophet Nathan. The answer comes in the form of a pun. "The Lord telleth thee that he will make thee an house. . . . And thine house and thy kingdom shall be established for ever before thee: thy throne shall be established for ever" (II Sam. 7:11-16). Solomon rather than David would build God a house (a place of worship), but God would build David a house (an eternal dynasty). Puns create a double meaning through the use of words that are identical or similar in sound but different in meaning.

Irony of all kinds is especially common in **satire**: corrective ridicule in literature. Irony is an ingredient of mockery, and satire typically has a mocking tone. The Old Testament prophetic books contain some strongly satirical passages. Isaiah, for example, ridicules the worship of idols, which must be made, carried about, and fastened in place by the worshiper. He contrasts idol worship with the worship of God, who both made and bears His people. "And even to your old age I am he; and even to hoar hairs will I carry you: I have made, and I will bear; even I will carry, and will deliver you" (Is. 46:4). It is ironic—contrary to what we would reasonably expect—that people prefer a religion that must be carried to one that carries them. Some works are satires themselves. In these, the ironic mode may continue throughout. Christ's story of the rich man and Lazarus satirizes the well-to-do religious

Punlike wordplay appears in the Lord's statement to Peter, "Thou art Peter *(petros)*, and upon this rock *(petra)* I will build my church" (Matt. 16:18).

leaders who prided themselves on their wealth, their descent from "father Abraham," and their knowledge of "Moses and the prophets" (Luke 16:19-31). In spite of these advantages, they were, like the rich man and his brethren, deaf to the voice of God and destined for hell. In this satirical story, irony controls almost every detail.

The selections in this unit illustrate these types and subtypes of irony. Identify as many of them as you can. Determine whether the irony is serious or humorous or both. In the case of verbal irony, show how the writer signals the reader that what he is reading is in the ironic mode.

Both of the following poems use situational irony as a device for arousing certain emotions in the reader. The intent in each case is to persuade rather than to entertain.

The Golf Links Lie So Near the Mill

Sarah N. Cleghorn

The golf links lie so near the mill
That almost every day
The working children can look out
And see the men at play.

OBJECTIVES

The students will be able to

- Analyze structural (persuasive verbal) irony.

- Discuss the advantage of structural irony over direct statement in persuasion.

FURTHER HELPS

Additional activity

Compile a current events album as a class. Have each student contribute a poem, paragraph, or short essay that uses some form of irony to discuss an event in the news. Have each one underline the example or examples of irony in his writing. Encourage students to maintain a Biblical perspective on the theme of their writing. Students may also wish to provide photos or art to go in the album.

Resources

David A. Fisher, *WORLD HISTORY for Christian Schools,* 2nd ed. (Greenville, S.C.: BJU Press, 1999).

John Hall Wheelock, *What Is Poetry?* (New York: Charles Scribner's Sons, 1963).

PREPARATION

"The Golf Links Lie So Near the Mill," "Earth"

Overview

The first short poem introduces situational irony. There is a paradoxical reversal of what would normally be expected—men working and children playing. "Earth" introduces what is sometimes called structural irony: verbal irony that extends throughout an entire work. The real meaning is the opposite of the literal. It also exhibits situational irony: the paradox of intelligent stupidity.

DISCUSSION

Introduction

Before beginning your discussion on the first poem, briefly discuss the child-labor laws to which the poem refers. For information, see BJU Press's *WORLD HISTORY for Christian Schools,* 2nd ed., page 454.

Analysis

"The Golf Links Lie So Near the Mill"

Read the poem aloud. Point out to the students that the irony consists in the juxtaposition of two activities: the playing men and working children. Something seems very wrong in a so-

ciety in which the children work so that the adults can enjoy themselves. The irony is meant to stir the reader's indignation. This indignation is directed toward the mill owners and middle-class smugness about the plight of the workers.

The words "almost every day" mean the mills were closed on Sundays and some holidays. (Point out that golf originated in Great Britain—specifically Scotland.)

Earth

John Hall Wheelock

"A planet doesn't explode of itself," said drily
The Martian astronomer, gazing off into the air—
"That they were able to do it is proof that highly
Intelligent beings must have been living there."

"Earth"

Read the poem aloud. In this poem Wheelock imagines a Martian astronomer witnessing the explosion of the earth and commenting on the scene in an impersonal, "scientific" way. The adverb "drily" is ambiguous. It can mean "matter-of-factly" and also "humorously in an off-hand, cleverly sarcastic way." Whatever the Martian's intention, we can be sure that Wheelock is not paying a compliment to human intelligence. A race that uses its technological advancement to destroy itself must be extremely clever but also incredibly stupid. This is the plain-prose meaning of the poem. The word "drily" is a signal to the reader that what he is reading may be in the ironic mode. The understated (low-keyed) response of the fictional astronomer ("gazing off into the air") intensifies the emotional impact. The simple phrase with which the poem ends—"must have been living there"—climaxes the horror (for Wheelock and his reader) of the death of a race.

Irony here intensifies emotion by communicating emotionally charged facts unemotionally. The fictional Martian serves the poem's purpose by giving us a distanced perspective on ourselves. Priorities would change if we could get God's view of our lives and circumstances. For the Christian the Bible provides such a view. Christians also understand that moral intelligence and the ability to live by it depend on the power of God in a life to defeat sin. A race in rebellion against its Creator needs more than cleverness to preserve itself. Intellectual abilities can be directed toward evil as well as good. Technology misapplied can be a great curse. The spiritual rebel eventually loses every good thing he has.

About the Author

John Hall Wheelock (1886-1978), American poet and editor, first experimented with poetry in grade school, transforming his Latin lessons into verse. His boyhood interest in poetry never left him, and he continued his literary activities until his death at 92. His poetry, pleasing in its rhythms, always had a simple, lyric quality.

In his poem "Earth" Wheelock typifies the concern of many unregenerate but thoughtful men. Unfortunately, his other writings prove that his solutions to the problems facing a technological age were based upon erroneous philosophies. Wheelock embraced the teachings of the Dutch philosopher Spinoza, a pantheist, who taught that man's reason could lead him not only to virtue but to ultimate perfection. In keeping with these views, Wheelock believed that human understanding and cooperation embodied in a unified world system could protect us against the "irrational" tendencies of man. History, of course, has repeatedly proved the foolishness of such beliefs.

About the Poems

1. What emotions is the author striving to evoke through the first poem?
2. Against whom are these emotions directed?
3. State the message of Wheelock's poem directly in prose.
4. What advantage does irony have over direct statement in persuasion?
5. Explain how this irony works.

Application

In Wheelock's poem "Earth" one proof of our human intelligence lies in our capacity to destroy ourselves. This irony also helps to convey Wheelock's moral: human intelligence does not guarantee common sense or virtue. Discuss this concept with the students. Have them think of other current trends that support this idea.

The Bible repeatedly illustrates the irony that great mental prowess is honored only when accompanied by lowliness of heart. Draw the students' attention to James 3:13-18. Does Wheelock's poem echo the Biblical principle that the use of the intellect without godliness results in destructive strife? *(yes)*

 About the Poems

1. *The poem uses irony to create a sense of indignation.*

2. *the mill owners and middle-class smugness*

3. *Answers may vary but should include the idea that a race that uses its technological advancement to destroy itself must be extremely clever but also incredibly stupid.*

4. *Answers may vary. Irony can often be used to humorous effect; it can also allow the audience to distance itself from what is being said.*

5. *Answers may vary. "The Golf Links" uses ironic, sly humor to provoke the mill owners and other adults to shame for their callousness toward the children's plight. "Earth" allows the reader to see human folly through someone else's eyes and not to feel personally rebuked. Irony of persuasion is very difficult to reply to; see Analysis section, pages 159-60.*

Note that the children already understand each other.

FURTHER HELPS

Additional activity

Note how the descriptions of the children's facial expressions throughout the story reveal what the children are thinking. Have the students bring their Bibles to class and look up as many verses as they can find dealing with man's countenance. Choose several references and discuss the context and application of each.

Resources

Malcom Foster, *Joyce Cary: A Biography* (Boston: Houghton Mifflin Company, 1968).

Charles G. Hoffman, *Joyce Cary: The Comedy of Freedom* (Pennsylvania: University of Pittsburgh Press, 1964).

Jack Wolkenfield, *Joyce Cary: The Developing Style* (New York: New York University Press, 1968).

A Special Occasion

Joyce Cary

Like the foregoing poems, Cary's story is written in a way that points up the paradoxical nature of a specific situation. Cary's intent, however, is not so much to evoke emotion as it is to broaden our perspective. By viewing an ordinary incident in an extraordinary way, he draws our attention to the potential problems of looking at a situation from a single viewpoint.

The nursery door opened and Nurse's voice said in the sugary tone which she used to little girl guests, 'Here you are, darling, and Tommy will show you all his toys.' A little brown-haired girl, in a silk party frock sticking out all round her legs like a lampshade, came in at the door, stopped, and stared at her host. Tom, a dark little boy, aged five, also in a party suit, blue linen knickers, and a silk shirt, stared back at the girl. Nurse had gone into the night nursery, next door, on her private affairs.

Tom, having stared at the girl for a long time as one would study a curiosity, rare and valuable, but extremely surprising, put his feet together, made three jumps forward and said, 'Hullo.'

The little girl turned her head over one shoulder and slowly revolved on one heel, as if trying to examine the back of her own frock. She then stooped suddenly, brushed the hem with her hand, and said, 'Hullo.'

Tom made another jump, turned round, pointed out of the window, and said in a loud voice something like 'twanky tweedle.' Both knew that neither the gesture nor the phrase was meant to convey meaning. They simply expressed the fact that for Tom this was an important and exciting, a very special occasion.

The little girl took a step forward, caught her frock in both hands as if about to make a curtsy, rose upon her toes, and said in a prim voice, 'I beg your pardon.'

They both gazed at each other for some minutes with sparkling eyes. Neither smiled, but it seemed that both were about to smile.

Tom then gave another incomprehensible shout, and ran round the table, sat down on the floor and began to play with a clockwork engine on a circular track. The little girl climbed on a tricycle and pedalled round the floor. 'I can ride your bike,' she said.

Tom paid no attention. He was trying how fast the engine could go without falling off the track.

The little girl took a picture book, sat down under the table with her back to Tom, and slowly, carefully, examined each page. 'It's got a crooked wheel,' Tom said, 'That's what it is.' The little girl made no answer. She was staring at the book with round eyes and a small pursed mouth—the expression of a nervous child at the zoo when the lions are just going to roar. Slowly and carefully she turned the next page. As it opened, her eyes became larger, her mouth more tightly pursed, as if she expected some creature to jump out at her.

'Tom.' Nurse, having completed her private business, came bustling in with the air of one restored to life after a dangerous illness. 'Tom, you naughty boy, is this the way you entertain

PREPARATION

"A Special Occasion"

Overview

Cary's story is a good example of situational irony. We know, and the children know, that Nurse completely misunderstands the budding friendship between Tom and the girl. Looking at a situation from a child's perspective, he "opens" our eyes that we might renew our vision and reminds us of a valuable lesson: not everyone views a situation the same way.

Potential problems

Cary was probably one of the most popular twentieth-century British authors. Although this selection is free of objectionable elements, we would not recommend his works on the whole for recreational reading.

DISCUSSION

Introduction

Ask the students whether they have ever been in a situation in which they discovered that another person's view of the situation was completely different from theirs. Comedy—as well your guests? Poor little Jenny, all by herself under the table.' The nurse was plump and middle-aged; an old-fashioned nanny.

'She's not by herself,' Tom said.

'Oh, Tom, that really is naughty of you. Where are all your nice manners? Get up, my dear, and play with her like a good boy.'

'I am playing with her,' Tom said, in a surly tone, and he gave Nurse a sidelong glance of anger.

'Now Tom, if you go on telling such stories, I shall know you are trying to be naughty. Get up now when I ask you.' She stooped, took Tom by the arm, and lifted him up. 'Come now, you must be polite, after you've asked her yourself and pestered for her all week.'

At this public disclosure, Tom instantly lost his temper and yelled, 'I didn't—I didn't—I won't—I won't.'

'Then I'll have to take poor little Jenny downstairs again to her mummy.'

'No—no—no.'

'Will you play with her, then?'

'No, I hate her—I never wanted her.'

At this the little girl rose and said, in precise indignant tones, 'He *is* naughty, isn't he?'

Tom flew at her, and seized her by the hair; the little girl at once uttered a loud scream, kicked him on the leg, and bit his arm. She was carried screaming to the door by Nurse, who, from there, issued sentence on Tom, 'I'm going straight to your father, as soon as he comes in.' Then she went out, banging the door.

Tom ran at the door and kicked it, rushed at the engine, picked it up and flung it against the wall. Then he howled at the top of his voice for five minutes. He intended to howl all day. He was suffering from a large and complicated grievance.

All at once the door opened and the little girl walked in. She had an air of immense self-satisfaction as if she had just done something very clever. She said in a tone demanding congratulation, 'I've come back.'

Tom gazed at her through his tears and gave a loud sob. Then he picked up the engine, sat down by the track. But the engine fell off at the first push. He gave another sob, looked at the wheels, and bent one of them straight.

The little girl lifted her party frock behind in order not to crush it, sat down under the table, and drew the book on her knee.

Tom tried the engine at high speed. His face was still set in the form of anger and

Discuss this sentence with the students. What is the "large and complicated grievance"? Why did Tom suddenly grow angry at Nurse and attack the girl? (*Nurse, once again demonstrating her poor understanding of the ways of children, humiliated him by stating in front of his visitor that he had "pestered for her [to come] all week." Then she added insult to injury by taking the girl away—all of this in spite of the fact that as far as Tom knew, they were having a fine time together.*)

paradox

as tragedy—can result from these situations. A good example of comedy arising from such misunderstanding is the classic Abbott and Costello skit "Who's on First?" If time permits, you may want to have several students perform this skit. (Be sure to check the skit for propriety before you allow students to perform it. As originally performed, the script includes at least one minced oath.)

Analysis

Use the "About the Story" questions (page 158) to show Cary's ability to use irony in communicating his message.

Application

Draw the students' attention to "About the Story" question 4 (page 158). In one or two paragraphs have them describe an ironic incident from their own experience. See **Writing Rubric 6-1: An Ironic Incident I.**

bitterness, but he forgot to sob. He exclaimed with surprise and pleased excitement, 'It's the lines too—where I trod on 'em.'

The little girl did not reply. Slowly, carefully, she opened the book in the middle and gazed at an elephant. Her eyes became immense, her lips minute. But suddenly, and, as it were, accidentally, she gave an enormous sigh of relief, of very special happiness.

About the Story

1. What are some clues Cary gives us to help us recognize that Tom and Jenny are becoming friends?
2. What problems arise when the nurse begins to evaluate the children's social interaction from an adult viewpoint?
3. What does the phrase "he forgot to sob" in the next to the last paragraph tell us?
4. In one or two paragraphs describe an ironic incident from your own experience.

About the Author

Joyce Cary (1888-1957) was born in Londonderry, a city in Northern Ireland, to parents of English descent. The family members were highly individualistic and memorable; Cary was to create in his novels similarly eccentric characters with strong personalities. Cary and his brother Jack got into innumerable boyish tussles and often had to be pulled apart by their Aunt Netta. Unlike the nanny in "A Special Occasion," however, Aunt Netta understood children's ways and realized that the boys harbored no malice toward each other.

Because he was raised by patient adults, Cary could write without bitterness about misunderstood children. His gift for humorous irony is evident in "A Special Occasion": the children do not appear to be getting along, but they are actually becoming acquainted. An important theme in Cary's fiction is the right of the individual to make his own choices and to express himself in his own way. Yet his stories also show that he recognizes the need for the restrictions of social institutions to guarantee optimum freedom.

About the Story

1. *Answers may vary but might include that "Tom . . . stared at the girl for a long time as one would study a curiosity, rare and valuable"; "Both knew that neither the gesture nor the phrase was meant to convey meaning. They simply expressed the fact that for Tom this was an important and exciting, a very special occasion"; "They both gazed at each other for some minutes with sparkling eyes."*

2. *She completely misinterprets the situation. What is "budding friendship" from the children's perspective is rudeness from hers.*

3. *It shows us that Tom's feelings of anger and shame have dissipated and he is again caught up in the excitement of having the little girl present.*

4. *Answers will vary; see Application section, page 157.*

Letter from a West Texas Constituent

J. B. Lee, Jr.

Verbal irony, like symbolism, can extend throughout a work; in such cases, the work must be read entirely on an implied level. It would be difficult to pick out sentence examples of irony in the following letter. The entire letter is in the ironic mode. J. B. Lee, Jr., "Potential Hog Raiser," is satirizing the federal government's farm subsidy program.

March 20, 1963

The Honorable Ed Foreman
House of Representatives
Congressional District #16
Washington 25, D.C.

Dear Sir:

My friend over in Terebone Parish received a $1,000 check from the government this year for not raising hogs. So I am going into the not-raising hogs business next year.

What I want to know is, in your opinion, what is the best kind of farm not to raise hogs on and the best kind of hogs not to raise? I would prefer not to raise Razorbacks, but if that is not a good breed not to raise, I will just as gladly not raise any Berkshires or Durocs.

The hardest work in this business is going to be in keeping an inventory of how many hogs I haven't raised.

My friend is very joyful about the future of his business. He has been raising hogs for more than 20 years and the best he ever made was $400, until this year, when he got $1,000 for not raising hogs.

If I can get $1,000 for not raising 50 hogs, then will I get $2,000 for not raising 100 hogs? I plan to operate on a small scale at first, holding myself down to 4,000 hogs which means I will have $80,000 coming from the government.

Now, another thing: these hogs I will not raise will not eat 100,000 bushels of corn. So will you pay me anything for not raising 100,000 bushels of corn not to feed the hogs I am not raising?

I want to get started as soon as possible as this seems to be a good time of year for not raising hogs.

One thing more, can I raise 10 or 12 hogs on the side while I am in the not-raising-hog-business just enough to get a few sides of bacon to eat?

Very truly yours,

J.B. Lee, Jr.
Potential Hog Raiser

FURTHER HELPS

Additional activities

1. Have students look for examples of irony used in letters to the editor, in news magazines, or on news websites.

2. Read aloud to the students other Frost poems that include irony. Examples would include "Mending Wall," "The Death of the Hired Man," "The Gift Outright," and many others.

PREPARATION

"Letter from a West Texas Constituent," "A Considerable Speck (Microscopic)"

Overview

The letter from the West Texas constituent is a full-blown example of structural (persuasive verbal) irony. The Frost poem links nicely with Wheelock's "Earth." Here the human being is not the subject of observation but the observer. And yet something of the mite's description reminds us of ourselves. Its actions show an almost human gamut of emotions. The conclusion, as in Wheelock's poem, pays a compliment to the creature's intelligence. The irony is targeted differently, however.

DISCUSSION

"Letter from a West Texas Constituent"

Introduction

Before discussing Mr. Lee's letter, share the following information with your students: agricultural price supports for American farmers greatly increased in the 1960s. Technological advances greatly increased productivity, threatening a disastrous fall in prices. Through a combination of approaches, the Commodity Credit Corporation, established in 1933, attempted to subsidize farm income while limiting production.

Analysis

Such government "solutions" have resulted in many such mock-serious inquiries. The one illustrated here is addressed to a congressman from a "potential hog raiser." We should be aware, however, of an undercurrent of deep disgust and even anger beneath the ridicule. There is a real seriousness beneath the mock seriousness of the surface meaning.

Comment on the advantage of irony in persuasion. It is very difficult for the opponent to reply to. It requires either counterirony or the reduction of the ironic meaning to plain statements and the refutation of them one by one.

A Considerable Speck (Microscopic)

Robert Frost

The exaggerated seriousness with which the poet treats this trivial incident gives the poem its humorously ironic tone.

A speck that would have been beneath my sight
On any but a paper sheet so white
Set off across what I had written there.
And I had idly poised my pen in air
To stop it with a period of ink   5
When something strange about it made me think.
This was no dust speck by my breathing blown,
But unmistakably a living mite
With inclinations it could call its own.
It paused as with suspicion of my pen,   10
And then came racing wildly on again
To where my manuscript was not yet dry;
Then paused again and either drank or smelt
With loathing, for again it turned to fly.
Plainly with an intelligence I dealt.   15
It seemed too tiny to have room for feet,
Yet must have had a set of them complete
To express how much it didn't want to die.
It ran with terror and with cunning crept.
It faltered: I could see it hesitate;   20
Then in the middle of the open sheet
Cower down in desperation to accept
Whatever I accorded it of fate.
I have none of the tenderer-than-thou
Collectivistic regimenting love*   25

Collectivistic . . . love: Socialistic liberal sentimentality

The device of the invented naive speaker offering his thoughts (or, in this case, requesting information) with the utmost sincerity and best of intentions is an old one. A master of this technique was Jonathan Swift.

"A Considerable Speck (Microscopic)"

Here Frost makes an educational event out of something most people would not even see. The poem takes us through the process of the event it describes. Frost has us peering at the speck on his page to see the movement he has embodied in it. The conclusion links it to the intelligence readers hope to find in the marks on a written or printed page. The target of the irony is writers (including himself) who write mindlessly. The irony is situational: that something so small could show intelligence and (by implication) that something so large and gifted with intelligence as man could so often show such unintelligence (see the last two lines). There is also irony in the heightened seriousness with which the incident is treated and rendered momentous. Frost's poetry typically finds significance in ordinary experience and common things.

Application

It takes more than facility with language to be a good poet or writer of any kind. Like Frost, one must be a keen observer, alert to things others fail to notice. Ask the students what they have witnessed and have found significant that no one else has noticed.

As time permits, have the students divide into groups. Have each group decide on an event or idea that is seemingly insignificant. Have them list several ways such an event might be viewed in a unique or more "in-depth" manner. Finally, have them compose either a poem or a paragraph describing the event or idea. Have each group share their final product with the class.

With which the modern world is being swept.
But this poor microscopic item now!
Since it was nothing I knew evil of
I let it lie there till I hope it slept.
I have a mind myself and recognize   30
Mind when I meet with it in any guise.
No one can know how glad I am to find
On any sheet the least display of mind.

The irony of the poem is revealed in the last two lines—the speaker often reads things by humans that show less intelligence than does this mite.

About the Author

In his later years, Robert Frost (1874-1963) acquired the reputation not only as New England's "poetic bard" but also as America's unofficial poet laureate. His poetry avoids the moral coarseness of Walt Whitman and displays more traditional form than do works by his contemporaries Carl Sandburg or E. E. Cummings.

Although his poetry was highly successful, his personal life was characterized by uncertainty and insecurity. Despite the aura of good-natured kindliness he displayed in his public life, his private life revealed another, less admirable side. He continually sought to build his own reputation, often by employing exaggerations and backbiting. Frost's family suffered greatly from his pride.

Frost did not like setting forth his beliefs systematically, but we can discover much of his philosophy by examining his poems. In his writing, he frequently encourages the use of human instinct as a moral guide. He also scoffs at the idea of an orderly world view. He does tell us, however, his purpose for writing. He states that "a poem ends in a clarification of life—a momentary stay against confusion." But as Frost readily admits, writing is at best a "momentary stay" against the feelings of helplessness and chaos that are an outgrowth of such beliefs.

About the Letter and Poem

1. According to J. B. Lee, Jr., how does the federal government's farm subsidy program work?
2. What are some clues that help you recognize that the entire letter is written in the ironic mode?
3. What is the point Mr. Lee is trying to make to the Honorable Ed Foreman?
4. The target of the irony in Robert Frost's poem is not the "speck." What is it?

About the Letter and Poem

1. *It pays people money not to raise hogs; in other words, it pays people to do nothing.*

2. *Answers may vary but might include nearly any sentence from the letter (such as the first sentence from the second paragraph) or a reference to the overly serious tone the writer takes toward his absurd topic.*

3. *He is making clear his contempt for what he considers to be wasteful government programs.*

4. *Writers who write mindlessly (see especially the last two lines).*

OBJECTIVES

The students will be able to

- Discuss hyperbole as a technique of humor.
- Discuss what the idea of the "lostness" of modern man means to a Christian.

Note Eastman's parallels between the fish and the humans, emphasized by highlighting in the teacher's edition. Ask students whether they can find a simile in the poem. *("They flow like water to and fro.")* Discuss why this is an appropriate comparison.

FURTHER HELPS

Additional activities

Have the students collect several examples of hyperbole from their own reading or discussions with others to share with the rest of the class (e.g., "I was so embarrassed I thought I would die!" "I am starving to death!").

Journal entry idea

Have the students take an ordinary experience they have

Scylla Toothless

Anonymous

Epigrams have often been used for mockery. What feature of Scylla is the real subject of the following one?

Scylla is toothless; yet when she was young,
She had both tooth enough, and too much tongue:
What should I now of Toothless Scylla say?
But that her tongue hath worn her teeth away.

At the Aquarium

Max Eastman

Notice that this poem uses irony to cause the reader to look closely at himself.

Serene the silver fishes glide,
Stern-lipped, and pale, and wonder-eyed;
As through the agèd deeps of ocean,
They glide with wan and wavy motion.
They have no pathway where they go,   5
They flow like water to and fro.
They watch with never-winking eyes,
They watch with staring, cold surprise,
The level people in the air,
The people peering, peering there,   10
Who wander also to and fro,
And know not why or where they go,
Yet have a wonder in their eyes,
Sometimes a pale and cold surprise.

PREPARATION

"Scylla Toothless," "At the Aquarium"

Overview

The first selection occupies a place in the irony unit because of its pretense of serious explanation. The implied meaning is the real one: Scylla talks too much.

Eastman's "At the Aquarium," like "Earth," uses an ironic reversal of perspective in which man is viewed by creatures that he feels, or would feel, superior to. The fish paradoxically see the human observers in the same way that the human observers see the fish.

Potential problems

In Eastman's poem the aquarium is a commercial aquarium, not a small home variety. There is no necessary evolutionary or naturalistic assumption here about a kinship between the animals and man. The poem is poetic fantasy.

DISCUSSION

"Scylla Toothless"

Introduction

Besides incongruity, another humorous technique is hyperbole. Have the students look up the definition of *hyperbole* (ironic overstatement) and come up with some examples of the technique from their own conversations and experiences. Ask them to find an example of hyperbole in "Scylla Toothless." *("her tongue hath worn her teeth away")*

Analysis

The poem purports to explain Scylla's lack of teeth. This mock explanation is an indirect (and humorous) way of condemning her habit of

About the Author

Max Eastman (1883-1969), American author and editor, spent his life trying to reconcile contradictory ideas. Eastman's first conflict was with organized religion. His mother, an ordained minister, was a rebellious, outspoken feminist who left her son a heritage of inconsistency. For example, she made him memorize Scripture but denied from the pulpit basic doctrines, such as the Trinity and the virgin birth. Eventually, Eastman completely rejected his family's "religion" and proudly proclaimed himself a pagan.

At Columbia University, under the influence of the humanistic educator John Dewey, Eastman denied the existence of absolute truth, asserting that man's reasoning powers should be used merely to better life here and now. According to Eastman, the ideal man shuns morality as a sham and a hindrance. His ideal man was one who followed his own decrees of right and wrong. From this arbitrary code of ethics came Eastman's most dangerous contradiction, the promotion of socialism and communism under the delusion that they emphasized human equality and individuality.

Ironically, later in life, Eastman bitterly attacked most of the ideas he had promoted as a youth. Although he was neither a superior writer nor a commanding social reformer, Eastman's life and writings are representative of twentieth-century man's illogical and inconsistent approach to the human condition. The irony of "At the Aquarium" echoes Eastman's view of life in the twentieth century.

About the Poems

1. What feature of Scylla is the real subject of the epigram?
2. How does this make the title ironic?
3. How does Eastman's poem cause the reader to look closely at himself?
4. Who are the watchers at the aquarium? Explain what is ironic about your answer.

had and transform it into a humorous essay by using hyperbole.

Resource

Milton Candor, *Max Eastman* (New York: Twayne Publishers, 1970).

---

malicious gossip. The poem is itself a hyperbole, an exaggerated account of a phenomenon, and therefore a form of verbal irony.

The name "Scylla" comes from classical mythology. Explain to the students that poets of earlier times gave classical names to friends and others whom they praised or dispraised. Ovid tells the story of Scylla in his *Metamorphoses*. Scylla was a beautiful girl turned into a hideous, carnivorous, many-headed, cave-dwelling, doglike creature of the straits of Messina. She snatched and devoured sailors whose ships sailed too close while attempting to avoid the terrible whirlpool of Charybdis on the opposite side. Hence the expression "between Scylla and Charybdis," which refers to opposing evils between which a proper course must be steered. Students are probably more

familiar with the phrase "between a rock and a hard place," which conveys the same idea. (Discussion of "At the Aquarium" continues after "About the Poems.")

 About the Poems

1. *The real subject of the poem is that Scylla talks too much; she is probably a malicious gossip.*

2. *The title is ironic in its humorous assumption that her toothlessness is a result of her tongue having worn away her teeth.*

3. *by giving the fish's view of the human spectators*

4. *Students may answer "the people"; however, the irony of the poem is that the fish are the watchers (lines 7-9).*

"At the Aquarium"

Ask the students whether they ever imagined at a zoo that the animals were studying them as they were studying the animals. This amusing fantasy is the basis of this quite serious poem.

This poem is a sonnet with an irregular (nontypical) rhyme scheme: couplets. It divides by its organization into the standard octave and sestet (8- and 6-line parts) of an Italian sonnet, though the division is not apparent syntactically (the sentence carries over from line 8 to line 9). The first eight lines describe the humans' view of the fish—wonder-eyed, looking surprised, wandering without path or purpose. The next (and last) six lines reverse the perspective, giving the fish's view of the human spectators. It is strangely identical. Floating in

"A Germ Destroyer"

Discuss the meaning of this passage: As in any bureaucracy, in some of these administrations the underling (the Private Secretary) does all the work for which the one in a position of prominence (the Viceroy) receives the credit.

paradox

Note how much this allusion reveals about both the Viceroy and Wonder. Wonder is so interested in expanding his own power that in heaven he will try to steal Peter's keys (cf. Matt. 16:18-19); but the Viceroy is well aware of what kind of person Wonder is and is letting him have his own way . . . for now. (You may wish to discuss the Biblical inaccuracies implicit in the Viceroy's statement.)

A Germ Destroyer

Rudyard Kipling

Important reversals and redirections in life sometimes result from what the world calls "coincidences." What kind of irony is produced by surprising "coincidences"?

As a general rule, it is inexpedient* to meddle with questions of State in a land where men are highly paid to work them out for you. This tale is a justifiable exception.

inexpedient: unnecessary and therefore unwise

Once in every five years, as you know, we indent for* a new Viceroy; and each Viceroy imports, with the rest of his baggage, a Private Secretary, who may or may not be the real Viceroy, just as Fate ordains. Fate looks after the Indian Empire because it is so big and so helpless.

indent for: order, requisition

There was a Viceroy once, who brought out with him a turbulent Private Secretary— a hard man with a soft manner and a morbid passion for work. This secretary was called Wonder—John Fennil Wonder. The Viceroy possessed no name—nothing but a string of counties and two-thirds of the alphabet after them. He said, in confidence, that he was the electroplated figure-head of a golden administration, and he watched in a dreamy, amused way Wonder's attempts to draw matters which were entirely outside his province into his own hands. "When we are all cherubim together," said His Excellency once, "my dear, good friend Wonder will head the conspiracy for stealing Peter's keys. *Then* I shall report him."

But, though the Viceroy did nothing to check Wonder's officiousness,* other people said unpleasant things. Maybe the Members of Council began it; but, finally all Simla agreed that there was "too much Wonder, and too little Viceroy" in that rule. Wonder was always quoting "His Excellency." It was "His Excellency this," "His Excellency that," "In the opinion of His Excellency," and so on. The Viceroy smiled; but he did not heed. He said that, so long as his old men squabbled with his "dear, good Wonder," they might be induced to leave the Immemorial East in peace.

officiousness: forwardness

That season, came up to Simla one of these crazy people with only a single idea. These are the men who make things move; but they are not nice to talk to. This man's name was Mellish, and he had lived for fifteen years on land of his own, in Lower Bengal, studying cholera. He held that cholera was a germ that propagated itself as it flew through a muggy atmosphere; and stuck in the branches of trees like a wool-flake. The germ could be rendered sterile, he said, by "Mellish's Own Invincible Fumigatory"—a heavy violet-black powder— "the result of fifteen years' scientific investigation, Sir!"

Inventors seem very much alike as a caste. They talk loudly, especially about "conspiracies of monopolists"; they beat upon the table with

the air (in their element as the fish in theirs), staring with wonder in their eyes and occasional "pale and cold surprise," wandering without knowledge of purpose, the humans must appear to the fish as the fish to the humans. This shift of perspective is ironic in its reversal of reader expectations and paradoxical point. Truth is found in the seemingly contradictory: humans, when viewed with detachment, are not very much different from the animals they pay to see. The poem comments poignantly on the lostness of modern man.

Application

Discuss with the students Eastman's concept of the lostness of modern man. Is his assessment accurate for those who have rejected God's

truth? How does this "lostness" exhibit itself in current society (e.g., drug and alcohol abuse in all levels of society, confusion on the true value of human life, apathetic response to values, emphasis on "what's in it for me," refusal to commit oneself, etc.)? What does Scripture have to say about the end times? *(cf. II Tim. 3:1-9, 12-13)* Are the characteristics of the end times consistent with the attitudes and values we see in today's society? *(yes)* What should be our response to such attitudes? *(The Christian must attempt to reach lost people with the saving knowledge of Christ.)* How can we help those who are deluded by such erroneous philosophies? *(by sharing the truth with them)* their fists; and they secrete fragments of their inventions about their persons.

Mellish said that there was a Medical "Ring" at Simla, headed by the Surgeon-General, who was in league, apparently, with all the Hospital Assistants in the Empire. I forgot exactly how he proved it, but it had something to do with "skulking up to the Hills";* and what Mellish wanted was the independent evidence* of the Viceroy—"Steward of our Most Gracious Majesty the Queen, Sir." So Mellish went up to Simla, with eighty-four pounds of Fumigatory in his trunk, to speak to the Viceroy and to show him the merits of the invention.

Hills: the hill district of the western Himalayas in which the town of Simla, a British military administrative center and officer's resort, was located
evidence: supporting testimony

But it is easier to see a Viceroy than to talk to him, unless you chance to be as important as Mellishe of Madras. He was a six-thousand-rupee man, so great that his daughters never "married." They "contracted alliances." He himself was not paid. He "received emoluments," and his journeys about the country were "tours of observation." His business was to stir up the people in Madras with a long pole—as you stir up tench* in a pond—and the people had to come up out of their comfortable old ways and gasp, "This Enlightenment and Progress. Isn't it fine!" Then they gave Mellishe statues and jasmine garlands, in the hope of getting rid of him.

tench: edible fish of Eurasia

Mellishe came up to Simla "to confer with the Viceroy." That was one of his perquisites.* The Viceroy knew nothing of Mellishe except

that he was "one of those middle-class deities who seem necessary to the spiritual comfort of this Paradise of the Middle-classes," and that, in all probability, he had "suggested, designed, founded, and endowed all the public institutions in Madras." Which proves that His Excellency, though dreamy, had experience of the ways of six-thousand-rupee men.

perquisites: extra benefits

Mellishe's name was E. Mellishe, and Mellish's name was E. Mellish, and they were both staying at the same hotel, and the Fate that looks after the Indian Empire ordained that Wonder should blunder and drop the final "e," that the Chaprassi* should help him, and that the note which ran:

> Dear Mr. Mellish,—Can you set aside your other engagements, and lunch with us at two tomorrow? His Excellency has an hour at your disposal then,

should be given to Mellish with the Fumigatory. He nearly wept with pride and delight, and at the appointed hour cantered to Peterhoff,* a big paper bag full of the Fumigatory in his coattail pockets. He had his chance, and he meant to make the most of it. Mellishe of Madras had been so portentously* solemn about his "conference," that Wonder had arranged for a private tiffin*—no A.-D.-C.'s,* no Wonder, no one but the Viceroy, who said plaintively that he feared being left alone with unmuzzled autocrats like the great Mellishe of Madras.

Chaprassi: chief servant
Peterhoff: palatial home of the Viceroy
portentously: awesomely, pompously
tiffin: luncheon
A.-D.-C.'s: aides-de-camp, officers serving as secretaries to high-ranking superiors

In other words, Mellish believes there is a conspiracy between medical professionals and the government to keep his discovery a secret, but that if he can show the Viceroy his Fumigatory, the Viceroy will listen.

Point out to students that Kipling is introducing another character here—note the slight difference in the spelling of the last name.

Note Kipling's humorous blending of metaphor, simile, and irony here.

The Viceroy's attitude toward Mellishe again shows him to be a keen observer of human nature. He uses hyperbole when referring to "middle-class deities . . . of the Paradise of the Middle-classes" and satire when giving Mellishe credit for everything good that had ever happened in Madras.

FURTHER HELPS

Additional activity

Have the students create a modern-day John Fennil Wonder and, using irony, write about another incident that might happen to him. Encourage them to keep Wonder's characterization in their writing consistent with that in the story. See **Writing Rubric 6-2: An Ironic Incident II.**

PREPARATION

"A Germ Destroyer"

Overview

"A Germ Destroyer" is another of Kipling's tales of life in British India. Notice the tongue-in-cheek tone at the beginning. There is humorous verbal as well as situational irony in the story. The student who reads rapidly or inattentively may miss the point of confusion that generates the action of the plot (Mellish vs. Mellishe). You may wish to call attention to it when making the assignment.

DISCUSSION

Introduction

Life is full of what some people call ironies of fate. This startling "coincidence" produces humor but also serious consequences for one person.

Analysis

The mix-up responsible for the wild confusion in this story produces an ironic reversal of expectation for the Viceroy as well as for the reader. The reader's learning the facts of the situation before the Viceroy creates dramatic irony, enhancing the sense of absurdity and the humor.

What characteristics of Wonder are indicated in paragraphs 3-4? *(inordinate ambition, pushiness, and toadyism)* What characteristics of the Viceroy are revealed in the same paragraphs? *(moderation, breadth, detachment, reasonableness, and sense of humor)* The two are moral and temperamental opposites. Wonder takes himself very seriously. The Viceroy does not take himself seriously—he enjoys belittling his importance though he does prove to have a definite sense of responsibility along with an awareness of limits. He is definitely a laid-back individual—the kind of administrator Kipling admired and felt was especially appropriate to the rule of India. He believes that in subjugating a proud people, less is often more.

Resource

The Best of C. S. Lewis, pp. 497-502, "The
Great Sin" from *Mere Christianity* (Michigan: Baker Book House, 1977).

But his guest did not bore the Viceroy. On
the contrary, he amused him. Mellish was
nervously anxious to go straight to his
Fumigatory, and talked at random until tiffin
was over and His Excellency asked him to
smoke. The Viceroy was pleased with Mellish
because he did not talk "shop."

As soon as the cheroots were lit, Mellish
spoke like a man; beginning with his cholera
theory, reviewing his fifteen years' "scientific
labors," the machinations of the "Simla Ring,"
and the excellence of his Fumigatory, while
the Viceroy watched him between half-shut
eyes and thought—"Evidently this is the wrong
tiger; but it is an original animal." Mellish's
hair was standing on end with excitement, and
he stammered. He began groping in his coat-
tails and, before the Viceroy knew what was
about to happen, he had tipped a bagful of
his powder into the big silver ashtray.

"J-j-judge for yourself, Sir," said Mellish.
"Y' Excellency shall judge for yourself!
Absolutely infallible, on my honor."

He plunged the lighted end of his cigar
into the powder, which began to smoke like
a volcano, and send up fat, greasy wreaths
of copper-colored smoke. In five seconds the
room was filled with a most pungent and
sickening stench—a reek that took fierce hold
of the trap of your windpipe and shut it. The
powder hissed and fizzed, and sent out blue
and green sparks, and the smoke rose till you
could neither see, nor breathe, nor gasp.
Mellish, however, was used to it.

"Nitrate of strontia," he shouted; "baryta,
bone meal *et cetera!* Thousand cubic feet
smoke per inch. Not a germ could live—not
a germ, Y' Excellency!"

But His Excellency had fled, and was

coughing at the foot of the stairs, while all
Peterhoff hummed like a hive. Red Lancers*
came in, and the head Chaprassi, who speaks
English, came in, and mace-bearers* came in,
and ladies ran downstairs screaming "Fire";
for the smoke was drifting through the house
and oozing out of the windows, and bellying
along the verandas, and wreathing and
writhing across the gardens. No one could enter
the room where Mellish was lecturing on his
Fumigatory, till that unspeakable powder had
burned itself out.

Red Lancers: palace guards
mace-bearers: ceremonial officials

Then an Aide-de-Camp, who desired the
V. C.,* rushed through the rolling clouds and
hauled Mellish into the hall. The Viceroy was
prostrate with laughter, and could only waggle
his hands feebly at Mellish, who was shaking
a fresh bagful of powder at him.

desired the V. C.: sought the Viceroy

"Glorious! Glorious!" sobbed His Excellency. "Not a germ, as you justly observe, could
exist! I can swear it. A magnificent success!"

Then he laughed till the tears came, and
Wonder, who had caught the real Mellishe at
the Mall, entered and was deeply shocked at
the scene. But the Viceroy was delighted,
because he saw that Wonder would presently
depart. Mellish with the Fumigatory was also
pleased, for he felt that he had smashed the
Simla Medical "Ring."

*   *   *   *   *

Few men could tell a story like His
Excellency when he took the trouble, and his

Notice a similar contrast between the Viceroy
and Mellish (a one-idea man) on the one hand
and Mellishe (a determined reformer of India)
on the other. Wonder, Mellish, and Mellishe are
a triumvirate of super-zealous, self-serving
fools. Notice how circumstances or "fate" (to
use Kipling's term) single-handedly (with little
assistance from the patient Viceroy) dispenses
with the three of them.

The concluding section of the story, which
serves with the first four paragraphs as its
frame, shows how the Viceroy gets rid of Wonder. Ask the students whether it is consistent
with his style of administration to handle the
problem this way. Ask them to describe this
style (unassertive, nonconfrontational) and this
particular strategy (indirect). Someone who

takes himself as seriously as Wonder does cannot stand ridicule, even of a good-natured sort.
Wonder was also perceptive enough to discern
the message of the "sub-tinkle": that his useful-
ness had ended.

The cryptic last sentences will probably need
elucidation. "My fault entirely" refers to the
cause of Wonder's health "giving way." This
fault—"My inconsistency"—has exasperated
Wonder into bad health, so the Viceroy explains with a "twinkle in his eye." We all, as well
as he and Wonder, know better. Wonder's character, along with the Viceroy's consistency of
inaction, did him in.

Application

Discuss with the students the characteristics of
those who are vain. Kipling makes clear in his
story that they are typically humorless and
oversensitive. See if the students can think of
other characters like those Kipling portrays.

Scripture, of course, has much to say about the
sin of pride. Look up several passages in Scripture that reveal the characteristics of a proud
man and show God's attitude toward such men
(cf. Prov. 11:2; 13:10; 16:18; 29:23; Dan.
4:37; Oba. 3; Mark 7:20-23; I John 2:16).
After reading these passages together, encourage students to examine their own hearts for
pride.

account of "my dear, good Wonder's friend with the powder" went the round of Simla, and flippant folk made Wonder unhappy by their remarks.

But His Excellency told the tale once too often—for Wonder. As he meant to do. It was at a Seepee Picnic. Wonder was sitting just behind the Viceroy.

"And I really thought for a moment," wound up His Excellency, "that my dear good Wonder had hired an assassin to clear his way to the throne!"

Everyone laughed; but there was a delicate sub-tinkle in the Viceroy's tone which Wonder understood. He found that his health was giving way, and the Viceroy allowed him to go, and presented him with a flaming "character"* for use at Home* among big people.

character: glowing recommendation
Home: back in England

"My fault entirely," said His Excellency, in after seasons, with a twinkle in his eye. "My inconsistency must always have been distasteful to such a masterly man."

About the Story

1. What kind of irony is produced by the surprising "coincidences" in Kipling's story?
2. Is the fall of the Viceroy's secretary due entirely to coincidence?
3. What else could have played a part in the secretary's downfall?
4. Who do you think is the main character in the story? Explain why you chose the character you did.

About the Story

1. *Primarily dramatic irony; students may also mention situational irony.*

2. *No, it is also a result of his inordinate ambition, pushiness, and toadyism.*

3. *Answers will vary; however, students should note that the Viceroy was well aware of what type of man Wonder was.*

4. *Answers may vary; however, students will most likely choose either Wonder or the Viceroy. Accept either answer as long as they can defend it from facts in the story.*

OBJECTIVE

The students will be able to

- Analyze and discuss situational irony in "The Grave Grass Quivers" and "Yet If His Majesty, Our Sovereign Lord."

Kantor uses foreshadowing to open the story. This heightens readers' interest in what will follow. We know murder has been committed—but whose? By whom?

Ask students what war this comment alludes to. *(World War I, since the story is set in 1921)*

The Grave Grass Quivers

Mackinlay Kantor

*The irony in this narrative is similar to that presented in "A Germ Destroyer"
by Kipling. In both selections the irony is produced by surprising "coincidences."
The tone of Kantor's story, however, is serious rather than humorous.*

We were alone, out there in the soft spring sunshine. There was no one to disturb us. We dug silently, carefully.

The clinging black earth came up at every shovelful—moist and alive with richness of the prairies. We had been digging for ten minutes, when my shovel struck something. It struck again, and something cracked.

After that, it wasn't long before we began to uncover things. "Murdered," Doc said, once, and then he didn't talk anymore.

It began in Doc Martindale's office, which, as soon as he retired, was to be my office, on a cool spring afternoon in 1921.

"How's it going?" asked Doc.

"I guess it'll be pretty slow here, to live," I said, childishly.

"Not much excitement," agreed Doc. He went to the door and picked up a copy of the *Cottonwood Herald* which a boy had just tossed over the banisters. . . . "Yes, local news is slow, pretty slow. There's a sample of a Cottonwood thriller."

It told of the plans for Arbor Day. The children of the public schools were going to set out some trees as a memorial to the local boys who had died in the World War.

. . . and selected as their choice, American elms. The trees will be planted on the Louis Wilson farm, above the Coon River. Mr. Wilson has agreed to donate a small plot of ground for this

---

PREPARATION

"The Grave Grass Quivers," "Yet If His Majesty, Our Sovereign Lord"

Overview

Kantor's "The Grave Grass Quivers" links well with "A Germ Destroyer." The irony of both stories is produced by a series of "coincidences." The resolution of Kantor's story, however, is serious rather than humorous. "Yet If His Majesty" illustrates irony of situation in a Biblical setting. Christ's coming to a world ignorant of and hostile toward Him is one of the great ironies of the ages. We would honor and show hospitality to an earthly ruler even if we disliked and disapproved of him. But we are

willing to rudely exclude and degrade the amiable King of heaven, the Lord Himself, when He comes to take up residence with us and within us.

DISCUSSION

"The Grave Grass Quivers"

Introduction

Read the headnote and story aloud in class.

Analysis

Have the students plot the action of the story, carefully noting the coincidences that compose the rising action. (For information on plotting stories see FUNDAMENTALS OF LITERATURE for

Christian Schools, pages 224-25.) You may also wish to compare the action of this story to that of "A Germ Destroyer." Notice, for example, the inciting moment in both stories: in Kipling's it is revealed in a note with a key misspelling (*Mellish* rather than *Mellishe*); in Kantor's story it is revealed in a newspaper article with a key piece of information (Goble's gift to the community). Continue your discussion of the story by asking the students to explain how Eli Goble's "gift" to the community is ironic. The irony arises from the fact that the gift is inconsistent with Goble's character. As the old doctor states, "He never lets go of a nickel until the Goddess of Liberty yells for mercy." Although the news article and Doc Martindale's reaction to the news are an excellent clue for us, we may not suspect Goble of any wrong-purpose. It is thought that these trees, standing on a high hill above the river and overlooking a majestic view of our city will be a fitting memorial.

Ceremonies are to begin at 2 P.M., and it is urged that all local people attend. Rev. J. Medley Williams of the Baptist Church will deliver a—

Doc pulled his gray beard and laughed. "A few meetings, a church social, once in a while a fire or an auto accident! Once in a blue moon we have a divorce. Life comes—and goes—without much hullabaloo."

Then I had to laugh also, and a bit sheepishly. "I guess I'm rather silly. Of course those are the important things in most people's lives. But I would like to get called in on a nice, exciting murder once in a while!"

Doc was silent for a moment. He appeared to be thinking heavily, as if he had taken me seriously. "Murders," he said, after a moment. "Once before the war, a Mexican worker stabbed his wife. Then back in '96, an insane farmer shot his neighbor. But, come to think of it, those are the only murders we've ever had here in all my years of practice." He seemed much impressed. "Think of that, think of that! Only two murders since 1861."

"And who," I inquired idly, "was murdered in 1861?"

He tugged at his beard again, and cleared his throat. "Well," he said, slowly, "it was my father and my brother."

"Oh." And I scarcely knew what to say. "I'm sorry, Doctor, I—"

"No matter." He shrugged. "It's a long time. I was just a boy then."

My curiosity was aroused. "What are the details, Doctor? That is, if you don't—"

"Oh, I don't mind. . . . Sit down and take it easy." It was several minutes before he began to talk.

"My brother Titus—he was a lot older—had run away from home when he was small, and gone West with some folks. He didn't come back until the spring of '61. And when he came, what a time!"

He laughed his short, dry laugh.

"Titus had struck it rich. He had about seven thousand dollars in gold with him.

"Pa and Titus decided to take the gold to Hamilton. There was a sort of bank opened up there, and the folks were afraid to risk keeping so much money around home.

"They were pretty careful, too, and didn't tell around town much about what they'd planned. They started out at night, figuring to get clear away from Cottonwood and the settlers who knew them, before daylight. Pa and Titus were strapping big men. They looked very strong, setting up on the board laid across the plank wagon box, and Titus carried a navy revolver on his hip and a Sharps rifle across his knees."

Doc Martindale shifted his fat, bumpy body in his wild swivel chair. "And that," he said, "was the last we ever saw them.

"On the evening of the second day after my folks left," Doc Martindale continued, "a farmer from the Salt Creek neighborhood rode up in front of our house, and said that he had seen our team down in a clump of willows by Little Hell Slough, hitched to a wagon, and that the men folks were not with the wagon. The team had been dragging around, and tried to go home, but they got hung up in the willows."

Old Doc was silent for several minutes.

"That was a terrible night," he said, simply. "Before we all got down to Little Hell Slough—most of the neighbors were with us—we found the team in those willows, pretty muddy and hungry, and tangled up in the harness, too.

"None of the stuff in the wagon had been taken except—sure: the gold was gone. The blankets were still there, and Titus's rifle, but his navy revolver wasn't anywhere around. And there was no other sign of Pa and Titus.

"I drove Ma and the girls home, in that

Ask students how many years back Doc is remembering. (sixty)

FURTHER HELPS

Additional activities

1. Have the students do a choral reading of the poem, "Yet If His Majesty, Our Sovereign Lord."

2. Review Units 4-6 with **Appendix O: Units 4, 5, 6 Review.**

 Journal entry idea
Have the students write a brief story with an ironic ending.

Resources

Albert C. Baugh, ed., *A Literary History of England,* 2nd ed. (New York: Prentice Hall, 1967).

Stanley J. Kunitz, ed., *Twentieth Century Authors* (New York: H. W. Wilson Company, 1979).

James Vinson, ed., *Contemporary Novelists,* 4th ed. (New York: St. Martin's Press, 1986).

doing when we first read of the incident. Many times, especially in a mystery story, we tend to see the significance of an action only after we know the resolution of the story. Ask at what point in the story students begin to suspect Eli Goble. Have them point to a specific quotation from the story that aroused their suspicions.

Finally, discuss the resolution of the story. Ask the students whether they are satisfied with the resolution. Some students may question the fact that Eli Goble is not imprisoned for the crime he committed. This may be a valid objection. Point out to them, however, that he is forced to make restitution. Also, it is evident that he has suffered from the guilt of his deed. "I've seen 'em—I've seen 'em. Always," he says. "Since I got old—they come back."

Discuss with the students the horrible disquietude that arises from guilt. The story of Joseph and his brothers is a good example. Joseph's brothers were afraid that he would wreak vengeance on them. Their fear made them suspicious even of Joseph's generosity. Joseph, however, reminds us of Christ. And like Christ, he assures his brothers that he forgives them. Their repentance and his forgiveness provide the relief for the weight of guilt. Remind the students that once they have confessed sin and turned from it, God does not intend them to be burdened by the guilt they may feel. As a matter of fact, Satan may use such guilt to attack their faith. Encourage them not to allow this to happen.

wagon. Ma sat there beside me on the board, stiff and solemn. Once she said, 'Georgie, if they're gone and gone for good, you'll get the man who did it. Won't you?' I began to cry, of course. I says, 'Yes, Ma. I'll take care of you always, Ma. . . . But if they're dead, it wasn't a man who killed 'em. It was men. One man wouldn't be a match for Titus alone.' "

Doc was buried in the thickening shadows of the office. I couldn't see his face any more.

"Then I went back with the men. We searched the river, up and down the hills around Cottonwood, too, clear down to the East Fork. And never found a thing.

"In that wagon there was just one clue—just one thing which made it certain in our minds that they were dead. That was a little spot of dried blood on the floor of the wagon, right behind the seat. About half as big as your hand. Seemed like, if they'd been shot off the wagon, there'd have been more blood. Then, too, the horses were a fairly young team and they might have cut loose and run away if any shooting had started.

"It was always the general opinion that the murderers had disposed of the bodies in the river. But, personally, I always hung to the idea that Titus and Pa were killed in some mysterious way, and their bodies buried. The fact is that the entire community searched for a week, and then gave it up. No other clue was ever discovered, and no further information of any kind was ever unearthed.

"I didn't quit searching for months. Eli Goble helped me, too; he worked like grim death. But we couldn't find a thing."

I asked, "Who was Eli Goble?"

There was a dull scraping of Doc's shoes on the floor. "Seems to me that you cashed a check this noon, boy. Where did you cash it?"

Somewhat perplexed, I told him. "At the bank across the street."

"Well, that's Eli Goble. And where are you living temporarily—until you can find rooms or an apartment to your liking?"

"At the—Oh, of course, Doctor. The Goble Hotel."

He chuckled. "Everything in this town's Goble, boy. He came here in '59 with a man named Goble, but that wasn't Eli's real name. He had heard that his folks came from Ohio, but didn't know anything about it. You see, his family was killed in the Mint Valley massacre, about 1840, and he had been kidnapped by the Indians. Lived with the Sioux until he was sixteen—could talk the language like a native, too. In fact, lots of folks used to think he was part Indian. But he wasn't. And during the search, he thought all the trailing experience he had had when among the Indians, might be of some account. But even that didn't help. We couldn't find a thing."

I said, slowly, "And he's rich, now?"

Doc sighed, and began to hunt around for the light switch. "Suspecting Eli Goble, are you?" He chuckled. "I don't believe anybody ever did, before. He never had a cent to his name for years after that. A few months later he enlisted in the army, served all through the war, and didn't come back here till 1867. In the meantime, through someone he met in the army, he had been trying to get track of his family. And eventually he succeeded. Found the original family, back in Ohio. He got what money was coming to him, brought it out here to Cottonwood, invested it carefully, and made good. He retained the name of Goble, for convenience's sake. Now he's almost ninety, but he's one of the richest men in the state, and one of the tightest. He never lets go of a nickel until the Goddess of Liberty yells for mercy."

The big yellow light hissed into being. It glared down on the white-enameled table, the glistening cabinets and instruments, the old desk and rows of books. Doc Martindale stood there in the middle of the office and nodded his head. "That's the story, boy. Real live mystery, just sixty years old this spring. . . ."

We were just putting on our hats, and Doc was struggling into his old brown slicker, when the telephone rang. Martindale took up the receiver. "Doctor Martindale speaking."

"Oh," he said, after a moment. "Well." And then he winked quickly at me above the telephone. "Did you use any of that stimulant I left last time? . . . Yes. I'm leaving the office, now, to go home, and I'll stop in. Yes."

He replaced the receiver on its hook. "Speak of the devil," he said. "Eli Goble's just had another heart attack. Nothing to get excited about. He has them frequently, but in between times he's up and down and around. We'll stop in to see him for a minute."

The Goble house was only a few minutes' drive from the main business streets. . . . Lights glowed from most of the windows, as we came up the sidewalk. "You can tell that Eli's flat on his back," said Doc. "If he was around, he wouldn't let them burn all that electricity."

The old man watched us from his pillow, with black-rimmed eyes, deeply sunk beneath the moldy fuzz of his eyebrows. . . . He was breathing heavily.

"Well, Eli. How do you feel? This is Dr. Patterson, Eli."

The old man seemed to glare broodingly at me.

"Don't feel—so—good," Goble managed with difficulty. "Plagued heart seems—like—played out on me."

Martindale began to open his bag. "Oh, nothing to worry about, Eli. We'll fix it up all right." He made a perfunctory* examination. "You'll feel better tomorrow, Eli. Sleep tight."

---

perfunctory: conducted routinely, with little interest or care

---

The old man mumbled and coughed; and we went down the shadowy stairway, through the gloomy, over-ornate hall, and out to the front door.

It was four o'clock the next afternoon when Doc Martindale and I arrived at the office, following a round of calls on widely separated cases. Beyond a few hasty reports to the girl whom Doc Martindale kept in his office during the mid-day hours, we had enjoyed no contact with the town of Cottonwood since 10 A.M.

When we returned in Doc's old touring car, it was to find the *Cottonwood Herald* spread on the table with plenty of black ink decorating the front page.

ELI GOBLE GIVES PARK TO CITY

Local Businessman and Pioneer Settler Decides on Memorial

Plans changed for Tomorrow's Dedication

At a special meeting of the city council this afternoon, it was unanimously agreed to accept the gift tendered by Eli Goble, revered Civil War veteran and early settler in Cottonwood, who today offered to give the town of Cottonwood some thirty acres of beautiful woodland, to be known as "Goble Memorial Park."

It is understood that Mr. Goble has been ill, and that is the reason for the delay in his plans.

"The grand old man of Crockett County" stipulated in the terms of his gift that the proposed Memorial Grove trees should be set out somewhere in the new park area. This necessitated a hasty change in plans. Instead of being planted on the north hill, on the Louis Wilson farm above the Coon River, the trees will be set out on the brow of the east hill, which is included in the thirty acres donated by Mr. Goble.

A big parade, forming in the city hall square, and proceeding across the east bridge toward the new park, will officially open Arbor Day ceremonies at two o'clock tomorrow afternoon. Following an invocation by Rev. J. Medley Williams, the Cottonwood city band will—

We leaned there, side by side with our hands upon the desk, and read that newspaper story.

Doc tapped the paper with his forefinger. "I'll go on record as saying," he declared, "that this is the first thing Eli Goble ever gave away

Note the irony used here. The narrator assumes Doc is speaking metaphorically; he is, of course, being quite literal.

in his life—at least the first thing in which there wasn't some chance of his getting value received out of it. And I don't see what he can get out of this, except glory. . . . Eli doesn't care a rap for glory. Listen to Editor Nollins calling him, 'the grand old man of Crockett County.' That's because Eli holds a mortgage on the *Herald* building."

Two patients drifted in for examination. When I left, an hour later, I looked back to see Doctor Martindale sitting there in his swivel chair, a tired hulk, still reading the *Cottonwood Herald.*

At five-thirty in the morning, Old Doc was beating on my door. I arose, startled, and feeling nothing short of peritonitis* or breech delivery could have made him summon me so insistently.

---

peritonitis: inflammation of the membrane lining the wall of the abdominal cavity

---

He came into the hotel room and waited while I threw on my clothes. "What is it?" I asked, between splashes of cold water.

"We're going out and do a little digging," he said.

I nodded. "Appendectomy? Or what?"

"Nothing so unimportant," Doc replied. And his eyes looked as if he had been awake all night—red-rimmed and circled. . . . "Real digging. No one will know where we are. If Mrs. Gustafson takes a notion to sink and die while we're away, she'll have to sink and die." He said it with seeming brutality. I was still too sleepy to press him for more details, or wonder what it was all about.

But when we got out to the curbing in front of the hotel, and I glanced into the rear seat of Doc's car, there lay two spades, a scoop-shovel and a pickax.

I turned with an exclamation of astonishment.

"Get in," said Doc. And I did, without any more words. He drove down Main Street,

north on Kowa Avenue, and under the Burlington viaduct.* We seemed to be heading north of town. Two minutes later our car was making the Coon River bridge rattle and bang in every loose joint.

---

viaduct: several arches used to carry a road or railroad across a valley or over another road or railroad

---

"This is the Louis Wilson farm," said Doc. "Hm. I reckon we can turn here past the Cedar school, and drive down the lane past the timber."

At the furthest corner of the cornfield we climbed out, taking the shovels and ax with us. Doc was breathing hoarsely, but the strange pallor* had left his face. . . . His eyes were bright and intent; there was something almost furious in their gleam.

---

pallor: severe paleness

He led me through a fringe of oak timberland, skirting two brushy ravines, and coming out on a sloping knoll* where one solitary oak tree stood, stunted and twisted by many winds. The grass beneath our feet was coarse, tangled, flat-bladed. Native prairie sod, without a doubt. . . . Far away, a band of crows was circling over the river, cawing with faint and raucous* cries.

---

knoll: a small rounded hill
raucous: harsh; disorderly

"This is the north hill," said Doc. "There's the town."

It was a very high hill, this bald mound on which we stood. Beneath us the Coon River swung in a flat band of glistening brown.

The thin, brittle grass of the barren hill was tufted with hundreds of pale, lilac-pastel flowers. The blossoms grew short, fuzzy stems; the petals shaded from white to purple, with a heart of yellow in each flower.

"They're beautiful," I said, "I never saw anything like them before. What are they?"

"Wind-flowers. Easter flowers. Or I guess the more modern name is pasque-flower. Pretty things, aren't they? One of the earliest we have around here. . . . Well, I'm going to get busy."

Doc dropped the shovel he was carrying, and I was just as willing to relinquish the heavy load in my own arms. I went over and sat down against the gnarled oak tree, which was the only tree on all that bald, brownish hill. A million facts and statements and conjectures seemed boiling in my brain; I could make nothing out of them.

Before my eyes, Doc Martindale was behaving in a very strange manner. He was walking slowly in vague, indefinite circles, his eyes staring at the ground in front of him. Occasionally he would move up beyond the brow of the hill and sweep the surrounding area with his eyes. I had the strange notion that Doctor George Martindale, after unloading the sad story of his youth, had taken two days in going deliberately and completely insane.

He thrust a small piece of stick into the ground, moved away, surveyed the spot carefully, and then came back to set up another stick, several feet from the first. He repeated this process two more times. He now had an uneven rectangle, eight or ten feet long, marked at its corners by bits of stick. "We'll try it here," he said.

Without another word, he removed his coat, lifted the pickax, and sent its point into the ground.

I cried, "Wait a minute! Won't people down in the town see us up here?"

"They'll think we're cows or pigs," said Doc.

And, as I have said before, we were alone—out there in the thin sunshine of early morning. We dug silently. Neither of us spoke a word. After Doc had penetrated some two feet in depth, at one side of the rectangle, he moved out toward the middle of the space he had marked. I followed, with my shovel.

We had been digging for about ten minutes, when we began to find things.

"Murdered," said Doc.

We were finding them, picking out discolored relics from the rich earth where they had lain so long. Tibiae, ribs . . . phalanges . . . the rusty remains of an ancient revolver.

Doc straightened up, and spoke to me gently. His face was set and strained; it might have been cast in iron. "There's a sheet and a grain sack or two in the car," he said. "Will you go over and bring them?"

I was glad of the opportunity to get away for a few minutes. When I came back, Doc had most of the bones covered with his coat. The knees of his trousers were dark and earthy; he had been kneeling in the loose mold of the grave, picking out the smaller fragments.

"I want a witness," he said, shortly. "Take a look at this." From beneath the coat he withdrew a human skull and turned it slowly for me to see. There was a complete and noticeable fracture, such as might have been caused by a blow of a sharp ax. "The other is the same way," he added, and replaced the skull tenderly.

Then I spoke for the first time. "Can you identify them?"

"Easily," he said. "There's a pocket-piece, the revolver, and knives and things. . . . The pocket-piece is the best bet. It's engraved with Pa's name. Not corroded at all. I rubbed it up and could read the engraving."

Wisely, he made no attempt to identify or isolate the separate skeletons. The bones made awkward bundles, in the grain sacks. We worked slowly, carrying them and the shovels back to the car. I was too stunned by the grim reality to ask any questions. We went away and left that uneven black hole in the middle of the blooming wind-flowers.

Back in town, we went to Doc Martindale's garage, behind his little house on Omaha Street, and left the bundles there. Then we hurried to the office; fortunately there had been no phone calls at either house or office. It was after seven o'clock, yet I had no desire for breakfast.

Doc sat at his desk and thumbed through a stack of old letters and notebooks. "Clell Howard's living in Long Beach," he muttered. "Got his address somewhere. . . . And Eph Spokesman is with his niece out in Portland. I've got to send telegrams right away." Then, strangely enough, he seemed to discover me standing there. "You go around and look at Mrs. Gustafson and that greenstick fracture and the little Walker boy; tell them I'm busy on an emergency case. Don't say a word to anybody."

"I won't," I promised.

He said, "And be sure you don't forget the parade. It forms at 2 P.M., at the city hall square. You'll want to see that." And then he turned back to his rummaging.

I had all of the bedfast patients bandaged and dosed and sprayed and examined before 1:30 P.M. At two o'clock I was standing, with a group of pleasant and gossipy citizens, on the steps of the Cottonwood city hall. The triangular "square" was blooming with the gay sweaters and dresses of hundreds of school children who darted wildly underfoot, seething and yelling in a mad half-holiday.

At twenty minutes after two, the crowd was somewhat impatient. There had been a large turn-out; the Boy Scouts were there, and the members of the American Legion, chafing and shifting in line. There was even a huge truck, splashed with vivid bunting, on which were the grove memorial elms all ready to be set out, their dirt-encrusted roots sticking from beneath the scarlet shimmer of flags, like so many claws.

This crowd was waiting for Eli Goble, albeit waiting impatiently. If a man was so kind as to give away thirty acres of land, one could at least expect him to show up for the dedication.

It was almost two-thirty before a big Cadillac touring car slid around the corner by Phillips's oil station, and the crowds in the vicinity began desultory* hand-clapping. Yes, it was Eli Goble. I could see that bearded, skeleton shape sitting hunched in the rear seat, a Navajo blanket across his knees. His narrow-eyed son, vice-president of the bank, was driving.

---

desultory: occurring randomly

Some fortunate fate had directed me to take up my station on those steps, above the mass of children. For I had a clear and unobstructed view of Doc Martindale, accompanied by a fat, pink-faced man who seemed very nervous emerging from a dark stairway across the street.

I vaulted over the concrete railing beside me, and shouldered through the knotted humanity. Once or twice I had a quick glance at Doc and the pink-faced man, over the heads of the crowd. They were walking rapidly toward the corner where the Goble car was parked; the pink-faced man was drawing a folded paper from his pocket, and he seemed more nervous than ever.

We reached the corner simultaneously. A benign citizen, who wore a white silk badge, "Chairman," fluttering from his coat, was leaning at the side of the car, conversing with Eli Goble and his son.

"Daniel," said Doc Martindale.

The chairman turned.

"Get up on the city hall steps," Doc directed him, "and announce to the crowd that Mr. Goble's physician refuses to allow him to participate in the exercises. Then get them started with their parade."

Daniel began to stammer and sputter.

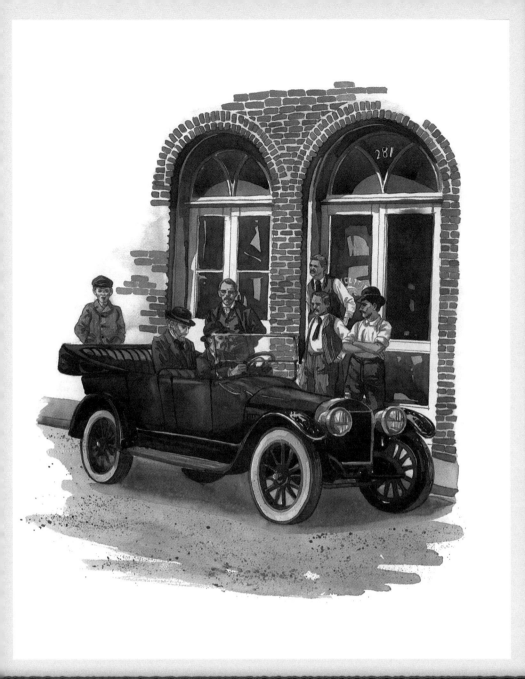

"Go 'long with you," ordered Doc, firmly. He opened the door of the back seat, and he and the pink-faced man slid in beside Eli Goble. And then Doc saw me standing there. "Get in the front seat, Dr. Patterson," he called, and before I knew it, I was sitting beside Vincent Goble, who was too excited even to bow.

"I don't understand this," he said importantly. "You're carrying things off with a very high hand, Doctor Martindale. It is my father's wish that—"

Doc's lips were thin and firm beneath his scraggly beard. "You keep your mouth shut, Vincent," he said. Vincent Goble gasped. "Drive around the corner on Queen Street, out of this crowd, and pull up at the curb."

The younger man's face was flaming with rage, but he obeyed the command. The Cadillac purred ahead, past the corner, past the alley, past the crowd. A block away it drew up beside the curb.

Vincent Goble and I swung around to face the trio in the back. Eli Goble sat in the middle, clutching and contracting his hands against the red triangles of his Navajo blanket.

"Go ahead, Ed," said Doctor Martindale.

The little pink-faced man gasped apologetically, and fluttered the folds of the paper in his hand. He began a whispered jumble of phrases: "As sheriff of Crockett County, it is my duty to place you, Eli Goble, under arrest. You are charged with the murder of Titus Martindale, and William Martindale, on or about the twenty-fourth of April, in the year 1861—"

Vincent Goble snarled. The old man still sat there, motionless except for the parchment hands which twisted in his lap. "Ain't true," he managed to whisper. "It—ain't true."

"You cowards!" cried his son. The banker's face was livid. "You'd devil the very life out of an old man with some crazy superstition like that! You'd—"

Doc Martindale said, "Drive up to the sheriff's office, Vincent. We want to talk things over."

"I won't! I—"

Ed Maxon, the sheriff, gulped fearfully. "Yes, Mr. Goble. That's right. Have to ask you to bring your father up to my office."

And so, we went. Vincent, muttering beneath his breath, Doc Martindale silent as a tomb, Ed Maxon twisting and rubbing a damp hand around his collar. And Eli Goble sitting there under the blanket, his eyes like black caverns, saying: "I—never done it. You'll see. I never done—that."

"You saw the gold at the house. And made up your mind—"

"No."

"You followed them out there on the east prairie. Or maybe you were lying there, waiting for them."

"I never—done it."

"Say, Doctor Martindale! If my father should have another heart attack and die while you're questioning him—"

"Now, Mr. Goble, you—"

"I'm a physician, Vincent. And Eli's my patient. I'll look out for him if he starts to faint. . . . Eli, you killed them from ambush."

"I never. Never did."

"Then you left the bodies in the wagon, took the team, and drove out to the north hill. It was a long drive—must have taken hours to get out there. But you figured that nobody ever went up there, and it was away from the beaten track, and would be a good place to hide the bodies."

"I—I—George, I'm an old man. I—"

"Martindale! You—"

"Sit down, Vincent, and shut up. I'm not going to fool with anybody today. . . . Let's take your pulse, Eli. . . . Hm. Guess you can stand it. All right. You buried them out on the north hill. Maybe you drove the wagon back and forth over the grave—an Indian trick. Trick you learned from the Sioux. And probably you scattered lots of grass and brush around."

"No. *No.*"

"Titus had his gun strapped on; you left them in the ground, just as they were. You didn't take anything out of the wagon except those buckskin bags. Then you drove over by Little Hell Slough. You left the team there, and skinned out. Took the gold somewhere and hid it probably."

"Ain't so. Lie."

"Then you laid low, and waited to join in the search. You were clever, Eli. You helped me search, too. Oh, how we searched! We even went right across that north hill. But we never saw anything that looked like a grave. . . . You kept it covered up. Eli. You were smart."

"Don't. . . . Don't talk so—I can't—"

"You let my father alone!—"

"Now, Mr. Goble. Please. Control yourself. Please—"

"You concluded that seven thousand dollars was a big fortune. Well, it was. Worth waiting for. So you enlisted in the army, took your chances—I'll give you credit for nerve there, Eli—and turned up after the war with that story about finding your relatives and your family property back in Ohio. Yes, you were smart."

"I never—never done it."

"Why did you give this park to the city?"

"Mmmmm. I—"

"The *Herald* carried that Arbor Day announcement, night before last. And right away you had a heart attack. And the next morning you came out with that gift to the city. *Provided*—"

"Vincent. Vincent. Make 'em let me—"

"I'll—"

"Here, hold him!"

"I've got him. Now, Mr. Goble, you'll have to sit down."

"Don't be a fool, Vincent. This is true—all true. It's taken me sixty years to find out, but I've found out. . . . You gave that park to the city of Cottonwood, Eli Goble *provided* that they set out the memorial grove over there, on the east hill, instead of the north hill. You didn't want anybody digging on the north hill, did you? It had never occurred to you to buy Louis Wilson's farm, so there wouldn't be a chance of people digging that ground up."

"No. . . . Don't talk so, George! . . . Old. I'm an old an'—"

"Well, it was the first thing you ever gave away, in your life. And it set me to thinking. I thought, 'Why didn't Eli want that memorial grove planted up there?' And then, I began to understand things. I went up there this morning. Doctor Patterson was with me—I have a witness to what I am now about to relate. He saw me dig; he saw me find things. I found *them,* Eli."

Vincent Goble was slumped forward, his head buried in his hands. Eli sat there in the sheriff's big chair, staring across the table. He seemed to be looking squarely through the opposite wall.

"They were murdered, Eli. Their skulls had been broken. A heavy, sharp blow at the back of each skull. I found them."

The old man's lips were gray and rubbery. He whispered, "No, I never done it. Can't prove it was me."

"A hatchet, Eli. Someone had thrown a hatchet—or maybe two hatchets, in quick succession. They were sitting on that wagon board, in the bright moonlight. It would have been easy for anyone who could throw a tomahawk."

Doc fumbled in the breast pocket of his coat, and brought out three folded squares of yellow paper. "I'll read to you all," he said calmly, "three telegrams. The first one I sent myself, early this morning, to Clell Howard, in Long Beach, California, and to Ephraim

Note the situational irony employed here—the murderer helped search for his victims.

Ironically, Goble's atypical generosity is his undoing.

Note the appropriateness of Goble's punishment—he must give away a million dollars to be used for saving lives.

Spokesman in Portland, Oregon. . . . Remember those names, Eli? . . . Clell was mayor here, once. And Eph Spokesman—everybody knew him. Here's my telegram: 'Please reply by wire completely at my expense. During the old days at Cottonwood, what man was skillful at throwing a knife or hatchet? Search your recollection and reply at once.'

"Here's the first reply I got. It came from Ephraim Spokesman's niece. Came about eleven o'clock. You can read it for yourself, gentlemen. It says, 'Uncle Eph very sick but says man named Goble was only one who could throw a hatchet. Wants to hear full details why you ask.'

"Along about eleven-forty-five, I got a telegram from Clell Howard. Here it is: 'Hello old neighbor regards to you. Am almost ninety but recall perfectly how I lost five dollars betting Eli Goble couldn't stick hatchet ten times in succession in a big tree by Halsey blacksmith shop.' "

The room was perfectly still, except for the hoarse sputtering in Eli Goble's throat. "No," he whispered tremulously. "No."

Doc Martindale pointed to the further corner of the dusty old room. There was a table, which none of us had noticed before, and on that table was a white sheet, rumpled and bulky. . . . "Eli," said Doc, quietly. "They're over there. In the corner."

The aged man stiffened in his chair. His back arched up, the shoulders quaking; his claw hands seemed wrenching a chunk of wood from the table in front of him.

"Father!" his son cried.

Eli Goble shook his head, and dropped back in his chair, his deep-set eyes dull with a flat, blue light. "The dead," he whispered. "They found me. . . . They're in this room. I done it. I killed them. Titus and Bill. Yes. Yes."

Vincent Goble dropped down, his head buried in his arms, and began to sob—big,

gulping sobs. The sheriff twisted nervously in his seat.

"George. You—you gonna send me to—prison? You gonna have them—hang me? I'm old . . . I done it. Yes."

Doc Martindale cleared his throat. "Yes, you are old, Eli. Lot older than I am. It's too late, now, to do anything about it. I told my mother I'd get the man, and—But I can't see what good it would do, now, to send you to jail or even try you for murder."

Sheriff Maxon wiped his forehead. "The law," he said shrilly, "the law must take its course! Eli Goble, you must—"

"No," said Old Doc derisively. "I'm running this show, Ed. Without me, without my testimony and the case I've built up, there isn't any show against Eli. I won't prosecute him, or furnish evidence."

Maxon shook his head and bit his lips.

"How much is your father worth?" asked Doc of Vincent Goble.

The banker lifted his face, on which the weary, baffled tears were still wet. "Couple of million, I guess."

"All yours," whispered Eli. "All yours. . . ."

"Maybe," Doc nodded. "Seven thousand dollars. Quite a nest egg in those days. Like fifty thousand, now. Or even more. . . . No, gentlemen. Money won't do me any good. It can't bring back Titus and my father. But it can still do good. Yes."

Eli Goble's eyes had closed, like dark windows on which ragged curtains had been drawn. "I've seen 'em—I've seen 'em. Always. Since I got old—they come back. . . . I had to give in. Yes."

"You'll go home," said Doc. "I'll give you something to put you to sleep. Then, after you have a little rest and get your strength back, you'll have a lawyer up at your house. . . . You will give, to this county in which you live, one million dollars for the purpose of founding and endowing a modern hospital, where every inhabitant can secure the best medical and surgical attention, free of charge. How does that sound?"

Head still buried in his arms, Vincent Goble nodded. His father had opened his eyes and was shivering, still staring through the blank wall ahead of him. "Yes. Anything. . . . I give—anything. But take me away. I want to go—home. . . . I'm old. I don't want to stay in—this room. I don't want to stay with—*them*."

After Eli Goble was in bed, and asleep, Doc and I came out into the damp warmth of the spring afternoon. Martindale looked ten years older than he did the day before. "After this," he said, "after everything is taken care of, I'll let things go. . . . You look after the practice beginning next Monday."

Our feet sounded flat and talkative, echoing on the long sidewalk. "One thing," I said. "I can't understand how you found the place. I can see how you reasoned out the rest—about the grove and about Eli Goble's not wanting the trees planted up there. But how did you know where to dig? We could have been up there for days, turning the soil."

"Wind-flowers," he said quietly. "They were scattered all over that hill. Beautiful, like you said. . . . But I knew enough to dig where there were no wind-flowers. The grass on that hill looked pretty much alike, all over, but there weren't any flowers growing in that place I marked off. Those little purple flowers are funny. They grow on native soil. You can't get them to grow where the sod has ever been turned."

About the Author

Mackinlay Kantor's (1904-1977) boyhood memories of Webster, Iowa, furnished him with rich material for his writing. The sturdy values of small-town life infused Kantor's writing with a sense of idealism and a touch of nostalgia for better, simpler days. Some critics have been quick to classify Kantor's writing as sentimental and didactic. Regardless of this criticism, Kantor still holds an important place in the development of the modern historical novel in America.

When Kantor was seventeen, his mother recruited his help in writing and editing the Webster newspaper. This internship kindled Kantor's writing ambitions and gave him needed experience in what he called "the daily necessity of writing words, words, words—handling them and managing them by the thousands, trying to learn how to put them together." But success came slowly. For many years, the struggling writer held down numerous odd jobs to support his family while he wrote and researched. The freshness and immediacy in Kantor's narrative style, however, gave his fiction the universal appeal that eventually insured his success.

Although Kantor is not a Christian writer, his best characters are often sincere, decent citizens with traditional American hopes and dreams. His most convincing characters learn the meaning of responsibility and sacrifice. Kantor's goal was to skillfully write realistic moral lessons that were entertaining.

Yet If His Majesty, Our Sovereign Lord

Anonymous

To most Englishmen in 1625, when "Yet If His Majesty" was written, there could be no more shocking irony than to situate an important person in a dishonorable place. The monarch referred to in the title and first line is either James I, who died in 1625, or his son Charles I, who succeeded him.

Yet if his majesty, our sovereign lord,
Should of his own accord
Friendly himself invite,
And say, "I'll be your guest tomorrow night,"
How should we stir ourselves, call and command   5
All hands to work! "Let no man idle stand.
Set me fine Spanish tables in the hall,
See they be fitted all;
Let there be room to eat,
And order taken that there want* no meat.   10   *want:* lack
See every sconce* and candlestick made bright,   *sconce:* wall-hung candleholder
That without tapers* they may give a light.   *tapers:* candles
Look to the presence:* are the carpets spread,   *presence:* throne area
The dais* o'er the head,   *dais:* canopy
The cushions in the chair,   15
And all the candles lighted on the stair?
Perfume the chambers, and in any case
Let each man give attendance in his place."
Thus if the king were coming would we do,
And 'twere good reason too;   20
For 'tis a duteous thing
To show all honor to an earthly king,
And, after all our travail and our cost,
So he be pleased, to think no labor lost.
But at the coming of the King of Heaven   25
All's set at six and seven:*   *set at six and seven:* in confusion
We wallow in our sin;
Christ cannot find a chamber in the inn.
We entertain him always like a stranger,
And, as at first, still* lodge him in the manger.   30   *still:* continually

"Yet If His Majesty, Our Sovereign Lord"

Christmas scenes of the divine Babe in a manger generally miss the point of the Biblical narrative. This poem shows discernment of the situation's irony and the continuing irony of our inhospitality toward Christ.

Notice how the poem gains by concreteness and specific detail. It gives us a clear picture of an English noble's house of the sixteenth and seventeenth centuries.

The ending perhaps alludes to Revelation 3:20 (note the ironic contrast between 3:20 and 3:21a). The point is that we, while condemning the innkeeper, do no better ourselves with the advantage of superior knowledge—a sad paradox.

The word *entertain* in the next-to-last line combines the meanings of (1) show hospitality toward (ironic here) and (2) treat. Notice the hyperbole in lines 11-12: to polish the brass so that it will give light even without candles.

Application

The two works in this lesson provide two valuable lessons for us: first, the great debt we owe to a forgiving Saviour who can not only cleanse us from sin but also free us from the burden of guilt; and second, the potential ingratitude of those who have received such favors. Discuss with the students how Christians often show ingratitude to the Saviour. Does the burden of guilt at times cause us to disbelieve God's willingness to forgive? Is that lack of trust one form of ingratitude? How can we protect ourselves from such attitudes?

About the Story and Poem

1. How is Eli Goble's "gift" to the community ironic?
2. At what point in the story do you begin to suspect Eli Goble?
3. Are you satisfied with the resolution of the story? Why or why not?
4. What is the point of the poem?
5. Both James I and Charles I, either of which could be the monarch referred to in the poem, antagonized their subjects. How does this dissatisfaction with the monarch add to the final irony of the poem?

 About the Story and Poem

1. *The gift is inconsistent with Goble's miserly character.*

2. *Answers may vary; students should, however, be able to point to a specific quotation from the story that aroused their suspicions.*

3. *Answers may vary; see Analysis section for further discussion.*

4. *We treat Christ little better than did the innkeeper in Bethlehem, even though we know who He is.*

5. *We honor even antagonistic earthly monarchs but fail to honor the perfect King of kings.*

FURTHER HELPS

Resource

"The Christian Teaching of English," Chapter 6 from *Christian Education: Its Mandate and Mission* (Greenville, S.C.: BJU Press, 1992).

Part III
The Forms of Literature

Exploring literature is a little like taking a journey to see the world. To understand what you see, you need a guidebook and a map. In Parts I and II you learned how to recognize literature by its special features and learned something about these features. You were given a guidebook. Now, to find your way around in literature, you will also need to be able to identify its common types or **genres.** That will require a map.

Let us suppose that we have before us a map of the world of literature we are about to explore. It is a recent map showing the unchanging natural features—the major land masses and their mountain ranges and great rivers. It also shows the artificial political boundaries that frequently and unpredictably change. The major types of literature are like continents and their natural subdivisions and bordering islands. They represent timeless categories of human experience and therefore do not change. The lesser types of literature may come and go, expand and diminish, like national boundaries or volcanic isles. They reflect particular national cultures or changing fashions within a culture. The once-popular *verse epistle* does not appear on a modern map of literature. Most noticeable is the absence of the long narrative poems: the *epic* and the *romance*. New forms such as the *dramatic monologue* and the *novel* have arisen to take their place.

Circling our imaginary globe horizontally is an equator dividing the world of literature into the northern and southern hemispheres of **poetry** and **prose.**

PREPARATION

The Forms of Literature

Introduction

Overview

This final major section introduces the students to the major types of genres. This section will not only help the students identify the various characteristics of each specific genre but will also provide them ample opportunity to apply what they have learned in the first two sections.

DISCUSSION

Introduction

Draw the students' attention to the analogy in the opening sentence of the essay. All of us have heard that reading is a good, inexpensive way to "travel." Through reading we can explore distant lands that would be impossible to actually visit. Ask the students for some examples of places they have "visited" through literature. Remind them of some of the locations from the stories covered thus far in this text: "Dawn in the Forest"; "The Spider and the Wasp" (tropics/southern U.S.); "All Day I Hear," "maggie and milly and molly and may" (seashore); "The Leak" (Atlantic Ocean); "The Fruits of Toil" (Newfoundland); "Snow-Bound" (New Eng-

land); "An Old-Fashioned Iowa Christmas"; "The Return of the Rangers" (Canada); "Cupid's Arrows," "A Germ Destroyer" (India); "Pigeon Feathers" (farm); "Earth" (outer space); "At the Aquarium"; "The Grave Grass Quivers" (western U.S.).

Analysis

Have the students read the essay together in class. To help the students get the most out of the geographic analogy, you may want to use the transparency provided in **Appendix P: The Forms of Literature I.**

If students find that the geographical analogy is a bit difficult, you may want to use **Appendix Q: The Forms of Literature II** for clarification.

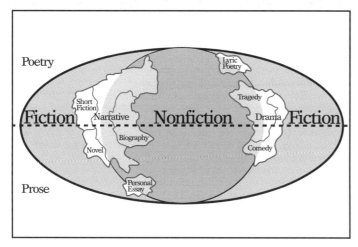

Circling the globe vertically is a meridian dividing it into the eastern and western hemispheres of **fiction** and **nonfiction.** Where these lines intersect on

Application

Scripture uses all of the genres mentioned in the introductory essay. Have the students identify examples of various genres illustrated in the Bible—the lyric poetry of Psalms and Isaiah, for example, or the narratives of Ruth, Jonah, and Esther. Discuss how each example reflects the characteristics of its particular genre.

the one side is a large land mass: the continent of *narrative*. Its upper half is within the hemisphere of poetry; its lower half, within that of prose. Literature contains both narrative poetry and narrative prose. The eastern side of the continent is within the hemisphere of nonfiction; the western, within that of fiction. Both narrative poetry and narrative prose may be either fictional or nonfictional. Along the eastern coast, extending above and below the equator, is the territory of biography. A nonfictional genre, it includes both poetry and prose. On the western side below the equator is the territory of the novel, a long fictional narrative in prose. Bordering on the novel to the north is the province of short fiction. It is divided by the equator, for short fictional narrative may be in either poetry or prose.

To the south of the mainland, in the territorial waters of narrative, is the large island of the *personal essay*. Though by definition autobiographical, it may include imaginary characters and incidents. It therefore lies on the meridian of fiction and nonfiction.

On the opposite side of the globe where the meridian intersects the equator is another large land mass: the continent of *drama*. Like narrative, drama includes both fiction and nonfiction, poetry and prose. The continent is bisected not only horizontally into poetic and prosaic drama by the equator and vertically into fictional and nonfictional drama by the meridian but also diagonally into the provinces of tragedy and comedy. Tragedies, plays ending unhappily, and comedies, plays ending happily, may be either fictional or nonfictional and in either poetry or prose.

Off the northern tip of the continent, in the territorial waters of drama, is the large island of *lyric poetry*. It lies on the meridian, for like a personal essay a lyric poem may contain fictional as well as nonfictional elements. As a personal expression it is in poetry what a personal essay is in prose. Its relation to drama may be unclear until we think of it as a speech delivered to an audience (the reader) by an actor alone on stage representing a character (the author). It is a confidential speech by means of which we "listen in" on an individual's private thoughts and enter his mental world.

The Bible provides divinely inspired examples of most of the main literary types. But some qualifications must be made. I and II Samuel may loosely be called biographical, as well as Ruth, Esther, and Jonah, for they focus on the lives of individuals and unfold their careers. The biographical narrative has gaps, however, for its goal is not so much the portrayal of a human being as the revealing of the person and work of God. The Gospel narratives reveal not so much the earthly life of a human being as His redeeming work as the Son of God. Drama is loosely represented in Scripture by the book of Job, of which the greater part is dialogue between Job and his three friends. The book is not intended for action, however, and the dialogue is set in a narrative frame. We approach the genre of the personal essay in Ecclesiastes and in the letters of Paul and others in the New Testament. Ecclesiastes, however, is mostly in poetry; and the epistles are not so much personal expressions of their authors as instructions to the churches. Biblical prose fiction consists of embedded allegorical stories—parables, fables, and analogies—rather than the fully formed tales of most artistic fiction. But the Scriptures abound with artfully shaped nonfictional narratives in prose and verse. The story of Joseph, as well as those of Ruth, Esther, and Jonah mentioned earlier, is a masterpiece of nonfictional narrative art. Psalms, Lamentations, and other Old Testament books contain lyric poems of incomparable beauty and power of expression.

These categories of literature, then, may be said to apply broadly to the Scriptures. Though the Bible is not merely a work of the human mind, it does show the larger contours of human literature, for it mirrors human life, the subject of literature. Genre classification is especially useful in the study of non-Biblical literature. All the genres mentioned above, with the exception of the novel and the drama, have in fact already appeared in the preceding units. In the remaining units we shall examine works of literature as examples of their genres, drawing on the content of the earlier sections when applicable.

7

UNIT SEVEN

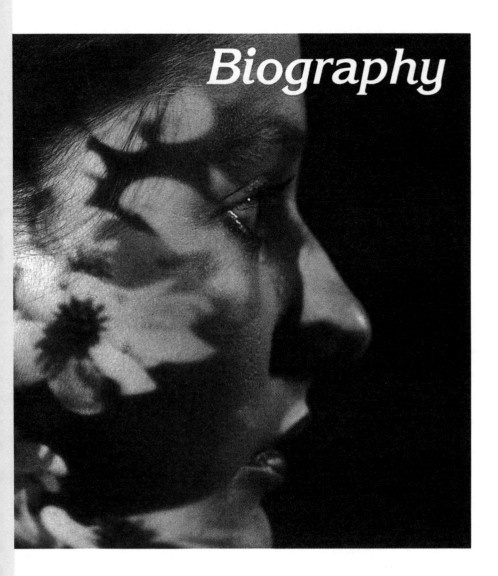

Biography

The word **biography** comes from two Greek words: *bios,* life, and *graphein,* to write. A full-scale biography is the history of the life of a person. It may be written by a contemporary of the subject or by a noncontemporary. In either case, good biography is written from a critical but usually sympathetic point of view and is artistically shaped. It often has a moral purpose.

When the subject of the biography is the writer himself, we are in the special area of **autobiography,** literally self-biography. The autobiographer offers an interpretation of his own life for the instruction or amusement of his reader or sometimes in defense of his reputation. Some public figures, such as Sir Winston Churchill, compile their personal recollections for publication after their deaths as *memoirs.* Memoirs usually focus on events and personalities of the author's public life rather than on the author's private self. They allow a less connected story line and more gossipy trivia than formal autobiography. However, their purpose is often of equal seriousness: that of self-explanation and self-justification. Even less connected than memoirs, but more strictly chronological, are the entries of a *diary* or *journal.* These are daily records of happenings and impressions of an individual, written to be read by him alone. The diary is usually more intimate than a journal. The journal is more likely to be kept for a specific professional purpose: for example, notes to be later worked up into a manuscript for publication.

Though certain Biblical narratives may loosely be called biographical, their scope is wider than a biography and their purpose extends beyond the revelation of a single human being. The Gospels, for example, are not so much biographies of Jesus as historical testimony: "the record that God gave of His Son" (I John 5:10). The book of Acts is not so much a biographical account of the ministries of Peter and Paul as a record of the acts of the Holy Spirit after the ascension of Christ. Certainly, it is true that none of the Biblical authors wrote to reveal himself. Paul used biographical summary (Gal. 1:13—2:21) and personal anecdote (II Cor. 12:2-4) in arguing his points, but these passages are stripped of personal detail not related to their purpose. Nehemiah is perhaps the most autobiographical of the Biblical books. It gives a rather personal account of what God put into the heart of its author to do and enabled him to accomplish (7:5; 13:30-31). And yet its style is closer to that of Biblical chronicle than to what we think of as autobiography today.

Biblical authors are the most self-effacing of writers, for their purpose is to reveal God, not themselves. But they do give fascinating glimpses of human personality and character in the process. The hallmark of great biography, illuminating detail, is everywhere evident in Scripture. What could serve better to emphasize the guilt of Saul and the certainty of God's judgment than the bleating of the sheep and the lowing of the oxen wickedly preserved by Saul (I Sam. 15:14)? What could better suggest the character of Daniel than his kneeling in prayer before the open window "as . . . aforetime" or the personality of Peter than his having to be roughly awakened by the angel

PREPARATION

Biography Introduction

Overview

This introduction helps the students understand the distinguishing marks of biographical and autobiographical writing. Although most Biblical narratives can only loosely be called biographical, their illuminating details give fascinating glimpses of human personality. This detail, everywhere evident in Scripture, is the key ingredient of a successful biography.

DISCUSSION

Introduction

Ask the students about biographies or autobiographies they have read, and have them share information they found interesting. For example, what made them read the work? Were they interested in the person or in the era in which the person lived? Did they feel that the book was well written? If so, what kept their interest? Did the book seem to have a greater purpose than simply providing information about a specific person? If so, what point did they feel the writer was trying to make?

Analysis

Read the introduction in class. To reinforce the differences among biography, autobiography, memoirs, journals, and diaries, use the examples that the students presented in the introductory discussions. You could also bring examples of each type of writing to class and have the students read them aloud. See also **Appendix R: Unit 7 Introduction Worksheet.** Following are several well-written works from which you or your students could choose excerpts to share with the class:

Biography

1. *Alone* by William Manchester. This is volume 2 of the three-part biography of Winston Churchill titled *The Last Lion.* Volume 2 cov-

the night before his scheduled execution and told to gird himself and put on his shoes (Acts 12:7-8)? What could better show the confusion of the disciples and the tender (and amused) regard of the Lord for them when, after His resurrection, He ate "a piece of broiled fish and of an honeycomb" to prove He had a real body (Luke 24:41-42)?

The basic unit of biography is the *anecdote,* a narrated memorable incident from the life of an important person. Autobiography draws its interest largely from the *personal anecdote,* an incident recollected by the author. The success of *Reader's Digest* and other popular periodicals depends largely on the universal appeal of the anecdote—for most of us are socially curious and find pleasure in reading about the doings of others. We also look for wisdom and inspiration in real-life stories of unusual courage and resourcefulness.

The following selections describe memorable days in the lives of their subjects. After you have read and discussed them, you may wish to share some examples from your own reading that your classmates might enjoy. Or you may wish to write an autobiographical anecdote of your own.

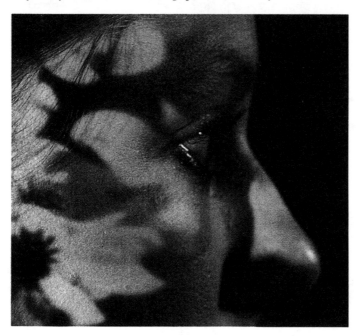

ers the years just before the outbreak of World War II, when the leaders of Western Europe ostracized Churchill as a "warmonger" and touted Hitler as a "gifted politician."

2. *C. T. Studd* by Norman Grubb. This is the biography of the gifted athlete from Cambridge who became a powerful force in opening China to the gospel in the late 1800s and early 1900s.

3. *The Triumph of Truth: A Life of Martin Luther* by Jean Henri Merle D'Aubigné, translated by Henry White. This lively biography testifies of the courage and faith of one of the greatest leaders of the Reformation (available from BJU Press).

4. *Lives* by Plutarch. This work, by one of the earliest noted biographers, includes biographical sketches of many famous historical figures. The one about Julius Caesar is included in this unit (pages 214-21).

5. *For God and His People: Ulrich Zwingli and the Swiss Reformation* by Jean Henri Merle D'Aubigné, translated by Henry White. This biography displays Zwingli's courage and heroism in the face of great opposition (available from BJU Press).

Autobiography

1. *The Little Woman* by Gladys Aylward as told to Christine Hunter. This is the autobiography of a courageous missionary to China during the Boxer Rebellion.

2. *Grace Abounding to the Chief of Sinners* by John Bunyan. This is the spiritual autobiography of the man who gave us *The Pilgrim's Progress.*

3. *Tortured for His Faith* by Haralan Popov. This autobiography vividly illustrates a courageous pastor's faith during his thirteen years of torture and imprisonment in the Soviet Union.

4. *Personal Narrative* by Jonathan Edwards. This is taken from the eight-volume work titled *The Works of President Edwards.* It traces Edwards's own spiritual awakening to the gospel of Christ.

Application

Discuss with the students the contrast between Biblical writers (and most writers of earlier centuries) and many twentieth- and twenty-first-century authors. Point out that writing has

"The Day the Dam Broke"

OBJECTIVE

The students will be able to

• Analyze how irony is used to create humor.

similes

allusion

metaphor

FURTHER HELPS

Additional activities

1. Read other humorous Thurber tales. "The Night the Bed Fell" is a good complement to "The Day the Dam Broke." Note that like the story in this text, the title is ironic: no bed falls in "The Night the Bed Fell." Be sure to pre-read any excerpts before reading them in class to make sure they are appropriate.

2. Read one of Thurber's fables, such as "The Little Girl and the Wolf" or "The Princess and the Tin Box." Discuss how they differ from "normal" fables.

The Day the Dam Broke

James Thurber

James Thurber published hundreds of humorous stories and essays drawing on his own experience. Many are critical of society, though usually in a playful way. Some are sheer fun.

The fact that we were all as safe as kittens under a cookstove did not assuage* in the least the fine despair and the grotesque desperation which seized upon the residents of the East Side when the cry spread like a grass fire that the dam had given way. Some of the most dignified, staid, cynical, and clear-thinking men in town abandoned their wives, stenographers, homes, and offices and ran east. There are few alarms in the world more terrifying than "The dam has broken!" There are few persons capable of stopping to reason when that clarion cry strikes upon their ears, even persons who live in towns no nearer than five hundred miles to a dam.

assuage: diminish

The Columbus, Ohio, broken-dam rumor began, as I recall it, about noon of March 12, 1913. High Street, the main canyon of trade, was loud with the placid hum of business and the buzzing of placid businessmen arguing, computing, wheedling, offering, refusing, compromising. Darius Conningway, one of the foremost corporation lawyers in the Middle West, was telling the Public Utilities Commission in the language of Julius Caesar that they might as well try to move the Northern star as to move him. Other men were making their little boasts and their little gestures. Suddenly somebody began to run.

It may be that he had simply remembered, all of a moment, an engagement to meet his wife, for which he was now frightfully late. Whatever it was, he ran east on Broad Street (probably toward the Maramor Restaurant, a favorite place for a man to meet his wife). Somebody else began to run, perhaps a newsboy in high spirits. Another man, a portly gentleman of affairs, broke into a trot. Inside of ten minutes, everybody on High Street, from the Union Depot to the Courthouse, was running. A loud mumble gradually crystallized into the dread word "dam." "The dam has broke!" The fear was put into words by a little old lady in an electric,* or by a traffic cop, or by a small boy: nobody knows who, nor does it now really matter. Two thousand people were abruptly in full flight. "Go east!" was the cry that arose—east away from the river, east to safety. "Go east! Go east! Go east!"

electric: electric automobile

Black streams of people flowed eastward down all the streets leading in that direction; these streams, whose headwaters were in the drygoods stores, office buildings, harness shops, movie theaters, were fed by trickles of housewives, children, servants, dogs, and cats, slipping out of the houses past which the main streams flowed, shouting and screaming. People ran out leaving fires burning and food

---

become increasingly myopic. "Self-expression" has become as important or even more important than communication. A Christian writer's first goal is not to express himself but to glorify God. This does not mean, of course, that personal experience is unimportant. Our experiences can, if used correctly, provide material that can benefit others. The works included in this unit, whether humorous or serious, have universal appeal. They also provide wisdom and inspiration.

 Review with the students the basic unit of biography, the anecdote. Then have each student write two or three paragraphs narrating a memorable incident from his own life. The anecdote can be serious or humorous. Regardless

of the tone, however, encourage the student to use the incident to make a valuable point. See **Writing Rubric 7-1: An Autobiographical Anecdote.**

PREPARATION

"The Day the Dam Broke"

Overview

This is only one of Thurber's many stories that both entertain and poke fun at society. Although the tone of the essay is playful, it does point out how easily the most "dignified, staid, and clear-thinking" people can be seized with panic (or any other emotion) in a crowd.

DISCUSSION

Introduction

Ask the students whether they have ever been in a crowd at the time an unusual incident occurred. If so, have them share their experiences and observations with the class. For example, some may have been in communities struck by tornadoes or particularly vicious storms. What were the reactions of the people? Was panic evident? Were there any deeds of heroism? Others may have been in situations in which people, like those in Thurber's essay, simply imagined they were in danger. Was the source of the chaos ever discovered? If so, what was it?

cooking and doors wide open. I remember, however, that my mother turned out all the fires and that she took with her a dozen eggs and two loaves of bread. It was her plan to make Memorial Hall, just two blocks away, and take refuge somewhere in the top of it, in one of the dusty rooms where war veterans met and where old battle flags and stage scenery were stored. But the seething throngs shouting, "Go east!" drew her along and the rest of us with her. When grandfather regained full consciousness, at Parsons Avenue, he turned upon the retreating mob like a vengeful prophet and exhorted the men to form ranks and stand off the Rebel dogs, but at length he, too, got the idea that the dam had broken and, roaring "Go east!" in his powerful voice, he caught up in one arm a small child and in the other a slight clerkish man of perhaps forty-two and we slowly began to gain on those ahead of us.

A scattering of firemen, policemen, and army officers in dress uniforms—there had been a review* at Fort Hayes, in the northern part of town—added color to the surging billows of people. "Go east!" cried a little child in a piping voice, as she ran past a porch on which drowsed a lieutenant-colonel of infantry. Used to quick decisions, trained to immediate obedience, the officer bounded off the porch and, running at full tilt, soon passed the child, bawling, "Go east!" The two of them emptied rapidly the houses of the little street they were on. "What is it? "What is it?" demanded a fat, waddling man who intercepted the colonel. The officer dropped behind and asked the little child what it was. "The dam has broke!" gasped the girl. "The dam has broke!" roared the colonel. "Go east! Go east!" He was soon leading, with the exhausted child in his arms, a fleeing company of three hundred persons who had gathered around him from livingrooms, shops, garages, backyards, and basements.

review: ceremonial presentation of troops

Nobody has ever been able to compute with any exactness how many people took part in the great rout of 1913, for the panic, which extended from the Winslow Bottling Works in the south end to Clintonville, six miles north, ended as abruptly as it began and the bobtail and ragtag and velvet-gowned groups of refugees melted away and slunk home, leaving the streets peaceful and deserted. The shouting, weeping, tangled evacuation of the city lasted not more than two hours in all. Some few people got as far as Reynoldsburg, twelve miles away; fifty or more reached the Country Club, eight miles away; most others gave up, exhausted, or climbed trees in Franklin Park, four miles out. Order was restored and fear dispelled finally by means of militiamen riding about in motor lorries bawling through megaphones: "The dam has *not* broken!" At first this tended only to add to the confusion and increase the panic, for many stampedes thought the soldiers were bellowing "The dam has now broken!" thus setting an official seal of authentication on the calamity.

All the time, the sun shone quietly and there was nowhere any sign of oncoming waters. A visitor in an airplane, looking down on the straggling, agitated masses of people below, would have been hard put to it to divine a reason for the phenomenon. It must have inspired, in such an observer, a peculiar kind of terror, like the sight of the *Marie Celeste,* abandoned at sea, its galley fires peacefully burning, its tranquil decks bright in the sunlight.

An aunt of mine, Aunt Edith Taylor, was in a movie theater on High Street, when, over and above the sound of the piano in the pit (a W. S. Hart picture was being shown), there rose the steadily increasing tromp of running feet. Persistent shouts rose above the tromping. An elderly man, sitting near my aunt, mumbled something, got out of his seat, and went up the aisle at a dogtrot. This started everybody.

simile, allusion, metaphor

Situational and dramatic irony: The lieutenant-colonel believes and obeys a little girl.

Irony: Initial attempts to calm the panic cause it to increase.

allusion

Resources

Charles S. Holmes, *The Clocks of Columbus: The Literary Career of James Thurber* (New York: Atheneum, 1972).

James Thurber, *Fables for Our Time and Famous Poems Illustrated* (New York: Harper-Collins Publishers, 1983).

James Thurber, *Further Fables for Our Time* (Simon and Schuster, 1978).

James Thurber, *My Life and Hard Times* (New York: HarperCollins Publishers, 1999).

Richard C. Tobias, *The Art of James Thurber* (Ohio: Ohio University Press, 1969).

Analysis

Thurber's essay might also be called a humorous anecdote. Much of the humor in the essay is created by irony. Notice that Thurber re-creates the situation in a way that highlights its paradoxical nature. The panic of the "Great Run," for example, is not brought about by the public outcry "The dam has broken!" but rather by someone running on the sidewalk. The fact that people jumped to the conclusion that there was danger is ironic. As Thurber points out, there are more plausible guesses about why someone might break into a run than that a dam has broken. The person could merely have remembered a forgotten appointment. Or perhaps he was simply "a newsboy in high spirits." These observations point out how ludicrous the

situation is. Notice, too, Thurber's description of his family's flight. His mother very logically collects food, turns off the appliances, and thinks through where she will "take refuge." All this rational planning becomes ridiculous in light of the irrational circumstances. After discussing these examples, see if the students can point out any other examples of irony.

The humor created by the paradoxical nature of the essay also allows Thurber to make a valuable point without offending. Thurber, of course, was having fun when he wrote his essay. But his playful tone was valuable as a teaching tool as well. We can glean a bit of wisdom from the essay. We see, for example, the dangers of jumping to conclusions, the influence of a crowd, and even the pitfalls of taking

ourselves too seriously (as in the case of Dr. Mallory). And all this is presented in such a lighthearted way that we actually enjoy the lessons.

Irony: A woman yells "Fire!" while townsfolk are running from (nonexistent) water.

Remind the students that the story is set in the days of silent movies. Note also the ironic choice of music played by the girl to accompany the film— ironic in light of what is happening outside the theater.

allusion

Note that people are running even though they have not heard the flood rumor. You may wish to comment on aspects of human nature that influence people to join a crowd or a mob.

allusion

In an instant the audience was jamming the aisle. "Fire!" shouted a woman who always expected to be burned up in a theater, but now the shouts outside were louder and coherent. "The dam has broke!" cried somebody. "Go east!" screamed a small woman in front of my aunt. And east they went, pushing and shoving and clawing, knocking women and children down, emerging finally into the street, torn and sprawling. Inside the theater, Bill Hart was calmly calling some desperado's bluff and the brave girl at the piano played "Row! Row! Row!" loudly. Outside, men were streaming across the Statehouse yard, others were climbing trees, a woman managed to get onto the "These Are My Jewels" statue, whose bronze figures of Sherman, Stanton, Grant, and Sheridan watched with cold unconcern the going to pieces of the capital city.

"I ran south to State Street, east on State to Third, south on Third to Town, and out east on Town," my Aunt Edith has written me. "A tall spare woman with grim eyes and a determined chin ran past me down the middle of the street. I was still uncertain as to what was the matter, in spite of all the shouting. I drew up alongside the woman with some effort, for although she was in her late fifties, she had a beautiful easy running form and seemed to be in excellent condition. 'What is it?' I puffed. She gave me a quick glance and then looked ahead again, stepping up her pace a trifle. 'Don't ask me, ask God!' she said.

"When I reached Grant Avenue, I was so spent that Dr. H. R. Mallory—you remember Dr. Mallory, the man with the white beard who looks like Robert Browning?—well, Dr. Mallory, whom I had drawn away from at

Application

Have the students read aloud in class the anecdotes they have written describing a humorous incident from their imagination or experience. (See "About the Essay" question 4.)

the corner of Fifth and Town, passed me. 'It's got us!' he shouted, and I felt sure that whatever it was *did* have us, for you know what conviction Dr. Mallory's statements have always carried. I didn't know at the time what he meant, but I found out later. There was a boy behind him on roller-skates, and Dr. Mallory mistook the swishing of the skates for the sound of rushing water. He eventually reached the Columbus School for Girls, at the corner of Parsons Avenue and Town Street, where he collapsed, expecting the cold frothing waters of the Scioto to sweep him into oblivion. The boy on skates swirled past him and Dr. Mallory realized for the first time what he had been running from. Looking up the street, he could see no signs of water, but nevertheless, after resting a few minutes, he jogged on east again. He caught up with me at Ohio Avenue, where we rested together. I should say that about seven hundred people passed us. A funny thing was that all of them were on foot. Nobody seemed to have had the courage to stop and start his car; but as I remember it, all cars had to be cranked in those days, which is probably the reason."

The next day, the city went about its business as if nothing had happened, but there was no joking. It was two years or more before you dared treat the breaking of the dam lightly. And even now, twenty years after, there are a few persons, like Dr. Mallory, who will shut up like a clam if you mention the Afternoon of the Great Run.

About the Essay

1. List several incidents from the essay which could be labeled ironic.
2. Into which category do you think this essay should be placed: (1) among those that were written as "critical of society" or (2) among those that were written for sheer fun?
3. Explain why you chose the category you did.
4. Write one or two paragraphs describing a humorous incident from either your imagination or your experience.

About the Author

James Thurber's (1894-1961) balance between comic pleasure and serious intent established him as one of the most popular writers of the twentieth century. He often used his writing to expose life's follies and voice his displeasure in current trends that rob us of our creativity and individuality. He especially despised the materialism fostered by our technological age. He exposes the follies of mankind by using humor and imagination, two defenses against pride and the misuse of reason.

Note the irony of distinguished Dr. Mallory's actions—he mistakes "swishing" roller-skates for water; he collapses at a school for girls; he continues running even after seeing "no signs of water."

Discuss this statement with the students. Why was there "no joking"? *(People were embarrassed, ashamed of their actions.)*

simile

 About the Essay

1. *Answers may vary but might include the title itself (because no dam breaks in the story); the way in which people jump to the conclusion that something awful has occurred because "somebody began to run"; and the way in which the narrator's mother carefully prepares for a nonexistent disaster.*

2. *Answers may vary.*

3. *Accept either answer if students can support it from the story. See the Analysis section, last paragraph, for further information.*

4. *Answers may vary.*

OBJECTIVES

The students will be able to

- Locate and discuss the use of imaginative comparison in biography.
- Analyze how an autobiographer interprets his own life for the instruction of others.

Note imagery used to draw contrasts between the sea and "a lake in the woods." Encourage students to note White's strong use of all types of sense imagery throughout the essay.

metaphors

FURTHER HELPS

Additional activities

1. Read aloud another essay from *The Collected Essays of E. B. White.*

2. White is recognized not only as an essayist but also as a classic children's author. Most of your students have probably read at least one of his classics (*Charlotte's Web, Stuart Little, The Trumpet of the Swan*). Having learned a bit about White from this autobiographical essay, read one of these classics aloud in class, or at least an excerpt from it. Discuss

A Slight Sound at Evening

E. B. White

The following excerpt is taken from The Points of My Compass, *by E. B. White. Unlike the Thurber selection, the tone of this essay is serious, almost melancholy in its nostalgic mood. Here, White does more than simply recount a specific event; he also endeavors to interpret that event. In so doing, he provides not only entertainment but also a bit of wisdom.*

One summer, along about 1904, my father rented a camp on a lake in Maine and took us all there for the month of August. We all got ringworm from some kittens and had to rub Pond's Extract on our arms and legs night and morning, and my father rolled over in a canoe with all his clothes on; but outside of that the vacation was a success and from then on none of us ever thought there was any place in the world like that lake in Maine. We returned summer after summer—always on August 1st for one month. I have since become a salt-water man, but sometimes in summer there are days when the restlessness of the tides and the fearful cold of the sea water and the incessant wind that blows across the afternoon and into the evening make me wish for the placidity of a lake in the woods. A few weeks ago this feeling got so strong I bought myself a couple of bass hooks and a spinner and returned to the lake where we used to go, for a week's fishing and to revisit old haunts.

I took along my son, who had never had any fresh water up his nose and who had seen lily pads only from train windows. On the journey over to the lake I began to wonder what it would be like. I wondered how time would have marred this unique, this holy spot—the coves and streams, the hills that the sun set behind, the camps and the paths behind the camps. I was sure that the tarred road would have found it out and I wondered in what other ways it would be desolated. It is strange how much you can remember about places like that once you allow your mind to return into the grooves that lead back. You remember one thing, and that suddenly reminds you of another thing. I guess I remembered clearest of all the early mornings, when the lake was cool and motionless, remembered how the bedroom smelled of the lumber it was made of and of the wet woods whose scent entered through the screen. The partitions in the camp were thin and did not extend clear to the top of the rooms, and as I was always the first up I would dress softly so as not to wake the others, and sneak out into the sweet outdoors and start out in the canoe, keeping close along the shore in the long shadows of the pines. I remembered being very careful never to rub my paddle against the gunwale for fear of disturbing the stillness of the cathedral.

The lake had never been what you would call a wild lake. There were cottages sprinkled around the shores, and it was in farming

PREPARATION

"A Slight Sound at Evening"

Overview

Like Thurber, White offers us a bit of wisdom while entertaining us. His tone, however, is serious and his lesson more universal.

DISCUSSION

Introduction

Ask the students to share some memorable vacation experiences. Does their family have a special place that they return to summer after summer as White's family did? Is it a lake? Or perhaps a cabin in the woods? What activities do they enjoy? Do they, like White, think they will want to continue their family "traditions"?

Analysis

Have the students jot down several illuminating details White gives about himself in the essay. Also, have them note what they think each specific quotation reveals about its author. Following are a few they might use:

"I have since become a salt-water man." (*White has changed his lifestyle since his boyhood. We could go further and say that this change indicates a certain amount of success, inferring that he is a writer who lives and works on the coast.*)

"I bought myself a couple of bass hooks and a spinner and returned to the lake where we used to go." (*White is, at least to some degree, a sentimental man.*)

"I took along my son . . . who had seen lily pads only from train windows." (*White and his family have done some traveling, but his son has never spent time at a quiet lake.*)

"I guess I remembered clearest of all the early mornings, . . . remembered how the bedroom smelled of the lumber it was made of and of the wet woods whose scent entered through the screen." (*White had always been a keen observer, a valuable trait for a writer.*)

There are many other quotations your students may point out. Some may reveal White's adventurous spirit. Others may show the melancholy or pensive side of his nature.

In addition to these illuminating details, White uses myriad imaginative comparisons to create his mood and add interest. When describing himself as a boy, he says, "I remembered being country although the shores of the lake were quite heavily wooded. Some of the cottages were owned by nearby farmers, and you would live at the shore and eat your meals at the farmhouse. That's what our family did. But although it wasn't wild, it was a fairly large and undisturbed lake and there were places in it which, to a child at least, seemed infinitely remote and primeval.

I was right about the tar: it led to within half a mile of the shore. But when I got back there, with my boy, and we settled into a camp near a farmhouse and into the kind of summertime I had known, I could tell that it was going to be pretty much the same as it had been before—I knew it, lying in bed the first morning, smelling the bedroom, and hearing the boy sneak quietly out and go off along the shore in a boat. I began to sustain the illusion that he was I, and therefore, by simple transposition, that I was my father. This sensation persisted, kept cropping up all the time we were there. It was not an entirely new feeling, but in this setting it grew much stronger. I seemed to be living a dual existence. I would be in the middle of some simple act, I would be picking up a bait box or laying down a table fork, or I would be saying something, and suddenly it would be not I but my father who was saying the words or making the gesture. It gave me a creepy sensation.

We went fishing the first morning. I felt the same damp moss covering the worms in the bait can, and saw the dragonfly alight on the tip of my rod as it hovered a few inches from the surface of the water. It was the arrival of this fly that convinced me beyond any doubt that everything was as it always had been, that the years were a mirage and there had been no years. The small waves were the same, chucking the rowboat under the chin as we fished at anchor, and the boat was the same boat, the same color green and the ribs broken in the same places, and under the floor-boards the same fresh-water leavings and debris—the dead helgramite,* the wisps of moss, the rusty discarded fishhook, the dried blood from yesterday's catch. We stared silently at the tips of our rods, at the dragonflies that came and went. I lowered the tip of mine into the water, tentatively, pensively dislodging the fly, which darted two feet away, poised, darted two feet back, and came to rest again a little farther up the rod. There had been no years between the ducking of this dragonfly and the other one—the one that was part of memory. I looked at the boy, who was silently watching his fly, and it was my hands that held his rod, my eyes watching. I felt dizzy and didn't know which rod I was at the end of.

---

helgramite: the large water larva of the dobson fly, frequently used as fishing bait; also spelled hellgrammite

---

We caught two bass, hauling them in briskly as though they were mackerel, pulling them over the side of the boat in a businesslike manner without any landing net, and stunning them with a blow on the back of the head. When we got back for a swim before lunch, the lake was exactly where we had left it, the same number of inches from the dock, and there was only the merest suggestion of a breeze. This seemed an utterly enchanted sea, this lake you could leave to its own devices for a few hours and come back to, and find that it had not stirred, this constant and trustworthy body of water. In the shallows, the dark, water-soaked sticks and twigs, smooth and old, were undulating in clusters on the bottom against the clean ribbed sand, and the track of the mussel was plain. A school of minnows swam by, each minnow with its small individual shadow, doubling the attendance, so clear and sharp in the sunlight. Some of the other campers were in swimming, along the shore, one of them with a cake of soap, and the water felt thin and clear and

with the students how knowing a bit about an author can in many cases help them better understand his fictional works. What characteristics of White can they find in these classics?

3. Have the students research another section of the country or a foreign country and share with the class at least one characteristic that seems dominant or unique to that area. Have them also give at least one example of the influence of this characteristic on the daily life of those who live there.

---

very careful never to rub my paddle against the gunwale for fear of disturbing the stillness of the cathedral." He also uses such comparisons to emphasize the unity of past and present. He tells us, "There had been no years between the ducking of this dragonfly and the other one—the one that was part of memory. . . . When we got back for a swim before lunch, the lake was exactly where we had left it, the same number of inches from the dock, and there was only the merest suggestion of a breeze. This seemed an utterly enchanted sea, this lake you could leave to its own devices for a few hours and come back to, and find that it had not stirred, this constant and trustworthy body of water." He also employs imaginative comparisons when drawing our attention to the only really significant difference between the past and present:

"The only thing that was wrong now, really, was the sound of the place, an unfamiliar nervous sound of the outboard motors. This was the note that jarred, the one thing that would sometimes break the illusion and set the years moving. In those summertimes all motors were inboard; and when they were at a little distance, the noise they made was a sedative, an ingredient of summer sleep." After noting these examples, have the students point out any others they found especially effective in creating the mood of the piece.

White vividly recounts this experience not simply to show us his adeptness at creating mood but also to draw our attention to a specific point. The last sentence in the essay states this point in a way that is almost poetic. Read the last sentence aloud. Then ask the students to restate White's idea in their own words. (See side margin notes, page 198.)

Application

Direct the students to complete **Appendix S: Tradition and the Bible.**

Ask students what they think the middle track was from and why it has vanished. *(It was a path made by horses pulling wagons; no one uses horses now.)*

Sound imagery supports the mood. Note also White's simile comparing the annoying sound of the outboards to the annoying sound of mosquitoes.

unsubstantial. Over the years there had been this person with the cake of soap, this cultist, and here he was. There had been no years.

Up to the farmhouse to dinner through teeming, dusty field, the road under our sneakers was only a two-track road. The middle track was missing, the one with the marks of the hooves and splotches of dried, flaky manure. There had always been three tracks to choose from in choosing which track to walk in; now the choice was narrowed down to two. For a moment I missed terribly the middle alternative. But the way led past the tennis court, and something about the way it lay there in the sun reassured me; the tape had loosened along the backline, the alleys were green with plantains and other weeds, and the net (installed in June and removed in September) sagged in the dry noon, and the whole place steamed with midday heat and hunger and emptiness. There was a choice of pie for dessert, and one was blueberry and one was apple, and the waitresses were the same country girls, there having been no passage of time, only the illusion of it as in a dropped curtain—the waitresses were still fifteen. . . .

Summertime, oh summertime, pattern of life indelible, the fadeproof lake, the woods unshatterable, the pasture with the sweetfern and the juniper forever and ever, summer without end; this was the background, and the life along the shore was the design, the cottages with their innocent and tranquil design, their tiny docks with the flagpole and the American flag floating against the white clouds in the blue sky, the little paths over the roots of the trees leading from camp to camp and the paths leading back to the outhouses and the can of lime for sprinkling, and at the souvenir counters at the store the miniature birch-bark canoes and the post cards that showed things looking a little better than they looked. This was the American family at play, escaping the city heat, wondering whether the newcomers

in the camp at the head of the cove were "common" or "nice," wondering whether it was true that people who drove up for Sunday dinner at the farmhouse were turned away because there wasn't enough chicken.

It seemed to me, as I kept remembering all this, that those times and those summers had been infinitely precious and worth saving. There had been jollity and peace and goodness. The arriving (at the beginning of August) had been so big a business in itself, at the railway station the farm wagon drawn up, the first smell of the pine-laden air, the first glimpse of the smiling farmer, and the great importance of the trunks and your father's enormous authority in such matters, and the feel of the wagon under you for the long ten-mile haul, and at the top of the last long hill catching the first view of the lake after eleven months of not seeing this cherished body of water. The shouts and cries of the other campers when they saw you, and the trunks to be unpacked, to give up their rich burden. (Arriving was less exciting nowadays, when you sneaked up in your car and parked it under a tree near the camp and took out the bags and in five minutes it was all over, no fuss, no loud wonderful fuss about trunks.)

Peace and goodness and jollity. The only thing that was wrong now, really, was the sound of the place, an unfamiliar nervous sound of the outboard motors. This was the note that jarred, the one thing that would sometimes break the illusion and set the years moving. In those other summertimes all motors were inboard; and when they were at a little distance, the noise they made was a sedative, an ingredient of summer sleep. They were one-cylinder and two-cylinder engines, and some were make-and-break and some were jump-spark, but they all made a sleepy sound across the lake. The one-lungers throbbed and fluttered, and the twin-cylinder ones purred and purred, and that was a quiet sound too. But now the campers all had outboards. In the daytime, in the hot mornings, these motors made a petulant,* irritable sound; at night, in the still evening when the afterglow lit the water, they whined about one's ears like mosquitoes. My boy loved our rented outboard, and his great desire was to achieve singlehanded mastery over it, and authority, and he soon learned the trick of choking it a little (but not too much), and the adjustment of the needle valve. Watching him I would remember the things you could do with the old one-cylinder engine with the heavy flywheel, how you could have it eating out of your hand if you really got close to it spiritually. Motor boats in those days didn't have clutches, and you would make a landing by shutting off the motor at the proper time and coasting in with a dead rudder. But there was a way of reversing them, if you learned the trick, by cutting the switch and putting it on again exactly on the final dying revolution of the flywheel, so that it would kick back against compression and begin reversing. Approaching a dock in a strong following breeze, it was difficult to slow up sufficiently by the ordinary coasting method, and if a boy felt he had complete mastery over his motor, he was tempted to keep it running beyond its time and then reverse it a few feet from the dock. It took a cool nerve, because if you threw the switch a twentieth of a second too soon you would catch the flywheel when it still had speed enough to go up past center, and the boat would leap ahead, charging bull-fashion at the dock.

---

petulant: unreasonably irritable

We had a good week at the camp. The bass were biting well and the sun shone endlessly, day after day. We would be tired at night and lie down in the accumulated heat of the little bedrooms after the long hot day and the breeze would stir almost imperceptibly outside and the smell of the swamp drift in through the rusty screens. Sleep would come easily and in the morning the red squirrel would be on the roof, tapping out his gay routine. I kept remembering everything, lying in bed in the mornings—the small steamboat that had a long rounded stern like the lip of a Ubangi, and how quietly she ran on the moonlight sails, when the older boys played their mandolins and the girls sang and we ate doughnuts dipped in sugar, . . . After breakfast we would go up to the store and the things were in the same place—the minnows in a bottle, the plugs and spinners disarranged and pawed over by the youngsters from the boys' camp, the fig newtons and the Beeman's gum. Outside, the road was tarred and cars stood in front of the store. Inside all was just as it had always been, except there was more Coca Cola and not so much Moxie and root beer and birch beer and sarsaparilla. We would walk out with a bottle of pop apiece and sometimes the pop would backfire up our noses and it hurt. We explored the streams, quietly, where the turtles slid off the sunny logs and dug their way into the soft bottom; and we lay on the town wharf and fed worms to the tame bass. Everywhere we went I had trouble making out which was I, the one walking at my side, the one walking in my pants.

Onc afternoon while we were there at the lake a thunderstorm came up. It was like the revival of an old melodrama that I had seen long ago with childish awe. The second-act climax of the drama of the electrical disturbance over a lake in America had not changed in any important respect. This was the big scene, still the big scene. The whole thing was so familiar, the first feeling of oppression and heat and a general air around camp of not wanting to go very far away. In a midafternoon (it was all the same) a curious darkening of the sky, and a lull in everything

metaphor, personification

White ends the essay with a poetic sentence that uses the metaphor of a strong chain linking generations to support his theme of the changelessness of the lake and the similarity of his son's experiences to his own.

that made life tick; and then the way the boats suddenly swung the other way at their moorings with the coming of a breeze out of the new quarter, and the premonitory* rumble. Then the kettle drum, then the snare, then the bass drum and cymbals, then crackling light against the dark, and the gods grinning and licking their chops in the hills. Afterward the calm, the rain steadily rustling in the calm lake, the return of light and hope and spirits, and the campers running out in joy and relief to go swimming in the rain, their bright cries perpetuating the deathless joke about how they were getting simply drenched, and the children screaming with delight at the new sensation of bathing in the rain, and the joke about getting drenched linking the generations in a strong indestructible chain.

premonitory: forewarning; foreboding

About the Essay

1. How were the boy's reactions to the lakeside visit similar to his father's?
2. How had the lake changed since White's boyhood?
3. List one imaginative comparison White uses in his essay.
4. What can we learn from the experience E. B. White recounts for us?

About the Author

E. B. White (1899-1985), essayist, poet, and fiction writer, displayed an admirable blend of keen wit, social insight, and gentle good-naturedness. White's name is often associated with that of his good friend James Thurber. The two men collaborated on a book and worked together for many years on the staff of the *New Yorker* magazine. After writing "The Talk of the Town" and the "Notes and Comments" sections of this weekly magazine for over a decade, White retired to a quiet farm in Maine, where he enjoyed the beauty of the countryside and obtained the privacy he craved. On the farm, White continued to write, contributing to a regular column in *Harper's Magazine* and free-lancing for the *New Yorker*. During this period White also produced several children's books, delightful tales such as *Charlotte's Web, Stuart Little,* and *The Trumpet of the Swan.* These stories not only added to White's already impressive literary output but also became well-loved children's classics.

About the Essay

1. *Answers may vary but might include "I knew it, lying in bed the first morning, . . . hearing the boy sneak quietly out and go off along the shore in a boat" (page 195);"I looked at the boy, who was silently watching his fly, and it was my hands that held his rod, my eyes watching" (page 195); "My boy loved our rented outboard, and his great desire was to achieve singlehanded mastery over it, and authority" (page 197); "After breakfast we would go up to the store and the things were in the same place—the minnows in a bottle, the plugs and spinners disarranged and pawed over" (page 197).*

2. *Answers may vary but might include the fact that the tarred road now comes closer to the lake (page 195); the road has changed from a three-track road (in which the middle track was caused by horses pulling wagons) to a two-track road (page 196); and the sound of outboard motors (page 196).*

3. *Answers may vary but might include references to the lake as a "holy spot" having "the stillness of a cathedral" (metaphor; page 194); "the years were a mirage" (metaphor; page 195); "The small waves were the same, chucking the rowboat under the chin" (personification; page 195). See Analysis section.*

4. *Answers may vary. One possible answer would be the way in which experiencing the beauty of nature "[links] the generations in a strong indestructible chain" (page 198).*

A Miserable Merry Christmas

Lincoln Steffens

Like White, Steffens recounts for us a boyhood experience that maintained its emotional impact for him even into adulthood. Notice, however, that in Steffens's selection all but the last paragraph is written from a child's perspective.

What interested me in our new neighborhood was not the school, nor the room I was to have in the house all to myself, but the stable which was built back of the house. My father let me direct the making of a stall, a little smaller than the other stalls, for my pony, and I prayed and hoped and my sister Lou believed that that meant that I would get the pony, perhaps for Christmas. I pointed out to her that there were three other stalls and no horses at all. This I said in order that she should answer it. She could not. My father, sounded,* said that someday we might have horses and a cow; meanwhile a stable added to the value of a house. "Someday" is a pain to a boy who lives in and knows only "now." My good little sisters, to comfort me, remarked that Christmas was coming, but Christmas was always coming and grownups were always talking about it, asking you what you wanted and then giving you what they wanted you to have. Though everybody knew what I wanted, I told them all again. My mother knew that I told God, too, every night, I wanted a pony, and to make sure that they understood, I declared that I wanted nothing else.

sounded: trying to learn how one feels about something

"Nothing but a pony?" my father asked.

"Nothing," I said.

"Not even a pair of high boots?"

That was hard. I did want boots, but I stuck to the pony. "No, not even boots."

"Nor candy? There ought to be something to fill your stocking with, and Santa Claus can't put a pony into a stocking."

That was true, and he couldn't lead a pony down the chimney either. But no: "All I want is a pony," I said. "If I can't have a pony, give me nothing, nothing."

Now, I had been looking myself for the pony I wanted, going to sales stables, inquiring of horsemen, and I had seen several that would do. My father let me "try" them. I tried so many ponies that I was learning fast to sit a horse. I chose several, but my father always found some fault with them. I was in despair. When Christmas was at hand I had given up hope of a pony, and on Christmas Eve I hung up my stocking along with my sisters, of whom, by the way, I now had three. I haven't mentioned them or their coming because, you understand, they were girls, and girls, young girls, counted for nothing in my manly life. They did not mind me either; they were so happy that Christmas Eve that I caught some

---

OBJECTIVE

The students will be able to

• Locate and analyze situational and dramatic irony used in an autobiography.

Discuss the paradoxical title with the students before they read the piece. Ask what they think it might mean and how it is effective as an attention-grabbing title.

FURTHER HELPS

Additional activities

Read another excerpt from Lincoln Steffens's *Autobiography*.

Journal entry idea

All of us can, like Steffens, vividly remember certain childhood experiences. In some cases, the experience seemed trivial or even humorous to others. But for some reason the event seemed momentous to us, and we remember every detail as if it happened yesterday. Have the students write about one such incident. Encourage them to remember exactly how they felt as a child.

Resources

Russel M. Horton, *Lincoln Steffens* (New York: Twayne Publishers, 1974).

Justin Kaplan, *Lincoln Steffens: A Biography* (New York: Simon and Schuster, 1974).

PREPARATION

"A Miserable Merry Christmas"

Overview

"A Miserable Merry Christmas" recounts one of the most significant events in Lincoln Steffens's life. It was a turning point for the young boy. In his *Autobiography* Steffens describes the freedom of a boy on horseback and the hours of imaginative play his romps through the countryside provided.

DISCUSSION

Introduction

Draw the students' attention to the paradoxical nature of the title of Steffens's story. Obviously, Steffens is trying to communicate the conflicting emotions of the event. Share such an event from your own experience, or have the students share some event that may have produced similar conflicting emotions. What was the outcome of the event? Were their feelings justified?

Analysis

The setting and theme of "A Miserable Merry Christmas" have much in common with Paul Engle's in "An Old-Fashioned Iowa Christmas." Both stories are about a childhood Christmas and are written from a young boy's perspective. Each also recounts an incident that maintained its effect into adulthood.

Unlike Engle's story, however, "A Miserable Merry Christmas" is more than a Christmas memory. The paradoxical nature of the incident gives it greater impact. There is, as mentioned earlier, the seeming contradiction of the title. But Steffens also uses situational irony. He repeatedly says that he wants nothing but a pony for Christmas; if he cannot have a pony, he wants nothing. But when it appears that he may indeed get nothing, his reaction shows us that he really never believed such a thing would happen. There is a direct contrast between what he expected to happen and what actually happened.

Situational irony: Lincoln said he wanted a pony or nothing—but when he gets nothing, he is heartbroken.

Dramatic irony: The reader knows (or at least suspects) that a pony is on the way because of the parents' actions—but the boy does not know.

metaphor

of their merriment. I speculated on what I'd get; I hung up the biggest stocking I had, and we all went reluctantly to bed to wait till morning. Not to sleep; not right away. We were told that we must not only sleep promptly, we must not wake up till seven-thirty the next morning—or if we did, we must not go to the fireplace for our Christmas. Impossible.

We did sleep that night, but we woke up at 6 A.M. We lay in our beds and debated through the open doors whether to obey till, say, half-past six. Then we bolted. I don't know who started it, but there was a rush. We all disobeyed; we raced to disobey and get first to the fireplace in the front room downstairs. And there they were, the gifts, all sorts of wonderful things, mixed-up piles of presents; only, as I disentangled the mess, I saw that my stocking was empty; it hung limp, not a thing in it, and under and around it—nothing. My sisters had knelt down, each by her pile of gifts; they were squealing with delight, till they looked up and saw me standing there in my nightgown with nothing. They left their piles to come to me and look with me at my empty place. Nothing. They felt my stocking: nothing.

I don't remember whether I cried at that moment, but my sisters did. They ran with me back to my bed, and there we all cried till I became indignant. That helped some. I got up, dressed, and, driving my sisters away, I went alone out into the yard, down to the stable, and there, all by myself, I wept. My mother came out to me by and by; she found me in my pony stall, sobbing on the floor, and she tried to comfort me. But I heard my father outside; he had come part way with her, and she was having some sort of angry quarrel with him. She tried to comfort me; besought me to come to breakfast. I could not; I wanted no comfort and no breakfast. She left me and went on into the house with sharp words for my father.

I don't know what kind of breakfast the family had. My sisters said it was "awful." They were ashamed to enjoy their own toys. They came to me, and I was rude. I ran away from them. I went around to the front of the house, sat down on the steps, and, the crying over, I ached. I was wronged, I was hurt—I can feel now what I felt then, and I am sure that if one could see the wounds upon our hearts, there would be found still upon mine a scar from that terrible Christmas morning. And my father, the practical joker, he must have been hurt, too, a little. I saw him looking out of the window. He was watching me or something for an hour or two, drawing back the curtain ever so little lest I catch him, but I saw his face, and I think I can see now the anxiety upon it, the worried impatience.

After—I don't know how long—surely an hour or two—I was brought to the climax of my agony by the sight of a man riding a pony down the street, a pony and a brand-new saddle, the most beautiful saddle I ever saw, and it was a boy's saddle; the man's feet were not in the stirrups; his legs were too long. The outfit was perfect; it was the realization of all my dreams, the answer to all my prayers. A fine new bridle, with a little curb bit. And the pony! As he drew near, I saw that the pony was really a small horse, what we called an Indian pony, a bay, with black mane and tail, and one white foot and a white star on his forehead. For such a horse as that, I would have given, I could have forgiven, anything.

But the man, a disheveled fellow with a blackened eye and a fresh-cut face, came along, reading the numbers on the houses, and, as my hopes—my impossible hopes—rose, he looked at our door and passed by, he and the pony, and the saddle and the bridle. Too much. I fell upon the steps, and having wept before, I broke now into such a flood of tears that I was a floating wreck when I heard a voice.

Steffens also provides dramatic irony in his essay. There is a contrast between what we know and what the boy knows. The interaction between father and mother reveals that, indeed, there is a pony for the boy. Although we are uncertain why it has not arrived, we are sure that it will arrive. In light of this knowledge, we sympathize with his despair but we are not overwhelmed by it as he is. In light of this, Steffens's last paragraph is even more interesting. Steffens says that on that particular boyhood Christmas he experienced the whole range of emotions. He says that "a grownup could hardly have stood it." Ask the students whether they think this is one reason Steffens—even though writing from a child's perspective—provides us with enough information to foreshadow the outcome. Could adults stand the emotional ups and downs of the story without some assurance of the outcome?

Application

See **Journal entry idea** under "Additional activities," page 199.

"Say, kid," it said, "do you know a boy named Lennie Steffens?"

I looked up. It was the man on the pony, back again, at our horse block.

"Yes," I sputtered through my tears. "That's me."

"Well," he said, "then this is your horse. I've been looking all over for you and your house. Why don't you put your number where it can be seen?"

"Get down," I said running out to him.

He went on saying something about "ought to have got here at seven o'clock; told me to bring the nag here and tie him to your post and leave him for you. But I got into a fight— and a hospital, and—"

"Get down," I said.

He got down, and he boosted me up to the saddle. He offered to fit the stirrups to me, but I didn't want him to. I wanted to ride.

"What's the matter with you?" he said angrily. "What you crying for? Don't you like the horse? He's a dandy, this horse. I know him of old. He's fine at cattle; he'll drive 'em alone."

I hardly heard, I could scarcely wait, but he persisted. He adjusted the stirrups, and then, finally, off I rode, slowly, at a walk, so happy, so thrilled, that I did not know what I was doing. I did not look back at the house or the man; I rode off up the street, taking note of everything—of the reins, of the pony's long mane, of the carved leather saddle. I had never seen anything so beautiful. And mine! I was going to ride up past Miss Kay's house. But I noticed on the horn of the saddle some stains like raindrops, so I turned and trotted home, not to the house but to the stable. There was the family, father, mother, sisters, all working for me, all happy. They had been putting in place the tools of my new business: blankets, currycomb, brush, pitchfork—everything, and there was hay in the loft.

"What did you come back so soon for?" somebody asked. "Why didn't you go on riding?"

I pointed to the stains. "I wasn't going to get my new saddle rained on," I said. And my father laughed.

"It isn't raining," he said. "Those are not raindrops."

"They are tears," my mother gasped, and she gave my father a look which sent him off to the house. Worse still, my mother offered to wipe away the tears still running out of my eyes. I gave her such a look as she had given him, and she went off after my father, drying her own tears. My sisters remained and we all unsaddled the pony, put on his halter, led him to his stall, tied and fed him. It began really to rain; so all the rest of that memorable day we curried and combed that pony. The girls plaited his mane, forelock, and tail, while I pitchforked hay to him and curried and brushed, curried and brushed. For a change we brought him out to drink; we led him up and down, blanketed like a race horse; we took turns at that. But the best, the most inexhaustible fun, was to clean him. When we went reluctantly to our midday Christmas dinner, we all smelt of horse, and my sisters had to wash their faces and hands. I was asked to, but I wouldn't, till my mother bade me look in the mirror. Then I washed up—quick. My face was caked with the muddy lines of tears that had coursed over my cheeks to my mouth. Having washed away that shame, I ate my dinner, and, as I ate, I grew hungrier and hungrier. It was my first meal that day, and as I filled up on the turkey and the stuffing, the cranberries and the pies, the fruit and the nuts—as I swelled, I could laugh. My mother said I still choked and sobbed now and then, but I laughed, too; I saw and enjoyed my sisters' presents till—I had to go out and attend to my pony, who was there, really and truly there, the promise, the beginning, of a happy double life. And—I went and looked to make sure— there was the saddle, too, and the bridle.

But that Christmas, which my father had planned so carefully, was it the best or the worst I ever knew? He often asked me that; I never could answer as a boy. I think now that it was both. It covered the whole distance from brokenhearted misery to bursting happiness—too fast. A grownup could hardly have stood it.

About the Essay

1. What is the one ironic incident in the story?
2. *An Iowa Christmas*, like this story, recounts a boy's memorable holiday. How are the two boys' experiences similar?
3. How are they different?
4. What is the significance of Steffens's title?

About the Author

In Lincoln Steffens's (1866-1936) *Autobiography*, the book from which "A Miserable Merry Christmas" is taken, Steffens tells us of two of his greatest passions: horses and books. "As a boy I would ride far, far away to some spot, give my pony a long rope to swing round on, and let him feed on the grass, while I sat and did nothing but muse. I read a great deal. Finding that books fed my fancies, I would take one along, and finding a quiet nook, I read. And my reading always gave me something to be. I liked to change the hero I was to the same thing on horseback, and once wholly in the part, I would remount my pony and be Napoleon, or Richard the Lion-hearted, or Byron, so completely that any actual happening would wake me up dazed as from a dreaming sleep."

Steffens spent much of his adult life as a reporter and editor of such widely read magazines as the *New York Evening Post* and *McClure's*. But his name was also linked with the "Muckrakers," a group of American writers in the early 1900s who endeavored to expose corruption in business and government. Steffens's influence and power were considerable. His impatience for change, however, caused him to support the fledgling communist movement. Steffens was just one of many well-meaning but naive writers who initially joined this movement, hoping it would accomplish the reforms for which they had so diligently worked.

Over ten years later, after much hardship and disillusionment, Steffens began his autobiography. His purpose in writing it was to give his son and others a chance to benefit from his lifetime of hard lessons. Steffens's initial title of the book, *A Life of Unlearning*, indicates the nature of those lessons.

About the Essay

1. *Answers may vary. Probably the most obvious example of irony is the situational irony in Steffens's saying that he wants nothing but a pony for Christmas; if he cannot have a pony, he wants nothing. But when it appears that he may indeed get nothing, his reaction shows us that he really never believed such a thing would happen. See Analysis section.*

2. *Both stories are about a childhood Christmas and are written from a young boy's perspective. Each also recounts an incident that maintained its effect into adulthood.*

3. *Steffens's story includes an emphasis on paradox that is lacking in Engle's. See Analysis section.*

4. *The title highlights the paradoxes of this Christmas for Steffens—"was it the best or the worst I ever knew? . . . It covered the whole distance from brokenhearted misery to bursting happiness" (page 202).*

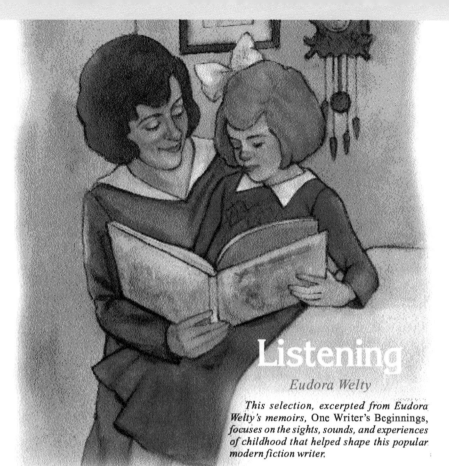

Listening

Eudora Welty

This selection, excerpted from Eudora Welty's memoirs, One Writer's Beginnings, *focuses on the sights, sounds, and experiences of childhood that helped shape this popular modern fiction writer.*

In our house on North Congress Street in Jackson, Mississippi, where I was born, the oldest of three children, in 1909, we grew up to the striking of clocks. There was a mission-style oak grandfather clock standing in the hall, which sent its gong-like strokes through the livingroom, diningroom, kitchen, and pantry, and up the sounding board of the stairwell. Through the night, it could find its way into our ears; sometimes, even on the sleeping porch, midnight could wake us up. My parents' bedroom had a smaller striking clock that answered it. Though the kitchen clock did nothing but show the time, the diningroom clock was a cuckoo clock with weights on long chains, on one of which my baby brother, after climbing on a chair to the top of the china closet, once succeeded in suspending the cat for a moment. I don't know whether or not my father's Ohio family, in having been Swiss

OBJECTIVES

The students will be able to

- Discuss the strong positive influence adults can have on children's imaginative gifts.
- Discuss the importance of a writer's being a keen observer.

Note how the selection starts with sound imagery, as is appropriate, considering the title. Have students look for examples of various types of imagery throughout. Note also that Welty's reference to the sound of the clocks is not thrown in merely for effect—she points out at the end of the first paragraph that it helped her become a better writer, teaching her about chronology.

FURTHER HELPS

Additional activity

Read another excerpt from Eudora Welty's autobiography, *One Writer's Beginnings.* You might also show the students some of the photographs in the book.

PREPARATION

"Listening"

Overview

This essay, like the previous one, reminds us how childhood experiences may affect our outlook. Welty, however, does not focus on a single event of great impact. She shares many experiences, all of which in some measure shaped her artistic outlook.

DISCUSSION

Introduction

One Writer's Beginnings appeared in 1983. Its great success amazed Welty. It is not surprising, however, when we remember that the origins of creativity have always fascinated us. Most of us enjoy finding out how artists, writers, and those in other creative fields accomplish their tasks.

We are all called on to be creative at one time or another. Daily problem solving often demands creative alternatives. Our hobbies are also usually creative. Discuss with the students some of their own creative endeavors. Ask them how they set about accomplishing such tasks.

Analysis

When thinking of painters or writers, we often imagine that they wait to begin working until they are inspired, but as one noted artist re-marked, "creativity lives at the mercy of self-discipline; without self-discipline creativity is just another flight of fancy." G. K. Chesterton, another author we have studied, also made an astute observation when he said, "Nothing sublime has ever arisen out of mere art. . . . There must always be a rich moral soil for any aesthetic growth."

Such rich "moral soil" was obviously in some measure evident in Welty's home. Self-discipline was also apparent. Have the students list at least one specific contribution Welty's mother made to her development. *(Her love of reading and her ability to empathize with characters in a story are two contributions she made.)* Have them also list at least one specific contribution Welty's father made to her development. *(His*

Resources

Elizabeth Evans, *Eudora Welty* (Crossroad, 1990).

Ruth Vande Kieft, *Eudora Welty* (Macmillan, 1987).

Eudora Welty, *One Writer's Beginnings* (Massachusetts: Harvard University Press, 1995).

---

back in the 1700s before the first three Welty brothers came to America, had anything to do with this; but we all of us have been time-minded all our lives. This was good at least for a future fiction writer, being able to learn so penetratingly, and almost first of all, about chronology. It was one of a good many things I learned almost without knowing it; it would be there when I needed it.

My father loved all instruments that would instruct and fascinate. His place to keep things was the drawer in the "library table" where lying on top of his folded maps was a telescope with brass extensions, to find the moon and the Big Dipper after supper in our front yard, and to keep appointments with eclipses. There was a folding Kodak that was brought out for Christmas, birthdays, and trips. In the back of the drawer you could find a magnifying glass, a kaleidoscope, and a gyroscope kept in a black buckram* box, which he would set dancing for us on a string pulled tight. He had also supplied himself with an assortment of puzzles composed of metal rings and intersecting links and keys chained together, impossible for the rest of us, however patiently shown, to take apart; he had an almost childlike love of the ingenious.

buckram: a rough cotton fabric heavily coated with glue

In time, a barometer was added to our diningroom wall; but we didn't really need it. My father had the country boy's accurate knowledge of the weather and its skies. He went out and stood on our front steps first thing in the morning and took a look at it and a sniff. He was a pretty good weather prophet.

"Well, I'm *not*," my mother would say with enormous self-satisfaction.

He told us children what to do if we were lost in a strange country. "Look for where the sky is brightest along the horizon," he said.

"That reflects the nearest river. Strike out for a river and you will find habitation." Eventualities were much on his mind. In his care for us children he cautioned us to take measures against such things as being struck by lightning. He drew us all away from the windows during the severe electrical storms that are common where we live. My mother stood apart, scoffing at caution as a character failing. "Why, I always loved a storm! High winds never bothered me in West Virginia! Just listen at that! I wasn't a bit afraid of a little lightning and thunder! I'd go out on the mountain and spread my arms wide and *run* in a good big storm!"

So I developed a strong meteorological* sensibility. In years ahead when I wrote stories, atmosphere took its influential role from the start. Commotion in the weather and the inner feelings aroused by such a hovering disturbance emerged connected in dramatic form. (I tried a tornado first, in a story called "The Winds.")

meteorological: dealing with the weather, especially weather conditions

From our earliest Christmas times, Santa Claus brought us toys that instruct boys and girls (separately) how to build things—stone blocks cut to the castle-building style, Tinker Toys, and Erector sets. Daddy made for us himself elaborate kites that needed to be taken miles out of town to a pasture long enough (and my father was not afraid of horses and cows watching) for him to run with and get up on a long cord to which my mother held the spindle, and then we children were given it to hold, tugging like something alive at our hands. They were beautiful, sound, shapely box kites, smelling delicately of office glue for their entire short lives. And of course, as soon as the boys attained anywhere near the right age, there was an electric train, the engine with its pea-sized working headlight, its line of cars, tracks equipped with switches, semaphores, its station, its bridges, and its tunnel, which

---

Application

Obviously, Eudora Welty's parents were a strong positive influence on her, playing a major role in helping her develop her considerable gifts. The very title of the chapter, "Listening," intimates that they made certain her childhood was full of sights and sounds that enabled her to better understand the world around her.

All of us have had the experience of "listening." We have had parents, teachers, or other adults who encouraged us to develop the gifts God has given us. Have each student write about one such experience. As in the case of Eudora Welty, it may not be one specific, overwhelming occurrence that each of us remembers most. It may be instead a simple word of encouragement or a prolonged example of consistent living. Such encouragement or behavior may have helped us recognize some quality in ourselves that we had never noticed before. Have the students not only relate the incident(s) but also tell how the realization brought on by the incident has changed or affected them. See **Writing Rubric 7-2: An Important Influence.**

blocked off all other traffic in the upstairs hall. Even from downstairs, and through the cries of excited children, the elegant rush and click of the train could be heard through the ceiling, running around and around its figure eight.

All of this, but especially the train, represents my father's fondest beliefs—in progress, in the future. With these gifts, he was preparing his children.

And so was my mother with her different gifts.

I learned from the age of two or three that any room in our house, at any time of day, was there to read in, or to be read to. My mother read to me. She'd read to me in the big bedroom in the mornings, when we were in her rocker together, which ticked in rhythm as we rocked, as though we had a cricket accompanying the story. She'd read to me in the diningroom on winter afternoons in front of the coal fire, with our cuckoo clock ending the story with "Cuckoo," and at night when I'd got in my own bed. I must have given her no peace. Sometimes she read to me in the kitchen while she sat churning, and the churning sobbed along with *any* story. It was my ambition to have her read to me while *I* churned; once she granted my wish, but she read off my story before I brought her butter. She was an expressive reader. When she was reading "Puss in Boots," for instance, it was impossible not to know that she distrusted *all* cats.

It had been startling and disappointing to me to find out that story books had been written by *people*, that books were not natural wonders, coming up of themselves like grass. Yet regardless of where they came from, I cannot remember a time when I was not in love with them—with the books themselves, cover and binding and the paper they were printed on, with their smell and their weight and with their possession in my arms, captured and carried off to myself. Still illiterate, I was ready for them, committed to all the reading I could give them.

Neither of my parents had come from homes that could afford to buy many books, but though it must have been something of a strain on his salary, as the youngest officer in a young insurance company, my father was all the while carefully selecting and ordering away for what he and Mother thought we children should grow up with. They bought first for the future.

Besides the bookcase in the livingroom, which was always called "the library," there were the encyclopedia tables and dictionary stand under windows in our diningroom. Here to help us grow up arguing around the diningroom table were the Unabridged Webster, the Columbia Encyclopedia, Compton's Pictured Encyclopedia, the Lincoln Library of Information, and later the Book of Knowledge. And the year we moved into our new house, there was room to celebrate it with the new 1925 edition of Britannica, which my father, his face always deliberately turned toward the future, was of course disposed to think better than any previous edition.

In "the library," inside the mission-style bookcase with its three diamond-latticed glass doors, with my father's Morris chair and the glass-shaped lamp on its table beside it, were books I could soon begin on—and I did, reading them all alike and as they came, straight down their rows, top shelf to bottom. There was the set of Stoddard's Lectures, in all its late nineteenth-century vocabulary and vignettes* of peasant life and quaint beliefs and customs, with matching halftone illustrations: Vesuvius erupting, Venice by moonlight, gypsies glimpsed by their campfires. I didn't know then the clue they were to my father's longing to see the rest of the world. I read straight through his other love-from-afar: the Victrola Book of the Opera, with opera after opera

onomatopoeia

Note onomatopoeia and simile here. Note also how the sound of one of the clocks reminds us of the opening of the essay.

simile

allusions

Merriam-Webster's Collegiate Dictionary, 10th ed. (1994), defines a morris chair this way: "[William *Morris*] (1900): an easy chair with adjustable back and removable cushions."

in synopsis, with portraits in costume of Melba, Caruso, Galli-Curci, and Geraldine Farrar, some of whose voices we could listen to on our Red Seal records.

---

vignettes: brief descriptions

My mother read secondarily for information; she sank as a hedonist* into novels. She read Dickens in the spirit in which she would have eloped with him. The novels of her girlhood that had stayed on in her imagination, besides those of Dickens and Scott and Robert Louis Stevenson, were *Jane Eyre, Trilby, The Woman in White, Green Mansions, King Solomon's Mines.* Marie Corelli's name would crop up but I understood she had gone out of favor with my mother, who had only kept *Ardath* out of loyalty. In time she absorbed herself in Galsworthy, Edith Wharton, above all in Thomas Mann of the *Joseph* volumes.

---

hedonist: one who believes pleasure is the chief good

St. Elmo was not in our house; I saw it often in other houses. This wildly popular Southern novel is where all the Edna Earles in our population started coming from. They're all named for the heroine, who succeeded in bringing a dissolute, sinning roué* and atheist of a lover (St. Elmo) to his knees. My mother was able to forgo it. But she remembered the classic advice given to rose growers on how to water their bushes long enough: "Take a chair and *St. Elmo.*"

---

roué: a wasted man

To both my parents I owe my early acquaintance with a beloved Mark Twain. There was a full set of Mark Twain and a short set of Ring Lardner in our bookcase, and those were the volumes that in time united us all, parents and children.

Reading everything that stood before me

was how I came upon a worn old book without a back that had belonged to my father as a child. It was called *Sanford and Merton.* Is there anyone left who recognizes it, I wonder? It is the famous moral tale written by Thomas Day in the 1780s, but of him no mention is made on the title page of *this* book; here it is *Sanford and Merton in Words of One Syllable* by Mary Godolphin. Here are the rich boy and the poor boy and Mr. Barlow, their teacher and interlocutor,* in long discourses alternating with dramatic scenes—danger and rescue allotted to the rich and the poor respectively. It may have only words of one syllable, but one of them is "quoth." It ends with not one but two morals, both engraved on rings: "Do what you ought, come what may," and "If we would be great, we must first learn to be good."

---

interlocutor: one who takes part in a conversation

This book was lacking its front cover, the back held on by strips of pasted paper, now turned golden, in several layers, and the pages stained, flecked, and tattered around the edges; its garish illustrations had come unattached but were preserved, laid in. I had the feeling even in my heedless childhood that this was the only book my father as a little boy had had of his own. He had held onto it, and might have gone to sleep on its coverless face: he had lost his mother when he was seven. My father had never made any mention to his own children of the book, but he had brought it along with him from Ohio to our house and shelved it in our bookcase.

My mother had brought from West Virginia that set of Dickens; those books looked sad, too—they had been through fire and water before I was born, she told me, and there they were, lined up—as I later realized, waiting for *me.*

I was presented, from as early as I can remember, with books of my own, which

appeared on my birthday and Christmas morning. Indeed, my parents could not give me books enough. They must have sacrificed to give me on my sixth or seventh birthday—it was after I became a reader for myself—the ten-volume set of *Our Wonder World*. These were beautifully made, heavy books I would lie down with on the floor in front of the diningroom hearth, and more often than the rest volume 5, *Every Child's Story Book,* was under my eyes. There were fairy tales—Grimm, Andersen, the English, the French, "Ali Baba and the Forty Thieves"; and there was Aesop and Reynard the Fox; there were the myths and legends, Robin Hood, King Arthur, and St. George and the Dragon, even the history of Joan of Arc; a whack of *Pilgrim's Progress* and a long piece of *Gulliver*. They all carried their classic illustrations. I located myself in these pages and could go straight to the stories and pictures I loved; very often "The Yellow Dwarf" was first choice, with Walter Crane's Yellow Dwarf in full color making his terrifying appearance flanked by turkeys. Now that volume is as worn and backless and hanging apart as my father's poor *Sanford and Merton*. The precious page with Edward Lear's "Jumblies" on it has been in danger of slipping out for all these years. One measure of my love for *Our Wonder World* was that for a long time I wondered if I would go through fire and water for it as my mother had done for Charles Dickens; and the only comfort was to think I could ask my mother to do it for me.

I believe I'm the only child I know of who grew up with this treasure in the house. I used to ask others, "Did you have *Our Wonder World?*" I'd have to tell them The Book of Knowledge could not hold a candle to it.

I live in gratitude to my parents for initiating me—and as early as I begged for it, without keeping me waiting—into knowledge of the word, into reading and spelling, by way of the alphabet. They taught it to me at home in time for me to begin to read before starting to school. I believe the alphabet is no longer considered an essential piece of equipment for traveling through life. In my day it was the keystone to knowledge. You learned the alphabet as you learned to count to ten, as you learned "Now I lay me" and the Lord's Prayer and your father's and mother's name and address and telephone number, all in case you were lost.

My love for the alphabet, which endures, grew out of reciting it but, before that, out of seeing the letters on the page. In my own story books, before I could read them for myself, I fell in love with various winding, enchanted-looking initials drawn by Walter Crane at the heads of fairy tales. In "Once upon a time," an "O" had a rabbit running it as a treadmill, his feet upon flowers. When the day came, years later, for me to see the Book of Kells, all the wizardry of letter, initial, and word swept over me a thousand times over, and the illumination, the gold, seemed a part of the word's beauty and holiness that had been there from the start.

About the Essay

1. List at least one specific contribution Welty's father made in shaping her as a writer.
2. List at least one contribution made by Welty's mother.
3. Why do you think the title of the first chapter of Welty's autobiographical work is "Listening"?
4. What one word would you use to describe Welty as she is in this selection?

---

4. *Answers may vary; accept any response that students can justify from details in the excerpt.*

 About the Essay

1. *Answers may vary but might include his curiosity, his love of teaching, and his gift for careful observation.*

2. *Answers may vary but might include her love of reading and her ability to empathize with characters in a story.*

3. *Answers may vary. It speaks of Welty's ability to absorb her surroundings through a variety of senses (most of us rely primarily on "seeing"); it also implies that Welty's parents made certain her childhood was full of sights and sounds that enabled her to better understand the world around her. See Application section.*

About the Author

Eudora Welty (1909-2001) was born in Jackson, Mississippi. Her parents exerted a strong, positive influence on their daughter's imagination, providing books, music, and the appeal of their own individuality. Our excerpt from Welty's autobiography, *One Writer's Beginnings,* was published in 1983. Its great success surprised even its author, but its acceptance should have been expected because the origins of creativity have always been fascinating to read.

Our excerpt, detailing some of the childhood experiences of this modest, reserved lady, represents only the beginning of the influence on her art. After high school, Welty continued her education and eventually finished at New York's Columbia University with training in advertising. During the Great Depression, she took a job with a radio station and later worked as a reporter-photographer on a government works project. This latter assignment provided valuable opportunities to meet, photograph, and describe the memorable "characters" who would later populate her stories.

Although Welty's first stories were pessimistic, focusing on man's solitude, she later showed a more positive outlook. It is unfortunate that no answer for man's true dilemma ever appears in her writing. Welty, believing that God was indifferent to man's needs, continued to portray characters who loved life but were frustrated by their inability to express this love or share it with others.

FURTHER HELPS

Additional activities

1. Read William Cullen Bryant's "Thanatopsis" aloud. (See *AMERICAN LITERATURE for Christian Schools,* pages 172-74.) Compare the view of death in Bryant's and Whittier's poems.

2. Have the students bring in other narrative poems. As a class, plot out the action of each poem.

Telling the Bees

John Greenleaf Whittier

This semiautobiographical poem appeared in April 1858 in the Atlantic Monthly *with the following note by the author: "A remarkable custom, brought from the Old Country, formerly prevailed in the rural districts of New England. On the death of a member of the family, the bees were at once informed of the event, and their hives dressed in mourning. This ceremonial was supposed to be necessary to prevent the swarms from leaving their hives and seeking a new home."*

Here is the place; right over the hill
    Runs the path I took;
You can see the gap in the old wall still,
    And the steppingstones in the shallow brook.

There is the house, with the gate red-barred,   5
    And the poplars tall;
Of the barn's brown length, and the cattle yard,
    And the white horns tossing above the wall.

There are the beehives ranged in the sun;
    And down by the brink   10
Of the brook are her poor flowers, weed-o'errun,
    Pansy and daffodil, rose and pink.

A year has gone, as the tortoise goes,
    Heavy and slow;
And the same rose blows,* and the same sun glows,   15
    And the same brook sings of* a year ago.

There's the same sweet clover-smell in the breeze;
    And the June sun warm
Tangles his wings of fire in the trees,
    Setting, as then, over Fernside farm.   20

rose blows: rosebush blooms
sings of: sings that song

PREPARATION

"Telling the Bees," "Verifying One's References"

Overview

Whittier's "Telling the Bees" is a good example of telling a story through poetry. Students seldom think of an author's using this genre to relate an actual incident. Whittier helps them see not only how this can be done, but how it can be done effectively. Kipling's "Verifying One's References" is a good example of "slice of life" writing. Using a single incident, he makes a simple but valuable point.

DISCUSSION

"Telling the Bees"

Introduction

You may want to introduce the poem by discussing with the students unusual rituals practiced by various cultures when someone dies. If you or any of your students have spent time on the mission field, discuss traditions held by those in other countries. Then read aloud both the headnote and Whittier's poem.

Analysis

Whittier's poem has all the elements of a good story. The speaker, a young man, begins by describing a lovely setting. But in stanza 3, line 11, the mood begins to change to one of

melancholy. Here he tells of an overgrown garden, a hint of the coming tragedy. There is also an ambiguous reference to "her" in the line, which heightens our interest. Although the lovely description is continued in stanzas 4 and 5, the images give us a sad or melancholy feeling: the year has been "heavy and slow" and the setting June sun "tangles his wings of fire in the trees." In stanza 6 Whittier piques our curiosity by revealing that the speaker is a lover describing a journey he had taken to see his love. The suspense builds in line 36 when the speaker tells us that "nothing [had] changed but the hives of the bees" and continues to build through stanza 12. The climax is in stanza 13. Here we learn that the bees are not being told about the old man. The first three lines of stanza 14 offer us a final moment of suspense.

I mind me how with a lover's care
　　From my Sunday coat
I brushed off the burrs, and smoothed my hair,
　　And cooled at the brookside my brow and throat.

Since we parted, a month had passed—　　　　　25
　　To love, a year;
Down through the beeches I looked at last
　　On the little red gate and the well-sweep* near.

I can see it all now—the slantwise rain
　　Of light through the leaves,　　　　　　30
The sundown's blaze on her windowpane,
　　The bloom of her roses under the eaves.

Just the same as a month before—
　　The house and the trees,
The barn's brown gable, the vine by the door—　　35
　　Nothing changed but the hives of bees.

Before them, under the garden wall,
　　Forward and back,
Went drearily singing the chore-girl small,
　　Draping each hive with a shred of black.　　40

Trembling, I listened: the summer sun
　　Had the chill of snow;
For I knew she was telling the bees of one
　　Gone on the journey we all must go!

Then I said to myself, "My Mary weeps　　　　45
　　For the dead today:
Haply her blind old grandsire sleeps
　　The fret and the pain of his age away."

But her dog whined low; on the doorway sill,
　　With his cane to his chin,　　　　　　50
The old man sat; and the chore-girl still
　　Sung to the bees stealing out and in.

And the song she was singing ever since
　　In my ear sounds on:
"Stay at home, pretty bees, fly not hence!　　55
　　Mistress Mary is dead and gone!"

well-sweep: long pole
on a pivot with a
bucket at one end

Note alliteration. Note also the poignancy of the speaker's actions here, in light of what follows.

Discuss these lines with the students. What meaning is compressed here? What ironic device is Whittier employing? *(The speaker and Mary have been apart for a month, but it seems to him to have been a year; hyperbole.)*

metaphors, paradoxes

Have students restate this stanza in their own words. *(The speaker thinks Mary's grandfather has died.)*

Resources

Raymond St. John, *AMERICAN LITERATURE for Christian Schools* (Greenville, S.C.: BJU Press, 1994).

Timothy Foote, "Fifty years on, 'O Best Beloved,' Kipling is making a comeback" from *Smithsonian,* January 1986.

The last line is the denouement: "Mistress Mary is dead and gone!"

Draw your students' attention to the vivid sensory images in the poem. Ask them to identify several and to choose the one they found most effective in communicating the mood of the poem.

Verifying One's References

Rudyard Kipling

"Verifying One's References"

Like Whittier, Kipling gives us a realistic "slice of life" in this short excerpt. Read the headnote and the excerpt aloud. Then draw the students' attention to "About the Poem and Essay" questions 2-4 (page 213).

Application

The styles of both Whittier and Kipling make "creating a mood" appear effortless. Such writing requires more skill than one might imagine. Have the students look back over journal entries they have written for this or other units. Have them rewrite at least one paragraph in which they consistently maintain a specific mood. Then have them read their paragraphs aloud to see whether the class can identify the mood they were trying to create.

Synecdoche: An eye represents a person who is watching and will tell others of the men's strange behavior.

simile

The fiction writer Rudyard Kipling was concerned with realism in his writing. In this excerpt from his autobiography, Something of Myself, *Kipling advised writers to check their facts. This is good advice for all who write on any subject. Certainly a high regard for accuracy should characterize the work of every Christian.*

In respect to verifying one's references, it is curious how loath a man is to take his own medicine. Once, on a Boxing Day, with hard frost coming greasily out of the ground, my friend, Sir John Bland-Sutton, the head of the College of Surgeons, came down to 'Bateman's' very full of a lecture which he was to deliver on 'gizzards.' We were settled before the fire after lunch, when he volunteered that So-and-so had said that if you hold a hen to your ear, you can hear the click in its gizzard of the little pebbles that help its digestion. 'Interesting,' said I. 'He's an authority.' 'Oh, yes, but'—a long pause—'have you any hens about here, Kipling?' I owned that I had, two hundred yards down a lane, but why not accept So-and-so? 'I can't,' said John simply, 'till I've tried it.' Remorselessly, he worried* me into taking him to the hens, who lived in an open shed in front of the gardener's cottage. As we skated over the glairy* ground, I saw an eye at the corner of the drawn-down Boxing-Day blind, and knew that my character* for sobriety would be blasted* all over the farms before nightfall. We caught an outraged pullet. John soothed her for a while (he said her pulse was a hundred and twenty-six), and held her to his ear. 'She clicks all right,' he announced. 'Listen.' I did, and there was a click enough for a lecture. '*Now* we can go back to the house,' I pleaded. 'Wait a bit. Let's catch that cock. He'll click better.' We caught him after a loud and long chase, and he clicked like a solitaire board.* I went home, my ears alive with parasites, so wrapped up in my own indignation that the fun of it escaped me. It had not been *my* verification, you see.

---

worried: agitated
glairy: glazed
character: reputation
blasted: blown to fragments
solitaire board: game board with holes for marbles or pegs

But John was right. Take nothing for granted if you can check it, even though that seem waste-work, and has nothing to do with the essentials of things. There are always men who by trade or calling know the fact or the inference that you put forth. If you are wrong by a hair in this, they argue: 'False in one thing, false in all.'

About the Poem and Essay

1. What is the surprise in Whittier's poem?
2. What is Kipling's initial reaction to his friend's request?
3. Why is this reaction ironic for a man in Kipling's profession?
4. What is meant by the phrase, "False in one thing, false in all"?

About the Poem and Essay

1. *that Mary, not the old man, has died*

2. *His initial reaction borders on irritation—he wants to accept the expert at his word.*

3. *As Kipling points out in the excerpt, a writer is held accountable for all of his facts. Readers are unforgiving of errors. Kipling, of all people, should have understood his friend's desire to "verify his references."*

4. *Answers may vary. In the discussion of this question, however, some reference should be made to the fact that a writer may have 99 facts out of 100 correct, but if a reader spots the one error, he will often disregard all that the author is saying.*

OBJECTIVES

The students will be able to

- Discuss how present context influences historical biography.

- Identify how a biography written by a contemporary can provide information not only on the historical figure but also on the era in which he lived.

- Discuss the importance of a biographer's including references to his subject's flaws even though he is sympathetic to his subject.

FURTHER HELPS

Additional activities

1. The following essays of Plutarch would make good complementary reading for "Life of Caesar." Choose one to read aloud: "How to Tell a Flatterer from a Friend," "Advice on Keeping Well," or "To an Uneducated Ruler" from *Moralia* or *Moral Essays*.

2. Numerous writers have been inspired and influenced by Plutarch. The most noted is William Shakespeare. Read

Life of Caesar

Plutarch

Bold and resourceful in battle, eloquent of speech, and humane toward his defeated opponents, Gaius Julius Caesar had all the qualities the Romans admired in a leader. Although personally ambitious, he also had the good of the people at heart. The story of his brilliant but tragic career is told by the late-Greek historian Plutarch—one of the earliest modern biographers. During a civil war of five years (45-40 B.C.), Caesar destroyed Pompey's armies in Spain, Greece, Egypt, and North Africa. Meanwhile, in Rome he was elected consul four times and dictator three times (a temporary office intended to preserve order during a time of civil confusion). After the civil war, Caesar was made dictator for life—a life, however, that was to end in two months by assassination. Caesar's death brought civil war once again and split the empire into three parts. Though his assassins had murdered him in the name of political liberty, the people of Rome pitied him. Caesar, they learned, had left each of them a sizable bequest in his will.

The legacy of Caesar extends far beyond his last will and testament. He left his surname to later emperors, to whom Caesar signified the height of imperial authority and grandeur. His legacy in literature is also monumental. The simple, clear style of his Gallic Wars and Civil Wars has given him a literary reputation equal to his military and political fame. The following story of his betrayal and assassination, later dramatized by Shakespeare, has stamped his character indelibly on the imagination of the world.

PREPARATION

"The Life of Caesar," "Sir Francis Drake"

Overview

The two selections in this lesson are biographical rather than autobiographical. Both Plutarch and Hayman were contemporaries of the men they wrote about. We, therefore, learn not only about Caesar and Drake but also about the times in which each lived.

DISCUSSION

Introduction

Introduce the lesson by discussing how present context colors our view of famous historical figures. (Our own presidents provide ample material for discussion.) This fact poses one of the greatest problems for historians. It is doubly difficult for the historian to put aside all personal bias and immerse himself in an objective examination of a figure from two or three hundred years ago. It may be difficult, for example, for an atheistic, twenty-first-century historian to understand the character of a man such as Francis Drake. The historian's bias may cause him to discount or misinterpret the importance of Drake's Christian beliefs.

Analysis

"Life of Caesar"

Julius Caesar is one of Plutarch's most effective examples of the well-rounded man. According to C. J. Gianakaris (for further information, see Resources section, page 215), "Caesar was psychologically aware of people and their needs and desires, as Plutarch stressed at the outset of his biography." Plutarch presents Caesar's accomplishments as the fruit of Caesar's character traits of self-discipline and drive. However, Gianakaris also observes that "without exception, in the heroes whose lives Plutarch traces there exist faults in character and judgment which run side by side with attributes of greatness. In the case of Caesar, Plutarch informs us, the most vocal opposition to him as a person

The period of those many expeditions in which he subdued Gaul showed Caesar to be a soldier and general not in the least inferior to any of the greatest commanders who have ever appeared at the heads of armies. The difficulty and extent of the country he subdued; the number and strength of the enemy he defeated; the wilderness and perfidiousness* of the tribes and his goodwill toward them; his clemency to the conquered; his gifts and kindnesses to his soldiers—what other general in history can match this? During the ten years he ultimately spent in Gaul, he captured eight hundred towns, subdued three hundred states, and, of the three million men who opposed him, he killed one million and captured another million.

perfidiousness: treachery

Caesar inspired his men with his own love of honor and passion for distinction. By generously distributing money and honors he showed that he was not heaping up wealth from the wars for his own luxury, but that it was a reward for valor. Moreover, there was no danger to which he did not willingly expose himself, no labor from which he shrank. Although the soldiers were not mystified by his contempt of danger, because they knew how much he coveted honor, they were astonished by his enduring so much hardship beyond his natural strength. For Caesar was of a slight build, had a soft and white skin, and was subject to epilepsy. However, he did not make his bodily weakness a pretext for ease, but rather used war as the best possible medicine; by fatiguing journeys, simple diet, frequent sleeping outdoors, and continual exercise, he fortified his body against all attacks. He slept generally in his chariot or while he was carried in a litter.* In the daytime he was thus carried to forts, garrisons, and camps, one servant sitting with him, who used to write down what he dictated as he went.

litter: a couch mounted on poles

After settling the affairs in Gaul, Caesar spent the winter by the Po,* in order to carry out his plans at Rome. He gave money to his candidates for office, so that they could corrupt the people and buy their votes and then, when elected, advance his own power. More significant was the fact that the most powerful men in Rome came to see him at Luca, among them Pompey and Crassus, and in all about two hundred senators. It was decided at Luca that Pompey and Crassus should be consuls the next year and that Caesar's command in Gaul should be extended another five years.

Po: a river in northern Italy

After this, Caesar returned to Gaul, where he found that German tribes had crossed the Rhine and stirred up revolts. So Caesar made this a pretext for invading the land of the Germans, being ambitious to be the first man to cross the Rhine with an army. He built a bridge across the river, though it was wide at this point. The current was swift and dashed trunks of trees against the foundations of the bridge. Caesar, however, drove great piles of wood into the bottom of the river just before the bridge, and these caught the trees and other things floating down and thus protected the bridge.

The bridge was completed in ten days. The Suevi, who were the most warlike people in all Germany, fled before his approach. After he had burned the countryside, Caesar returned to Gaul eighteen days later.

Caesar's expedition to Britain was the most famous example of his courage. He was the first who brought a navy into the western ocean or who sailed into the Atlantic with an army to make war. Historians had actually doubted the existence of the island, considering it a mere name or piece of fiction, and so Caesar may be said to have carried the Roman Empire

Shakespeare's *Julius Caesar* and note similarities and differences between Shakespeare's and Plutarch's accounts. See BJU Press's *Julius Caesar Teacher's Edition* for further information. (See Resources section.)

3. Read aloud from C. J. Gianakaris's biography of Plutarch (see Resources section). This is a highly recommended critical biography written in a readable style.

4. Have the students find out more about the English Sea Dogs.

5. In this unit you have read some biographies or autobiographies of different people. As a class, discuss some insights that you have gained about these people. Or assign each person to a group of students and let them discuss the biography/autobiography together and finally report their conclusions to the class.

Resources

C. J. Gianakaris, *Plutarch* (New York: Twayne Publishers, 1970).

Donna Hess, *Julius Caesar Teacher's Edition* (Greenville, S.C.: BJU Press, 1999).

derived from his obvious passion for royal power." This passion led to Caesar's premature death. Still, Plutarch remarked that "the measure of life is its excellence, not its length in years." Plutarch was to enjoy both, exuberant and active, right up to his death.

Have the students make two lists to contrast Julius Caesar's character strengths and weaknesses. See **Appendix T: Caesar's Character.**

Draw your students' attention to the fact that some of the traits might be considered strengths as well as weaknesses. Caesar's kindness in rewarding his soldiers, for example, might have led to his surrounding himself with sycophants and other men of weak character.

beyond the limits of the known world. He crossed twice from Gaul and fought several battles. But he did not win much for himself, since the islanders were very poor. Accordingly, he took hostages from the king and, after imposing a tribute, left Britain.

Caesar's troops were now so numerous that he had to distribute them in various camps for winter quarters. Then, according to custom, he went to Italy. Scattered revolts brought him back soon to Gaul; and, in the course of the winter, he visited every part of the country. But after a while, the seeds of war, which had long since been secretly sown by the most powerful men in those warlike nations, broke forth into the greatest and most dangerous war that was ever fought there. More men had gathered for it, youthful and vigorous and well armed; they had much money; their towns were strongly fortified. Besides, it was winter, and the rivers were frozen, the woods were covered with snow, paths were obliterated, and there were overflowing marshes. It seemed unlikely, therefore, that Caesar would march against the rebels. The general who was in supreme command of the rebels was Vercingetorix, chief of the Arverni.

But Caesar was gifted above all other men with the faculty of making the right use of everything in war, and especially in seizing the right moment. Therefore, as soon as he heard of the revolt, he advanced quickly in the terrible weather with his army. In fact, in the time that it would have taken an ordinary messenger to cover the distance, Caesar appeared with all his army, ravaged the country, reduced outposts, and captured towns.

Even the Haedui, who had hitherto been friends of the Roman people and had been honored by them, joined the rebels. Accordingly Caesar struck out for the land of the Sequani, who were his friends. At this point tens of thousands of the enemy set upon him, but after much slaughter he won a victory.

The rest of the enemy fled with Vercingetorix into a town called Alesia. Caesar besieged it, though the height of the walls and the number of defenders made it appear impregnable. Then suddenly, from outside the walls, Caesar was assailed by a greater danger than can be described. For the best men of Gaul, picked out of each nation and well-armed, came to the relief of Alesia. There were 300,000 of these men, and inside the town were 170,000 more. And so Caesar was shut up between the two forces. He now built two walls, one toward the town, and the other against the relieving army, for he knew that he would be ruined if the enemy joined forces.

The danger that Caesar underwent at Alesia justly gained him great honor and gave him the opportunity of showing his valor as no other contest had done. But it seems extraordinary that he was able to defeat thousands of men outside the town without those inside being able to see it. Even the Romans guarding the wall next to the town did not know of it, until finally they heard the cries of the men and women inside who spied the Roman soldiers carrying into their camp great quantities of shields adorned with gold and silver, and breastplates stained with blood, besides cups and tents made in the Gallic fashion. Just as fast as that did a vast army vanish like a ghost or dream, most of them being killed on the spot.

At last those who were in Alesia surrendered. Vercingetorix put on his best armor, adorned his horse, and rode out of the gates to Caesar; then he dismounted and threw off his armor and remained quietly sitting at Caesar's feet until he was led away for triumph in Rome.

Back in Gaul, Caesar had received letters announcing that his daughter Julia, Pompey's wife, had died in childbirth; soon afterward the child also died. Both Caesar and Pompey were much affected by Julia's death; as were also their friends, for they felt that the alliance was broken which had kept the troubled state in peace.

Caesar had long ago resolved upon Pompey's overthrow, as had Pompey, for that matter, on his. The fear of Crassus had kept them in peace, but Crassus had recently been killed. And so, if one of them wished to make himself the greatest man in Rome, he had only to overthrow the other.

Rome itself was now the scene of election riots and murders. Some thought that the only hope lay in monarchy. Others tried to reconcile Pompey and Caesar, but they would not yield, and finally two of Caesar's friends—Antony and Curio—were driven out of the senate house with insults. This gave Caesar the chance to inflame his soldiers, for he showed them two reputable Romans of authority who had been forced to escape in a hired wagon, dressed as slaves.

Caesar was now in Gaul on the southern side of the Alps, with 300 cavalry and 5,000 infantry; the rest of his army was beyond the Alps, with orders to follow. But Caesar felt that here, at the beginning of his design, he did not need large forces; he planned, rather, to astound his enemies with the speed and boldness of his plan. This particular day he spent in public as a spectator at gladiatorial games. Then, a little before night, he dressed and went into the hall and chatted for some time with those he had invited to supper. When it began to grow dark, he rose from the table and made his excuses to the company. Then he and a few friends drove off in hired wagons, some going one way and some another—so that no one could suspect what they were up to—until at last he came to the River Rubicon, which divides Cisalpine Gaul* from Italy proper.

Cisalpine Gaul: Gaul south of the Alps

Caesar now began to reflect upon the danger, and he wavered when he considered the greatness of the enterprise. He checked himself and halted while he turned things over in his mind. He discussed the matter at some length with friends who were with him, estimating how many calamities his passing of that small river would bring on mankind and what a tale about it would be transmitted to posterity. At last, in a sort of passion, throwing aside calculation and abandoning himself to what might come, he used the proverb of people entering upon dangerous attempts, "The die is cast," and crossed the river. He then pushed south as fast as possible.

Wide gates, so to speak, were now thrown open to let in war upon every land and sea. Men and women fled, in their consternation, from one town of Italy to another. The city of Rome was overrun with a deluge of people flying in from all the neighboring places. Magistrates could no longer govern, nor could the eloquence of an orator quiet the mob.

Pompey at this time had more forces than Caesar. But he did not think clearly and believed false reports that Caesar was close at hand. He was carried away by the general panic. And so he issued an edict that the city was in a state of anarchy* and left it, ordering the senators to follow him unless they preferred tyranny to their country and liberty.

anarchy: lawlessness

Pompey fled south all the way to Brundisium and shipped the consuls and soldiers across the Adriatic Sea. He himself soon followed, on Caesar's approach. But Caesar could not pursue him, since he had no boats, and therefore turned back to Rome. He had made himself master of all Italy, without bloodshed, in sixty days.

Caesar arranged things in Rome and then went off to Spain, so that no enemy would be left behind him when he marched against

Discuss with the students the proverb based on this event, "crossing the Rubicon." Ask them what they think this statement means today metaphorically. *(making a momentous decision that cannot be retracted)* Why does it have this meaning? *(It alludes to this decision of Caesar's—to start a civil war in an attempt to overthrow Pompey, his rival for complete power in Rome.)*

Although the tone here is quite different, ask students what other selection in this unit shows powerful people allowing themselves to be "carried away by the general panic." *("The Day the Dam Broke")*

Note Plutarch's references to omens here and below. Discuss with the students the foolishness of trusting in supposed "signs" and superstitions.

metaphors

Pompey. Back in Rome, he stopped only briefly and then hastened with all speed to Brundisium. It was the beginning of January and the winter storms made it difficult for him to transport his troops across the Adriatic. Finally this was done, and Caesar was joined by Antony and other friends. After several skirmishes, both Pompey and Caesar moved their armies into Greece.

The two armies now encamped at Pharsalus, in Thessaly.* Pompey was still against fighting, because of certain omens. His friends, on the other hand, acted as if they had already won the battle, and some even sent messages to Rome to rent houses for them fit for consuls and praetors,* so sure were they of themselves. The cavalry was especially anxious to fight, being splendidly armed and mounted on fine horses; also, they numbered 7,000 to Caesar's 1,000. Similarly, Pompey had 45,000 infantry to Caesar's 22,000.

Thessaly: an ancient division of northern Greece
praetors: magistrates just below the rank of consul

Caesar collected together his soldiers and told them that reinforcements were on the way, but they called out to him not to wait. As soon as the sacrifices had been made to the gods, the seer* told him that within three days he would come to a decisive action.

seer: prophet

The night before the battle, as Caesar was making the rounds about midnight, there was a light seen in the heavens, very bright and flaming, which seemed to pass over Caesar's camp and fall into Pompey's. In the morning, Caesar's soldiers saw panic among the enemy.

The signal for battle was now given on both sides. Pompey ordered the infantry not to break their order, but to stand their ground and receive the enemy's first attack till they came within a javelin's throw. Caesar, in his own writings, blames Pompey's generalship in this regard. Pompey should have realized, says Caesar, how the first encounter, when made on the run, gives weight to the blows and actually fires the men's spirits into a flame.

While the infantry was engaged on the flank, Pompey's cavalry rode up confidently and opened their ranks wide, so that they could surround Caesar's right wing. At this very moment, Caesar's six cohorts* of infantry, which he had moved up from the rear and had stationed behind his right wing, rushed out and attacked the cavalry. They now followed the special instructions which Caesar had given them. This was that they were not to throw their javelins from a distance nor were they to strike at the legs and thighs of the enemy. They must aim at their faces. Caesar had noted that most of Pompey's men were young, not accustomed to battles and wounds; they were naturally vain, being in the flower of their youth, and would not wish to risk either death now or a scar for the future. And that is the way it worked out. For Pompey's cavalry could not stand the sight of javelins, but turned and covered their faces. Now in disorder, they fled and ruined everything. With Pompey's cavalry beaten back, Caesar's men outflanked the infantry and cut it to pieces.

cohorts: division of a legion containing several hundred men each

When Pompey, who was commanding the other wing of his army, saw the cavalry broken and fleeing, he was no longer himself. He forgot that he was Pompey the Great and, like someone whom the gods have deprived of his senses, retired to his tent. He did not say a word, but just sat there, until his whole army was routed and the enemy appeared upon the defenses which had been thrown before his camp. Then he seemed to recover his senses, and with the words, "What, are they in the camp too?" he took off his general's uniform and put on ordinary clothes. He then stole off and made his way to Egypt.

After the victory Caesar pardoned his opponents, including Brutus—who afterward was to kill him. He then set off in pursuit of Pompey, but when he reached Alexandria, in Egypt, he learned that Pompey had been murdered. This caused Caesar to weep, for, as he wrote his friends in Rome, his greatest desire was always to save the lives of fellow citizens who had fought against him.

Caesar passed on to Syria and Asia Minor. At Zela, in Pontus,* he destroyed Pharnaces,* an enemy of Rome, and sent the senate a message that expressed the promptness and rapidity of his action: "I came, I saw, I conquered."

Pontus: a country of Asia Minor on the Black Sea
Pharnaces: king of Pontus

His victories brought war at long last to an end. Triumphs, banquets, and other celebrations were held in Rome on a magnificent scale. But a census of people showed that Rome's population had declined from 320,000 to 150,000. So great a waste had the civil wars made in Rome alone, to say nothing of the other parts of Italy and the provinces.

The Romans, hoping that the government of a single person would give them time to breathe after so many civil wars and calamities, made Caesar dictator for life. This was an out-and-out tyranny, for his power was both absolute and perpetual. But Caesar was moderate and even gave offices to those who had fought against him, such as Brutus and Cassius. He entertained the common people with more feasting and free gifts of grain and founded colonies at Carthage and Corinth, which Rome had destroyed a century earlier. The colonies provided a good place for his soldiers to settle.

Caesar was born to do great things, and had a passion for honor. His noble exploits merely inflamed him with a passion to accomplish even more. But Caesar's desire to be king brought on him open and mortal hatred.

One day, when a festival was being celebrated in the Forum, Caesar was dressed in his triumphal robe and seated on a golden chair at the speaker's platform, or rostra. Antony, who was then consul, came up to Caesar and offered him a diadem* wreathed with laurel. There was a slight shout of approval from the crowd, and when Caesar refused it, there was universal applause. It was offered a second time and again refused, and again applauded. Caesar, finding that this idea could not succeed, ordered the diadem to be carried into the Capitol.

diadem: ornamental headband

Such matters made the multitude think of Marcus Brutus, whose paternal ancestor centuries earlier had slain the last of Rome's kings. But the honors and favors he had received from Caesar took the edge off Brutus's desire to overthrow the new monarchy. Those who looked on Brutus to effect the change would put papers near his official chair, with sentences such as, "You are asleep, Brutus," "You are no longer Brutus." Cassius, too, because of a private grudge against Caesar, was eager to be done with him. Caesar had his suspicions of Cassius and once remarked to a friend, "What do you think Cassius is aiming at? I don't like him; he looks so pale." He added that he feared pale, lean fellows, meaning Cassius and Brutus.

Fate, however, is to all appearances more unavoidable than expected. Many strange prodigies* and apparitions were now observed. As to the lights in the heavens, the noises heard in the night, and the wild birds which perched in the Forum, these are perhaps not worth noticing in a case as great as this. But, it is also said that a seer warned Caesar to watch

Discuss this attribute of Caesar's personality. Ask students whether they think pardoning opponents and saving lives of those who had fought against him was a strength or a weakness. Those who view it as a strength might cite forgiveness as a virtue. Those who cite it as a weakness might point out that Caesar was murdered by one whom he had pardoned.

In Latin, *"Veni, vidi, vici"*—an oft-quoted (and sometimes parodied) statement. (For a list of common and not-so-common Latin words, phrases, and sentences, go to bjup.com.)

Point out to students that this is the same location referred to in Paul's letters to the Corinthians.

for a great danger on the Ides of March.* When this day arrived, Caesar met the seer as he was going into the senate house and said jokingly to him, "Well, the Ides of March have come." The seer answered calmly, "Yes, they have come, but they are not yet past."

prodigies: omens
Ides of March: March 15

The day before his assassination, Caesar dined with Lepidus. As he was signing some letters at the table, the question came up as to what kind of death was best. Caesar answered immediately, "A sudden one." Later, when he was in bed, all the doors and the windows of the house flew open together; he was startled at the noise and the light which broke into the room, and he sat up in bed. By the light of the moon he could see his wife, Calpurnia, fast asleep, but he also heard her utter in her dream some indistinct words and inarticulate groans. Later on, she said that she had been dreaming that she was weeping over Caesar, holding him butchered in her arms.

In the morning, Calpurnia urged Caesar to postpone the meeting of the senate to another day, but he would not hear of it. After he left his house, a teacher of Greek philosophy, who knew of the conspiracy, slipped Caesar a piece of paper and said, "Read this Caesar, alone and quickly." Caesar tried to read it, but could not, on account of the crowd pressing in on him. But he kept the note in his hand till he entered the senate.

All these things might happen by chance. But the place that was destined for the scene of the murder—where the senate was then meeting—was the same in which Pompey's statue stood. A supernatural force seemed to guide affairs to this spot. In fact, just before the murder, Cassius looked at Pompey's statue and silently implored his aid.

When Caesar entered, the senate rose in respect, and then some of the confederates pressed up to him, pretending that they had petitions. As he seated himself, Cimber seized his toga and pulled it down from his neck, which was the signal for assault. Casca gave him the first cut in the neck, neither a mortal nor a dangerous blow, for he was probably too nervous, here at the beginning. Caesar immediately turned around and seized the dagger and kept hold on it. And both cried out, Caesar in Latin, "Vile Casca, what does this mean?" And Casca in Greek, to his brother, "Brother, help!"

The conspirators now closed in on Caesar from every side, with their drawn daggers in their hands. No matter which way Caesar turned, he was met with blows; on all sides he was surrounded by wild beasts. The conspirators had agreed that each of them should make a stab at Caesar. And so Brutus also stabbed him. When Caesar saw Brutus's dagger, he covered his face with his toga and let himself fall at the foot of the pedestal on which Pompey's statue stood. It seemed as if Pompey himself had presided, as it were, over the revenge of his enemy, who lay here at his feet and breathed out his last with twenty-three wounds in his body.

The senators, who had not been part of the conspiracy, now fled out of the doors and filled the people with so much alarm that some shut up their houses, and others left their shops. Everyone seemed to run this way and that. Antony and Lepidus, Caesar's most faithful friends, who had been kept out of the senate house during the murder, sneaked off and hid in friends' houses. Brutus and his followers, still hot from their deed, marched in a body from the senate house to the Capitol and called on people, as they passed them, to resume their liberty.

Next day, Brutus and the others came down from the Capitol and addressed the people, who showed by their silence that they pitied Caesar and respected Brutus. Then the senate passed an amnesty* for what was past and took steps to reconcile all parties. The senate ordered that Caesar should receive divine honors, and that no act of his was to be revoked. At the same time, it gave Brutus and his followers the command of provinces and other important posts. And so, people thought that everything had been brought to a happy conclusion.

amnesty: general pardon

But when Caesar's will was opened and it was found that he had left a considerable legacy to each Roman citizen, and then when his body was carried through the Forum all mangled with wounds, the people could contain themselves no longer. They heaped together a pile of benches, railings, and tables, and then set Caesar's corpse on top and set fire to it all.*

set . . . all: Bodies of rich or great men were cremated rather than buried.

Caesar died in his fifty-sixth year, not having survived Pompey by much more than four years. The empire and power which he sought through his life with so much risk, he finally achieved with much difficulty, but he got little from it except glory. But the great genius,* which attended him through his lifetime, even after his death remained the avenger of his murder, pursuing through every sea and land all those connected with it and allowing none to escape.

genius: presiding spirit

The most remarkable of mere human coincidences was that which befell Cassius, who, when he was defeated by Antony and Octavian* at Philippi, killed himself with the same dagger which he had used against Caesar; Brutus also committed suicide after that battle. But the most extraordinary supernatural happenings were the great comet, which shone very bright for seven nights after Caesar's death and then disappeared, and the dimness of the sun. The sun remained pale and dull all that year, never really shining at sunrise and not giving much heat. Consequently, the air was damp and the fruits never properly ripened.

Octavian: Caesar's grandnephew and adopted son, later Augustus Caesar

About the Author

The Greek writer-orator Plutarch (c. A.D. 46-c. 120) was the most famous and influential biographer of ancient times. Born into a wealthy Greek family, Plutarch enjoyed the privileges of an extensive education and a prominent social standing. His keen memory and diligently kept notebooks provided him with a rich mine of biographical, historical, and cultural material. Plutarch transformed this material into biographical sketches and essays, teaching moral truth and encouraging upright living. Although informative, his writing is artful, displaying the characteristic marks of literature. Most noticeable is his use of imaginative comparison to illustrate moral precepts. His writing bears out his own assertion that his primary goal was not to record facts but to examine "the signs of the soul [or character] in men."

Discuss the concluding paragraphs of the account with students. Possible topics:

1. Suppose a group of senators banded together today to stab the president to death. How would public reaction be different from what it was in Caesar's day? Why would it be different? How might it be the same? *(Answers may vary.)*

2. Again the idea of omens and "signs" comes up here. Discuss the repeated references throughout the account to such events. What do students think of these occurrences? *(Possible responses include that they never really happened—although Plutarch's apparently reliable relating of events would belie that; that they were mere coincidences; or that they were signs from the Lord to turn people's hearts from wickedness.)*

Sir Francis Drake

Robert Hayman

One of England's greatest naval heroes was Sir Francis Drake. During his famous voyage around the world (1577-80), Drake attacked Spanish ships and towns and brought back an immense treasure in gold and precious stones. His purpose was to disrupt Spanish commerce and weaken Spain's grip on the New World. Drake was known as a devout Christian who would not tolerate evil among his men and regularly led them in worship aboard ship. The following poetic tribute does not exaggerate the goodness of his character and reputation. The almost humorous despair of the poet adds luster to the portrait of his hero.

The Dragon that our seas did raise his crest*
And brought back heaps of gold unto his nest,
Unto his foes more terrible than thunder,
Glory of his age, after-ages' wonder,
Excelling all those that excelled before—   5
It's feared we shall have none such any more—
Effecting all, he sole did undertake,
Valiant, just, wise, mild, honest, godly Drake.
This man when I was little I did meet
As he was walking up Totnes' long street.*   10
He asked me whose I was. I answered him.

Dragon . . . crest: whose crest our seas did raise (drake is a form of the word dragon)

Totnes: a town on a hill above the river Dart about eight miles upriver from the seaport Dartmouth in Devonshire.

"Sir Francis Drake"

Although your students may have studied Plutarch, the author of the previous selection, they are probably unfamiliar with Robert Hayman, the contemporary of Drake and the author of this poem. Before examining the poem, therefore, you may want to have them read the note on Hayman in the "About the Author" section.

Next read the headnote and poem aloud. (Point out to students that Drake was not a pirate; he was acting on behalf of the English crown in his attacks on Spanish commerce.) Then have the students give a brief character description of Drake based on what they have learned about him from the poem. Point out the Biblical allusion in line 18. "His gifts, Elias-like," alludes to the prophet Elijah, whose gifts were both praiseworthy and awe-inspiring. Draw the students' attention to II Kings 2. Discuss with the students how this passage sheds light on Hayman's allusion. Point out that the author is expressing his wish that Drake's myriad gifts could be passed on to him as Elijah's were to his successor, Elisha. He goes on to say, however, that he does not believe this to be possible.

Having studied Caesar and Drake, ask your students which they would most like to emulate. Have them also explain why they made the choice they did.

Application

Scripture often uses negative examples to teach us positive lessons. Jonah, the prodigal son (as well as the elder brother in the parable), and King Saul are just a few examples. Have the students choose one such character from the Bible and do a character study. Following their study, have them share with the class the most important lesson they learned from their character analysis.

He asked me if his good friend were within.
A fair red orange in his hand he had;
He gave it me, whereof I was right glad,
Takes and kissed me, and prays, "God bless my boy,"   15
Which I record with comfort to this day.
Could he on me have breathèd with his breath
His gifts, Elias-like, after his death,
Then had I been enabled for to do
Many brave things I have a heart unto.   20
I have as great desire as e'er had he
To joy, annoy, friends, foes; but 'twill not be.

About the Essay and Poem

1. What are Caesar's sympathetic traits that Plutarch brings out in this essay?
2. Does Plutarch also provide us with a glimpse at Caesar's flaws?
3. Why do you think Plutarch chose to write about this famous commander? Did he have a specific moral purpose?
4. What is the Biblical allusion used in Hayman's poem about Drake?
5. How would you compare the two great commanders Caesar and Drake? Which would you like to emulate?

About the Author

Robert Hayman (d. 1631?) was born in Devonshire, England. As a gentleman of the ruling class, he was expected to be skilled in the fine arts, including the art of composing verse. By 1621 he had earned a reputation as a poet of quality.

For a time, Hayman served as governor of the Harbour Grace settlement in Newfoundland, but by 1628 he had returned to England. After returning to his homeland, he published a book whose title is absurdly long. It reads in part as follows: "*Quodlibets,* lately come over from Britaniola, Old Newfoundland. Epigrams and other small parcels, both morall and divine. The first foure books being the authors owne. . . ." The collection included translations of John Owen, the epigrammatist, and François Rabelais, the French satirist. After his book was published, Hayman moved to British Guiana. No evidence exists that he ever returned to England.

About the Essay and Poem

1. *Answers will vary but may include his self-discipline and drive, his kindness to his soldiers, his courage, and so on. See Analysis section, pages 214-25.*

2. *Yes—his penchant for luxury, his physical infirmities, his superstition, his pride. See Analysis section.*

3. *Answers may vary. Plutarch knew Caesar was a great leader and wanted him to be remembered throughout history. He wanted to write an accurate record of this great man's strengths as well as weaknesses so that succeeding generations could learn from him.*

4. *"His gift, Elias-like" alludes to the prophet Elijah, whose gifts were both praiseworthy and awe-inspiring (cf. II Kings 2). See Analysis section, page 222.*

5. *Answers may vary. Allow any response that the students can support from details in the essay and poem.*

UNIT EIGHT

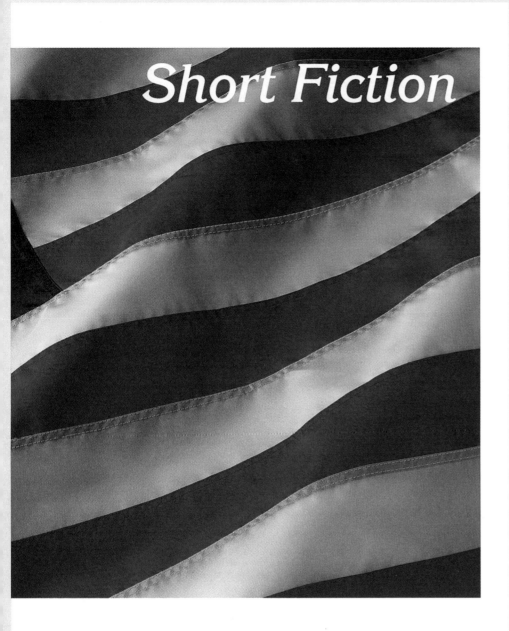

Short Fiction

OBJECTIVES

The students will be able to

- Defend fiction's potential for teaching valuable truths.
- Analyze the organization of a work of fiction.
- Interpret and evaluate fiction.

FURTHER HELPS

Additional activity

Choose one of the following excerpts from John Bunyan's *The Pilgrim's Progress:* Christian and Faithful at Vanity Fair, Christian and Hopeful sleeping in By-path Meadow and their subsequent capture by Giant Despair, the pilgrims' journey through the country of Conceit. Discuss with the students the universal truths Bunyan presents through these fictional episodes. Remind the students that many writers of fiction, even those who are not guided by God's Word, are endeavoring to present universal truths. Christian readers must therefore develop discernment when approaching any literature, short fiction included.

Resource

Grace Collins Hargis, *The Pilgrim's Progress Teacher's Guide* (Greenville, S.C.: BJU Press, 2002).

A work of fiction is an imagined story. It may be written in poetry—as a ballad, for instance—or in prose. It may be short, as in the case of the prose tale. Or it may be long, as in the case of the novel. But all fiction is imagined rather than literally true, and for this reason its value has at times been questioned. When we read tales of adventure that never happened with persons who never existed, are we not escaping reality? Are not those who enjoy novels preferring falsehood to truth? Isn't fiction really a lie?

First, let us realize that fiction does not pretend to tell the truth in an ordinary sense. Therefore, it does not necessarily lie. Second, fiction *does* claim to tell the truth in a deeper sense. It offers what the author considers basic truths about man and his life in the world. Like biography, it aims not only to please the reader but also to inform and improve him. A parable or a fable, for example, may be just as true, in what it teaches about life, as the most accurate news release. In fact, it may summarize more of life. It may set forth a moral or spiritual principle more consistently. It may show God's dealings with man more clearly. Notice the importance of *may* in these statements. The truth and value of fiction depend on the accuracy with which it represents man and the world. This accuracy depends upon the agreement of the author's imagination with the Word of God.

One of the liveliest imaginations ever given by God to a human being belonged to John Bunyan. Silenced from preaching in pulpits, he continued to preach by his pen. We can read in his spiritual autobiography, *Grace Abounding to the Chief of Sinners,* a factual account of events leading up to and following his conversion. We can read in his fictional narrative *The Pilgrim's Progress* an equally true, though unhistorical, account of the same process. As an allegory of the Christian life, *The Pilgrim's Progress* charts the experience not only of Bunyan but also of every faithful believer who has struggled in his journey through the world toward the Celestial City. Bunyan's writing reminds us that a fictional narrative need be no less true to life than a nonfictional one. It may very well be more—for it displays general human experience rather than just the life of an individual man.

Before Bunyan, most narrative fiction was written in poetry. Epics, romances, and verse tales were the standard fictional genres. Though fictional poetic narrative still appears, most popular fiction is now written in prose. Modern prose fiction divides into the territories of the novel and the short story. The novel, which emerged as a genre in the eighteenth century, differs from most earlier long fiction not only by being written in prose but also by focusing on the actions of ordinary people. The short story, an even more recent form, is less ambitious in length and complexity.

The basic unit of all narrative is the *incident.* In biography it takes the form of the *anecdote.* In prose fiction it is known as an *episode,* if the story contains more than one. The short story usually contains, or at least focuses on, a single incident. Earlier events are summarized as introductory background

---

PREPARATION

Short Fiction Introduction

Overview

This essay explains the potential value and the specific characteristics of fictional writing. If your students have used FUNDAMENTALS OF LITERATURE *for Christian Schools* in ninth grade, much of the material in this introduction will be review for them.

DISCUSSION

Introduction

Discuss with the students fictional stories or poems that they especially liked from previous units. Ask them to explain why they liked each work. Was it the topic that sparked their interest? Did they find themselves "caught up" in the mood of the piece? Did the work accurately represent man and his world? Did the work broaden their outlook on life? What else did they learn from the selection?

Analysis

Read the introduction aloud in class. You may want students to fill in **Appendix U: Short Fiction Crossword,** which reviews terms covered in the introduction. Using the same stories and poems that the students chose to open the discussion, have them jot down answers to the following questions:

1. How are the episodes in the story or poem organized?

2. What is the most important incident in the story?

3. Did the work use the technique of flashback? If so, what important information was included in the flashback?

4. What was the central conflict of the story or poem?

5. Was this conflict internal or external?

6. Who was the protagonist?

7. Who was the antagonist?

8. What was the setting of the work?

9. Did the setting play a major part in the work? Did it help establish a specific atmosphere or mood? Give an example.

Have the students share the information about their stories. As stated in the introduction, de-

or inserted later parenthetically as **flashback.** The novel contains many incidents. These connect to form the **plot.** The arrangement of incidents in a plot may be chronological (in order of occurrence) or nonchronological or may be a blend of these. A typical plot begins with an incident of high interest; focuses on a series of crucial episodes, linked by lesser incidents; and climaxes with an incident containing a surprising revelation. The conclusion normally follows shortly.

Good writers control the flow of information to the reader or to the characters in order to provide for climactic disclosure. In a story of suspense such as "The Sire de Maletroit's Door," character and reader are surprised or relieved by the outcome. In a story of dramatic irony such as "A Germ Destroyer," only the character is surprised or relieved. The reader has been put "in the know" by the author beforehand. Some of the most memorable incidents of disclosure appear in the Bible: Joseph's revelation of his identity to his brothers (Genesis 45), Ruth's of hers to Boaz (Ruth 3), and Esther's of hers to Haman and Ahasuerus (Esther 7). These historical narratives are among the world's great examples of dramatic irony, for the reader knows the identities from the beginning.

The most astonishing incident of disclosure in all literature, human or divine, is the event recorded in the Gospels in which God punished His own Son for the sins of mankind. The Gospel narrative, to one who did not know the outcome, would be powerfully suspenseful. The climactic incident of the crucifixion solves the problems of the preceding narrative—and of all human life—in a completely unsuspected though perfectly suitable way. To one who does know the outcome, the narrative generates the sublimest dramatic irony. Neither the rulers of Israel nor the disciples had any comprehension of what would happen or, when it was happening, of the meaning of it all. The very efforts of Christ's enemies to defeat Him brought His plan to completion. Their hatred of Him enabled His love for them to succeed.

Essential to plot is **conflict.** The central character contends with forces that may defeat and even destroy him. In "The Adventure of the Speckled Band," Sherlock Holmes struggles against an adversary of extraordinary strength and intelligence, Grimesby Roylott. Hardy's Tony Kytes grapples with an awkward circumstance, though comic and of his own making. The basketball player in "Foul Shot" seeks mental mastery of the physical laws determining the arc of a successful throw. The opponent of the central character may be therefore a person, a situation, or a natural force. In these cases the conflict is said to be **external,** outside the protagonist. The conflict may also be **internal.** A person's worst enemy may be himself. Bradbury's drummer boy struggles not only with the enemy but more importantly with his own fears. Even in a courageous, mature person, such as Crane's infantry captain, love may strive with anger, pity with duty, patience with zeal.

The characters of a story are often distinguished as major and minor,

termining the tone of a work is the most important, and often the most difficult, task in analysis. But we need to understand the tone of a work before we can properly evaluate and apply its theme. Choose one (or more, as time permits) of the stories just discussed. The information provided should enable the students to determine the tone of the work.

Application

Finally, have the students jot down what they believe to be the central idea of their story and have them evaluate this idea in the light of Scripture. The questions provided in the last paragraph of the introductory essay can help them in their evaluation. Once they have completed their evaluation, ask them to apply what they have learned from the story to a contemporary situation. Have them share their ideas with the class.

static and developing, flat and round. The chief or main character is known as the **protagonist,** literally the "first actor." His opponent (whether a person, a force, or a situation) is the **antagonist.** Static characters remain the same during the course of a story. Developing characters change, perhaps maturing in self-control, social feelings, or understanding of life. They may undergo a moral education, learning through hard experience the truth about themselves and the world and gaining certain virtues. Flat characters have little individuality—few distinguishing physical or psychological traits. Round characters are presented in greater detail as individuals, usually with some inward complexity. Most novels use characters of each type.

Obviously a story must take place at a certain time and place. We need therefore to identify its **setting.** Writers choose their settings carefully with a regard to possible associations in the reader's mind. The old mansion in "A Gray Sleeve" may suggest, with its occupants, something of the fading strength and splendor of the South. The dark afternoon is appropriate to the dismal business of war, as Crane perceived it. These both combine to create a sensation of gloom. Crane's story shows how physical location in space and time can contribute to **atmosphere,** the emotion pervading a story.

The atmosphere of a story is sometimes confused with its **tone.** Whereas atmosphere is the emotion shared by the characters and the reader, tone is the attitude of approval or disapproval toward a character, event, situation, or idea that the reader is meant to share with the author. Simply defined, tone is the attitude of a work toward its subject. This attitude may be stated. More often, though, it is not. Crane does not tell us his attitude toward war—toward military duty and honor. He leaves that attitude to be inferred from the pattern and details of the narrative. The soldiers' charge appears ridiculous when we consider the weakness of the fortification, an old house, and the helplessness of its defenders: an old man, a wounded youth, and a young girl. The captain seems confused and indecisive, pulled in one direction by humanitarian concern and in another by military duty.

Determining the tone of a work is the most important, and often the most difficult, task in analysis. We need to know how the work judges a questionable action, such as the captain's swerving from duty, before we can judge the work. The Bible describes evil actions but leaves no doubt what our attitude toward those actions should be. It does not leave us in moral confusion. Good fiction likewise does not, directly or by implication, call good evil or evil good. It does not leave moral questions unanswered. Its moral viewpoint is that of the Scriptures.

Fiction then needs to be judged as strictly by standards of truth as nonfiction. There is no subtler persuasion than that which occurs in a well-written serious work of fiction. We will need to ask of a story whether God—the Biblical God—is present and active, at least by implication, in its imaginary world. Is there "a Providence that shapes our ends, rough hew them as we may," as Shakespeare has Hamlet say? Do characters' actions have moral consequences? Is evil condemned and good approved? Authors set out to influence their readers in a total way—intellectually, emotionally, and spiritually—to embrace their views of the world. The discerning Christian approves of fiction that is neither *cynical* (denying the possibility of happiness and goodness) nor *sentimental* (denying the possibility of unhappiness and evil) but Biblically *realistic* (affirming the possibility of happiness and goodness as man acts in accordance with the will of God).

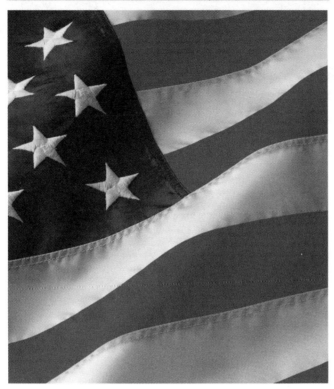

"The Sire de Maletroit's Door,"
"Lady Clare"

Emphasize this statement with the students before they read the story. Fiction written during the Romantic period (1789-1832) bases its plot on emotion rather than realism.

metonymy (swaggering walk represents pride)

safe-conduct: "protection given a person passing through a military zone or occupied area" (*Merriam-Webster's Collegiate Dictionary*, 10th ed., 1994)

FURTHER HELPS

Additional activities

1. Have a student find out the meaning of *maletroit* (narrow-mindedness, meanness, evil) and *blanche* (white, indicating purity or goodness). Note that the color white reappears in "Lady Clare," symbolizing the same thing.

The Sire de Maletroit's Door

Robert Louis Stevenson

"The Sire de Maletroit's Door" is a delightful Romantic adventure set in fifteenth-century France. It is among the earliest examples of modern short fiction. In this story, Stevenson's characters and scenes are realistically drawn. His plot, however, is typically Romantic, relying on incidents that are emotionally dynamic rather than rationally controlled.

Denis de Beaulieu was not yet two-and-twenty, but he counted himself a grown man, and a very accomplished cavalier into the bargain. Lads were early formed in that rough, warfaring epoch; and when one has been in a pitched battle and a dozen raids, has killed one's man in an honorable fashion, and knows a thing or two of strategy and mankind, a certain swagger in the gait is surely pardoned. He had put up his horse with due care, and supped with due deliberation; and then, in a very agreeable frame of mind, went out to pay a visit in the gray of the evening. It was not a very wise proceeding on the young man's part. He would have done better to remain beside the fire or go decently to bed. For the town was full of troops of Burgundy and England* under a mixed command; and though Denis was there on safe-conduct, his safe-conduct was like to serve him little on a chance encounter.

Burgundy and England: The Duke of Burgundy, a Frenchman, was an ally of England for a time.

It was September, 1429; the weather had fallen sharp; a flighty, piping wind, laden with

---

PREPARATION

"The Sire de Maletroit's Door,"
"Lady Clare"

Overview

Both the selections in this lesson are Romantic in style. Thus, the characters and action of these works provide an interesting contrast to the more realistic selections that the students have read thus far.

Potential problems

The words "Sire de Maletroit" are pronounced *seer dø maløtrwa (ø— French* **feu***).*

DISCUSSION

"The Sire de Maletroit's Door"

Introduction

"The Sire de Maletroit's Door," written in 1878, is one of the earliest modern English short stories. It is in many ways characteristic of Romantic writing. The setting is typically distant in time, the perspective is almost eccentric, and the atmosphere is emotionally turbulent. (For more information on the Romantic movement, see *BRITISH LITERATURE for Christian Schools*, pages 504-15.)

Before the students read the story, tell them to be prepared to discuss its ending afterwards. Is it what they expected? Tell them that although

it may not be the type of ending today's readers might expect, it is an appropriate ending for fiction written during the Romantic period. Then have the students read the story either silently or aloud.

Analysis

After the students have read the story, discuss it with them. Although the characters are drawn realistically enough to make the action convincing, they are still Romantic types: the distressed maiden, the cruel uncle, and the noble hero. Have the students compare them to the characters from "The Leak" (pp. 30-40). How do the characters differ? Which of the characters seem more like people you could meet on the street? What about the conflicts that em-showers, beat about the township; and the dead leaves ran riot along the streets. Here and there a window was already lighted up, and the noise of men-at-arms, making merry over supper within, came forth in fits and was swallowed up and carried away by the wind. The night fell swiftly; the flag of England, fluttering on the spire top, grew even fainter and fainter against the flying clouds,—a black speck like a swallow in the tumultuous, leaden chaos of the sky. As the night fell the wind rose and began to hoot under archways and roar amid the tree-tops in the valley below the town.

Denis de Beaulieu walked fast and was soon knocking at his friend's door; but though he promised himself to stay only a little while and make an early return, his welcome was so pleasant, and he found so much to delay him, that it was already long past midnight before he said good-bye upon the threshold. The wind had fallen again in the meanwhile; the night was as black as the grave; not a star, nor a glimmer of moonshine, slipped through the canopy of cloud. Denis was ill acquainted with the intricate lanes of Chateau Landon; even by daylight he had found some trouble in picking his way; and in this absolute darkness he soon lost it altogether. He was certain of one thing only,—to keep mounting the hill; for his friend's house lay at the lower end, or tail, of Chateau Landon, while the inn was up at the head, under the great church spire. With this clue to go upon he stumbled and groped forward, now breathing more freely in the open places where there was a good slice of sky overhead, now feeling along the wall in stifling closes.* It is an eerie and mysterious position to be thus submerged in opaque blackness in an almost unknown town. The silence is terrifying in its possibilities. The touch of cold window bars to the exploring hand startles the man like a touch of a toad; the inequalities of the pavement shake his heart into his mouth; a piece of denser darkness

threatens an ambush or a chasm in the pathway; and where the air is brighter, the houses put on strange and bewildering appearances, as if to lead him further from his way. For Denis, who had to regain his inn without attracting notice, there was real danger as well as mere discomfort in the walk, and he went warily and boldly at once, and at every corner paused to make an observation.

stifling closes: narrow passageways or alleys

He had been for some time threading a lane so narrow that he could touch a wall with either hand, when it began to open out and go sharply downward. Plainly this lay no longer in the direction of his inn, but the hope of a little more light tempted him forward to reconnoitre.* The land ended in a terrace with a bartizan wall,* which gave an outlook between high houses, as out of an embrasure,* into the valley lying dark and formless several hundred feet below. Denis looked down, and could discern a few tree-tops waving and a single speck of brightness where the river ran across a weir.* The weather was clearing up, and the sky had lightened, so as to show the outline of heavier clouds and the dark margin of the hills. By the uncertain glimmer the house on his left hand should be a place of some pretensions; it was surmounted by several pinnacles and turret-tops; the round stern of a chapel, with a fringe of flying buttresses,* projected boldly from the main block, and the door was sheltered under a deep porch carved with figures and overhung by two long gargoyles.* The windows of the chapel gleamed through their intricate tracery with a light as of many tapers, and threw out the buttresses and the peaked roof in a more intense blackness against the sky. It was plainly the mansion of some great family of the neighborhood, and as it reminded Denis of a town house of his own at Bourges, he stood for some time gazing up at it and mentally gauging the skill of the

Encourage the students to note details throughout that were discussed in the unit introduction: plot, conflict (both external and internal), protagonist and antagonist, setting, atmosphere, and tone.

2. Give the students some background information about the time in which this story occurs. It takes place during the Hundred Years' War (1338-1453). This war was waged by the English on French soil, beginning with King Edward III of England, who claimed the French crown in 1337. At first the English won several decisive battles and French territory. In return for additional French territory, Edward relinquished his claim to the French crown. Under a strong French king, Charles V, by 1380 France regained much of her territory. However, when Charles died, civil war broke out in France. King Henry V, who came to the English throne in 1414, took advantage of the French civil war by invading Normandy in 1415. With the Battle of Agincourt, the English gained control of Normandy. The territory of Burgundy was not gained. At the time of the story, the

broil the characters in these two stories? Which one seems more "lifelike"? (*Most students will agree that "The Leak" is a more realistic, believable story in any area.*)

Following this discussion, point out to the students that a writer who creates realistic characters is not necessarily superior to the writer who chooses to be less realistic in his approach. Less realistic characters are often used to represent specific human emotions, virtues, or vices. Consequently, these characters are usually timeless: they bear no marks of time or place. Dickens's characters are good examples. We would never expect to meet a person exactly like Scrooge or Tiny Tim on the street. We do, however, recognize the universal traits these characters represent: Scrooge (miserli-

ness), Tiny Tim (longsuffering). We've seen these traits a hundred times. Dickens's gift for creating such characters is one reason he is still so popular; his writing is timeless. This same appeal is found in Stevenson's writing. Blanche and Denis are symbols of courtly love: Denis is handsome, noble, swashbuckling, and willing to die for the beautiful Blanche; Blanche is beautiful, demure, brave, and easily moved by a noble lord.

The reader knows that Denis's falling into the Sire's trap is a mere coincidence. This heightens the dramatic irony throughout the rest of the story.

English and Burgundians controlled France. Of course, the English were trying to take Burgundy. At Orleans, Joan of Arc encouraged the French forces so much that they won against the English. She was captured and then burned at the stake, but the French succeeded in driving the English totally out of France.

3. Show the students pictures of a chateau, a gargoyle, and/or a buttress.

4. Have the students contrast the Sire and Blanche. They could make two columns and briefly list the differences.

Sire	Blanche
old	young
strong, powerful	helpless
arrogant, bold	shy
evil	kind

5. Ask students to compare/contrast Blanche and Denis with Lady Clare and Lord Ronald.

---

architects and the consideration* of the two families.

---

reconnoitre: to make a careful inspection of
bartizan wall: a small overhanging wall
embrasure: an opening in a wall for a door, window, or gun position
weir: a fence or dam placed in a stream or river to retain fish or divert the water
flying buttresses: masonry structures to brace a roof or arch
gargoyles: grotesquely carved water spouts projecting from a roof gutter
consideration: high regard or importance

There seemed to be no issue* to the terrace but the land by which he had reached it; he could only retrace his steps, but he had gained some notion of his whereabouts, and hoped by this means to hit the main thoroughfare and speedily regain the inn. He was reckoning without that chapter of accidents which was to make this night memorable above all others in his career; for he had not gone back above a hundred yards before he saw a light coming to meet him and heard loud voices speaking together in the echoing narrows of the lane. It was a party of men-at-arms going the night round with torches. Denis assured himself that they had all been making free with the wine-bowl and were in no mood to be particular about safe-conducts or the niceties of chivalrous war. It was as like as not that they would kill him like a dog and leave him where he fell. The situation was both inspiring and frightening. Their own torches would conceal him from sight, he reflected; and he hoped that they would drown the noise of his footsteps with their own empty voices. If he were but fleet and silent, he might evade their notice altogether.

---

issue: outlet

Unfortunately, as he turned to beat a retreat, his foot rolled upon a pebble; he fell against the wall with an ejaculation, and his sword rung loudly on the stones. Two or three

voices demanded who went there—some in French, some in English; but Denis made no reply, and ran the faster down the lane. Once upon the terrace, he paused to look back. They still kept calling after him and just then began to double the pace in pursuit, with a considerable clank of armor and great tossing of the torchlight to and fro in the narrow jaws of the passage.

Denis cast a look around and darted into the porch. There he might escape observation, or—if that were too much to expect—was in a capital posture whether for parley* or defense. So thinking, he drew his sword and tried to set his back against the door. To his surprise it yielded behind his weight and, though he turned in a moment, continued to swing back on oiled and noiseless hinges until it stood wide open on a black interior. When things fall out opportunely for the person concerned, he is not apt to be critical about how or why, his own immediate personal convenience seeming a sufficient reason for the strangest oddities and revolutions in our sublunary* things; and so Denis, without a moment's hesitation, stepped within and partly closed the door behind him to conceal his place of refuge. Nothing was further from his thoughts than to close it altogether; but for some inexplicable reason—perhaps by a spring or a weight—the ponderous mass of oak whipped itself out of his fingers and clanked to, with a formidable rumble and a noise like the falling of an automatic bar.

---

parley: discussion
sublunary: of this earth

The round,* at that very moment, debouched upon the terrace* and proceeded to summon him with shouts and curses. He heard them ferreting in the dark corners; the stock of a lance even rattled along the outer surface of the door behind which he stood; but these gentlemen were in too high a humor to be long delayed, and soon made off down a corkscrew pathway which had escaped Denis's observation, and passed out of sight and hearing along the battlements of the town.

round: group of soldiers making the night round
debouched . . . terrace: moved from the confined alley onto the terrace

Denis breathed again. He gave them a few minutes' grace for fear of accidents, and then groped about for some means of opening the door and slipping forth again. The inner surface was quite smooth,—not a handle, not a moulding, not a projection of any sort. He got his finger-nails round the edges and pulled, but the mass was immovable. He shook it, it was as firm as a rock. Denis de Beaulieu frowned and gave vent to a little noiseless whistle. What ailed the door, he wondered. Why was it open? How came it to shut so easily and so effectually after him? There was something obscure and underhand about all this, that was little to the young man's fancy. It looked like a snare in such a quiet by-street and in a house of so prosperous and even noble an exterior. And yet—snare or no snare, intentionally or unintentionally—here he was, prettily trapped; and for the life of him he could see no way out of it again. The darkness began to weigh upon him. He gave ear; all was silent without, but within and close by he seemed to catch a faint sighing, a faint sobbing rustle, a little stealthy creak—as though many persons were at his side, holding themselves quite still, and governing even their respiration with extreme slyness. The idea went to his vitals with a shock, and he faced about suddenly as if to defend his life. Then, for the first time he became aware of a light about the level of his eyes and at some distance in the interior of the house—a vertical thread of light, widening toward the bottom, such as might escape between two wings of arras* over a doorway.

arras: a tapestry usually hung on the wall

To see anything was a relief to Denis; it was like a piece of solid ground to a man laboring in a morass;* his mind seized upon it with avidity,* and he stood staring at it trying to piece together some logical conception of his surroundings. Plainly there was a flight of steps ascending from his own level to that of this illuminated doorway, and indeed he thought he could make out another thread of light, as fine as a needle and as faint as phosphorescence, which might very well be reflected along the polished wood of a handrail. Since he had begun to suspect that he was not alone, his heart had continued to beat with smothering violence, and an intolerable desire for action of any sort had possessed itself of his spirit. He was in deadly peril, he believed. What could be more natural than to mount the staircase, lift the curtain, and confront his difficulty at once? At least he would be dealing with something tangible; at least he would no longer be in the dark. He stepped slowly forward with outstretched hands, until his foot struck the bottom step; then he rapidly scaled the stairs, stood for a moment to compose his expression, lifted the arras, and went in.

morass: soggy ground
avidity: eagerness

He found himself in a large apartment of polished stone. There were three doors, one on each of three sides, all similarly curtained with tapestry. The fourth side was occupied by two large windows and a great stone chimney-piece, carved with arms of the Maletroits. Denis recognized the bearings and was gratified to find himself in such good hands. The room was strongly illuminated, but it contained little furniture except a heavy table and a chair or two, the hearth was innocent of fire, and the pavement was but sparsely strewn with rushes clearly many days old.

similes

Rushes (marsh plants) were commonly strewn on floors of houses in the Middle Ages.

similes, paradoxes

allusion to women in Leonardo da Vinci's paintings

situational irony

On a high chair beside the chimney, and directly facing Denis as he entered, sat a little old gentleman in a fur tippet.* He sat with his legs crossed and his hands folded, and a cup of spiced wine stood by his elbow on a bracket on the wall. His countenance had a strong masculine cast,—not properly human, but such as we see in the bull, the goat, or the domestic boar,—something equivocal* and wheedling, something greedy, brutal, and dangerous. The upper lip was inordinately full, as though swollen by a blow or a toothache; and the smile, the peaked eyebrows, and the small, strong eyes were quaintly and almost comically evil in expression. Beautiful white hair hung straight all round his head, like a saint's, and fell in a single curl upon the tippet. His beard and moustache were the pink of venerable sweetness. Age, probably in consequence of inordinate precautions, had left no mark upon his hands; and the Maletroit hand was famous. It would be difficult to imagine anything at once so fleshy and so delicate in design; the tapered, sensual fingers were like those of one of Leonardo's women; the fork of the thumb made a dimpled protuberance* when closed; the nails were perfectly shaped, and of a dead, surprising whiteness. It rendered his aspect tenfold more redoubtable* that a man with hands like these should keep them devoutly folded like a virgin martyr,—that a man with so intent and startling expression of face should sit patiently on his seat and contemplate people with an unwinking stare, like a god, or a god's statue. His quiescence* seemed ironical and treacherous, it fitted so poorly with his looks.

tippet: a scarf for the shoulders
equivocal: capable of misleading
protuberance: bulge
redoubtable: arousing fear
quiescence: inactiveness

Such was Alain, Sire de Maletroit. Denis and he looked silently at each other

for a second or two.

"Pray step in," said the Sire de Maletroit. "I have been expecting you all the evening."

He had not risen, but he accompanied his words with a smile and a slight but courteous inclination of the head. Partly from the smile, partly from the strange musical murmur with which the sire prefaced his observation, Denis felt a strong shudder of disgust go through his marrow. And what with disgust and honest confusion of mind, he could scarcely get words together in reply.

"I fear," he said, "that this is a double accident. I am not the person you suppose me. It seems you were looking for a visit; but for my part, nothing was further from my thoughts—nothing could be more contrary to my wishes—than this intrusion."

"Well, well," replied the old gentleman indulgently, "here you are, which is the main point. Seat yourself, my friend, and put yourself entirely at your ease. We shall arrange our little affairs presently."

Denis perceived that the matter was still complicated with some misconception, and he hastened to continue his explanations.

"Your door," he began.

"About my door?" asked the other, raising his peaked eyebrows. "A little piece of ingenuity." And he shrugged his shoulders. "A hospitable fancy! By your own account, you were not desirous of making my acquaintance. We old people look for such reluctance now and then; when it touches our honor, we cast about until we find some way of overcoming it. You arrive uninvited, but believe me, very welcome."

"You persist in error, sir," said Denis. "There can be no question between you and me. I am a stranger in this countryside. My name is Denis damoiseau* de Beaulieu. If you see me in your house it is only—"

damoiseau: a young nobleman not yet made a knight

"My young friend," interrupted the other, "you will permit me to have my own ideas on that subject. They probably differ from yours at the present moment," he added with a leer, "but time will show which of us is in the right."

Denis was convinced he had to do with a lunatic. He seated himself with a shrug, content to wait the upshot, and a pause ensued, during which he thought he could distinguish a hurried gabbling as of a prayer from behind the arras immediately opposite him. Sometimes there seemed to be but one person engaged, sometimes two; and the vehemence of the voice, low as it was, seemed to indicate either great haste or an agony of spirit. It occurred to him that this piece of tapestry covered the entrance to the chapel he had noticed from without.

The old gentleman meanwhile surveyed Denis from head to foot with a smile, and from time to time emitted little noises like a bird or a mouse, which seemed to indicate a high degree of satisfaction. This state of matters became rapidly insupportable; and Denis, to put an end to it, remarked politely that the wind had gone down.

The old gentleman fell into a fit of silent laughter, so prolonged and violent that he became quite red in the face. Denis got upon his feet at once, and put on his hat with a flourish.

"Sir," he said, "if you are in your wits, you have affronted me grossly. If you are out of them, I flatter myself I can find better employment for my brains than to talk with lunatics. My conscience is clear; you have made a fool of me from the first moment; you have refused to hear my explanations; and now there is no power under God will make me stay here any longer; and if I cannot make my way out in a more decent fashion, I will hack your door in pieces with my sword."

The Sire de Maletroit raised his right hand and wagged it at Denis with the fore and little fingers extended.

"My dear nephew," he said, "sit down."

"Nephew!" retorted Denis, "You lie in your throat"; and he snapped his fingers in his face.

"Sit down, you rogue!" cried the old gentleman, in a sudden, harsh voice, like the barking of a dog. "Do you fancy," he went on, "that when I had made my little contrivance for the door I had stopped short with that? If you prefer to be bound hand and foot till your bones ache, rise and try to go away. If you choose to remain a free young buck, agreeably conversing with an old gentleman—why, sit where you are in peace, and God be with you."

"Do you mean I am a prisoner?" demanded Denis.

"I state the facts," replied the other. "I would rather leave the conclusion to yourself."

Denis sat down again. Externally he managed to keep pretty calm, but within, he was now boiling with anger, now chilled with apprehension. He no longer felt convinced that he was dealing with a madman. And if the old gentleman was sane, what had he to look for? What absurd or tragical adventure was he to assume?

While he was thus unpleasantly reflecting, the arras that overhung the chapel door was raised, and a tall priest in his robes came forth, and, giving a long, keen stare at Denis, said something in an undertone to Sire de Maletroit.

"She is in a better frame of spirit?" asked the latter.

"She is more resigned, messire," replied the priest.

"Now, the Lord help her, she is hard to please!" sneered the old gentleman. "A likely stripling—not ill-born—and of her own choosing, too! Why, what more would the jade* have?"

---

jade: willful young lady

There are at least two layers of irony in the Sire's statement. (1) Yes, the Sire and Denis have different ideas as to why Denis is there; but Denis truly is not the man the Sire thinks he is. (2) "Time will show which of us is in the right"—the Sire ends up being "right" about Denis and Blanche in a way, but neither Denis nor the reader expects him to be right at this point.

hyperbole, irony

simile

These words describing Denis are ironic—he is not the man of Blanche's choosing . . . yet.

"The situation is not usual for a young damsel," said the other, "and somewhat trying to her blushes."

"She should have thought of that before she began to dance! It was none of my choosing; but since she is in it, she shall carry it to the end." And then addressing Denis, "Monsieur de Beaulieu," he asked, "may I present you my niece? She has been waiting your arrival, I may say, with even greater impatience than myself."

Denis had resigned himself with a good grace—all he desired to know was the worst of it as speedily as possible; so he rose at once, and bowed in acquiescence. The Sire de Maletroit followed his example and limped, with the assistance of the chaplain's arm, toward the chapel door. The priest pulled aside the arras, and all three entered. The building had considerable architectural pretensions. A light groining* sprung from six stout columns, and hung down in two rich pendants from the center of the vault. The place terminated behind the altar in a round end, embossed and honeycombed with a superfluity* of ornament in relief, and pierced by many little windows shaped like stars, trefoils,* or wheels. These windows were imperfectly glazed, so that the night air circulated freely in the chapel. The tapers, of which there must have been half a hundred burning on the altar, were unmercifully blown about; and the light went through many different phases of brilliancy and semi-eclipse. On the steps in front of the altar knelt a young girl richly attired as a bride. A chill settled over Denis as he observed her costume; he fought with desperate energy against the conclusion that was being thrust upon his mind; it could not—it should not—be as he feared.

groining: curved edge formed at the meeting of two vaults
superfluity: excess
trefoils: architectural forms having the appearance of three leaflets

"Blanche," said the sire, in his most flute-like tones, "I have brought a friend to see you, my little girl; turn round and give him your pretty hand. It is good to be devout; but it is necessary to be polite, my niece."

The girl rose to her feet and turned towards the newcomers. She moved all of a piece; and shame and exhaustion were expressed in every line of her fresh young face; she kept her eyes upon the pavement, as she came slowly forward. In the course of her advance her eyes fell upon Denis de Beaulieu's feet—feet of which he was justly vain, be it remarked, and wore in the most elegant accoutrement even while travelling. She paused—startled, as if his yellow boots had conveyed some shocking meaning—and glanced suddenly up into the wearer's countenance. Their eyes met; shame gave place to horror and terror in her looks; the blood left her lips; with a piercing scream she covered her face with her hands and sank upon the chapel floor.

"That is not the man!" she cried. "My uncle, that is not the man!"

The Sire de Maletroit chirped agreeably. "Of course not," he said; "I expected as much. It was so unfortunate you could not remember his name."

"Indeed," she cried, "indeed, I have never so much as set eyes upon him—I never wish to see him again. Sir," she said, turning to Denis, "if you are a gentleman, you will bear me out. Have I ever seen you—have you ever seen me—before this accursed hour?"

"To speak for myself, I have never had that pleasure," answered the young man. "This is the first time, messire, that I have met with your engaging niece."

The old gentleman shrugged his shoulders.

"I am distressed to hear it," he said. "But it is never too late to begin. I had little more acquaintance with my own late lady ere I married her; which proves," he added, with a grimace, "that these impromptu marriages

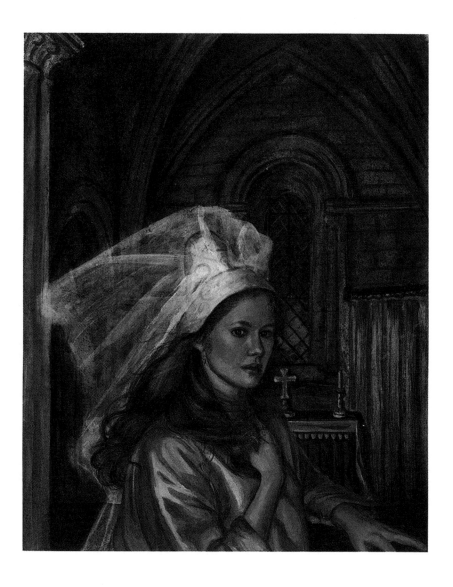

Ask students why, in spite of Blanche's and Denis's protestations, the Sire thinks Denis is the man Blanche had secretly planned to meet. *(He thinks they are lying—they are saying exactly what two lovers would say to protect each other.)*

synecdoche

may often produce an excellent understanding in the long run. As the bridegroom is to have a voice in the matter, I will give him two hours to make up for lost time before we proceed with the ceremony." And he turned toward the door, followed by the clergyman.

The girl was on her feet in a moment. "My uncle, you cannot be in earnest," she said. "I declare before God I will stab myself rather than be forced on that young man. The heart rises at it; God forbids such marriages; you dishonor your white hair. Oh, my uncle, pity me! There is not a woman in all the world but would prefer death to such a nuptial. Is it possible," she added, faltering—"is it possible that you do not believe me—that you still think this"—and she pointed at Denis with a tremor of anger and contempt—"that you still think *this* to be the man?"

"Frankly," said the old gentleman, pausing on the threshold, "I do. But let me explain to you once for all, Blanche de Maletroit, my way of thinking about the affair. When you took it into your head to dishonor my family and the name I have borne, in peace and war, for more than threescore years, you forfeited, not only the right to question my designs, but that of looking me in the face. If your father had been alive, he would have spat on you and turned you out of doors. His was the hand of iron. You may bless your God you have only to deal with the hand of velvet, mademoiselle. It was my duty to get you married without delay. Out of pure good-will I have tried to find your own gallant for you. And I believe I have succeeded. But Blanche de Maletroit, if I have not, I care not one jackstraw.* So let me recommend you to be polite to our young friend: for, upon my word, your next groom may be less appetizing."

---

jackstraw: thin stick used in the game of jackstraw

And with that he went out, with the chaplain at his heels; and the arras fell behind the pair.

The girl turned upon Denis with flashing eyes.

"And what, sir," she demanded, "may be the meaning of all this?"

"Heaven knows," returned Denis, gloomily. "I am a prisoner in this house, which seems full of mad people. More I know not; and nothing do I understand."

He told her as briefly as he could. "For the rest," he added, "perhaps you will follow my example, and tell me the answer to all these riddles, and what is like to be the end of it."

She stood silent for a little, and he could see her lips tremble and her tearless eyes burn with a feverish luster. Then she pressed her forehead in both hands.

"Alas, how my head aches!" she said, wearily, "to say nothing of my poor heart! But it is due to you to know my story, unmaidenly as it must seem. I am called Blanche de Maletroit; I have been without father or mother for—oh! for as long as I can recollect, and indeed I have been most unhappy all my life. Three months ago a young captain began to stand near me every day in church. I could see that I pleased him; I am much to blame, but I was so glad that anyone should love me; and when he passed me a letter, I took it home with me and read it with great pleasure. Since that time he has written many. He was so anxious to speak with me, poor fellow! and kept asking me to leave the door open some evening that we might have two words upon the stair. For he knew how much my uncle trusted me." She gave something like a sob at that, and it was a moment before she could go on. "My uncle is a hard man, but he is very shrewd," she said at last. "He has performed many feats in war, and was a great person at court, and much trusted by Queen Isabeau in old days. How he came to suspect me I cannot tell; but it is hard to keep anything from his knowledge; and this morning, as we came from mass, he took my hand in his, forced it open, and read my little billet,* walking by my side all the while.

billet: short letter

"When he finished, he gave it back to me with great politeness. It contained another request to have the door left open; and this has been the ruin of us all. My uncle kept me strictly in my room until evening, and then ordered me to dress myself as you see me— a hard mockery for a young girl, do you not think so? I suppose, when he could not prevail with me to tell him the young captain's name, he must have laid a trap for him; into which, alas! you have fallen. I looked for much confusion; for how could I tell whether he was willing to take me for his wife on these sharp terms? He might have been trifling with me from the first, or I might have made myself too cheap in his eyes. But truly I had not looked for such a shameful punishment as this! I could not think that God would let a girl be so disgraced before a young man. And now I tell you all; and I can scarcely hope that you will not despise me."

Denis made her a respectful inclination.

"Madam," he said, "you have honored me by your confidence. It remains for me to prove that I am not unworthy of the honor. Is Messire de Maletroit at hand?"

"I believe he is writing in the salle* without," she answered.

salle: sitting room

"May I lead you thither, madam?" asked Denis offering his hand with his most courtly bearing.

She accepted it, and the pair passed out of the chapel, Blanche in a very drooping and shamefaced condition, but Denis strutting and ruffling in the consciousness of a mission, and the boyish certainty of accomplishing it with honor.

The Sire de Maletroit rose to meet them with an ironical obeisance.

"Sir," said Denis, with the grandest possible air, "I believe I am to have some say in the matter of this marriage; and let me tell you at once, I will be no party to forcing the inclination of this young lady. Had it been freely offered to me, I should have been proud to accept her hand, for I perceive she is as good as she is beautiful; but as things are, I have now the honor, messire, of refusing."

Blanche looked at him with gratitude in her eyes; but the old gentleman only smiled and smiled, until his smile grew positively sickening to Denis.

"I am afraid," he said, "Monsieur de Beaulieu, that you do not perfectly understand the choice I have offered you. Follow me, I beseech you, to this window." And he led the way to one of the large windows which stood open on the night. "You observe," he went on, "there is an iron ring in the upper masonry, and reeved through that a very efficacious rope. Now, mark my words: if you should find your disinclination to my niece's person insurmountable, I shall have you hanged out of this window before sunrise. I shall only proceed to such an extremity with the greatest regret, you may believe me. For it is not at all your death that I desire, but my niece's establishment in life. At the same time, it must come to that if you prove obstinate. Your family, Monsieur de Beaulieu, is very well in its way, but if you sprung from Charlemagne,* you should not refuse the hand of a Maletroit with impunity— not if she had been as common as the Paris road—not if she was as hideous as the gargoyle over my door. Neither my niece nor you, nor my own private feelings, move me at all in this matter. The honor of my house has been compromised; I believe you to be the guilty person, at least you are now in the secret; and

Ask the students how the Sire's obeisance (bow) would be "ironical." *(A bow shows honor to another, yet the Sire does not trust or respect either of the young people.)*

Denis carries off the duties of a Romantic hero well: he will not disgrace the lady by forcing her into marriage, but neither will he humiliate her in his refusal ("Had it been freely offered to me, I should have been proud to accept her hand").

allusion

Here the Sire makes clear Denis's choice, and Denis's conflict becomes both internal and external. Note the Sire's reason for this (in Blanche's encouraging of the young man at church and inviting him to sneak into her home, she has dishonored the family name). Note also his use of metaphor to state his cruel design.

"Retainers" means "servants." Note use of metaphor here as well.

hyperbole

you can hardly wonder if I request you to wipe out the stain. If you will not, your blood be on your own head! It will be no great satisfaction to me to have your interesting relics kicking their heels in the breeze below my windows, but half a loaf is better than no bread, and if I cannot cure the dishonor, I shall at least stop the scandal."

Charlemagne: emperor who laid the basis for the Holy Roman Empire (742?–814)

There was a pause.

"I believe there are other ways of settling such imbroglios* among gentlemen," said Denis. "You wear a sword, and I hear you have used it with distinction."

---

imbroglios: disagreements

The Sire de Maletroit made a signal to the chaplain, who crossed the room with long, silent strides and raised the arras over the third of the three doors. It was only a moment before he let it fall again; but Denis had time to see a dusky passage full of armed men.

"When I was a little younger, I should have been delighted to honor you, Monsieur de Beaulieu," said Sire Alain; "but I am now too old. Faithful retainers are the sinews of age, and I must employ the strength I have. This is one of the hardest things to swallow as a man grows up in years, but with a little patience even this becomes habitual. You and the lady seem to prefer the salle for what remains of your two hours; and as I have no desire to cross your preference, I shall resign it to your use with all the pleasure in the world. No haste!" he added, holding up his hand, as he saw a dangerous look come into Denis de Beaulieu's face. "If your mind revolts against hanging, it will be time enough two hours hence to throw yourself out the window or upon the pikes of my retainers. Two hours of life are always two hours. A great many things may turn up in even as little a while as that. And, besides, if I understand her appearance, my niece has something to say to you. You will not disfigure your last hours by a want of politeness to a lady?"

Denis looked at Blanche, and she made him an imploring gesture.

It is likely that the old gentleman was hugely pleased at this symptom of an understanding, for he smiled on both and added sweetly, "If you will give me your word of honor Monsieur de Beaulieu, to await my return at the end of the two hours before attempting anything desperate, I shall withdraw my retainers and let you speak in greater privacy with mademoiselle."

Denis again glanced at the girl, who seemed to beseech him to agree.

"I give you my word of honor," he said.

Messire de Maletroit bowed and proceeded to limp about the apartment, clearing his throat the while with that odd musical chirp which had already grown so irritating in the ears of Denis de Beaulieu. He first possessed himself of some papers which lay upon the table; then he went to the mouth of the passage and appeared to give an order to the men behind the arras; and lastly he hobbled out through the door by which Denis had come in, turning upon the threshold to address a last smiling bow to the young couple, and followed by the chaplain with a hand-lamp.

No sooner were they alone than Blanche advanced toward Denis with her hands extended. Her face was flushed and excited, and her eyes shone with tears.

"You shall not die!" she cried, "you shall marry me after all."

"You seem to think, madam," replied Denis, "that I stand much in fear of death."

"Oh, no, no," she said, "I see you are no poltroon.* It is for my own sake—I could not bear to have you slain for such a scruple."

poltroon: horrible coward

"I am afraid," returned Denis, "that you underrate the difficulty, madam. What you may be too generous to refuse I may be too proud to accept. In a moment of noble feeling toward me, you forget what you perhaps owe to others."

He had the decency to keep his eyes on the floor as he said this, and after he had finished, so as not to spy upon her confusion. She stood silent for a moment, then walked suddenly away, and falling on her uncle's chair, fairly burst out sobbing. Denis was in the acme of embarrassment. He looked round, as if to seek for inspiration, and seeing a stool, plumped down upon it for something to do. There he sat, playing with the guard of his rapier, and wishing himself dead a thousand times over, and buried in the nastiest kitchen-heap in France. His eyes wandered round the apartment, but found nothing to arrest them. There were such wide spaces between the furniture, the light fell so badly and cheerlessly over all, the dark outside air looked in so coldly through the windows, that he thought he had never seen a church so vast, nor a tomb so melancholy. The regular sobs of Blanche de Maletroit measured out the time like the ticking of a clock. He read the device upon the shield over and over again, until his eyes became obscured; he stared into shadowy corners until he imagined they were swarming with horrible animals; and every now and again he awoke with a start, to remember that his last two hours were running, and death was on the march.

Oftener and oftener, as the time went on, did his glance settle on the girl herself. Her face was bowed forward and covered with her hands, and she was shaken at intervals by the convulsive hiccough of grief. Even thus she was not an unpleasant object to dwell upon, so plump and yet so fine, with a warm brown skin, and the most beautiful hair, Denis thought, in the whole world of womankind. Her hands were like her uncle's; but they were more in place at the end of her young arms, and looked infinitely soft and caressing. He remembered how her blue eyes had shone upon him, full of anger, pity, and innocence. And the more he dwelt on her perfections, the uglier death looked, and the more deeply was he smitten with penitence at her continued tears. Now he felt that no man could have the courage to leave a world which contained so beautiful a creature; and now he would have given forty minutes of his last hour to have unsaid his cruel speech.

Suddenly a hoarse and ragged peal of cockcrow rose to their ears from the dark valley below the windows. And this shattering noise in the silence of all around was like a light in a dark place, and shook them both out of their reflections.

"Alas, can I do nothing to help you?" she said, looking up.

"Madam," replied Denis, with a fine irrelevancy, "if I have said anything to wound you, believe me, it was for your own sake and not for mine."

She thanked him with a tearful look.

"I feel your position cruelly," he went on. "The world has been bitter hard on you. Your uncle is a disgrace to mankind. Believe me, madam, there is no young gentleman in all France but would be glad of my opportunity, to die in doing you a momentary service."

"I know already that you can be very brave and generous," she answered. "What I *want* to know is whether I can serve you—now or afterward," she added with a quaver.

"Most certainly," he answered, with a smile. "Let me sit beside you as if I were a friend, instead of a foolish intruder; try to forget how awkwardly we are placed to one another; make my last moments go pleasantly; and you will do me the chief service possible."

Ask students to explain Denis's meaning here. (*He is referring obliquely to the young captain whom Blanche was expecting.*)

personification

understatement

"You are very gallant," she added, with a yet deeper sadness "—very gallant—and it somehow pains me. But draw nearer, if you please; and if you find anything to say to me, you will at least make certain of a very friendly listener. Ah! Monsieur de Beaulieu," she broke forth—"ah! Monsieur de Beaulieu, how can I look you in the face?" And she fell to weeping again with a renewed effusion.

"Madam," said Denis, taking her hand in both of his, "reflect on the little time I have before me, and the great bitterness into which I am cast by the sight of your distress. Spare me, in my last moments, the spectacle of what I cannot cure even with the sacrifice of my life."

"I am very selfish," answered Blanche. "I will be braver, Monsieur de Beaulieu, for your sake. But think if I can do you no kindness in the future—if you have no friends to whom I could carry your adieus. Charge me as heavily as you can; every burden will lighten, by so little, the invaluable gratitude I owe you. Put in my power to do something more for you than weep."

"My mother is married again, and has a young family to care for. My brother Guichard will inherit my fiefs;* and if I am not in error, that will content him amply for my death. Life is a little vapor that passeth away, as we are told by the holy scriptures. When a man is in a fair way and sees all life open in front of him, he seems to himself to make a very important figure in the world. His horse whinnies to him; the trumpets blow and the girls look out of windows as he rides into town before his company; he receives many assurances of trust and regard,—sometimes by express in a letter, sometimes face to face, with persons of great consequence falling on his neck. It is not wonderful if his head is turned for a time. But once he is dead, were he as brave as Hercules or as wise as Solomon, he is soon forgotten. It is not ten years since my father fell, with many other knights around him, in a very fierce encounter, and I do not think that any one of them, nor as much as the name of the fight, is now remembered. No, no, madam, the nearer you come to it, you see that death is a dark and dusty corner, where a man gets into his tomb and has the door shut after him till the judgment day. I have a few friends just now, and once I am dead shall have none."

---

fiefs: lands in a family estate

"Ah, Monsieur de Beaulieu!" she exclaimed, "you forget Blanche de Maletroit."

"You have a sweet nature, madam, and you are pleased to estimate a little service far beyond its worth."

"It is not that," she answered. "You mistake me if you think I am easily touched by my own concerns. I say so because you are the noblest man I have ever met,—because I recognize in you a spirit that would have made even a common person famous in the land."

"And yet here I die in a mousetrap, with no more noise about it than my own squeaking," answered he.

A look of pain crossed her face, and she was silent for a little while. Then a light came into her eyes, and with a smile she spoke again.

"I cannot have my champion think meanly of himself. Anyone who gives his life for another will be met in paradise by all the heralds and angels of the Lord God. And you have no such cause to hang your head. For— Pray, do you think me beautiful?" she asked, with a deep flush.

"Indeed, madam, I do," he said.

"I am glad of that," she answered heartily. "Do you think there are many men in France who have been asked in marriage by a beautiful maiden—with her own lips—and who have refused her to her face? I know you men would half despise such a triumph; but believe me, we women know more of what is precious in love. There is nothing that should set a person higher in his own esteem; and we women would prize nothing more dearly."

"You are very good," he said; "but you cannot make me forget that I was asked in pity and not for love."

"I am not so sure of that," she replied holding down her head. "Hear me to an end, Monsieur de Beaulieu. I know how you despise me; I feel you are right to do so; I am too poor a creature to occupy one thought of your mind, although, alas! you must die for me this morning. But when I asked you to marry me, indeed, and indeed, it was because I respected and admired you, and loved you with my whole soul, from the very moment that you took my part against my uncle. If you had seen yourself, and how noble you looked, you would pity rather than despise me. And now," she went on, hurriedly checking him with her hand, "although I have laid aside all reserve and told you so much, remember that I know your sentiments toward me already. I would not, believe me, being nobly born, weary you with importunities* into consent. I too have a pride of my own; and I declare if you should now go back from your word already given, I would no more marry you than I would marry my uncle's groom."

---

importunities: persistent requests

Denis smiled a little bitterly.

"It is a small love," he said, "that shies at a little pride."

She made no answer, although she probably had her own thoughts.

"Come hither to the window," he said with a sigh. "Here is the dawn."

And indeed the dawn was already beginning. The hollow of the sky was full of essential daylight, colorless and clean; and the valley underneath was flooded with a gray

reflection. A few thin vapors clung in the coves of the forest or lay along the winding course of the river. The scene disengaged* a surprising effect of stillness, which was hardly interrupted when the cocks began once more to crow among the steadings.* Perhaps the same fellow who had made so horrid a clamor in the darkness, not half an hour before, now sent

Blanche means, "Even knowing all about me and my inviting the captain here, you would still marry me?" Denis again proves himself the chivalrous Romantic hero by freely and completely forgiving her. If students find the ending too facile, too pat, remind them that it is a completely appropriate conclusion for a story written in the Romantic tradition—its climax culminates in emotion rather than in reality.

up the merriest cheer to greet the coming day. A little wind went bustling and eddying among the tree-tops underneath the windows. And still the daylight kept flooding insensibly out of the east, which was soon to grow incandescent and cast up that red-hot cannon-ball, the rising sun.

---

disengaged: caused
steadings: farm buildings and outbuildings

Denis looked out over all this with a bit of a shiver. He had taken her hand, and retained it in his almost unconsciously.

"Has the day begun already?" she said; and then, illogically enough: "the night has been so long! Alas! what shall we say to my uncle when he returns?"

"What you will," said Denis, and he pressed her fingers in his.

She was silent.

"Blanche," he said, with a swift, uncertain, passionate utterance, "you have seen whether I fear death. You must know well enough that I would as gladly leap out of that window into the empty air as to lay a finger on you without your free and full consent. But if you care for me at all, do not let me lose my life in a misapprehension, for I love you better than the whole world; and though I will die for you blithely, it would be like all the joys of paradise to live on and spend my life in your service."

As he stopped speaking a bell began to ring loudly in the interior of the house, and a clatter of armor in the corridor showed that the retainers were returning to their post, and the two hours were at an end.

"After all that you have heard?" she whispered, leaning toward him.

"I have heard nothing," he replied.

"The captain's name was Florimond de Champdivers," she said in his ear.

"I did not hear it," he answered, taking her in his arms and wiping away her tears.

A melodious chirping was audible behind, followed by a beautiful chuckle, and the voice of Messire de Maletroit wished his new nephew a good morning.

Lady Clare

Alfred, Lord Tennyson

In this narrative poem Lady Clare seems almost to welcome the painful revelation from her nurse as a means of testing the love of Lord Ronald.

It was the time when lilies blow,*
    And clouds are highest up in air,
Lord Ronald brought a lily-white doe
    To give his cousin, Lady Clare.

I trow* they did not part in scorn: 5
    Lovers long-betrothed were they:
They two will wed the morrow morn—
    God's blessing on the day!

"He does not love me for my birth,
    Nor for my lands so broad and fair;   10
He loves me for my own true worth,
    And that is well," said Lady Clare.

In there came old Alice the nurse,
    Said, "Who was this that went from thee?"
"It was my cousin," said Lady Clare,   15
    "Tomorrow he weds with me."

"O God be thanked!" said Alice the nurse,
    "That all comes round so just and fair:
Lord Ronald is heir of all your lands,
    And you are *not* the Lady Clare."   20

"Are ye out of your mind, my nurse, my nurse,"
    Said Lady Clare, "that ye speak so wild?"
"As God's above," said Alice the nurse,
    "I speak the truth: you are my child.

blow: bloom

trow: can imagine

White represents purity (cf. "Blanche" in the previous story)—in this case, the purity of Lady Clare.

understatement

"Lady Clare"

Although it is poetry, the action and characterization in Tennyson's "Lady Clare" have much in common with Stevenson's story. Read the headnote and poem aloud. Then compare Tennyson's poem to Stevenson's story. Are the settings similar? *(yes)* How are the circumstances of Lady Clare and Lord Ronald like those of Denis and Blanche? *(They are Romantic types who act nobly in trying circumstances.)* How are Lord Ronald and Denis alike? How are they different? How are Lady Clare and Blanche alike? How are they different? *(Accept any answers to these questions that students can defend from the selections.)*

Application

In both the story and the poem, the characters find themselves in circumstances that initially seem intolerable. By the end of each story, however, they find the circumstances not only tolerable but even desirable. The Bible also has examples of such situations. For example, when the Lord informed His disciples that He must suffer and die at the hands of the Jews, Peter—finding such a thought intolerable—cried out, "Be it far from thee, Lord!" Of course, the Lord rebuked him sternly (Matt. 16:21-23). It was not until after the Resurrection that Peter realized that this "unbearable set of circumstances" was both essential and desirable. There are also instances in Scripture in which an apparently desirable situation in real-ity became intolerable. Samson's experiences are a good example here (Judges 13–16).

 Ask the students to write about a real or fictional experience in which an "intolerable" situation turned out to be much better than they had anticipated. Or perhaps they might write about a real or fictional time when someone was placed in a situation he or she believed desirable, only to discover it intolerable. See **Writing Rubric 8-1: Situation and Circumstance.** Remind students that as they write they should be mindful of the dramatic and situational irony inherent in such a story.

The Nurse encourages her daughter not to tell Lord Ronald the truth. Discuss with the students whether they think this is wise or poor advice. *(Poor advice—she is encouraging Clare to deceive her fiancé.)*

Metonymy: The throwing aside of these accoutrements symbolizes her unwillingness to pose as a "lady" (in the English social rank sense of the word) when she is not one.

"The old earl's daughter died at my breast;   25
  I speak the truth, as I live by bread!
I buried her like my own sweet child,
  And put my child in her stead."

"Falsely, falsely have ye done,
  O mother," she said, "if this be true,   30
To keep the best man under the sun
  So many years from his due."*

his due: the land that he rightfully should have inherited on the death of the heir

"Nay now, my child," said Alice the nurse,
  "But keep the secret of your life,
And all you have will be Lord Ronald's,   35
  When you are man and wife."

"If I'm a beggar born," she said,
  "I will speak out, for I dare not lie.
Pull off, pull off, the brooch of gold,
  And fling the diamond necklace by."   40

"Nay now, my child," said Alice the nurse,
  "But keep the secret all you can."
She said, "Not so: but I will know
  If there be any faith in man."

"Nay now, what faith?" said Alice the nurse,   45
  "The man will cleave unto his right."
"And he shall have it," the lady replied,
  "Though I should die tonight."

"Yet give one kiss to your mother dear,
  Alas, my child, I sinned for thee."   50
"O mother, mother, mother," she said,
  "So strange it seems to me."

"Yet here's a kiss for my mother dear,
  My mother dear, if these be so,
And lay your hand upon my head,   55
  And bless me, mother, ere I go."

She clad herself in a russet gown,*
  She was no longer Lady Clare:
She went by dale,* and she went by down,*
  With a single rose in her hair.   60

russet gown: gown of coarse brown homespun cloth
dale: valley down: hill

The lily-white doe Lord Ronald had brought
    Leaped up from where she lay,
Dropped her head in the maiden's hand,
    And followed her all the way.

Down stepped Lord Ronald from his tower: 65
    "O Lady Clare, you shame your worth!
Why come you dressed like a village maid,
    That are the flower of the earth?"

"If I come dressed like a village maid,
    I am but as my fortunes are: 70
I am a beggar born," she said,
    "And not the Lady Clare."

"Play me no tricks," said Lord Ronald,
    "For I am yours in word and in deed;
Play me no tricks," said Lord Ronald,   75
    "Your riddle is hard to read."

O, and proudly stood she up!
    Her heart within her did not fail;
She looked into Lord Ronald's eyes,
    And told him all her nurse's tale.   80

He laughed a laugh of merry scorn:
    He turned and kissed her where she stood:
"If you are not the heiress born,
    And I," said he, "the next in blood—

"If you are not the heiress born,   85
    And I," said he, "the lawful heir,
We two will wed tomorrow morn,
    And you shall still be Lady Clare."

About the Story and Poem

1. Plot the action of Stevenson's story.
2. How would you say the action characterizes the Romantic era?
3. Does the fictional story in Tennyson's poem express a truth? Support your answer.
4. What ambiguity is found in the title of the poem?
5. What figure of irony appears in line 5 of the poem?

Her purity—far more important than the station of her birth—comes with her on her fateful visit to her fiancé.

Symbolism: Ronald steps "down" to accept Clare.

metaphor, hyperbole

paradox

About the Story and Poem

1. *Inciting moment: Denis, running from the men-at-arms, enters the Sire de Maletroit's door. Rising action: Denis finds himself a prisoner; he meets the Sire de Maletroit and Blanche and is given his choice—to marry Blanche or be hanged; he and Blanche discuss their situation. Climax: Denis admits his love for Blanche and asks her hand in marriage. Falling action: The bell rings, the retainers return, and Blanche confesses the name of her former beau. Denouement: "Messire de Maletroit [wishes] his new nephew a good morning." For a more complete discussion of plot, see BJU Press's* Fundamentals of Literature, *pages 224-25.*

2. *Answers may vary but should include the elements of a handsome hero, unafraid of death; a distressed maiden who is in the power of her cruel uncle; and the idea that love can overcome all obstacles.*

3. *Answers may vary. Students might point out that the Lord can use a difficult situation for His own glory. Some might also mention that those who are spiritually born again are similar to Lady Clare—lifted from a position of disgrace and shame by our loving Lord.*

4. *Though in the heart of Lord Ronald, Clare has always been a lady, the title is ambiguous because we learn that Lady Clare is not truly a "lady" by birth; however, when the poem ends, we learn that she will become Lady Clare the next morning.*

5. *understatement (See page 150.)*

OBJECTIVES

The students will be able to

- Discuss the significance of point of view in detective fiction.

- Analyze and discuss characteristics of mystery fiction that make it popular and intriguing.

foreshadowing

That is, the year 1883.

FURTHER HELPS

Additional activities

1. Read aloud another of Doyle's stories—perhaps "The Red-Headed League." Or you may want to choose a favorite mystery story by another writer.

2. Additional questions for discussion: What does the opening of the story tell us about the relationship between Holmes and Watson? *(They are long-time friends who respect one another.)* What makes Watson a good storyteller? *(Answers may vary but might include his careful description and recording of events. The fact*

The Adventure of the Speckled Band

Sir Arthur Conan Doyle

"The Adventure of the Speckled Band" is in many ways a typical Conan Doyle detective story: Watson narrates how his friend, the master sleuth Sherlock Holmes, uses his extraordinary deductive powers to unravel a seemingly impossible mystery. This story, however, is more artfully constructed than other Holmes mysteries. Notice, for example, how quickly the author draws us into the conflict. Notice, too, how deftly he maintains a high level of suspense until the very end of his narrative.

On glancing over my notes of the seventy odd cases in which I have during the last eight years studied the methods of my friend Sherlock Holmes, I find many tragic, some comic, a large number merely strange, but none commonplace; for, working as he did rather for the love of his art than for the acquirement of wealth, he refused to associate himself with any investigation which did not tend towards the unusual, and even the fantastic. Of all these varied cases, however, I cannot recall any which presented more singular features than that which was associated with the well-known Surrey family of the Roylotts of Stoke Moran. The events in question occurred in the early days of my association with Holmes, when we were sharing rooms as bachelors in Baker Street. It is possible that I might have placed them upon record before, but a promise of secrecy was made at the time, from which I have only been freed during the last month by the untimely death of the lady to whom the pledge was given. It is perhaps as well that the facts should now come to light, for I have reasons to know that there were widespread rumors as to the death of Dr. Grimesby Roylott which tend to make the matter even more terrible than the truth.

It was early in April in the year '83 that I woke one morning to find Sherlock Holmes standing, fully dressed, by the side of my bed. He was a late riser, as a rule, and as the clock on the mantlepiece showed me that it was only a quarter past seven, I blinked up at him in some surprise, and perhaps just a little resentment, for I was myself regular in my habits.

"Very sorry to knock you up,* Watson," said he, "but it's the common lot this morning. Mrs. Hudson has been knocked up, she retorted upon me, and I on you."

knock . . . up: Wake up; the phrase is derived from an old custom whereby a designated person awakened the people of a neighborhood by knocking at their doors.

"What is it, then—a fire?"

"No; a client. It seems that a young lady has arrived in a considerable state of excitement, who insists upon seeing me. She is waiting now in the sitting room. Now, when young ladies wander about the metropolis at this hour of the morning, and knock sleepy people up out of their beds, I presume that

PREPARATION

"The Adventure of the Speckled Band"

Overview

"The Adventure of the Speckled Band" is one of Doyle's most artful detective stories. The plot is well constructed and the details of the story are integral in maintaining the high level of suspense.

DISCUSSION

Introduction

Ask the students about mystery stories they have read. Discuss with them why they liked such stories. Was it the suspense? Or the ingenuity of the master sleuth ? Did they enjoy trying to figure out who the villain was before the end of the story? Or did they prefer to be kept in suspense until the last possible moment? Were they usually successful in guessing who the villain was? Did their success or failure affect their enjoyment of the story?

Analysis

Doyle does a masterful job of plunging us into the middle of the conflict and maintaining our interest until the very end of the story. In this story, we know from the start who the villain is; we simply need to figure out how he accomplished his villainy. Doyle does a good job of making that a difficult task.

After the students complete the reading of the story, have the class discuss the action by answering the following questions:

1. What is the story's inciting moment? *(Helen Stoner's plea for help from Sherlock Holmes)*

2. What is the climax of the story? *(Holmes and Watson's vigil at Stoke Moran and their subsequent battle with the speckled band)*

it is something very pressing which they have to communicate. Should it prove to be an interesting case, you would, I am sure, wish to follow it from the outset. I thought, at any rate, that I should call you and give you the chance."

"My dear fellow, I would not miss it for anything."

I had no keener pleasure than in following Holmes in his professional investigations, and in admiring the rapid deductions, as swift as intuitions, and yet always founded on a logical basis, with which he unraveled the problems which were submitted to him. I rapidly threw on my clothes and was ready in a few minutes to accompany my friend down to the sitting room. A lady dressed in black and heavily veiled, who had been sitting in the window, rose as we entered.

"Good-morning, madam," said Holmes cheerily. "My name is Sherlock Holmes. This is my intimate friend and associate, Dr. Watson, before whom you can speak as freely as before myself. Ha! I am glad to see that Mrs. Hudson has had the good sense to light the fire. Draw up to it, and I shall order you a cup of hot coffee, for I observe that you are shivering."

"It is not cold which makes me shiver," said the woman in a low voice, changing her seat as requested.

"What, then?"

"It is fear, Mr. Holmes. It is terror." She raised her veil as she spoke, and we could see that she was indeed in a pitiable state of agitation, her face all drawn and gray, with restless, frightened eyes, like those of some hunted animal. Her features and figure were those of a woman of thirty, but her hair was shot with premature gray, and her expression was weary and haggard. Sherlock Holmes ran her over with one of his quick, all-comprehensive glances.

"You must not fear," said he soothingly,

bending forward and patting her forearm. "We shall soon set matters right, I have no doubt. You have come in by train this morning, I see."

"You know me, then?"

"No, but I observe the second half of a return ticket in the palm of your left glove. You must have started early, and yet you had a good drive in a dogcart, along heavy roads, before you reached the station."

The lady gave a violent start and stared in bewilderment at my companion.

"There is no mystery, my dear madam," said he, smiling. "The left arm of your jacket is spattered with mud in no less than seven places. The marks are perfectly fresh. There is no vehicle save a dogcart which throws up mud in that way, and then only when you sit on the left-hand side of the driver."

"Whatever your reasons may be, you are perfectly correct," said she. "I started from home before six, reached Leatherhead at twenty past, and came in by the first train. Sir, I can stand this strain no longer; I shall go mad if it continues. I have no one to turn to—none, save only one, who cares for me, and he, poor fellow, can be of little aid. I have heard of you, Mr. Holmes; I have heard of you from Mrs. Farintosh, whom you helped in the hour of her sore need. It was from her that I had your address. Oh, sir, do you not think that you could help me, too, and at least throw a little light through the dense darkness which surrounds me? At present it is out of my power to reward you for your services, but in a month or six weeks I shall be married, with the control of my own income, and then at least you shall not find me ungrateful."

Holmes turned to his desk and, unlocking it, drew out a small casebook, which he consulted.

"Farintosh," said he. "Ah, yes, I recall the case; it was concerned with an opal tiara. I think it was before your time, Watson. I can

simile

Such comments are typical of Holmes throughout Doyle's stories. He is able to deduce much about everyone he meets by picking up on clues that the average person would overlook.

She is referring here to her fiancé.

metaphor

that he, as well as the readers, holds Holmes in awe also contributes to his appeal as a narrator.) How does Helen Stoner's description of her stepfather differ from what Holmes deduces of the man's character? (She is unwilling to admit that he had been physically abusive with her.) Describe Holmes's method as an investigator. (Answers may vary but might include his ability to deduce events from seemingly insignificant clues; his physical strength and fearlessness; his willingness to put himself in danger to solve a crime.) Which of the characters in the story are round characters (well developed)? (Holmes and Watson) Which are one-dimensional? (Helen Stoner and Dr. Roylott)

Resource

Arthur Conan Doyle, *The Complete Sherlock Holmes* (Bantam Doubleday Dell, 1998).

3. What significant details are revealed in Helen Stoner's story to Watson and Holmes? *(Julia Stoner's sudden death before her marriage, the description of the inquest following her death, Dr. Roylott's heritage, Roylott's time and trouble in India, his erratic behavior at Stoke Moran and the subsequent brawls with his neighbors, his menagerie, Mrs. Roylott's will, the recent engagement of Helen Stoner, the unexpected "remodeling" of Stoke Moran)*

Draw the students' attention to how Doyle uses Helen Stoner's story to reveal his characters. Notice, for example, how much we learn about Holmes's deductive powers. Watson, although he is fascinated by Holmes's cases and enjoys his part in them immensely, does not have the deductive powers of the master sleuth.

Of course, limiting Watson's "powers" allows him to narrate the story without disclosing the outcome. The reader can identify with Watson, for he too is kept in the dark until the last possible moment. We also learn much about Dr. Roylott, the villain. Before we ever see this man, we are convinced that he is vicious. Have the students identify one specific quotation from the story that convinced them of Roylott's treachery.

4. What one detail is included in Helen Stoner's story that initially seems significant but later proves to be only a "red herring" (a clue that seems important but actually distracts the reader from the truly important clues)? *(Roylott's association with the gypsies)*

5. List the significant actions that occur be-

tween the inciting moment and the climax. *(Dr. Roylott's rude visit, Watson and Holmes's afternoon visit to Stoke Moran, Miss Stoner's successful "escape" from her sister's room, and Holmes and Watson's successful, undetected entry into Stoke Moran)*

6. How is the conflict resolved? *(Roylott is killed by "the speckled band"—an example of poetic justice.)*

Application

Following your discussion of the story's details, draw the students' attention to Psalm 7:12-16. Discuss how the principles of this passage are illustrated in the resolution of the story. See how many other contemporary applications of this principle the students can find.

This is another reference to her fiancé. Note that her statements reveal her conflicts to be external and internal.

Here begins a carefully crafted flash-back, which extends to page 253.

metaphor

only say, madam, that I shall be happy to devote the same care to your case as I did to that of your friend. As to reward, my profession is its own reward; but you are at liberty to defray whatever expenses I may be put to, at the time which suits you best. And now I beg that you will lay before us everything that may help us in forming an opinion upon the matter."

"Alas!" replied our visitor, "the very horror of my situation lies in the fact that my fears are so vague, and my suspicions depend so entirely upon small points, which might seem trivial to another, that even he to whom of all others I have a right to look for help and advice looks upon all that I tell him about it as the fancies of a nervous woman. He does not say so, but I can read it from his soothing answers and averted eyes. But I have heard, Mr. Holmes, that you can see deeply into the manifold wickedness of the human heart. You may advise me how to walk amid the dangers which encompass me."

"I am all attention, madam."

"My name is Helen Stoner, and I am living with my stepfather, who is the last survivor of one of the oldest Saxon families in England, the Roylotts of Stoke Moran, on the western border of Surrey."

Holmes nodded his head. "The name is familiar to me," said he.

"The family was at one time among the richest in England, and the estates extended over the borders into Berkshire in the north, and Hampshire in the west. In the last century, however, four successive heirs were of a dissolute and wasteful disposition, and the family ruin was eventually completed by a gambler in the days of the Regency.* Nothing was left save a few acres of ground, and the two-hundred-year-old house, which is itself crushed under a heavy mortgage. The last squire dragged out his existence there, living the horrible life of an aristocratic pauper; but

his only son, my stepfather, seeing that he must adapt himself to the new conditions, obtained an advance from a relative, which enabled him to take a medical degree and went out to Calcutta, where, by his professional skill and his force of character, he established a large practice. In a fit of anger, however, caused by some robberies which had been perpetrated in the house, he beat his native butler to death and narrowly escaped a capital sentence. As it was, he suffered a long term of imprisonment and afterwards returned to England a morose and disappointed man.

Regency: the period (1811–20) when George III was declared incompetent and the Prince of Wales ruled as regent

"When Dr. Roylott was in India he married my mother, Mrs. Stoner, the young widow of Major-General Stoner, of the Bengal Artillery. My sister Julia and I were twins, and we were only two years old at the time of my mother's remarriage. She had a considerable sum of money—not less than £1000 a year—and this she bequeathed to Dr. Roylott entirely while we resided with him, with a provision that a certain annual sum should be allowed to each of us in the event of our marriage. Shortly after our return to England my mother died—she was killed eight years ago in a railway accident near Crewe. Dr. Roylott then abandoned his attempts to establish himself in practice in London and took us to live with him in the old ancestral house at Stoke Moran. The money which my mother had left was enough for all our wants, and there seemed to be no obstacle to our happiness.

"But a terrible change came over our stepfather about this time. Instead of making friends and exchanging visits with our neighbors, who had at first been overjoyed to see a Roylott of Stoke Moran back in the old family seat, he shut himself up in his house and seldom came out save to indulge in ferocious quarrels with whoever might cross his path. Violence of temper approaching to mania has been hereditary in the men of the family, and in my stepfather's case it had, I believe, been intensified by his long residence in the tropics. A series of disgraceful brawls took place, two of which ended in the police court, until at last he became the terror of the village, and the folks would fly at his approach, for he is a man of immense strength, and absolutely uncontrollable in his anger.

"Last week he hurled the local blacksmith over a parapet into a stream, and it was only by paying over all the money which I could gather together that I was able to avert another public exposure. He had no friends at all save the wandering gypsies, and he would give these vagabonds leave to encamp upon the few acres of bramble-covered land which represent the family estate, and would accept in return the hospitality of their tents, wandering away with them sometimes for weeks on end. He has a passion also for Indian animals, which are sent over to him by a correspondent, and he has at this moment a cheetah and a baboon, which wander freely over his grounds and are feared by the villagers almost as much as their master.

"You can imagine from what I say that my poor sister Julia and I had no great pleasure in our lives. No servant would stay with us, and for a long time we did all the work of the house. She was but thirty at the time of her death, and yet her hair had already begun to whiten, even as mine has."

"Your sister is dead, then?"

"She died just two years ago, and it is of her death that I wish to speak to you. You can understand that, living the life which I have described, we were little likely to see anyone of our own age and position. We had, however, an aunt, my mother's maiden sister, Miss Honoria Westphail, who lives near Harrow, and we were occasionally allowed to pay short visits at this lady's house. Julia went there at Christmas two years ago, and met there a half-pay major of marines, to whom she became engaged. My stepfather learned of the engagement when my sister returned and offered no objection to the marriage; but within a fortnight of the day which had been fixed for the wedding, the terrible event occurred which has deprived me of my only companion."

Sherlock Holmes had been leaning back in his chair with his eyes closed and his head sunk in a cushion, but he half opened his lids now and glanced across at his visitor.

"Pray be precise as to details," he said.

"It is easy for me to be so, for every event of that dreadful time is seared into my memory. The manor house is, as I have already said, very old, and only one wing is now inhabited. The bedrooms in this wing are on the ground floor, the sitting rooms being in the central block of the buildings. Of these bedrooms the first is Dr. Roylott's, the second my sister's, and the third my own. There is no communication between them, but they all open out into the same corridor. Do I make myself plain?"

"Perfectly so."

"The windows of the three rooms open out upon the lawn. That fatal night Dr. Roylott had gone to his room early, though we knew that he had not retired to rest, for my sister was troubled by the smell of the strong Indian cigars which it was his custom to smoke. She left her room, therefore, and came into mine, where she sat for some time, chatting about her approaching wedding. At eleven o'clock she rose to leave me, but she paused at the door and looked back.

" 'Tell me, Helen,' said she, 'have you ever heard anyone whistle in the dead of night?'

" 'Never,' said I.

" 'I suppose that you could not possibly whistle, yourself, in your sleep?'

" 'Certainly not. But why?'

Notice how Doyle increases the atmosphere of suspense and impending doom by repeated references to potentially dangerous elements—the gypsies, the cheetah, the baboon, and Dr. Roylott himself.

personification

simile

" 'Because during the last few nights I have always, about three in the morning, heard a low, clear whistle. I am a light sleeper, and it has awakened me. I cannot tell where it came from—perhaps from the next room, perhaps from the lawn. I thought that I would just ask you whether you had heard it.'

" 'No, I have not. It must be those wretched gypsies in the plantation.'

" 'Very likely. And yet if it were on the lawn, I wonder that you did not hear it also.'

" 'Ah, but I sleep more heavily than you.'

" 'Well, it is of no great consequence, at any rate.' She smiled back at me, closed my door, and a few moments later I heard her key turn in the lock."

"Indeed," said Holmes. "Was it your custom always to lock yourselves in at night?"

"Always."

"And why?"

"I think that I mentioned to you that the doctor kept a cheetah and a baboon. We had no feeling of security unless our doors were locked."

"Quite so. Pray proceed with your statement."

"I could not sleep that night. A vague feeling of impending misfortune impressed me. My sister and I, you will recollect, were twins, and you know how subtle are the links which bind two souls which are so closely allied. It was a wild night. The wind was howling outside, and the rain was beating and splashing against the windows. Suddenly, amid all the hubbub of the gale, there burst forth the wild scream of a terrified woman. I knew that it was my sister's voice. I sprang from my bed, wrapped a shawl round me, and rushed into the corridor. As I opened my door I seemed to hear a low whistle, such as my sister had described, and a few moments later a clanging sound, as if a mass of metal had fallen. As I ran down the passage, my sister's door was unlocked, and revolved slowly upon its hinges.

I stared at it horror-stricken, not knowing what was about to issue from it. By the light of the corridor-lamp I saw my sister appear at the opening, her face blanched with terror, her hands groping for help, her whole figure swaying to and fro like that of a drunkard. I ran to her and threw my arms round her, but at that moment her knees seemed to give way and she fell to the ground. She writhed as one who is in terrible pain, and her limbs were dreadfully convulsed. At first I thought that she had not recognized me, but as I bent over her she suddenly shrieked out in a voice which I shall never forget, 'Oh Helen! Helen! It was the band! The speckled band!' There was something else which she would fain have said, and she stabbed with her finger into the air in the direction of the doctor's room, but a fresh convulsion seized her and choked her words. I rushed out, calling loudly for my stepfather, and I met him hastening from his room in his dressing gown. When he reached my sister's side she was unconscious, and though he sent for medical aid from the village, all efforts were in vain, for she slowly sank and died without having recovered her consciousness. Such was the dreadful end of my beloved sister."

"One moment," said Holmes; "are you sure about this whistle and metallic sound. Could you swear to it?"

"That was what the county coroner asked me at the inquiry. It is my strong impression that I heard it, and yet, among the crash of the gale and the creaking of an old house, I may possibly have been deceived."

"Was your sister dressed?"

"No, she was in her night dress. In her right hand was found the charred stump of a match, and in her left a matchbox."

"Showing that she had struck a light and looked about her when the alarm took place. That is important. And what conclusions did the coroner come to?"

"He investigated the case with great care, for Dr. Roylott's conduct had long been notorious in the county, but he was unable to find any satisfactory cause of death. My evidence showed that the door had been fastened upon the inner side, and the windows were blocked by old-fashioned shutters with broad iron bars, which were secured every night. The walls were carefully sounded and were shown to be quite solid all round, and the flooring was also thoroughly examined, with the same result. The chimney is wide, but is barred up by four large staples. It is certain, therefore, that my sister was quite alone when she met her end. Besides, there were no marks of any violence upon her."

"How about poison?"

"The doctors examined her for it, but without success."

"What do you think this unfortunate lady died of, then?"

"It is my belief that she died of pure fear and nervous shock, though what it was that frightened her I cannot imagine."

"Were there gypsies in the plantation at the time?"

Having a character become the victim of murder when apparently alone in a locked room is a staple of much detective fiction.

This explanation of the meaning of "the speckled band" is a red herring—an incident, explanation, or clue inserted into the story to draw the reader's attention away from the real solution to the mystery.

metaphor

"Yes, there are nearly always some there."

"Ah, and what did you gather from this allusion to a band—a speckled band?"

"Sometimes I have thought that it was merely the wild talk of delirium, sometimes that it may have referred to some band of people, perhaps to these very gypsies in the plantation. I do not know whether the spotted handkerchiefs which so many of them wear over their heads might have suggested the strange adjective which she used."

Holmes shook his head like a man who is far from being satisfied.

"These are very deep waters," said he; "pray go on with your narrative."

"Two years have passed since then, and my life has been until lately lonelier than ever. A month ago, however, a dear friend, whom I have known for many years, had done me the honor to ask my hand in marriage. His name is Armitage—Percy Armitage—the second son of Mr. Armitage, of Crane Water, near Reading. My stepfather has offered no opposition to the match, and we are to be married in the course of the spring. Two days ago some repairs were started in the west wing of the building, and my bedroom wall has been pierced, so that I have had to move into the chamber in which my sister died, and to sleep in the very bed in which she slept. Imagine, then, my thrill of terror when last night, as I lay awake, thinking over her terrible fate, I suddenly heard in the silence of the night the low whistle which had been the herald of her own death. I sprang up and lit the lamp, but nothing was to be seen in the room. I was too shaken to go to bed again, however, so I dressed, and as soon as it was daylight I slipped down, got a dogcart at the Crown Inn, which is opposite, and drove to Leatherhead, from whence I have come on this morning with the one object of seeing you and asking your advice."

"You have done wisely," said my friend.

"But have you told me all?"

"Yes, all."

"Miss Roylott, you have not. You are screening your stepfather."

"Why, what do you mean?"

For answer Holmes pushed back the frill of black lace which fringed the hand that lay upon our visitor's knee. Five little livid spots, the marks of four fingers and a thumb, were printed upon the white wrist.

"You have been cruelly used," said Holmes.

The lady colored deeply and covered over her injured wrist. "He is a hard man," she said, "and perhaps he hardly knows his own strength."

There was a long silence, during which Holmes leaned his chin upon his hands and stared into the crackling fire.

"This is very deep business," he said at last. "There are a thousand details which I should desire to know before I decide upon our course of action. Yet we have not a moment to lose. If we were to come to Stoke Moran today, would it be possible for us to see over these rooms without the knowledge of your stepfather?"

"As it happens, he spoke of coming into town today upon some most important business. It is probable that he will be away all day, and that there would be nothing to disturb you. We have a housekeeper now, but she is old and foolish, and I could easily get her out of the way."

"Excellent. You are not averse to this trip, Watson?"

"By no means."

"Then we shall both come. What are you going to do yourself?"

"I have one or two things which I would wish to do now that I am in town. But I shall return by the twelve o'clock train, so as to be there in time for your coming."

"And you may expect us early in the afternoon. I have myself some small business

Doyle again introduces red herrings here: the gypsy "band" and a wrong assumption regarding the metallic sound.

matters to attend to. Will you not wait and breakfast?"

"No, I must go. My heart is lightened already since I have confided my trouble to you. I shall look forward to seeing you again this afternoon." She dropped her thick black veil over her face and glided from the room.

"It seems to me to be a most dark and sinister business."

"Dark enough and sinister enough."

"Yet if the lady is correct in saying that the flooring and walls are sound, and that the door, window, and chimney are impassable, then her sister must have been undoubtedly alone when she met her mysterious end."

"What becomes, then, of these nocturnal whistles, and what of the very peculiar words of the dying woman?"

"I cannot think."

"When you combine the ideas of whistles at night, the presence of a band of gypsies who are on intimate terms with this old doctor, the fact that we have every reason to believe that the doctor has an interest in preventing his stepdaughter's marriage, the dying allusion to a band, and, finally, the fact that Miss Helen Stoner heard a metallic clang, which might have been caused by one of those metal bars that secured the shutters falling back into its place, I think that there is good ground to think that the mystery may be cleared along those lines."

"But what, then, did the gypsies do?"

"I cannot imagine."

"I see many objections to such a theory."

"And so do I. It is precisely for that reason that we are going to Stoke Moran this day. I want to see whether the objections are fatal, or if they may be explained away. But what in the name of—!"

The ejaculation had been drawn from my companion by the fact that our door had been suddenly dashed open, and that a huge man had framed himself in the aperture. His costume was a peculiar mixture of the professional and of the agricultural, having a black top hat, a long frock coat, and a pair of high gaiters, with a hunting crop swinging in his hand. So tall was he that his hat actually brushed the cross bar of the doorway, and his breadth seemed to span it across from side to side. A large face, seared with a thousand wrinkles, burned yellow with the sun, and marked with every evil passion, was turned from one to the other of us, while his deep-set, bile-shot eyes, and his high, thin, fleshless nose, gave him somewhat the resemblance to a fierce old bird of prey.

"Which of you is Holmes?" asked this apparition.

"My name, sir; but you have the advantage of me," said my companion quietly.

"I am Dr. Grimesby Roylott, of Stoke Moran."

"Indeed, Doctor," said Holmes blandly. "Pray take a seat."

"I will do nothing of the kind. My step-daughter has been here. I have traced her. What has she been saying to you?"

"It is a little cold for the time of year," said Holmes.

"What has she been saying to you?" screamed the old man furiously.

"But I have heard that the crocuses promise well," continued my companion imperturbably.

"Ha! You put me off, do you?" said our new visitor, taking a step forward and shaking his hunting crop. "I know you, you scoundrel! I have heard of you before. You are Holmes, the meddler."

My friend smiled.

"Holmes, the busybody!"

His smile broadened.

"Holmes, the Scotland Yard Jack-in-office!"

Holmes chuckled heartily. "Your conversation is most entertaining," said he. "When you go out close the door, for there is a decided draught."

"I will go when I have had my say. Don't you dare to meddle with my affairs. I know that Miss Stoner has been here. I traced her! I am a dangerous man to fall foul of! See here." He stepped swiftly forward, seized the poker, and bent it into a curve with his huge brown hands.

"See that you keep yourself out of my grip," he snarled, and hurling the twisted poker into the fireplace he strode out of the room.

"He seems a very amiable person," said Holmes, laughing. "I am not quite so bulky, but if he had remained I might have shown him that my grip was not much more feeble than his own." As he spoke he picked up the steel poker and, with a sudden effort, straightened it out again.

"Fancy his having the insolence to confound me with the official detective force! This incident gives zest to our investigation, however, and I only trust that our little friend will not suffer from her imprudence in allowing this brute to trace her. And now, Watson, we shall order breakfast, and afterwards I shall walk down to Doctors' Commons,* where I hope to get some data which may help us in this matter."

Doctors' Commons: a place in London used as an official storage place for wills and other deeds

---

It was nearly one o'clock when Sherlock Holmes returned from his excursion. He held in his hand a sheet of blue paper, scrawled over with notes and figures.

"I have seen the will of the deceased wife," said he. "To determine its exact meaning I have been obliged to work out the present prices of the investments with which it is concerned. The total income, which at the time of the wife's death was little short of £1100, is now, through the fall in agricultural prices, not more than £750. Each daughter can claim an income of £250, in case of marriage. It is evident, therefore, that if both girls had married, this beauty would have had a mere pittance, while even one of them would cripple him to a very serious extent. My morning's work has not been wasted, since it has proved that he has the very strongest motives for standing in the way of anything of the sort. And now, Watson, this is too serious for dawdling, especially as the old man is aware that we are interesting ourselves in his affairs; so if you are ready, we shall call a cab and drive to Waterloo. I should be very much obliged if you would slip your revolver into your pocket. A handgun is an excellent argument with gentlemen who can twist steel pokers into knots. That and a toothbrush are, I think, all that we need."

At Waterloo we were fortunate in catching a train for Leatherhead, where we hired a trap* at the station inn and drove for four or five miles through the lovely Surrey lanes. It was a perfect day, with a bright sun and a few fleecy clouds in the heavens. The trees and wayside hedges were just throwing out their first green shoots, and the air was full of the pleasant smell of the moist earth. To me at least there was a strange contrast between the sweet promise of the spring and this sinister quest upon which we were engaged. My companion sat in the front of the trap, his arms folded, his hat pulled down over his eyes, and his chin sunk down upon his breast, buried in the deepest thought. Suddenly, however, he started, tapped me on the shoulder, and pointed over the meadows.

---

trap: small coach drawn by horses

"Look there!" said he.

A heavily timbered park stretched up in a gentle slope, thickening into a grove at the highest point. From amid the branches there jutted out the gray gables and high roof-tree of a very old mansion.

"Stoke Moran?" said he.

"Yes, sir, that be the house of Dr. Grimesby Roylott," remarked the driver.

"There is some building going on there," said Holmes; "that is where we are going."

"There's the village," said the driver, pointing to a cluster of roofs some distance to the left; "but if you want to get to the house, you'll find it shorter to get over this stile, and so by the foot path over the fields. There it is, where the lady is walking."

"And the lady, I fancy, is Miss Stoner," observed Holmes, shading his eyes. "Yes, I think we had better do as you suggest."

We got off, paid our fare, and the trap rattled back on its way to Leatherhead.

"I thought it as well," said Holmes as we climbed the stile, "that this fellow should think we had come here as architects, or on some definite business. It may stop his gossip. Good afternoon, Miss Stoner. You see that we have been as good as our word."

Our client of the morning hurried forward to meet us with a face which spoke her joy. "I have been waiting so eagerly for you," she cried, shaking hands with us warmly. "All has turned out splendidly. Dr. Roylott has gone to town, and it is unlikely that he will be back before evening."

"We have had the pleasure of making the doctor's acquaintance," said Holmes, and in a few words he sketched out what had occurred. Miss Stoner turned white to the lips as she listened.

"Good heavens!" she cried, "he has followed me, then?"

"So it appears."

"He is so cunning that I never know when I am safe from him. What will he say when he returns?"

"He must guard himself, for he may find that there is someone more cunning than himself upon his track. You must lock yourself up from him tonight. If he is violent, we shall take you away to your aunt's at Harrow. Now, we must make the best use of our time, so kindly take us at once to the rooms which we are to examine."

The building was of gray, lichen-blotched stone, with a high central portion and two curving wings, like the claws of a crab, thrown out on each side. In one of these wings the windows were broken and blocked with wooden boards, while the roof was partly caved in, a picture of ruin. The central portion was in little better repair, but the right hand block was comparatively modern, and the blinds in the windows, with the blue smoke curling up from the chimneys, showed that this was where the family resided. Some scaffolding had been erected against the end wall, and the stone work had been broken into, but there were no signs of any workmen at the moment of our visit. Holmes walked slowly up and down the ill-trimmed lawn and examined with deep attention the outsides of the windows.

"This, I take it, belongs to the room in which you used to sleep, the center one to your sister's, and the one next to the main building to Dr. Roylott's chamber?"

"Exactly so. But I am now sleeping in the middle one."

"Pending the alterations, as I understand. By the way, there does not seem to be any very pressing need for repairs at that end wall."

"There were none. I believe that it was an excuse to move me from my room."

"Ah! that is suggestive. Now, on the other side of this narrow wing runs the corridor from which these three rooms open. There are windows in it, of course?"

"Yes, but very small ones. Too narrow for anyone to pass through."

"As you both locked your doors at night, your rooms were unapproachable from that side. Now, would you have the kindness to go into your room and bar your shutters?"

Miss Stoner did so, and Holmes, after a careful examination through the open window, endeavored in every way to force the shutter open, but without success. There was no slit through which a knife could be passed to raise the bar. Then with his lens he tested the hinges, but they were of solid iron, built firmly into the massive masonry. "Hum!" said he, scratching his chin in some perplexity, "my theory certainly presents some difficulties. No one could pass these shutters if they were bolted. Well, we shall see if the inside throws any light upon the matter."

A small side door led into the whitewashed corridor from which the three bedrooms opened. Holmes refused to examine the third chamber, so we passed at once to the second, that in which Miss Stoner was now sleeping, and in which her sister had met her fate. It was a homely little room, with a low ceiling and a gaping fireplace, after the fashion of old country houses. A brown chest of drawers stood in one corner, a narrow white counter-paned bed in another, and a dressing table on the left hand side of the window. These articles, with two small wicker-work chairs, made up all the furniture in the room save for a square of Wilton carpet in the center. The boards round and the paneling of the walls were of brown, worm-eaten oak, so old and discolored that it may have dated from the original building of the house. Holmes drew one of the chairs into a corner and sat silent, while his eyes traveled round and round and up and down, taking in every detail of the apartment.

"Where does that bell communicate with?" he asked at last, pointing to a thick bell-rope which hung down beside the bed, the tassel actually lying upon the pillow.

"It goes to the housekeeper's room."

"It looks newer than the other things?"

"Yes, it was only put there a couple of years ago."

"Your sister asked for it, I suppose?"

"No. I never heard of her using it. We used always to get what we wanted for ourselves."

"Indeed, it seemed unnecessary to put so nice a bell-pull there. You will excuse me a few minutes while I satisfy myself as to this floor." He threw himself down upon his face with his lens in his hand and crawled swiftly backward and forward, examining minutely the cracks between the boards. Then he did the same with the wood work with which the chamber was paneled. Finally he walked over to the bed and spent some time in staring at it and in running his eye up and down the wall. Finally he took the bell-rope in his hand and gave it a brisk tug.

"Why, it's a dummy," said he.

"Won't it ring?"

"No, it is not even attached to a wire. This is very interesting. You can see now that it is fastened to a hook just above where the little opening for the ventilator is."

"How very absurd! I never noticed that before."

"Very strange!" muttered Holmes, pulling at the rope. "There are one or two very singular points about this room. For example, what a fool a builder must be to open a ventilator into another room, when, with the same trouble, he might have communicated with the outside air!"

"That is also quite modern," said the lady.

"Done about the same time as the bell-rope?" remarked Holmes.

"Yes, there were several little changes carried out about that time."

"They seem to have been of a most interesting character—dummy bell-ropes, and ventilators which do not ventilate. With your permission, Miss Stoner, we shall now carry our researches into the inner apartment."

Dr. Grimesby Roylott's chamber was larger than that of his stepdaughter, but was as plainly furnished. A camp bed, a small wooden shelf full of books, mostly of a technical character, an armchair beside the bed, a plain wooden chair against the wall, a round table, and a large iron safe were the principal things which met the eye. Holmes walked slowly round and examined each and all of them with the keenest interest.

"What's in here?" he asked tapping the safe.

"My stepfather's business papers."

"Oh! you have seen inside, then?"

"Only once, some years ago. I remember that it was full of papers."

"There isn't a cat in it, for example?"

"No. What a strange idea!"

"Well, look at this!" he took up a small saucer of milk which stood on the top of it.

"No; we don't keep a cat but there is a cheetah and a baboon."

"Ah, yes, of course! Well, a cheetah is just a big cat, and yet a saucer of milk does not go very far in satisfying its wants, I dare say. There is one point which I should wish to determine." He squatted down in front of the wooden chair and examined the seat of it with the greatest attention.

"Thank you. That is quite settled," said he, rising and putting his lens in his pocket. "Hello! Here is something interesting!"

The object which had caught his eye was a small dog lash* hung on one corner of the bed. The lash, however, was curled upon itself and tied so as to make a loop of whipcord.

lash: leash

"What do you make of that, Watson?"

"It's a common enough lash. But I don't know why it should be tied."

"That is not quite so common, is it? Ah, me! It's a wicked world, and when a clever man turns his brains to crime it is the worst of all. I think that I have seen enough now, Miss Stoner, and with your permission we shall walk out upon the lawn."

I had never seen my friend's face so grim or his brow so dark as it was when we turned from the scene of this investigation. We had walked several times up and down the lawn, neither Miss Stoner nor myself liking to break in upon his thoughts before he roused himself from his reverie.

"It is very essential, Miss Stoner," said he, "that you should absolutely follow my advice in every respect."

"I shall most certainly do so."

"The matter is too serious for any hesitation. Your life may depend upon your compliance."

"I assure you that I am in your hands."

"In the first place, both my friend and I must spend the night in your room."

Both Miss Stoner and I gazed at him in astonishment.

"Yes, it must be so. Let me explain. I believe that that is the village inn over there?"

"Yes, that is the Crown."

"Very good. Your windows would be visible from there?"

"Certainly."

"You must confine yourself to your room, on pretence of a headache, when your stepfather comes back. Then when you hear him retire for the night, you must open the shutters of your window, undo the hasp, put your lamp there as a signal to us, and then withdraw quietly with everything you are likely to want into the room which you used to occupy. I have no doubt that, in spite of the repairs, you could manage there for one night."

"Oh, yes, easily."

"The rest you will leave in our hands."

"But what will you do?"

"We shall spend the night in your room, and we shall investigate the cause of this noise which has disturbed you."

"I believe, Mr. Holmes, that you have already made up your mind," said Miss Stoner, laying her hand upon my companion's sleeve.

"Perhaps I have."

"Then for pity's sake, tell me what was the cause of my sister's death."

Foreshadowing: Through Watson's eyes we have seen all that Holmes has seen and heard all he has heard, yet we realize that he comprehends far more about what has happened and what will happen than we do.

synecdoche

"I should prefer to have clearer proofs before I speak."

"You can at least tell me whether my own thought is correct, and if she died from some sudden fright."

"No, I do not think so. I think that there was probably some more tangible cause. And now, Miss Stoner, we must leave you, for if Dr. Roylott returned and saw us our journey would be in vain. Goodbye, and be brave, for if you will do what I have told you you may rest assured that we shall soon drive away the dangers that threaten you."

Sherlock Holmes and I had no difficulty in engaging a bedroom and sitting room at the Crown Inn. They were on the upper floor, and from our window we could command a view of the avenue gate, and of the inhabited wing of Stoke Moran Manor House. At dusk we saw Dr. Grimesby Roylott drive past, his huge form looming up beside the little figure of the lad who drove him. The boy had some slight difficulty in undoing the heavy iron gates, and we heard the hoarse roar of the doctor's voice and saw the fury with which he shook his clinched fists at him. The trap drove on, and a few minutes later we saw a sudden light spring up among the trees as the lamp was lit in one of the sitting rooms.

"Do you know, Watson," said Holmes as we sat together in the gathering darkness, "I have really some scruples as to taking you tonight. There is a distinct element of danger."

"Can I be of assistance?"

"Your presence might be invaluable."

"Then I shall certainly come."

"It is very kind of you."

"You speak of danger. You have evidently seen more in these rooms than was visible to me."

"No, but I fancy that I may have deduced a little more. I imagine that you saw all that I did."

I saw nothing remarkable save the bell-rope, and what purpose that could answer I confess is more than I imagine."

"You saw the ventilator, too?"

"Yes, but I do not think that it is such a very unusual thing to have a small opening between two rooms. It was so small that a rat could hardly pass through."

"I knew that we should find a ventilator before ever we came to Stoke Moran."

"My dear Holmes!"

"Oh, yes, I did. You remember in her statement she said that her sister could smell Dr. Roylott's cigar. Now, of course that suggested at once that there must be a communication between the two rooms. It could only be a small one, or it would have been remarked upon at the coroner's inquiry. I deduced a ventilator."

"But what harm can there be in that?"

"Well, there is at least a curious coincidence of dates. A ventilator is made, a cord is hung, and a lady who sleeps in a bed dies. Does that not strike you?"

"I cannot as yet see any connection."

"Did you observe anything very peculiar about that bed?"

"No."

"It was clamped to the floor. Did you ever see a bed fastened like that before?"

"I cannot say that I have."

"The lady could not move her bed. It must always be in the same relative position to the ventilator and to the rope—or so we may call it, since it was clearly never meant for a bell pull."

"Holmes," I cried, "I seem to see dimly what you are hinting at. We are only just in time to prevent some subtle and horrible crime."

"Subtle enough and horrible enough. When a doctor does go wrong he is the first of criminals. He has nerve and he has knowledge. Palmer and Pritchard were among the heads of their profession. This man strikes even deeper, but I think, Watson, that we shall be able to strike deeper still. But we shall have horrors enough before the night is over."

About nine o'clock the light among the trees was extinguished, and all was dark in the direction of the Manor house. Two hours passed slowly away, and then, suddenly, just at the stroke of eleven, a single bright light shone out right in front of us.

"That is our signal," said Holmes, springing to his feet; "it comes from the middle window."

As we passed out he exchanged a few words with the landlord, explaining that we were going on a late visit to an acquaintance, and that it was possible that we might spend the night there. A moment later we were out on the dark road, a chill wind blowing in our faces, and one yellow light twinkling in front of us through the gloom to guide us on our somber errand.

There was little difficulty in entering the grounds, for unrepaired breaches gaped in the old park wall. Making our way among the trees, we reached the lawn, crossed it, and were about to enter through the window when out from a clump of laurel bushes there darted what seemed to be a hideous and distorted child, who threw itself upon the grass with writhing limbs and then ran swiftly across the lawn into the darkness.

"Did you see it?" I whispered.

Holmes was for the moment as startled as I. His hand closed like a vise upon my wrist in agitation. Then he broke into a low laugh and put his lips to my ear.

"It is a nice household," he murmured. "That is the baboon."

I had forgotten the strange pets which the doctor affected. There was a cheetah, too; perhaps we might find it upon our shoulders at any moment. I confess that I felt easier in my mind when, after following Holmes's example and slipping off my shoes, I found myself inside the bedroom. My companion

Note that it was around 3 A.M. when Julia heard the whistle (page 252).

A dark lantern is "a lantern that can be closed to conceal the light" (*Merriam-Webster's Collegiate Dictionary*, 10th ed., 1994).

noiselessly closed the shutters, moved the lamp onto the table, and cast his eyes round the room. All was as we had seen it in the daytime. Then creeping up to me and making a trumpet of his hand, he whispered into my ear again so gently that it was all that I could do to distinguish the words:

"The least sound would be fatal to our plans."

I nodded to show that I had heard.

"We must sit without light. He would see it through the ventilator."

I nodded again.

"Do not go to sleep; your very life may depend upon it. Have your pistol ready in case we should need it. I will sit on the side of the bed, and you in that chair."

I took out my revolver and laid it on the corner of the table.

Holmes had brought up a long thin cane, and this he placed upon the bed beside him. By it he laid the box of matches and the stump of a candle. Then he turned down the lamp, and we were left in darkness.

How shall I ever forget that dreadful vigil? I could not hear a sound, not even the drawing of a breath, and yet I knew that my companion sat open-eyed, within a few feet of me, in the same state of nervous tension in which I was myself. The shutters cut off the least ray of light, and we waited in absolute darkness. From outside came the occasional cry of a night bird, and once at our very window a long drawn catlike whine, which told us that the cheetah was indeed at liberty. Far away we could hear the deep tones of the parish clock, which boomed out every quarter of an hour. How long they seemed, those quarters! Twelve struck, and one and two and three, and still we sat waiting silently for whatever might befall.

Suddenly there was a momentary gleam of a light in the direction of the ventilator, which vanished immediately, but was suc-ceeded by a strong smell of burning oil and heated metal. Someone in the next room had lit a dark lantern. I heard a gentle sound of movement, and then all was silent once more, though the smell grew stronger. For half an hour I sat with straining ears. Then suddenly another sound became audible—a very gentle, soothing sound, like that of a small jet stream escaping continually from a kettle. The instant that we heard it, Holmes sprang from the bed, struck a match, and lashed furiously with his cane at the bell-pull.

"You see it, Watson?" he yelled. "You see it?"

But I saw nothing. At the moment when Holmes struck the light I heard a low, clear whistle, but the sudden glare flashing into my weary eyes made it impossible for me to tell what it was at which my friend lashed so savagely. I could, however, see that his face was deadly pale and filled with horror and loathing.

He had ceased to strike and was gazing up at the ventilator when suddenly there broke from the silence of the night the most horrible cry to which I have ever listened. It swelled up louder and louder, a hoarse yell of pain and fear and anger all mingled in the one dreadful shriek. They say that away down in the village, and even in the distant parsonage, that cry raised the sleepers from their beds. It struck cold to our hearts, and I stood gazing at Holmes, and he at me, until the last echoes of it had died away into the silence from which it rose.

"What can it mean?" I gasped.

"It means that it is all over," Holmes answered. "And perhaps, after all, it is for the best. Take your pistol, and we will enter Dr. Roylott's room."

With a grave face he lit the lamp and led the way down the corridor. Twice he struck at the chamber door without any reply from within. Then he turned the handle and entered,

I at his heels, with the cocked pistol in my hand.

It was a singular sight which met our eyes. On the table stood a dark lantern with the shutter half open, throwing a brilliant light upon the iron safe, the door of which was ajar. Beside the table, on the wooden chair, sat Dr. Grimesby Roylott, clad in a long gray dressing gown, his bare ankles protruding beneath, and his feet thrust into red heelless Turkish slippers. Across his lap lay the short stock with the long lash which we had noticed during the day. His chin was cocked upward and his eyes were fixed in a dreadful rigid stare at the corner of the ceiling. Round his brow he had a peculiar yellow band, with brownish speckles, which seemed to be bound tightly round his head. As we entered he made neither sound nor motion.

"The band! the speckled band!" whispered Holmes.

I took a step forward. In an instant his strange headgear began to move, and there reared itself from among his hair the squat diamond-shaped head and puffed neck of a loathsome serpent.

"It is a swamp adder!" cried Holmes; "the deadliest snake in India. He has died within ten seconds of being bitten. Violence does, in truth, recoil upon the violent, and the schemer falls into the pit which he digs for another. Let us thrust this creature back into its den, and we can then remove Miss Stoner to some place of shelter and let the county police know what has happened."

As he spoke he drew the dog-whip swiftly from the dead man's lap, and throwing the noose round the reptile's neck he drew it from its horrid perch and, carrying it at arm's length, threw it into the iron safe, which he closed upon it.

Such are the true facts of the death of Dr. Grimesby Roylott, of Stoke Moran. It is not necessary that I should prolong a narrative which has already run to too great a length by telling how we broke the sad news to the terrified girl, how we conveyed her by the morning train to the care of her good aunt at Harrow, of how the slow process of official inquiry came to the conclusion that the doctor met his fate while discreetly playing with a dangerous pet. The little which I had yet to learn of the case was told me by Sherlock Holmes as we traveled back next day.

"I had," said he, "come to an entirely erroneous conclusion which shows, my dear Watson, how dangerous it always is to reason from insufficient data. The presence of the gypsies, and the use of the word 'band,' which was used by the poor girl, no doubt to explain the appearance which she had caught a hurried glimpse of by the light of her match, were sufficient to put me upon an entirely wrong scent. I can only claim the merit that I instantly reconsidered my position when, however, it became clear to me that whatever danger threatened an occupant of the room could not come either from the window or the door. My attention was speedily drawn, as I have already remarked to you, to this ventilator, and to the bell-rope which hung down to the bed. The discovery that this was a dummy, and that the bed was clamped to the floor, instantly gave rise to the suspicion that the rope was there as a bridge for something passing through the hole and coming to the bed. The idea of a snake instantly occurred to me, and when I coupled it with my knowledge that the doctor was furnished with a supply of creatures from India, I felt that I was probably on the right track. The idea of using a form of poison which could not possibly be discovered by any chemical test was just such a one as would occur to a clever and ruthless man who had had an Eastern training. The rapidity with which such a poison would take effect would also, from his point of view, be an advantage.

Biblical allusion (Prov. 28:10)

Note that the "official inquiry" comes to the wrong conclusion about exactly how Dr. Roylott died. Discuss with the students how and why this could occur. (Perhaps Holmes desired to keep his role in the events a secret. However, it is more likely that he suppressed his evidence in order to spare Helen Stoner further pain and embarrassment. See also Watson's reference in the first paragraph of the story to having promised a lady [no doubt Helen Stoner] to keep the facts a secret. At any rate, it is apparent that Holmes and Watson were not forthcoming with the truth about the events—something Christians cannot defend.)

Note that Holmes's summary here (the denouement) achieves what a masterful mystery writer seeks to achieve—it clearly explains all the facts of the story that up until now had mystified the readers.

Holmes's examination of the chair and his conclusion reached from looking at it are typical. In "The Red-Headed League," Holmes interviews a man not to hear what he has to say but to examine "the knees of his trousers." And in "Silver Blaze," Holmes and Watson have one of their best-known exchanges. Watson speaks first.

"Is there any point to which you would wish to draw my attention?"

"To the curious incident of the dog in the night-time."

"The dog did nothing in the night-time."

"That was the curious incident."

It would be a sharp-eyed coroner, indeed, who could distinguish the two little dark punctures which would show where the poison fangs had done their work. Then I thought of the whistle. Of course he must recall the snake before the morning light revealed it to the victim. He had trained it, probably by use of the milk which we saw, to return to him when summoned. He would put it through this ventilator at the hour that he thought best, with the certainty that it would crawl down the rope and land on the bed. It might or might not bite the occupant, perhaps she might escape every night for a week, but sooner or later she must fall victim.

"I had come to these conclusions before ever I had entered his room. An inspection of his chair showed me this: he had been in the habit of standing on it, which of course would be necessary in order that he should reach the ventilator. The sight of the safe, the saucer of milk, and the loop of whipcord were enough to finally dispel any doubts which may have remained. The metallic clang heard by Miss Stoner was obviously caused by her stepfather hastily closing the door of his safe upon its terrible occupant. Having once made up my mind, you know the steps which I took in order to put the matter to the proof. I heard the creature hiss as I have no doubt that you did also, and I instantly lit the light and attacked it."

"With the result of driving it through the ventilator."

"And also with the result of causing it to turn upon its master at the other side. Some of the blows of my cane came home and roused its snakish temper, so that it flew upon the first person it saw. In this way I am no doubt indirectly responsible for Dr. Grimesby Roylott's death, and I cannot say that it is likely to weigh very heavily upon my conscience."

About the Story

1. What story element is introduced to divert readers' (and Holmes's) attention from the real cause of the crime?
2. At what point are we convinced of Dr. Roylott's treachery?
3. What advantage is there in having Watson rather than Holmes narrate the story?
4. Did Holmes intend for the "speckled band" to attack Dr. Roylott? Support your answer with quotations from the story.
5. List at least three characteristics you can think of that help make mysteries like "The Speckled Band" enjoyable to read.

 About the Story

1. *the band of gypsies*

2. *Answers may vary; require students to support their response with a quotation from the story.*

3. *Because he lacks Holmes's deductive powers, he can narrate the story without disclosing the outcome. He is also, therefore, easier for the reader to identify with.*

4. *Answers may vary; require students to support their response with a quotation from the story.*

5. *Answers may vary but might include suspense; the desire to be fooled; the enjoyment of solving an intellectual puzzle; the thrill of experiencing danger and adventure vicariously.*

The Drummer Boy of Shiloh

Ray Bradbury

Shiloh, one of the bloodiest battles of America's bloodiest war, had some 23,000 casualties. These statistics are not surprising since almost 80 per cent of the men who fought in this early Civil War battle had never been in combat. Many did not even know how to fire their guns.

In this selection, a commanding general who clearly understands the tragedies of war speaks frankly to a young drummer boy. He does so, however, in a way that inspires the fainthearted youth. Notice Bradbury's use of imaginative comparison, sound and syntax, and symbol. These literary elements help make his story memorable and moving.

In the April night, more than once, blossoms fell from the orchard tree and lighted with rustling taps on the drumhead. At midnight a peach stone, left miraculously on a branch through winter, flicked by a bird, fell swift and unseen; it struck once, like panic, and jerked the boy upright. In silence he listened to his own heart ruffle away, away—at last gone from his ears and back in his chest again.

After that he turned the drum on its side, where its great lunar face peered at him whenever he opened his eyes.

His face, alert or at rest, was solemn. It was a solemn time and a solemn night for a boy just turned fourteen in the peach orchard near Owl Creek, not far from the church at Shiloh.

". . . thirty-one . . . thirty-two . . . thirty-three." Unable to see, he stopped counting.

Beyond the thirty-three familiar shadows, forty thousand men, exhausted by nervous expectation and unable to sleep for romantic dreams of battles yet unfought, lay crazily askew in their uniforms. A mile farther on, another army was strewn helter-skelter, turning slowly, basting themselves with the thought of what they would do when the time came— a leap, a yell, a blind plunge their strategy, raw youth their protection and benediction.

Now and again the boy heard a vast wind come up that gently stirred the air. But he knew what it was—the army here, the army there, whispering to itself in the dark. Some men talking to others, others murmuring to themselves, and all so quiet it was like a natural element arisen from South or North with the motion of the earth toward dawn.

What the men whispered the boy could only guess, and he guessed that it was "Me, I'm the one, I'm the one of all the rest who won't die. I'll live through it. I'll go home. The band will play. And I'll be there to hear it."

"Yes," thought the boy, "that's all very well for them, they can give as good as they get!"

For with the careless bones of the young men, harvested by night and bindled* around campfires, were the similarly strewn steel bones

OBJECTIVES

The students will be able to

- Differentiate between internal and external conflict.
- Locate examples of imaginative comparison, sound and syntax, and symbol.

onomatopoeia, sound imagery, simile

personification, metaphor ("lunar face")

metaphor

Joby's conflict is an internal one.

PREPARATION

"The Drummer Boy of Shiloh"

Overview

"The Drummer Boy of Shiloh" is a moving story of a young boy's internal struggle on the eve of a historic battle. Although Bradbury is best known for his science fiction, this story is not science fiction; but its deft use of images and symbols is distinctly "Bradburyan."

Potential problems

Although this story is free of objectionable elements, much of Bradbury's writing contains erroneous philosophical and religious views. It would, there-fore, be unwise to encourage indiscriminate recreational reading of Bradbury.

DISCUSSION

Introduction

Ask the students what they know about the Battle of Shiloh. They may remember it from their study of the Civil War in history class. The headnote provides some information. For additional information, you may want to have one of the students look up the battle in a reference book and share this information with the rest of the class (cf. BJU Press's UNITED STATES HISTORY *for Christian Schools,* page 299).

Analysis

Although the setting of the story is war, this external conflict merely serves to highlight Joby's internal struggle. It is this struggle that is the central conflict of the story. Bradbury makes this struggle memorable and moving through his use of images, sounds, and symbols. Read the story aloud in class.

Following the reading, have the students take a few minutes to skim the story and jot down several images, sounds, and symbols that they can find. Following are several examples:

1. "rustling taps on the drumhead" (page 265; sound imagery, onomatopoeia)

2. "a peach stone . . . struck once, like panic" (page 265; simile)

Note Bradbury's meaning tucked neatly into poetic language: Each soldier has a "shield" from death in his own mind based on "family devotion, . . . patriotism, and cocksure immortality," but also backed up by his weapons. The drummer boy has no weapons, so the intangible protections mentioned above are scant comfort. (Note that "Minié" can be pronounced "mini" or "mini-ay"; it is named after its inventor, French army officer Claude Étienne Minié.)

metaphor

touch imagery, onomatopoeia

FURTHER HELPS

Additional activities

1. Have the students research any Civil War landmarks in their area. If time permits, visit these historic sites.

2. Give information about the Battle of Shiloh. It occurred April 6-7, 1862, near Savannah, Tennessee. It is also called the Battle of Pittsburg Landing. The generals for the North were Grant and Buell. Johnston was the general for the South, but he was killed in the battle and then replaced by Beauregard. The battle received its name from a nearby church called Shiloh Church.

---

of their rifles with bayonets fixed like eternal lightning lost in the orchard grass.

bindled: bound together

"Me," thought the boy, "*I got only a drum, two sticks to beat it, and no shield.*"

There wasn't a man-boy on this ground tonight who did not have a shield he cast, riveted, or carved himself on his way to his first attack, compounded of remote but nonetheless firm and fiery family devotion, flag-blown patriotism, and cocksure* immortality, strengthened by the touchstone of very real gunpowder, ramrod, Minié ball,* and flint. But without these last, the boy felt his family move yet farther off in the dark, as if one of those great prairie-burning trains had chanted them away, never to return—leaving him with his drum, which was worse than a toy in a game to be played tomorrow or someday much too soon.

cocksure: certain
Minié ball: rifle bullet

The boy turned on his side. A moth brushed his face, but it was peach blossom. A peach blossom flicked him, but it was a moth. Nothing stayed put. Nothing had a name. Nothing was as it once was.

If he stayed very still when the dawn came up and the soldiers put on their bravery with their caps, perhaps they might go away, the war with them, and not notice him lying small here, no more than a toy himself.

"Well, by thunder now," said a voice. The boy shut his eyes to hide inside himself, but it was too late. Someone, walking by in the night, stood over him. "Well," said the voice quietly, "here's a soldier crying *before* the fight. Good. Get it over. Won't be time once it all starts."

And the voice was about to move on when the boy, startled, touched the drum at his elbow. The man above, hearing this, stopped. The boy could feel his eyes, sense him slowly bending near. A hand must have come down out of the night, for there was a little *rat-tat* as the fingernails brushed and the man's breath fanned the boy's face.

"Why, it's the drummer boy, isn't it?"

The boy nodded, not knowing if his nod was seen. "Sir, is that you?" he said.

"I assume it is." The man's knees cracked as he bent still closer. He smelled as all fathers should smell, of salt-sweat, horse and boot leather, and the earth he walked upon. He had many eyes. No, not eyes, brass buttons that watched the boy.

He could only be, and was, the general. "What's your name, boy?" he asked.

"Joby, sir," whispered the boy, starting to sit up.

"All right, Joby, don't stir." A hand pressed his chest gently, and the boy relaxed. "How long you been with us, Joby?"

"Three weeks, sir."

"Run off from home or join legitimate, boy?"

Silence.

"Fool question," said the general. "Do you shave yet, boy? Even more of a fool. There's your cheek, fell right off the tree from overhead. And the others here, not much older. Raw, raw, the lot of you. You ready for tomorrow or the next day, Joby?"

"I think so, sir."

"You want to cry some more, go on ahead. I did the same last night."

"You, sir?"

"God's truth. Thinking of everything ahead. Both sides figuring the other side will just give up, and soon, and the war done in weeks and us all home. Well, that's not how it's going to be. And maybe that's why I cried."

"Yes, sir," said Joby.

The general must have taken out a cigar now, for the dark was suddenly filled with the

---

3. he listened to his own heart ruffle away, away" (page 265; sound imagery, onomatopoeia)

4. the drum's "great lunar face peered at him" (page 265; personification)

5. "another army was strewn helter-skelter, turning slowly, basting themselves" (page 265; metaphor)

6. "the army here, the army there, whispering to itself in the dark" (page 265; sound imagery)

7. "the careless bones of the young men, harvested by night and bindled around campfires" (page 265; metonymy [bones represent the soldiers], metaphor)

8. "strewn steel bones of their rifles with bayonets fixed like eternal lightning lost in the orchard grass" (pages 265-66; alliteration, metaphor, simile)

9. "no more than a toy himself" (page 266; metaphor)

10. "The boy could feel his eyes, sense him slowly bending near. A hand must have come down out of the night, for there was a little rat-tat as the fingernails brushed and the man's breath fanned the boy's face." (page 266; touch imagery, onomatopoeia)

11. "You are the heart of the army." (page 267; metaphor)

12. Both the drum and the peach blossoms are symbols in the story. The drum symbolizes Joby's youth and defenselessness (drum/toy). The peach blossoms also symbolize youth and defenselessness (springtime/delicacy). Point out to the students that these two symbolic images provide a frame for the story. Ask them why they think Bradbury chose to open and close his story this way. (*Answers may vary but might focus on the fact that these images bring home the tragedy of war by emphasizing its effect on someone young and innocent.*)

Bradbury credits this effective use of metaphor to his childhood immersion in the classics, especially mythology. According to Wayne L. Johnson (see Resource section), "when describing an object or situation, Bradbury will often use a different metaphor or simile for each part, as if moving a spotlight over the thing, building it up in our minds out of a number of separate pictures. Each picture will have a

Indian smell of tobacco—unlighted yet, but chewed as the man thought what next to say.

"It's going to be a crazy time," said the general. "Counting both sides, there's a hundred thousand men—give or take a few thousand—out there tonight, not one as can spit a sparrow off a tree or knows a horse clod from a Minié ball. Stand up, bare the breast, ask to be a target, thank them, and sit down, that's us, that's them. We should turn tail and train four months; they should do the same. But here we are, taken with spring fever and thinking it blood lust, taking our sulphur* with cannons instead of with molasses, as it should be—going to be a hero, going to live forever. And I can see all them over there nodding agreement, save the other way around. It's wrong, boy, it's wrong as a head put on hindside front and a man marching backward through life. Sometime this week more innocents will get shot out of pure Cherokee enthusiasm than ever got shot before. Owl Creek was full of boys splashing around in the noonday sun just a few hours ago. I fear it will be full of boys again, just floating, at sundown tomorrow, not caring where the current takes them."

sulphur: medicine

The general stopped and made a little pile of winter leaves and twigs in the dark, as if he might at any moment strike fire to them to see his way through the coming days when the sun might not show its face because of what was happening here and just beyond.

The boy watched the hand stirring the leaves and opened his lips to say something, but did not say it. The general heard the boy's breath and spoke himself.

"Why am I telling you this? That's what you wanted to ask, eh? Well, when you got a bunch of wild horses on a loose rein somewhere, somehow you got to bring order, rein them in. These lads, fresh out of the milkshed, don't know what I know; and I can't tell them—men actually die in war. So each is his own army. I got to make one army of them. And for that, boy, I need you."

"Me!" the boy's lips barely twitched.

"You, boy" said the general quietly. "You are the heart of the army. Think about that. You are the heart of the army. Listen to me, now."

And lying there, Joby listened. And the general spoke. If he, Joby, beat slow tomorrow, the heart would beat slow in the men. They would lag by the wayside. They would drowse in the fields on their muskets. They would sleep forever after that—in those same fields, their hearts slowed by a drummer boy and stopped by enemy lead.

But if he beat a sure, steady, ever-faster rhythm, then, then, their knees would come up in a long line down over that hill, one knee after the other, like a wave on the ocean shore. Had he seen the ocean ever—seen the waves rolling in like a well-ordered cavalry charge to the sand? Well, that was it, that's what he wanted; that's what he needed. Joby was his right hand and his left. He gave the orders, but Joby set the pace.

So bring the right knee up and the right foot out and the left knee up and the left foot out, one following the other in good time, in brisk time. Move the blood up the body, and make the head proud and the spine stiff and the jaw resolute. Focus the eye and set the teeth; flare the nostril and tighten the hands; put steel armor all over the men, for blood moving fast in them does indeed make men feel as if they'd put on steel. He must keep at it, at it! Long and steady, steady and long! Then, even though shot or torn, those wounds got in hot blood—in blood he'd helped stir—would feel less pain. If their blood was cold, it would be more than slaughter: it would be

personification

Have students note how this metaphor is carried forward through the next several paragraphs.

metaphor

simile

Note reiteration of the idea of being shielded from death. Joby learns here that he is part of the soldiers' symbolic shield. Trying to defeat Grant's army, the Confederates attacked on April 6. Grant's surprised troops were pushed back that day, but by April 7 the outnumbered Confederates were repelled and withdrew to Corinth, Mississippi.

3. Have the students research one of the other famous Civil War battlefields (e.g., Gettysburg, Antietam) and write their own story about the battle.

Journal entry idea
Speculate on what happened to the drummer boy the next day.

Resource
Wayne L. Johnson, *Ray Bradbury* (New York: Frederick Ungar, 1980).

different emotional tint according to the metaphor used, so that the complete image has an emotional as well as visual richness."

This is certainly true of this story. Discuss with the students the emotional mood established by Bradbury's use of images.

As in "The Drummer Boy of Shiloh," Bradbury's characters often perceive reality in a new and different way when they change their point of view. How does the general encourage Joby to see the battle? How does this perspective resolve his internal struggle? *(After the general's talk, Joby is led to imagine himself "general of the army when the general's left behind." He is thus emboldened by his imagination to face the fear of dying and to act in a calm, resolute manner. The reader is left, however, with a lingering sense of the* author's anxiety provided by the recurring use of the two symbols.)

Application

Read the following paragraph from the story: "The boy turned on his side. A moth brushed his face, but it was a peach blossom. A peach blossom flicked him, but it was a moth. Nothing stayed put. Nothing had a name. Nothing was as it once was" (page 266). This unsettling paragraph mirrors not only Joby's turmoil but Bradbury's as well. The fears produced by the seeming uncertainties of life are clearly articulated in this paragraph. Discuss with the students how prevalent such feelings are. Have them provide the Biblical answer to such unsettling views.

murderous nightmare and pain best not told and no one to guess.

The general spoke and stopped, letting his breath slack off. Then, after a moment, he said, "So there you are, that's it. Will you do that, boy? Do you know now you're general of the army when the general's left behind?"

The boy nodded mutely.

"You'll run them through for me then, boy?"

"Yes, sir."

"Good. And, God willing, many nights from tonight, many years from now, when you're as old or far much older than me, when they ask you what you did in this awful time, you will tell them—one part humble and one part proud—I was the drummer boy at the battle of Owl Creek or of the Tennessee River, or maybe they'll just name it after the church there. I was the drummer boy at Shiloh. Good grief, that has a beat and sound to it fitting for Mr. Longfellow. 'I was the drummer boy at Shiloh.' Who will ever hear those words and not know you, boy, or what you thought this night, or what you'll think tomorrow or the next day when we must get up on our legs and move."

The general stood up. "Well, then, God bless you, boy. Good night."

"Good night, sir." And brass, boot polish, salt-sweat, and leather, the man moved away through the grass.

Joby lay for a moment staring, but unable to see where the man had gone. He swallowed. He wiped his eyes. He cleared his throat. He settled himself. Then, at last, very slowly and firmly, he turned the drum so it faced up toward the sky.

He lay next to it, his arm around it, feeling the tremor, the touch, the muted thunder as all the rest of the April night in the year 1862, near the Tennessee River, not far from the Owl Creek, very close to the church named Shiloh, the peach blossoms fell on the drum.

About the Story

1. What one imaginative comparison in Bradbury's story did you find most effective in contributing to the mood of the story?
2. List four sounds or onomatopoetic words that Bradbury uses which help convey his mood?
3. What object could also be a symbol in the story?
4. What do you think this object represents?

About the Author

Ray Bradbury (1920-) has always considered himself a self-taught writer, and he counsels would-be writers to learn by constant practice. As a young man, he set himself the goal of writing at least one thousand words per day, a practice he has continued much of his adult life. His childhood reading included classical mythology and Edgar Rice Burroughs's adventure tales. His aunt introduced him to the world of imaginative literature by reading Frank Baum's "Oz" books to him. From these and other childhood favorites, Bradbury developed a love for imaginative literature.

At twenty-one, he sold his first story. Since then, hundreds of his short stories have been published in nationally known magazines and anthologies. Bradbury's writing can best be classified as "fantasy." Although he is often categorized as a science-fiction writer, most of his references to technology are romantic and visionary rather than scientific. Bradbury's impressionistic, often dream-like scenes are the result of his abundant use of metaphors. His descriptive phrases build up memorable images that linger in the mind long after the story is read.

A frequent theme in Bradbury's stories is the dehumanizing effects of modern society and science on the human imagination. Although Bradbury makes several good points in his writing, he tends to deify the imagination, rejecting the God who gave him his imaginative faculties. In Bradbury's mind God is "that dreary old bore . . . who sat around writing up life transcripts and noticing dead sparrows." For Bradbury, survival is the ultimate goal. "For the dream of mankind," he says, "has been to someday kill death." As Christians we have more than our own imaginations to help us understand the darker aspects of life and to endure what is difficult or painful. Our first and best source of guidance and strength is the Lord Jesus Christ. Although Bradbury's powers of imagination are exceptional and admirable, they are ultimately fruitless if not used in the service of God who bestowed them.

*About
the Story*

1. *Answers may vary. Make sure the students' answers are indeed imaginative comparisons (metaphor, simile, etc.) and not another literary device.*

2. *Answers may vary but might include "whispering," "murmuring," "flicked," "rustling taps."*

3. *Either the drum or the peach blossoms would be an acceptable answer.*

4. *The drum and peach blossoms symbolize youth and defenselessness. See also Analysis section (page 266).*

"A Gray Sleeve," "Barbara Frietchie"

FURTHER HELPS

Additional activities

1. Read several excerpts from Crane's most popular novel, *The Red Badge of Courage*. Discuss with the students how this story, like "A Gray Sleeve," reflects Crane's philosophy. Preview sections you plan to read aloud for appropriateness.

2. Have the students do a storyboard of Whittier's poem.

3. Have the students do some additional research on Stonewall Jackson. He provides an excellent example of godly character and superb military leadership.

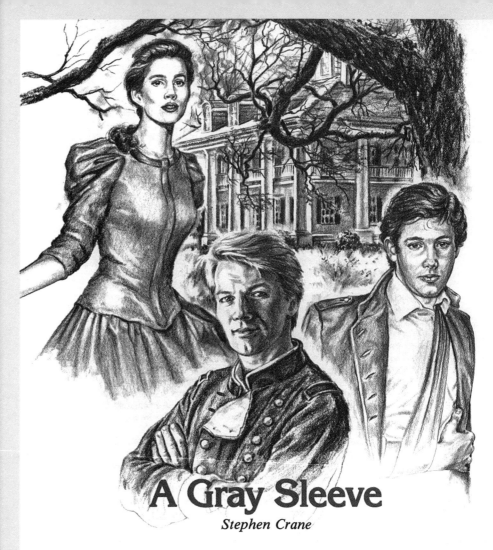

A Gray Sleeve
Stephen Crane

Union blue meets Confederate gray in this story—but not in a way we are led to expect. The real struggle proves not to be a military one. A sudden decline from the lofty to the ridiculous after a building up of suspense is known as anticlimax. *Notice the anticlimactic elements in the story.*

DISCUSSION

"A Gray Sleeve," "Barbara Frietchie"

Introduction

Like James Joyce (Unit 2), Crane artfully uses sound and syntax to create a mood. Critic Frank Bergon (see Resources section) said of Crane that "in terms of language and syntax, Crane's style is one which interprets life as fragmented and unpredictable, something about which it is difficult to form express conclusions."

Analysis

"A Gray Sleeve"

The feeling of uncertainty generated by "A Gray Sleeve" is due in large part to the words Crane chooses. Notice for example how many verbs Crane uses that indicate either indistinct vision or a vague studiousness. Forms of "look" appear approximately twenty times, "eyes" and "see" about eight times. Over a dozen instances of verbs such as "watch," "glance," "glare," "gaze," "gape," and "study" occur.

Also point out that Crane is noted for his copious use of words such as "seem," "might," and "maybe." Bergen recognizes that "Crane's use of these words for events normally taken for granted creates an indefiniteness of statement

that he further increases through his penchant for negatives." In this story negatives such as "not" occur about fifty times, "no" and its derivative forms approximately two dozen times. "Never" occurs six times. Tell the students that the greatest concentration of negatives occurs at the time of greatest uncertainty in the story. Then have them identify this point. *(the end of the story, page 279)*

These word choices, typical of Crane's style, also reflect his world-view. Crane believed that man was destined to assert himself futilely before an indifferent universe. As a result, his characters often find themselves in situations in which they feel insignificant and unable to communicate. There are several passages in our selection that reflect these characteristics. Have

1

"It looks as if it might rain this afternoon," remarked the lieutenant of artillery.

"So it does," the infantry captain assented. He glanced casually at the sky. When his eyes had lowered to the green-shadowed landscape before him, he said fretfully: "I wish those fellows out yonder would quit pelting at us. They've been at it since noon."

At the edge of a grove of maples, across wide fields, there occasionally appeared little puffs of smoke of a dull hue in this gloom of sky which expressed an impending rain. The long wave of blue and steel in the field moved uneasily at the eternal barking of the faraway sharpshooters, and the men, leaning upon their rifles, stared at the grove of maples. Once a private turned to borrow some tobacco from a comrade in the rear rank, but, with his hand still stretched out, he continued to twist his head and glance at the distant trees. He was afraid the enemy would shoot him at a time when he was not looking.

Suddenly the artillery officer said, "See what's coming!"

Along the rear of the brigade of infantry a column of cavalry was sweeping at a hard gallop. A lieutenant, riding some yards to the right of the column, bawled furiously at the four troopers just at the rear of the colors. They had lost distance and made a little gap, but at the shouts of the lieutenant they urged their horses forward. The bugler, careering along behind the captain of the troop, fought and tugged like a wrestler to keep his frantic animal from bolting far ahead of the column.

On the springy turf the innumerable hoofs thundered in a swift storm of sound. In the brown faces of the troopers their eyes were set like bits of flashing steel.

The long line of the infantry regiments standing at ease underwent a sudden movement at the rush of the passing squadron. The foot soldiers turned their heads to gaze at the torrent of horses and men.

The yellow folds of the flag fluttered back in silken, shuddering waves, as if it were a reluctant thing. Occasionally a giant spring of a charger would rear the firm and sturdy figure of a soldier suddenly head and shoulders above his comrades. Over the noise of the scudding* hoofs could be heard the creaking of leather trappings, the jingle and clank of steel, and the tense, low-toned commands or appeals of the men to their horses. And the horses were mad with the headlong sweep of this movement. Powerful underjaws bent back and straightened so that the bits were clamped as rigidly as vises upon the teeth, and glistening necks arched in desperate resistance to the hands on the bridles. Swinging their heads in rage at the granite laws of their lives, which compelled even their angers and their ardors to chosen directions and chosen paces, their flight was as a flight of harnessed demons.

scudding: swiftly and easily running

The captain's bay kept its pace at the head of the squadron with the lithe bounds of a thoroughbred, and this horse was proud as a chief at the roaring trample of his fellows behind him. The captain's glance was calmly upon the grove of maples whence the sharpshooters of the enemy had been picking at the blue line. He seemed to be reflecting. He stolidly rose and fell with the plunges of his horse in all the indifference of a deacon's figure seated plumply in church. And it occurred to many of the watching infantry to wonder why this officer could remain imperturbable and reflective when his squadron was thundering and swarming behind him like the rushing of a flood.

The column swung in a saber-curve toward a break in a fence, and dashed into a roadway. Once a little plank bridge was encountered,

---

The first sentence typifies the tentative, uncertain nature of much of the dialogue in the story. See Analysis section.

Note the almost humorous situational irony evident in the private's action.

similes

metaphor, simile, personification

metaphor

Resources

Frank Bergon, *Stephen Crane's Artistry* (New York: Columbia University Press, 1975).

Wilson Follett, *The Collected Poems of Stephen Crane* (New York: Alfred Knopf, 1977).

---

the students identify some of these passages. Following are a few examples:

1. "He wore an air of being deeply wretched and ashamed. There was a silence." (Page 276; the silences scattered throughout the story give the situation a sense of poignancy.)

2. "The captain took her hand, and then he blushed, for he found himself unable to formulate a sentence that applied in any way to the situation." (page 278)

3. "He loosened his grasp presently, for he was ashamed to hold it so long without saying anything clever." (page 278)

4. "He evidently had something enormously important to say to her, but it seemed that he could not manage it." (page 279)

Draw the students' attention to the title of the story, which focuses our attention on one detail. Ask the students why they think Crane titled the story as he did. Point out that it draws our attention to the theme: the power of vague hints to confuse or mislead. The hint of a gray sleeve at an empty window causes the Yankee soldiers to assume that the eerie white house is full of Confederates. In the course of their investigation, the troop members lose track of their original quarry and discover only an old man, a wounded soldier, and a young girl. The swaggering confidence of the infantry captain fades into ridiculous indecision as he confronts the young lady. The empty pistol she holds behind her back is a tangible symbol of the powerful but empty significance of the false signal (the gray sleeve) at the window.

Point out the progression of movement in the final scene. As the troops leave, the captain once again sees a hint of movement at the window. He returns to the girl and receives her promise of future attentions. But this, like the gray sleeve, proves misleading, for she calls him back to retract her promise. The captain's hope turns to limp dejection, which is made more moving by the girl's sorry attempt to reiterate her empty promise.

similes

cf. "The Listeners," pages 290-91

and the sound of the hoofs upon it was like the long roll of many drums. An old captain in the infantry turned to his first lieutenant and made a remark which was a compound of bitter disparagement of cavalry in general and soldierly admiration of this particular troop.

Suddenly the bugle sounded, and the column halted with a jolting upheaval amid sharp, brief cries. A moment later the men had tumbled from their horses and, carbines in hand, were running in a swarm toward the grove of maples. In the road one of every four of the troopers was standing with braced legs, and pulling and hauling at the bridles of four frenzied horses.

The captain was running awkwardly in his boots. He held his saber low, so that the point often threatened to catch in the turf. His yellow hair ruffled out from under his faded cap. "Go in hard now!" he roared, in a voice of hoarse fury. His face was violently red.

The troopers threw themselves upon the grove like wolves upon a great animal. Along the whole front of the woods there was the dry crackling of musketry, with bitter, swift flashes and smoke that writhed like stung phantoms. The troopers yelled shrilly and spanged bullets low into the foliage.

For a moment, when near the woods, the line almost halted. The men struggled and fought for a time like swimmers encountering a powerful current. Then with a supreme effort they went on again. They dashed madly at the grove, whose foliage, from the high light of the field, was as inscrutable as a wall.

Then suddenly each detail of the calm trees became apparent, and with a few more frantic leaps the men were in the cool gloom of the woods. There was a heavy odor as from burned paper. Wisps of gray smoke wound upward. The men halted; and, grimy, perspiring, and puffing, they searched the recesses of the woods with eager, fierce glances. Figures could be seen flitting afar off. A dozen carbines rattled at them in an angry volley.

During this pause the captain strode along the line, his face lit with a broad smile of contentment. "When he sends this crowd to do anything, I guess he'll find we do it pretty sharp," he said to the grinning lieutenant.

"Say, they didn't stand that rush a minute, did they?" said the subaltern.* Both officers were profoundly dusty in their uniforms, and their faces were soiled like those of two urchins.

---

subaltern: assisting officer

Out in the grass behind them were three tumbled and silent forms.

Presently the line moved forward again. The men went from tree to tree like hunters stalking game. Some at the left of the line fired occasionally, and those at the right gazed curiously in that direction. The men still breathed heavily from their scramble across the field.

Of a sudden a trooper halted and said: "Hello! there's a house!" Everyone paused. The men turned to look at their leader.

The captain stretched his neck and swung his head from side to side. "By George, it is a house!" he said.

Through the wealth of leaves there vaguely loomed the form of a large white house. These troopers, brown-faced from many days of campaigning, each feature of them telling of their placid confidence and courage, were stopped abruptly by the appearance of this house. There was some subtle suggestion—some tale of an unknown thing—which watched them from they knew not what part of it.

A rail fence girded a wide lawn of tangled grass. Seven pines stood along a driveway which led from two distant posts of a vanished gate. The blue-clothed troopers moved forward until they stood at the fence, peering over it.

The captain put one hand on the top rail and seemed to be about to climb the fence, when suddenly he hesitated and said in a low voice: "Watson, what do you think of it?"

The lieutenant stared at the house. "I don't know!" he replied.

The captain pondered. It happened that the whole company had turned a gaze of profound awe and doubt upon this edifice which confronted them. The men were very silent.

At last the captain swore and said: "We are certainly a pack of fools. Old deserted house halting a company of Union cavalry, and making us gape like babies!"

"Yes, but there's something—something—" insisted the subaltern in half a stammer.

"Well, if there's 'something—something' in there, I'll get it out," said the captain. "Send Sharpe clean around to the other side with about twelve men, so we will sure bag your 'something—something,' and I'll take a few of the boys and find out what's in the thing!"

He chose the nearest eight men for his "storming party," as the lieutenant called it. After he had waited some minutes for the others to get into position, he said "Come ahead" to his eight men, and climbed the fence.

The brighter light of the tangled lawn made him suddenly feel tremendously apparent, and he wondered if there could be some mystic thing in the house which was regarding this approach. His men trudged silently at his back. They stared at the windows and lost themselves in deep speculations as to the probability of there being, perhaps, eyes behind the blinds—malignant eyes, piercing eyes.

Suddenly a corporal in the party gave vent to a startled exclamation and half threw his carbine into position. The captain turned quickly, and the corporal said: "I saw an arm move the blinds. An arm with a gray sleeve!"

"Don't be a fool, Jones, now!" said the captain sharply.

"I swear—" began the corporal, but the captain silenced him.

When they arrived at the front of the house, the troopers paused, while the captain went softly up the front steps. He stood before the large front door and studied it. Some crickets chirped in the long grass, and the nearest pine could be heard in its endless sighs. One of the privates moved uneasily, and his foot crunched the gravel. Suddenly the captain swore angrily and kicked the door with a loud crash. It flew open.

simile ("like a child"), metaphor ("raid")

The captain was prepared for a literal external conflict. Instead he is faced with an internal one—what to do now that his "adversary" is a young woman.

similes

Note that her eyes reveal that she is lying. (See Analysis section, first paragraph, page 270.)

2

The bright light of the day flashed into the old house when the captain angrily kicked open the door. He was aware of a wide hallway carpeted with matting and extending deep into the dwelling. There was also an old walnut hat rack and a little marble-topped table with a vase and two books upon it. Farther back was a great venerable fireplace containing dreary ashes.

But directly in front of the captain was a young girl. The flying open of the door had obviously been an utter astonishment to her, and she remained transfixed there in the middle of the floor, staring at the captain with wide eyes.

She was like a child caught at the time of a raid upon the cake. She wavered to and fro upon her feet, and held her hands behind her. There were two little points of terror in her eyes, as she gazed up at the young captain in dusty blue, with his reddish, bronze complexion, his yellow hair, his bright saber held threateningly.

These two remained motionless and silent, simply staring at each other for some moments.

The captain felt his rage fade out of him and leave his mind limp. He had been violently angry, because this house had made him feel hesitant, wary. He did not like to be wary. He liked to feel confident, sure. So he had kicked the door open, and had been prepared to march in like a soldier of wrath.

But now he began, for one thing, to wonder if his uniform was so dusty and old in appearance. Moreover, he had a feeling that his face was covered with a compound of dust, grime, and perspiration. He took a step forward and said, "I didn't mean to frighten you." But his voice was coarse from his battle-howling. It seemed to him to have hempen fibers in it.

The girl's breath came in little, quick gasps, and she looked at him as she would have looked at a serpent.

"I didn't mean to frighten you," he said again.

The girl, still with her hands behind her, began to back away.

"Is there anyone else in the house?" he went on, while slowly following her. "I don't wish to disturb you, but we had a fight with some rebel skirmishers in the woods, and I thought maybe some of them might have come in here. In fact, I was pretty sure of it. Are there any of them here?"

The girl looked at him and said, "No!" He wondered why extreme agitation made the eyes of some women so limpid and bright.

"Who is here besides yourself?"

By this time his pursuit had driven her to the end of the hall, and she remained there with her back to the wall and her hands still behind her. When she answered this question, she did not look at him, but down at the floor. She cleared her voice and then said, "There is no one here."

"No one?"

She lifted her eyes to him in that appeal that the human being must make even to falling trees, crashing boulders, the sea in a storm, and said, "No, no, there is no one here." He could plainly see her tremble.

Of a sudden he bethought him that she continually kept her hands behind her. As he recalled her air when first discovered, he remembered she appeared precisely as a child detected at one of the crimes of childhood. Moreover, she had always backed away from him. He thought now that she was concealing something which was an evidence of the presence of the enemy in the house.

"What are you holding behind you?" he said suddenly.

She gave a little quick moan, as if some grim hand had throttled her.

"What are you holding behind you?"

"Oh, nothing—please. I am not holding anything behind me; indeed I'm not."

"Very well. Hold your hands out in front of you, then."

"Oh, indeed, I'm not holding anything behind me. Indeed I'm not."

"Well," he began. Then he paused, and remained for a moment dubious. Finally, he laughed. "Well, I shall have my men search the house, anyhow. I'm sorry to trouble you, but I feel sure that there is someone here whom we want." He turned to the corporal, who, with the other men, was gaping quietly in at the door, and said: "Jones, go through the house."

As for himself, he remained planted in front of the girl, for she evidently did not dare to move and allow him to see what she held so carefully behind her back. So she was his prisoner.

The men rummaged around on the ground floor of the house. Sometimes the captain called to them. "Try that closet." "Is there any cellar?" But they found no one, and at last they went trooping toward the stairs which led to the second floor.

But at this movement on the part of the men the girl uttered a cry—a cry of such fright and appeal that the men paused. "Oh, don't go up there! Please don't go up there!—ple—ease! There is no one there! Indeed—indeed there is not! Oh, ple—ease!"

"Go on, Jones," said the captain calmly.

The obedient corporal made a preliminary step, and the girl bounded toward the stairs with another cry.

As she passed him, the captain caught sight of that which she had concealed behind her back, and which she had forgotten in this supreme moment. It was a pistol.

She ran to the first step and, standing there, faced the men, one hand extended with perpendicular palm, and the other holding the pistol at her side. "Oh, please, don't go up

there! Nobody is there—indeed, there is not! P-l-e-a-s-e!" Then suddenly she sank swiftly down upon the step and, huddling forlornly, began to weep in the agony and with the convulsive tremors of an infant. The pistol fell from her fingers and rattled down to the floor.

The astonished troopers looked at their astonished captain. There was a short silence.

Finally, the captain stopped and picked up the pistol. It was a heavy weapon of the army pattern. He ascertained that it was empty.

He leaned toward the shaking girl and said gently, "Will you tell me what you were going to do with this pistol?"

He had to repeat the question a number of times, but at last a muffled voice said, "Nothing."

"Nothing!" He insisted quietly upon a further answer. At the tender tones of the captain's voice, the phlegmatic corporal turned and winked gravely at the man next to him.

"Won't you tell me?"

The girl shook her head.

"Please tell me!"

The silent privates were moving their feet uneasily and wondering how long they were to wait.

The captain said: "Please, won't you tell me?"

Then the girl's voice began in stricken tones, half coherent, and amid violent sobbing: "It was grandpa's. He—he—he said he was going to shoot anybody who came in here—he didn't care if there were thousands of 'em. And—and I know he would, and I was afraid they'd kill him. And so—and—so I stole away his pistol—and I was going to hide it when you—you—you kicked open the door."

The men straightened up and looked at each other. The girl began to weep again.

The captain mopped his brow. He peered down at the girl. He mopped his brow again. Suddenly he said: "Ah, don't cry like that."

He moved restlessly and looked down at

his boots. He mopped his brow again.

Then he gripped the corporal by the arm and dragged him some yards back from the others. "Jones," he said, in an intensely earnest voice, "will you tell me what I am going to do?"

The corporal's countenance became illuminated with satisfaction at being thus requested to advise his superior officer. He adopted an air of great thought, and finally said: "Well, of course, the feller with the gray sleeve must be upstairs, and we must get past the girl and up there somehow. Suppose I take her by the arm and lead her—"

"What!" interrupted the captain from between his clenched teeth. As he turned away from the corporal, he said fiercely over his shoulder: "You touch that girl and I'll split your skull!"

3

The corporal looked after his captain with an expression of mingled amazement, grief, and philosophy. He seemed to be saying to himself that there unfortunately were times, after all, when one could not rely upon the most reliable of men. When he returned to the group he found the captain bending over the girl saying: "Why is it that you don't want us to search upstairs?"

The girl's head was buried in her crossed arms. Locks of her hair had escaped from their fastenings, and these fell upon her shoulder.

"Won't you tell me?"

The corporal here winked again at the man next to him.

"Because," the girl moaned—"because—there isn't anybody up there."

The captain at last said timidly: "Well, I'm afraid—I'm afraid we'll have to—"

The girl sprang to her feet again, and implored him with her hands. She looked deep into his eyes with her glance, which was at this time like that of the fawn when it says

to the hunter, "Have mercy upon me!"

These two stood regarding each other. The captain's foot was on the bottom step, but he seemed to be shrinking. He wore an air of being deeply wretched and ashamed. There was a silence.

Suddenly the corporal said in a quick, low tone: "Look out, captain!"

All turned their eyes swiftly toward the head of the stairs. There had appeared there a youth in a gray uniform. He stood looking coolly down at them. No word was said by the troopers. The girl gave vent to a little wail of desolation. "Oh. Harry!"

He began slowly to descend the stairs. His right arm was in a white sling, and there were some fresh bloodstains upon the cloth. His face was rigid and deathly pale, but his eyes flashed like lights. The girl was again moaning in an utterly dreary fashion, as the youth came slowly down toward the silent men in blue.

Six steps from the bottom of the flight he halted and said, "I reckon it's me you're looking for."

The troopers had crowded forward a trifle and, posed in lithe, nervous attitudes, were watching him like cats. The captain remained unmoved. At the youth's question he merely nodded his head and said, "Yes."

The young man in gray looked down at the girl, and then, in the same even tone, which now, however, seemed to vibrate with suppressed fury, he said: "And is that any reason why you should insult my sister?"

At this sentence, the girl intervened, desperately, between the young man in gray and the officer in blue. "Oh, don't, Harry, don't! He was good to me! He was good to me, Harry—indeed he was!"

The youth came on in his quiet, erect fashion until the girl could have touched either of the men with her hand, for the captain still remained with his foot upon the first step. She continually repeated: "Oh, Harry! Oh, Harry!"

The youth in gray maneuvered to glare into the captain's face, first over one shoulder of the girl and then over the other. In a voice that rang like metal, he said: "You are armed and unwounded, while I have no weapons and am wounded; but—"

The captain had stepped back and sheathed his saber. The eyes of these two men were gleaming fire, but otherwise the captain's countenance was imperturbable. He said: "You are mistaken. You have no reason to—"

"You lie!"

All save the captain and the youth in gray started in an electric movement. These two

words crackled in the air like shattered glass. There was a breathless silence.

The captain cleared his throat. His look at the youth contained a quality of singular and terrible ferocity, but he said in his stolid tone: "I don't suppose you mean what you say now."

Upon his arm he had felt the pressure of some unconscious little fingers. The girl was leaning against the wall as if she no longer knew how to keep her balance, but those fingers—he held his arm very still. She murmured: "Oh, Harry, don't! He was good to me—indeed he was!"

The corporal had come forward until he in a measure confronted the youth in gray, for he saw those fingers upon the captain's arm, and he knew that sometimes very strong men were not able to move hand nor foot under such conditions.

The youth had suddenly seemed to become weak. He breathed heavily and clung to the rail. He was glaring at the captain, and apparently summoning all his will power to combat his weakness. The corporal addressed him with profound straightforwardness: "Don't you be a fool!" The youth turned toward him so fiercely that the corporal threw up a knee and an elbow like a boy who expects to be cuffed.

The girl pleaded with the captain: "You won't hurt him, will you? He don't know what he's saying. He's wounded, you know. Please don't mind him!"

"I won't touch him," said the captain, with rather extraordinary earnestness; "don't you worry about him at all. I won't touch him!"

Then he looked at her, and the girl suddenly withdrew her fingers from his arm.

The corporal contemplated the top of the stairs, and remarked without surprise: "There's another of 'em coming!"

An old man was clambering down the stairs with much speed. He waved a cane wildly.

similes

Note the symbolic positioning of the girl—between her Confederate brother and the Yankee officer.

The corporal's awkward, effete action here symbolizes the awkwardness of the whole situation.

"Get out of my house, you thieves! Get out! I won't have you cross my threshold! Get out!" he mumbled and wagged his head in an old man's fury. It was plainly his intention to assault them.

And so it occurred that a young girl became engaged in protecting a stalwart captain, fully armed, and with eight grim troopers at his back, from the attack of an old man with a walking stick!

A blush passed over the temples and brow of the captain, and he looked particularly savage and weary. Despite the girl's efforts, he suddenly faced the old man.

"Look here," he said distinctly, "we came in because we had been fighting in the woods yonder, and we concluded that some of the enemy were in this house, especially when we saw a gray sleeve at the window. But this young man is wounded, and I have nothing to say to him. I will even take it for granted that there are no others like him upstairs. We will go away, leaving your house just as we found it! And we are no more thieves and rascals than you are!"

The old man simply roared: "I haven't got a cow nor a pig nor a chicken on the place! Your soldiers have stolen everything they could carry away. They have torn down half my fences for firewood. This afternoon some of your accursed bullets even broke my windowpanes!"

The girl had been faltering: "Grandpa! Oh, grandpa!"

The captain looked at the girl. She returned his glance from the shadow of the old man's shoulder. After studying her face a moment, he said: "Well, we will go now." He strode toward the door, and his men clanked docilely after him.

At this time there was the sound of harsh cries and rushing footsteps from without. The door flew open, and a whirlwind composed of bluecoated troopers came in with a swoop.

It was headed by the lieutenant. "Oh, here you are!" he cried, catching his breath. "We thought—Oh, look at the girl!"

The captain said intensely: "Shut up, you fool!"

The men settled to a halt with a crash and a bang. There could be heard the dulled sound of many hoofs outside the house.

"Did you order up the horses?" inquired the captain.

"Yes. We thought—"

"Well, then, let's get out of here," interrupted the captain morosely.

The men began to filter out into the open air. The youth in gray had been hanging dismally to the railing of the stairway. He was now climbing slowly up to the second floor. The old man was addressing himself directly to the serene corporal.

"Not a chicken on the place!" he cried.

"Well, I didn't take your chickens, did I?"

"No, maybe you didn't but—"

The captain crossed the hall and stood before the girl in rather a culprit's fashion. "You are not angry at me, are you?" he asked timidly.

"No," she said. She hesitated a moment, and then suddenly held out her hand. "You were good to me—and I'm—much obliged."

The captain took her hand, and then he blushed, for he found himself unable to formulate a sentence that applied in any way to the situation.

She did not seem to heed that hand for a time.

He loosened his grasp presently, for he was ashamed to hold it so long without saying anything clever. At last, with an air of charging an entrenched brigade, he contrived to say: "I would rather do anything than frighten or trouble you."

His brow was warmly perspiring. He had a sense of being hideous in his dusty uniform and with his grimy face.

She said, "Oh, I'm so glad it was you instead

of somebody who might have—might have hurt brother Harry and grandpa!"

He told her, "I wouldn't have hurt 'em for anything!"

There was a little silence.

"Well, good-by!" he said at last.

"Good-by!"

He walked toward the door past the old man, who was scolding at the vanishing figure of the corporal. The captain looked back. She had remained there watching him.

At the bugle's order, the troopers standing beside their horses swung briskly into the saddle. The lieutenant said to the first sergeant: "Williams, did they ever meet before?"

"Hanged if I know!"

"Well, say—"

The captain saw a curtain move at one of the windows. He cantered from his position at the head of the column and steered his horse between two flower beds.

"Well, good-by!"

The squadron trampled slowly past.

"Good-by!"

They shook hands.

He evidently had something enormously important to say to her, but it seemed that he could not manage it. He struggled heroically. The bay charger, with his great mystically solemn eyes, looked around the corner of his shoulder at the girl.

The captain studied a pine tree. The girl inspected the grass beneath the window. The captain said hoarsely: "I don't suppose—I don't suppose—I'll ever see you again!"

She looked at him affrightedly and shrank back from the window. He seemed to have woefully expected a reception of this kind for his question. He gave her instantly a glance of appeal.

She said: "Why, no, I don't suppose we will."

"Never?"

"Why, no, 'tain't possible. You—you are a—Yankee!"

"Oh, I know it, but—" Eventually he continued: "Well, some day, you know, when there's no more fighting, we might—" he observed that she had again withdrawn suddenly into the shadow, so he said: "Well, good-by!"

When he held her fingers she bowed her head, and he saw a pink blush steal over the curves of her cheek and neck.

"Am I never going to see you again?"

She made no reply.

"Never?" he repeated.

After a long time, he bent over to hear a faint reply: "Sometimes—when there are no troops in the neighborhood—grandpa don't mind if I—walk over as far as that old oak tree yonder—in the afternoons."

It appeared that the captain's grip was very strong, for she uttered an exclamation and looked at her fingers as if she expected to find them mere fragments. He rode away.

The bay horse leaped a flower bed. They were almost to the drive, when the girl uttered a panic-stricken cry.

The captain wheeled his horse violently, and upon his return journey went straight through a flower bed.

The girl clasped her hands. She beseeched him wildly with her eyes. "Oh, please, don't believe it! I never walk to the old oak tree. Indeed I don't! I never—never—never walk there."

The bridle drooped on the bay charger's neck. The captain's figure seemed limp. With an expression of profound dejection and gloom he stared off at where the leaden sky met the dark green line of the woods. The long impending rain began to fall with a mournful patter, drop and drop. There was a silence.

At last a low voice said, "Well, I might—sometimes I might—perhaps—but only once in a great while—I might walk to the old tree—in the afternoons."

Discuss with students whether they think the awkwardness and uncertainty of the captain's parting from the girl might symbolize the "awkwardness" and difficulty of the North and South reuniting after the war.

Hamlin Garland (1860-1940) was a famous novelist and short story writer. See "Under the Lion's Paw" in BJU Press's *FUNDAMENTALS OF LITERATURE for Christian Schools* (pages 51-62) for an example of his work.

Though many lines are exceptions, the poem is generally written in trochaic tetrameter (see pages 26-27). Paired lines of rhyme such as this are called couplets.

alliteration

allusion, simile

About the Author

Stephen Crane (1871-1900) was the last of fourteen children born to a Methodist minister in New Jersey. While Crane was still a teenager, his older brother provided him with opportunities to write short news reports. Journalism held great appeal for Crane, not only as an outlet for his writing skills but also as a way to earn a living. Unfortunately, his highly imaginative style of reporting was not what the newspaper editors wanted. For a time, Crane tried to produce cut-and-dried factual reports. But this was unrewarding, both personally and financially. His attempts to privately publish and promote his first novel were unproductive. Eventually, Hamlin Garland helped the struggling young writer to gain the attention of the literary world.

Crane's second novel, *The Red Badge of Courage,* established his reputation as a leader in the modern realistic movement of American fiction. Like the short story "A Gray Sleeve," the topic of the book is war. Unlike our selection, however, *The Red Badge of Courage* presents a grim view of battle through the eyes of a young soldier, Henry Fleming. Like much of Crane's work, it is naturalistic fiction which emphasizes the darker, more depressing aspects of life.

Barbara Frietchie
John Greenleaf Whittier

In the legend that forms the basis of "Barbara Frietchie," as in Crane's "A Gray Sleeve," a woman outfaces a military commander.

Up from the meadows rich with corn,
Clear in the cool September morn,

The clustered spires of Frederick stand
Green-walled by the hills of Maryland.

Round about them orchards sweep,   5
Apple and peach tree fruited deep,

Fair as the garden of the Lord
To the eyes of the famished rebel horde,

"Barbara Frietchie"

The characters in Whittier's poem are the complete antithesis to those in Crane's story. Read the headnote and poem aloud. Then have the students compare the Confederate Stonewall Jackson with Crane's Yankee captain. Both unexpectedly find themselves facing female adversaries. Unlike the captain, Jackson's manner is confident and his actions decisive. The same can be said of Barbara Frietchie. She is not feigning bravery; she is truly courageous, ready to die if necessary for her values.

By the end of Crane's story we sympathize with the characters. They do not, however, evoke our admiration as do the characters in Whittier's poem. Jackson and Frietchie, like the captain and the girl, are two of a kind, and we admire both of them. We sense, too, that Whittier admired them. We are less sure about Crane's view of the captain and the girl. His "voice" remains ambivalent like the characters he creates.

Application

Share with the students the following information about Crane's beliefs. The author's belief in an indifferent god was coupled with a deep hatred for the true God of the Scripture. Especially repugnant to Crane was God's attribute of divine justice. Crane would accept only the merciful aspects of God's nature. This is not to imply that Crane was blind to man's faults. He recognized both man's depravity and his weakness. Although he accepted God's view of man, Crane refused to accept God's revelation of Himself. Crane chose instead to view God as an unreasonable, vain, and petty god who mockingly eludes those who seek him. He states emphatically, "God is cold." Crane is only one of many men who fail to grasp the true nature of God. Although we feel great compassion for such men, we must emphatically refute their beliefs. Discuss with the students how they would deal with someone like Crane. What portions of Scripture would they show him? *(cf. John 3:16; 1 John 4:8)* What personal experiences would they share with him?

On that pleasant morn of the early fall
When Lee marched over the mountain wall;

Over the mountains winding down,
Horse and foot, into Frederick town.

Forty flags with their silver stars,
Forty flags with their crimson bars,

Flapped in the morning wind: the sun   15
Of noon looked down, and saw not one.

Up rose old Barbara Frietchie then,
Bowed with fourscore years and ten;

Bravest of all in Frederick town,
She took up the flag the men hauled down;   20

In her attic window the staff she set,
To show that one heart was loyal yet.

Up the street came the rebel tread.
Stonewall Jackson riding ahead.

Under his slouched hat left and right   25
He glanced; the old flag met his sight.

"Halt!"—the dust-brown ranks stood fast,
"Fire"—out blazed the rifle blast.

It shivered the window, pane and sash;
It rent the banner with seam and gash.   30

Quick as it fell, from the broken staff
Dame Barbara snatched the silken scarf.

She leaned far out on the window sill,
And shook it forth with a royal will.

"Shoot, if you must, this old gray head,   35
But spare your country's flag," she said.

A shade of sadness, a blush of shame,
Over the face of the leader came;

allusions

Ask students what Barbara Frietchie's
age is. *(ninety)*

Note similarity here to "A Gray
Sleeve."

simile

personification

symbolism, metonymy (flag = freedom, peace, order, beauty)

The nobler nature within him stirred
To life at that woman's deed and word;   40

"Who touches a hair of yon gray head
Dies like a dog! March on!" he said.

All day long through Frederick street
Sounded the tread of marching feet:

All day long that free flag tossed   45
Over the heads of the rebel host.

Ever its torn folds rose and fell
On the loyal winds that loved it well;

And through the hill-gaps sunset light
Shone over it with a warm good-night.   50

Barbara Frietchie's work is o'er,
And the Rebel rides on his raids no more.

Honor to her! and let a tear
Fall, for her sake, on Stonewall's bier.

Over Barbara Frietchie's grave,   55
Flag of Freedom and Union, wave!

Peace and order and beauty draw
Round thy symbol of light and law;

And ever the stars above look down
On thy stars below in Frederick town!   60

About the Story and Poem

1. What is the actual struggle in Crane's story, "A Gray Sleeve"?
2. In the story, whose responses to the situation contrast with those of the captain?
3. Compare the response of the Confederate Stonewall Jackson with the response of Crane's Union captain.
4. Is the source of the two men's shame the same?
5. Are both responses approved by the authors? Support your answers with quotations from the texts.

About the Story and Poem

1. *Answers may vary but might include the struggle within the captain's mind about what to do in this awkward situation.*

2. *Answers may vary; students may suggest either the young lady's or her brother's.*

3. *Answers may vary; both men are put to shame by the unexpected response of a brave woman.*

4. *yes*

5. *Yes, both Crane and Whittier seem to imply that they approve of the man's responses. The captain's kind treatment of the girl and Whittier's comment that "the nobler nature within [Jackson] stirred" would be two examples to support that claim. Accept others as well.*

Tony Kytes, the Arch-Deceiver

Thomas Hardy

Hardy's novels and tales give a sense of the past. Their stories are set against a background of undisturbed nature and primitive customs in the Dorsetshire heathlands. This short narrative is typical in its fusing of conflict and characters with setting. The lightheartedness of the story, however, is an exception to the somber tone that marks much of Hardy's work. Notice the structuring of the story—its phases and the ironies that result.

I shall never forget Tony's face. 'Twas a little, round, firm, tight face, with a seam here and there left by the smallpox, but not enough to hurt his looks in a woman's eye, though he'd had it badish when he was a little boy. So very serious looking and unsmiling 'a was, that young man, that it really seemed as if he couldn't laugh at all without great pain to his conscience. He looked very hard at a small speck in your eye when talking to 'ee. And there was no more sign of a whisker or beard on Tony Kytes's face than on the palm of my hand. He used to sing "The Tailor's Breeches" with a religious manner, as if it were a hymn.

He was quite the women's favorite, and in return for their likings he loved 'em in shoals.*

shoals: large groups

But in course of time Tony got fixed down to one in particular, Milly Richards, a nice, light, tender little thing; and it was soon said that they were engaged to be married. One Saturday he had been to market to do business for his father, and was driving home the wagon in the afternoon. When he reached the foot of the very hill we shall be going over in ten minutes who should he see waiting for him at the top but Unity Sallet, a handsome girl, one of the young women he'd been very tender toward before he'd got engaged to Milly.

As soon as Tony came up to her she said, "My dear Tony, will you give me a lift home?"

"That I will, darling," said Tony. "You don't suppose I could refuse 'ee?"

She smiled a smile, and up she hopped, and on drove Tony.

"Tony," she says, in a sort of tender chide, "why did ye desert me for that other one? In what is she better than I? I should have made 'ee a finer wife, and a more loving one too. 'Tisn't girls that are so easily won at first that are the best. Think how long we've known each other—ever since we were children almost—now haven't we, Tony?"

"Yes, that we have," says Tony, a-struck with the truth o't.

"And you've never seen anything in me to complain of, have ye, Tony? Now tell the truth to me?"

"I never have, upon my life," says Tony.

"And—can you say I'm not pretty, Tony? Now look at me!"

OBJECTIVES

The students will be able to

- Analyze and state the lesson that "Tony Kytes, the Arch-Deceiver" teaches (liars do not prosper).
- Identify the three-part structure of "Tony Kytes, the Arch-Deceiver," which characterizes many of Hardy's tales.

Note that Hardy does not tell us that they were engaged but that people *said* they were engaged. This uncertainty recurs through the story.

Hardy inserts this comment to add to the conversational tone of the story—as though we were riding along with the narrator in a wagon.

FURTHER HELPS

Additional activities

Point out the way in which Hardy uses Milly, Unity, and Hannah to divide the plot into three parts. Another of Hardy's stories that bears his careful three-part structure is "The Three Strangers." You may wish to read this story aloud to see whether the students can plot the action.

PREPARATION

"Tony Kytes, the Arch-Deceiver"

Overview

The tone of this story, unlike many of Hardy's other works, is lighthearted, even whimsical. It is a tale of a naive youth who, though easily swayed by feminine charm, seems oblivious to the true virtues of womanhood.

Potential problems

Due to the pessimistic view of some of Hardy's stories, it would be unwise to encourage indiscriminate recreational reading of his works.

DISCUSSION

Introduction

Briefly discuss with the students the purposes and value of humor. Ask them to think of some humorous stories they have heard or read (including ones they may have read in this text ["What Stumped the Bluejays," "Cupid's Arrows," "A Special Occasion," "A Germ Destroyer," "The Day the Dam Broke"] or in other literature studies). These types of stories, though enjoyable, have a point to make. Ask the students what value they see in using humor to teach a lesson. Point out, for example, that such writing tends to use stock characters—characters who are stereotypes and without much depth or complication of character.

Although we can recognize certain universal traits in these characters, they seem less personal. This objectivity allows the writer to make his point without offending his readers.

Analysis

In this story, Hardy is trying to teach us a valuable lesson in an enjoyable way. Before we can discern this lesson, however, we must look at the story's conflict, characters, and plot. After the students have read the story, ask them first to identify the central conflict. *(Whom will Tony marry?)* Then have them describe each of the characters in one or two words. Draw the students' attention to the fact that the action in the story can be organized around the three female characters. Have the students plot the

Journal entry idea

Have the students write about a humorous situation like the one in Hardy's tale. The entry can either be based on personal experience or be completely imaginary. Encourage them to use the humor in the story to teach a point.

He let his eyes light upon her for a long while. "I really can't," says he. "In fact, I never knowed you was so pretty before!"

"Prettier than she?"

What Tony would have said to that nobody knows, for before he could speak, what should he see ahead, over the hedge past the turning, but a feather he knew well—the feather in Milly's hat—she to whom he had been thinking of putting the question as to giving out the banns* that very week.

---

banns: an announcement of an intended marriage

"Unity," says he, as mild as he could, "here's Milly coming. Now I shall catch it mightily if she sees 'ee riding here with me; and if you get down she'll be turning the corner in a moment, and, seeing 'ee in the road, she'll know we've been coming on together. Now, dearest Unity, will ye, to avoid all unpleasantness, which I know ye can't bear any more than I, will ye lie down in the back part of the wagon, and let me cover you over with the tarpaulin till Milly has passed? It will all be done in a minute. Do!—and I'll think over what we've said; and perhaps I shall put a loving question to you, after all, instead of to Milly. 'Tisn't true that it is all settled between her and me."

Well, Unity Sallet agreed, and lay down at the back end of the wagon, and Tony covered her over, so that the wagon seemed to be empty but for the loose tarpaulin; and then he drove on to meet Milly.

"My dear Tony!" cries Milly, looking up with a pout at him as he came near. "How long you've been coming home! Just as if I didn't live at Upper Longpuddle at all! And I've come to meet you as you asked me to do, and to ride back with you, and talk over our future home—since you asked me, and I promised. But I shouldn't have come else, Mr. Tony!"

"Ay, my dear, I did ask ye—to be sure I did, now I think of it—but I had quite forgot it. To ride back with me, did you say, dear Milly?"

"Well of course! What can I do else? Surely you don't want me to walk, now I've come all this way?"

"O, no, no! I was thinking you might be going to town to meet your mother. I saw her there—and she looked as if she might be expecting 'ee."

"O no; she's just home. She came across the fields, and so got back before you."

"Ah! I didn't know that," says Tony. And there was no help for it but to take her up beside him.

They talked on very pleasantly, and looked at the trees, and beasts, and birds, and insects, and at the ploughmen at work in the fields, till presently who should they see looking out of the upper window of a house that stood beside the road they were following, but Hannah Jolliver, another young beauty of the place at that time, and the very first woman that Tony had fallen in love with—before Milly and before Unity, in fact—the one that he had almost arranged to marry instead of Milly. She was a much more dashing girl than Milly Richards, though he'd not thought much of her of late. The house Hannah was looking from was her aunt's.

"My dear Milly—my coming wife, as I may call 'ee," says Tony in his modest way, and not so loud that Unity could overhear, "I see a young woman alooking out of window, who I think may accost me. The fact is, Milly, she had a notion that I was wishing to marry her, and since she's discovered I've promised another, and a prettier than she, I'm rather afeared of her temper if she sees us together. Now, Milly, would you do me a favor—my coming wife, as I may say?"

"Certainly, dearest Tony," says she.

"Then would ye creep under the empty

---

action of the story (noting the inciting moment, the rising action, the climax, and the resolution). Having looked at these details, have the students state the theme in their own words. Finally, discuss with them what Hardy is teaching by this theme. See **Appendix V: "Tony Kytes, the Arch-Deceiver" Analysis** to help with these ideas.

Application

Although humor can be used as a valuable teaching tool, it must be used wisely, for it also has the potential to become biting cynicism. Mark Twain provides a good example. As a humorous writer he provided much valuable insight in his early works. He became increasingly bitter, however, and this bitterness began to show in his writing. His later works are not only philosophically unsound but are also biting. Such humor produces a scornful smirk rather than a good-natured laugh.

Scripture has much to say about both laughter and scorn. Divide the class into two or more groups and assign each group one of these two topics. Have students use a concordance to find various passages relating to these characteristics. Have each group share what they have learned.

sacks just here in front of the wagon, and hide there out of sight till we've passed the house? She hasn't seen us yet. You see, we ought to live in peace and good-will since 'tis almost Christmas, and 'twill prevent angry passions rising, which we always should do."

"I don't mind, to oblige you, Tony," Milly said; and though she didn't care much about doing it, she crept under, and crouched down just behind the seat, Unity being snug at the other end. So they drove on till they got near the road-side cottage. Hannah had soon seen him coming, and waited at the window, looking down upon him. She tossed her head a little disdainful and smiled off-hand.

"Well, aren't you going to be civil enough to ask me to ride home with you!" she says, seeing that he was for driving past with a nod and a smile.

"Ah, to be sure! What was I thinking of?" said Tony, in a flutter. "But you seem as if you was staying at your aunt's?"

"No, I am not," she said. "Don't you see I have my bonnet and jacket on? I have only called to see her on my way home. How can you be so stupid, Tony?"

"In that case—ah—of course you must come along wi' me," says Tony, feeling a dim sort of sweat rising up inside his clothes. And he reined in the horse, and waited till she'd come downstairs, and then helped her up beside him. He drove on again, his face as long as a face that was a round one by nature well could be.

Hannah looked round sideways into his eyes. "This is nice, isn't it, Tony?" she says. "I like riding with you."

Tony looked back into her eyes. "And I with you," he said after a while. In short, having considered her, he warmed up, and the more he looked at her the more he liked her, till he couldn't for the life of him think why he had ever said a word about marriage to Milly or Unity while Hannah Jolliver was in

question. So they sat a little closer and closer, their feet upon the footboard and their shoulders touching, and Tony thought over and over again how handsome Hannah was. He spoke tenderer and tenderer, and called her "dear Hannah" in a whisper at last.

"You've settled it with Milly by this time, I suppose," said she.

"N—no, not exactly."

"What? How low you talk, Tony."

"Yes—I've a kind of hoarseness. I said, not exactly."

"I suppose you mean to?"

"Well, as to that—" His eyes rested on her face, and hers on his. He wondered how he could have been such a fool, as not to follow up Hannah. "My sweet, Hannah!" he burst out, taking her hand, not being really able to help it, and forgetting Milly and Unity, and all the world besides. "Settled it? I don't think I have!"

"Hark!" said Hannah.

"What?" says Tony, letting go her hand.

"Surely I heard a little sort of screaming squeak under those sacks? Why, you've been carrying corn, and there's mice in this wagon, I declare!" She began to haul up the tails of her gown.

"Oh no; 'tis the axle," said Tony in an assuring way. "It do go like that sometimes in dry weather."

"Perhaps it was. . . . Well now, to be quite honest, dear Tony, do you like her better than me? Because—because, although I've held off so independent, I'll own at last that I do like 'ee, Tony, to tell the truth; and I wouldn't say no if you asked me—you know what."

Tony was so won over by this pretty offering mood of a girl who had been quite the reverse (Hannah had a backward way with her at times, if you can mind) that he just glanced behind, and then whispered very soft, "I haven't quite promised her, and I think I can get out of it, and ask you that question

you speak of."

"Throw over Milly?—all to marry me! How delightful!" broke out Hannah, quite loud, clapping her hands.

At this time there was a real squeak—an angry, spiteful squeak, and afterward a long moan, as if something had broke its heart, and a movement of the empty sacks.

"Something's there!" said Hannah, starting up.

"It's nothing, really," says Tony in a soothing voice, and praying inwardly for a way out of this. "I wouldn't tell 'ee at first, because I wouldn't frighten 'ee. But, Hannah, I've a couple of ferrets* in a bag under there, for rabbiting, and they quarrel sometimes. I don't wish it knowed, as 'twould be called poaching. Oh, they can't get out, bless ye—you are quite safe! And—and—what a fine day it is, isn't it Hannah, for this time of year? Be you going to market next Saturday? How is your aunt now?" And so on, says Tony, to keep her from talking any more about love in Milly's hearing.

---

ferrets: small, weasel-like animals trained to hunt rats or rabbits

---

But he found his work cut out for him, and wondering again how he should get out of this ticklish business, he looked about for a chance. Nearing home he saw his father in a field not far off, holding up his hand as if he wished to speak to Tony.

"Would you mind taking the reins a moment, Hannah," he said, much relieved, "while I go and find out what father wants?"

She consented, and away he hastened into the field, only too glad to get breathing time. He found that his father was looking at him with rather a stern eye.

"Come, come, Tony," says old Mr. Kytes, as soon as his son was alongside him, "this won't do, you know."

"What?" says Tony.

"Why, if you mean to marry Milly Richards, do it, and there's an end o't. But don't go driving about the country with Jolliver's daughter and making a scandal. I won't have such things done."

"I only asked her—that is, she asked me, to ride home."

"She? Why, now, if it had been Milly, 'twould have been quite proper; but you and Hannah Jolliver going about by yourselves—"

"Milly's there too, father."

"Milly? Where?"

"Under the corn-sacks! Yes, the truth is, father, I've got rather into a nunny-watch, I'm afeared! Unity Sallet is there too—yes, at the other end, under the tarpaulin. All three are in that wagon, and what to do with 'em I know no more than the dead! The best plan is, as I'm thinking, to speak out loud and plain to one of 'em before the rest, and that will settle it; not but what 'twill cause 'em to kick up a bit of a miff, for certain. Now which would you marry, father, if you was in my place?"

"Whichever of 'em did *not* ask to ride with thee."

"That was Milly, I'm bound to say, as she only mounted by my invitation. But Milly—"

"Then stick to Milly, she's the best. . . . But look at that!"

His father pointed toward the wagon. "She can't hold that horse in. You shouldn't have left the reins in her hands. Run on and take the horse's head, or there'll be some accident to them maids!"

Tony's horse, in fact, in spite of Hannah's tugging at the reins, had started on his way at a brisk walking pace, being very anxious to get back to the stable, for he had had a long day out. Without another word Tony rushed away from his father to overtake the horse.

Now of all things that could have happened to wean him from Milly there was nothing so powerful as his father's recommending her. No; it could not be Milly, after all. Hannah

This is not a very complimentary explanation as far as Milly and Unity are concerned.

Ask students to remember another story in this unit in which an adult is concerned that the romantic escapades of a young person will bring scandal on the family. *("The Sire de Maletroit's Door")*

Tony once again demonstrates, in spite of his popularity with women, that he does not understand them at all.

Irony: Hannah may not have known Tony had two other women in the wagon, but she certainly knew he was a deceiver willing to drop Milly for her. Remind students that if someone they are interested in romantically is a liar to others, he or she will lie to the one he or she loves as well.

simile

must be the one, since he could not marry all three. This he thought while running after the wagon. But queer things were happening inside it.

It was, of course, Milly who screamed under the sack-bags, being obliged to let off her bitter rage and shame in that way at what Tony was saying, and never daring to show, for very pride and dread o' being laughed at, that she was in hiding. She became more and more restless, and in twisting her self about, what did she see but another woman's foot and white stocking close to her head. It quite frightened her, not knowing that Unity Sallet was in the wagon likewise. But after the fright was over she determined to get to the bottom of all this, and she crept and crept along the bed of the wagon, under the tarpaulin, like a snake, when lo and behold she came face to face with Unity.

"Well, if this isn't disgraceful!" says Milly in a raging whisper to Unity.

" 'Tis," says Unity, "to see you hiding in a young man's wagon like this, and no great character belonging to either of ye!"

"Mind what you are saying!" replied Milly, getting louder. "I am engaged to be married to him, and haven't I a right to be here? What right have you, I should like to know? What has he been promising you? A pretty lot of nonsense I expect! But what Tony says to other women is mere wind, and no concern to me!"

"Don't you be too sure!" says Unity. "He's going to have Hannah, and not you, nor me either; I could hear that."

Now at these strange voices sounding from under the cloth Hannah was thunderstruck a'most into a swound; and it was just at this time that the horse moved on. Hannah tugged away wildly, not knowing what she was doing; and as the quarrel rose louder and louder Hannah got so horrified that she let go the reins altogether. The horse went at his own pace, and coming to the corner where we turn round to drop down the hill to Lower Longpuddle he turned too quick, the off wheels went up the bank, the wagon rose sideways till it was quite on edge upon the near axles, and out rolled the three maidens into the road in a heap.

When Tony came up, frightened and breathless, he was relieved to see that none of his darlings was hurt, beyond a few scratches from the bramble hedge. But he was rather alarmed when he heard how they were going at one another.

"Don't ye quarrel my dears—don't ye!" says he, taking off his hat out of respect to 'em. And then he would have kissed them all round, as fair and square as a man could, but they were in too much of a taking to let him, and screeched and sobbed till they was quite spent.

"Now I'll speak out honest, because I ought to," says Tony, as soon as he could get heard. "And this is the truth," says he. "I've asked Hannah to be mine, and she is willing, and we are going to put up the banns next—"

Tony had not noticed that Hannah's father was coming up behind, nor had he noticed that Hannah's face was beginning to bleed from the scratch of a bramble. Hannah had seen her father, and had run to him, crying worse than ever.

"My daughter is *not* willing, sir!" says Mr. Jolliver hot and strong. "Be you willing, Hannah? I ask ye to have spirit enough to refuse him."

"I have spirit, and I do refuse him!" says Hannah, partly because her father was there, and partly, too, in a tantrum because of the discovery, and the scratch on her face. "Little did I think when I was so soft with him just now that I was talking to such a false deceiver!"

"What, you won't have me, Hannah?" says Tony, his jaw hanging down like a dead man's.

"Never—I would sooner marry no—nobody at all!" she gasped out, though with her heart in her throat, for she would not have refused Tony if he had asked her quietly, and her father had not been there, and her face had not been scratched by the bramble. And having said that, away she walked upon her father's arm, thinking and hoping he would ask her again.

Tony didn't know what to say next. Milly was sobbing her heart out; but as father had strongly recommended her he couldn't feel inclined that way. So he turned to Unity.

"Well, will you, Unity dear, be mine?" he says.

"Take her leavings? Not I!" says Unity. "I'd scorn it!" And away walks Unity Sallet likewise, though she looked back when she'd gone some way, to see if he was following her.

So there at last were left Milly and Tony by themselves, she was crying in watery streams, and Tony looking like a tree struck by lightning.

"Well, Milly," he says at last, going up to her, "it do seem as if fate had ordained that it should be you and I, or nobody. And what must be must be, I suppose. Hey, Milly?"

"If you like, Tony. You didn't really mean what you said to them?"

"Not a word of it!" declares Tony, bringing down his fist upon his palm.

And then he kissed her, and put the wagon to rights, and they mounted together; and their banns were put up the very next Sunday. I was not able to go to their wedding, but it was a rare party they had, by all account.

About the Story

1. Describe Tony Kytes in two or three sentences.
2. How does Tony's predicament compare with Denis de Beaulieu's in "The Sire de Maletroit's Door"?
3. Why do you think Hardy chose the title he did?
4. What point does this story make?

About the Story

1. *Answers will vary but may include adjectives such as appealing, deceptive, proud, self-deceived, naive.*

2. *Answers may vary; both men are trapped in an awkward situation concerning the opposite sex. However, unlike Denis, Tony creates the difficulty himself.*

3. *Answers may vary; the title is ironic—Tony actually ends up deceiving no one.*

4. *Answers may vary but should include that liars do not prosper.*

OBJECTIVES

The students will be able to

- Discuss the symbolism used in "The Listeners."
- Explain how an author creates suspense.
- Analyze and discuss the despair in de la Mare's poem as a philosophy prevalent in modern literature.

onomatopoeia, alliteration, assonance (ferny, bird, turret)

FURTHER HELPS

Additional activities

1. Discuss what John Ciardi said about "The Listeners" in the April 4, 1964, edition of the *Saturday Review.* It is "a powerful dream-sequence presented in words that are far more important for their connotations than for their denotations."

2. Discuss an exciting sports event with the class. Talk about what makes the sport exciting. Notice the verbs Hoey uses in "Foul Shot" to convey action: *seeks out, soothes, drums, measures, raises, balances, calms, breathes, crouches.* Now have the students write about a sports event using vivid verbs.

The Listeners

Walter de la Mare

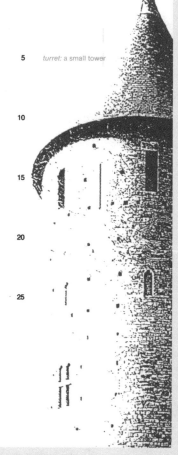

Sometimes a story succeeds because of what it does not tell us. "The Listeners" teases our imaginations to supply missing details—or ponder the mystery. Notice that the less a story explains, the more it can suggest and symbolize.

"Is there anybody there?" said the Traveler,
    Knocking on the moonlit door;
And his horse in the silence champed the grasses
    Of the forest's ferny floor.
And a bird flew up out of the turret,*   5   *turret: a small tower*
    Above the Traveler's head:
And he smote upon the door again a second time;
    "Is there anybody there?" he said.
But no one descended to the Traveler;
    No head from the leaf-fringed sill   10
Leaned over and looked into his gray eyes,
    Where he stood perplexed and still.
But only a host of phantom listeners
    That dwelt in the lone house then
Stood listening in the quiet of the moonlight   15
    To that voice from the world of men:
Stood thronging the faint moonbeams on their dark stair
    That goes down to the empty hall,
Hearkening in an air stirred and shaken
    By the lonely Traveler's call.   20
And he felt in his heart their strangeness,
    Their stillness answering his cry,
While his horse moved, cropping the dark turf,
    'Neath the starred and leafy sky;
For he suddenly smote on the door, even   25
    Louder, and lifted his head:—
"Tell them I came, and no one answered,
    That I kept my word," he said.

PREPARATION

"The Listeners," "Foul Shot"

Overview

De la Mare's "The Listeners" provides not only a good review of imagery and symbol but also an opportunity for developing discernment in students. Despair, characteristic of much modern literature, is artfully interwoven in the poem. Hoey's poem, like de la Mare's, raises the readers' curiosity to a level of suspense. But unlike "The Listeners," "Foul Shot" is a simple narrative.

Potential problems

The references to "phantom listeners" in the poem may prove problematic to some. Remind students that The "listeners" are symbolic of the unknown. De la Mare is not trying to prove the existence of ghosts.

DISCUSSION

"The Listeners"

Analysis

Read aloud the "About the Author" note on Walter de la Mare (page 291). Draw the students' attention to de la Mare's use of the "dreamy, imaginative side of existence as a means of discovering truth about life." This selection, typical in this regard, is also the poet's most anthologized piece. Although we can enjoy the poem as a simple narrative, its imagery offers deeper, richer meaning upon closer examination. Read the headnote and poem aloud.

Like most of de la Mare's poetic settings, "The Listeners" presents an isolated, chilling night landscape. The reader is not told where the traveler is from nor where he is headed. Notice that the traveler is nowhere presented as actually having a message to relate. Several times, however, he appears to be questioning (ll. 1, 8, 12, 22, 27). In line with de la Mare's view of God and society, only stillness (l. 22) and

Never the least stir made the listeners,
  Though every word he spake
Fell echoing through the shadowiness of the still house
  From the one man left awake:
Aye, they heard his foot upon the stirrup,
  And the sound of iron on stone,
And how the silence surged softly backward,
  When the plunging hoofs were gone.

About the Author

Henry C. Duffin introduces Walter de la Mare (1873-1956) as a poet "with spade and pick-axe digging up the queer side of things." Certainly de la Mare's writing deals with the strange and the uncanny. Yet he cannot be compared with a writer such as Edgar Allan Poe, whose primary goal was to create an atmosphere of terror or strangeness. Instead, de la Mare explored the dreamy, imaginative side of existence as a means of discovering truth about life. His tone is gentler than Poe's. De la Mare wrote numerous poems for or about children. Yet they appeal to all ages with their lyricism and deceptively simple style.

De la Mare saw the universe as devoid of a caring, controlling God. To him, humanity suffers from the inexplicable action of "fate." In this respect, he strongly resembles Thomas Hardy (see page 73). His rejection of Christianity was well known.

Nevertheless, de la Mare does make some valid observations about modern man. Although he was to all appearances a very ordinary, conservative Englishman, his mind was keenly aware of the spiritual as opposed to the strictly materialistic side of life. He shows insight into the connection between our sinful nature and our hidden imaginings, a relationship that the Scriptures had long ago revealed.

i.e., alive

alliteration (/s/ sounds), consonance (/n/ and /ng/)

3. Look at another poem about a sport (e.g., "The Double-Play" by Robert Wallace).

4. To review all the short fiction, have a "True/False contest." Ask each student to write some brief information about an element such as the setting, characters, plot, or climax of one of the fiction pieces. (You may want to assign a specific piece or specific pieces to groups to assure a well-rounded review.) Tell the students they may give only accurate information, or they may mix inaccurate information with accurate information. Students then take turns reading theirs aloud. Each class member writes "true" or "false" on his own paper. The originator of the statement reads the correct answer, and each class member checks his own. Then the next student reads his statement, and so on. The student with the most correct answers after all students have read and given their answers is the winner of the contest.

---

strangeness (l. 21) answer. Look again at the traveler's exclamation to "Tell them I came, and no one answered, / That I kept my word." The traveler tries to preserve his integrity and sincerity as a "quester"; he "keeps his word" but is unrewarded.

In de la Mare, houses represent death and ultimate reality. In lines 2 and 7, the traveler knocks on the door. The door has long been used as a symbol of access to truth. Unfortunately, de la Mare presents the door as "locked." "The Listeners" is one of the most poignant pictures of unregenerate man's spiritual longing.

Aside from the house and the door there are several other interesting images, such as the horse-and-rider motif. The figure of a mounted knight errant on a noble quest goes back to chivalric romances. Line 10 contains another familiar image: "the leaf-fringed sill," or window. De la Mare frequently presents eyes and windows as mirrors of the soul and of ultimate reality. Notice that no "head from the leaf-fringed sill / Leaned over and looked into his gray eyes." In de la Mare's eerie world, no human or supernatural response ensues. Throughout his work, de la Mare intended to present a universe in which ultimate truth would always be a mystery and we would always remain thwarted seekers.

As John Hall Wheelock (see Resources section), author of "Earth," stated, "'The Listeners' is an example of skilled metaphor. The entire poem might be said to be a single complex metaphor." Wheelock labels the simple narrative in this poem as "surface." He goes on to say that "at the same time that these surfaces are engaging our attention, their underlying power as metaphors, as symbols, is communicating almost unconsciously, to those capable of receiving it, the actual substance of the poem."

Alliteration; note also assonance (soothes, uniform).

Journal entry idea

Notice the atmosphere in "The Listeners" and tell how the poet creates it.

Journal entry idea

Describe an action in a sport like Hoey does. Use shape, if possible, to emphasize the sport's action.

Resources

Henry Charles Duffin, *Walter de la Mare, a Study of His Poetry* (M.S.G. House, 1970).

Walter de la Mare, *Come Hither: A Collection of Rhymes and Poems for the Young of All Ages* (New York: Alfred Knopf, 1963).

Doris Ross McCrosson, *Walter de la Mare* (New York: Twayne Publishers, 1966).

John Hall Wheelock, *What Is Poetry?* (New York: Charles Scribner's Sons, 1963).

Foul Shot

Edwin A. Hoey

Most narrative involves some kind of conflict. When the outcome of a conflict remains in doubt, the reader's curiosity and anxiety may rise to a level known as suspense. Authors sometimes allow suspense to build until nearly the end of the story.

With two 60's stuck on the scoreboard
And two seconds hanging on the clock,
The solemn boy in the center of eyes,
Squeezed by silence,
Seeks out the line with his feet,   5
Soothes his hands along his uniform,
Gently drums the ball against the floor,
Then measures the waiting net,
Raises the ball on his right hand,
Balances it with his left,   10
Calms it with fingertips,
Breathes,
Crouches,
Waits,
And then through a stretching of stillness,   15
Nudges it upward.

"Foul Shot"

Read aloud the headnote and poem. Like de la Mare, Hoey endeavors to raise our curiosity and anxiety to a level known as suspense. His technique is the same as de la Mare's—withholding information from us. Is this technique as successful in this simple narrative as it is in de la Mare's more complex piece? Do we want to read on to the end of the poem?

One significant difference between "The Listeners" and "Foul Shot" is that in the latter we eventually do obtain the information we desire. Ask the students to identify the point at which the outcome of the poem becomes clear. Also draw their attention to the shape of Hoey's poem. Ask the students why they think Hoey shaped the poem as he did.

Finally, ask the students which poem they like better, "The Listeners" or "Foul Shot." Have them give the rationale for their preference. Is the topic of the poem a major factor?

Application

The thoughtful Christian reader needs to be aware that modern authors such as de la Mare have developed a strange mixture of hopelessness and pride concerning ultimate truth. God and those who have the truth are presented as "silent" and "strange." Yet the Bible clearly shows that man can discover truth if he approaches God with a humble heart, accepting God's terms (Isa. 57:15).

The Bible, like de la Mare, uses the door as a symbol. Have the students look up several passages in which the door is used symbolically (cf. John 10:1-18; Acts 14:27; I Cor. 16:8-9; II Cor. 2:12-13; Col. 4:2-4; James 5:9; Rev. 3:7-8, 20). How does the Scripture's use of this symbol differ from de la Mare's? *(New Testament symbolic references to a door nearly always picture it as open, a means of access to better knowledge of the Lord.)*

The ball
Slides up and out,
Lands,
Leans,   20
Wobbles,
Wavers,
Hesitates,
Exasperates,
Plays it coy   25
Until every face begs with unsounding screams—

And then

    And then

        And then,

Right before ROAR-UP,   30
Dives down and through.

About the Poems

1. What are we *not* told about the incident in Walter de la Mare's poem, "The Listeners"?
2. How does this withholding of information add interest?
3. What few facts are made clear in de la Mare's poem?
4. At what point in Hoey's poem does the outcome become clear?
5. Was Hoey successful in building suspense in "Foul Shot"?

About the Poems

1. *We are not told where the traveler is from nor where he is going; accept other answers as well.*

2. *Answers may vary; the withholding of information adds to the aura of suspense and mystery.*

3. *Answers may vary but might include that the traveler came in fulfillment of a promise, received no response, and then left.*

4. *lines 30 and 31*

5. *Answers may vary, but most will say yes.*

9
UNIT NINE

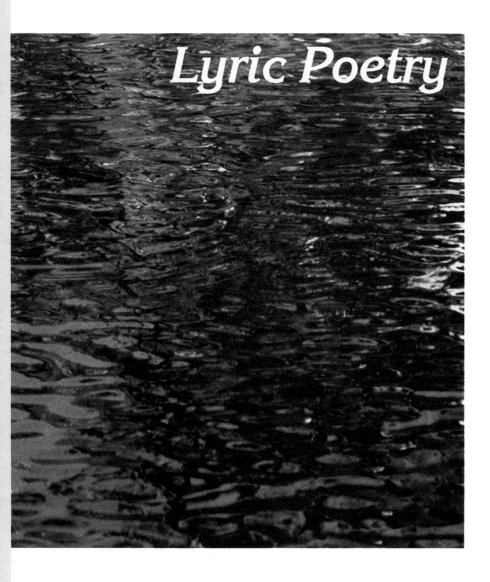

Lyric Poetry

Lyric Poetry Introduction,
"Rattlesnake"

OBJECTIVES

The students will be able to

- Identify the characteristics of lyric poetry.
- Explain Chávez's use of images and sound.

FURTHER HELPS

Additional activities

1. Give the students a copy of a lyric poem with several words omitted. Have the students choose words and fill in the blanks. Then share the author's original words with the class.

2. Study one of the psalms together, noting how the psalm illustrates the characteristics of good lyric poetry.

Resource

Charlton Ogburn, "What's the Use of Poetry?" *Reader's Digest,* December 1982.

Of all the genres, the lyric is the most difficult to define. A lyric poem can tell a story, like a narrative poem, and have dialogue, like a drama. It can draw from the whole range of human emotions and experience. It can be formal—an ode, for instance—or informal. It can be melodious—"lyrical"—or quite unmelodious. Some modern literary theorists almost despair of defining it at all.

On our map of the genres, the lyric lies in the territorial waters of the drama. It shows some resemblances to the drama in its form and in its content. In a typical lyric poem the poet, like an actor, speaks his thoughts aloud to himself. These thoughts, as in a soliloquy, are "overheard" by his audience of readers. The poem may be considered, then, a kind of speech lifted out of the drama of an individual mind, a speech in which an actor, alone on stage, verbalizes his thoughts to an audience he pretends not to notice. Whether the poet speaks in his own voice or in the voice of a character he has invented, the lyric poem suggests a background of personal experience and resonates with the intensity of a speech in a dramatic setting.

In content the lyric poem "stages" an incident—the props, costumes, and even actors being supplied by the imagination. Whether anecdotal, descriptive, or directly analytical, or a little of each, the lyric poem internalizes human experience. A lyric poem assumes that what is going on inside a person is just as real and important as what is going on outside.

The psalms show most of the moods and forms possible to the lyric. They range from anguished cries (Pss. 6, 12, 22, 38, 42, 51, 69) to joyous exuberance (21, 30, 34, 47, 48) to sober reflection (8, 46, 87, 91). They include earnest exhortation (24, 29, 37, 82, 99, 103) and informal instruction (78, 119, 127, 128). Some are highly schematic (1, 107, 114, 119, 136), others relatively free in form (37, 40, 53). The psalmist may be identified (41, 50) or unidentified. His specific circumstances may be stated (51, 52, 54) or unstated. Typically the poem shows the psalmist responding to, triumphing over, or meditating upon a time of stress. It is a speech resulting from an action or a situation. The action or situation is implied more often than stated. We hear only the words of the human protagonist and his God. The words are written to be sung. In the hymns of Israel as well as in the hymns of the church today, the lyric has distilled the inner experience of God's people. By means of the lyric this experience has been incorporated into the worship of God.

Obviously lyric poetry can be written to reveal God, rather than just to display self. Though the psalms do not lack references to the psalmist, they abound in references to God. Many are prayers. Their purpose is to glorify their divine rather than human creator. So it is with the life of every believer. Paul wrote to the Ephesians, "For we are his workmanship [literally *poem*], created in Christ Jesus unto good works, which God hath before ordained that we should walk in them" (Eph. 2:10).

PREPARATION

Lyric Poetry Introduction, "Rattlesnake"

Overview

Although lyric poetry can be difficult to define, the analogies and examples in the introductory essay should help the students understand the characteristics of the genre. The selection by Chávez is a good opening for the unit; it provides a fairly straightforward illustration of the elements inherent in a good lyric poem.

Potential problems

Some students may be unfamiliar with cloisonné. Bring a piece of cloisonné jewelry to class for the students to see. *Merriam-Webster's Collegiate Dictionary,* tenth edition (1994) defines it as "a style of enamel decoration in which the enamel is applied and fired in raised cells (as soldered wires) on a usu. metal background."

DISCUSSION

Introduction

Read the introductory essay aloud. Draw the students' attention to the analogy between drama and lyric poetry. Keeping this analogy in mind, read "Rattlesnake" aloud to them. Then discuss with the students characteristics of lyric poetry that are highlighted in the teacher's edition on page 296. Discuss with them how each is fulfilled in "Rattlesnake."

Analysis

Chávez's poem reinforces the dramatic analogy. Unlike many of the poems from previous units, this poem does not make us feel that the speaker is addressing us. We feel instead that we are overhearing his thoughts. It is as if he has unexpectedly come upon a rattlesnake and, arrested by its beauty, stops to study the creature. We sense an intensity, an immediacy, a drama in the tone of the poem.

Draw the students' attention to the contrast between stanzas one and two. Ask the students to identify any words or phrases in stanza one that describe the snake favorably. *(line of beauty,*

Rattlesnake

Fray Angélico Chávez

In the following poem Fray Angélico Chávez creates startling images. Notice the metaphors and similes in the poem. Notice, too, the difference between the two stanzas. The first is a vivid description of the rattlesnake; the second, the poet's personal response. In the first he observes; in the second he reacts.

Line of beauty scrawled alive
by God's finger on the sand,
diamond-patterned inlaid band
scrolling inward like a hive—

stay away,
crawl-created,
articulated
coil of cloisonné!

---

diamond-patterned, inlaid band) Then read this stanza aloud. Notice that the words almost roll off the tongue, creating an easy rhythm, a sense of slow movement. The speaker seems spellbound by the beauty of God's creature. Point out, however, that the picture Chávez creates through his images is one of inward, contracting movement. In line 1 we have the impression that the snake is "scrawled" full-length in the sand, but by line 4 it is "scrolling inward." This image, one of coiling as if to strike, prepares us for the abrupt change in thought in stanza two.

Read stanza two aloud. Draw the students' attention to the short line, the difficult juxtaposition of words, and the frequent use of the hard *c* sound. The sound and syntax reinforce the speaker's mood. He has awakened to the danger; attraction has given way to revulsion. The last line, however, combines the two moods. Ask the students to identify the word in this line which shows us that, although alert to the danger, the speaker is yet fascinated by the rattlesnake's beauty. *(cloisonné)*

 Application

Divide the class into several small groups. Have each group identify another of God's creatures that might evoke the same "mixed feelings" presented in Chávez's poem. Then have each group write its own short poem, contrasting these emotions. Remind them that the speaker should be "thinking aloud," not addressing the reader. See **Writing Rubric 9-1: A Lively Lyric.**

About the Poem

1. Which imaginative comparisons seem to describe the snake favorably?
2. Which imaginative comparisons seem to describe the rattlesnake unfavorably?
3. Identify at least one sound device Chávez uses in his poem.
4. Notice the last line of stanza one. How does this line prepare us for the first line of stanza two?

About the Author

Fray Angélico Chávez (1910-1996), a Franciscan missionary in the southwestern United States, was a gifted poet and painter. Born in New Mexico, Chávez was influenced early in life by his Catholic teachers. In 1937 he was ordained and took the religious name Fray Angélico in admiration of the fifteenth-century Italian religious painter. Chávez worked in the Indian missions in the Southwest as well as among Spanish-speaking people. The poetry he wrote during this time won the admiration of area authors, who encouraged Chávez to publish.

Chávez's first volume of poetry, *Clothed with the Sun,* takes its name from a passage in Revelation. Like much of Chávez's poetry, it reflects both his familiarity with the Scripture and his artistic appreciation of the beauties of the southwestern desert. His poetry also reflects his sense of line and balance. "Rattlesnake" clearly illustrates Chávez's keen ability to create visual images that illustrate his appreciation of God's design in creation.

 About the Poem

1. *"Line of beauty," "by God's finger," "diamond-patterned inlaid band," "cloisonné"*

2. *"scrawled alive," "scrolling inward like a hive," "crawl-created, / articulated / coil"*

3. *alliteration ("crawl-created" "coil of cloisonné"); assonance (line, alive, by, diamond, like, hive; stay, away, created, articulated, cloisonné); rhyme (alive, hive; sand, band; stay, away, cloisonné; created, articulated); consonance (/d/)*

4. *It implies that the snake is coiling ("like a hive"), ready to strike.*

March for a One-Man Band

David Wagoner

Wagoner effectively uses sound and syntax to reinforce content. His poem seems to be more than a description; it is almost a "performance," one in which the reader can see and "hear" the one-man band on the march.

He's *a boom a blat* in the uniform

Of an army *tweedledy* band *a toot*

Complete with medals *a honk* cornet

Against *a thump* one side of his lips

And the other stuck with *a sloop a tweet*

A whistle *a crash* on top of *a crash*

A helmet *a crash* a cymbal a drum

At his *bumbledy* knee and a *rimshot* flag

A click he stands at attention *a wheeze*

And plays the Irrational Anthem *bang.*

OBJECTIVES

The students will be able to

- Explain the value of wordplay in a poem.
- Write a humorous onomatopoetic poem as a class.

FURTHER HELPS

Additional activity

Like Wagoner, Poe uses the sounds of words to focus our attention on real sounds. Have the students compare Wagoner's poem with Edgar Allan Poe's "The Bells."

PREPARATION

"March for a One-Man Band"

Overview

Wagoner's poem is both a visual and an aural "experience." As the headnote points out, it is almost a performance. The images and sound devices should make it an enjoyable selection for the students.

DISCUSSION

Introduction

Ask the students whether they have ever seen a one-man band. Let those who have describe what they saw. How did the one-man band sound? What impressions do they have of the experience? Did they enjoy it or find it annoying?

Analysis

Read the poem aloud or have a student do so. You may then want to read it again, this time asking a group or groups of students to "interrupt" each time an onomatopoetic phrase is used. Discuss the fact that Wagoner has successfully re-created the awkwardness and humor inherent when one person endeavors to play several instruments. Then have the students analyze the poem by using the questions at the end of the selection. (See page 300.)

Application

As a class, write a humorous poem using as many devices of sound as you can. When you have finished writing, you may want to share the poem with other classes and/or display all of them on a bulletin board.

About the Poem

1. Notice the italicized words. What instruments do you think are represented by these words?
2. Identify at least three sound devices Wagoner uses in his poem.
3. Do you think the poet is entertained or annoyed by the performance of a one-man band?
4. Why do you think the poet used "Irrational Anthem" rather than "National Anthem"?

About the Author

David Wagoner (1926-) was born in Massillon, Ohio, and received his education at Pennsylvania State University and Indiana University. While a student, he was greatly influenced by Theodore Roethke, professor and modern poet. Like Roethke, Wagoner went on to become both a university professor and a writer.

Wagoner is well respected among modern poets for his ability to reanimate familiar or worn-out language, using the sound and the rhythm of words to paint dramatic scenes for his reader. His poems, which are a blend of the simple and the serious, display great energy. Our poetic selection is a good example of Wagoner's artistry.

The themes in Wagoner's works are less admirable than his artistic form. In much of his work we find the individual struggling to retain meaning in a senseless, chaotic world. In Wagoner's opinion, the primary sources of blame for man's woes are the constrictions and demands of family and country. Society is Wagoner's favorite scapegoat for man's condition. The troubled characters in his novels are typically portrayed as helpless victims of circumstance, not as willfully rebellious or in need of a Saviour. They seem curiously disjointed, isolated, and absurd, as does the fumbling one-man band.

 About the Poem

1. *Answers may vary, but some possibilities are various drums, horns, whistles, cymbals, triangles, pipes, sticks, etc. Point out to the students that these words provide the "melody" of the band. Wagoner also uses an irregular choppy rhythm, the lack of rhyme, and various sound devices to reinforce the wretchedly halting attempt of the one-man band to create music.*

2. *There are myriad sound devices. Following are some examples: alliteration—boom/blat/bang, toot/tweet; onomatopoeia—boom, blat, toot, honk, thump, tweet; assonance—boom/toot/ sloop, blat/bang, wheeze/tweet; consonance— toot/complete/coronet, cymbal/drum/bum-bledy/rimshot. Take time to reread the poem aloud, leaving out all of the italicized words. Point out that even if we remove the "melody" of the poem, we still have a visual description of the man himself.*

3. *Answers will vary. Be sure, however, that the students use specific references from the poem to support their view; both views could be supported.*

4. *This wordplay reinforces the tongue-in-cheek attitude of the poem. The cacophony produced by the one-man band playing the national anthem can hardly be recognized as a patriotic "celebration."*

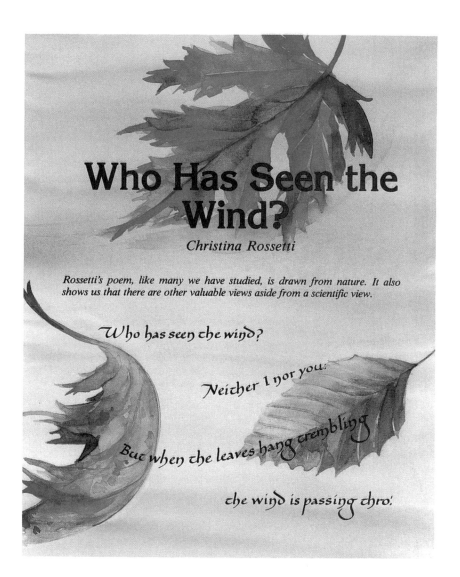

Who Has Seen the Wind?

Christina Rossetti

Rossetti's poem, like many we have studied, is drawn from nature. It also shows us that there are other valuable views aside from a scientific view.

Who has seen the wind?

Neither I nor you:

But when the leaves hang trembling

the wind is passing thro'.

DISCUSSION

"Who Has Seen the Wind?"

Introduction

Before reading the poem, read aloud the "About the Author" section on page 303. Point out to students that Rossetti was a dedicated Christian. They may be familiar with another of her poems, often quoted or sung at Christmas. You may want to share the following stanza with the class. Point out the clear Christian message as well as the allusions (shepherd, wise man) and metonymy (heart = soul, life).

What can I give Him,
 Poor as I am?
If I were a shepherd
 I would bring a lamb,

If I were a wise man
 I would do my part,—
Yet what I can I give Him,
 Give my heart.

Analysis

Read the poem on pages 301-2 aloud. Then have the students use the questions at the end of the selection to analyze the poem. (See page 303.)

Application

There were times in Rossetti's life when her purity and plainness of speech, dress, and manners drew sharp criticism. In response to the criticism, she wrote the following passage in her devotional *Letter and Spirit*.

True, all our lives long we shall be bound to restrain our soul and keep it low; but what then? For the books we now forbear to read we shall one day be endowed with wisdom and knowledge. For the music we will not listen to, we shall join in the song of the redeemed. For the pictures from which we turn, we shall gaze unabashed on the Beatific Vision. For the companionship we shun, we shall be welcomed with angelic society and the communion of triumphant saints. For the amusements we avoid, we shall keep the supreme jubilee. For the pleasures we miss, we shall abide in the rapture of heaven. It cannot be much of a hardship to dress modestly at a small cost, rather than richly and fashionably, if with conviction we are awaiting the white robes of the redeemed.

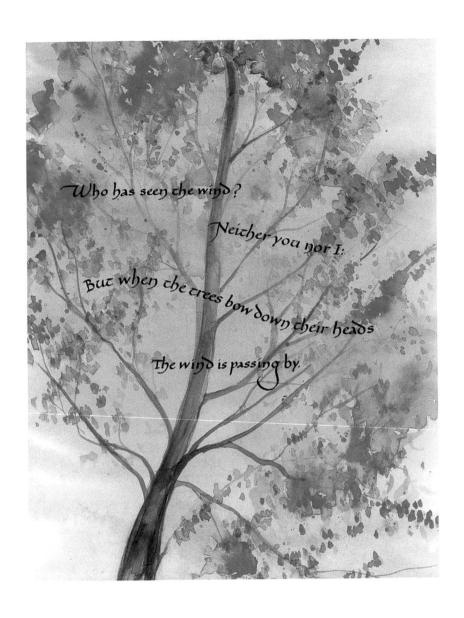

Who has seen the wind?

Neither you nor I:

But when the trees bow down their heads

The wind is passing by.

Discuss with the students Rossetti's response. Do students agree with Rossetti, that there are many things that the world accepts to which dedicated Christians should not expose themselves? Are they keeping their lives pure because of love for the Lord and a desire to be a good testimony? If they are criticized for righteous living—perhaps, at times, even by other Christians—do they have a godly response as did Christina Rossetti?

About the Poem

1. Though we have never seen the wind, what are some proofs of its existence?
2. Identify the personification in the poem.
3. What is the allusion in the poem?
4. What point does the poem make?

About the Author

Christina Rossetti (1830-1894) was part of the famous and talented Rossetti family of England. Her father had been exiled from his native country, Italy, because of his influence as a patriot and nationalistic poet. Her devout and dignified mother, formerly a governess, was an example of godly piety to her daughter Christina. Christina enjoyed an atmosphere of refined culture and education in her parents' home, where she remained all her life.

In the best traditions of lyric poetry, Rossetti's carefully crafted poems deal with the realities of life and death, the love of God and of others, and the joys and mysteries of nature. The sensitivity and depth of her writing are in part due to her many personal trials. The heavy responsibilities of caring for her mother and aging maiden aunts greatly weighed upon her. There were financial worries as well. Also, neither of the men who proposed marriage to Rossetti shared her sturdy Christian faith and practice; thus, she chose to remain single. The loneliness she faced is often reflected in her poems. But stronger than her loneliness was her total confidence in and submission to her Lord and Saviour. Rossetti filled her mind and heart with Scripture. She gained from it a unique appreciation of the sustaining and sacrificial love of God. Her poetry and uplifting devotional literature are the natural overflow of her complete dependence upon God.

About the Poem

1. *Many proofs of the wind occur daily but draw little notice. Of course, there is the rustling of the wind in the trees as Rossetti notes. We can also see the surface waves on bodies of water. We not only see these effects but also hear them. The whistling of the wind under the door is another example of hearing the wind. Seasonal smells are also carried on the wind; it is the wind that brings the aroma of fresh-cut grass and blooming flowers. We also feel the wind; there are the gentle breezes of spring as well as the biting winds of winter. Although we have never "seen" the wind, our senses affirm its existence.*

2. *"the trees bow down their heads"*

3. *Line 7 alludes to the trees or nature "bowing down," or worshiping, the Creator. Scripture is replete with support for this allusion. As Psalm 19 points out, all nature attests to the power and majesty of God. Rossetti may also have been alluding to Christ's words in John 3:8: "The wind bloweth where it listeth, and thou hearest the sound thereof, but canst not tell whence it cometh, and whither it goeth: so is every one that is born of the Spirit."*

4. *"Sight" is not the sole criterion for the existence of something. Many flippantly remark that they do not believe in God because they have never seen Him. Rossetti's poem points out the absurdity of such comments. Draw the students' attention to Hebrews 11. Ask them what is meant in verse 1 by "evidence." When we think of evidence, we think of something tangible, concrete. Faith, like the wind, does have tangible, concrete effects. The writer of Hebrews records those effects in the remainder of chapter 11.*

"The Windows"

FURTHER HELPS

Additional activities

1. Have the students find several pictures of stained glass windows to bring to class.

2. Herbert compares man to cracked glass. Ask the students to locate comparisons God makes in Scripture of man and objects/animals.

3. Read aloud several other poems by George Herbert. The following are found in BJU Press texts.

   "Our life is hid with Christ in God" in *Excursions in Literature,* 2nd ed., page 306 (eighth-grade text).

   "The Altar" in *Fundamentals of Literature,* page 302 (ninth-grade text).

   "Redemption," "Love," "Aaron," "Denial," and "Virtue" in *British Literature,* pages 306-10 (twelfth-grade text).

The Windows

George Herbert

George Herbert, devout Anglican parson and lyric poet of the first rank, dedicated his poetic gifts to God. Before his early death, he completed a collection of lyric poems entitled The Temple. *This collection represents Christian experience symbolically in terms of the structure and furnishings of an English church.*

Salvation, designed and executed by Hiemer and Co. in Patterson, New Jersey, The Bob Jones University Collection.

PREPARATION

"The Windows"

Overview

Herbert's selection illustrates how lyric poetry, though personal, can express universal ideas and profound emotion. Like Rossetti's, Herbert's "personal expression" provides readers with valuable food for thought.

DISCUSSION

Introduction

Discuss briefly how this poem resembles a psalm (a hymn to God). As in many of the psalms, we hear the speaker of the poem in private conversation with his heavenly Father. The poem also displays the wide range of emotion we see in many of David's songs. The speaker bemoans, for example, his weak condition; yet at the same time he rejoices in his position in Christ.

Analysis

Read the headnote and the poem aloud in class. Then have the students use the questions at the end of the selection to continue their analysis of the poem. (See page 305.)

Application

Have each student give a brief (5-8 minute) devotional for the class on a metaphor, simile, or personification found in Scripture. Encourage students to go beyond merely explaining the imaginative comparison; they also need to make an application to their audience's lives— i.e., what is the Bible telling us to *do* in this passage? (For review on the steps in writing a devotional see *WRITING AND GRAMMAR 9,* 2nd ed., pages 206-7.)

Lord, how can man preach thy eternal word?
　　He is a brittle crazy*glass:

crazy: crazed, cracked

Yet in thy temple thou dost him afford
　　This glorious and transcendent place,
　　To be a window through thy grace.

But when thou dost anneal*in glass thy story,
　　Making thy life to shine within

anneal: heat in order to add colors

The holy Preacher's; then the light and glory
　　More revrend grows, and more doth win:
　　Which else shows watrish, bleak, and thin.

Doctrine and life, colors and light*in one

The correspondences are reversed: doctrine (expository preaching)=light; life (Christ within the preacher)=colors.

　　When they combine and mingle, bring
A strong regard and awe:　but speech alone
　　Doth vanish like a flaring thing,
　　And in the ear, not conscience ring.

About the Poem

1. What metaphor is developed in Herbert's poem?
2. Explain the metaphor as it is developed in the poem.
3. What was the original function of stained-glass church windows?
4. What is the significance of this original function to the poem?

About the Poem

1. *The preacher of God's Word is likened to a stained glass window.*

2. *It might be best to have the class outline on the chalkboard the images and what they represent. The following ideas should be covered somewhere in the outline: The poet first uses the metaphor to illustrate man's weakness in ll. 1 and 2. Man's inner nature is brittle like glass, and thus able to be cracked. This wordplay here also implies not only man's weakness (being cracked) but also his penchant for being irrational (crazed). The poet goes on to focus on the place wherein the glass is "housed." A stained glass window is usually housed in a magnificent cathedral. So too we, though cracked and brittle, are afforded a place in God's house. This stanza also points to why we are housed in God's sacred edifice. Like the stained glass windows in a cathedral, we are permitted to "enhance by color and light" God's rich grace. Stanza 2 points to the fact that the hotter the furnace that prepares the glass, the brighter the colors produced. So, too, the greater the suffering, the brighter the testimony of those who bear witness of Christ. Stanza 3 brings the metaphor to a climax, combining the ideas and images presented in the first two stanzas.*

3. *Stained glass was part of the architectural development in the Middle Ages. It became important "when the ingenious use of a structural skeleton made it possible to eliminate much of the wall. For both mosaic and stained glass, as developed in the western world, a realistic approach to the representation of man and nature was inappropriate. Their purpose was to enhance by color and light and stylized figures the spiritual meaning of a sacred edifice and to set before the visitor the timeless forms of the supernaturalized world" (Encyclopaedia Britannica).*

4. *The students may have already answered this question in the discussion of question 2. If not, have them make the application here.*

OBJECTIVES

The students will be able to

- Discuss the use of metaphor, imagery, and sound devices.
- Write a descriptive paragraph or poem using sensory images to describe an exhilarating experience.

FURTHER HELPS

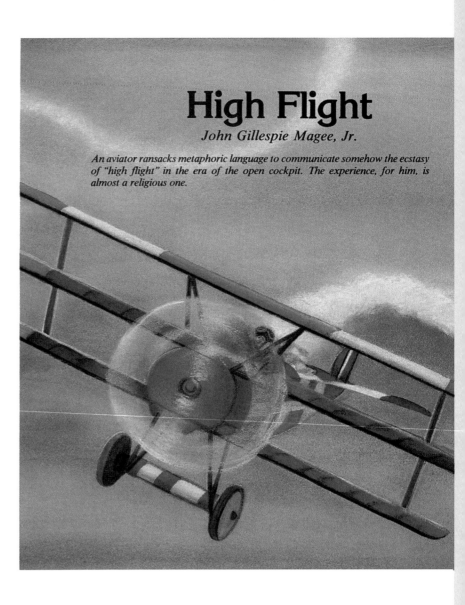

Journal entry idea
Have the students write a descriptive paragraph or poem about an exhilarating activity they have experienced. Remind them to use as many sense images as they can. Remind them of the various techniques previous poets in this unit used to create mood. Chávez's use of the hard *c* is one example; Wagoner's irregular, choppy rhythm is another. Encourage the students to try their hand at such techniques.

High Flight

John Gillespie Magee, Jr.

An aviator ransacks metaphoric language to communicate somehow the ecstasy of "high flight" in the era of the open cockpit. The experience, for him, is almost a religious one.

DISCUSSION

"High Flight"

Introduction

Most of the students have probably flown either in a commercial airliner or in a private plane. Ask them if they enjoy flying. For those who do like to fly, what do they enjoy most? Is it the spectacular scenery? Or perhaps is it the feeling of freedom that flying sometimes evokes? Do any of the students have their pilot's license? Do any plan to get their license in the future? For those who plan to become pilots one day, find out what first got them interested in flying.

Analysis

Have a student read the poem and headnote aloud. Tell the students that this poem was published in 1942 during World War II. Its author, a member of the Royal Canadian Air Force, was killed in action in 1941. He was only nineteen at the time. Remind the students that at this time, few people flew regularly and space travel was unheard of. These facts give clearer insight into Magee's descriptions. Notice, for example, line 13 in which he speaks of "The high *untrespassed* sanctity of space." You may also want to inform students that the poem gained fame again in 1986 when, after the space shuttle *Challenger* exploded, killing seven astronauts, President Reagan read from the poem on national television.

Continue your discussion of the poem, using the questions at the end of the selection. (See page 307.)

Application

See "Further helps" above.

OH, I HAVE SLIPPED THE SURLY BONDS OF EARTH,
AND DANCED THE SKIES ON LAUGHTER-SILVERED WINGS;
SUNWARD I'VE CLIMBED AND JOINED THE TUMBLING MIRTH
OF SUN-SPLIT CLOUDS—AND DONE A HUNDRED THINGS
YOU HAVE NOT DREAMED OF—WHEELED AND SOARED AND SWUNG
HIGH IN THE SUNLIT SILENCE. HOV'RING THERE,
I'VE CHASED THE SHOUTING WIND ALONG AND FLUNG
MY EAGER CRAFT THROUGH FOOTLESS HALLS OF AIR.
UP, UP THE LONG DELIRIOUS, BURNING BLUE
I'VE TOPPED THE WIND-SWEPT HEIGHTS WITH EASY GRACE,
WHERE NEVER LARK, OR EVEN EAGLE, FLEW;
AND, WHILE WITH SILENT, LIFTING MIND I'VE TROD
THE HIGH UNTRESPASSED SANCTITY OF SPACE,
PUT OUT MY HAND, AND TOUCHED THE FACE OF GOD.

About the Poem

1. How is the last metaphor appropriate?
2. List two specific images you think are particularly vivid.
3. Identify an example of the following:
   a. alliteration
   b. onomatopoeia
   c. personification
4. What is the point of the poem?
5. What specifically do you think the author is trying to say in the last line of the poem?

About the Poem

1. *Answers may vary. The students should refer in some way, however, to the building of the poem to a crescendo. The description becomes increasingly spectacular and awesome. It is reasonable that such a magnificent scene culminates in a picture of "the face of God." In essence, all the magnificent aspects of creation declare and reflect the glory of "God's face."*

2. *Some examples are "danced on laughter-silvered wings," "tumbling mirth of sun-split clouds," "shouting wind," "footless halls of air," and "burning blue."*

3. a. alliteration: *"slipped the surly bonds," "sunlit silence," "burning blue," "sanctity of space"*

   b. onomatopoeia: *Explain to the students that onomatopoeia need not be limited to words like boom or bang, whose pronunciation suggests their meaning. In the hands of a poet it can be more subtle. He can give us words whose sound and sense work together. Slipped is one example; notice that the sound of the word and its action seem to fit together. Flung is another example. Have the students find other words they feel would illustrate this broader concept.*

   c. personification: *"tumbling mirth," "shouting wind," "eager craft"*

4. *to describe the exhilarating, awe-inspiring joy of flying*

5. *Answers may vary.*

"The Wise Old Apple Tree in Spring"

FURTHER HELPS

Additional activities

Compare Hillyer's "orchard men of time" with the father in Udpike's story "Pigeon Feathers."

Decisions recalled or in progress are among the most interesting subjects of lyric poetry. A poem may simply present a decision. Or it may analyze it, investigating its causes and consequences or showing the conflict leading up to it.

The Wise Old Apple Tree in Spring

Robert Hillyer

The wise old apple tree in spring,
Though split and hollow, makes a crown
Of such fantastic blossoming
We cannot let them cut it down.
It bears no fruit, but honeybees   5
Prefer it to the other trees.

The orchard man chalks his mark
And says, "This empty shell must go."
We nod and rub it off the bark
As soon as he goes down the row.   10
Each spring he looks bewildered. "Queer,
I thought I marked this thing last year."

Ten orchard men have come and gone
Since first I saw my grandfather
Slyly erase it. I'm the one   15
To do it now. As I defer
The showy veteran's removal
My grandson nods his full approval.

Like mine, my fellow ancient's roots
Are deep in the last century   20
From which our memories send shoots
For all our grandchildren to see
How spring, inviting bloom and rhyme,
Defeats the orchard men of time.

PREPARATION

"The Wise Old Apple Tree in Spring"

Overview

"The Wise Old Apple Tree in Spring" is typical of Hillyer's work—technically flawless. Its theme, like several poems from earlier units, reminds us that things in life need not always have a specific, utilitarian purpose to be valuable.

DISCUSSION

Introduction

Most students have probably seen an apple tree in spring. Some may not have noticed it, however. You may want to show them some pic-tures or have several students give their own description of an apple tree in bloom.

Analysis

Read the headnote and poem aloud. Initiate your discussion using the "About the Poem" questions (page 309).

Application

Hillyer's poem presents a decision. It also investigates the causes and consequences of the decision. Have the students write their own poem. The poem should present not only a decision (as stanzas 1-3 of Hillyer's poem do) but go on to include the causes and consequences of the decision (as stanza 4 of Hillyer's poem does). See **Writing Rubric 9-2: Causes and Consequences.**

As time permits, have the students share these poems with the class. You may wish to have each student provide an illustration for his poem. You could then compile these poems (and others the students have written throughout the year) in a class notebook. You may want to have the students choose for the notebook two or three of their favorite poems from those they have written.

About the Poem

1. Explain the decisions involving trees in "The Wise Old Apple Tree in Spring."
2. What do these decisions reveal about the poet's view of trees?
3. Who do you think are the "orchard men of time"?
4. What does the poem reveal of the poet's view of life?

About the Author

"The Wise Old Apple Tree in Spring" reflects the calm tone and temper of a conservative poet. Robert Hillyer's (1895-1961) desire to create beautiful, orderly poetry is praise-worthy, especially in a modern poet. Hillyer's attitude toward traditional literary values strongly resembles the attachment of the speaker in our selection to a well-loved landmark. This poem, like Hillyer's other works, aptly illustrates his philosophy: Poetry can and should keep alive that which is beautiful and worthwhile for the enjoyment of posterity.

About the Poem

1. The first "decision" is implied by the speaker when he affirms his acceptance of the tree's aesthetic value. The second "decision" is that of the orchard man who, blinded to the value of beauty, decides that the tree is worthless. The speaker "nullifies" the orchard man's decision by rubbing off the mark. This cyclical process is continued for several generations.

2. The poet believes that the aesthetic beauty of the apple tree, the "fantastic blossoming," is as profitable as its fruit bearing.

3. They are those who value only those things that can provide immediate, concrete gratification. Creativity has no place in their world. Point out to the students that man "made in the image of God" should have a correct appreciation for beauty and creativity. Man's capacity to discern and appreciate beauty is as distinctive as his capacity to reason. Both are God-given.

4. The poet values beauty as much as, if not more than, simple utilitarianism. Like the poets, musicians, and artists of all the ages, he believes that man's soul as well as his body must be fed. One of the ways God provides such "food" for us is through His creation.

OBJECTIVE

The students will be able to

• Analyze the metaphoric meaning of this poem from a Biblical perspective.

Traveling Through the Dark

William Stafford

This irregular sonnet (notice the **approximate rhyme***) shows the speaker in a moral dilemma. His reverence for life and strong sense of responsibility cause him to weigh the choices carefully. There seems to be no right thing to do. He feels that he is being watched and that much depends on his decision.*

Traveling through the dark I found a deer
dead on the edge of Wilson River road.
It is usually best to roll them into the canyon:
that road is narrow; to swerve might make more dead.

By glow of the tail-light I stumbled back of the car   5
and stood by the heap, a doe, a recent killing;
she had stiffened already, almost cold.
I dragged her off; she was large in the belly.

My fingers touching her side brought me the reason—
her side was warm; her fawn lay there waiting,   10
alive, still, never to be born.
Beside that mountain road I hesitated.

The car aimed ahead its lowered parking lights;
under the hood purred the steady engine.
I stood in the glare of the warm exhaust turning red;   15
around our group I could hear the wilderness listen.

I thought hard for us all—my only swerving—,
then pushed her over the edge into the river.

PREPARATION

"Traveling Through the Dark"

Overview

Stafford's writing style is lyrical and retains a flavor of everyday conversation. Stafford was once quoted as saying, "My poetry seems to me direct and communicative, with some oddity and variety. It is usually not formal. It is much like talk, with some enchancement." "Traveling Through the Dark" is not an exception. The tone of the poem is conversational, the setting colloquial. The theme, however, is much more complex, even profound.

Potential problems

William Stafford's writing does not point to Christ as the Light of the world and the Guide through life's darkness. But his poetry does present thought-provoking ethical challenges.

DISCUSSION

Introduction

Read the headnote and poem aloud. Then discuss and fill in together **Appendix W: "Traveling Through the Dark" Analysis.**

Analysis

The speaker in "Traveling Through the Dark" faces a moral dilemma and resolves it as best he can. Nevertheless, his decision does not erase his sense of respectful awe spawned by his "life-and-death" encounter. Draw the students' attention to the phrase the "road is narrow." In light of the symbolic meaning of the poem, is there an allusion here? *(perhaps to Matthew 7:13-14)* As time permits, use the following phrases to evoke further discussion of the metaphorical meaning of the poem: "to swerve might make more dead," "I stumbled back of the car," "Beside that mountain road I hesitated," "I stood in the glare of the warm exhaust turning red," "then pushed her over the edge into the river."

About the Poem

1. Describe the dilemma facing the speaker.
2. What word recurs at the end of the poem with enriched meaning?
3. Does the title have additional meaning when you have finished reading the poem?
4. What would you have done if you had faced the speaker's dilemma?

About the Author

William Edgar Stafford (1914-1993) was born and reared in Kansas, where he enjoyed a happy childhood in small rural towns and the countryside. His love and respect for life, especially wildlife, was nurtured during these quiet years. When he went away to graduate school, and, later, with the onset of the Second World War, Stafford's peaceful vision of life was shattered. His personal beliefs caused him to refuse military service, choosing instead to serve in a public-works division. Stafford spent most of the war years in these camps, where he recalled that "we fought forest fires, built trails and roads, and terraced eroding land." When the war ended, Stafford continued his public service in religious charity organizations. One of Stafford's positions was that of educational secretary. He later took a teaching position in the English department of Oregon's Lewis and Clark College.

William Stafford received many awards and grants, most notably the 1962 National Book Award for Poetry for his *Traveling Through the Dark*. The men who presented this award to Stafford described his work as "both tough and gentle." These qualities are evident in our selection, the title poem from this book. The speaker in "Traveling Through the Dark" faces a moral dilemma and resolves it to the best of his ability. Nevertheless, his decision does not erase his sense of respectful awe before the forces of life and death he has encountered.

Continue your discussion with the "About the Poem" questions (page 311).

Application

Discuss with the students similar situations they might face someday or may have already faced in life—situations in which they might have to make a difficult, unpleasant decision where the right answer is not clear. Perhaps you could share experience from your own life in this regard. How does our Christian faith help us make decisions in such situations? Or if the situation is beyond our control, how does it help us endure uncertainty and apparent helplessness?

 About the Poem

1. *The speaker has to decide what, if anything, can be done with the deer that—though dead—still carries her living fawn.*

2. *edge*

3. *Once the reader has finished, he should recognize not only the literal but also the symbolic meaning of the title. The speaker in Stafford's poem is traveling through a moral as well as a physical darkness, where no easy answers are available. Questions must be decided quickly and without outside help. Traveling heedless and headlong through life may appear to be the safest, easiest way to behave. But sometimes a moral dilemma arises that forces one person to swerve aside and "think for us all."*

4. *Answers will vary.*

"Dust of Snow," "The Span of Life"

FURTHER HELPS

Additional activities

1. Ask artistically inclined students to draw a picture illustrating either of these poems or perhaps another poem in the unit. Display the art on a bulletin board.

2. Read other poems from Frost's book *New Hampshire*. Throughout this book Frost employs this ambivalent snow imagery. Some examples you may want to include are "Stopping by Woods on a Snowy Evening," "Good-by and Keep Cold" (snow as a protector), and "The Onset" (snow as the process of death and assurance of renewed spring).

3. Share another short poem that talks about snow with the class. A good one is "Night," by Sara Teasdale.

4. If you can obtain one, listen to a recording of Frost reading his own poetry. A video of Kennedy's inauguration might include Frost's reading of "The Gift Outright."

Birds enjoy dusting themselves to be rid of vermin. In the first of these poems by Robert Frost, a crow dusts a man—the poet. Notice that the first poem focuses on the poet's reaction to the event rather than on the event itself. The second poem contrasts two mental images of a dog, present and past.

Dust of Snow
Robert Frost

The way a crow
Shook down on me
The dust of snow
From a hemlock tree
Has given my heart
A change of mood
And saved some part
Of a day I had rued.

PREPARATION

"Dust of Snow," "The Span of Life"

Overview

These selections are characteristic of Frost's poetry. The first, "Dust of Snow," uses his recurrent snow imagery. The theme is also typical of Frost. The second, "The Span of Life," is an excellent example of his artful style.

DISCUSSION

Introduction

Snow imagery abounds in Frost's *New Hampshire*, from which the first selection is taken. The winter season, as many of our previous se-lections have shown (see selections in Units 2 and 3), can evoke a great variety of moods and images. Have the students think of several moods and images that winter has evoked for them.

Analysis

"Dust of Snow"

The theme of this first poem is a recurrent Frost theme: making the best of a situation by appreciating nature's gifts of beauty and humor. Notice that it is the element of surprise or un-expectedness that buoys the speaker's spirit and alters his mood and outlook.

Frost wrote "Dust of Snow" at Stone Cottage, his farm and the family haven in Vermont.

Though the poet's first years at the farm were fraught with personal and financial worries, Frost was reveling in his newfound gift for writing compact, expressive verse. Notice that the poem consists of only one sentence, divided into two four-line stanzas of iambic dimeter.

The snow that shook down from a hemlock tree is both an antidote for "rue" (deep sorrow of conscience) and also a symbol for death, coldness, and defeat. Point out to the students that there is a common hemlock native to New England that is a beautiful and valuable ever-green. There is also, however, a poisonous hem-lock, a deadly herb originally used in Greece for capital punishment. The snow from the hemlock tree reduces the narrator's pride and self-pity but also comforts him.

The Span of Life

Robert Frost

The old dog barks backward without getting up;
I can remember when he was a pup.

About the Poems

1. What was the poet's reaction in "Dust of Snow"?
2. Describe the pacing of line one in "The Span of Life."
3. Describe the pacing of line two in "The Span of Life."
4. How does the pacing of these lines support the contrast of images presented?

5. **Review game for Units 7, 8, and 9:** Make large cards with different characters' names from each unit on each card. Place a name card on a student's back. Do not let him see the card. Have the player turn his back to the class so that they can see the character's name. The player is then allowed to ask not more than five yes-or-no questions of the group to gather details. If he succeeds in guessing the character's name, he is given another card. If not, another person takes his place.

Resources

"Robert Frost: An Introduction," *Literary Cavalcade,* Vol. 38, No. 1, October 1985.

Dorothy Judd, *Robert Frost: Contours of Belief* (Ohio: Ohio University Press, 1984).

James L. Potter, *Robert Frost Handbook* (Pennsylvania: Pennsylvania State University Press, 1980).

"The Span of Life"

This simple but profound poem comes from Frost's Pulitzer Prize-winning *A Further Range.* Draw the students' attention to the rhythm and sound of the first line by reading it aloud. Point out that its short words and consonant sounds mimic the barking of a dog. Read the second line aloud. Frost's use of dactyllic feet causes the line to bounce along like a pup at play. Have the students count the number of words in the poem. *(8 per line for a total of 16)* Ask them how many one-syllable words there are *(12)* and how many two-syllable words. *(3)* Which is the only three-syllable word in the poem? *(remember)* Why is this appropriate? *(The theme of the poem is the rapid passage of time.)*

Application

In "Dust of Snow" Frost transforms an everyday happening into something special. He shows how little things can change one's mood or outlook. Look at Proverbs 12:25 together. Discuss with the students how Christians can encourage others and help to change their outlook. Following this discussion, you may want to have the students write a short two-line poem like "The Span of Life," expressing poetically one of the ideas derived from your discussion.

Q&A About the Poems

1. *His heart is lifted by the effects of the crow's action.*

2. *The pacing causes the line to sound like a dog barking.*

3. *The rhythm causes the line to bounce along like a pup.*

4. *The first line speaks of the tiredness of the old dog—that everything is more of a struggle now. The second line evokes a feeling of nostalgia.*

10

UNIT TEN

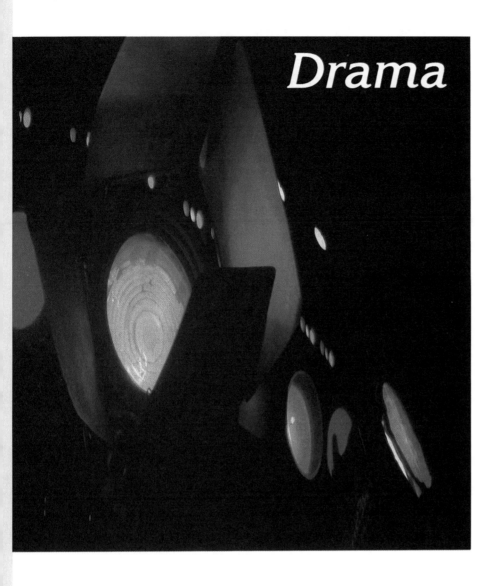

Drama

OBJECTIVES

The students will be able to

• Find examples of and discuss the theme of haste in *Romeo and Juliet.*

• Discuss whether fate of free will predominates in the action of *Romeo and Juliet.*

FURTHER HELPS

Additional activities

1. Have students fill in answers to **Appendix X: Romeo and Juliet Review** either during their reading of the play (note that act and scene numbers are given with each question) or fill it in together as a class after completing the play. This could serve as a test review as well.

2. For a review game after studying the play, make up a "Who's Who?" game. Each student locates a quote from the play describing a character in the play. Then divide the class into two teams. Team A reads one of their quotes, and Team B must tell whom Team A is describing in order to receive a point. Team B then has a turn. The team with the most correct answers for the descriptive quotes wins. Another way to play would be to have students quote characters and

Literary historians believe drama to be among the oldest of the genres. It probably has existed as long as man himself. Certainly it is among the most popular. Almost everybody at one time or another has helped act out a story. Children are born actors. They like to show as well as tell what happened at a birthday party or on the way home from school. Even adults enjoy skits, charades, masquerades, or other forms of play-acting and pretending. Performing the parts of characters, real or imagined, involves speaker and listener more fully in the story than can narrative alone.

Drama, strictly speaking, becomes a literary form only when it is deprived of its basic attributes. For drama—an acted story—requires actors and an audience. It is composed for performance and exists as a performance. What we read in print is only the actors' script. Therefore, unlike the more purely literary genres, it requires the participation of more than just the author to succeed or even to exist. A director and set designer, actors, stage hands, costume designers and seamstresses, even ushers all must cooperate to bring a play before an audience. The playwright cannot do it by himself. Even when read as literature, drama requires greater cooperation to succeed than do the other genres. The reader must become the stage director, scene and costume designer, stage hand, and casting director if the play is to go on. He must stage the action in his mind, with appropriate sets, props, costumes, gestures, and vocal intonations. In the twentieth century such action is more likely to be experienced mentally as a film than as a play. But there are advantages in visualizing a stage with costumed actors, scenery, and props as our imaginary background. Drama takes its shape from the expectations of the audience for which it is written.

These expectations are influenced by the physical structure of the theaters to which the audience is accustomed. The modern "picture-frame stage" opens for the audience a window on the fictional world created by the author. The audience is, as it were, spying on life. The characters are expected to behave realistically—as ordinary persons do when viewed through the windows of our houses or automobiles. The Elizabethan outdoor "platform stage," extending into the audience and rising in tiered balconies at the rear, tended to rub out the line between actor and spectator. The audience was physically close to the action. In prologues, epilogues, soliloquies, asides, and other speeches directed or half-directed to the audience, the spectators were recognized as co-participants with the actors in the dramatic illusion.

> Thou seest we are not all alone unhappy:
> This wide and universal theater
> Presents more woeful pageants than the scene
> Wherein we play.

These lines from Shakespeare's *As You Like It,* spoken by a banished duke to a bitter courtier, refer to the discovery of two hungry wanderers nearby in the forest. They also, by the proper gesture, could be made to include

See **Appendix X:** *Romeo and Juliet*
Review for a depiction of the Globe
stage.

the audience seated in the actual theater (the word *theater* literally denotes
the world), whose faces, postures, and clothes indicate various degrees of good
or evil fortune. Or, on the other hand, half-facing the audience, the duke
could be made to address both the courtier and the audience, assuring all
present that others suffer as well as they. In either case, the audience is brought
through the window or picture frame (like Alice through the looking-glass)
to mingle with the characters.

Our enjoyment of Shakespeare's *Romeo and Juliet* is increased greatly
by our understanding something of the Elizabethan theater. It was simple
and adaptable. The balcony immediately above the stage floor served as the
balcony of Juliet's room from which Juliet is overheard by Romeo in the
garden (II.ii). The shop of the apothecary (V.i) would be suggested by the
balcony and a curtained recess: living quarters above (from which he is hailed
by Romeo) and place of business below. Separate action could be going on
simultaneously on more than one level. In scene four of act three Capulet
consoles Paris about the interruption of his courtship of Juliet by Tybalt's
death and the need to scale down their plans for the wedding. In scene five
Romeo and Juliet, now married, come from her room onto the balcony speaking
their final words of farewell. Their presence is doubtless visible above throughout
the preceding scene while Capulet is discussing the wedding with Paris below.
Stage location thus creates one of the most notable ironies in Elizabethan
drama.

Not only irony but also all the other elements of literature we have studied
are powerfully present in the play. Notice that most of the play is in poetry—
usually unrhymed but poetry nonetheless. Romeo, on finding Juliet beautifully
preserved in death (she is only unconscious), exclaims:

> O my love, my wife,
> Death, that hath suck'd the honey of thy breath
> Hath had no power yet upon thy beauty.
> Thou art not conquer'd; beauty's ensign yet
> Is crimson in thy lips and in thy cheeks,
> And death's pale flag is not advanced there. (V.iii.92-7)

Romeo's words compare death to a bee and to a military conqueror. The
face of Juliet is both a flower and a battlefield on which beauty is contending
with death. The comparisons are rich in meaning. The Bible speaks of the
sting of death (I Cor. 15:55-56). Romeo expands the Biblical metaphor into
a compliment. Death, approaching Juliet, forgot to sting her. Distracted by
the beauty of her face and the fragrance of her breath, it instead sucked the
nectar of her breath (stopped her breathing). It kissed her and left her radiant
as before. The paleness of death's horse in Revelation 6:8 is extended to death's
military banner, the "ensign" of his advance. Beauty's red banner—the crimson
of her lips and cheeks—has not been displaced by the pale banner of death—
the bloodless white or gray of his victims. Beauty therefore has escaped death
by both deception and force.

have others guess which character
spoke the line. Students should seek
for quotations that include some sort
of clue to the character's identity
(e.g., "My only love sprung from my
only hate!") rather than those that are
trivial or needlessly obscure.

3. Divide the class into groups. Have
each group characterize one person
in the play, being sure to note specific passages. One member of the
group then gives the findings to the
class.

4. Have someone who has directed or
acted in a play talk to your class
about the experience.

5. Prepare a scene from the play and
present this dramatization to another
school or to your own student body
or parent/teacher association.

6. Assign parts and read the play aloud.

7. Make a mural of several key scenes in
the play (e.g., Capulet's ball, the balcony scene, Mercutio's death, the Capulets' vault).

8. Have a student write an "on-the-
spot" report about an event in the
play. Instruct him to write the report
as if it were to be presented for a television or radio broadcast.

9. Play some music from the Elizabethan period. Consult *The
Timetables of History* (available from

10. Ask a student to give an explanation or interpretation of a specific soliloquy such as Juliet's in Act II, Scene ii.

11. Ask several students to prepare a Shakespearean display before you begin the study of Shakespeare and *Romeo and Juliet*. Let them use pictures and information you have plus anything else they can send for, locate from other teachers or students, download from the Internet, or find in a library. Students may wish to make a scale model of the Globe Theatre, based on the drawing in **Appendix X:** *Romeo and Juliet* **Review** and other sources.

12. Have a student read the myth "Pyramus and Thisbe" from *Mythology* by Edith Hamilton or another mythology book. Then ask the student to compare Romeo and Juliet with Pyramus and Thisbe. You may also wish to present Shakespeare's hilarious parody of Pyramus and Thisbe, found in Act V of *A Midsummer Night's Dream.*

13. The text discusses irony in Unit 6. See if the students recognize ironic happenings in the play. Have them keep a list of ironic events as they occur in the play. *(Examples: A boy and girl from enemy families fall in love; Romeo kills Tybalt, his wife's cousin; Paris wants Friar Lawrence to perform his marriage to Juliet, but the Friar has already married Romeo and Juliet; Friar John does not deliver the message to Romeo*

The theme of the play concerns youth—its strengths and limitations, its dreams and disappointments, its dangers and splendors. Youth is a time of crucial choices and decisions. The consequences of these choices and decisions often continue throughout life. They may be foreseeable or unforeseeable. Often they are foreseen by the old but unforeseen by the young. The play is about choosing, especially in love—its mystery, its finality, and its need for wise judgment. "I stand on sudden haste," declares Romeo. "Wisely and slow," replies the Friar; "they stumble that run fast" (II.iii.83-4).

The play is also therefore about responsibility. Who are responsible for the deaths of Romeo and Juliet? The feuding houses? Tybalt? the Friar? Romeo and Juliet themselves? Must a person accept responsibility for unwise behavior to which he was provoked? Can more than one person be responsible for an act? Notice the frequent mention of tempering or temperance—that is, of balance and self-control.

Notice also the care with which Shakespeare establishes the tone of the play concerning the love of Romeo and Juliet. The play stresses the worthiness of the relationship. The Friar will have no part in Romeo's business until he is convinced that Romeo's desire for Juliet is genuine and chaste (II.iii). Romeo and Juliet do not appear in Juliet's room or in any other room alone until after they have been married by the Friar. Romeo does wrong in killing Tybalt (III.i) and Paris (V.iii), and both lovers err in taking their lives at the end (V.iii). But the provocation is strong, and the play is both condemning and forgiving. Though drama excludes the author's speaking voice (he cannot tell us what to think about the characters or incidents), it implies the author's judgments in various ways. The Friar and the Prince seem to be spokesmen for the attitudes that Shakespeare would have us adopt toward the lovers and the course of events.

Though the Bible does not offer examples of drama intended for stage performance, the book of Job has been adapted for the stage. Also the Song of Solomon is in dialogue form and has been analyzed as drama. It is interesting that these two books treat the central questions raised by *Romeo and Juliet.* Eliphaz, Bildad, and Zophar attribute Job's sufferings to secret, unconfessed sin. God, they say, does not punish the good or prosper the wicked. He takes a personal interest in His creatures and deals with them reasonably and predictably. Job, they insist, slanders God by contending otherwise. Elihu replies that God's ways are mysterious, unknowable. The good may suffer, the wicked may prosper. Only a proud man thinks that he can understand God's ways or that he has any claim on God's attention. Job, says Elihu, is arrogant in judging God by a human standard. Each view is true up to a point but distorts the character of God by excluding the other. The voice of God in chapters 38-41 expresses both sides of His nature. God cares for the smallest of His creatures and yet is ultimately incomprehensible. He is both good and great, both personally attentive and transcendent. It follows that the situations of life are not the result of blind forces acting haphazardly. There are no such things as "star-crossed lovers." Everyone's "fate" is the product of his own will interacting with God's. Everyone must take responsibility for his own life's decisions and choices.

The Song of Solomon glorifies chaste love between man and woman. The speakers are the king and his bride. The story, implied, is of love—romantic love—fulfilled in marriage. The theme—the excellence and permanence of love—is identical to that in *Romeo and Juliet*. It is stated near the end.

> Set me as a seal upon thine heart, as a seal upon thine arm: for love is strong as death; jealousy is cruel as the grave: the coals thereof are coals of fire, which hath a most vehement flame. Many waters cannot quench love, neither can the floods drown it: if a man would give all the substance of his house for love, it would utterly be contemned. (8:6-7)

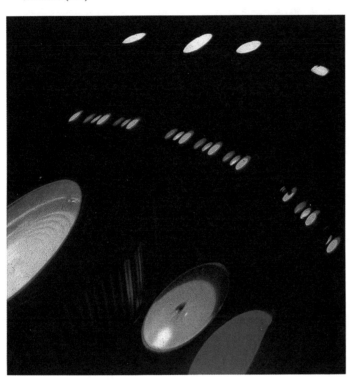

explaining what has happened to Juliet; Romeo kills himself shortly before Juliet awakens and Friar Lawrence arrives.)

14. Ask the students to look for puns as they read the play (e.g., as Mercutio is dying he says, "Ask for me tomorrow, and you shall find me a grave man").

Essay Suggestions

Allow students to choose from the list of essay ideas below, or assign them as you see fit. See **Writing Rubric 10-1: Dissecting a Drama** for help in grading the essays. Students must support their ideas with evidence from the play itself.

1. According to the sonnet which precedes Act I of the play, Romeo and Juliet are "star-cross'd lovers." This initial allusion to astrology is followed in the text of the play by numerous references to fate, fortune, and the stars. List these allusions as you read the play. What effect do they have on your impression of the final outcome of the action for the main characters? What effect does the prologue have on the audience's perception of the plot from the very beginning?

2. One important theme of the play, haste, is closely related to the play's economical time scheme. Describe the way in which Shakespeare uses this recurring motif through the plot and/or imagery of several scenes of the play.

3. The Friar proposes four different

credible plans to enable the young lovers to be happily united, but each is in turn thwarted. Describe each plan and its subsequent frustration. What does Shakespeare thus suggest about the destiny of the "star-cross'd lovers"? What does he suggest about man's exercise of his own free will to direct his destiny? (For information regarding the Friar's four plans, see teacher's edition pages 383-84.)

4. Shakespeare complements his characterization of Romeo by surrounding him with other young men who are similar to Romeo in certain respects and different from him in others. What can we conclude about Romeo by analyzing the characters of Benvolio, Paris, Mercutio, and Tybalt? Consider the words and actions of each as well as the final outcome of the plot for each.

5. The character of Juliet is defined in part by her relationship to her mother and to the Nurse. In what matters is she ruled by her mother's advice? In what matters does she reject her mother's views? At what point does she separate herself from the Nurse? How is Juliet similar to and different from her mother and the Nurse in her attitudes toward love, marriage, and men in general?

6. Discuss the effect of Shakespeare's use of the recurring imagery of light and darkness (and day and night) by commenting on its function in several scenes in the play. Does Shakespeare use light and darkness in this context in a conventional poetic sense?

The Tragedy of Romeo and Juliet

William Shakespeare

The facts of Shakespeare's life do very little to illuminate his writing. Born in Stratford, England, to a prominent merchant and later town official, he had the advantage of very good training in the village school. Taught by an Oxford M.A., the school offered today's equivalent of an undergraduate major in the Latin classics. Exactly when the teen-age William left Stratford for London and joined the Lord Chamberlain's players is not known. During the late 1500s and early 1600s (the main portion of his career) he averaged writing almost two plays a year while acting and helping administer the affairs of the company. The best of these plays are considered among the highest achievements of human art. They are also among the most interesting, as you may already have discovered. A stockholder as well as actor and playwright in his company, Shakespeare knew how important it was to please the nonliterary members of the audience as well as the highly educated minority. The performances had to entertain in order to show a profit. All the evidence indicates that they did.

Though we do not know much about Shakespeare's personal life, we do know a great deal about what he read; and that knowledge is much more important for our understanding of his writing. The curriculum of the Elizabethan "grammar school" (the grammar studied was, of course, Latin) was fairly well standardized, and reflections of his classroom reading appear constantly in his plays. Of the standard Latin works assigned, a favorite was the Metamorphoses *of the Roman poet Ovid, a veritable library of classical mythology containing tales of miraculous transformations. Ovid's story of Pyramus and Thisbe, the unfortunate eloping lovers of ancient Babylon, furnished the basic plot of* Romeo and Juliet *and also of* A Midsummer Night's Dream, *written the same year (1595). Chief among the works with which Shakespeare was well acquainted was the Bible, read publicly every day in the Elizabethan church and school. Its influence is shown in the abundance of Biblical allusions and verbal echoes in the plays and the reflection of Biblical truth in their themes.*

The Tragedy of Romeo and Juliet, by William Shakespeare, Bob Jones University Classic Players.
(Each of the photographs in Unit 10 is from this production.)

in five plays; *Romeo and Juliet* is the only tragedy among them. In fact, his authorship of this particular prologue may be doubtful, for it does not appear with the text in the First Folio. It is, however, a typical prologue in its function: it lays the scene of the action, refers to the plot in general terms, and calls attention to the audience's relationships to the actors and the drama. Notice the reference in line 12 to the duration of the performance: "the two hours traffic of our stage." Since *Romeo* is three thousand lines long, it could not have been performed in only two hours—that is, at the rate of two hundred words per minute.

This prologue is the first of three sonnets embedded in *Romeo.* It is English in form, rhyming *ababcdcdefefgg* and consisting of three quatrains

and a couplet. (The other two sonnets in the play are Romeo and Juliet's first conversation, at I.v.93-106, and the prologue to Act II.)

For the interpreter of *Romeo and Juliet,* the prologue to Act I is among the most difficult passages in the play. Taken literally, it denies free will to Romeo and Juliet, whom it labels "star-cross'd lovers." The play as a whole, however, weighs free will against fate. As students read the play, have them consider these important questions: Why do Romeo and Juliet have to die? Are they helpless victims of fate? Are they doomed from the beginning of the play? Do their deaths come about as a result of their own actions? What freewill choices do they make? What character weaknesses does Shakespeare attribute to them?

Characters

The Montague Household and Friends

Montague
Lady Montague
Romeo, their son
Balthasar, Romeo's servant
Benvolio, Montague's nephew and friend to Romeo
Mercutio, Romeo's friend and kinsman to Prince Escalus
Abram, servant

The Capulet Household and Friends

Capulet
Lady Capulet
Juliet, their daughter
Nurse, Juliet's attendant
Peter, Nurse's servant
Tybalt, Lady Capulet's nephew
Sampson, servant
Gregory, servant
Potpan, servant
Clown, servant
Old Capulet, Capulet's cousin
Paris, noble suitor to Juliet
Petruchio, a (mute) follower of Tybalt

Neutral Parties

Chorus
Escalus, Prince of Verona
Friar Lawrence, Franciscan counselor to Romeo and Juliet
Friar John, Franciscan priest
An Apothecary of Mantua
Citizens of Verona, Gentlemen and Ladies of both houses, Pages, Maskers, Torch-bearers, Musicians, Guards, Watchmen, Servants, Attendants

Setting

Place: Verona and Mantua, Italy
Time: Early Fourteenth Century

Note with students the clear example of foreshadowing here. Shakespeare is such a master of his art that he can give away the ending of the play in the first fourteen lines and still hold our attention for all the acts to follow. Note that all types of imaginative comparison (metaphors, similes, etc.) as well as sound devices (alliteration, consonance, etc.), and irony abound in the play; most of them are not marked in this teacher's edition.

Encourage students to notice how little time passes during the play's events.

Act I

Prologue

*Enter Chorus.**

CHORUS   Two households, both alike in dignity,
In fair Verona, where we lay our scene,
From ancient grudge break to new mutiny,*
Where civil* blood makes civil hands unclean.
From forth the fatal loins of these two foes   5
A pair of star-cross'd* lovers take their life;
Whose misadventur'd piteous overthrows*
Doth with their death bury their parents' strife.
The fearful passage* of their death-mark'd love
And the continuance of their parents' rage,   10
Which, but their children's end, nought could remove,
Is now the two hours traffic* of our stage;
The which if you with patient ears attend,
What here shall miss,* our toil shall strive to mend.*

Exit Chorus.

Chorus: An actor who summarizes in general terms the play and comments on its moral significance
mutiny: fighting
civil: citizens'

star-cross'd: doomed by having been born under the wrong astrological signs
overthrows: fates
passage: course

traffic: subject

What . . . miss: What we perform ineffectually *mend:* make better (in future performances)

Scene I

Time: Sunday morning
Place: A public street in Verona

Jesting leads to quarreling between the servants of Capulet and Montague, rekindling an ancient feud. The Prince stills the commotion, sternly warning both houses not to break the peace again. Romeo's parents discuss with Benvolio their son's recent bizarre behavior. Romeo himself explains that he is scorned by one he loves, Rosaline.

Enter SAMPSON and GREGORY, with swords and bucklers, of the house of Capulet.

SAMPSON   Gregory, on my word, we'll not carry coals.*

carry coals: take insults graciously

Act I, Scene i

In the beginning of this two-part scene the Montague-Capulet feud is introduced. Significantly, the servants, not the nobility, of the two houses quarrel and then fight. Notice that Tybalt is the only nonservant who is involved in the actual fighting in the street. Shakespeare instantly characterizes this young man as hotheaded and impetuous by his very first lines (ll. 35-36). Tybalt's fiery indignation is directed toward Benvolio, another young man and the one who serves as a dramatic foil to Tybalt. Benvolio's first words, "Part, fools!" also summarize his role in the play as peacemaker and normative character among the youths.

Shakespeare employs two literary symbols with which his audience would have been familiar in his introduction of Capulet. The old man enters in his nightgown, a symbol of violated domestic peace and dignity. And he wields a rusty sword, one that has not been used in a very long time. Throughout the play Capulet suggests that he has no desire to see an old feud, the original grievance of which is never mentioned, reactivated. Notice that it is the young, not the old, who keep the feud alive. In our own day this play is usually produced as an argument for determinism, the philosophy that man is merely a product of his heredity and environment. Certainly a close reading of the text does not justify such an interpretation.

The entrance of Montague reinforced for Shakespeare's audience the comic tone with which the scene begins, although the humor may be lost to modern audiences: he is a man unable to break loose from the hold of his wife (ll. 49-50). Once the Prince enters, the scene includes a medley of characters representing all ages and social ranks—young/old, servant/prince. The feud comes and goes in the first hundred lines of the scene. Through it Shakespeare introduces tragic potential in a comic context. We laugh as Capulet and Montague, too old to fight, are chided by their wives, but we also recognize the as-yet-undeveloped possibility of a feud, which, at this point in the action, only Tybalt takes seriously.

In the second part of Scene i, Shakespeare shifts his focus from the all-inclusive street brawl to the solitary figure of Romeo. The play is unusual among Shakespeare's works in its depic-

GREGORY	No, for then we should be colliers.
SAMPSON	I mean, and we be in choler,* we'll draw.*
GREGORY	Ay, while you live, draw your neck out of collar.*
SAMPSON	I strike quickly, being mov'd.
GREGORY	But thou art not quickly mov'd to strike.
SAMPSON	A dog of the house of Montague moves me.
GREGORY	To move is to stir, and to be valiant is to stand; therefore, if thou art mov'd, thou run'st away.
SAMPSON	A dog of that house shall move me to stand! I will take the wall* of any man or maid of Montague's.
GREGORY	That shows thee a weak slave, for weakest goes to the wall.* Draw thy tool, here comes two of the house of Montagues.
	Enter two other Servants, ABRAM and BALTHASAR.
SAMPSON	My naked weapon is out. Quarrel, I will back thee.
GREGORY	How, turn thy back and run?
SAMPSON	Fear me not.
GREGORY	I fear thee!
SAMPSON	Let us take the law of our sides; let them begin.
GREGORY	I will frown as I pass by and let them take it as they list.
SAMPSON	Nay, as they dare.
GREGORY	Do you quarrel, sir?
ABRAM	Quarrel, sir? No, sir.
SAMPSON	But if you do, sir, I am for you. I serve as good a man as you.

5

10

15

20

25

choler: anger *draw:* make our swords ready
draw . . . collar: avoid being hanged

take . . . wall: force to the gutterside of the walk

goes . . . wall: yields

---

tion of two complete family units: parents and son and parents and daughter. Romeo's parents here discuss with his friend Benvolio his recent bizarre behavior. Lines 88-125 establish through poetic imagery and symbolism Romeo's lovesickness. Shakespeare also introduces the play's major imagery, light and darkness, in this part of the scene. Romeo initially closes himself away from all light, for he does not want to acknowledge the truth that the woman for whom he pines will never reciprocate his love. Why? *(See ll. 184 ff. She is forsworn to love; she has purposed never to marry.)* Once he meets Juliet, however, Romeo is attracted to light; the disappointed suitor experiences true love.

Although Rosaline never appears as a character in the play, Romeo's attitudes toward her are the focus of Shakespeare's initial depiction of a protagonist who is a developing character. In his relationship to Rosaline, Romeo is a courtly lover: one who is willing to become an abject slave for a disdainful mistress; one who pines, cries, and displays symptoms of physical illness because he is scorned. Such a man is a comic butt in Shakespeare's plays, for even if he succeeds in obtaining the hand of the woman he pursues in marriage, misery is his lot. (Compare Lucentio in *The Taming of the Shrew* and Silvius in *As You Like It.* See also Sonnet 130, which satirizes courtly love poetry. Contrast it with Sonnet 147.)

Shakespeare also associates Romeo's pining for Rosaline with the carpe diem theme from medieval literature. Such profane works urge the reader to "seize the day," or to enjoy the pleasures of youth, for after a short season he will be too old to do so, or, in the case of a woman, she will no longer be attractive to men. Shakespeare "Christianizes" this old hedonistic theme by applying it in this scene to the context of marrying and perpetuating one's good qualities through offspring. (Compare Shakespeare's sonnets, particularly the first seventeen, all of which are carpe diem pieces urging the poet's patron, Southampton, to marry.) Romeo quips that in sparing herself (i.e., refusing marriage), Rosaline actually squanders herself because when she dies, she will leave behind no little Rosalines to carry on her line of beauty.

Benvolio's and Tybalt's roles as peacemaker and rabble-rouser respectively
are revealed in their first lines.

ABRAM	No better?	
SAMPSON	Well, sir.	
	Enter BENVOLIO.	
GREGORY	Say "better," here comes one of my master's kinsmen.	
SAMPSON	Yes, better, sir.	
ABRAM	You lie.	30
SAMPSON	Draw if you be men. Gregory, remember thy washing* blow.	*washing:* swashing, swordsmanlike
	They fight.	
BENVOLIO	Part, fools! Put up your swords, you know not what you do.	
	Enter TYBALT.	
TYBALT	What, art thou drawn among these heartless hinds?* Turn thee, Benvolio, look upon thy death.	35 *heartless hinds:* cowards; also a pun on female deer (hinds) that have no male (hart) to protect them
BENVOLIO	I do but keep the peace. Put up thy sword Or manage it to part these men with me.	
TYBALT	What, drawn and talk of peace? I hate the word As I hate hell, all Montagues, and thee. Have* at thee, coward!	40 *Have:* Thrust
	They fight. Enter three or four CITIZENS with clubs or partisans.	
CITIZENS	Clubs, bills,* and partisans!* Strike! Beat them down! Down with the Capulets! Down with the Montagues!	*bills:* billhooks *partisans:* broadheaded spears about nine feet long
	Enter old CAPULET in his gown, and his wife LADY CAPULET.	
CAPULET	What noise is this? Give me my sword, ho!	45

Appropriately, Romeo expresses his excessive love for Rosaline in an exaggerated, flowery poetic style. Notice the string of oxymorons that he uses in lines 146-51. (*Oxymoron* literally means "acutely silly." It is a figure of speech which combines contradictory elements.) Later in the play Juliet too will employ such a series (cf. III.ii.60-70; ask students to watch for the context and determine its significance in Shakespeare's characterization of Juliet). It is appropriate that Romeo so describe his immature, selfish love for Rosaline because her feeling for him is the opposite of his for her. This love is a phantom love, one which never materializes; hence, Rosaline never appears onstage (although she is among the guests invited to Capulet's ball). Shakespeare's intent in depicting Romeo's love for Rosaline is comic.

Finally, in the second part of Scene i Shakespeare introduces both the fictional time scheme of the play and the theme of love's relationship to the passing of time. At line 131 the dialogue establishes the time of the present action as 9:00 A.M. On the basis of specific day-of-the-week allusions in later scenes, we can thus conclude that Act I, Scene i begins on Sunday morning before 9:00 A.M. For each scene we can then pinpoint a fictional day of the week and time of day. The Prince's final words in the last scene are spoken at sunrise on Friday. Notice that at the point in Scene i at which Shakespeare first alludes to time of day (l. 131), he immediately introduces the idea that the time that a person spends away from the one he loves passes slowly, but the time that he

spends with his love always seems "short" (ll. 131-34). Trace this theme throughout the play.

LADY CAP.   A crutch, a crutch! Why call you for a sword?

CAPULET   My sword, I say! Old Montague is come,
            And flourishes his blade in spite of me.

            Enter old MONTAGUE and his wife LADY MONTAGUE.

MONTAGUE   Thou villain* Capulet!—*(To LADY MONTAGUE.)* hold me   villain: peasant, low-
            not, let me go.   born fellow

LADY MON.   Thou shalt not stir one foot to see a foe.   50

            Enter PRINCE ESCALUS with his train.

PRINCE   Rebellious subjects, enemies to peace,
            Profaners of this neighbor-stained steel—*   Profaners . . . steel:
            Will they not hear?—Who ho, you men, you beasts   Irreverent users of
            That quench the fire of your pernicious rage   weapons, stained
            With purple* fountains issuing from your veins—   55   with neighbors'
            On pain of torture, from those bloody hands   blood
            Throw your mistempered* weapons to the ground,   purple: blood-colored
            And hear the sentence* of your moved prince.
            Three civil brawls, bred of an airy word   mistempered: illforged
            By thee, old Capulet and Montague,   60   sentence: decision
            Have thrice disturb'd the quiet of our streets
            And made Verona's ancient citizens   Cast by: Throw aside
            Cast by* their grave beseeming ornaments*   ornaments: dignified
                                                                        apparel

To wield old partisans in hands as old,
Cank'red* with peace, to part your cank'red* hate   65   *Cank'red*: Rusted
If ever you disturb our streets again   *cank'red*: biting,
Your lives shall pay the forfeit of the peace.   corrosive
For this time all the rest depart away.
You, Capulet, shall go along with me,
And Montague, come you this afternoon,   70
To know our farther pleasure in this case,
To old Free-town, our common judgment-place.
Once more, on pain of death, all men depart.

Exeunt all but MONTAGUE, LADY MONTAGUE, *and*
BENVOLIO.

MONTAGUE   Who set this ancient quarrel new abroach?*   *abroach*: astir
           Speak, nephew; were you by when it began?   75

BENVOLIO   Here were the servants of your adversary
           And yours, close fighting ere I did approach.
           I drew to part them. In the instant came
           The fiery Tybalt with his sword prepar'd,
           Which, as he breath'd defiance to my ears,   80
           He swung about his head and cut the winds,
           Who, nothing hurt withal,* hiss'd him in scorn.   *withal*: by it
           While we were interchanging thrusts and blows,
           Came more and more and fought on part and part
           Till the Prince came, who parted either part.   85

LADY MON. O, where is Romeo? Saw you him today?
           Right glad I am he was not at this fray.*   *fray*: brawl

BENVOLIO   Madam, an hour before the worshipp'd sun
           Peer'd forth the golden window of the east,
           A troubled mind drew me from company,   90
           Where, underneath the grove of sycamore
           That westward rooteth from this city side,*   *city side*: side of the
           So early walking did I see your son.   city
           Towards him I made,* but he was ware* of me,   *made*: went *ware*:
           And stole into the covert* of the wood.   95   wary, cautious
           I, measuring his affections by my own,   *covert*: protecting
           Which then most sought where most might not be found,*   cover
           Being one too many by my weary self,   *where . . . found*: i.e.,
           Pursued my humour* not pursuing his,   sought privacy
           And gladly shunn'd who gladly fled from me.   100 *Pursued . . . humour*:
                                                                  Followed my
                                                                  inclination

MONTAGUE	Many a morning hath he there been seen,	
	With tears augmenting* the fresh morning's dew,	*augmenting:* increasing
	Adding to clouds more clouds with his deep sighs,	
	But all so soon as the all-cheering sun	
	Should in the farthest east begin to draw	105
	The shady curtains from Aurora's* bed,	*Aurora:* Goddess of the dawn
	Away from light steals home my heavy son,	
	And private in his chamber pens himself,	
	Shuts up his windows, locks fair daylight out,	
	And makes himself an artificial night.	110
	Black and portendous* must this humour* prove,	*portendous:* ominous *humour:* disposition
	Unless good counsel may the cause remove.	
BENVOLIO	My noble uncle, do you know the cause?	
MONTAGUE	I neither know it nor can learn of him.	
BENVOLIO	Have you importun'd* him by any means?	115 *importun'd:* pressed
MONTAGUE	Both by myself and many other friends,	
	But he, his own affections' counsellor,	
	Is to himself (I will not say how true)	
	But to himself so secret and so close,	
	So far from sounding and discovery	120
	As is the bud bit with an envious* worm	*envious:* malicious, spiteful
	Ere he can spread his sweet leaves to the air	
	Or dedicate his beauty to the same.	
	Could we but learn from whence his sorrows grow,	
	We would as willingly give cure as know.	125
	Enter ROMEO.	
BENVOLIO	See where he comes. So please you step aside;	
	I'll know his grievance or be much denied.*	*much denied:* refused after much urging
MONTAGUE	I would thou wert so happy* by thy stay*	*happy:* fortunate *stay:* lingering
	To hear true shrift.* Come, madam, let's away.	*shrift:* confession
	Exit MONTAGUE and LADY MONTAGUE.	
BENVOLIO	Good morrow, cousin.	
ROMEO	Is the day so young?	130

BENVOLIO	But new strook nine.	
ROMEO	Ay me, sad hours seem long. Was that my father that went hence so fast?	
BENVOLIO	It was. What sadness lengthens Romeo's hours?	
ROMEO	Not having that which, having, makes them short.	
BENVOLIO	In love?	135
ROMEO	Out—	
BENVOLIO	Of love?	
ROMEO	Out of her favor where I am in love.	
BENVOLIO	Alas that love, so gentle in his view, Should be so tyrannous and rough in proof!*	140

proof: experience

ROMEO	Alas that love, whose view is muffled still,*
	Should without eyes see pathways to his will!*
	Where shall we dine? O me! what fray was here?
	Yet tell me not, for I have heard it all:
	Here's much to do with hate, but more with love.

145

view . . . still: face is always covered
pathways . . . will: ways to accomplish what he wants

	Why then, O brawling love! O loving hate!
	O any thing, of nothing first creat'd!*
	O heavy lightness, serious vanity,
	Misshapen chaos of* well-seeming forms,
	Feather of lead, bright smoke, cold fire, sick health,
	Still-waking sleep, that is not what it is!
	This love feel I, that feel no love in this.*
	Dost thou not laugh?

150

any . . . creat'd: All things were created by God out of nothing, *ex nihilo.*
Misshapen . . . of: That which is made without shape
that . . . this: that have no love in return

BENVOLIO	No, coz, I rather weep.
ROMEO	Good heart, at what?
BENVOLIO	At thy good heart's oppression.
ROMEO	Why, such is love's transgression.
	Griefs of mine own lie heavy in my breast,
	Which thou wilt propagate* to have* it press'd
	With more of thine. This love that thou hast shown

155

propagate: increase *to have:* by having

	Doth add more grief to too much of mine own.	
	Love is a smoke made with the fume of sighs,	160
	Being purg'd,* a fire sparkling in lovers' eyes,	
	Being vex'd, a sea nourish'd with lovers' tears.	
	What is it else? a madness most discreet,	
	A choking gall* and a persevering sweet.	
	Farewell, my coz.	

purg'd: rid of smoke (love is)

gall: bitterness

BENVOLIO   Soft,* I will go along;   165
And if you leave me so, you do me wrong.

Soft: Not so fast

ROMEO   Tut, I have lost myself. I am not here:
This is not Romeo, he's some other where.

BENVOLIO   Tell me in sadness,* who is that you love?

sadness: seriousness (Romeo deliberately misconstrues it as "heaviness of spirit," the usual meaning today.)

ROMEO   In sadness, cousin, I do love a woman.   170

BENVOLIO   I aim'd so near* when I suppos'd you lov'd.

aimed . . . near: supposed so

ROMEO   A right good markman! And she's fair I love.

BENVOLIO   A right fair mark, fair coz, is soonest hit.

ROMEO   Well, in that hit you miss: she'll not be hit
With Cupid's arrow: She hath Dian's wit;*   175
O, she is rich in beauty, only poor
That, when she dies, with beauty dies her store.*

Dian's wit: The mind of Diana, goddess of chastity
with . . . store: Her stock of beauty will die (she will leave no offspring to continue it).
chaste: unmarried

BENVOLIO   Then she hath sworn that she will still live chaste?*

ROMEO   She hath, and in that sparing makes huge waste;
For beauty starv'd with* her severity   180
Cuts beauty off from all posterity.
She is too fair,* too wise, wisely too fair,
To merit bliss* by making me despair.
She hath forsworn* to love, and in that vow
Do I live dead that live to tell it now.   185

starv'd with: not reproduced because of

fair: (1) just (2) beautiful
merit bliss: earn her own salvation
forsworn: sworn not to

BENVOLIO   Be rul'd by me; forget to think of her.

ROMEO   O, teach me how I should forget to think.

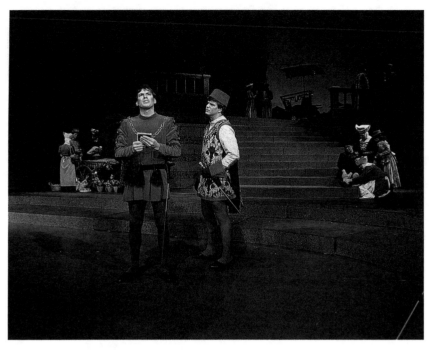

BENVOLIO	By giving liberty unto thine eyes:		
	Examine other beauties.*		*Examine . . . beauties:* Take notice of other beautiful girls.
ROMEO	'Tis the way		
	To call hers exquisite in question more.*	190	*in . . . more:* by comparing her beauty to others'
	He that is strooken blind cannot forget		
	The precious treasure of his eyesight lost.		
	Show me a mistress that is passing fair,*		*passing fair:* surpassingly beautiful
	What doth her beauty serve but as a note		
	Where I may read who pass'd* that passing* fair?	195	*pass'd:* surpassed *passing:* surpassingly
	Farewell, thou canst not teach me to forget.		
BENVOLIO	I'll pay that doctrine* or else die in debt.*		*pay . . . doctrine:* teach (you) that lesson *in debt:* without having fulfilled my obligations to you

Exeunt.

Montague and Capulet both wish to keep the peace; it is the younger generation that keeps the feud alive.

The emphasis on Juliet's youth (she is thirteen) helps support the immaturity of her hasty, often unwise, actions and decisions throughout the play.

Scene II

Time: Sunday afternoon
Place: A street

Capulet responds encouragingly to Paris's request for Juliet's hand in marriage. He then sends a servant out to invite kinsmen and friends to a feast. Unable to read, the servant encounters Romeo, who reads the list for him. Learning that Rosaline is among the guests, Romeo is persuaded by Benvolio to go to the feast uninvited.

Enter CAPULET, COUNTY PARIS, and the CLOWN, Capulet's servant.

CAPULET	But Montague is bound* as well as I,	*bound:* pledged
	In penalty alike, and 'tis not hard, I think,	
	For men so old as we to keep the peace.	
PARIS	Of honorable reckoning* are you both,	*reckoning:* reputation
	And pity 'tis you liv'd at odds so long. 5	
	But now, my lord, what say you to my suit?	
CAPULET	But saying o'er what I have said before:	
	My child is yet a stranger* in the world;	*stranger:* newcomer
	She hath not seen the change of fourteen years.	
	Let two more summers wither in their pride 10	
	Ere we may think her ripe to be a bride.	
PARIS	Younger than she are happy mothers made.	
CAPULET	And too soon marr'd are those so early made.	
	Earth hath swallowed all my hopes but she;	
	She's the hopeful lady of my earth.* 15	*hopeful . . . earth:* (1) hope for which I exist (2) heir to all I own (3) person who will carry on my line
	But woo her, gentle Paris; get her heart.	
	My will to her consent is but a part;	
	And she agreed,* within her scope of choice	*And . . . agreed:* If she agrees
	Lies my consent and fair according voice.*	*according voice:* agreement
	This night I hold an old accustom'd feast, 20	
	Whereto I have invited many a guest	

Act I, Scene ii

Whereas Scene i ends with a discussion of Montague family matters, Scene ii begins with the Capulet affairs. Lines 1-3 are evidence that the old men do not wish to keep the feud alive. Read lines 9-10 to determine Juliet's age. (This is further clarified in I.iii.6-18; she is thirteen.) Shakespeare reduced it from other contemporary versions of the plot (eighteen in one source and sixteen in another) to the earliest age at which English girls were marriageable. Why do you suppose he did so? (Consider both plot and characterization in answering this question.) At lines 14-15 Shakespeare employs microcosm imagery to describe Capulet's special relationship to his only child. The playwright found in the father-daughter relationship powerful material for characterization and imagery throughout his career. Capulet says that Juliet, as his heir and the one who will perpetuate his family line, is the center of his little world. Notice that Capulet is a sympathetic character here. Although he is carrying out his paternal responsibility to find a good husband for his daughter, he does not want to rush her or to finalize a match without her consent (ll. 10-19). Notice Capulet's dealings with the young people in the play. His motives are good, but his attempts at restraining them ironically serve only to urge them on, for he becomes angry himself.

The first coincidence of the plot occurs at lines 30 and following: a servant sent to invite guests to Capulet's feast cannot read; therefore, he stops "the learned" (ironically, a group of rowdy young men) for assistance. What important event results from this coincidental encounter? Notice that Benvolio, again acting as normative character among the young men, delivers a speech of rhymed commonplaces (ll. 33-38) to Romeo.

Analyze the Capulet guest list at lines 52-58. What is ironic about its including the names of Mercutio and Rosaline? Do you think that Shakespeare was merely careless with regard to small details or that he implies here that the feud has not actually set up inviolable social barriers? *(Answers may vary. Some students may note that on page 322 Mercutio is described as a "kinsman to Prince Escalus." That important familial relationship could have gotten him an invitation.)*

This is the first coincidence in the play: because the servant cannot read, the Montagues find out about the Capulets' ball.

Such as I love, and you, among the store
One more, most welcome, makes my number more.
At my poor house look to behold this night
Earth-treading* stars that make dark heaven light.   25   *Earth-treading:* Moving above the earth
Come go with me. *(To servant.)* Go, sirrah, trudge about
Through fair Verona; find those persons out
Whose names are written there and to them say
My house and welcome on their pleasure stay.*   *on . . . stay:* wait for their arrival

Exit with PARIS.

SERVANT   I am sent to find those persons whose names are here   30
writ, and can never find what names the writing person
hath here writ. I must to the learned. In good time!*   *In . . . time:* What good timing!

Enter BENVOLIO and ROMEO.

BENVOLIO   Tut, man, one fire burns out another's burning;
One pain is less'ned by another's anguish;
Turn giddy,* and be holp* by backward turning;*   35   *Turn giddy:* Become dizzy *holp:* helped *backward turning:* turning in reverse
One desperate grief cures with another's languish.
Take thou some new infection to thy eye,
And the rank poison of the old will die.

ROMEO   Your plantan* leaf is excellent for that.   *plantan:* plantain, a medicinal plant

BENVOLIO   For what, I pray thee?

ROMEO   For your broken shin.   40

BENVOLIO   Why, Romeo, art thou mad?*   *mad:* insane

ROMEO   Not mad, but bound more than a madman is,
Shut up in prison, kept without my food,
Whipt and tormented and—God-den*, good fellow.   *God-den:* Good evening (used after noon)

SERVANT   God gi'* God-den. I pray, sir, can you read?   45   *gi':* give you

ROMEO   Ay, mine own fortune in my misery.

SERVANT   Perhaps you have learn'd it without book.*   *without book:* by heart
But I pray, can you read any thing you see?

ROMEO   Ay, if I know the letters and the language.

SERVANT	Ye say honestly, rest you merry!*	50

rest . . . merry: farewell

ROMEO	Stay, fellow, I can read.	
	(He reads the letter.) "Signior Martino and his wife and	
	daughters; Count Anselme and his beauteous sisters; the	
	lady widow of Vitruvio; Signior Placentio and his lovely	
	nieces; Mercutio and his brother Valentine; mine uncle	55
	Capulet, his wife, and daughters; my fair niece Rosaline	
	and Livia; Signior Valentio and his cousin Tybalt; Lucio	
	and the lively Helena."	
	A fair assembly. Whither should they come?	

SERVANT	Up.	60

ROMEO	Whither? To supper.

SERVANT	To our house.

ROMEO	Whose house?

SERVANT	My master's.

ROMEO	Indeed I should have asked you that before.	65

SERVANT	Now I'll tell you without asking. My master is the great
	rich Capulet, and if you be not of the house of Montagues,
	I pray come and crush* a cup of wine. Rest you merry!

crush: drink

Exit SERVANT.

BENVOLIO	At this same feast of Capulet's	
	Sups the fair Rosaline, whom thou so lovest,	70
	With all the admired beauties of Verona.	
	Go thither, and with unattainted* eye	
	Compare her face with some that I shall show,	
	And I will make thee think thy swan a crow.	

unattainted: unbiased

ROMEO	One fairer than my love! The all-seeing sun	75
	Ne'er saw her match since first the world begun.	

BENVOLIO	Tut, you saw her fair, none else being by,	
	Herself pois'd* with herself in either eye;	
	But in that crystal scales let there be weigh'd	
	Your lady's love against some other maid	80

pois'd: balanced

That I will show you shining at this feast,
And she shall scant* show well that now seems best.   *scant:* scarcely

ROMEO   I'll go along no such sight to be shown,
But to rejoice in splendor of mine own.

Exeunt.

Scene III

Time: Sunday afternoon
Place: A room in Capulet's house

Lady Capulet and the Nurse encourage the hesitant Juliet to receive Paris's proposal favorably.

Enter LADY CAPULET and NURSE.

LADY CAP.   Nurse, where's my daughter? Call her forth to me.

NURSE   I bade her come. What, lamb! What, ladybird!*   *ladybird:* sweetheart
Where's this girl? What, Juliet!

Enter JULIET.

JULIET   How now, who calls?

NURSE   Your mother.

JULIET   Madam, I am here; what is your will?   5

LADY CAP.   This is the matter. Nurse, give leave a while;
We must talk in secret. Nurse, come back again;
I have rememb'red me, thou's hear* our counsel.*   *thou's hear:* thou shalt
Thou knowest my daughter's of a pretty age.   hear *counsel:* private
                                                conversation

NURSE   Faith, I can tell her age unto an hour.   10

LADY CAP.   She's not fourteen.

Act I, Scene iii

This is a scene of exposition with regard to Juliet. It focuses on her relationship to Lady Capulet and the Nurse. One way in which Shakespeare defines the character of Juliet is by depicting these two older women as foils to her, not so much in physical appearance (although the differences between Juliet and the Nurse would have been a source of comedy for Shakespeare's audience) as in attitudes toward love, marriage, and men in general. The subject which in this scene effects their comments along these lines is Paris. The two older women see love as physical attraction and marriage as a means of self-advancement. Does Juliet ultimately adopt their values? *(no)*

The age of Lady Capulet is a matter of critical dispute which hinges on the reading of line 37. Some versions of the play read "I was your mother," and others, "I was a mother." What is the difference in terms of Shakespeare's characterization of Lady Capulet? *(If Juliet were born when Lady Capulet was Juliet's current age, Lady Capulet is roughly twenty-six years old. Yet in V.iii.208, she refers to her "old age." Probably, then, "I was a mother" is the more likely reading.)* In quartos 2-6 her speeches in this scene are prefixed *Old Lady.*

NURSE	I'll lay fourteen of my teeth—		
	And yet, to my teen* be it spoken, I have but four—		*teen:* sorrow
	She's not fourteen. How long is it now		
	To Lammas-tide?*	15	*Lammas-tide:* August 1, a church festival in honor of harvest (and thus a symbol of early ripening); thus the action of the play is set in July.

LADY CAP.   A fortnight and odd days.

NURSE	Even or odd, of all days in the year,	
	Come Lammas-eve at night shall she be fourteen.	
	Susan and she—God rest all Christian souls!—	
	Were of an age. Well, Susan is with God;	20
	She was too good for me. But as I said,	
	On Lammas-eve at night she shall be fourteen.	
	'Tis since the earthquake now eleven years,	
	And she was wean'd—I never shall forget it—	

LADY CAP.   Enough of this, I pray thee hold thy peace.   25

NURSE	Peace, I have done. God mark thee to his grace!	
	Thou wast the prettiest babe that e'er I nurs'd.	
	An* might I live to see thee married once,	*An:* If
	I have my wish.	

LADY CAP.	Indeed, that "marry" is the very theme	30
	I came to talk of. Tell me, daughter Juliet,	
	How stands your dispositions to be married?	

JULIET   It is an honor that I dream not of.

LADY CAP.	Well, think of marriage now; younger than you,	
	Here in Verona, ladies of esteem,	35
	Are made already mothers. By my count,	
	I was your mother much upon these years*	*much . . . years:* about the same age
	That you are now a maid. Thus then in brief,	
	The valiant Paris seeks you for his love.	

| NURSE | A man, young lady! Lady, such a man | 40 |
| | As all the world—why, he's a man of wax.* | *man . . . wax:* perfect of feature, like a wax model |

LADY CAP.   Verona's summer hath not such a flower.

NURSE   Nay, he's a flower, in faith, a very flower.

LADY CAP.	What say you? Can you love the gentleman?	
	This night you shall behold him at our feast; 45	
	Read o'er the volume of young Paris' face,	
	And find delight writ there with beauty's pen;	
	Examine every married* lineament	*married:* matched, symmetrical
	And see how one another lends content;*	*content:* This phrase continues the book metaphor.
	And what obscured in this fair volume lies 50	
	Find written in the margent* of his eyes.	*margent:* margin (which in books often supplied commentary
	This precious book of love, this unbound lover,	
	To beautify him only lacks a cover.*	*cover:* binding; i.e., the binding of marriage vows
	The fish lives in the sea, and 'tis much pride	
	For fair without* the fair within* to hide. 55	*fair without:* outward beauty *fair within:* inward beauty
	That book in many's eyes doth share the glory	
	That in gold clasps* locks in the golden story;	*gold clasps:* (1)the lock of a book (2)wedding rings
	So shall you share all that he doth possess,	
	By having him, making yourself no less.	
	Speak briefly, can you like of Paris' love? 60	

JULIET	I'll look* to like, if looking liking move;*	*look:* expect *move:* arouse
	But no more deep will I endart* mine eye	*endart:* shoot forth
	Than your consent gives strength to make it fly.	

Enter CLOWN.

CLOWN	Madam, the guests are come, supper serv'd up, you call'd,	
	my young lady ask'd for, the nurse curs'd in the pantry, 65	
	and every thing in extremity. I must hence to wait; I	
	beseech you follow straight.	

Exit CLOWN.

LADY CAP.	We follow thee. Juliet, the County* stays.*	*County:* Count, i.e., Paris *stays:* waits for you

Exeunt.

Scene IV

Time: Sunday evening
Place: A street near Capulet's house

Masked, Romeo and his friends go to Capulet's feast in an exuberant, frolicsome mood.

Act I, Scene iv

This scene is built around Mercutio's Queen Mab speech (ll. 29-72). Carefully consider the lines by Romeo which precede and follow it. Just before Romeo meets Juliet (in the next scene), Shakespeare reinforces for the audience the immature quality of his affection for Rosaline. Mercutio's famous lines about the creative power of the imagination and the shallowness of wish-fulfillment dreams are directly applicable to Romeo, a vain dreamer at this point in the play. In light of Mercutio's import, we do not take very seriously Romeo's musings about fatal omens at the end of the scene. The play to this point remains pure comedy.

Enter ROMEO, MERCUTIO, BENVOLIO, with five or six other MASKERS,* and TORCH-BEARERS.

ROMEO | What, shall this speech be spoke for our excuse?*
Or shall we go in without apology?

BENVOLIO | The date is out of such prolixity:*
We'll have no Cupid* hoodwink'd* with a scarf,
Bearing a Tartar's painted bow of lath,*   5
Scaring the ladies like a crow-keeper,*
Nor no without-book* prologue, faintly spoke
After the prompter, for our entrance;
But let them measure us by what they will;
We'll measure them a measure* and be gone.   10

ROMEO | Give me a torch; I am not for this ambling.
Being but heavy,* I will bear the light.

MERCUTIO | Nay, gentle Romeo, we must have you dance.

ROMEO | Not I, believe me. You have dancing shoes
With nimble soles; I have a soul of lead   15
So stakes me to the ground I cannot move.

MERCUTIO | You are a lover; borrow Cupid's wings,
And soar with them above a common bound.*

ROMEO | I am too sore enpierced with his shaft
To soar with his light feathers and so bound   20
I cannot bound a pitch* above dull woe.
Under love's heavy burden do I sink. *(Puts on a mask.)*
A torch for me. Let wantons light of heart
Tickle the senseless rushes* with their heels.

MERCUTIO | Why, may one ask?   25

ROMEO | I dreamt a dream tonight.

MERCUTIO | And so did I.

ROMEO | Well, what was yours?

MERCUTIO | That dreamers often lie.

maskers: those wearing masks, participants in either a masquerade or a masque
shall . . . excuse: Shall we have a presenter introduce us with a speech?
The . . . prolixity: Long introductions are outdated.
Cupid: Boy dressed as Cupid (to present us) *hoodwink'd:* blindfolded
Tartar's . . . lath: Short, curved, lip-shaped archer's bow
crow-keeper: scarecrow
without-book: unmemorized
measure . . . measure: deal them out a dance
heavy: low in spirits

common bound: dancing leap

pitch: leap

rushes: floor covering

ROMEO	In bed asleep while they do dream things true.

MERCUTIO O then I see Queen Mab hath been with you.
She is the fairies' midwife, and she comes   30
In shape no bigger than an agot-stone*
On the forefinger of an alderman,*
Drawn with a team of little atomies*
Athwart men's noses as they lie asleep.
Her wagon spokes made of long spinners'* legs,   35
The cover of the wings of grasshoppers;
The traces* of the smallest spider web;
The collars of the moonshine's wat'ry beams;
Her whip of cricket's bone, the lash of films;*
Her wagoner a small grey-coated gnat,   40
Not half so big as a round little worm
Prick'd from the lazy finger of a maid.*
Her chariot is an empty hazel-nut,
Made by the joiner* squirrel or old grub,
Time out a' mind* the fairies' coachmakers.   45
And in this state* she gallops night by night
Through lovers' brains, and then they dream of love;
O'er courtiers' knees, that dream on cur'sies* straight;*
O'er lawyers' fingers, who straight dream on fees;
O'er ladies' lips, who straight on kisses dream,   50
Which oft the angry Mab with blisters plagues
Because their breaths with sweetmeats tainted are.
Sometime she gallops o'er a courtier's nose,
And then dreams he of smelling out a suit;*
And sometime comes she with a tithe-pig's tail*   55
Tickling a parson's nose as 'a lies asleep;
Then he dreams of another benefice.*
Sometime she driveth o'er a soldier's neck,
And then dreams he of cutting foreign throats,
Of breaches,* ambuscadoes,* Spanish blades,*   60
Of healths five fathom deep; and then anon*
Drums in his ear, at which he starts* and wakes,
And being thus frighted, swears a prayer or two
And sleeps again.

ROMEO   Peace, peace, Mercutio, peace!
Thou talk'st of nothing.

MERCUTIO   True, I talk of dreams,   65
Which are the children of an idle brain,

Margin glosses:

agot-stone: agate
alderman: member of the town council
atomies: tiny creatures

spinners': daddy-long-legs'

traces: harness

films: thin membranous coating

the . . . maid: According to folklore, worms grew in the fingers of lazy girls.
joiner: carpenter
Time . . . mind: Since time began
state: splendor

cur'sies: curtsies, bows *straight:* immediately

smelling . . . suit: finding a client
tithe-pig's tail: tail of a pig used in payment of a church tithe
benefice: ecclesiastical appointment

breaches: breaking down *ambuscadoes:* ambushes *Spanish blades:* fine swords
anon: immediately
starts: jumps up

Begot of nothing but vain fantasy,
Which is as thin of substance as the air
And more inconstant than the wind, who woos
Even now the frozen bosom of the north,   70
And, being anger'd,* puffs away from thence,
Turning his side to the dew-dropping south.

anger'd: i.e., because
he cannot thaw the
North

BENVOLIO   This wind you talk of blows us from ourselves:
            Supper is done, and we shall come too late.

ROMEO   I fear too early, for my mind misgives   75
            Some consequence yet hanging in the stars
            Shall bitterly begin his fearful date
            With this night's revels,* and expire the term*
            Of a despised life clos'd in my breast
            By some vile forfeit of untimely* death.   80

revels: merry making
expire . . . term:
bring the end, in the
sense of the forfei-
ture of an unpaid
mortgage
untimely: premature

But He that hath the steerage of my course
Direct my sail! On, lusty gentleman!

BENVOLIO   Strike, drum.

Exeunt.

Scene V

Time: Sunday evening
Place: A hall in Capulet's house

*Capulet welcomes his guests and then chides Tybalt for being offended by
the intrusion of Romeo and his friends. Unaware of each other's identity,
Romeo and Juliet meet and fall in love.*

SERVINGMEN come forth with napkins.

SERVANT 1   Where's Potpan that he helps not to take away? He shift a
trencher?* he scrape a trencher?

> *trencher:* wooden platter

SERVANT 2   When good manners shall lie all in one or two men's
hands, and they unwash'd too, 'tis a foul thing.

SERVANT 1   Away with the joint-stools;* remove the court-cubberd;*   5
look to the plate.* Good thou, save me a piece of
marchpane,* and as thou loves me, let the porter let in
Susan Grindstone and Nell.

> *joint-stools:* folding stools *court-cubberd:* sideboard *plate:* silver flatware *marchpane:* marzipan (molded cake made with almond paste)

Exit SERVANT 2.

Anthony and Potpan!

Enter ANTHONY and POTPAN.

ANTHONY   Ay, boy, ready.   10

SERVANT 1   You are look'd for and call'd for ask'd for and sought for
in the great chamber.

POTPAN   We cannot be here and there too. Cheerly, boys, be brisk a
while, and the longer liver take all.*

> *the . . . all:* enjoy life while it lasts

Act I, Scene v

The scene opens with a brief humorous exchange among the servingmen and moves to a section in which Shakespeare enriches the characterization of Capulet. On the basis of his exchange with an old man of his family (ll. 28-40), what is his approximate age? *(Capulet and Old Capulet debate whether it has been twenty-five or thirty years since they "mask'd"; Capulet must be at least forty.)* In his dealings with Tybalt (ll. 54-92), what are his intentions? In reality, what is the effect of his words to Tybalt? *(He attempts to keep peace; he ends up enraging Tybalt further.)* Notice that ironically as he seeks to control Tybalt's rage, he becomes enraged himself. As a host, Capulet is complimented, not offended, that uninvited guests have appeared at his feast.

Tybalt, hotheaded as he is, takes the intrusion as occasion for revenge.

Romeo falls in love with Juliet at first sight of her. On Shakespeare's stage such a love usually proved to be a lasting one, although the course of its development was not free from difficulties. In this context Tybalt hears Romeo at approximately the same moment Romeo sees Juliet. Thus Shakespeare creates a complicated stage moment in which hate intrudes upon a scene of love. Theme and structure—the relationship of love to hate—become one.

Romeo and Juliet's first conversation (ll. 93-106) forms an embedded sonnet. What is the rhyme scheme of these fourteen lines? *(ababcbcbdedeff)* The poem is built around a central image: Romeo is a pilgrim, or one who

travels in quest of a religious goal. Juliet is the shrine at which he seeks to worship; she is also the statue of a saint. Romeo prays to her, and she grants his request for a kiss, symbolizing their mutuality in love.

The scene ends with first Romeo's and then Juliet's discovery of the other's identity. Juliet expresses her reaction in the form of a paradox: "My only love sprung from my only hate!" (l. 134). Shakespeare's paradoxes in this play function to reinforce the characterization of the protagonists and their perception of love and hate as irreconcilable forces.

Exit SERVANT 1, ANTHONY, and POTPAN. Enter CAPULET,
LADY CAPULET, JULIET, TYBALT, NURSE, SERVINGMEN,
GENTLEMEN, LADIES, and MASKERS.

CAPULET   Welcome, gentlemen! Ladies that have their toes   15
                Unplagu'd with corns will have a bout* with you.
                Ah, my mistresses, which of you all
                Will now deny to dance? She that makes dainty,*
                She I'll swear, hath corns. Am I come near ye now?
                Welcome, gentlemen! I have seen the day   20
                That I have worn a visor and could tell
                A whispering tale in a fair lady's ear,
                Such as would please; 'tis gone, 'tis gone, 'tis gone.
                You are welcome, gentlemen! Come musicians, play.

                Musicians play, and they dance.

                A hall, a hall,* give room! And foot it, girls!   25
                More light, you knaves, and turn the tables up*
                And quench the fire; the room is grown too hot.
                Ah, sirrah, this unlook'd-for sport comes well.
                Nay, sit, nay, sit, good cousin Capulet,
                For you and I are past our dancing days.   30
                How long is't now since last yourself and I
                Were in mask?

OLD CAP.   By my count, thirty years.

CAPULET   What, man? 'tis not so much, 'tis not so much:
                'Tis since the nuptial of Lucentio,   35
                Come Pentecost* as quickly as it will,
                Some five and twenty years, and then we mask'd.

OLD CAP.   'Tis more, 'tis more. His son is elder, sir;
                His son is thirty.

CAPULET   Will you tell me that?
                His son was but a ward* two years ago.   40

ROMEO   *(To SERVANT.)* What lady's that which doth enrich the hand
                Of yonder knight?

SERVANT 2   I know not, sir.

will . . . bout: will
   dance a measure

makes dainty: refuses

A . . . hall: Clear the
   floor
turn . . . up: stack the
   tables

Pentecost: Church
   festival on the sev
   enth Sunday after
   Easter

ward: minor

ROMEO	O, she doth teach the torches to burn bright!		
	It seems she hangs upon the cheek of night	45	
	As a rich jewel in an Ethiop's ear—		
	Beauty too rich for use, for earth too dear!		
	So shows a snowy dove trooping* with crows		*trooping:* moving in a throng
	As yonder lady o'er her fellows shows.		
	The measure* done, I'll watch her place of stand,	50	*measure:* dance
	And touching hers, make blessed my rude* hand.		*rude:* rough
	Did my heart love till now? Forswear it, sight!		
	For I ne'er saw true beauty till this night.		
TYBALT	This, by his voice, should be a Montague.		
	Fetch me my rapier, boy. What dares the slave	55	
	Come hither, cover'd with an antic face,*		*antic face:* grotesque mask
	To fleer* and scorn at our solemnity?*		*fleer:* mock *solemnity:* celebration
	Now by the stock and honor of my kin,		
	To strike him dead I hold it not a sin.		
CAPULET	Why, how now, kinsman, wherefore storm you so?	60	
TYBALT	Uncle, this is a Montague, our foe;		
	A villain that is hither come in spite		
	To scorn at our solemnity this night.		
CAPULET	Young Romeo is it?		
TYBALT	'Tis he, that villain Romeo.		
CAPULET	Content thee, gentle coz, let him alone,	65	
	'A bears him like a portly* gentleman;		*portly:* well-mannered
	And to say truth, Verona brags of him		
	To be a virtuous and well-govern'd youth.		
	I would not for the wealth of all this town		
	Here in my house do him disparagement;*	70	*disparagement:* disrespect
	Therefore be patient; take no note of him;		
	It is my will, the which if thou respect,		
	Show a fair presence and put off these frowns,		
	An ill-beseeming semblance* for a feast.		*ill-beseeming semblance:* inappropriate appearance
TYBALT	It fits when such a villain is a guest.	75	
	I'll not endure him.		

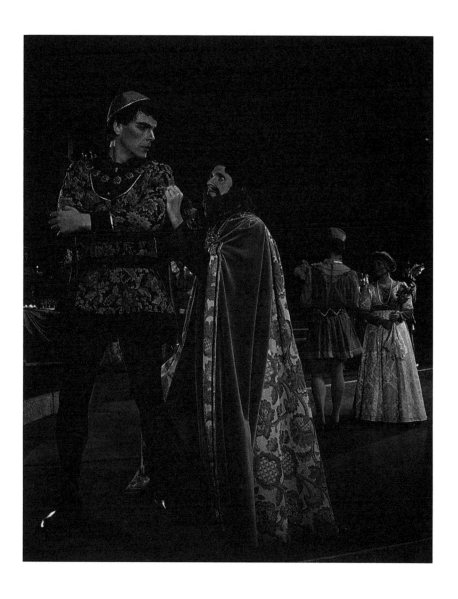

This embedded sonnet incorporates religious symbolism to emphasize the purity of Romeo and Juliet's love.

CAPULET   He shall be endured.
What, goodman boy?* I say he shall, go to!
Am I the master here, or you? Go to!*
You'll not endure him! God shall mend my soul,
You'll make a mutiny among my guests!   80
You will set cock-a-hoop!* You'll be the man!*

goodman boy: a double insult: goodman is a commoner; boy, a contemptuous term
Go to: Come, come!
cock-a-hoop: everything in disorder
You'll . . . man: You merely play at being a man.

TYBALT   Why, uncle, 'tis a shame.

CAPULET   Go to, go to,
You are a saucy boy. Is't so indeed?
This trick* will scath* you, I know what.*
You must contrary* me! Go to, 'tis time.—*   85
Well said, my hearts!—You are a princox,* go,
Be quiet, or—More light, more light!—For shame,
I'll make you quiet, what!—Cheerly, my hearts!

trick: foolish behavior *scath:* harm *what:* i.e., what will happen to you
contrary: be contrary to *'tis time:* i.e., that you learned a lesson
princox: impudent boy

TYBALT   Patience perforce* with willful choler meeting
Makes my flesh tremble in their different greeting.   90
I will withdraw, but this intrusion shall,
Now seeming sweet, convert to bitt'rest gall.

perforce: of necessity

Exit TYBALT.

ROMEO   *(To JULIET.)* If I profane* with my unworthiest hand
This holy shrine,* the gentle fine is this:
My lips, two blushing pilgrims,* ready stand   95
To smooth that rough touch with a tender kiss.

profane: treat irreverently
This . . . shrine: Juliet's hand
pilgrims: those who for penance go on a journey to a holy place

JULIET   Good pilgrim, you do wrong your hand too much,*
Which mannerly devotion shows* in this:
For saints have hands that pilgrims' hands do touch,
And palm to palm is holy palmers'* kiss.   100

wrong . . . much: accuse your hand of a sin it did not commit
which . . . shows: i.e., which has shown
palmers': pilgrims', those who brought back palm boughs from a pilgrimage to Jerusalem

ROMEO   Have not saints lips, and holy palmers too?

JULIET   Ay, pilgrim, lips that they must use in pray'r.

ROMEO   O then, dear saint, let lips do what hands do:
They pray; grant thou,* lest faith turn to despair.

grant thou: i.e., my request for a kiss

JULIET   Saints do not move,* though grant* for prayers' sake.   105

move: insinuate an action *grant:* they grant

ROMEO   Then move not while my prayer's effect I take.
               Thus from my lips, by thine, my sin is purg'd.

               They kiss.

NURSE   Madam, your mother craves a word with you.

ROMEO   What is her mother?

NURSE   Indeed, bachelor,
               Her mother is the lady of the house,   110
               And a good lady, and a wise and virtuous.
               I nurs'd her daughter that you talk'd withal.

ROMEO   Is she a Capulet?
               O dear account!* My life is my foe's debt.*

account: costly reckoning *my . . . debt* in my enemy's power

BENVOLIO	Away, be gone; the sport is at the best.*	115

Away . . . best: "Quit while you are winning."

ROMEO	Ay, so I fear, the more is my unrest.

CAPULET
Nay, gentlemen, prepare not to be gone.
We have a trifling foolish banquet towards.*

towards: on the way

Is it e'en so? Why then I thank you all.
I thank you, honest gentlemen, good night.   120
More torches here! Come on, then let's to bed.
Ah, sirrah, by my fay,* it waxes* late;

fay: faith *waxes:* grows

I'll to my rest.

Exeunt all but JULIET and NURSE.

JULIET   Come hither, nurse. What is yond gentleman?

NURSE   The son and heir of old Tiberio.   125

JULIET   What's he that now is going out of door?

NURSE   Lady, that, I think, be young Petruchio.

JULIET   What's he that follows here, that would not dance?

NURSE   I know not.

JULIET   Go ask his name. *(Aside.)* If he be married,   130
My grave is like to be my wedding-bed.*

My . . . wedding-bed: i.e., I'll go to my grave unmarried.

NURSE   His name is Romeo, and a Montague,
The only son of our great enemy.

JULIET   My only love sprung from my only hate!
Too early seen unknown* and known too late!   135
Prodigious* birth of love it is to me
That I must love a loathed enemy.

Too . . . unknown: Seen before known *Prodigious:* Ominous

NURSE   What's this? what's this?

JULIET   A rhyme I learnt even now
Of one I danc'd withal. *(One calls within, "Juliet!")*

NURSE   Anon, anon!
Come let's away, the strangers all are gone.   140

Exeunt.

About the Play

1. What do the following quotations reveal about the older generation's attitude toward the ancient feud between the Montagues and the Capulets?
   a. *Lady Montague to her husband, Scene i:* "Thou shalt not stir one foot to seek a foe."
   b. *Old Capulet to Paris, Scene ii:* "But Montague is bound as well as I, / In penalty alike, and 'tis not hard, I think, / For men so old as we to keep the peace."
   c. *Old Capulet to Tybalt, Scene v:* "Content thee, gentle coz, let him [Romeo] alone. / 'A bears him like a portly gentleman; / And to say truth, Verona brags of him / To be a virtuous and well-govern'd youth. / I would not for the wealth of all this town / Here in my house do him disparagement."
2. What do the following quotations reveal about the younger generation's attitude toward the ancient feud?
   a. *Gregory to Sampson, Scene i:* "Draw thy tool; here comes two of the house of Montagues. / I will frown as I pass by and let them take it as they list."
   b. *Tybalt to Benvolio:* "What, drawn and talk of peace? I hate the word / As I hate hell, all Montagues, and thee. / Have at thee, coward!"
   c. *Capulet and Tybalt, Scene v:* Capulet: "Therefore be patient; take no note of him; / It is my will, the which if thou respect, / Show a fair presence and put off these frowns, / An ill-beseeming semblance for a feast." Tybalt: "It fits when such a villain is a guest. / I'll not endure him." Capulet: "He shall be endured. / What, goodman boy? I say he shall, go to. Am I the master here or you? Go to!"
3. In light of these attitudes, who would you say is keeping the feud alive— the older or the younger generation?
4. Taking into account what others say about Romeo, Romeo's actions, and his dialogue, how would you describe his behavior in Scene i?
5. What causes him to behave in such a manner?
6. What do you think of his behavior?

*About
the Play*

1. *Each quotation reveals the older generation's desire to let the feud die.*

2. *Each quotation reveals the younger generation's desire to keep the feud alive.*

3. *the younger generation*

4. *Answers may vary but might include that he is lovesick, rather immature, and moody.*

5. *the fact that he loves Rosaline and knows his love will remain unrequited*

6. *Answers will vary. Hopefully students will recognize his immaturity and the fact that his love for Rosaline is really mere infatuation.*

Note that the Prologue is an embedded sonnet.

Prologue

Enter Chorus.

CHORUS Now old desire* doth in his death-bed lie,
And young affection gapes* to be his heir.
That fair* for which love groan'd for and would die,
With tender Juliet match'd is now not fair.
Now Romeo is belov'd and loves again, 5
Alike* bewitched by the charm of looks;
But to his foe suppos'd he must complain,*
And she steal love's sweet bait from fearful* hooks.
Being held a foe, he may not have access
To breathe such vows as lovers use* to swear, 10
And she as much in love, her means much less
To meet her new-beloved any where.
But passion lends them power, time means, to meet,
Temp'ring* extremities* with extreme sweet.

old desire: i.e.,
Romeo's infatuation
with Rosaline
gapes: yearns
fair: beauty

Alike: Equally

But . . . complain: i.e.,
he must attribute his
love to his foe
fearful: dangerous

use: are accustomed

Temp'ring: Moderating
extremities: pain

Exit.

Scene I

Time: Sunday evening (very late)
Place: Capulet's orchard

*To escape the company of his friends, Romeo unwittingly enters Capulet's
orchard. Cloaked in darkness, he listens as Mercutio and Benvolio, ignorant
of Romeo's love for Juliet, jest about his love for Rosaline.*

Enter ROMEO alone.

ROMEO Can I go forward when my heart is here?
Turn back, dull earth,* and find thy center* out.

dull earth: i.e.,
Romeo's body *cen-
ter:* i.e., Juliet is the
center—the core—of
his being.

Enter BENVOLIO with MERCUTIO. ROMEO withdraws.

Prologue

The third and final embedded sonnet, this prologue contributes nothing to Shakespeare's
plot, theme, or characterization.

Act II, Scene i

The scene opens with one of ten soliloquies by
Romeo in Act II. (A soliloquy is a speech in
which a character reveals to the audience his or
her private thoughts.) Notice the microcosm
image at line 2. Romeo, like Capulet (at
I.ii.14-15), describes Juliet as the center of his
world. The soliloquies in this play, unlike those
in Shakespeare's mature tragedies, do not reveal any inner struggle on the part of the protagonists; nor do they depict them in the
process of decision making. These speeches
serve instead to establish rapport between
Romeo and Juliet and the audience—in other
words, to make them highly sympathetic characters by emphasizing their good intentions.
Other ways in which the playwright makes
these protagonists sympathetic are the foils to
them (Romeo/Mercutio, Tybalt, Paris; Juliet/
Rosaline); the dilemmas they face (Juliet's parents' harshness, her break with the Nurse, the
Friar's desertion of her in the tomb, Romeo's
banishment, the quarantine); and the feud.

BENVOLIO	Romeo! My cousin Romeo! Romeo!
MERCUTIO	He is wise And, on my life, hath stol'n him home to bed.
BENVOLIO	He ran this way and leapt this orchard wall. 5 Call, good Mercutio.
MERCUTIO	Nay, I'll conjure* too. Romeo! humours! madman! passion! lover! Appear thou in the likeness of a sigh!
BENVOLIO	Come, he hath hid himself among these trees To be consorted with* the humourous* night. 10 Blind is his love and best befits the dark.
MERCUTIO	If love be blind, love cannot hit the mark.* Romeo, good night, I'll to my truckle-bed.* This field-bed is too cold for me to sleep. Come, shall we go?
BENVOLIO	Go then, for 'tis in vain 15 To seek him here that means not to be found.

conjure: call up a spirit

be . . . with: keep company with
humourous: damp

If . . . mark: An allusion to the naughty, blind Cupid, who shoots arrows aimlessly
truckle-bed: trundle bed

Exeunt.

Scene II

Time: Sunday evening (very late)
Place: Capulet's orchard

After Benvolio and Mercutio depart, Romeo overhears Juliet describing her love for him along with her fear of her family's opposition to their union. Gathering courage, he reveals his presence—and his love—to her. The two pledge their unending love and make plans to wed.

Romeo comes forward.

ROMEO	He jests at scars that never felt a wound.

Enter JULIET above at her window. ROMEO advances.

Act II, Scene ii

In the opening speech Romeo describes Juliet as a source of great light, his true love. His worst fears are that she, like Rosaline, will be a devotee of Diana, the virgin goddess of the moon. (You might ask students whether they recall another selection in this text which makes allusion to Diana *[Cupid's Arrows]*.) To Shakespeare's audience the moon was a symbol of the cold, the far-off, the distant, and hence, of chastity. It also symbolized envy and fickleness. Juliet's soliloquy at lines 32-35 is the only soliloquy in Shakespeare's plays overheard by another character. Line 32 ("O Romeo, Romeo, wherefore art thou Romeo?") is undoubtedly the play's most famous and most misunderstood line. Ask students to paraphrase its meaning. Then point out the gloss beside the line; Juliet is not asking where Romeo is but *why* ("wherefore") he was born a Montague. Juliet, as the soliloquy continues, argues that a word (i.e., the name Romeo) is only a code or signal; it is not to be equated with reality. Words are worth only the value we assign to them. Stereotypes do not apply to matters of the heart.

At lines 65-68 Shakespeare suggests that love enables one to accomplish seemingly impossible tasks, a theme that he develops fully in *The Tempest.* What symbolism operates in lines 108-10? Note that at lines 114-18 the imagery of haste converges with the light theme in Juliet's pun on the word *lightning.* What is the paradox of love's "bounty" (ll. 131-33)? *(The more love one gives, the more one has.)* Notice also the emphasis once again on time near the end of the scene (ll. 164-72).

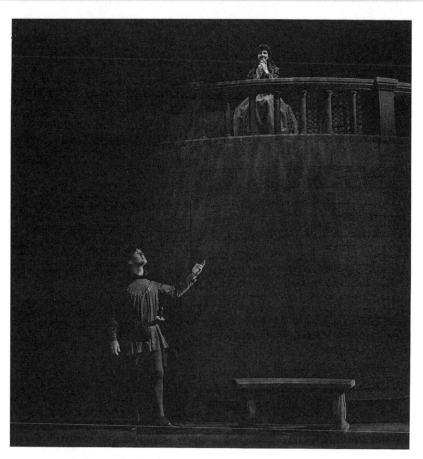

But soft, what light through yonder window breaks?
It is the east, and Juliet is the sun.
Arise, fair sun, and kill the envious moon,*
Who is already sick and pale with grief   5
That thou, her maid, art far more fair than she.
Be not her maid, since she is envious;
Her vestal livery* is but sick and green,
And none but fools* do wear it; cast it off.
It is my lady, O, it is my love!   10
She speaks, yet she says nothing; what of that?

moon: i.e., Diana, goddess of the moon and of chastity

vestal livery: maiden dress
fools: jesters whose multicolored costumes included green

Her eye discourses;* I will answer it.
I am too bold; 'tis not to me she speaks.
Two of the fairest stars in all the heaven,
Having some business, do entreat her eyes   15
To twinkle in their spheres till they return.
What if her eyes were there, they in her head?
The brightness of her cheek would shame those stars
As daylight doth a lamp; her eyes in heaven
Would through the airy region stream so bright   20
That birds would sing and think it were not night.
See how she leans her cheek upon her hand!
O that I were a glove upon that hand
That I might touch that cheek!

discourses: speaks

JULIET   Ay me!

ROMEO   She speaks!
O, speak again, bright angel, for thou art   25
As glorious to this night, being o'er my head,
As is a winged messenger of heaven
Unto the white up-turned wond'ring eyes
Of mortals that fall back to gaze on him
When he bestrides the lazy puffing clouds   30
And sails upon the bosom of the air.

JULIET   O Romeo, Romeo, wherefore art thou Romeo?*
Deny thy father and refuse thy name;
Or if thou wilt not, be but sworn my love,
And I'll no longer be a Capulet.   35

wherefore . . . Romeo:
i.e., why are you
called Romeo (and
thus a Montague)

ROMEO   (Aside.) Shall I hear more, or shall I speak at this?

JULIET   'Tis but thy name that is my enemy;
Thou art thyself, though not a Montague.*
What's Montague? It is nor hand nor foot,
Nor arm nor face, nor any other part.   40
O, be some other name belonging to a man.
What's in a name? That which we call a rose
By any other name would smell as sweet;
So Romeo would, were he not Romeo call'd,
Retain that dear* perfection which he owes*   45
Without that title Romeo. Doff* thy name,
And for thy name, which is not part of thee,
Take all myself.

though . . . Montague:
i.e., though you
were to change your
name

dear: previous *owes:*
owns
Doff: Discard

ROMEO	I take thee at thy word.		
	Call me but love, and I'll be new baptiz'd;*		*be . . . baptiz'd:* acquire a new name
	Henceforth I never will be Romeo.	50	

JULIET   What man art thou that thus bescreen'd in night
So stumblest* on my counsel?*   *stumblest:* overhears
                                                                 counsel: private
                                                                 thoughts

ROMEO   By a name
I know not how to tell thee who I am.
My name, dear saint, is hateful to myself,
Because it is an enemy to thee.   55
Had I it written, I would tear the word.

JULIET   My ears have yet not drunk a hundred words
Of thy tongue's uttering, yet I know the sound.
Art thou not Romeo and a Montague?

ROMEO   Neither, fair maid, if either thee dislike.   60

JULIET   How camest thou hither, tell me, and wherefore?
The orchard walls are high and hard to climb
And the place death, considering who thou art,
If any of my kinsmen find thee here.

ROMEO   With love's light wings did I o'erperch* these walls,   65   *o'erperch:* fly over
For stony limits cannot hold love out,
And what love can do, that dares love attempt;
Therefore thy kinsmen are no stop to me.

JULIET   If they do see thee, they will murder thee.

ROMEO   Alack, there lies more peril in thine eye   70
Than twenty of their swords! Look thou but sweet,
And I am proof against* their enmity.   *proof against:* invulnerable to

JULIET   I would not for the world they saw thee here.

ROMEO   I have night's cloak to hide me from their eyes,
And but* thou love me, let them find me here;   75   *but:* if only
My life were better ended by their hate
Than death prorogued,* wanting of* thy love.   *prorogued:* delayed
                                                               wanting of: lacking

JULIET   By whose direction foundst thou out this place?

ROMEO	By love, that first did prompt me to inquire;
	He lent me counsel, and I lent him eyes. 80
	I am no pilot,* yet wert thou as far
	As that vast shore wash'd with the farthest sea,
	I should adventure* for such merchandise.
JULIET	Thou knowest the mask of night is on my face,
	Else would a maiden blush bepaint my cheek 85
	For that which thou hast heard me speak tonight.
	Fain* would I dwell on form, fain, fain, deny
	What I have spoke, but farewell compliment!*
	Dost thou love me? I know thou wilt say "Ay,"
	And I will take thy word; yet if thou swear'st, 90
	Thou mayest prove false: at lovers' perjuries*
	They say Jove laughs. O gentle Romeo,
	If thou dost love, pronounce it faithfully;
	Or if thou thinkest I am too quickly won,
	I'll frown and be perverse and say thee nay 95
	So* thou wilt woo, but else not for the world.
	In truth, fair Montague, I am too fond,*
	And therefore thou mayest think my behavior light,*
	But trust me, gentleman, I'll prove more true
	Than those that have more coying* to be strange.* 100
	I should have been more strange, I must confess,
	But that thou overheard'st, ere I was ware,*
	My true-love passion; therefore pardon me
	And not impute this yielding* to light* love,
	Which the dark night hath so discovered. 105
ROMEO	Lady, by yonder blessed moon I vow,
	That tips with silver all these fruit-tree tops—
JULIET	O, swear not by the moon, th' inconstant moon
	That monthly changes in her circled orb,*
	Lest that thy love prove likewise variable. 110
ROMEO	What shall I swear by?
JULIET	Do not swear at all;
	Or if thou wilt, swear by thy gracious self,
	And I'll believe thee.
ROMEO	If my heart's dear love—

pilot: merchant-venturer

adventure: take a risk

Fain: Gladly

compliment: social rules

perjuries: broken promises

So: So long as

fond: foolish

light: silly

coying: skill in acting coy *strange:* distant, reserved
ware: aware

this yielding: my candor *light:* insubstantial

orb: orbit

JULIET	Swear not at all. Though I do joy in thee,	
	I have no joy of this contract* tonight.	115
	It is too rash, too unadvis'd,* too sudden,	
	Too like the lightning, which doth cease to be	
	Ere one can say it lightens. Sweet good night!	
	This bud of love, by summer's ripening breath,	
	May prove a beauteous flow'r when next we meet.	120
	Good night, good night! As sweet repose and rest	
	Come to thy heart as that within my breast!	

contract: exchange of promises
unadvis'd: imprudent

ROMEO   O, wilt thou leave me so unsatisfied?

JULIET   What satisfaction canst thou have tonight?

ROMEO   Th' exchange of thy love's faithful vow for mine.   125

JULIET   I gave thee mine before thou didst request it;
And yet I would it were to give again.

ROMEO   Woulds't thou withdraw it? For what purpose, love?

JULIET	But to be frank* and give it thee again,	
	And yet I wish but for the thing I have.	130
	My bounty* is as boundless as the sea,	
	My love as deep; the more I give to thee,	
	The more I have, for both are infinite.	

frank: freely generous

bounty: store of love

NURSE calls from within.

I hear some noise within; dear love, adieu!
Anon, good nurse! Sweet Montague, be true.   135
Stay but a little; I will come again.

Exit JULIET.

ROMEO   O blessed, blessed night! I am afeard,
Being in night, all this is but a dream
Too flattering-sweet to be substantial.

Enter JULIET above.

JULIET	Three words, dear Romeo, and good night indeed.	140
	If that thy bent of love* be honorable,	
	Thy purpose marriage, send me word tomorrow	

bent . . . love: intentions with regard to love

By one that I'll procure* to come to thee,   *procure:* hire
Where and what time thou wilt perform the rite;
And all my fortunes at thy foot I'll lay   145
And follow thee my lord throughout the world.

NURSE calls "Madam!" from within.

I come, anon. But if thou meanest not well,
I do beseech thee—

NURSE calls "Madam!" again.

               By and by, I come—
To cease thy strife, and leave me to my grief.
Tomorrow will I send.

ROMEO   So thrive my soul—   150

JULIET   A thousand times good night!

Exit JULIET.

ROMEO   A thousand times the worse, to want* thy light.   *want:* lack
Love goes toward love as schoolboys from their books,
But love from love, toward school with heavy looks.

Enter JULIET again.

JULIET   Hist, Romeo, hist! O, for a falc'ner's voice   155
To lure this tassel-gentle* back again!   *tassel-gentle:* tercel-
Bondage is hoarse and may not speak aloud,   gentle, or male hawk
Else would I tear the cave where Echo* lies   used in falconry by
And make her airy tongue more hoarse than mine   the nobility
With repetition of my Romeo's name. Romeo!   160   *Echo:* A nymph who
                                    pined for her love
                                    until only her voice
                                    remained

ROMEO   It* is my soul that calls upon my name.   *It:* i.e., Juliet
How silver-sweet sound lovers' tongues by night,
Like softest music to attending ears!

Romeo!

           My madam?

                   What a'clock tomorrow
Shall I send to thee?

| ROMEO | By the hour of nine. | 165 |

| JULIET | I will not fail. 'Tis twenty year till then. |
| | I have forgot why I did call thee back. |

| ROMEO | Let me stand here till thou remember it. |

| JULIET | I shall forget, to have thee still* stand there, | *still:* forever |
| | Rememb'ring how I love thy company. | 170 |

| ROMEO | And I'll still stay, to have thee still forget, |
| | Forgetting any other home but this. |

JULIET	'Tis almost morning; I would have thee gone—
	And yet no farther than a wanton's* bird,	*wanton's:* spoiled child's
	That lets it hop a little from its hand,	175
	Like a poor prisoner in his twisted gyves,*	*gyves:* fetters
	And with a silken thread plucks it back again,
	So loving-jealous of his liberty.

| ROMEO | I would I were thy bird. |

JULIET	Sweet, so would I,
	Yet I should kill thee with much cherishing.	180
	Good night, good night! Parting is such sweet sorrow
	That I shall say good night till it be morrow.*	*morrow:* morning

Exit JULIET.

ROMEO	Sleep dwell upon thine eyes, peace in thy breast!
	Would I were sleep and peace, so sweet to rest!
	Hence will I to my ghostly sire's* close cell,*	185	*ghostly sire's:* spiritual father's *close cell:* small room
	His help to crave and my dear hap* to tell.		*dear hap:* good (or costly) fortune

Exit.

Scene III

Time: Monday morning
Place: Friar Lawrence's cell

The meditations of Friar Lawrence are interrupted by Romeo, who announces his new love for Juliet. Once convinced of the genuineness of this affection,

Act II, Scene iii

Although the play is set in late medieval Italy (traditionally at the beginning of the fourteenth century), Shakespeare is not consistent in his depiction of a Catholic society. The opening speech reveals the Friar's knowledge of herbs, poisons, and medicine. Why is it important that the playwright establish this character's competence in such matters? What plot event do these lines foreshadow? *(The Friar later supplies the "distilling liquor" that causes Juliet to appear dead [IV.i.91-120].)* What is the time of the action of this scene? *(Monday morning)*

The last eight lines of the Friar's speech embody the hierarchy theme: God has created an orderly universe in which every entity, animate or inanimate, has a preordained function. Ironi-cally just as the Friar mentions the possibility of the abuse of such functions, Romeo, who will ultimately take his own life by means of poison, enters. The last four lines of the Friar's speech allude to the dual nature of man. The "two such opposed kings [which] encamp them still in man" are reason and passion.

Notice the Friar's concern for Romeo's chastity (ll. 29-38). The play does not advocate double standards. It promotes the fulfillment of true love in marriage. The final couplet (the whole scene is rhymed) embodies the haste theme in the context of the Friar's admonishing Romeo against impetuosity; thus it is a crucial passage in terms of both Shakespeare's theme and characterization.

The Friar speaks here of the dual nature of man: reason and passion.

the Friar agrees to marry Romeo and Juliet secretly in the hope that their love will reconcile their families' hatred.

Enter FRIAR LAWRENCE alone, with a basket.

FRIAR L.	The grey-ey'd morn smiles on the frowning night,	
	Check'ring the eastern clouds with streaks of light,	
	From darkness flecked* like a drunkard reels	*flecked:* spotted
	From forth day's path and Titan's fiery wheels.*	*Titan's . . . wheels:* The chariot of the sun
	Now ere the sun advance his burning eye	5
	The day to cheer and night's dank dew to dry,	
	I must up-fill this osier cage* of ours	*osier cage:* willow basket
	With baleful* weeds and precious-juiced flowers.	*baleful:* poisonous
	O, mickle* is the powerful grace* that lies	*mickle:* very great *powerful grace:* gracious healing power
	In plants, herbs, stones, and their true qualities;	10
	For naught so vile* that on the earth doth live	*vile:* held in low esteem
	But to the earth some special good doth give;	
	Nor aught so good but, strain'd* from that fair use,*	*strain'd:* forced *fair use:* proper function
	Revolts from true birth,* stumbling on abuse.*	*true birth:* natural purpose *stumbling . . . abuse:* falling into misuse
	Virtue itself turns vice, being misapplied,	15
	And vice sometime by action dignified.*	*dignified:* may become virtue

Enter ROMEO.

	Within the infant rind* of this weak flower	*rind:* bud
	Poison hath residence and medicine power;	
	For this, being smelt, with that part* cheers each part,*	*that part:* the odor *part:* i.e., of the body
	Being tasted, stays* all senses with the heart.*	20 *slays:* stops *with . . . heart:* along with the heart
	Two such opposed kings encamp them still*	*still:* always
	In man as well as herbs, grace and rude will;	
	And where the worser is predominant,	
	Full soon the canker* death eats up that plant.	*canker:* destructive worm
ROMEO	Good morrow, father.	
FRIAR L.	*Benedicite!**	25 *Benedicite:* Bless you!
	What early tongue so sweet saluteth me?	
	Young son, it argues* a distempered* head	*argues:* reflects *distempered:* disturbed
	So soon to bid good morrow to thy bed.*	*So . . . bed:* To be up so early (at dawn)
	Care keeps his watch in every old man's eye,	
	And where care lodges, sleep will never lie;	30
	But where unbruised* youth with unstuff'd* brain	*unbruised:* uninjured by the cares of life *unstuff'd:* unburdened
	Doth couch his limbs, there golden sleep doth reign.	
	Therefore thy earliness doth me assure	

	Thou art up-rous'd with some distemp'rature;*		*distemp'rature:*
	Or if not so, then here I hit it right—	35	ailment
	Our Romeo hath not been in bed tonight.		

ROMEO   That last is true—the sweeter rest was mine.

FRIAR L.   God pardon sin! Was thou with Rosaline?

ROMEO   With Rosaline? my ghostly father, no!
                I have forgot that name and that name's woe.   40

FRIAR L.   That's my good son, but where hast thou been then?

ROMEO   I'll tell thee ere thou ask it me again.
                I have been feasting with mine enemy,
                Where on a sudden one hath wounded me
                That's by me wounded; both our remedies   45
                Within thy help* and holy physic* lies.
                I bear no hatred, blessed man, for lo
                My intercession likewise steads* my foe.

Within . . . help: Power to heal *physic:* medicine *steads:* helps

FRIAR L.   Be plain, good son, and homely* in thy drift,*
                Riddling confession finds but riddling shrift.*   50

homely: simple *drift:* current of meaning *shrift:* absolution (declaration of forgiveness)

ROMEO   Then plainly know my heart's dear love is set
                On the fair daughter of rich Capulet.
                As mine on hers, so hers is set on mine
                And all combin'd, save what thou must combine
                By holy marriage. When and where and how   55
                We met, we woo'd, and made exchange of vow
                I'll tell thee as we pass, but this I pray,
                That thou consent to marry us today.

FRIAR L.   O what a change is here!
                Is Rosaline, that thou didst love so dear,   60
                So soon forsaken? Young men's love then lies
                Not truly in their hearts but in their eyes.
                The sun not yet thy sighs from heaven clears,*   *clears:* dries
                Thy old groans yet ringing in mine ancient ears;
                Lo here upon thy cheek the stain doth sit   65
                Of an old tear that is not wash'd off yet.
                  If e'er thou wast thyself and these woes thine,
                Thou and these woes were all for Rosaline.

And art thou chang'd? Pronounce this sentence* then:
Women may fall when there's no strength in men.*   70

ROMEO   Thou chidst* me oft for loving Rosaline.

FRIAR L.   For doting, not for loving, pupil mine.

ROMEO   And badst me bury love.

FRIAR L.   Not in a grave
To lay one in, another out to have.

ROMEO   I pray thee chide me not. Her I love now   75
Doth grace for grace and love for love allow;*
The other did not so.

FRIAR L.   O, she* knew well
Thy love did read by rote that could not spell.*
But come, young waverer, come go with me.
In one respect I'll thy assistant be;   80
For this alliance may so happy prove
To turn your households' rancor* to pure love.

ROMEO   O, let us hence. I stand* on sudden haste.

FRIAR L.   Wisely and slow, they stumble that run fast.

Exeunt.

Scene IV

Time: Monday morning
Place: A street

Again the object of his friends' jesting, Romeo is met by Juliet's Nurse who has been sent to confirm the young couple's wedding plans.

Enter BENVOLIO and MERCUTIO.

MERCUTIO   Where should this Romeo be?
Came he not home tonight?

BENVOLIO   Not to his father's; I spoke with his man.

Glosses:
sentence: wise saying
Women . . . men: Women may be excused for fickleness when men are so weak.
chidst: scolded
Doth . . . allow: Reciprocates my love
she: Rosaline
did . . . spell: was imitative rather than genuine
rancor: hatred
stand: insist; am set

Act II, Scene iv

Just as the preceding scene embodies an important announcement—that Romeo is in love with Juliet—this scene makes an important announcement—that Tybalt has challenged Romeo to fight. Note that it is a human agent, not fate, that is about to interfere in the young lovers' plans.

In describing Tybalt, Mercutio mocks him as a student at a prestigious academy of martial arts (ll. 18-24). Ironically, Mercutio directs his resentment of Tybalt toward the very quality that also characterizes him: both young men are quarrelsome.

As the Nurse comes to speak with Romeo about his marrying Juliet, the young men make the Nurse a subject for mockery (ll. 34-55). They begin by punning on her size and outlandish dress: her arrival is comparable to the appearance of a ship in harbor. Then they match her malapropism, *confidence* for *conference* at line 49 and *indite* for *invite* (l. 50). In the final segment of the scene Shakespeare depicts the Nurse as comic in her tediousness and inefficiency as a message-carrier, a trait that will culminate in Scene v.

MERCUTIO	Why, that same pale hard-hearted wench, that Rosaline, Torments him so, that he will sure run mad.	5
BENVOLIO	Tybalt, the kinsman to old Capulet, Hath sent a letter to his father's house.	
MERCUTIO	A challenge, on my life.	
BENVOLIO	Romeo will answer it.	
MERCUTIO	Any man that can write may answer a letter.	10
BENVOLIO	Nay, he will answer the letter's master, how he dares, being dar'd.	
MERCUTIO	Alas, poor Romeo, he is already dead, stabb'd with a white wench's black eye, run through the ear with a love-song, the very pin* of his heart cleft with the blind bow-boy's butt-shaft;* and is he a man to encounter Tybalt?	15
BENVOLIO	Why, what is Tybalt?	
MERCUTIO	More than Prince of Cats.* O, he's the courageous captain of compliments. He fights as you sing prick-song,* keeps time, distance, and proportion;* he rests his minim* rests, one, two, and the third in your bosom: the very butcher of a silk button,* a duellist, a duellist; a gentleman of the very first house,* of the first and second cause.* Ah, the immortal *passado,* the *punto reverso,* the *hay!**	20
BENVOLIO	Here comes Romeo, here comes Romeo.	25
MERCUTIO	Signor Romeo, *bon jour!* there's a French salutation to your French slop.* You gave us the counterfeit* fairly last night.	
ROMEO	Good morrow to you both. What counterfeit did I give you?	30
MERCUTIO	The slip,* sir, the slip, can you not conceive?	
ROMEO	Pardon, good Mercutio, my business was great, and in such a case as mine a man may strain courtesy.*	

Enter NURSE and her servant PETER.

pin: peg at the center of an archery target
blind . . . shaft: blunt arrow used for practice, here associated with Cupid

Prince . . . of Cats: The king of cats in the folktale *Reynard the Fox* is named Tibalt.
as . . . prick-song: like a polished singer who sings by music, not rote
proportion: rhythm
minim: short
the . . . button: an expert swordsman, one able to pluck a button off his opponent's doublet
first house: best school (of fencing)
of . . . cause: ready on the earliest acceptable occasions for dueling
passado: forward thrust punto reverso: backhanded thrust
hay: home thrust
slop: sloppy trousers (Romeo has the neglectful appearance of a suffering lover.)
gave . . . counterfeit: (1)eluded us (2)gave us false coins (slips)

ROMEO	Here's a goodly gear!* A sail, a sail!*
MERCUTIO	Two, two: a shirt and a smock.*
NURSE	Peter!
PETER	Anon!*
NURSE	My fan, Peter.
MERCUTIO	Good Peter, to hide her face, for her fan's the fairer face.
NURSE	Out upon you, what a man are you?
ROMEO	One, gentlewoman, that God hath made, himself to mar.
NURSE	By my troth, it is well said; "for himself to mar," quoth 'a! Gentleman, can any of you tell me where I may find the young Romeo?
ROMEO	I can tell you, but young Romeo will be older when you have found him than he was when you sought him. I am the youngest of that name, for fault of a worse.
NURSE	If you be he, sir, I desire some confidence* with you.
BENVOLIO	She will indite* him to some supper.
MERCUTIO	Romeo, will you come to your father's? We'll to dinner thither.
ROMEO	I will follow you.
MERCUTIO	Farewell, ancient lady, farewell, *(singing)* "lady, lady, lady."

Exeunt MERCUTIO and BENVOLIO.

NURSE	I pray you, sir, what saucy merchant* was this that was so full of his ropery?*
ROMEO	A gentleman, nurse, that loves to hear himself talk and will speak more in a minute than he will stand to* in a month.

35

40

45

50

55

60

slip: pun on counter-
feit coins
strain courtesy: break
the rules of etiquette
gear: matter referring
to Mercutio's jesting;
equipment, clothing,
referring mockingly
to the Nurse's
appearance
sail: call indicating the
appearance of a
ship, here referring
to the Nurse's size
and outlandish
regalia
shirt . . . smock: i.e., a
man and a woman
Anon: Right here

confidence: malapro-
pism for conference,
private conversation
indite: malapropism
for invite, said in
mockery

merchant: fellow
ropery: knavery, mischief

stand to: apply himself
manfully to (as in a
fight or contest)

NURSE	Scurvy knave!* *(She turns to Romeo.)* Pray you, sir, a word: and as I told you, my young lady bid me inquire you out. What she bid me say I will keep to myself. But first let me tell ye, if ye should lead her in a fool's paradise,* as they say, it were a very gross kind of behavior, as they say; for the gentlewoman is young; and therefore, if you should deal double with her, truly it were an ill thing to be off'red to any gentlewoman, and a very weak dealing.		*Scurvy knave:* Worthless rascal, spoken of Mercutio
		65	*lead . . . paradise:* deceive her
ROMEO	Nurse, commend me* to thy lady and mistress. I protest* to thee—	70	*commend me:* give my regards *protest:* affirm
NURSE	Good heart, and, i' faith, I will tell her as much. O, she will be a joyful woman.		
ROMEO	What wilt thou tell her, nurse? Thou dost not mark* me.		*mark:* listen to
NURSE	I will tell her, sir, that you do protest, which, as I take it, is a gentleman-like offer.	75	
ROMEO	Bid her devise Some means to come to shrift this afternoon, And there she shall at Friar Lawrence' cell Be shriv'd and married. Here is for thy pains.*	80	*pains:* service (of carrying the message)
NURSE	No, truly, sir, not a penny.		
ROMEO	Go to, I say you shall.		
NURSE	This afternoon, sir? Well, she shall be there.		
ROMEO	And stay, good nurse, behind the abbey wall. Within this hour my man shall be with thee And bring thee cords made like a tackled stair,* Which to the high top-gallant* of my joy Must be my convoy* in the secret night. Farewell, be trusty, and I'll quit* thy pains. Farewell, commend me to thy mistress.	85	*tackled stair:* rope ladder *top-gallant:* highest mast of a ship *convoy:* means of passage (to Juliet's chamber) *quit:* requite, repay
		90	
NURSE	Now God in heaven bless thee! Hark you, sir.		
ROMEO	What say'st thou, my dear nurse?		

NURSE	Is your man secret? Did you ne'er hear say, "Two may keep counsel, putting one away"?*		*Two . . . away:* Two may keep a secret, subtracting one.
ROMEO	Warrant thee,* my man's as true as steel.	95	*Warrant thee:* I assure you
NURSE	Well, sir, my mistress is the sweetest lady—O, O! when 'twas a little prating thing—O, there is a nobleman in town, one Paris, that would fain lay knife aboard;* but she, good soul, had as lieve* see a toad, a very toad, as see him. I anger her sometimes and tell her that Paris is the properer* man, but I'll warrant you, when I say so, she looks as pale as any clout* in the versal* world.	100	*lay . . . aboard:* claim Juliet *lieve:* soon *properer:* more handsome *clout:* white cloth (Cf. "as white as a sheet") *versal:* universal, entire
ROMEO	Commend me to thy lady.		
NURSE	Ay, a thousand times.		
	Exit ROMEO.		
	Peter!	105	
PETER	Anon!		
NURSE	Before, and apace.*		*apace:* quickly
	Exeunt.		

Scene V

Time: Monday noon
Place: Capulet's house

Juliet awaits the return of her tardy nurse, who reveals only gradually the information she has just received from Romeo.

Enter JULIET.

JULIET	The clock strook nine when I did send the nurse; In half an hour she promised to return. Perchance she cannot meet him—that's not so. O, she is lame! Love's heralds should be thoughts, Which ten times faster glides than the sun's beams, Driving back shadows over low'ring* hills;	5	*low'ring:* frowning

Act II, Scene v

The opening speech, one of Shakespeare's most famous soliloquies for a female character, deals with both the time scheme of the plot and the love and haste themes in imagery that is dramatically functional. As a comic messenger, one who cannot get to the point of her communication, the Nurse keeps the anxious Juliet waiting for some forty lines for Romeo's reply concerning the details of their wedding.

Therefore do nimble-pinion'd* doves draw Love
And therefore hath the wind-swift Cupid wings.
Now is the sun upon the highmost hill
Of this day's journey, and from nine till twelve   10
Is three long hours, yet she is not come.
Had she affections and warm youthful blood,
She would be as swift in motion as a ball;
My words would bandy* her to my sweet love
And his to me.   15
But old folks—many feign as they were dead,
Unwieldy,* slow, heavy, and pale as lead.
O, there she comes!

nimble-pinion'd:
quick-winged
(Venus's chariot was
drawn by doves.)

bandy: toss

Unwieldy: Clumsy

Enter NURSE and PETER.

      O honey nurse, what news?
Hast thou met with him? Send thy man away.

NURSE Peter, stay at the gate.   20

Exit PETER.

JULIET Now good, sweet nurse—why look'st thou so sad?
Though news be sad, yet tell them merrily;
If good, thou shamest the music of sweet news
By playing it to me with so sour a face.

NURSE I am a-weary; give me leave a while.   25
Fie, how my bones ache! What a jaunce* have I!

jaunce: jostling
journey

JULIET I would thou hadst my bones and I thy news.
Nay, come, I pray thee speak, good, good nurse, speak.

NURSE O, fie! what haste! Can you not stay awhile?
Do you not see that I am out of breath?   30

JULIET How art thou out of breath when thou hast breath
To say to me that thou art out of breath?
The excuse that thou dost make in this delay
Is longer than the tale thou dost excuse.
Is thy news good or bad? Answer to that.   35
Say either, and I'll stay the circumstance.*
Let me be satisfied: is't good or bad?

stay . . . circumstance:
wait for the details

NURSE   Well, you have made a simple choice, you know not how
to choose a man. Romeo! No, not he. He is not the flower
of courtesy,* but I'll warrant him, as gentle as a lamb.   40
Go thy ways, wench, serve God. What, have you din'd at
home?

*flower . . . of cour-
tesy:* perfect
gentleman

JULIET   No, no! But all this did I know before.
What says he of our marriage? what of that?

NURSE   O, how my head aches! What a head have I!   45
It beats as it would fall in twenty pieces.
My back a' t' other side—ah, my back, my back!
Beshrew your heart for sending me about
To catch my death with jauncing up and down!

JULIET	I' faith, I am sorry that thou art not well.	50	
	Sweet, sweet, sweet nurse, tell me, what says my love?		
NURSE	Your love says, like an honest* gentleman,		*honest:* honorable
	An' a courteous and a kind and a handsome,		
	And, I warrant, a virtuous—Where is your mother?		
JULIET	Where is my mother! why, she is within!	55	
	Where should she be? How oddly thou repliest!		
	"Your love says like an honest gentleman,		
	'Where is your mother?' "		
NURSE	Is this the poultice for my aching bones?		
	Hencefoward do your messages yourself.	60	
JULIET	Here's such a coil! Come, what says Romeo?		
NURSE	Have you got leave to go to shrift today?		
JULIET	I have.		
NURSE	Then hie* you hence to Friar Lawrence' cell,		*hie:* hurry
	There stays a husband to make you a wife.	65	
	Now comes the wanton* blood up in your cheeks;		*wanton:* unruly, impetuous
	They'll be scarlet straight at any news.*		*scarlet . . . news:* You have always blushed easily.
	Hie you to church; I must another way		
	To fetch a ladder, by the which your love		
	Must climb a bird's nest soon when it is dark.	70	
	Go, I'll to dinner; hie you to the cell.		
JULIET	Hie to high fortune! Honest nurse, farewell.		

Exeunt.

Scene VI

Time: Monday afternoon
Place: Friar Lawrence's cell

Juliet meets Romeo and Friar Lawrence for the wedding.

Enter FRIAR LAWRENCE and ROMEO.

Act II, Scene vi

The Friar in his opening speech expresses his concern that heaven will bless the marriage that he is about to perform. Romeo's reply embodies both the love and time themes. The Friar's next speech (ll. 8-15) is important thematically, for it is an attempt to restrain the young, impetuous lovers. It also develops the haste theme. Immediately following these lines admonishing the protagonist to slow down, the stage directions in an early edition of the play read, "Enter Juliet rather fast and embraceth Romeo." The Friar's lines that end the scene again reveal his concern for the young lovers' purity. The actual wedding between Romeo and Juliet takes place offstage. To depict such a holy ceremony onstage would have profaned it. In only one context, *Much Ado About Nothing* (Act IV, Scene i), does Shakespeare use any actual lines from the marriage vows onstage, and there the Friar delivers only the first line, "If any of you know any inward impediment why you should not be conjoin'd, . . ." before the wedding is broken off.

Romeo and Juliet has occasionally been misinterpreted by Christian students as a work that glorifies fornication. Quite to the contrary, it promotes the sanctity of the marriage relationship. Romeo and Juliet are together onstage "alive" only four times, for a total of about fourteen minutes' playing time: (1) they meet at Capulet's ball, (2) they court during the balcony scene, (3) they marry (offstage) at the Friar's cell, and (4) they part (Act III, Scene v) after having been together on their wedding night.

Shakespeare carefully accounts for their time from their first meeting on Sunday evening until their wedding on Monday afternoon, and the Friar, who views fornication with the same seriousness in men as in women, at the end of this scene states that he will not leave Romeo and Juliet alone together until they have been married. (See also Prospero's admonition to his daughter and prospective son-in-law in *The Tempest,* Act IV, Scene i, ll. 13-23. This passage suggests that the heavens withhold the blessings of domestic peace and fertility from those who during courtship "give dalliance / Too much the rein" [ll. 51-52].)

FRIAR L.   So smile the heavens upon this holy act
             That after-hours with sorrow chide us not.

ROMEO   Amen, amen! But come what sorrow can,
             It cannot countervail* the exchange of joy   *countervail*: equal
             That one short minute gives me in her sight.   5
             Do thou but close our hands with holy words;
             Then love-devouring death do what he dare;
             It is enough I may but call her mine.

FRIAR L.   These violent delights have violent ends
             And in their triumph die like fire and powder,   10
             Which as they kiss consume. The sweetest honey
             Is loathsome* in his own deliciousness   *loathesome*: repulsive
             And in the taste confounds* the appetite.   *confounds*: destroys
             Therefore love moderately; long love doth so.
             Too swift arrives as tardy as too slow.   15

Enter JULIET somewhat fast and embraces ROMEO.

Here comes the lady. O, so light of foot
Will ne'er wear out the everlasting flint;*
A lover may bestride the gossamers*
That idles in the wanton summer air
And yet not fall; so light is vanity.* 20

everlasting flint: hard stone (upon which Juliet walks)
gossamers: thin webs spun by spiders
vanity: empty, vain worldly pleasures

JULIET   Good even* to my ghostly confessor.

even: evening

FRIAR L.   Romeo shall thank thee, daughter, for us both.

JULIET   As much* to him, else in his thanks too much.

As much: the same greeting

ROMEO   Ah, Juliet, if the measure of thy joy
Be heap'd like mine and that* thy skill be more 25
To blazon* it, then sweeten with thy breath
This neighbor air and let rich music's tongue
Unfold the imagin'd happiness that both
Receive in either by this dear* encounter.

that: if
blazon: proclaim

dear: precious (with a secondary, ominous meaning of costly)

JULIET   Conceit,* more rich in matter than in words, 30
Brags of* his substance, not of ornament.
They are but beggars that can count their worth,
But my true love is grown to such excess
I cannot sum up sum* of half my wealth.

Conceit: Thought
Brags of: Takes pride in

sum . . . sum: calculate the sum

FRIAR L.   Come, come with me, and we will make short work, 35
For by your leaves* you shall not stay alone
Till Holy Church incorporate two in one.

For . . . leaves: Pardon me for insisting

Exeunt.

About the Play

1. List at least two specific differences between the love relationship of Romeo/ Rosaline and Romeo/Juliet. Support your answer with quotations from the text.
2. What is Friar Lawrence's motivation for consenting to marry Romeo and Juliet?
3. What is the significance of Friar Lawrence's statement "Wisely and slow; they stumble that run fast"?
4. How would you describe the nurse? Defend your answer with specific quotations from the text.
5. Compare Friar Lawrence, who counsels Romeo, with the Nurse, who counsels Juliet.

About the Play

1. *Answers may vary but might include that Juliet returns Romeo's love and that they are from feuding houses. Accept any reasonable answers that students can support from the text.*

2. *He hopes the marriage may "turn your households' rancor to pure love" (II.iii.82).*

3. *His words have a double meaning: (1) a literal one, since Romeo is urging him to hurry; (2) a symbolic one—he is urging Romeo not to rush into marriage.*

4. *Answers may vary; she loves Juliet a great deal (I.iii.27); she is a comic character (II.iv.49; also II.v); she is talkative (II.iv.61-69, 96-102).*

5. *Answers will vary. Lawrence seems more trustworthy and dependable; he bases his willingness to marry the two on a desire to end the feud. The Nurse seems to think little beyond Juliet's happiness.*

Act II

Scene I

Time: Monday afternoon
Place: A street

The young men of the opposing houses quarrel. When Romeo tries to ignore Tybalt's insults, Mercutio takes up the challenge. Romeo attempts to stop their fight, but in so doing, he obscures Mercutio's view of Tybalt, who then kills Mercutio and flees.

Enter MERCUTIO, BENVOLIO, PAGE, and MEN.

BENVOLIO	I pray thee, good Mercutio, let's retire. The day is hot, the Capulets abroad, And if we meet, we shall not 'scape a brawl; For now these hot days is the mad blood stirring.	
MERCUTIO	Thou art like one of these fellows that, when he enters 5 the confines of a tavern, claps me his sword upon the table and says, "God send me no need of thee!" and by the operation of the second cup draws* him on the drawer* when indeed there is no need.	*draws:* i.e., draws his sword *drawer:* tapster
BENVOLIO	Am I like such a fellow? 10	
MERCUTIO	Come, come, thou are as hot a Jack in thy mood as any in Italy and as soon mov'd to be moody* and as soon moody to be mov'd.	*moody:* angry
BENVOLIO	And what to?	
MERCUTIO	Nay, and there were two such we should have none 15 shortly, for one would kill the other. Thou? Why, thou wilt quarrel with a man that hath a hair more or a hair less in his beard than thou hast. Thou wilt quarrel with a man for cracking nuts, having no other reason but because thou hast hazel eyes. What eye but such an eye would 20 spy out such a quarrel? Thy head is as full of quarrels as an egg is full of meat,* and yet thy head hath been beaten as	*meat:* food

Act III, Scene i

As the scene opens, Romeo's young friends reinforce for the audience the seasonal setting of the play. This can be established as the month of July from the Nurse and Lady Capulet's discussion of Juliet's age in relationship to Lammas-tide, or August 1, in Act I, Scene iii. (Interestingly, they talk about Juliet's "ripeness" for marriage in terms of the festival in celebration of the first ripe corn.) According to Sir Thomas Smith in *The Commonwealth of England*, 1583, "In the warm time people for the most part be more unruly." Probably it is for purposes of characterization that Shakespeare changed the Christmas setting in his source to July.

The opening segment of the scene also reinforces Mercutio's propensity for quarreling established in Act II, Scene iv. Whereas Tybalt forthrightly states that he likes to fight, Mercutio only accuses others of being pugnacious. In contrast to these two young men, Benvolio (his name literally means "of good will") is a peacemaker. Notice that at lines 45-48 he suggests alternatives to public fighting, which the Prince has forbidden.

Romeo enters the scene a more mature man than he was in the preceding acts. Although he refuses to fight Tybalt, his attempt to restrain Tybalt and Mercutio as they fight has an ironic effect; he steps between them and unwittingly blocks Mercutio's view of Tybalt, leaving his friend unable to defend himself. Tybalt thrusts under Romeo's arm and kills Mercutio. Thus fate intrudes upon the action, for Romeo's good intentions lead to the death of his friend. This part of the plot is Shakespeare's own invention, not found in his sources. Shakespeare employs Mercutio's death as the motivation for Romeo's murder of Tybalt. In the sources, during a fray between the two bands, Tybalt attacks Romeo, who then kills the attacker in self-defense. In Shakespeare's more complicated plot, fate intervenes as Romeo attempts to make peace; Romeo seeks Tybalt to avenge his friend's death; and both Tybalt and Mercutio die as a result of their own doings. Ironically, however, both are also ignorant of the love of Romeo and Juliet.

addle* as an egg for quarreling. Thou hast quarrel'd with a man for coughing in the street because he hath waken'd thy dog that hath lain asleep in the sun. Didst thou not 25 fall out with a tailor for wearing his new doublet* before Easter;* with another for tying his new shoes with old riband? And yet thou wilt tutor me from* quarreling!

BENVOLIO   And* I were so apt to quarrel as thou art, any man should buy the fee-simple* of my life for an hour and a 30 quarter.*

MERCUTIO   The fee-simple! O simple!

Enter TYBALT, PETRUCHIO, and others.*

BENVOLIO   By my head, here comes the Capulets.

MERCUTIO   By my heel, I care not.

TYBALT   Follow me close, for I will speak to them. Gentlemen, 35 good e'en, a word with one of you.

MERCUTIO   And but one word with one of us? Couple it with something; make it a word and a blow.

TYBALT   You shall find me apt enough to that, sir, and you will give me occasion. 40

MERCUTIO   Could you not take some occasion without giving?

TYBALT   Mercutio, thou consort'st* with Romeo—

MERCUTIO   Consort! What, dost thou make us minstrels? And thou make minstrels of us, look to hear nothing but discords.

BENVOLIO   We talk here in the public haunt of men. 45 Either withdraw unto some private place And reason coldly* of your grievances Or else depart; here all eyes gaze on us.

MERCUTIO   Men's eyes were made to look, and let them gaze; I will not budge for no man's pleasure, I. 50

Enter ROMEO.

addle: muddled, rotten

doublet: coat

before Easter: during Lent, when only dismal dress was allowed by the Catholic church
tutor . . . from: persuade me against
And: If
fee-simple: absolute ownership
an . . . quarter: i.e., a small sum, the pay for a small amount of work
Petruchio: a "ghost" character, or one whom Shakespeare intended to develop but wound up giving no lines

consort'st: (1) keep company (2) perform music

reason coldly: discuss calmly

The climax of the play, or turning point in the action for the main characters, is Romeo's killing Tybalt. This event is a point of no return for both Romeo and Juliet. Up to this point nothing has occurred in the action that would preclude a happy ending for the young lovers. In a sense this play might be classified a comitragedy because beyond the midpoint of the action there is still the possibility of a happy ending. No villain has plotted the undoing of the protagonists, and they have not doomed themselves by consciously entering into a course of evil action. Shakespeare is careful not to consign the young lovers to the machinations of fate. Romeo and Juliet ultimately suffer the consequences of their own freewill decisions. What major character weakness does Shakespeare attribute to them both? *(See analy-sis of Act II, Scenes iii and vi; they are hasty, impetuous.)*

Analyze Benvolio's account of the fray at lines 147-70. Is it accurate? *(yes)* What theme does Shakespeare convey here? *(haste, impetuosity)* After reporting the events of the climax scene to the Prince, Benvolio does not appear again in the play. The functions he has performed, reporting on the other young men's behavior (in Acts I and III) and restraining them, are no longer needed.

TYBALT	Well, peace be with you, sir, here comes my man.*	*my man:* the man I'm looking for
MERCUTIO	But I'll be hang'd, sir, if he wear your livery.* Indeed, go before to field;* he'll be your follower; Your worship* in that sense may call him "man."	*livery:* servant's uniform (Mercutio deliberately misinterprets *man* as *servant.*) *go . . . field:* arrive first at the site of a duel *your worship:* term of polite address to a noble man, used ironically by Mercutio to address Tybalt
TYBALT	Romeo, the hate I bear thee can afford 55 No better term than this: thou art a villain.	
ROMEO	Tybalt, the reason that I have to love thee Doth much excuse* the appertaining rage* To* such a greeting. Villain am I none; Therefore farewell. See thou know'st me not. 60	*excuse:* justify the absence of *appertaining rage:* angry response *To:* Appropriate to
TYBALT	Boy, this shall not excuse the injuries That thou hast done me; therefore turn and draw.	
ROMEO	I do protest I never injured thee But love thee better than thou canst devise.* Till thou shalt know the reason of my love, 65 And so, good Capulet—which name I tender* As dearly as mine own—be satisfied.	*devise:* understand *tender:* care for
MERCUTIO	O calm, dishonorable, vile submission! *Alla Staccato** carries it away.* *(He draws.)* Tybalt, you rat-catcher,* will you walk? 70	*Alla staccato:* "with the thrust" (a scornful designation of Tybalt, the technical swordsman) *carries . . . away:* wins *rat-catcher:* i.e., Prince of Cats
TYBALT	What wouldst thou have with me?	
MERCUTIO	Good King of Cats, nothing but one of your nine lives; that I mean to make bold withal, and as you shall use me hereafter, dry-beat* the rest of the eight. Will you pluck your sword out of his pilcher* by the ears?* Make haste, 75 lest mine be about your ears ere it* be out.	*dry-beat:* bruise *pilcher:* scabbard *by . . .ears:* i.e., so reluctantly *it:* i.e., your sword
TYBALT	I am for you.	
ROMEO	Gentle, Mercutio, put thy rapier up.	
MERCUTIO	Come, sir, your *passado.**	*passado:* lunge
	They fight.	

ROMEO	Draw, Benvolio; beat down their weapons.	80
	Gentlemen, for shame, forbear this outrage!	
	Tybalt, Mercutio, the Prince expressly hath	
	Forbid this bandying* in Verona streets.	*bandying:* quarreling

ROMEO steps between them.

Hold Tybalt! Good Mercutio!

TYBALT stabs MERCUTIO. Exeunt TYBALT and his followers.

MERCUTIO	I am hurt.	
	A plague a' your houses! I am sped.*	85
	Is he gone and hath nothing?*	*sped:* mortally wounded
		nothing: no injury

BENVOLIO	What, art thou hurt?	
MERCUTIO	Ay, ay, a scratch, a scratch, but, 'tis enough. Where is my page? Go, villain,* fetch a surgeon.	*villain:* fellow

Exit PAGE.

ROMEO	Courage, man; the hurt cannot be much.	

MERCUTIO No, 'tis not so deep as a well nor so wide as a church- 90
door, but 'tis enough; 'twill serve. Ask for me tomorrow,
and you shall find me a grave man. I am pepper'd,* I *pepper'd:* shot to
warrant, for this world. A plague a' both your houses! pieces
What! A dog, a rat, a mouse, a cat, to scratch a man to
death! A braggart, a rogue, a villain that fights by the 95
book of arithmetic!* Why came you between us? I was *book . . . arithmetic:*
hurt under your arm. fencing text

ROMEO I thought all for the best.

MERCUTIO Help me into some house, Benvolio,
Or I shall faint. A plague a' both your houses! 100
They have made worms' meat of me. I have it,
And soundly. To your houses!

Exeunt MERCUTIO and BENVOLIO.

ROMEO This gentleman, the Prince's near ally,* *ally:* kinsman
My very friend, hath got this mortal hurt
In my behalf; my reputation stain'd 105
With Tybalt's slander—Tybalt, that an hour
Hath been my cousin! O sweet Juliet,
Thy beauty hath made me effeminate* *effeminate;* weak of
And in my temper* soft'ned valor's steel!* will
temper: composition,
make up *valor's*
steel: my courage

Enter BENVOLIO.

BENVOLIO O Romeo, Romeo, brave Mercutio is dead! 110
That gallant spirit hath aspir'd* the clouds, *aspir'd:* risen to
Which too untimely here did scorn the earth.

ROMEO This day's black fate on moe* days doth depend.* *moe:* more *depend:*
This but begins; the woe others must end. extends its influence

Enter TYBALT.

BENVOLIO   Here comes the furious Tybalt back again.   115

ROMEO   He gone in triumph, and Mercutio slain!
            Away to heaven, respective lenity,*   *respective lenity:* con-
            And fire and fury be my conduct now!   siderations of being
            Now, Tybalt, take the "villain" back again   mild
            That late thou gavest me, for Mercutio's soul   120
            Is but a little way above our heads,
            Staying* for thine to keep company.   *Staying:* Waiting
            Either thou or I or both must go with him.

TYBALT	Thou wretched boy that didst consort him here Shalt with him hence.
ROMEO	This shall determine that. 125

(They fight; TYBALT falls.)

BENVOLIO	Romeo, away, be gone! The citizens are up and Tybalt slain. Stand not amazed. The Prince will doom thee death If thou art taken. Hence be gone away!
ROMEO	O, I am fortune's fool!* 130

fool: plaything; the helpless victim of fortune

BENVOLIO	Why dost thou stay?

Exit ROMEO. Enter CITIZENS.

CITIZEN 1	Which way ran he that kill'd Mercutio? Tybalt, that murderer, which way ran he?
BENVOLIO	There lies that Tybalt.
CITIZEN 1	Up, sir, go with me; I charge thee in the Prince's name, obey. 135

Enter PRINCE, OLD MONTAGUE, CAPULET, their WIVES, and all.

PRINCE	Where are the vile beginners of this fray?
BENVOLIO	O noble Prince, I can discover* all The unlucky manage* of this fatal brawl: There lies the man, slain by Romeo, That slew thy kinsman, brave Mercutio. 140

discover: reveal

manage: circumstance

LADY CAP.	Tybalt, my cousin! O my brother's child! O Prince! O cousin! O husband! O, the blood is spill'd Of my dear kinsman! Prince, as thou art true, For blood of ours shed blood of Montague. O cousin, cousin! 145
PRINCE	Benvolio, who began this bloody fray?

BENVOLIO   Tybalt, here slain, whom Romeo's hand did slay!
Romeo that spoke him fair, bid him bethink*
How nice* the quarrel was, and urg'd withal*
Your high displeasure; all this, uttered   150
With gentle breath, calm look, knees humbly bowed,
Could not take truce with* the unruly spleen*
Of Tybalt, deaf to peace, but that he tilts
With piercing steel at bold Mercutio's breast,
Who, all as hot, turns deadly point to point   155
And, with a martial scorn, with one hand beats
Cold death aside and with the other sends
It back to Tybalt, whose dexterity*
Retorts* it. Romeo he cries aloud,
"Hold, friends! Friends, part!" and swifter than his
    tongue   160
His agile arm beats down their fatal* points
And 'twixt them rushes, underneath whose arm
An envious* thrust from Tybalt hit the life
Of stout Mercutio, and then Tybalt fled;
But by and by comes back to Romeo,   165
Who had but newly entertain'd* revenge,
And to't they go like lightning, for ere I
Could draw to part them was stout Tybalt slain;
And as he fell, did Romeo turn and fly.
This is the truth, or let Benvolio die.   170

LADY CAP.   He is a kinsman to the Montague.
Affection makes him false; he speaks not true.
Some twenty of them fought in this black strife,
And all those twenty could but kill one life.
I beg for justice, which thou, Prince, must give: 175
Romeo slew Tybalt; Romeo must not live.

PRINCE   Romeo slew him; he slew Mercutio;
Who now the price of his dear blood doth owe?

MONTAGUE   Not Romeo, Prince: he was Mercutio's friend.
His fault concludes but what the law should end: 180
The life of Tybalt.

PRINCE   And for that offense
Immediately we do exile him hence.
I have an interest* in your heart's proceeding.
My blood for your rude brawls doth lie a-bleeding;

bethink: consider

nice: trivial *urg'd
  withal:* emphasized
  also

take . . . with: calm
  spleen: seat (bodily
  source) of anger

dexterity: skill

Retorts: Returns

fatal: deadly

envious: malicious

entertain'd: thought of

interest: personal
  involvement

But I'll amerce* you with so strong a fine   185   *amerce:* punish (by
That you shall all repent the loss of mine.   fine)
I will be deaf to pleading and excuses,
Nor tears nor prayers shall purchase out abuses;*   *purchase . . . abuses:*
Therefore use none. Let Romeo hence in haste,   pay for your
Else when he is found, that hour is his last.   190   transgressions
Bear hence this body and attend our will;*   *attend . . . will:* come
Mercy but murders,* pardoning those that kill.   to hear my pro-
                                                                     nouncement of
                                                                     judgment
                    Exeunt.   *but murders:* encour-
                                                                     ages others to
                                                                     murder

Scene II

Time: Monday afternoon
Place: Capulet's house

Juliet, eagerly awaiting her husband's arrival at her chamber, is told by the
Nurse that Romeo has murdered Tybalt and been banished. Torn between
love for her husband and her cousin, she sends the Nurse to summon Romeo.

Enter JULIET alone.

JULIET   Gallop apace, you fiery-footed steeds,
                Toward Phoebus'* lodging; such a wagoner   *Phoebus':* The sun's,
                As Phaeton would whip you to the west*   Phoebus Apollo
                And bring in cloudy night immediately.   succeeded the Titan
                Come, night, come, Romeo, come, thou day in night, 5   Helios as sun god.
                For thou wilt lie upon the wings of night,   The boy Phaeton
                Whiter than new snow upon a raven's back.   insisted on driving
                Come, gentle night, come, loving, black-brow'd night.   the chariot (wagon)
                Give me my Romeo, and when he shall die,   of his father, god of
                Take him and cut him out in little stars,   10   the sun, and thus
                And he will make the face of heaven so fine   destroyed himself.
                That all the world will be in love with night   *whip . . . west:* i.e.,
                And pay no worship to the garish* sun.   make the sun set
                O, I have bought the mansion of a love
                But not possess'd it; and though I am sold,   15 *garish:* gaudy
                Not yet enjoy'd. So tedious is this day
                As is the night before some festival
                To an impatient child that hath new robes
                And may not wear them. O, here comes my nurse,

Act III, Scene ii

The scene opens with another of Juliet's famous soliloquies. The speech is full of Shakespeare's classical learning. Juliet alludes to mythology in the beginning of the soliloquy and then in the middle portion to Renaissance falconry. In lines 8-13 she paraphrases a passage from *Metamorphoses,* describing Romeo's apotheosis into "little stars" in terms derived from Ovid's account of the glorification of Caesar. Yet Shakespeare's allusions and imagery in this speech heighten the drama of the scene rather than detract from it. Which of the play's themes are united in this passage? *(the love of Juliet and Romeo, haste)* How does the speech reinforce the playwright's characterization of Juliet? *(It emphasizes her true love for Romeo.)*

The Nurse arrives once again with information that is important to Juliet, yet she cannot get to the point of her communication. Notice her exaggerated reactions to Tybalt's death. These lines foreshadow her response to Juliet's "death" in Act IV, Scene v. Her linguistic limitations are an important feature of Shakespeare's comic characterization. Why are lines 46-48 humorous? *(It is highly doubtful that the young, quarrelsome Tybalt was "the best friend [the Nurse] had.")*

Juliet's reaction upon discovering that Romeo has killed Tybalt is a rare speech in this play in its depiction of internal struggle. Like Romeo in Act I, Scene i, Juliet feels the pull of antithetical emotions: she loves Romeo, yet she hates him. Appropriately, to express such feelings, she employs a string of oxymorons (cf. I.i.146-51). In her response to this speech, the Nurse voices a negative attitude toward men in general. Juliet quickly recovers her wits, however, and turns her attention to Romeo's present woe, banishment, and makes plans to be with him.

Enter NURSE, wringing her hands, with the ladder of cords in her lap.

And she brings news; and every tongue that speaks   20
But Romeo's name speaks heavenly eloquence.
Now, nurse, what news? What hast thou there? the cords
That Romeo bid thee fetch?

NURSE   Ay, ay, the cords.

JULIET   Ay, me, what news? Why dost thou wring thy hands?

NURSE   Alack the day, he's dead, he's dead, he's dead!   25
We are undone, lady, we are undone!
Alack the day, he's gone, he's kill'd, he's dead!

JULIET   Can heaven be so envious?*   *envious:* spiteful

NURSE   Romeo can,
Though heaven cannot. O Romeo, Romeo!
Who ever would have thought it Romeo?   30

JULIET   Hath Romeo slain himself? Say thou but ay,
And that bare vowel *I* shall poison more
Than the death-darting eye of cockatrice.*   *cockatrice:* a mythical
I am not I, if there be such an ay,   serpent that could
Or those* eyes shut, that make thee answer ay. 35   kill by its glance
If he be slain, say ay, or if not, no.   *those:* Romeo's
Brief sounds determine of* my weal or woe.   *determine of:* establish
                                                       definitely

NURSE   I saw the wound here on his manly breast.
A piteous corse,* a bloody, piteous corse,   *corse:* corpse
Pale, pale as ashes, all bedaub'd in blood,   40
All in gore blood; I sounded* at the sight.   *sounded:* swooned;
                                                       fainted

JULIET   O, break, my heart! Poor bankrout,* break at once! *bankrout:* bankrupt
To prison, eyes, ne'er look on liberty!
Vile earth,* to earth* resign;* end motion here   *earth:* Juliet's body
And thou and Romeo press one heavy bier!   45   *earth:* the soil *resign:*
                                                       surrender

NURSE   O Tybalt, Tybalt, the best friend I had!
O courteous Tybalt, honest gentleman,
That ever I should live to see thee dead!

JULIET	What storm is this that blows so contrary?
	Is Romeo slaught'red? And is Tybalt dead? 50
	My dearest cousin and my dearer lord?
	Then, dreadful trumpet, sound the general doom,*
	For who is living if those two are gone?
NURSE	Tybalt is gone and Romeo banished;*
	Romeo that killed him, he is banished. 55
JULIET	O Nurse, did Romeo's hand shed Tybalt's blood?
NURSE	It did, it did. Alas the day, it did!
	O serpent heart hid with a flow'ring* face!
	Did ever dragon keep* so fair a cave?
JULIET	Beautiful tyrant! fiend angelical! 60
	Dove-feather'd raven! wolvish ravening lamb!
	Despised substance* of divinest show!*
	Just opposite to what thou justly* seem'st,
	A dimmed saint, an honorable villain!
	O nature, what hadst thou to do in hell 65
	When thou didst bower* the spirit of a fiend
	In mortal paradise of such sweet flesh?
	Was ever book containing such vile matter
	So fairly bound? O that deceit should dwell
	In such a gorgeous palace!
NURSE	There's no trust, 70
	No faith, no honesty in men, all perjur'd,
	All forsworn,* all naught,* all dissemblers.*
	Ah, where's my man? Give me some aqua-vitae.*
	These griefs, these woes, these sorrows make me old.
	Shame come to Romeo!
JULIET	Blister'd be thy tongue 75
	For such a wish! He was not born to shame.
	Upon his brow shame is asham'd to sit;
	For 'tis a throne where honor may be crown'd
	Sole monarch of the universal earth.
	O, what a beast was I to chide at him! 80
NURSE	Will you speak well of him that kill'd your cousin?

the . . . doom: universal judgment (Rev. 11:15)

banished: exiled, forced to leave his city by official decree

flow'ring: fair

keep: dwell in

substance: reality
show: appearance
justly: rightly

bower: lodge

forsworn: disloyal, false *naught:* wicked *dissemblers:* hypocrites
aqua-vitae: a strong drink used as medicine

JULIET	Shall I speak ill of him that is my husband?
	Ah, poor my lord, what tongue shall smooth thy name
	When I, thy three-hours' wife, have mangled it?
	But wherefore, villain, didst thou kill my cousin? 85
	That villain cousin would have kill'd my husband.
	Back, foolish tears, back to your native spring;
	Your tributary drops belong to* woe,
	Which you, mistaking, offer up to joy.*
	My husband lives that Tybalt would have slain, 90
	And Tybalt's dead that would have slain my husband.
	All is comfort; wherefore weep I then?
	Some word there was, worser than Tybalt's death
	That murder'd me; I would forget it fain,
	But O, it presses to my memory 95
	Like damned* guilty deeds to sinners' minds:
	"Tybalt is dead, and Romeo is banished."
	That "banished," that one word "banished"
	Hath slain* ten thousand Tybalts. Tybalt's death
	Was woe enough if it had ended there; 100
	Or if sour woe delights in fellowship*
	And needly* will be rank'd with other griefs,
	Why followed not when she said, "Tybalt's dead,"
	Thy father or thy mother, nay, or both,
	Which modern* lamentation might have moved? 105
	But with a rearward* following Tybalt's death,
	"Romeo is banished," to speak that word
	Is father, mother, Tybalt, Romeo, Juliet,
	All slain, all dead: "Romeo is banished!"
	There is no end, no limit, measure, bound 110
	In that word's* death; no words can that woe sound.
	Where is my father and my mother, nurse?
NURSE	Weeping and wailing over Tybalt's corse.
	Will you go to them? I will bring you thither.
JULIET	Wash they his wounds with tears? Mine shall be spent,* 115
	When* theirs are dry, for Romeo's banishment.
	Take up those cords. Poor ropes, you are beguil'd,*
	Both you and I, for Romeo is exil'd.
NURSE	Hie to your chamber. I'll find Romeo
	To comfort you. I wot* well where he is. 120
	Hark ye, your Romeo will be here at night.
	I'll to him; he is hid at Lawrence's cell.

Your . . . to: You should function in *joy:* i.e., the occasion of Romeo's survival

damned: damnable

Hath slain: Carries the emotional force of the deaths of *delights . . . fellowship.* ushers in other woes *needly:* of necessity

modern: moderate, not excessive *rearward:* rear guard (literally a group of soldiers that follow)

that word's: i.e., Romeo's

spent: used up *When:* i.e., only when *beguil'd:* cheated

wot: know

| JULIET | O, find him! Give this ring to my true knight
And bid him come to take his last farewell. | |

Exeunt.

Scene III

Time: Monday afternoon
Place: Friar Lawrence's cell

Friar Lawrence informs Romeo of his banishment and tries to console him. The Nurse also informs Romeo of Juliet's predicament and gives him a ring from Juliet.

Enter FRIAR LAWRENCE.

| FRIAR L. | Romeo, come forth, come forth, thou fearful man.
Affliction is enamor'd of* thy parts,*
And thou art wedded to calamity. | | *enamor'd of:* charmed
by *parts:* good fea-
tures, qualities |

Enter ROMEO.

| ROMEO | Father, what news? What is the Prince's doom?*
What sorrow craves acquaintance at my hand?*
That I yet know not? | 5 | *doom:* judicial deci-
sion, sentence
craves . . . hand: waits
to make
acquaintance |

| FRIAR L. | Too familiar
Is my dear son with such sour company!
I bring thee tidings of the Prince's doom. | | |

| ROMEO | What less than doomsday is the Prince's doom? | | |

| FRIAR L. | A gentler judgment vanish'd* from his lips—
Not body's death but body's banishment. | 10 | *vanish'd:* escaped |

| ROMEO | Ha, banishment? Be merciful: say "death";
For exile hath more terror in his look,
Much more than death. Do not say "banishment"! | | |

| FRIAR L. | Here from Verona art thou banished.
Be patient, for the world is broad and wide. | 15 | |

Act III, Scene iii

At the beginning of the scene Friar Lawrence announces to Romeo the Prince's sentence of banishment. The rest of the scene consists of the Friar's and later the Nurse's attempts to deal with Romeo's very immature response to this penalty. Notice that the Friar deals with Romeo in spiritual terms, first charging him with the sin of ingratitude and then pointing out the merciful nature of the Prince's sentence.

Notice the stage directions below line 108. When Romeo threatens suicide, the Nurse "snatches the dagger away." Suicide is always condemned before it occurs on Shakespeare's stage. According to Renaissance theologians, a Christian is prevented by the Holy Spirit from committing suicide. The person who commits suicide goes to hell, for he has killed both body and soul. He is not permitted a Christian funeral or burial. (Thus the charge of suicide brings great grief to the family of one who has died.) Shakespeare's audience certainly knew this doctrine, but he does not remind them of it onstage.

At lines 135-44, what blessings does the Friar admonish Romeo to "count"? (*Juliet is alive; Tybalt did not kill him; he is exiled, not under a death sentence.*) Such a list of blessings suggests that fate is not against Romeo. Shakespeare further argues for man's free will in this scene as the Friar at lines 146-58 proposes a plan to enable Romeo to see Juliet once again. Throughout the play the character of the Friar, a figure of good counsel, implies that man can direct his destiny. He also attempts to cure social ills by natural means (cf. his famous speech at the beginning of II.iii). During the course of the plot he proposes four credible plans for the union of Romeo and Juliet and the consequent reconciliation of the Capulets and Montagues. As each plan is in turn foiled, he devises another: (1) He marries Romeo and Juliet secretly, intending later to announce the marriage and see the feud resolved. This plan is foiled by Romeo's murder of Tybalt. (2) He proposes that Romeo go to Mantua and that Juliet join him there later (III.iii.146-58). This plan is foiled by Capulet's insistence that Juliet marry Paris. (3) He proposes the potion plan (IV.i.89-120), which is foiled by the quarantine of Friar John. (4) He plans to arrive at the Capulet

ROMEO	There is no world without* Verona's walls		*without:* outside
	But purgatory, torture, pain itself.		
	Hence "banished" is banish'd from the world,		
	And world's exile is death. Then "banished"	20	
	Is death mistermed. Calling death "banished,"		
	Thou cut'st my head off with a golden axe		
	And smilest upon the stroke that murders me.		
FRIAR L.	O deadly sin! O rude unthankfulness!		*Thy . . . death:*
	Thy fault our law calls death;* but the kind Prince,	25	According to our
	Taking thy part, hath rush'd* aside the law		laws, you have com-mitted a capital
	And turn'd that black word "death" to "banishment."		offense.
	This is dear mercy, and thou seest it not.		*rush'd:* pushed

tomb before Juliet awakens, to write to inform Romeo that she is alive, and to keep her at his cell until Romeo can come for her (V.ii.24-30). This plan fails simply because Romeo arrives at the tomb and commits suicide before the Friar gets there. Even in the face of this final failure the Friar has a plan: the widowed Juliet should go to live in a convent (V.iii.157-58).

Notice the Nurse's comic reaction to the Friar's good counsel (ll. 159-60). As the play goes on, Shakespeare will reveal the extent to which she is his ironic counterpart, or evil counsel. The Nurse is a near-literal mother to Juliet, for she provided her physical nourishment as a young child. (See I.iii.17-29.) On the other hand, the Friar is Romeo's spiritual ("ghostly") father.

ROMEO	'Tis torture and not mercy. Heaven is here	
	Where Juliet lives, and every cat and dog	30
	And little mouse, every unworthy thing	
	Live here in heaven and may look on her,	
	But Romeo may not. More validity,*	*validity:* dignity
	More honorable state, more courtship lives	
	In carrion* flies than Romeo. They may seize	35 *carrion:* flesh-eating
	On the white wonder of dear Juliet's hand	
	And steal immortal blessing from her lips,	
	Who, even in pure and vestal modesty,	
	Still* blush, as thinking their own kisses* sin.	*Still:* Continually
	But Romeo may not; he is banished.	40 *kisses:* contact with each other
	This may flies do, but I from this must fly.	
	They are free men, but I am banished.	
	And sayest thou yet that exile is not death?	
	Hadst thou no poison mix'd, no sharp-ground knife,	
	No sudden mean* of death, though ne'er so mean,*	45 *mean:* means *mean:* base, lowly
	But "banished" to kill me? "Banished"?	
	O friar, the damned use that word in hell;	
	Howling attends it. How hast thou the heart,	
	Being a divine,* a ghostly confessor,	*divine:* learned clergyman
	A sin-absolver, and my friend profess'd,	50
	To mangle me with that word "banished"?	
FRIAR L.	Then fond* madman, hear me a little speak.	*fond:* foolish
ROMEO	O, thou wilt speak again of banishment.	
FRIAR L.	I'll give thee armor to keep off that word:	
	Adversity's sweet milk, philosophy,	55
	To comfort thee though thou art banished.	
ROMEO	Yet "banished"? Hang up philosophy!	
	Unless philosophy can make a Juliet,	
	Displant* a town, reverse a prince's doom,	*Displant:* Transplant
	It helps not, it prevails not. Talk no more.	60
FRIAR L.	O then I see that madmen have no ears.	
ROMEO	How should they when that wise men have no eyes?	
FRIAR L.	Let me dispute* with thee of thy estate.*	*dispute:* discuss *estate:* situation

ROMEO	Thou canst not speak of that thou dost not feel.
	Wert thou as young as I, Juliet thy love, 65
	An hour but married, Tybalt murdered,
	Doting like me and like me banished,
	Then mightest thou speak; then mightest thou tear thy hair
	And fall upon the ground as I do now,
	Taking the measure of* an unmade grave. 70

Taking . . . of: Measuring for

NURSE knocks within.

FRIAR L.	Arise; one knocks. Good Romeo, hide thyself.
ROMEO	Not I, unless the breath of heartsick groans
	Mist-like infold* me from the search of eyes.

infold: obscure, hide

Knock.

FRIAR L.	Hark how they knock!—Who's there?—Romeo, arise;
	Thou wilt be taken.—Stay a while!*—Stand up! 75

Stay . . . while: Wait a moment!

Loud knock.

Run to my study by and by! Good man,
What simpleness* is this? I come, I come!

simpleness: foolishness

Knock.

Who knocks so hard? Whence come you? What's your
will?

NURSE	Let me come in, and you shall know my errand.
	I come from Juliet.
FRIAR L.	Welcome then! 80

Enter NURSE.

NURSE	O holy friar, O, tell me, holy friar,
	Where's my lady's lord? Where's Romeo?
FRIAR L.	There on the ground, with his own tears made drunk.
NURSE	O, he is even in my mistress' case,
	Just in her case, O woeful sympathy!* 85

sympathy: affinity

Piteous predicament! Even so lies she,
Blubb'ring and weeping, weeping and blubb'ring.
Stand up, stand up, stand, and* you be a man.

and: if

For Juliet's sake, for her sake rise and stand.
Why should you fall into so deep an O?*   90

O: Groaning fit

ROMEO   Nurse!

NURSE   Ah, sir, ah, sir, death's the end of all.

ROMEO   Spakest thou of Juliet? How is it with her?
Doth not she think me an old* murderer,

old: hardened

Now I have stain'd the childhood of our joy   95
With blood removed but little from her own?*

removed . . . own: i.e., of her cousin Tybalt

Where is she? And how doth she? And what says
My conceal'd lady* to our cancell'd love?

conceal'd lady: secret wife

NURSE   O, she says nothing, sir, but weeps and weeps
And now falls on her bed and then starts up   100
And Tybalt calls and then on Romeo cries
And then falls down again.

ROMEO   As if that name,
Shot from the deadly level* of a gun,

level: aim

Did murder her as that name's cursed hand
Murder'd her kinsman? O, tell me, friar, tell me,   105
In what vile part of this anatomy
Doth my name lodge? Tell me that I may sack*

sack: destroy

That hateful mansion.

He offers to stab himself, and the NURSE *snatches the dagger away.*

FRIAR L.   Hold thy desperate hand!
Art thou a man? Thy form cries out thou art;
Thy tears are womanish; thy wild acts denote   110
The unreasonable fury of a beast.
Unseemly* woman in* a seeming* man
And ill-beseeming* beast in seeming both,*
Thou hast amaz'd me! By my holy order*
I thought thy disposition better temper'd.*   115

Unseemly: Improper
in: in the form of
seeming: what seems to be a
ill-beseeming: unnatural *seeming both:* seeming to be both (woman and beast)
holy order: priestly vows
temper'd: made up

Hast thou slain Tybalt? Wilt thou slay thyself
And slay thy lady that in thy life lives
By doing cursed hate upon thyself?

Why railest thou on thy birth, the heaven and earth?*
Since birth and heaven and earth all three do meet   120
In thee at once, which thou at once wouldst lose.
Fie, fie, thou shamest thy shape, thy love, thy wit,*
Which* like a usurer* abound'st in all
And usest none in that true use* indeed
Which should bedeck thy shape, thy love, thy wit.   125
Thy noble shape is but a form of wax,*
Digressing* from the valor of man;
Thy dear love sworn but hollow perjury,
Killing that love which thou hast vow'd to cherish;
Thy wit, that ornament to shape and love,   130
Misshapen* in the conduct* of them both,*
Like powder in a skilless soldier's flask,*
Is set afire by thine own ignorance
And thou dismemb'red with thine own defense.*
What, rouse thee, man! Thy Juliet is alive,   135
For whose dear sake thou was but lately dead:*
There art thou happy.* Tybalt would kill thee,
But thou slewest Tybalt: there art thou happy.
The law that threaten'd death becomes thy friend
And turns it to exile: there art thou happy.   140
A pack of blessings lights upon thy back;
Happiness courts thee in her best array,
But like a mishaved* and sullen wench,
Thou frownst upon thy fortune and thy love.
Take heed, take heed, for such die miserable.   145
Go get thee to thy love as was decreed;*
Ascend her chamber; hence and comfort her.
But look thou stay not till the watch be set,*
For then thou canst not pass to Mantua,
Where thou shalt live till we find a time   150
To blaze* your marriage, reconcile your friends,*
Beg pardon of the Prince, and call thee back
With twenty hundred thousand times more joy
Than thou went'st forth in lamentation.
Go before, nurse; commend me to thy lady,   155
And bid her hasten all the house to bed,
Which heavy sorrow makes them apt unto.*
Romeo is coming.

NURSE   O how I could have stay'd here all the night
To hear good counsel. O, what learning is!   160
My lord, I'll tell my lady you will come.

---

heaven . . . earth: i.e., soul and body

wit: intelligence

Which: For you
usurer: moneylender charging high interest (Usury was illegal in Shakespeare's England.)
that . . . use: the way in which God intended it to be used
form . . . wax: wax figure, a shell without a manly substance
Digressing: Turning aside
Misshapen: Deformed
conduct: guidance
them both: i.e., shape (appearance) and love
flask: powderhorn
defense: means of defense
thou . . . dead: you wished to die
happy: fortunate

mishaved: misbehaved

decreed: planned

watch . . . set: guard be posted and the city gates shut

blaze: announce
friends: relations (kin and in-laws)

apt unto: likely to do

ROMEO Do so, and bid my sweet prepare to chide.

NURSE offers to go and then turns again.

NURSE Here, sir, a ring she bid me give you, sir.
Hie you, make haste, for it grows very late.

ROMEO How well my comfort is reviv'd by this!   165

Exit NURSE.

FRIAR L. Go hence; good night; and here stands all your state:*   *here . . . state:* your well-being depends entirely on this
Either be gone before the watch is set
Or by the break of day disguise from hence.
Sojourn* in Mantua. I'll find out* your man,   *Sojourn:* Reside *find out:* locate
And he shall signify from time to time   170
Every good hap* to you that chances* here.   *hap:* happening *chances:* occurs
Give me thy hand. 'Tis late; farewell; good night.

ROMEO But that a joy past joy calls out on me,
It was a grief so brief to part with thee.
Farewell.   175

Exeunt.

Scene IV

Time: Monday evening
Place: Capulet's house

The Capulets make plans with Paris for Juliet's marriage.

Enter CAPULET, LADY CAPULET, and PARIS.

CAPULET Things have fall'n out, sir, so unluckily
That we have had no time to move our daughter.*   *move . . . daughter:* persuade our daughter to accept your proposal
Look you, she lov'd her kinsman Tybalt dearly,
And so did I. Well, we were born to die.
'Tis very late; she'll not come down tonight.   5
I promise you, but for your company
I would have been abed an hour ago.

PARIS	These times of woe afford no times to woo.
	Madam, good night. Commend me to your daughter.

LADY CAP.	I will, and know her mind early tomorrow.	10
	Tonight she's mewed up to* her heaviness.	

mewed . . . to: shut up with (Mews were houses in which hawks slept.)

PARIS begins to exit, but CAPULET calls him again.

CAPULET	Sir Paris, I will make a desperate tender*	
	Of my child's love. I think she will be rul'd	
	In all respects by me; nay more, I doubt it not.	
	Wife, go you to her ere you go to bed;	15
	Acquaint her here of my son* Paris' love.	
	And bid her—mark you me?—on We'n'sday next—	
	But soft, what day is this?	

desperate tender: bold offer

son: future son-in-law

PARIS	Monday, my lord.

CAPULET	Monday! Ha, ha! Well, We'n'sday is too soon.	
	A' Thursday let it be—a' Thursday, tell her,	20
	She shall be married to this noble earl.	
	Will you be ready? Do you like this haste?	
	We'll keep no great ado*—a friend or two,	
	For hark you, Tybalt being slain so late,	
	It may be thought we held him carelessly,	25
	Being our kinsman, if we revel much.	
	Therefore we'll have some half a dozen friends	
	And there an end. But what say you to Thursday?	

ado: hustle and bustle

PARIS	My lord, I would that Thursday were tomorrow.

CAPULET	Well, get you gone; a' Thursday be it then.	30
	Go you to Juliet ere you go to bed;	
	Prepare her, wife, against this wedding day.	
	Farewell, my lord. Light to my chamber, ho!	
	Afore me! It is so very late that we	
	May call it early by and by. Good night.	35

Exeunt.

Scene V

Time: Early Tuesday morning
Place: Juliet's balcony

Romeo and Juliet bid each other farewell as he leaves for exile in Mantua. Lady Capulet at first encourages Juliet to marry Paris, but when she fails to embrace the idea, Capulet angrily insists that she follow his wishes in the matter. The Nurse loses Juliet's respect when she counsels her to ignore her marriage to Romeo and marry again.

Enter ROMEO and JULIET aloft at the window.

JULIET	Wilt thou be gone? It is not yet near day.
	It was the nightingale and not the lark
	That pierc'd the fearful hollow of thine ear.
	Nightly she sings on yond pomegranate tree.
	Believe me, love, it was the nightingale.

       5

ROMEO	It was the lark, the herald of the morn,
	No nightingale. Look, love, what envious streaks*
	Do lace the severing clouds in yonder east.
	Night's candles are burnt out, and jocund* day
	Stands tiptoe on the misty mountain tops.
	I must be gone and live or stay and die.

       streaks: i.e., early
       morning light

       jocund: merry

       10

JULIET	Yond light is not daylight; I know it, I.
	It is some meteor that the sun exhales*
	To be to thee this night a torchbearer
	And light thee on thy way to Mantua.
	Therefore stay yet; thou need'st not to be gone.

       exhales: gives off

       15

ROMEO	Let me be ta'en; let me be put to death;
	I am content so thou wilt have it so.
	I'll say yon grey is not the morning's eye;
	'Tis but the pale reflex* of Cynthia's* brow;
	Nor that is not the lark whose notes do beat
	The vaulty* heaven so high above our heads.
	I have more care* to stay than will to go.
	Come, death, and welcome! Juliet wills it so.
	How is't, my soul?* Let's talk; it is not day.

       20   *reflex:* reflection *Cynthia's:* the moon's

       vaulty: arched
       care: desire

       25   *soul:* i.e., Juliet

JULIET	It is, it is! Hie hence, be gone, away!

Act III, Scene v

The subject of the lovers' argument that dominates this scene, known as the "lark-nightingale scene," is time. These two birds are commonly found in Renaissance literature. The nightingale is representative of night (cf. "the Nightingale and the Glowworm," pages 133-35); the lark is a harbinger of day (cf. "How to Get Things Done," page 452—"When tomorrow comes, I am up with one of the older and more sluggish larks"). Notice Shakespeare's skillful interweaving of the major light-dark imagery with theme, plot, characterization, and time scheme in this scene. What is the irony at line 51? *(The next time Juliet sees Romeo, he will be dead.)* What is foreshadowed at lines 54-57? *(Romeo's death)* Line 59 alludes to Elizabethan medicinal theory that every sigh of a lover dries up a drop of his heart's blood.

Lady Capulet, ignorant of Juliet's love for Romeo, tries to lift her daughter's spirits as she voices the Renaissance attitude toward grief at the death of a loved one, that it should be moderate, not excessive. At the same time she reveals her own inordinate desire to avenge Tybalt's death. Capulet sees the solution to Juliet's present problem in a plan of action rather than theoretical advice: she will marry Paris immediately. Both parents become enraged when their daughter does not accept the plan. They accuse her of ingratitude and rail at her to the extreme of stating that they wish she were dead (Lady Capulet, l. 141) or that she had never been born (Capulet, ll. 165-69). (Is

it any wonder that Juliet herself acts according to passion rather than reason?) Although the Capulets' motive is the welfare of their child, they become cruel and abusive in their attempts to force her to do what they perceive as right. Parents and daughter have failed to communicate. Shakespeare obviously embodies the "generation gap" theme in this play. The failure of the young people (i.e., Romeo, Juliet, Tybalt, Mercutio, and Paris) to communicate with *each other* produces more severe consequences, however, than the "generation gap."

Notice Capulet's description of Paris at lines 175-81. Because the love of Romeo and Juliet is so attractive to the audience, it would be easy for them to see Paris in a negative light. To do so is counter to Shakespeare's intentions,

	It is the lark that sings so out of tune,		
	Straining harsh discords and unpleasing sharps.*		*sharps:* shrill sounds
	Some say the lark makes sweet division.*		*division:* variations on a melody
	This doth not so, for she divideth us.	30	
	Some say the lark and loathèd toad change eyes;*		*change eyes:* exchange eyes, or fall in love
	O now I would they had chang'd voices too,		*affray:* frighten away
	Since arm from arm that voice doth us affray,*		
	Hunting thee hence with hunt's-up* to the day.		*hunt's-up:* a song to waken hunters or newly-weds, who customarily had a formal hunt on the morning after their wedding
	O now be gone; more light and light it grows.	35	

ROMEO   More light and light, more dark and dark our woes!

Enter NURSE hastily.

NURSE   Madam!

JULIET   Nurse?

NURSE   Your lady mother is coming to your chamber.
            The day is broke;* be wary; look about.   40   *is broke:* has dawned

Exit.

JULIET   Then, window, let day in and let life out.

ROMEO   Farewell, farewell! One kiss, and I'll descend.

He goes down.

JULIET   Art thou gone so, my lord, my love, my friend!
            I must hear from thee every day in the hour,
            For in a minute there are many days.   45
            O, by this count I shall be much in years
            Ere I again behold my Romeo!

ROMEO   Farewell!
            I will omit* no opportunity   *omit:* fail to take advantage of
            That may convey my greetings, love, to thee.   50

JULIET   O, think'st thou we shall ever meet again?

ROMEO   I doubt it not, and all these woes shall serve
            For sweet discourses* in our times to come.   *discourses:* subjects of conversation

however. Paris is young, attractive, and prominent, a seemingly perfect match for Juliet. There is no reason to believe that he would intrude on the love of Romeo and Juliet if he knew about it.

Ask the students what evil advice the Nurse gives Juliet at the end of the scene. How does Juliet react? From what source does Juliet decide to seek further counsel? What desperate course of action does she consider in the final couplet? *(The Nurse advises Juliet to marry Paris—that is, to commit bigamy. Juliet's first, seemingly positive, response is ironic; once the Nurse leaves, she reveals her repugnance for the Nurse's advice. Juliet decides to go to the Friar for advice. She considers suicide as a solution if all else fails.)*

JULIET	Husband, I have an ill-diving* soul!	*ill-diving:* full of evil premonitions
	Methinks I see thee now, thou art so low, 55	
	As one dead in the bottom of a tomb.	
	Either my eyesight fails or thou lookest pale.	
ROMEO	And trust me, love, in my eye so do you;	
	Dry* sorrow drinks* our blood. Adieu, adieu!	*Dry:* Thirsty *drinks:* dries up
	Exit.	
JULIET	O Fortune, Fortune, all men call thee fickle. 60	
	If thou art fickle, what dost thou with him	
	That is renown'd for faith? Be fickle, Fortune;	
	For then I hope thou wilt not keep him long	
	But send him back.	
LADY CAP.	*(Within.)* Ho, daughter, are you up?	
JULIET	Who is't that calls? It is my lady mother. 65	
	Is she not down so late, or up so early?	
	What unaccustom'd cause* procures* her hither?	*unaccustom'd cause:* unusual circumstance *procures:* brings
	She goes down from the window. Enter LADY CAPULET.	
LADY CAP.	Why, how now, Juliet?	
JULIET	Madam, I am not well.	
LADY CAP.	Evermore weeping for your cousin's death?	
	What, wilt thou wash him from his grave with tears? 70	
	And if thou couldst, thou couldst not make him live;	
	Therefore have done. Some grief shows much of love,	
	But much of grief shows still some want of wit.*	*want . . . wit:* lack of intelligence
JULIET	Yet let me weep for such a feeling* loss.	*feeling:* deeply felt
LADY CAP.	So shall you feel the loss but not the friend 75	
	Which you weep for.	
JULIET	Feeling so the loss,	
	I cannot choose but ever weep the friend.	
LADY CAP.	Well, girl, thou weep'st not so much for his death	
	As that the villain lives which slaughter'd him.	

personification (more precisely, an example of apostrophe), alliteration

JULIET	What villain, madam?	80
LADY CAP.	That same villain Romeo.	
JULIET	*(Aside.)* Villain and he be many miles asunder.— God pardon him! I do with all my heart, And yet no man like* he doth grieve my heart.	*like:* as much as
LADY CAP.	That is because the traitor murderer lives.	85
JULIET	Ay, madam, from the reach of these my hands. Would none but I might venge my cousin's death!	
LADY CAP.	We will have vengeance for it; fear thou not. Then weep no more. I'll send to one in Mantua, Where that same banish'd runagate* doth live, Shall give him such an unaccustom'd dram* That he shall soon keep Tybalt company; And then I hope thou wilt be satisfied.	90 *runagate:* renegade *unaccustom'd dram:* poison
JULIET	Indeed I never shall be satisfied With Romeo till I behold him—dead— Is my poor heart so for a kinsman vex'd. Madam, if you could find out but a man To bear a poison, I would temper it, That Romeo should upon receipt thereof Soon sleep in quiet. O how my heart abhors To hear him nam'd and cannot come to him To wreak the love I bore my cousin Upon his body* that hath slaughter'd him.	95 100 *Upon . . . body:* Upon the body of him
LADY CAP.	Find thou the means, and I'll find such a man. But now I'll tell thee joyful tidings, girl.	105
JULIET	And joy comes well in such a needy time. What are they, I beseech your ladyship?	
LADY CAP.	Well, well, thou hast a careful* father, child, One who, to put thee from thy heaviness,* Hath sorted out a sudden* day of joy That thou expects not nor I look'd not for.	*careful:* concerned *heaviness:* grief 110 *sudden:* imminent
JULIET	Madam, in happy time, what day is that?	

LADY CAP.	Indeed, my child, early next Thursday morn
	The gallant, young, and noble gentleman,
	The County Paris, at Saint Peter's Church 115
	Shall happily make thee there a joyful bride.
JULIET	No; at Saint Peter's Church or any place
	He shall not make me there a joyful bride.
	I wonder at this haste, that I must wed
	Ere he that should be husband comes to woo. 120
	I pray you tell my lord and father, madam,
	I will not marry yet, and when I do, I swear
	It shall be Romeo, whom you know I hate,
	Rather than Paris. These are news indeed!
LADY CAP.	Here comes your father; tell him so yourself 125
	And see how he will take it at your hands.

Enter CAPULET and NURSE.

CAPULET	When the sun sets, the earth doth drizzle dew,	
	But for the sunset of my brother's son	
	It rains downright.	
	How now, a conduit,* girl? What, still in tears? 130	*conduit:* fountain
	Evermore show'ring? In one little body	
	Thou resemblest a bark,* a sea, a wind;	*bark:* any sailing vessel
	For still thy eyes, which I may call the sea,	
	Do ebb and flow with tears. The bark thy body is,	
	Sailing in this salt flood; the winds, thy sighs, 135	
	Who, raging with thy tears and they with them,	
	Without a sudden calm* will overset	*Without . . . calm:* Unless they (the winds) suddenly calm
	Thy tempest-tossed body. How now, wife?	
	Have you delivered to her our decree?	
LADY CAP.	Ay, sir, but she will none, she gives you thanks.* 140	*she . . . thanks:* i.e., she replies, "No, thanks."
	I would the fool were married to her grave!	
CAPULET	Soft, take me with you;* take me with you, wife.	*take . . . you:* explain what you mean
	How, will she none? Doth she not give us thanks?	
	Is she not proud?* Doth she not count her* blest,	*proud:* overjoyed *her:* herself
	Unworthy as she is, that we have wrought* 145	*wrought:* gotten
	So worthy a gentleman to be her bride?*	*bride:* bridegroom
JULIET	Not proud you have, but thankful that you have.	
	Proud can I never be of what I hate,	
	But thankful even for hate that is meant love.	

CAPULET	How now, how now, chopp'd logic!* What is this?	150	*chopp'd logic:* faulty reasoning
	"Proud" and "I thank you" and "I thank you not,"		
	And yet "not proud," mistress minion* you?		*minion:* impudent, spoiled girl
	Thank me no thankings nor proud me no prouds,		
	But fettle* your fine joints 'gainst* Thursday next		*fettle:* prepare *'gainst:* for
	To go with Paris to Saint Peter's Church,	155	
	Or I will drag thee on a hurdle* thither.		*hurdle:* frame for carrying criminals to execution
	Out, you green-sickness carrion!* Out, you baggage,		*green-sickness carrion:* anemic flesh
	You tallow* face!		*tallow:* pale

LADY CAP.   Fie, fie. What, are you mad?

JULIET   Good father, I beseech you on my knees,
          Hear me with patience but to speak a word.   160

She kneels down.

CAPULET	Hang thee, young baggage! Disobedient wretch!		
	I tell thee what: get thee to church a' Thursday,		
	Or never after look me in the face.		
	Speak not, reply not, do not answer me!		
	My fingers itch.* Wife, we scarce thought us blest	165	*My . . . itch:* I have an overwhelming urge to thrash her.
	That God had lent us but this only child,		
	But now I see this one is one too much		
	And that we have a curse in having her,		
	Out on her, hilding!*		*hilding:* good-for-nothing
NURSE	God in heaven, bless her!		
	You are to blame, my lord, to rate* her so.	170	*rate:* berate, scold
CAPULET	And why, my Lady Wisdom? Hold your tongue,		
	Good Prudence. Smatter* with your gossips.* Go!		*Smatter:* Chatter *gossips:* old-women friends
NURSE	I speak no treason.		
CAPULET	Peace, you mumbling fool!		
	Utter your gravity* o'er a gossip's bowl,		*gravity:* advice
	For here we need it not. Day, night, early, late,	175	
	At home, abroad, still* my care hath been		*still:* always
	To have her match'd; and having now provided		
	A gentleman of noble parentage,		
	Of fair demesnes,* youthful and nobly train'd,		*demesnes:* domains, estates
	Stuff'd, as they say, with honorable parts,	180	
	Proportion'd as one's thought would wish a man,		
	And then to have a wretched puling* fool,		*puling:* whimpering
	A whining mammet,* in her fortunes tender,*		*mammet:* doll, puppet *in . . . tender:* young and vulnerable in her fate
	To answer, "I'll wed not; I cannot love;		
	I am too young, I pray you pardon me."	185	
	But and you will not wed, I'll pardon you.*		*I'll . . . you:* used ironically as I'll excuse you from the house
	Graze where you will; you shall not house* with me.		*do . . . use:* am not accustomed
	Look to't, think on't, I do not use* to jest.		*advise:* think it over
	Thursday is near; lay hand on heart; advise.*		
	And you be mine, I'll give you to my friend;	190	
	And you be not, hang, beg, starve, die in the streets;		
	For by my soul I'll ne'er acknowledge thee,		
	Nor what is mine shall never do thee good.		
	Trust to't, bethink you; I'll not be forsworn.		

Exit.

JULIET	Is there no pity sitting in the clouds	195
	That sees into the bottom of my grief?	
	O sweet my mother, cast me not away!	
	Delay this marriage for a month, a week,	
	Or if you do not, make a bridal bed	
	In that dim monument* where Tybalt lies.	200

monument: tomb

LADY CAP.	Talk not to me, for I'll not speak a word.
	Do as thou wilt, for I have done with thee.

Exit.

JULIET	O nurse, O nurse, how shall this be prevented?	
	My husband is on earth, my faith* in heaven.	
	How shall that faith return again to earth	205
	Unless that husband send it me from heaven	
	By leaving earth?* Comfort me, counsel me!	
	Alack, alack, that heaven should practice strategems*	
	Upon so soft a subject as myself!	
	What say'st thou? Has thou not a word of joy?	210
	Some comfort, nurse.	

faith: marriage vows

How . . . leaving earth: How can I marry again unless my present husband dies?

strategems: devious schemes

NURSE	Faith, here it is.	
	Romeo is banished, and all the world* to nothing	
	That he dares ne'er come back to challenge you,	
	Or if he do, it needs must be by stealth.*	
	Then since the case so stands as now it doth,	215
	I think it best you married with the County.	
	O, he's a lovely gentleman!	
	Romeo's a dish-clout* to him.* An eagle, madam,	
	Hath not so green, so quick, so fair an eye	
	As Paris hath. Beshrow* my very heart,	220
	I think you are happy in this second match,	
	For it excels your first; or if it did not,	
	Your first is dead, or 'twere as good he were	
	As living here* and you no use of him.	

all . . . world: I'll bet the world

stealth: covert means

dish-clout: dishrag *to him:* compared to him

Beshrow: A curse upon

here: i.e., on earth

JULIET	Speak'st thou from thy heart?

NURSE	And from my soul too,	225
	Else beshrew them both.	

JULIET	Amen!

NURSE	What?
JULIET	Well thou hast comforted me marvelous much.
	Go in and tell my lady I am gone,
	Having displeas'd my father, to Lawrence's cell
	To make confession and to be absolv'd. 230
NURSE	Well, I will, and this is wisely done.

Exit.

JULIET	*(She looks after the* NURSE.*)*
	Ancient damnation! O most wicked fiend!
	Is it more sin to wish me thus forsworn
	Or to dispraise my lord with that same tongue
	Which she hath prais'd him with above compare 235
	So many thousand times? Go, counselor.
	Thou and my bosom* henceforth shall be twain.*
	I'll to the friar to know his remedy.
	If all else fail, myself have power to die.

bosom: innermost thoughts *twain:* separated

Exit.

About the Play

1. Contrast Benvolio with the following characters:
   a. Romeo
   b. Mercutio
   c. Tybalt
2. What does Mercutio's speech on page 375, lines 90-102, tell you about him?
3. Describe Juliet's dilemma in Scene ii.
4. What do Juliet's parents believe to be the cause of her excessive grief?
5. Describe Romeo's reaction to the Prince's pronouncement of banishment.
6. What do you think of his reaction?
7. What does the Nurse counsel Juliet to do regarding Paris? What do you think of her counsel?

About the Play

1. *Benvolio is a peacemaker; Romeo's attempts to be a peacemaker result in Mercutio's death. Mercutio accuses others of being pugnacious, and Tybalt admits that he likes to fight; both of them are contrasts to Benvolio.*

2. *He has a gift for wit, even in death, but his humor betrays an underlying bitterness. He blames Romeo for his death and later curses both the Montagues and the Capulets.*

3. *She is torn between her love for her husband and her cousin.*

4. *the death of Tybalt, her cousin*

5. *He overreacts with anger, bitterness, and despair—to the point of threatening to stab himself.*

6. *It reveals his immaturity—the Prince has been lenient in his sentence.*

7. *She counsels Juliet to marry Paris even though she is already married to Romeo. This is, obviously, terribly unscriptural counsel.*

Act IV

Scene I

Time: Tuesday
Place: Friar Lawrence's cell

Paris makes arrangements with Friar Lawrence for his wedding to Juliet. She pays passing courtesies to Paris upon his departure and then entreats the Friar to help her escape marriage to him. Friar Lawrence formulates the potion plan.

Enter FRIAR LAWRENCE and PARIS.

FRIAR L.	On Thursday, sir? The time is very short.
PARIS	My father Capulet will have it so, And I am nothing slow to slack his haste.*
FRIAR L.	You say you do not know the lady's mind? Uneven* is the course; I like it not.
PARIS	Immoderately she weeps for Tybalt's death, And therefore have I little talk'd of love, For Venus smiles not in a house of tears. Now, sir, her father counts it dangerous That she do give her sorrow so much sway And in his wisdom hastes our marriage To stop the inundation* of her tears, Which, too much minded* by herself alone, May be put from her by society.* Now do you know the reason for this haste.
FRIAR L.	*(Aside.)* I would I knew not why it should be slowed.— Look, sir, here comes the lady toward my cell.

Enter JULIET.

PARIS	Happily met, my lady and my wife!
JULIET	That may be, sir, when I may be a wife.

Marginal glosses:

nothing . . . haste: not hesitant myself so I am not given to slowing him down

5   *Uneven:* Irregular

10

inundation: flood

minded: thought about

society: companionship (i.e., that of Paris)

15

Act IV, Scene i

At this scene Shakespeare begins the rapid acceleration of his plot. The time scheme and haste theme once again converge as the scene opens. At the Friar's cell Juliet must play up to Paris's courtesies. Once he leaves, she threatens suicide, but the Friar persuades her as he has persuaded Romeo to adopt a rational course of action. What are the details of the "potion plan"? *(He gives her a potion that will mimic death for forty-two hours. Her body will be taken to the family's cemetery vault. In the meantime, the Friar will write to Romeo; the two men will rescue her from the vault and the couple will escape to Mantua.)*

PARIS	That may be, must be, love, on Thursday next.	20
JULIET	What must be shall be.	
FRIAR L.	That's a certain text.	
PARIS	Come you to make confession to this father?	

JULIET	To answer that I should* confess to you.	*should:* would need to
PARIS	Do not deny to him that you love me.	
JULIET	I will confess to you that I love him.	25
PARIS	So will ye, I am sure, that you love me.	
JULIET	If I do so, it will be of more price,* Being spoke behind your back, than to your face.	*price:* value
PARIS	Poor soul, thy face is much abus'd with tears.	
JULIET	The tears have got small victory by that, For it was bad enough before their spite.	30
PARIS	Thou wrong'st it more than tears with that report.	
JULIET	That is no slander, sir, which is a truth, And what I spake, I spake it to* my face.	*to:* concerning
PARIS	Thy face is mine, and thou hast sland'red it.	35
JULIET	It may be so, for it is not mine own. Are you at leisure, holy father, now, Or shall I come to you at evening mass?	
FRIAR L.	My leisure serves me, pensive* daughter, now. My lord, we must entreat* the time alone.	*pensive:* sad *entreat:* beg to have
PARIS	God shield* I should disturb devotion.* Juliet, on Thursday early I will rouse ye. Till then adieu, and keep this holy kiss.	*shield:* forbid *devotion:* prayers
	Exit.	
JULIET	O, shut the door, and when thou hast done so, Come weep with me, past hope, past care, past help!	45
FRIAR L.	O Juliet, I already know thy grief.* It strains me past the compass* of my wits. I hear thou must, and nothing may prorogue* it, On Thursday next be married to this County.	*thy grief:* the cause of thy grief *compass:* boundary *prorogue:* postpone

JULIET	Tell me not, Friar, that thou hearest of this	50	
	Unless thou tell me how I may prevent it.		
	If in thy wisdom thou canst give no help,		
	Do thou but call my resolution wise,		
	And with this knife I'll help it presently.*		*presently:* immediately
	God join'd my heart and Romeo's, thou our hands,	55	
	And ere this hand, by thee to Romeo's seal'd,		
	Shall be the label* to another deed*		*label:* seal *deed:* legal document
	Or my true heart with treacherous revolt		
	Turn to another,* this shall slay them both.*		*another:* i.e., man *both:* i.e., hand and heart
	Therefore out of thy long-experienc'd time	60	
	Give me some present counsel, or, behold,		
	'Twixt my extremes* and me this bloody knife		*extremes:* dire plight
	Shall play the umpeer,* arbitrating that		*umpeer:* umpire
	Which the commission* of thy years and art*		*commission:* authority *art:* skill
	Could to no issue* of true honor bring.	65	*issue:* outcome, conclusion
	Be not so long to speak. I long to die		
	If what thou speak'st speak not of remedy.		
FRIAR L.	Hold, daughter! I do spy a kind of hope		
	Which craves as desperate an execution*		*craves . . . execution:* necessitates a course of action
	As that is desperate which we would prevent.	70	
	If rather than to marry County Paris		
	Thou hast the strength of will to slay thyself,		
	Then is it likely thou wilt undertake		
	A thing like death to chide away this shame,		
	That cop'st with* Death himself to scape from it;	75	*That . . . with:* (a plan) that deals with
	And if thou darest, I'll give thee remedy.*		*remedy:* the plan
JULIET	O, bid me leap, rather than marry Paris,		
	From off the battlements* of any tower		*battlements:* top wall
	Or walk in thievish ways,* or bid me lurk		*thievish ways:* places where thieves lurk
	Where serpents are; chain me with roaring bears	80	
	Or hide me nightly in a charnel house*		*charnel house:* storage place for bones of the dead
	O'ercover'd quite with dead men's rattling bones,		
	With reeky* shanks and yellow chapless* skulls;		*reeky:* stinking *chapless:* jawless
	Or bid me go into a new-made grave		
	And hide me with a dead man in his shroud—	85	
	Things that, to hear them told, have made me tremble—		
	And I will do it without fear or doubt,		
	To live an unstain'd wife to my sweet love.		
FRIAR L.	Hold then. Go home, be merry, give consent		
	To marry Paris. We'n'sday is tomorrow;	90	

Tomorrow night look that thou lie alone;
Let not the nurse lie with thee in thy chamber.
Take thou this vial, being then in bed,
And this distilling* liquor* drink thou off,
When presently through all thy veins shall run 95
A cold and drowsy humor;* for no pulse
Shall keep his native progress* but surcease.*
No warmth, no breath shall testify thou livest.
The roses in thy lips and cheeks shall fade
To many ashes, thy eyes' windows* fall 100
Like death when he shuts up the day of life.
Each part, depriv'd of supple government,*
Shall, stiff and stark and cold, appear like death,
And in this borrowed likeness of shrunk death

distilling: permeating
liquor: liquid

humor: moisture

native progress: natural progression *surcease:* cease

eyes' windows: i.e., eyelids

supple government: control of movement

	Thou shalt continue two and forty hours	105

Thou shalt continue two and forty hours   105
And then awake as from a pleasant sleep.
Now when the bridegroom in the morning comes
To rouse thee from thy bed, there art thou dead.
Then as the manner of our country is,
In thy best robes, uncovered on the bier,   110
Thou shalt be borne to that same ancient vault
Where all the kindred of the Capulets lie.
In the meantime, against* thou shalt awake   *against*: before
Shall Romeo by my letters know our drift*   *drift*: purpose
And hither shall he come, an' he and I   115
Will watch thy waking, and that very night
Shall Romeo bear thee hence to Mantua.
And this shall free thee from this present shame,
If no inconstant toy* nor womanish fear   *inconstant toy*: wavering fancy
Abate thy valor* in the acting it.   120   *Abate . . . valor*: Lessen your courage

JULIET   Give me, give me! O tell me not to fear!

FRIAR L.   Hold, get you gone. Be strong and prosperous
In this resolve.* I'll send a friar with speed   *resolve*: decision
To Mantua with letters to thy lord.

JULIET   Love, give me strength! And strength shall help afford.* 125   *afford*: (me) carry out the deed
Farewell, dear father.

Exeunt.

Scene II

Time: Tuesday, near night
Place: A hall in Capulet's house

Capulet prepares for Juliet's marriage to Paris on Thursday but moves the date up to Wednesday when Juliet, returning from the Friar's cell, pretends to yield to his will.

Enter CAPULET, LADY CAPULET, NURSE, and SERVANTS.

CAPULET   So many guests invite as here are writ.

Exit SERVANT 1.

Act IV, Scene ii

This scene allows for the passage of time between Juliet's collaboration with the Friar on the potion plan and the actual enactment of it. The scene also adds to the general atmosphere of haste that Shakespeare wants to maintain. Day has passed very quickly; night is near. Keep in mind that Juliet's feigning filial submission represents transgression against order and hierarchy, a sin that does not go unpunished in Shakespeare's works. What major change does Capulet make in his plans for Juliet's wedding? *(He moves it from Thursday to Wednesday—the very next morning.)*

	Sirrah, go hire me twenty cunning* cooks.		*cunning:* expert
SERVANT 2	You shall have none ill, sir, for I'll try if they can lick their fingers.		
CAPULET	How canst thou try them so?*	5	*try . . . so:* discern their ability by such a test
SERVANT 2	Well, sir, 'tis an ill cook that cannot lick his own fingers; therefore he that cannot lick his fingers goes not with me.		
CAPULET	Go, be gone.		

Exit SERVANT 2.

	We shall be much unfurnish'd* for this time. What, is my daughter gone to Friar Lawrence?	10	*unfurnish'd:* unprepared
NURSE	Ay, forsooth.*		*forsooth:* indeed
CAPULET	Well, he may chance to do some good on her. A peevish* self-will'd harlotry* it is.		*peevish:* silly *harlotry:* good-for-nothing girl

Enter JULIET.

NURSE	See where she comes from shrift with merry look.		
CAPULET	How now, my headstrong, where have you been gadding?	15	
JULIET	Where I have learnt me to repent of sin Of disobedient opposition To you and your behests* and am enjoin'd By holy Lawrence to fall prostrate here To beg your pardon. *(She kneels down.)* Pardon, I beseech you! Henceforward I am ever rul'd by you.	20	*behests:* commands
CAPULET	Send for the County. Tell him this. I'll have this knot knit up tomorrow morning.		
JULIET	I met the youthful lord at Lawrence' cell And gave him what becomed* love I might, Not stepping o'er the bounds of modesty .	25	*becomed:* befitting

CAPULET	Why, I am glad on't. This is well; stand up.
	This is as't should be. Let me see the County;
	Ay, indeed, go, I say, and fetch him hither.	30
	Now afore God, this reverend holy friar,
	All our whole city is much bound to him.

JULIET	Nurse, will you go with me into my closet*	*closet:* private room
	To help me sort such needful ornaments
	As you think fit to furnish me tomorrow?	35

LADY CAP.	No, not till Thursday. There is time enough.

CAPULET	Go, nurse, go with her. We'll to church tomorrow.

Exeunt JULIET and NURSE.

LADY CAP.	We shall be short in our provision.*	*provision:* i.e., for the
	'Tis now near night.	wedding feast

CAPULET	Tush, I will stir about,
	And all things shall be well, I warrant thee, wife.	40
	Go thou to Juliet; help to deck her up.
	I'll not to bed tonight; let me alone.*	*let . . . alone:* allow
	I'll play huswife for this once. What ho!	me to take care of
	They are all forth. Well, I will walk myself	everything
	To County Paris to prepare him up	45
	Against* tomorrow. My heart is wondrous light,	*Against:* For
	Since this same wayward girl is so reclaim'd.

Exeunt.

Scene III

Time: Tuesday evening
Place: Juliet's chamber

After her mother and the Nurse leave her alone for the night, Juliet takes the potion prepared by Friar Lawrence.

Enter JULIET and NURSE.

JULIET	Ay, those attires are best, but, gentle nurse,

Act IV, Scene iii

The main business of this scene is Juliet's soliloquy, a piece in which Shakespeare brilliantly captures the fears of a young girl faced with two wholly undesirable alternatives. What are her fears? *(See ll. 21-23 [that the potion will not work at all]; ll. 24-27 [that the potion is poison and will kill her]; ll. 30-32 [that she might awaken alone in the tomb]; ll. 33-35 [that she might suffocate in the vault]; ll. 36-54 [that she might awake in the vault, go mad, and kill herself]; ll. 55-58 [that she might see Tybalt's ghost]).* Why does Juliet place a dagger beside her? What does this foreshadow? *(She places the dagger there to kill herself in case the potion does not put her to sleep and she is thus forced to marry Paris. It foreshadows her suicide at the end of the play.)*

I pray thee leave me to myself tonight,
For I have need of many orisons* *orisons:* prayers
To move the heavens to smile upon my state,
Which, well thou knowest, is cross* and full of sin. 5 *cross:* perverse

Enter LADY CAPULET.

LADY CAP. What, are you busy, ho? Need you my help?

JULIET No, madam, we have cull'd* such necessaries *cull'd:* selected
As are behooveful* for our state* tomorrow. *behooveful:* suitable
So please you, let me now be left alone *state:* ceremony
And let the nurse this night sit up with you, 10
For I am sure you have your hands full all
In this so sudden business.

LADY CAP. Good night.
Get thee to bed and rest, for thou hast need.

Exeunt LADY CAPULET and NURSE.

JULIET Farewell! God knows when we shall meet again.
I have a faint* cold fear thrills* through my veins 15 *faint:* that which pro-
That almost freezes up the heat of life. duces faintness
I'll call them back again to comfort me. *thrills:* that pierces
Nurse!—What should she do here?
My dismal* scene I needs must act alone. *dismal:* dreadful
Come, vial. 20
What if this mixture do not work at all?
Shall I be married then tomorrow morning?
No, no, this shall forbid it. Lie thou there.

She places a dagger beside her bed.

What if it be a poison which the friar
Subtly hath minist'red to have me dead 25
Lest in this marriage he should be dishonor'd
Because he married me before to Romeo?
I fear it is, and yet methinks it should not,
For he hath still* been tried* a holy man. *still:* always *tried:*
How if, when I am laid into the tomb, 30 proved
I wake before the time that Romeo
Come to redeem me? There's a fearful point!
Shall I not then be stifled* in the vault, *stifled:* suffocated

To whose foul mouth no healthsome air breathes in,
And there die strangled ere my Romeo comes?   35
Or if I live, is it not very like
The horrible conceit* of death and night   *conceit: fantastic
Together with the terror of the place—   thought
As in a vault, an ancient receptacle,
Where for this many hundred years the bones   40
Of all my buried ancestors are pack'd,
Where bloody Tybalt, yet but green* in earth,   *green: newly buried
Lies fest'ring in his shroud, where, as they say,
At some hours in the night spirits resort—
Alack, alack, is it not like that I   45
So early waking—what with loathsome smells
And shrikes* like mandrakes* torn out of the earth,   *shrikes: shrieks *man-
That living mortals, hearing them, run mad—   drakes: plants with
O, if I wake, shall I not be distraught,   forked roots thought
Environed with all these hideous fears,   50   to resemble a man;
And madly play with my forefathers' joints   said to shriek when
And pluck the mangled Tybalt from his shroud   pulled from the
And in this rage, with some great kinsman's bone   earth, causing the
As with a club, dash out my desp'rate brains?   hearer to become
O, look! Methinks I see my cousin's ghost   55   insane or die
Seeking out Romeo, that did spit* his body   *spit: stab
Upon a rapier's point. Stay, Tybalt, stay!
Romeo, Romeo, Romeo! Here's drink. I drink to thee.

She falls upon her bed within the curtains.

Scene IV

Time: Early Wednesday morning
Place: A hall in Capulet's house

Capulet and the servants complete the wedding preparations.

Enter LADY CAPULET and NURSE with herbs.

LADY CAP.   Hold, take these keys and fetch more spices, nurse.

NURSE   They call for dates and quinces in the pastry.*   *pastry: pantry

Enter CAPULET.

Act IV, Scene iv

This is another scene that serves mainly to
mark the passage of time. What is the precise
time setting? *(3:00 A.M.; l. 4)* Who is Angelica?
(Lady Capulet; l. 5) Which character admonishes
the others to "make haste"? *(Capulet)*

CAPULET	Come, stir, stir, stir! The second cock hath crowed;
	The curfew bell hath rung; 'tis three a' clock.
	Look to the bak'd meats, good Angelica; 5
	Spare not for cost.

LADY CAP.	Go, you cot-queen,* go.
	Get you to bed. Faith, you'll be sick tomorrow
	For this night's watching.*

cot-queen: man who does woman's work

watching: staying awake

CAPULET	No, not a whit. What, I have watch'd ere now
	All night for lesser cause and ne'er been sick. 10

Exeunt LADY CAPULET and NURSE.

CAPULET	A jealous hood,* a jealous hood!

hood: person

Enter three or four servants with spits and logs and baskets.

SERVANT 1	Things for the cook, sir, but I know not what.

CAPULET	Make haste, make haste.

Exit SERVANT 1.

	Sirrah, fetch drier logs.
	Call Peter; he will show thee where they are. 15

SERVANT 2	I have a head, sir, that will find out logs
	And never trouble Peter for the matter.

CAPULET	Thou shalt be logger-head. Sirrah, 'tis day;
	The County will be here with music straight,
	For so he said he would. *(Music plays within.)* I hear him
	near. 20
	Nurse! Wife! What ho! What, nurse, I say!

Enter NURSE.

	Go waken Juliet; go and trim her up.
	I'll go and chat with Paris. Hie, make haste,
	Make haste! The bridegroom he is come already.
	Make haste, I say. 25

Exeunt.

Scene V

Time: Early Wednesday morning
Place: Juliet's chamber

The Nurse discovers Juliet's "death," and great lamentation follows. The Friar assures Juliet's family and Paris of God's providence; and the musicians, turning from wedding to funeral song, jest with Peter.

Enter NURSE above.

NURSE	Mistress! What, mistress! Juliet!—Fast,* I warrant her. She—

Fast: Fast asleep

Why, lamb! Why, lady! Fie, you slug-a-bed!
Why, love, I say madam! Sweetheart! Why, bride!
What, not a word? How sound is she asleep!
I needs must wake her. Madam, madam, madam!   5

Draws back the curtains around Juliet's bed.

What, dress'd and in your clothes and down again?
I must needs wake you. Lady, lady, lady!
Alas, alas! Help, help! My lady's dead!
O, weraday* that ever I was born!

weraday: alas

Some aqua-vitae, ho! My lord! My lady!   10

Enter LADY CAPULET.

LADY CAP.   What noise is here?

NURSE   O lamentable day!

LADY CAP.   What is the matter?

NURSE   Look, look! O heavy day!

LADY CAP.   O me, O me, my child, my only life!
Revive, look up, or I will die with thee!
Help, help! Call help.   15

Enter CAPULET.

CAPULET   For shame, bring Juliet forth! Her lord is come.

Act IV, Scene v

This is a difficult scene for modern audiences to relate to because it operates on two different and opposite emotional levels. The audience has a knowledge of events of which the characters onstage are ignorant (dramatic irony). Therefore, Shakespeare depicts the Capulet household's grief at the "death" of Juliet in terms that would have been comic to his audience. A master of psychology, he knew that he could not expect the audience to mourn twice for her passing, so he makes them laugh here instead. The major character who evokes audience laughter in this scene is the Nurse, beginning at lines 8-10 as she calls to awaken Juliet on the morning of her wedding to Paris. Her limited linguistic ability is manifested in some of the

same phrases that she has used as a comic messenger in earlier scenes and in her inability to use synonyms. Exaggeration is her stock in trade.

At line 34, Lady Capulet begins a formal stage eulogy for Juliet. Notice that she employs four adjectives before the word *day*. According to stage tradition, another character can participate in a eulogy by emulating the formal pattern established in the opening of the eulogy. The Nurse's attempt to join in this eulogy is the major source of comic relief in the scene (ll. 40-45). Both Capulet and Paris, in contrast, make articulate contributions to the speech in honor of Juliet. (See ll. 46-55.)

In the next segment of the scene the Friar comforts the other characters, citing a few

favorite Renaissance clichés about death. Shakespeare does not intend that the audience view the Friar as hypocritical in this pose; he has the protagonists' best interests at heart.

Notice the stage directions below line 87. As the Nurse closes the curtains around Juliet's bed, she delocalizes the scene, and the Musicians take over. At the entrance of these hirelings the humor of the scene becomes obvious even to modern audiences. The Musicians are indifferent to the grief of the family. They can make music for wedding or burial alike. The scene may well have been a comic highlight for Shakespeare's audience. The stage directions in an early edition below line 90 read "Enter Will Kempe" rather than "Enter Peter." The very sight of Kempe, Shakespeare's chief

NURSE	She's dead, deceased; she's dead, alack the day!
LADY CAP.	Hah, let me see her. Out alas, she's cold. Her blood is settled, and her joints are stiff; Life and these lips have long been separated. 20 Death lies on her like an untimely frost Upon the sweetest flower of all the field.
NURSE	O lamentable day!
LADY CAP.	O woeful time!
CAPULET	Death, that hath ta'en her hence to make me wail, Ties up my tongue and will not let me speak. 25

Enter FRIAR LAWRENCE and PARIS with MUSICIANS.

FRIAR L.	Come, is the bride ready to go to church?
CAPULET	Ready to go but never to return.— O son, the night before thy wedding day Hath Death lain with thy wife. Death is my heir; My daughter he hath wedded. I will die 30 And leave him all: life, living,* all is Death's.
PARIS	Have I thought long* to see this morning's face, And doth it give me such a sight as this?
LADY CAP.	Accurs'd, unhappy, wretched, hateful day! Most miserable hour that e'er time saw 35 In lasting labor of his pilgrimage! But one, poor one, one poor and loving child, But one thing to rejoice and solace in, And cruel Death hath catch'd* it from my sight!

All cry out at once and wring their hands.

NURSE	O woe! O woeful, woeful, woeful day! 40 Most lamentable day, most woeful day That ever, ever I did yet behold! O day, O day, O day, O hateful day! Never was seen so black a day as this. O woeful day, O woeful day! 45

living: possessions

thought long: been impatient

catch'd: taken

company clown until 1590, would have ensured a mood of laughter. What is the comic significance of the names Simon Catling, Hugh Rebick, and James Soundpost (ll. 115-19)? *(See marginal glosses, page 415.)*

PARIS   Beguil'd, divorced, wronged, spited, slain!   Beguil'd: Cheated
             Most detestable Death, by thee beguil'd,
             By cruel, cruel, thee quite overthrown!
             O love, O life! Not life, but love in death!

CAPULET   Despis'd, distressed, hated, martyr'd, kill'd!   50
             Uncomfortable* time, why cam'st thou now   Uncomfortable:
             To murder, murder our solemnity?*   Comfortless
                                                                 solemnity: celebration
             O child, O child! My soul and not my child!
             Dead art thou! Alack, my child is dead,
             And with my child my joys are buried.   55

FRIAR L.   Peace, ho, for shame! Confusion! Cure lives not
             In these confusions. Heaven and yourself
             Had part in this fair maid; now heaven hath all,
             And all the better is it for the maid.
             Your part in her you could not keep from death, 60
             But heaven keeps his part in eternal life.
             The most you sought was her promotion,*   promotion: translation
             In these confusions.* Heaven and yourself   to heaven
             For 'twas your heaven she should be advanc'd.   confusions: disorder
             And weep ye now, seeing she is advanc'd   65
             Above the clouds as high as heaven itself?
             O, in this love* you love your child so ill   in . . . love: by show-
             That you run mad, seeing that she is well.   ing your love
                                                                   through such
             She's not well married that lives married long,   lamentation
             But she's best married that dies married young. 70
             Dry up your tears and stick your rosemary*   rosemary: fragrant
             On this fair corse, and as the custom is,   herb, whose sprigs
             And in her best array bear her to church;   symbolized remem-
                                                                   brance and were
             For though some nature bids us all lament,   strewn at both fun-
             Yet nature's tears are reason's merriment.*   75   erals and weddings
                                                                 nature's . . . merriment:
                                                                     The human side of
                                                                     man mourns for that
                                                                     which makes his
                                                                     reason rejoice.
CAPULET   All things that we ordained festival*   ordained festival:
             Turn from their office to black funeral: intended for our
             Our instruments to melancholy bells;   festivities
             Our wedding cheer* to a sad burial feast;   cheer: food
             Our solemn hymns to sullen dirges* change;   80 dirges: funeral songs
             Our bridal flowers serve for a buried corse;
             And all things change them to the contrary.

FRIAR L.   Sir, go you in, and madam, go with him;
             And go, Sir Paris. Every one prepare
             To follow this fair corse unto her grave.   85

The heavens do low'r* upon you for some ill;*
Move them no more by crossing their high will.

low'r: frown *ill:* sin

Exeunt all but NURSE *and the* MUSICIANS, *casting rosemary on* JULIET *and shutting the curtains.*

MUSIC. 1   Faith, we may put up our pipes* and be gone.

put . . . pipes: These musicians are string players, not pipers.

NURSE   Honest good fellows, ah, put up, put up.
For well you know this is a pitiful case.   90

Exit NURSE.

MUSIC. 1   Ay, by my troth, the case may be amended.*

amended: (1) The instrument case might well be repaired. (2) The situation can be made better.

PETER   Musicians, O musicians, "Heart's ease,*" "Heart's ease"!
O, and you will have me live, play "Heart's ease."

"Heart's ease:" the name of a popular tune

MUSIC. 1   Why "Heart's ease"?

PETER   O, musicians, because my heart itself plays "My heart   95
is full," O play me some merry dump* to comfort me.

dump: sad tune

MUSIC. 1   Not a dump we; 'tis not time to play now.

PETER   You will not then?

MUSIC. 1   No.

PETER   I will then give it you soundly.   100

MUSIC. 1   What will you give us?

PETER   No money, on my faith, but a gleek;*
I will give you the minstrel.*

gleek: gibe, witty taunt
give . . . minstrel: call you rascals

MUSIC. 1   Then will I give you the serving-creature.

PETER   Then will I lay the serving-creature's dagger on your   105
pate.* I will carry no crotchets.* I'll *re* you, I'll *fa* you. Do
you note* me?

pate: head

crotchets: (1) quarter notes (2) fanciful notions

note: observe, with a pun on musical notes

MUSIC. 1	And you *re* us and *fa* us, you note* us.
MUSIC. 2	Pray you put up your dagger and put out* your wit.

PETER	Then have at you with my wit! I will dry-beat you with 110
	an iron wit and put up my iron dagger. Answer me like men:
	    "When griping griefs the heart doth wound,
	    Then music with her silver sound"—
	why "silver sound"? Why "music with her silver sound"?
	What say you, Simon Catling?* 115

MUSIC. 1	Forsooth, sir, because silver hath a sweet sound.
PETER	Pretty! What say you, Hugh Rebick?*
MUSIC. 2	I say "silver sound" because musicians sound* for silver.
PETER	Pretty too! What say you, James Soundpost?*
MUSIC. 3	Faith, I know not what to say. 120
PETER	O, I cry you mercy,* you are the singer. I will say* for you. It is "music with her silver sound" because musicians have no gold for sounding.* "Then music with her silver sound With speedy help doth lend redress."* 125
	Exit.
MUSIC. 1	What a pestilent knave is this same!
MUSIC. 2	Hang him, Jack! Come we'll in here. Tarry for the mourners and stay* dinner.
	Exeunt.

note: make music of

put out: exhibit

Simon Catling: Name suggestive of a lute string, which was made of cat gut

Hugh Rebick: Name suggestive of three-stringed instrument, prototype of the violin

sound: make music

James Soundpost: Name suggestive of a component part of a stringed instrument

cry . . . mercy: beg your pardon *say:* speak

sounding: speaking

redress: aid

stay: stay for

About the Play

1. How much time has passed since the opening of the play?
2. Why is the length of this time lapse significant?
3. Plot out Romeo and Juliet's actions and reactions up to this point.
4. Review these actions and reactions. If you had to identify one "tragic flaw" in the young lovers, what would it be?

*About
the Play*

1. *Act I opens on Sunday morning; Act IV takes place on Tuesday and Wednesday of the same week.*

2. *The plot is accelerating: Sunday and Monday are covered in Acts I, II, and III; we cover two days in Act IV alone.*

3. *Romeo: grieves for Rosaline; falls in love with Juliet; marries her; causes the death of Mercutio; kills Tybalt; is banished. Juliet: falls in love with Romeo; marries him; grieves for Tybalt; agrees to the potion plan.*

4. *They are driven by haste and their emotions.*

Act V

Scene I

Time: Thursday
Place: A street in Mantua

Balthasar informs Romeo of Juliet's "death." Refusing to be separated from his love, Romeo persuades an apothecary to sell him illegal poison.

Enter ROMEO.

ROMEO	If I may trust the flattering truth of sleep*		*the . . . sleep:* i.e., exaggeratedly favorable dreams
	My dreams presage* some joyful news at hand.		*presage:* foretell
	My bosom's lord* sits lightly in his throne,		*bosom's lord:* i.e., the heart
	And all this day an unaccustom'd spirit		
	Lifts me above the ground with cheerful thoughts.	5	
	I dreamt my lady came and found me dead—		
	Strange dream, that gives a dead man leave* to think—		*gives . . . leave:* permits a dead man
	And breath'd such life with kisses in my lips		
	That I reviv'd and was an emperor.		
	Ah me, how sweet is love itself possess'd*	10	*how . . . possess'd:* love itself is possessed of such sweetness
	When but love's shadows* are so rich in joy!		*love's shadows:* dreams of love

Enter BALTHASAR, Romeo's man.

	News from Verona! How now, Balthasar?		
	Dost thou not bring me letters from the friar?		
	How doth my lady? Is my father well?		
	How fares my Juliet? That I ask again,	15	
	For nothing can be ill if she be well.		
BALTHASAR	Then she is well, and nothing can be ill:		
	Her body sleeps in Capel's monument		
	And her immortal part with angels lives.		
	I saw her laid low in her kindred's vault	20	
	And presently took post* to tell it you.		*took post:* engaged relays of fast horses
	O, pardon me for bringing these ill news,		
	Since you did leave it for my office,* sir.		*office:* duty
ROMEO	Is it e'en so? Then I defy you, stars!		
	Thou knowest my lodging. Get me ink and paper	25	
	And hire post horses; I will hence tonight.		

Act V, Scene i

Notice the dramatic irony of Romeo's speech that opens this scene. No sooner has he described a dream of his miraculous reunion with Juliet than Balthasar enters to announce Juliet's "death." Throughout Act V references to fate and fortune and ironic coincidences are prominent. In the earlier acts of the play Shakespeare's emphasis, however, is on Romeo's and Juliet's exercise of free will.

What plan does Romeo formulate without the Friar's good counsel? *(He will return to Verona, go to Juliet's tomb, and kill himself there.)* Carefully examine Shakespeare's depiction of the Apothecary. At first he will not consent to the illegal sale of poison to Romeo. On what basis does Romeo persuade him to break Mantua's laws?

(the Apothecary's poverty) What is the penalty for such a crime? *(death)* At line 75, the Apothecary states that in selling the poison he has not exercised his free will. Is he being truthful? *(no)* What, according to Romeo, is the irony of the Apothecary's exchanging poison for gold? *(Gold is itself a "poison.")* As the scene ends, Romeo states that to him this poison is a restorative, or a means of renewal, for he will be reunited with Juliet in death.

BALTHASAR	I beseech you, sir, have patience.	
	Your looks are pale and wild and do import*	*import*: indicate, show the possibility of
	Some misadventure.*	*misadventure*: misfortune

ROMEO   Tush, thou art deceiv'd
Leave me and do the thing I bid thee do.   30
Hast thou no letters to me from the friar?

BALTHASAR   No, my good lord.

ROMEO   No matter. Get thee gone
And hire these horses; I'll be with thee straight.

Exit BALTHASAR.

Well, Juliet, I will lie with thee tonight.
Let's see for means.* O mischief, thou art swift   35
To enter in the thoughts of desperate* men!
I do remember an apothecary—
And hereabouts 'a dwells—which late I noted
In tatt'red weeds,* with overwhelming brows,*
Culling of simples.* Meager* were his looks;   40
Sharp misery had worn him to the bones.
And in his needy shop a tortoise hung,
An alligator stuff'd, and other skins
Of ill-shap'd fishes, and about his shelves
A beggarly account* of empty boxes,   45
Green earthen pots, bladders,* and musty seeds.
Remnants of packthread* and old cakes of roses*
Were thinly scattered to make up a show.
Noting this penury* to myself I said,
"And if a man did need a poison now,   50
Whose sale is present death* in Mantua,
Here lives a caitiff* wretch would sell it him."
O, this same thought did but forerun* my need,
And this same needy man must sell it me.
As I remember, this should be the house.   55
Being holiday, the beggar's shop is shut.
What ho, apothecary!

Enter APOTHECARY.

APOTH.   Who calls so loud?

means: a way to accomplish the aforementioned purpose
desperate: those devoid of hope
weeds: clothes
with . . . brows: giving a frowning appearance
Culling . . . simples: Selecting medicinal herbs *Meager*: Poor

beggarly account: pitifully small collection
bladders: pouches
packthread: twine
cakes . . . roses: roses pressed for the making of perfume
penury: poverty
is . . . death: subjects the seller to immediate capital punishment
caitiff: miserable
forerun: go before

metonymy (gold = greed)

ROMEO	Come hither, man. I see that thou art poor.	
	Hold, there is forty ducats;* let me have	ducats: gold coins
	A dram of poison, such soon-speeding gear* 60	soon-speeding gear: fast-acting stuff
	As will disperse itself through all the veins	
	That the weary taker's life may fall dead	
	And that the trunk may be discharg'd of breath	
	As violently as hasty powder fir'd	
	Doth hurry from the fatal cannon's womb. 65	
APOTH.	Such mortal* drugs I have, but Mantua's law	mortal: lethal
	Is death to any he that utters* them.	utters: sells
ROMEO	Art thou so bare and full of wretchedness	
	And fearest to die? Famine is in thy cheeks;	
	Need and opposition starveth in thy eyes; 70	
	Contempt and beggary hangs upon thy back.*	Contempt . . . back: Contemptible poverty is evident in thy poor clothing.
	The world is not thy friend, nor the world's law;	
	The world affords no law to make thee rich.	
	Then be not poor, but break it,* and take this.	it: i.e., the law
APOTH.	My poverty but not my will consents. 75	
ROMEO	I pay thy poverty and not thy will.	
APOTH.	Put this in any liquid thing you will	
	And drink it off, and if you had the strength	
	Of twenty men, it would dispatch you straight.*	dispatch . . . straight: kill you immediately
ROMEO	There is thy gold, worse poison to men's souls, 80	
	Doing more murders in this loathsome world	
	Than these poor compounds that thou mayest not sell.	
	I sell thee poison; thou hast sold me none.	
	Farewell! Buy food, and get thyself in flesh.*	get . . . flesh: fatten yourself

Exit APOTHECARY.

	Come, cordial* and not poison, go with me 85	cordial: restorative drink; literally a stimulant to the heart (used ironically here)
	To Juliet's grave, for there I must use thee.	

Exit.

personification (cf. "The Masque of the
Red Death," pp. 139-44)

Scene II

Time: Thursday evening
Place: Friar Lawrence's cell

*Friar John, just returned from Mantua, reports that a quarantine has prevented
his delivering to Romeo the message that Juliet's "death" is only temporary.
Friar Lawrence quickly leaves to go to the tomb so that he can be with
Juliet until Romeo arrives.*

Enter FRIAR JOHN.

FRIAR J.   Holy Franciscan brother! Brother, ho!

Enter FRIAR LAWRENCE.

FRIAR L.   This same should be the voice of Friar John.
Welcome from Mantua! What says Romeo?
Or if his mind be writ, give me his letter.

FRIAR J.   Going to find a barefoot brother out,   5
One of our order to associate* me   *associate:* go with (the Franciscan toward Mantua)
Here in this city visiting the sick
And finding him, the searchers of the town,*   *searchers . . . town:* quarantine officers
Suspecting that we both were in a house
Where the infectious pestilence* did reign,   10   *pestilence:* plague
Seal'd up the doors and would not let us forth,
So that my speed to Mantua there was stay'd.   *stayed:* delayed

FRIAR L.   Who bare my letter then to Romeo?

FRIAR J.   I could not send it—here it is again—
Nor get a messenger to bring it thee,   15
So fearful were they of infection.

FRIAR L.   Unhappy fortune! By my brotherhood,*   *brotherhood:* office as a friar
The letter was not nice* but full of charge   *nice:* trivial
Of dear import, and the neglecting it
May do much danger. Friar John, go hence.   20
Get me an iron crow* and bring it straight   *iron crow:* crowbar
Unto my cell.

FRIAR J.   Brother, I'll go and bring it thee.

Exit.

Act V, Scene ii

The most crucial coincidence of the plot occurs
in this scene. What are the circumstances of
Friar John's quarantine? *(While searching for a
fellow monk to accompany him to Mantua, he was
quarantined in a house where authorities suspected
the plague. He never went to Mantua.)* The ironic
significance of Capulet's moving Juliet's wedding to Paris from Thursday to Wednesday also
becomes apparent here, for if Juliet had taken
the potion a day later, the Friar would have had
more time to get his message to Romeo. The
scene ends with the Friar's fourth credible
plan.

FRIAR L.　Now must I to the monument alone.
　　　　　Within this three hours will fair Juliet wake.　　　25
　　　　　She will beshrew me much that Romeo
　　　　　Hath had no notice of these accidents;*　　　　　　*accidents: dire events
　　　　　But I will write again to Mantua
　　　　　And keep her at my cell till Romeo come—
　　　　　Poor living corse, clos'd in a dead man's tomb!　　30

Exit.

Scene III

Time: Late Thursday evening
Place: The Capulets' tomb

*Paris encounters Romeo, who he assumes has come to desecrate the grave
of Tybalt. In self-defense Romeo kills Paris. Purposing to join Juliet in
death, Romeo drinks poison and dies just moments before Juliet awakens.
Friar Lawrence fails in his attempt to persuade Juliet to flee with him. Seeing Romeo dead, Juliet, too, kills herself. Watchmen discover what has
happened at the Capulet monument. The Prince reconstructs the tragic
events of the deaths of Paris, Romeo, and Juliet and then denounces the
hate of the Capulets and Montagues that has brought their children to such
a lamentable end. The penitent Capulet and Montague are reconciled, and
each promises to erect a gold statue in memory of the other's child and in
token of the death of their vile enmity.*

Enter PARIS, and PAGE 2 with flowers and sweet water.

PARIS　　Give me thy torch, boy. Hence and stand aloof
　　　　　Yet put it out, for I would not be seen.
　　　　　Under yond yew trees lay thee all along,*　　　　　*all along: stretched out
　　　　　Holding thy ear close to the hollow ground.
　　　　　So shall not foot upon the churchyard tread,　　　5
　　　　　Being loose, unfirm with digging up of graves,
　　　　　But thou shalt hear it. Whistle then to me
　　　　　As signal that thou hearest something approach.
　　　　　Give me those flowers. Do as I bid thee. Go!

PAGE 2　　I am almost afraid to stand alone　　　　　　　10
　　　　　Here in the churchyard, yet I will adventure.*　　　*adventure: take the risk
　　　　　　　　　　　　　　　　　　　　　　　　　　　　　　　　(of doing so)

PAGE 2 retires. PARIS strews the tomb with flowers.

Act V, Scene iii

On Shakespeare's stage this final scene was
probably not played in the study; most theater
historians believe that the Capulet family tomb
was represented by a large portable property.
Paris's timing in arriving to bestow flowers on
Juliet's grave is another large coincidence of
the plot. He does not appear in this scene in
Shakespeare's sources. Notice that Paris is characterized by a persistence in love and an ignorance of Romeo and Juliet's love. Ironically, it
is these very two qualities—persistence in love
and ignorance of the truth—that lead to
Romeo's death as well.

Follow the details of the plot closely in this
scene. What piece of evidence does Romeo
leave with Balthasar (ll. 24-25)? *(a letter for his*

father) Why does Paris believe Romeo has come
to the tomb (ll. 50-54)? *(to desecrate the Ca-*
pulets' tomb, especially Tybalt's body) Notice that at
line 60 Romeo refers to Paris as a "youth." He
and Romeo are of approximately the same age.
He is another of the young men in the play
who is an ironic foil to Romeo, yet the two
share some crucial qualities as well, and they
die for the same cause. Romeo is more mature
in this scene than earlier. He is resolute. He
does not want to fight Paris. In this instance he
does kill in self-defense.

Notice Shakespeare's use of light in this scene,
beginning at line 1, and notice also the light-
and-dark imagery throughout. The final allusion
to light comes in the Prince's closing speech at
lines 306-7. How does Shakespeare finally

unite the play's light and dark imagery with the
time scheme, plot, and theme? *(Friday morning*
is dawning. This joins the themes of time and haste
[the play's action opens on Sunday morning] and
light / dark imagery.)

Shakespeare departs from his sources in the
timing of Romeo's death before Juliet awakens
from her potion-induced sleep. He thus avoids
the potential remorse and despair of such a
melodramatic scene.

According to some critics of the play, the
Friar's actions in the last scene are inconsistent
with Shakespeare's earlier characterization of
him. At lines 132 and 136-37 he is fearful. He
proposes a final plan at lines 154-58, an attempt to salvage Juliet's life from a desperate
situation, but then exits saying, "I dare no

PARIS	Sweet flower, with flowers thy bridal bed I strew.	
	Sweet tomb that in thy circuit dost contain	
	The perfect model of eternity,	
	Fair Juliet, that with angels dost remain,	15
	Accept this latest favor at my hands,	
	That living honored thee, and being dead,	
	With funeral praises do adorn thy tomb.	

PAGE 2 whistles and calls.

	The boy gives warning something doth approach.	
	What cursed foot wanders this way tonight	20
	To cross* my obsequies* and true love's rite?	
	What, with a torch? Muffle me, night, awhile.	

cross: thwart obse-
quies: rites for the
dead

*PARIS retires. Enter ROMEO and BALTHASAR with a torch,
a mattock, and a crow of iron.*

ROMEO	Give me that mattock and the wrenching iron.	
	Hold, take this letter; early in the morning	
	See thou deliver it to my lord and father.	25
	Give me the light. Upon my life I charge thee	
	Whate'er thou hearest or seest, stand all aloof*	
	And do not interrupt me in my course.	
	Why I descend into this bed of death	
	Is partly to behold my lady's face	30
	But chiefly to take thence from her dead finger	
	A precious ring—a ring that I must use	
	In dear employment.* Therefore hence be gone.	
	But if thou, jealous, dost return to pry	
	In what I farther shall intend to do,	35
	By heaven I will tear thee joint by joint	
	And strew this hungry churchyard with thy limbs.	
	The time and my intents are savage wild,	
	More fierce and more inexorable* far	
	Than empty* tigers or the roaring sea.	40

aloof: aside

dear employment:
urgent business

inexorable: unyielding

empty: hungry

| BALTHASAR | I will be gone, sir, and not trouble ye. | |

| ROMEO | So shalt thou show me friendship. Take thou that; | |
| | Live and be prosperous, and farewell, good fellow. | |

| BALTHASAR | *(Aside.)* For all this same, I'll hide me hereabout. | |
| | His looks I fear,* and his intents I doubt.* | 45 |

fear: am anxious
about doubt:
suspect

longer stay" (l. 160). Some critics suggest that the Friar at this point actually wants Juliet to commit suicide in order to cover his part in the tragic events. Others see him as cowardly in leaving Juliet alone at this point. Neither view is supported by a close reading of the play. The Friar has no motives for leaving; motivation to Shakespeare in this case is expendable in the interest of plot. Ask students their opinions: Would Shakespeare have created a better plot by having Juliet live out her days in a nunnery?

Juliet's death is even swifter than Romeo's. At lines 164-67 she too refers to poison as a restorative. The dramatic irony which Shakespeare points out through her realization at line 167 that Romeo has just died is perhaps the most poignant passage in the play.

After Juliet's death the stage begins to fill as party after party of characters enter for the finale. Notice Shakespeare's characterization of Montague in his first two speeches. What has happened to Lady Montague (ll. 211-12)? *(Grief over Romeo's banishment has killed her.)* Why does Montague reproach Romeo (ll. 215-16)? *(for preceding his father in death)*

The Prince reconstructs the sequence of events leading to the tragic deaths of Romeo and Juliet. What three witnesses does he call? *(Friar Lawrence, Balthasar, Paris's page)* What evidence does Romeo's letter present? *(It verifies the Friar's story.)* According to the Prince, why have these events occurred (ll. 292-96)? *(because of the hatred of the Capulets and Montagues and because of the Prince's "winking at [the] discords")*

What personal loss has he sustained as a result of the action of the plot (ll. 295-96)? *(He has "lost a brace of kinsmen.")* Who are the "brace of kinsmen" to whom he alludes? *(Mercutio and Paris)* Notice that he refers to punishment for those involved in and privy to the events only in vague terms (ll. 296, 309).

Which does Shakespeare finally emphasize, retribution or reconciliation? Why? Most critics point out that in *Romeo and Juliet* the old are ultimately reconciled through the love and sacrifice of the young. Such a view fails to take into consideration, however, the ironic nature of the outcome of the plot. The ending is not what Romeo and Juliet have intended. Critics also imply that the deaths of the young— Mercutio, Tybalt, Paris, Romeo, and Juliet—

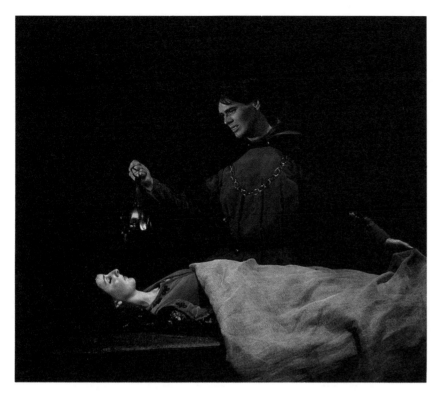

ROMEO	Thou detestable maw,* thou womb of death,	*maw:* mouth (of the tomb)
	Gorg'd with the dearest morsel of the earth,	
	Thus I enforce thy rotten jaws to open	
	And in despite I'll cram thee with more food.	*in despite:* for spite

ROMEO opens the tomb.

PARIS	This is that banish'd haughty Montague	50
	That murd'red my love's cousin, with which grief	
	It is supposed the fair creature died,	
	And here is come to do some villainous shame	
	To the dead bodies. I will apprehend* him.	*apprehend:* arrest

occur because of the hate of the old. Does a close reading of the play support this critical view (cf. quotations cited in the "About the Play" section at the end of Act I)? *(The play seems to support, rather, the free will of the young and the suffering for their own impetuosity. The older generation is tired of the feud.)*

	Stop thy unhallowed toil,* vile Montague!	55	*unhallowed toil:* unholy work
	Can vengeance be pursued further than death?		
	Condemned villain, I do apprehend thee.		
	Obey and go with me, for thou must die.		
ROMEO	I must indeed and therefore came I hither.		
	Good gentle youth, tempt not a desp'rate man.	60	
	Fly hence and leave me; think upon these gone,*		*these gone:* i.e., the dead
	Let them affright thee. I beseech thee, youth,		
	Put not another sin upon my head		
	By urging* me to fury.* O, be gone!		*urging:* provoking *fury:* rage
	By heaven I love thee better than myself,	65	
	For I come hither arm'd against myself.		
	Stay not; be gone; live; and hereafter say		
	A madman's mercy bid thee run away.		
PARIS	I do defy thy commiseration*		*commiseration:* expression of sympathy
	And apprehend thee for a felon here.	70	
ROMEO	Wilt thou provoke me? Then have at thee, boy!		
	They fight.		
PAGE 2	Help, help! They fight! I will go call the watch.*		*watch:* watchmen
	Exit.		
PARIS	O, I am slain! If thou be merciful,		
	Open the tomb; lay me with Juliet.		
	PARIS dies.		
ROMEO	In faith, I will. Let me peruse* this face:	75	*peruse:* examine closely
	Mercutio's kinsman, noble County Paris!		
	What said my man* when my betossed soul		*man:* servant (Balthasar)
	Did not attend* him as we rode? I think		*attend:* pay attention to
	He told me Paris should* have married Juliet.		
	Said he not so, or did I dream it so?	80	*should:* was to
	Or am I mad, hearing him talk of Juliet,		
	To think it was so? O, give me thy hand,		
	One writ with me in sour misfortune's book!		
	I'll bury thee in a triumphant grave.		
	A grave? O no, a lanthorn,* slaught'red youth;	85	*lanthorn:* lantern

See page 317 for an analysis of these lines.

For here lies Juliet, and her beauty makes
This vault a feasting presence* full of light.

feasting presence: brightly lit, festive hall

ROMEO drags PARIS into the tomb.

Death, lie thou there, by a dead man interr'd.*
How oft when men are at the point of death
Have they been merry, which their keepers* call   90
A lightning before death! O how may I
Call this a lightning?* O my love, my wife,
Death that hath suck'd the honey of thy breath
Hath no power yet upon thy beauty.
Thou art not conquer'd; beauty's ensign* yet   95
Is crimson in thy lips and in thy cheeks,
And death's pale flag is not advanced* there.
Tybalt, liest thou there in thy bloody sheet?
O, what more favor can I do to thee
Than with that hand that cut thy youth in twain*   100
To sunder* his that was thine enemy?
Forgive me, cousin! Ah, dear Juliet,
Why art thou yet so fair? Shall I believe
That unsubstantial* Death is amorous
And that the lean abhorred monster keeps   105
Thee here in dark to be his paramour?
For fear of that I still will stay with thee
And never from this palace of dim night
Depart again. Here, here will I remain
With worms that are thy chambermaids; O, here   110
Will I set up my everlasting rest
And shake the yoke of inauspicious* stars
From this world-wearied flesh. Eyes, look your last!
Arms, take your last embrace! And lips, O you
The doors of breath seal with a righteous kiss,   115
A dateless bargain* to engrossing* death!
Come, bitter conduct; come, unsavory guide!
Thou desperate pilot, now at once run on
The dashing rocks thy seasick weary bark!
Here's to my love! *(He drinks.)* O true apothecary,   120
Thy drugs are quick. Thus with a kiss I die.

by . . . interr'd: i.e., buried by one who is himself about to die
keepers: jailers

lightning: an uplifting of the spirits said to occur before death

ensign: military banner

advanced: raised

cut . . . twain: caused you to die
sunder: cut off

unsubstantial: having not bodily form

inauspicious: hostile

dateless bargain: unending contract
engrossing: all-encompassing

ROMEO dies. Enter FRIAR LAWRENCE with lanthorn, crow, and spade.

FRIAR L.	Saint Francis be my speed!* How oft tonight Have my old feet stumbled at graves!* Who's there?	speed: aid Have . . . graves: Such was thought an evil omen in Shakespeare's day.
BALTHASAR	Here's one, a friend and one that knows you well.	
FRIAR L.	Bliss be upon you! Tell me, good friend, 125 What torch is yond that vainly lends his light To grubs and eyeless skulls? As I discern, It burneth in the Capels' monument.	
BALTHASAR	It doth so, holy sir, and there's my master, One that you love.	
FRIAR L.	Who is it?	
BALTHASAR	Romeo. 130	
FRIAR L.	How long hath he been there?	
BALTHASAR	Full half an hour.	
FRIAR L.	Go with me to the vault.	
BALTHASAR	I dare not, sir. My master knows not but I am gone hence And fearfully did menace* me with death If I did stay to look on his intents. 135	menace: threaten
FRIAR L.	Stay then; I'll go alone. Fear comes upon me. O, much I fear some ill unthrifty* thing.	unthrifty: unlucky
BALTHASAR	As I did sleep under this yew tree here, I dreamt my master and another fought And that my master slew him.	
FRIAR L.	Romeo! 140	

FRIAR stoops and looks on the blood and weapons.

Alack, alack, what blood is this which stains
The stony entrance of this sepulchre?
What mean these masterless and gory swords
To lie discolor'd by this place of peace?

Enters the tomb.

	Romeo, O pale! Who else? What, Paris too,	145	
	And steep'd in blood? Ah, what an unkind* hour		*unkind:* cruel
	Is guilty of this lamentable chance?		
	The lady stirs.		

JULIET rises.

JULIET   O comfortable* friar! Where is my lord?
        I do remember well where I should be,   150
        And there I am. Where is my Romeo?

comfortable: comfort-
giving

Noise from outside.

FRIAR L.   I hear some noise, lady. Come from that nest
        Of death, contagion, and unnatural sleep.
        A greater power than we can contradict*
        Hath thwarted our intents. Come, come away.   155

A . . . contradict: i.e.,
Providence

Thy husband in thy bosom there lies dead
And Paris too. Come, I'll dispose of thee
Among a sisterhood of holy nuns.
Stay not to question, for the watch is coming.
Come go, good Juliet; I dare no longer stay.   160

Exit.

JULIET   Go get thee hence, for I will not away.
              What's here? A cup clos'd in my true love's hand?
              Poison, I see, hath been his timeless* end.   *timeless:* untimely
              O churl,* drunk all and left no friendly drop   *churl:* miser; stingy
              To help me after?* I will kiss thy lips.   165   person
              Haply* some poison yet doth hang on them   *help . . . after:* allow
              To make me die with a restorative.   me to follow you in
                                                                             death
                                                                             Haply: Perhaps

              She kisses ROMEO.

              Thy lips are warm.

WATCH. 1   *(Within.)* Lead, boy. Which way?

JULIET   Yea, noise? Then I'll be brief. O happy dagger,   170
              This is thy sheath. There rust, and let me die.

              She stabs herself and dies, falling on Romeo's corpse.
              Enter PAGE 2 and WATCHMEN.

PAGE 2   This is the place, there where the torch doth burn.

WATCH. 1   The ground is bloody; search about the churchyard.
              Go, some of you; whoe'er you find attach.*   *attach:* arrest

              Exeunt some WATCHMEN.

              Pitiful sight! Here lies the County slain   175
              And Juliet, bleeding, warm, and newly dead,
              Who hath here lain these two days buried.
              Go tell the Prince; run to the Capulets;
              Raise up the Montagues; some others search.

              Exeunt others.

	We see the ground whereon these woes* do lie,	180	woes: woeful creatures
	But the true ground* of all these piteous woes*		ground: cause woes: woeful events
	We cannot without circumstance descry.*		descry: discern

Enter some of the WATCHMEN and BALTHASAR.

WATCH. 2   Here's Romeo's man. We found him in the churchyard.

WATCH. 1   Hold him in safety* till the Prince come hither.   *safety:* security

Enter FRIAR LAWRENCE and another WATCHMAN.

WATCH. 3   Here is a friar that trembles, sighs, and weeps.   185
We took this mattock and this spade from him
As he was coming from the churchyard's side.

WATCH. 1   A great suspicion.* Stay* the friar too.   *suspicion:* cause for suspicion *Stay:* Detain

Enter PRINCE ESCALUS and attendants.

PRINCE   What misadventure is so early up
That calls our person from our morning rest?   190

Enter CAPULET, LADY CAPULET, and others.

CAPULET   What should it be that they so shriek abroad?

LADY CAP.   O, the people in the street cry "Romeo,"
Some "Juliet," and some "Paris," and all run
With open outcry toward our monument.

PRINCE   What fear is this which startles in your ears?   195

WATCH. 1   Sovereign, here lies the County Paris slain,
And Romeo dead, and Juliet, dead before,
Warm and new kill'd.

PRINCE   Search, seek, and know how this foul murder comes.

WATCH. 1   Here is a friar and slaughter'd Romeo's man   200
With instruments upon them fit to open
These dead men's tombs.

CAPULET   O heavens! O wife, look how our daughter bleeds!

	This dagger hath mista'en, for lo his house*	
	Is empty on the back of Montague*	205
	And is mis-sheathed in my daughter's bosom!	

house: i.e., sheath

on . . . Montague: Men conventionally wore daggers on their backs.

LADY CAP. O me, this sight of death is as a bell
          That warns my old age to a sepulchre.

Enter MONTAGUE and others.

PRINCE Come, Montague, for thou art early up
          To see thy son and heir more early down.   210

MONTAGUE Alas, my liege, my wife is dead tonight;
          Grief of my son's exile hath stopp'd her breath.
          What further woe conspires against mine age?

PRINCE Look and thou shalt see.

MONTAGUE O thou untaught!* What manners is in this,   215
          To press* before thy father to a grave?

untaught: ill-mannered

press: rush forward

PRINCE Seal up the mouth of outrage* for a while
          Till we can clear these ambiguities
          And know their spring, their head, their true descent,*
          And then will I be general of your woes*   220
          And lead you even to death. Meantime forbear
          And let mischance be slave to patience.
          Bring forth the parties of suspicion.

mouth . . . outrage: violent outcry

descent: origin

general . . . woes: your leader in mourning these woes

FRIAR L. I am the greatest, able to do least
          Yet most suspected, as the time and place   225
          Doth make against me, of this direful murder;
          And here I stand both to impeach* and purge*
          Myself condemned and myself excus'd.*

impeach: accuse
purge: exonerate
Myself . . . excus'd: I am both guilty and innocent.

PRINCE Then say at once what thou dost know in this.

FRIAR L. I will be brief, for my short date of breath*   230
          Is not so long as is a tedious tale.
          Romeo, there dead, was husband to that Juliet,
          And she, there dead that's Romeo's faithful wife.
          I married them, and their stol'n marriage day
          Was Tybalt's doomsday, whose untimely death   235
          Banish'd the new-made bridegroom from this city,

short . . . breath: brief remaining lifespan

For whom, and not for Tybalt, Juliet pin'd.
You, to remove that siege of grief from her,
Betroth'd and would have married her perforce*
To County Paris. Then comes she to me   240
And with wild looks bid me devise some mean
To rid her from this second marriage,
Or in my cell there would she kill herself.
Then gave I her (so tutor'd by my art*)
A sleeping potion which so took effect   245
As I intended, for it wrought on her
The form of death. Meantime I writ to Romeo
That he should hither come as this* dire night
To help to take her from her borrowed grave,
Being the time the potion's force should cease.   250
But he which bore my letter, Friar John,
Was stayed by accident* and yesternight
Return'd my letter back. Then all alone
At the prefixed hour of her waking
Came I to take her from her kindred's vault,   255
Meaning to keep her closely* at my cell
Till I conveniently could send to Romeo.
But when I came some minute ere the time
Of her awakening, here untimely lay
The noble Paris and true Romeo dead.   260
She wakes, and I entreated her come forth
And bear this work of heaven with patience.*
But then a noise did scare me from the tomb,
And she, too desperate, would not go with me,
But as it seems, did violence on herself.   265
All this I know, and to the marriage
Her nurse is privy;* and if aught in this
Miscarried* by my fault, let my old life
Be sacrific'd some hour before his time
Unto the rigor of severest law.   270

PRINCE   We still have known thee for a holy man.
              Where's Romeo's man? What can he say to this?

BALTHASAR   I brought my master news of Juliet's death,
              And then in post* he came from Mantua
              To this same place, to this same monument.   275
              This letter he early bid me give his father
              And threaten'd me with death, going in the vault,
              If I departed not and left him there.

perforce: by compulsion

art: skill with herbs

as this: this very

stayed . . . accident: delayed by chance

closely: secretly

patience: fortitude

privy: knowledgeable (concerning these secret matters)
Miscarried: Went wrong

in post: speedily, by horse

PRINCE   Give me the letter. I will look on it.
              Where is the County's page that rais'd the watch?   280
              Sirrah, what made your master* in this place?

PAGE 2   He came with flowers to strew his lady's grave
              And bid me stand aloof, and so I did.
              Anon comes one with light to ope the tomb,
              And by and by my master drew on him,   285
              And then I ran away to call the watch.

PRINCE   This letter doth make good the friar's words,
              Their course of love, the tidings of her death;
              And here he writes that he did buy a poison
              Of a poor 'pothecary and therewithal   290
              Came to this vault to die and lie with Juliet.
              Where be these enemies? Capulet! Montague!
              See what a scourge* is laid upon your hate
              That heaven finds means to kill your joys* with* love.
              And I, for winking at* your discords, too   295
              Have lost a brace of* kinsmen. All are punish'd.

CAPULET   O brother Montague, give me thy hand.
              This is my daughter's jointure,* for no more
              Can I demand.

MONTAGUE   But I can give thee more,
              For I will raise her statue in pure gold,   300
              The whiles* Verona by that name is known,
              There shall no figure at such a rate* be set
              As that of true and faithful Juliet.

CAPULET   As rich shall Romeo's* by his lady's lie,
              Poor sacrifices of our enmity!*   305

PRINCE   A glooming* peace this morning with it brings.
              The sun for sorrow will not show his head.
              Go hence to have more talk of these sad things.
              Some shall be pardon'd and some punished.
              For never was a story of more woe   310
              Than this of Juliet and her Romeo.

                                          Exeunt.

made . . . master: did
   your master do

scourge: punishment
kill . . . joys: (1) kill
   your children (2)
   make you unhappy,
   i.e., punish you *with:*
   by means of
winking at: closing my
   eyes to
a . . . of: two (Mercu-
   tio and Paris)
jointure: wifely inherit-
   ance (as a result of
   Romeo's death, i.e.,
   the reconciliation of
   Montague with
   Capulet)

whiles: as long as

rate: (1) value (2) cost

Romeo's: a statue of
   Romeo
enmity: hatred,
   hostility

glooming: cloudy

About the Play

1. There are several "coincidences" in the plot. Identify at least two of these coincidences.
2. What does Romeo decide to do when he hears of Juliet's "death"?
3. What happens to Romeo's mother?
4. Philip Sidney once said that the purpose of literature is "to delight and to instruct." The value of *Romeo and Juliet* as entertaining drama is clear. But how does the play also "instruct"? List at least three things the drama teaches us.

 *About
the Play*

1. *Answers may vary but might include (from Act V) Friar John's having been quarantined; Romeo's dying moments before Juliet awakes. (For further discussion of coincidences in the play see teacher's edition pages 333-34, 420-21.)*

2. *to go to her grave and kill himself*

3. *She dies of "grief of [her] son's exile."*

4. *Answers may vary. The most obvious lessons include a warning against haste in important decisions; the danger of deceiving one's parents; the harmful outworkings of long-held bitterness.*

UNIT ELEVEN

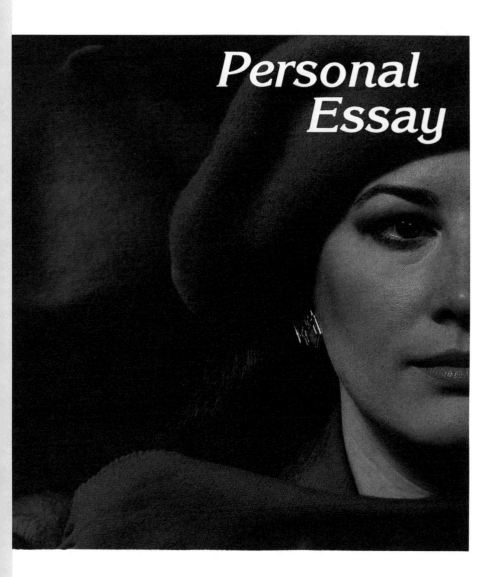

Personal Essay

FURTHER HELPS

Additional activities

1. Read other nonfiction pieces to the class. Help students see that nonfiction is interesting. Share newspaper articles, informative articles from magazines, excerpts from biographies, or essays about a relevant teen subject. Then ask them to bring nonfiction articles to class to read aloud.

2. James Thurber ("The Day the Dam Broke," pp. 190-93) is another popular essayist. Your students might enjoy "The Spreading 'You Know'" from *Lanterns and Lances,* "Memorial" from *My World—And Welcome to It,* or an essay from *My Life and Hard Times.* As always, preview the essay before presenting it to the class.

3. Ask some students who have participated in sporting events such as the one in the essay to tell the class members about it.

The personal essay is of all the genres the one the unskilled writer is most likely to try with some success. Yet it is among the most difficult to master. Its quirky movement—with sudden breaks in thought, parenthetical interruptions, and afterthoughts—give it the appearance of informal chat. But mere chat it is not. Its appearance is deceptively simple.

In this respect the personal essay is very much like a letter. Its style can be fancy but is usually relaxed and unpretentious. It is addressed to an individual—to *you,* the reader, rather than to readers as a whole. The reader is taken into the confidence, as it were, of the author, who shares some of his experience and thoughts in a more or less disconnected way. But, to the writer, the end is always in view. The randomness is only apparent.

You will notice that the personal essay, on our map of the genres, is situated in the territorial waters of narrative. It has close ties with the autobiographical anecdote. The personal essay typically begins with an anecdote and concludes with some kind of comment. The comment may relate to conduct or attitude or may be a general observation on life. It is usually stated in the author's own voice. The anecdote therefore becomes an illustration of a point. The anecdote-with-comment from *Something of Myself* by Rudyard Kipling in Unit 7 could very easily be expanded into a personal essay on the subject of checking one's facts. Though from an autobiography, the selection contains all the basic ingredients of the personal essay.

The personal essay is in some ways the prose counterpart of the lyric poem. Notice that the two are positioned correspondingly on our map of the genres. Each gives a personal view of life and the world. Each typically relates a mental incident from the author's private world and comments upon it. Both are versatile and flexible, able to include many of the elements, modes, and techniques of the other genres. The personal essay may contain dialogue, formal description, analogy, and even allegory. Its moods range from vivacious to seriously reflective, keenly earnest to subdued. It may reenact a suspenseful experience, or calmly reminisce. In either case (and the second is more common), it has a point to make. The point is made all the more effectively because the reader while being taught is also being entertained.

Though the personal essay as such does not appear in the Bible, its strategy is well represented there. The Lord's stories of the good Samaritan (Luke 10:30-36) and the rich man in hell (Luke 16:19-31) make their points indirectly but powerfully. Paul in his epistles often argues from personal experience (Rom. 7, II Cor. 11-12, Gal. 1-2). The personal essay similarly lends itself to deadly serious persuasion. No subject is too weighty or purpose too urgent for its use. Its offhand manner catches the reader with his guard down. It is therefore a greatly effective vehicle for the Christian witness. We need to learn how to use it well.

PREPARATION

Personal Essay Introduction, "Crossing the Bar on a Fiberglas Pole"

Overview

Having studied Units 7 and 9, the students should find this unit on personal essay somewhat familiar. The techniques used in writing autobiography and lyric poetry are also used in writing a personal essay. Dubber, for example, approaches his subject much as a lyric poet would. The style and topic of his essay should also be appealing to a high school audience.

DISCUSSION

Introduction

Read the introduction aloud. Draw the students' attention to the characteristics shared by the personal essay and the lyric poem. Keeping these characteristics in mind, read Dubber's essay.

Analysis

"Crossing the Bar on a Fiberglas Pole"

Point out to the students that, like the lyric poet, Dubber relates to us a mental incident from his private world and comments on it. In this case, we do not feel that the author is "addressing" us. We feel rather that he is having a private conversation. This essay, like many lyric poems, seems almost like a soliloquy. It is highly personal. Have the students point out several specific references from the essay that reinforce these facts. Notice, for example, the frequent use of "I."

4. Have an experienced pole-vaulter demonstrate his or her skill for your class on the athletic field. Encourage the students to ask questions about equipment, techniques, and so on.

5. Have the student look up sports-related allusions in the Bible. Discuss these as a class. (*cf. Ps. 19:5; Eccles. 9:11; Jer. 12:5; Joel 2:4; Rom. 9:16; I Cor. 9:24, 26, 27; Gal. 2:2; 5:7; Phil. 2:16; Heb. 12:1*)

Journal entry idea

Explain in an informal essay the physical manipulations and/or sensations involved in an activity. It may be a sports activity or another activity such as mowing the grass. Try to describe all these senses: what you see, what you hear, what you smell, what you feel.

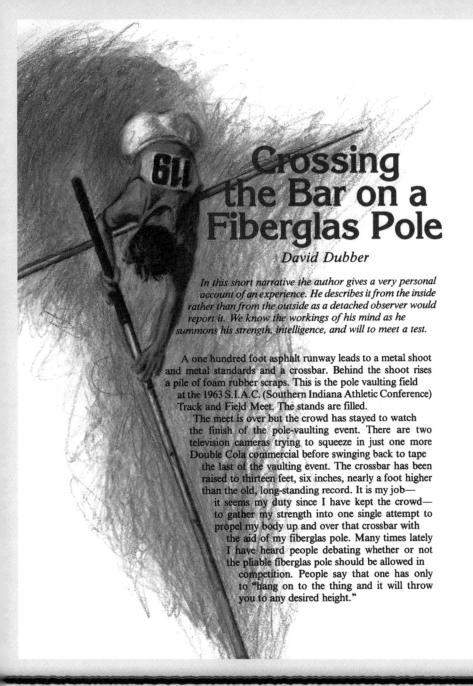

Crossing the Bar on a Fiberglas Pole

David Dubber

In this short narrative the author gives a very personal account of an experience. He describes it from the inside rather than from the outside as a detached observer would report it. We know the workings of his mind as he summons his strength, intelligence, and will to meet a test.

A one hundred foot asphalt runway leads to a metal shoot and metal standards and a crossbar. Behind the shoot rises a pile of foam rubber scraps. This is the pole vaulting field at the 1963 S.I.A.C. (Southern Indiana Athletic Conference) Track and Field Meet. The stands are filled.

The meet is over but the crowd has stayed to watch the finish of the pole-vaulting event. There are two television cameras trying to squeeze in just one more Double Cola commercial before swinging back to tape the last of the vaulting event. The crossbar has been raised to thirteen feet, six inches, nearly a foot higher than the old, long-standing record. It is my job— it seems my duty since I have kept the crowd— to gather my strength into one single attempt to propel my body up and over that crossbar with the aid of my fiberglas pole. Many times lately I have heard people debating whether or not the pliable fiberglas pole should be allowed in competition. People say that one has only to "hang on to the thing and it will throw you to any desired height."

Have the students continue their analysis of the essay using the "About the Essay" questions (page 439).

Application

Following their analysis, the students should be able to see the clear similarities between Dubber's approach to his subject matter and a lyric poet's approach. As a class or in groups, have the students use Dubber's essay as a basis for a poem. Students may want to review "Foul Shot" (pp. 292-93) for ideas.

As an alternative, you may want them to write a poem or personal essay based on their own personal athletic experience. Remind them, however, that like Dubber's essay, their writings should make a point.

These recollections bring me much bitterness as I stand before my trial. I am developing a fatalistic attitude toward this towering height and wish I had never come out for track, or at least I wish I had never heard of this silly "bending" pole. But it is too late to untwine this tightly woven cord; the crowd is waiting. I completely dismiss distracting thoughts and put all my powers, mental and physical, into this one leap.

Mentally I run through the particulars of the vault. I have counted my steps down to the tape mark on the runway where my left foot is to hit the runway for the last time. I must remember to keep my body loose to conserve strength. I must also remember to strike my left foot on the mark hard enough to give me a four-foot jump on the pole before switching my balance and strength to my hands; otherwise I will not get off the ground. It must be a quick and trained reflex that is well routed in the grooves of my mind.

Now the crowd is dead silent. I count ten as I leave the world—seeing only the runway and crossbar directly ahead, believing only that I will succeed in clearing the bar, hearing only the beating of my own heart. Slowly I begin an easy jog down the runway as the pole I cling to bounces slightly in front of me in a syncopation of my steps. Gradually my speed picks up until my body attains a swift glide. The tip of the pole descends as I approach the shoot. Although my main concern is making good contact between the end of my pole and the shoot, I am also watching the tape marking. After a few years' practice, a vaulter learns to compensate for any misjudgment the last few strides before he reaches the shoot. Through some inexplicable mechanism the vaulter's subconscious tells his body how much to shorten or lengthen the stride in order to hit the take-off mark. Just as the tip of my pole touches the backstop of the shoot, I push the pole straight forward and with one final bound I smack the pavement with the ball of my left foot and straighten my half bent leg with a great thrust to give me my height on the pole.

All my weight shifts to my hands, and as the angle of the pole increases toward the vertical, my body climbs to about three-fourths the height of the crossbar. As I come up I throw my head back toward the ground causing my hips to sweep upward until my feet pass through my line of vision and on, one foot further, so that I am now completely upside down. The pole bends suddenly to about four feet from the ground, and my body, remaining in the inverted position, falls rapidly with it. In my upside down position, all the stress is put on the abdominal area of the body. The tension wrenches the stomach and the intestines. The pole now stops its bend and starts to reflex back up to a straight position, but my body is still falling straight downward. At this moment the strain multiplies as my body is brought to an abrupt stop and then starts back in the opposite direction. The inverted position must be maintained. Unbelievable pressure is put on the abdominal area. My hands and fingers clench the pole like wrenches. Just as the deep-sea pole comes alive in the hands of a fisherman when he has hooked a fighting sailfish, this pole strains to pull from me as it jiggles violently from side to side. I feel I can't hold on any longer. In my fury to keep from losing the pole I wish the people who had said one merely has to "hang on" to the fiberglas pole for the ride could take my place now and try "hanging on" to this monster. I feel the muscle fibers along my stomach straining to the point of popping, and my numb fingers seem to be slipping off the rising pole; but suddenly, my body ceases to resist and rises upward toward the stars.

I am amazed to realize that I am still on the pole. My body writhes slowly to the left, and my feet come up to the crossbar. My body continues turning as the bar passes under my shins, knees, thighs, and my body stops in a half-twist as the crossbar stands directly under my waist. At this point I lock my arms in a half-bent position, the pole begins its final slight bend. My waist is approximately three feet higher than my hands and well above the crossbar. The slight bend of the pole lowers my body four to six inches. I keep my arms locked in bent position as again the pressure mounts on my tight, quivering stomach muscles. As the pole becomes a straight line, I straighten my arms out keeping my head forward and down, my body arched into a parabola around the crossbar. I stiffen my arms, and the fingertips, tired and pained, become the only things supporting my weight on the pole. I push off with my stiff fingertips, pulling my elbows up, back, and over; I throw my head back as my weak fingers barely clear the bar. I let go of all tension and let my body fall easily, down, and backward—sinking into the soft white mass, seeing only the dark blue sky. Wait! Not only the dark blue sky, but also a crossbar lying across the tops of two standards up there in the heavens, quivering a bit perhaps, but not falling, not in a thousand years. The hundred or so people who have gathered around the pit rush to pick me up as the masses in the stands exhale a roar. I look back at the pole lying over there alone, still, and I know what a marvelous monster it is to ride.

About the Essay

1. Would you say the style of this essay is formal or informal?
2. What is the mood of this essay?
3. At what point in the essay does the author capture your interest?
4. The description in the essay is not just for its own sake. A point is being made. What is the point?

 About the Essay

1. *Although the structure of the essay is tight, the syntax and style are informal. Point out, for example, the journalistic, "blow by blow" description.*

2. *Dubber's highly personal, detailed description of the incident gives it an intensity that reinforces the serious mood of the piece. This intensity serves to focus the reader's attention, to make us—like Dubber—rule out all other distractions until we are "over the bar."*

3. *Answers will vary. In answering, however, encourage the students to give a specific quotation from the essay.*

4. *It is not the pole but the vaulter who determines the success or failure of a jump.*

metaphor, mathematical allusion

hyperbole

alliteration, metaphor

OBJECTIVE

The students will be able to

• *Write a personal essay.*

Ask students to name a story they have studied this year in which exactly this event occurs. (*"The Sire de Maletroit's Door"*)

allusions

metaphor

FURTHER HELPS

Additional activities

1. Have students read brief paragraphs in the essay such as the second paragraph on the right-hand side of page 440. After they read the paragraph, ask them to give its main idea. You may want to list four alternatives for them. Alternatives for that paragraph could be as follows:

   a. Life goes by quickly.
   b. We do not realize all we have to be thankful for in life.
   c. No one thinks of death while he is in good health.
   d. Live life to the fullest.

   In this case *b* would be the best choice for the main idea.

Three Days to See

Helen Keller

Helen Keller's familiar style reinforces the personal tone of her essay, an essay clearly written to you—the individual reader. Like Dubber's, her purpose is not simply to entertain; it is to make a specific point.

All of us have read thrilling stories in which the hero had only a limited and specified time to live. Sometimes it was as long as a year; sometimes as short as twenty-four hours. But always we were interested in discovering just how the doomed man chose to spend his last days or his last hours. I speak, of course, of free men who have a choice, not condemned criminals whose sphere of activities is strictly delimited.

Such stories set us thinking, wondering what we should do under similar circumstances. What events, what experiences, what associations should we crowd into those last hours as mortal beings? What happiness should we find in reviewing the past, what regrets?

Sometimes I have thought it would be an excellent rule to live each day as if we should die tomorrow. Such an attitude would emphasize sharply the values of life. We should live each day with a gentleness, a vigor, and a keenness of appreciation which are often lost when time stretches before us in the constant panorama of more days and months and years to come. There are those, of course, who would adopt the epicurean* motto of "Eat, drink, and be merry," but most people would be chastened by the certainty of impending death.

epicurean: one devoted to a life of pleasure

In stories, the doomed hero is usually saved at the last minute by some stroke of fortune, but almost always his sense of values is changed. He becomes more appreciative of the meaning of life and its permanent spiritual values. It has often been noted that those who live, or have lived, in the shadow of death bring a mellow sweetness to everything they do.

Most of us, however, take life for granted. We know that one day we must die, but usually we picture that day as far in the future. When we are in buoyant health, death is all but unimaginable. We seldom think of it. The days stretch out in an endless vista. So we go about our petty tasks, hardly aware of our listless attitude toward life.

The same lethargy, I am afraid, characterizes the use of all our faculties and senses. Only the deaf appreciate hearing, only the blind realize the manifold blessings that lie in sight. Particularly does this observation apply to those who have lost sight and hearing in adult life. But those who have never suffered impairment of sight or hearing seldom make the fullest use of these blessed faculties. Their eyes and ears take in all sights and sounds hazily, without concentration, and with little appreciation. It is the same old story of not being grateful for what we have until we lose it, of not being conscious of health until we are ill.

PREPARATION

"Three Days to See"

Overview

The mood and purpose of Keller's personal essay is, like Dubber's, serious. Her style, however, is less intense. Her essay is a good example of how the anecdote, often used in autobiographical writing, might also be effectively used in this genre.

DISCUSSION

Introduction

Before reading the essay together as a class, introduce it with the same "test" Keller used for her sighted friends. Have the students answer the questions on **Appendix Y: How Observant Are You?** Have fun with the activity and generate good discussion from it, but make the point of the activity clear: sighted people take their vision for granted. We all take many blessings for granted.

Analysis

Read the first few paragraphs of the essay aloud. Draw the students' attention to the fact that Keller begins her essay with an anecdote—one, by the way, that is universally compelling. We can also discern from the content of the anecdote that Keller, like Dubber, has a serious point to make. Continue reading the essay either aloud or silently. Then discuss it by answering the "About the Essay" questions (page 449).

Application

As mentioned, Keller's "theme" is both universal and compelling. Have the students write a short essay titled "If I Had Only Three Days to ____." They should fill this blank in with a verb of their choosing (other than "see"): *hear, walk, run, talk,* or even something such as *fly.* Each student's essay may be serious or humorous, depending on what approach he believes is best. Essays written by any disabled students should be especially compelling. See **Writing Rubric 11-1: An Enlightening Essay.**

I have often thought it would be a blessing if each human being were stricken blind and deaf for a few days at some time during his early adult life. Darkness would make him more appreciative of sight; silence would teach him the joys of sound.

Now and then I have tested my seeing friends to discover what they see. Recently I was visited by a very good friend who had just returned from a long walk in the woods, and I asked her what she had observed. "Nothing in particular," she replied. I might have been incredulous* had I not been accustomed to such responses, for long ago I became convinced that the seeing see little.

incredulous: unbelieving

How was it possible, I asked myself, to walk for an hour through the woods and see nothing worthy of note? I who cannot see find hundreds of things to interest me through mere touch. I feel the delicate symmetry of a leaf. I pass my hands lovingly about the smooth skin of a silver birch, or the rough shaggy bark of a pine. In spring I touch the branches of trees hopefully in search of a bud, the first sign of awakening Nature after her winter's sleep. I feel the delightful, velvety texture of a flower, and discover its remarkable convolutions;* and something of the miracle of Nature is revealed to me. Occasionally, if I am very fortunate, I place my hand gently on a small tree and feel the happy quiver of a bird in full song. I am delighted to have the cool waters of a brook rush through my open fingers. To me a lush carpet of pine needles or spongy grass is more welcome than the most luxurious Persian rug. To me the pageant of seasons is a thrilling and unending drama, the action of which streams through my finger tips.

convolutions: folds

At times my heart cries out with longing to see all these things. If I can get so much pleasure from mere touch, how much more beauty must be revealed by sight. Yet, those who have eyes apparently see little. The panorama of color and action which fills the world is taken for granted. It is human, perhaps, to appreciate little that which we have and to long for that which we have not, but it is a great pity that in the world of light the gift of sight is used only as a mere convenience rather than as a means of adding fullness to life.

If I were the president of a university I should establish a compulsory course in "How to Use Your Eyes." The professor would try to show his pupils how they could add joy to their lives by really seeing what passes unnoticed before them. He would try to awake their dormant and sluggish faculties.

Perhaps I can best illustrate by imagining what I should most like to see if I were given the use of my eyes, say, for just three days. And while I am imagining, suppose you, too, set your mind to work on the problem of how you would use your own eyes if you had only three more days to see. If with the oncoming darkness of the third night you knew that the sun would never rise for you again, how would you spend those three precious intervening days? What would you most want to let your gaze rest upon?

I, naturally, should want most to see the things which have become dear to me through my years of darkness. You, too, would want to let your eyes rest long on the things that have become dear to you so that you could take the memory of them with you into the night that loomed before you.

If, by some miracle, I were granted three seeing days, to be followed by a relapse into darkness, I should divide the period into three parts.

Note imagery, alliteration, personification, and metaphor in this paragraph.

You may wish to discuss this statement with the students. How is it true of children? of teens? of adults?

pun

Thus, after her introduction, Keller sets up for readers the structure of the rest of the essay.

2. Have the students do additional research on other types of physical disabilities. Have them research, for example, some of the problems a deaf person might face on a daily basis.

3. Have a disabled person come speak to the class. Dedicated Christians who glorify God through their infirmities make powerful speakers.

4. Encourage students to read Helen Keller's autobiography (*The Story of My Life*) and/or the play based on her childhood (*The Miracle Worker*) when "Anne Sullivan . . . opened the outer world" to her. Note that Miss Keller did not claim to be a born-again Christian. Students will need to examine her philosophical tenets from a Biblical perspective.

As time permits, have the students share their essays with the class. Discuss with them how their Christian outlook affected their response to the topic. If this "effect" is not explicit in any essays, have them rework the essay in order to show how their view of life would affect the choices they made in the essay.

metaphor, personification

synecdoche, allusion

Resources

Gibson, William, *The Miracle Worker* (Bantam Books, 1994).

Keller, Helen, *The Story of My Life* (Doubleday, 1991).

The First Day

On the first day, I should want to see the people whose kindness and gentleness and companionship have made my life worth living. First I should like to gaze long upon the face of my dear teacher, Mrs. Anne Sullivan Macy, who came to me when I was a child and opened the outer world to me. I should want not merely to see the outline of her face, so that I could cherish it in my memory, but to study that face and find in it the living evidence of the sympathetic tenderness and patience with which she accomplished the difficult task of my education. I should like to see in her eyes that strength of character which has enabled her to stand firm in the face of difficulties, and that compassion for all humanity which she has revealed to me so often.

I do not know what it is to see into the heart of a friend through that "window of the soul," the eye. I can only "see" through my finger tips the outline of a face. I can detect laughter, sorrow, and many other obvious emotions. I know my friends from the feel of their faces. But I cannot really picture their personalities by touch. I know their personalities, of course, through other means, through the thoughts they express to me, through whatever of their actions are revealed to me. But I am denied that deeper understanding of them which I am sure would come through sight of them, through watching their reactions to various expressed thoughts and circumstances, through noting the immediate and fleeting reactions of their eyes and countenance.

Friends who are near to me I know well, because through the months and years they reveal themselves to me in all their phases; but of casual friends I have only an incomplete impression, an impression gained from a handclasp, from spoken words which I take from their lips with my finger tips, or which they tap into the palm of my hand.

How much easier, how much more satisfying it is for you who can see to grasp quickly the essential qualities of another person by watching the subtleties of expression, the quiver of a muscle, the flutter of a hand. But does it ever occur to you to use your sight to see into the inner nature of a friend or acquaintance? Do not most of you seeing people grasp casually the outward features of a face and let it go at that?

For instance, can you describe accurately the faces of five good friends? Some of you can, but many cannot. As an experiment, I have questioned husbands of long standing about the color of their wives' eyes, and often they express embarrassed confusion and admit that they do not know. And, incidentally, it is a chronic complaint of wives that their husbands do not notice new dresses, new hats, and changes in household arrangements.

The eyes of seeing persons soon become accustomed to the routine of their surroundings, and they actually see only the startling and spectacular. But even in viewing the most spectacular sights the eyes are lazy. Court records reveal every day how inaccurately "eyewitnesses" see. A given event will be "seen" in several different ways by as many witnesses. Some see more than others, but few see everything that is within the range of their vision.

Oh, the things that I should see if I had the power of sight for just three days!

The first day would be a busy one. I should call to me all my dear friends and look long into their faces, imprinting upon my mind the outward evidences of the beauty that is within them. I should let my eyes rest, too, on the face of a baby, so that I could catch a vision of the eager, innocent beauty which precedes the individual's consciousness of the conflicts which life develops.

And I should like to look into the loyal, trusting eyes of my dogs—the grave, canny little Scottie, Darkie, and the stalwart, understanding great Dane, Helga, whose warm, tender, and playful friendships are so comforting to me.

On that busy first day I should also view the small simple things of my home. I want to see the warm colors in the rugs under my feet, the pictures on the walls, the intimate trifles that transform a house into a home. My eyes would rest respectfully on the books in raised type which I have read, but they would be more eagerly interested in the printed books which seeing people can read, for during the long night of my life the books I have read and those which have been read to me have built themselves into a great shining lighthouse, revealing to me the deepest channels of human life and the human spirit.

In the afternoon of that first seeing day, I should take a long walk in the woods and intoxicate my eyes on the beauties of the world of Nature, trying desperately to absorb in a few hours the vast splendor which is constantly unfolding itself to those who can see. On the way home from my woodland jaunt my path would lie near a farm so that I might see the patient horses plowing in the field (perhaps I should see only a tractor!) and the serene content of men living close to the soil. And I should pray for the glory of a colorful sunset.

When dusk had fallen, I should experience the double delight of being able to see by artificial light, which the genius of man has created to extend the power of his sight when Nature decrees darkness.

In the night of that first day of sight, I should not be able to sleep, so full would be my mind of the memories of the day.

The Second Day

The next day—the second day of sight—I should arise with the dawn and see the thrilling miracle by which night is transformed into day. I should behold with awe the magnificent panorama of light with which the sun awakens the sleeping earth.

This day I should devote to a hasty glimpse of the world, past and present. I should want to see the pageant of man's progress, the kaleidoscope of the ages. How can so much be compressed into one day? Through the museums, of course. Often I have visited the New York Museum of Natural History to touch with my hands many of the objects there exhibited, but I have longed to see with my eyes the condensed history of the earth and its inhabitants displayed there—animals and the races of men pictured in their native environment.

I wonder how many readers of this article have viewed this panorama of the face of living things as pictured in that inspiring museum. Many, of course, have not had the opportunity, but I am sure that many who *have* had the opportunity have not made use of it. There, indeed, is a place to use your eyes. You who see can spend many fruitful days there, but I, with my imaginary three days of sight, could only take a hasty glimpse, and pass on.

My next stop would be the Metropolitan Museum of Art, for just as the Museum of Natural History reveals the material aspects of the world, so does the Metropolitan show the myriad facets of the human spirit. Throughout the history of humanity the urge to artistic expression has been almost as powerful as the urge for food, shelter, and procreation. And here, in the vast chambers of the Metropolitan Museum, is unfolded before me the spirit of Egypt, Greece, and Rome, as expressed in their art. I know well

Hamlet by William Shakespeare (Bob Jones University Classic Players)

through my hands the sculptured gods and goddesses of the ancient Nile-land. I have felt copies of Parthenon friezes,* and I have sensed the rhythmic beauty of charging Athenian warriors. Apollos and Venuses and the Wingèd Victory of Samothrace* are friends of my finger tips. The gnarled, bearded features of Homer* are dear to me, for he, too, knew blindness.

Parthenon friezes: decorated or sculptured scenes on the walls of this Greek temple
Wingèd Victory of Samothrace: Greek goddess of victory
Homer: Greek poet

My hands have lingered upon the living marble of Roman sculpture as well as that of later generations. I have passed my hands over a plaster cast of Michelangelo's inspiring and heroic Moses; I have sensed the power of Rodin;* I have been awed by the devoted spirit of Gothic wood carving. These arts which can be touched have meaning for me, but even they were meant to be seen rather than felt, and I can only guess at the beauty which remains hidden from me. I can admire the simple lines of a Greek vase, but its figured decorations are lost to me.

Rodin: (1840-1917) French sculptor

So on this, my second day of sight, I should try to probe into the soul of man through his art. The things I knew through touch I should now see. More splendid still, the whole magnificent world of painting would be opened to me, from the Italian Primitives, with their serene religious devotion, to the Moderns, with their feverish visions. I should look deep into the canvases of Raphael, Leonardo da Vinci, Titian, Rembrandt. I should want to feast my eyes upon the warm colors of Veronese, study the mysteries of El Greco,* catch a new vision of Nature from Corot.* Oh, there is so much rich meaning and beauty in the art of the ages for you who have eyes to see!

El Greco: (1541? - 1614?) Spanish artist and architect
Corot: (1796-1875) French painter

Upon my short visit to this temple of art I should not be able to review a fraction of that great world of art which is open to you. I should be able to get only a superficial impression. Artists tell me that for a deep and true appreciation of art one must educate the eye. One must learn through experience to weigh the merits of line, of composition, of form and color. If I had eyes, how happily would I embark upon so fascinating a study! Yet I am told that, to many of you who have eyes to see, the world of art is a dark night, unexplored and unilluminated.

It would be with extreme reluctance that I should leave the Metropolitan Museum, which contains the key to beauty—a beauty so neglected. Seeing persons, however, do not need a Metropolitan to find this key to beauty. The same key lies waiting in smaller museums, and in books on the shelves of even small libraries. But naturally, in my limited time of imaginary sight, I should choose the place where the key unlocks the greatest treasures in the shortest time.

The evening of my second day of sight I should spend at a theater. Even now I often attend theatrical performances of all sorts, but the action of the play must be spelled into my hand by a companion. But how I should like to see with my own eyes the fascinating figure of Hamlet, or the gusty Falstaff* amid colorful Elizabethan trappings! How I should like to follow each movement of the graceful Hamlet, each strut of the hearty Falstaff! And since I could see only one play, I should be confronted by a many-horned dilemma, for there are scores of plays I should want to see. You who have eyes can see any you like. How many of you, I wonder, when you gaze at a play or any spectacle, realize and give thanks

Allusion; note the many allusions in the following paragraphs.

metaphor

Note how Keller reviews the essay for the reader before going on to her third major point.

paradox ("lacy . . . steel")

onomatopoeia, personification, alliteration

metaphor, alliteration, simile

for the miracle of sight which enables you to enjoy its color, grace, and movement?

Falstaff: jovial character in Shakespeare's *Henry IV* and *Merry Wives of Windsor*

I cannot enjoy the beauty of rhythmic movement except in a sphere restricted to the touch of my hands. I can vision only dimly the grace of a Pavlova*, although I know something of the delight of rhythm, for often I can sense the beat of music as it vibrates through the floor. I can well imagine that cadenced* motion must be one of the most pleasing sights in the world. I have been able to gather something of this by tracing with my fingers the lines in sculptured marble; if this static grace can be so lovely, how much more acute must be the thrill of seeing grace in motion.

Pavlova: (1885-1931) Anna Pavlova, Russian dancer
cadenced: balanced

One of my dearest memories is of the time when Joseph Jefferson* allowed me to touch his face and hands as he went through some of the gestures of his beloved Rip Van Winkle. I was able to catch thus a meager glimpse of the world of drama, and I shall never forget the delight of that moment. But, oh, how much I must miss, and how much pleasure you seeing ones can derive from watching and hearing the interplay of speech and movement, in the unfolding of a dramatic performance! If I could see only one play, I should know how to picture in my mind the action of a hundred plays which I have read or had transferred to me through the medium of the manual alphabet.

Joseph Jefferson: (1829-1905) American actor

So, through the evening of my second imaginary day of sight, the great figures of dramatic literature would crowd sleep from my eyes.

The Third Day

The following morning, I should again greet the dawn, anxious to discover new delights, for I am sure that, for those who have eyes which really see, the dawn of each day must be a perpetually new revelation of beauty.

This, according to the terms of my imagined miracle, is to be my third and last day of light. I shall have no time to waste in regrets or longings; there is too much to see. The first day I devoted to my friends, animate and inanimate. The second revealed to me the history of man and Nature. Today I shall spend in the workaday world of the present, amid the haunts of men going about the business of life. And where can one find so many activities and conditions of men as in New York? So the city becomes my destination.

I start from my home in the quiet little suburb of Forest Hills, Long Island. Here, surrounded by green lawns, trees, and flowers, are neat little houses, happy with the voices and movements of wives and children, havens of peaceful rest for men who toil in the city. I drive across the lacy structure of steel which spans the East River, and I get a new and startling vision of the power and ingenuity* of the mind of man. Busy boats chug and scurry about the river—racy speedboats, stolid, snorting tugs. If I had long days of sight ahead, I should spend many of them watching the delightful activity upon the river.

ingenuity: inventiveness

I look ahead, and before me rise the fantastic towers of New York, a city that seems to have stepped from the pages of a fairy story. What an awe-inspiring sight, these glittering spires, these vast banks of stone and steel—structures such as the gods might build for themselves! This animated picture is a part of

Remind students that when Keller was writing, this was the tallest structure in the world.

metaphor

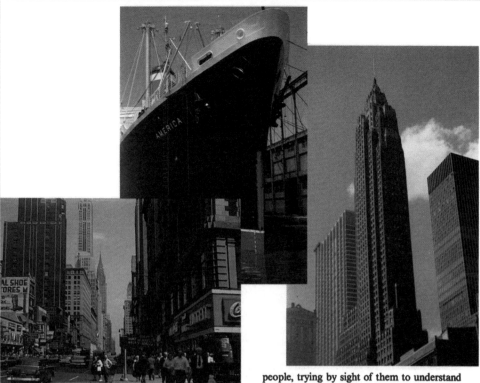

the lives of millions of people every day. How many, I wonder, give it so much as a second glance? Very few, I fear. Their eyes are blind to this magnificent sight because it is so familiar to them.

I hurry to the top of one of those gigantic structures, the Empire State Building, for there, a short time ago, I "saw" the city below through the eyes of my secretary. I am anxious to compare my fancy with reality. I am sure I should not be disappointed in the panorama spread out before me, for to me it would be a vision of another world.

Now I begin my rounds of the city. First, I stand at a busy corner, merely looking at people, trying by sight of them to understand something of their lives. I see smiles, and I am happy. I see serious determination, and I am proud. I see suffering, and I am compassionate.

I stroll down Fifth Avenue. I throw my eyes out of focus so that I see no particular object but only a seething kaleidoscope of color. I am certain that the colors of women's dresses moving in a throng must be a gorgeous spectacle of which I should never tire. But perhaps if I had sight I should be like most other women—too interested in styles and the cut of individual dresses to give much attention to the splendor of color in the mass. And I am convinced, too, that I should become an inveterate* window shopper, for it must be a delight to the eye to view the myriad articles of beauty on display.

inveterate: habitual

From Fifth Avenue I make a tour of the city—to Park Avenue, to the slums, to factories, to parks where children play. I take a stay-at-home trip abroad by visiting the foreign quarters. Always my eyes are open wide to all the sights of both happiness and misery so that I may probe deep and add to my understanding of how people work and live. My heart is full of the images of people and things. My eye passes lightly over no single trifle; it strives to touch and hold closely each thing its gaze rests upon. Some sights are pleasant, filling the heart with happiness; but some are miserably pathetic. To these latter I do not shut my eyes, for they, too, are part of life. To close the eye on them is to close the heart and mind.

My third day of sight is drawing to an end. Perhaps there are many serious pursuits to which I should devote the few remaining hours, but I am afraid that on the evening of that last day I should again run away to the theater, to a hilariously funny play, so that I might appreciate the overtones of comedy in the human spirit.

At midnight my temporary respite from blindness would cease, and permanent night would close in on me again. Naturally in those three short days I should not have seen all I wanted to see. Only when darkness had again descended upon me should I realize how much I had left unseen. But my mind would be so crowded with glorious memories that I should have little time for regrets. Thereafter the touch of every object would bring a glowing memory of how that object looked.

Perhaps this short outline of how I should spend three days of sight does not agree with the program you would set for yourself if you knew that you were about to be stricken blind. I am, however, sure that if you actually faced that fate, your eyes would open to things you had never seen before, storing up memories for the long night ahead. You would use your eyes as never before. Everything you saw would become dear to you. Your eyes would touch and embrace every object that came within your range of vision. Then, at last, you would really see, and a new world of beauty would open itself before you.

I who am blind can give one hint to those who see—one admonition to those who would make full use of the gift of sight: Use your eyes as if tomorrow you would be stricken blind. And the same method can be applied to the other senses. Hear the music of voices, the song of a bird, the mighty strains of an orchestra, as if you would be stricken deaf tomorrow. Touch each object you want to touch as if tomorrow your tactile sense would fail. Smell the perfume of flowers, taste with relish each morsel, as if tomorrow you could never smell and taste again. Make the most of every sense; glory in all the facets of pleasure and beauty which the world reveals to you through the several means of contact which Nature provides. But of all the senses, I am sure that sight must be the most delightful.

About the Essay

1. What is the author's purpose in writing this essay?
2. Do you think she is successful in accomplishing her purpose? Support your answer.
3. Identify at least one point the author makes that particularly impresses you.
4. How does the mood of this essay differ from the mood of the Dubber selection?

About the Essay

make concrete something that, until this point, seemed too abstract to be personal?

1. *She wants us to stop, to think, and to remember how important it is that we "Make the most of every sense; [and] glory in all the facets of pleasure and beauty which the world reveals to [us] through the several means of contact which Nature provides."*

2. *Answers will vary, but be sure that the students provide specific quotations from the essay to support their views.*

3. *Answers will vary. You may wish to have the students tell not only what impressed them but why it impressed them. For example, did the point reinforce some previous experience? Or did it perhaps*

4. *Although Keller's essay is as serious as Dubber's, there is a distinct difference between the intensity in this essay and that of the last one. Keller seems to be speaking to each of us individually. Her conversation, therefore, though compelling, seems more relaxed. There is a comfortable "distance" between the reader and writer. Instead of feeling as if we are eavesdropping, we feel as if we are seated beside the author, engaged in friendly conversation. This added "distance" is appropriate for the universal point she will make at the end. Keller's essay is broader in scope than Dubber's.*

About the Author

Helen Keller (1880-1968) is one of the world's best-loved heroines. Her life story is one of triumph over enormous obstacles. An illness in infancy left her blind and deaf, shut off from her loving family. Her inability to communicate effectively and her parents' frustration with her violent temper prompted the Kellers to seek a teacher. "The most important day I remember in all my life," recalls Keller, "is the one on which my teacher, Anne Mansfield Sullivan, came to me."

Annie Sullivan was the ideal person to bring Helen out of her physical prison. Abandoned in childhood and almost completely blind, she could empathize with Helen's deepest frustrations. She won Helen's affection through her firmness and diligence. The breakthrough came on a sultry day in spring. The seven-year-old Helen finally realized that every object had a name and that she could communicate by using words spelled into her hand by Miss Sullivan. The world of ideas was now open to her.

The next few years were full of learning and excitement for both teacher and pupil. Learning to read Braille print, mastering writing, even uttering her first words were great triumphs for Helen. But the greatest challenge for Helen and her teacher still lay ahead of them. Helen insisted that she was going to college. At that time, no blind and deaf person had ever graduated from a university. College for Helen required twice the normal time and effort. Few college textbooks existed in Braille. Helen's graduation with honors was also Miss Sullivan's triumph.

After college, the industrialist-millionaire Andrew Carnegie offered to support Helen with a comfortable allowance, enabling her to embark on a writing career. Her inspiring essay "Three Days to See" reflects her sensitivity, her cultured mind, and her flowing prose style. Because she was cut off from the world of senses, she felt very keenly "the separateness between soul and body" and the existence of "the eyes within her eyes."

┌─────────────────────────────┐
│ **OBJECTIVES** │
│ ───────────── │
│ *The students will be able to* │
│ • Define *parody*. │
│ • Analyze essays in order to │
│   discuss their purpose. │
└─────────────────────────────┘

Dissipated means used up, wasted. Notice how Benchley sets the stage for the rest of the essay in the first two sentences—he is making fun of himself. He does, of course, none of the things he claims to do in the second paragraph. (See About the Author section, page 453, for further examples of this type of Benchley humor.)

allusions

FURTHER HELPS

Additional activities

1. Encourage students to make a list of activities they need to accomplish in a day or a week. At the end of the day or week, have them evaluate themselves. Which activities did they do first? last? Why? What distractions did they have? Did they have a "method" to accomplish their task? Use this as an opportunity to discuss the pernicious nature of procrastination.

How to Get Things Done

Robert Benchley

If this essay, originally published in the Chicago Tribune *in 1930, were not in the ironic mode, it might be entitled "Procrastination." Even professional writers such as the humorist Benchley sometimes find it hard to get down to the business of writing.*

A great many people have come up to me and asked me how I manage to get so much work done and still keep looking so dissipated. My answer is "Don't you wish you knew?" and a pretty good answer it is, too, when you consider that nine times out of ten I didn't hear the original question.

But the fact remains that hundreds of thousands of people throughout the country are wondering how I have time to do all my painting, engineering, writing and philanthropic work when, according to the rotogravure sections and society notes I spend all my time riding to hounds, going to fancy-dress balls disguised as Louis XIV or spelling out *Greetings to California* in formation with three thousand Los Angeles school children. "All work and all play," they say.

The secret of my incredible energy and efficiency in getting work done is a simple one. I have based it very deliberately on a well-known psychological principle and have refined it so that it is now almost *too* refined. I shall have to begin coarsening it up again pretty soon.

The psychological principle is this: anyone can do any amount of work, provided it isn't the work he is supposed to be doing at the moment.

Let us see how this works out in practice. Let us say that I have five things which have to be done before the end of the week: (1) a basketful of letters to be answered, some of them dating from October, 1928, (2) some bookshelves to be put up and arranged with books (3) a haircut to get (4) a pile of scientific magazines to go through and clip (I am collecting all references to tropical fish that I can find, with the idea of some day buying myself one) and (5) an article to write for this paper.

Now. With these five tasks staring me in the face on Monday morning, it is little wonder that I go right back to bed as soon as I have had breakfast, in order to store up health and strength for the almost superhuman expenditure of energy that is to come. *Mens sana in corpore sano** is my motto, and, not even to be funny, am I going to believe that I don't know what the Latin means. I feel that the least that I can do is to treat my body right when it has to supply fuel for an insatiable mind like mine.

Mens sana in corpore sano: "a sound mind in a sound body," quotation from Juvenal

PREPARATION

"How to Get Things Done," "On the Road Again with Recorded Books"

Overview

Both the Benchley and the Hardison essays are informal and "chatty." They are, however, also persuasive. Benchley makes a good point about procrastination, and Hardison presents the advantages of listening to recorded books while traveling. The selections show how the personal essay might be used as a tool for persuasion.

DISCUSSION

Introduction

Bring to class several political cartoons or caricatures. Ask the class what ideas or leaders are being lampooned in these examples.

Analysis

"How to Get Things Done"

Point out to the students that the purpose of Benchley's article is much like the purpose of the political cartoonist. He is poking fun at something; in so doing he is writing what we call a parody. A parody is a humorous imitation of a serious work. Benchley's essay might be called a parody of all the "self-help" articles that have flooded the market for years. He takes a

serious subject (procrastination) and gives us a ridiculous solution (make a list backwards). To alert us to the fact that he is writing a parody, Benchley uses verbal irony. Have the students continue their analysis of the selection using the "About the Essay" questions (page 453).

As I lie in bed on Monday morning storing up strength, I make out a schedule. "What do I have to do first?" I ask myself. Well, those letters really should be answered and the pile of scientific magazines should be clipped. And here is where my secret process comes in. Instead of putting them first on the list of things which have to be done, I put them last. I practice a little deception on myself and say: "First you must write that article for the newspaper." I even say this out loud (being careful that nobody hears me, otherwise they would *keep* me in bed) and try to fool myself into really believing that I must do the article that day and that the other things can wait. I sometimes go so far in this self-deception as to make out a list in pencil, with "No. 1. Newspaper article" underlined in red. (The underlining in red is rather difficult, as there is never a red pencil on the table beside the bed, unless I have taken one to bed with me on Sunday night.)

Then, when everything is lined up, I bound out of bed and have lunch. I find that a good, heavy lunch, with some sort of glutinous dessert, is good preparation for the day's work as it keeps one from getting nervous and excitable. We workers must keep cool and calm, otherwise we would just throw away our time in jumping about and fidgeting.

I then seat myself at my desk with my typewriter before me and sharpen five pencils. (The sharp pencils are for poking holes in the desk-blotter, and a pencil has to be pretty sharp to do that. I find that I can't get more than six holes out of one pencil.) Following this I say to myself (again out loud, if it is practical) "Now, old man! Get at this article!"

Gradually the scheme begins to work. My eye catches the pile of magazines, which I have artfully placed on a nearby table beforehand. I write my name and address at the top of the sheet of paper in the typewriter and then sink back. The magazines being within reach (also part of the plot) I look to see if anyone is watching me and get one off the top of the pile. Hello, what's this! In the very first one is an article by Dr. William Beebe, illustrated by horrifying photographs! Pushing my chair away from my desk, I am soon hard at work clipping.

One of the interesting things about the Argyopelius, or "Silver Hatchet" fish, I find, is that it has eyes in its wrists. I would have been sufficiently surprised just to find out that a fish had wrists, but to learn that it has eyes in them is a discovery so astounding that I am hardly able to cut out the picture. What a lot one learns simply by thumbing through the illustrated weeklies! It is hard work, though, and many a weaker spirit would give it up half-done, but when there is something else of "more importance" to be finished (you see, I still keep up the deception, letting myself go on thinking that the newspaper article is of more importance) no work is too hard or too onerous* to keep one busy.

---
onerous: burdensome

Thus, before the afternoon is half over, I have gone through the scientific magazines and have a neat pile of clippings (including one of a Viper Fish which I wish you could see. You would die laughing). Then it is back to the grind of the newspaper article.

This time I get as far as the title, which I write down with considerable satisfaction until I find that I have misspelled one word terribly, so that the whole sheet of paper has to come out and a fresh one be inserted. As I am doing this, my eye catches the basket of letters.

Now, if there is one thing that I hate to do (and there is, you may be sure) it is to write letters. But somehow, with the magazine article before me waiting to be done, I am seized with an epistolary fervor which amounts to a craving, and I slyly sneak the first of the

verbal irony

Dr. William Beebe (1877-1962) was an American "naturalist and explorer who helped design the bathysphere" (*American Heritage Dictionary,* 3rd ed., 1993). Ask students how this allusion ties in to Benchley's search for articles.

Verbal irony: The newspaper article is, of course, of more importance than clipping out fish pictures.

hyperbole

"Of or associated with letters or the writing of letters" (*American Heritage Dictionary,* 3rd ed., 1993). Compare New Testament *epistles* or an *epistolary* novel.

2. Read other humorous Benchley essays.

3. Check out a recorded short story or novel from the public library or rent one. Play one that has a good reader in order to make the listening more enjoyable.

4. See if a few students would be interested in reading children's books for the younger children in the school in order to increase the children's appreciation of storytelling.

Benchley is making a joke on the aphorism "up with the larks"—which means getting up quite early (cf. page 391).

metaphor

verbal irony

Journal entry idea

Using their answers from "About the Story" question four (page 453), have the students write their own essay. Encourage them to maintain the informal, chatty style Benchley and Hardison maintain in their essays. Require them to do an outline before they begin writing. Remind them that the content of their opening anecdote should reinforce the style of the article. As time permits, have the students share their essays. You might also want to collect their articles into a personal essay notebook. Such a notebook might be a good way for class members to get to know a little more about each other.

unanswered letters out of the basket. I figure out in my mind that I will get more into the swing of writing the article if I practice a little on a few letters. The first one, anyway, I really must answer. True, it is from a friend in Antwerp asking me to look him up when I am in Europe in the summer of 1929, so he can't actually be watching the incoming boats for an answer, but I owe something to politeness after all. So instead of putting a fresh sheet of copy-paper into the typewriter, I slip in one of my handsome bits of personal stationery and dash off a note to my friend in Antwerp. Then, being well in the letter-writing mood, I clean up the entire batch. I feel a little guilty about the article, but the pile of freshly stamped envelopes and the neat bundle of clippings on tropical fish do much to salve my conscience. Tomorrow I will do the article, and no fooling this time either.

When tomorrow comes I am up with one of the older and more sluggish larks. A fresh sheet of copy-paper in the machine, and my name and address neatly printed at the top, and all before eleven A.M.! "A human dynamo" is the name I think up for myself. I have decided to write something about snake charming and am already more than satisfied with the title "These Snake-Charming People." But, in order to write about snake charming, one has to know a little about its history, and where should one go to find history but a book? Maybe in that pile of books in the corner is one on snake charming! Nobody could point the finger of scorn at me if I went over to those books for the avowed purpose of research work for the matter at hand. No writer could be supposed to carry all that information in his head.

So, with a perfectly clear conscience, I leave my desk for a few minutes and begin glancing over the titles of the books. Of course, it is difficult to find any book, much less one on snake charming, in a pile which has been standing in the corner for weeks. What really is needed is for them to be on a shelf where their titles will be visible at a glance. And there is the shelf, standing beside the pile of books! It seems almost like a divine command written in the sky: "If you want to finish that article, first put up the shelf and arrange the books on it!" Nothing could be clearer or more logical.

In order to put up the shelf, the laws of physics have decreed that there must be nails, a hammer and some sort of brackets to hold it up on the wall. You can't just wet a shelf with your tongue and stick it up. And, as there are no nails or brackets in the house (or, if there are, they are probably hidden somewhere) the next thing to do is put on my hat and go out to buy them. Much as it disturbs me to put off the actual start of the article, I feel that I am doing only what is in the line of duty to put on my hat and go out to buy nails and brackets. And, as I put on my hat, I realize to my chagrin that I need a haircut badly. I can kill two birds with one stone, or at least with two, and stop in at the barber's on the way back. I will feel all the more like writing after a turn in the fresh air. Any doctor would tell me that.

So in a few hours I return, spick and span and smelling of lilac, bearing nails, brackets, the evening papers and some crackers and peanut butter. Then it's ho! for a quick snack and a glance through the evening papers (there might be something in them which would alter what I was going to write about snake charming) and in no time at all the shelf is up, slightly crooked but up, and the books are arranged in a neat row in alphabetical order and all ready for almost instantaneous reference. There does not happen to be one on snake charming among them, but there is a very interesting one containing some Hogarth prints and one which will bear even closer inspection dealing with the growth of the Motion Picture, illustrated with "stills" from famous productions. A really remarkable industry, the motion pictures. I might want to write an article on it sometime. Not today, probably, for it is six o'clock and there is still the one on snake charming to finish up first. Tomorrow morning sharp! Yes, *sir!*

And so, you see, in two days I have done four of the things I had to do, simply by making believe that it was the fifth that I *must* do. And the next day, I fix up something else, like taking down the bookshelf and putting it somewhere else, that I *have* to do, and then I get the fifth one done.

The only trouble is that, at this rate, I will soon run out of things to do, and will be forced to get at that newspaper article first thing Monday morning.

About the Essay

1. Humorous exaggeration is often the first signal of the ironic mode. Where does irony first appear in the article?
2. Have you ever used Benchley's "method" of getting things done?
3. Identify one allusion Benchley uses.
4. What point, if any, is Benchley trying to make?

About the Author

According to a 1941 *Current Biography* sketch "Benchley (1889-1945) himself claims that he was born on the Isle of Wight, September 15, 1807, shipped as a cabin boy on the *Florence J. Marble* in 1815, wrote *Tale of Two Cities* in 1820, married Princess Anastasia of Portugal in 1831 (children: Prince Rupprecht and several little girls) was buried in Westminster Abbey in 1871." This "biographical sketch" provides a taste of Benchley's gift for preposterous nonsense. Benchley's "merry madness," however, displays method; his literary style is professional and polished. He wrote fifteen collections of humorous personal essays.

Benchley had a genius for turning the frustrations of the average middle-class American into delightful comic material. He gained a solid reputation as a highly original humorist. His versatility and wit were evident even in his undergraduate days at Harvard. He strictly abstained from the common vices of his classmates. Benchley chose instead to employ his talent for humor in the school's plays and comic magazine. After college, Benchley took several unfulfilling jobs until his introduction into journalism on the staff of the *New York Tribune* in 1916.

After World War I, Benchley served as editor and contributor to a succession of well-known periodicals. He was also noted for his work on the stage and in film and radio. Despite his public success, however, Benchley never felt as if he had taken full advantage of his opportunities to excel as a writer. He resembled his own characters in his penchant for procrastination. But he always had time for people, and he had many devoted friends. Benchley's whimsical advice on "how to get things done" fits well with the challenging motto he kept over his desk: "The work can wait."

About the Essay

1. *The opening sentence alerts us to the fact that Benchley is not expecting us to take him seriously.*

2. *Answers will vary. Point out, however, that most of us find Benchley's article humorous because we recognize certain "procrastination" techniques we have used. Of course, Benchley doesn't seriously believe that his suggestions are a viable "method" of getting things done; they are rather evidences of our tendencies to avoid getting things accomplished.*

3. *There are several allusions; the two most obvious are the reference to Louis XIV and the quotation from Juvenal, Mens sana in corpore sano. After*

the students have identified the allusion, ask them to identify what point the allusion supports.

4. *Answers may vary. Their answers should, however, make some reference to the fact that Benchley is really pointing out that the only way to get anything done is to do it. Interwoven into this major point is the implication that procrastination is a painful pitfall in accomplishing any task.*

simile

Allusion; note the subtle contrast between the writer's son's taste in listening and that proposed by the writer. Were the writer and his wife to listen to their son's cassettes while traveling, would the trip be as enjoyable? Would any of the favorable effects described later in the essay be realized? Note also the many allusions in the following paragraphs.

metaphor

On the Road Again with Recorded Books

O. B. Hardison, Jr.

Hardison's essay, like Benchley's, appears deceptively simple. A close look at the selection, however, reveals that it is a carefully constructed piece. Notice, for example, how the opening anecdote illustrates the concluding point. Notice, too, the range of moods Hardison creates while making his point.

Last May my wife announced that we were going to drive to Canada in July. It looked like a long way. She said distance is all in the mind. She had read an ad for books on cassette that explained how they make the longest drive seem short. So why didn't I get busy and install a cassette deck in our station wagon like the one our son had in his sports car? A week later, I disentangled myself from a spaghetti-like mass of wires and pushed a Johnny Cash cassette (borrowed from my son's sports car) into the slot. To my astonishment, the cassette played. "I Fell into a Burning Ring of Fire" blasted through the neighborhood in full-throated stereo.

Next, the books.

You can rent books on cassette from Recorded Books in Clinton, Maryland, and you can buy them at many local bookstores. Some public libraries also carry them.

The list of titles is staggering. You can learn Portuguese, brush up on your management skills, relive Custer's Last Stand, or select anything in the way of fiction from a thriller by Eric Ambler to Mark Twain's *Adventures of Huckleberry Finn.*

Lots of tapes are abridged. If you want every word your author wrote, read the fine print on the label to make sure it's all there. Another tip. The narrators are usually pretty good, but there are rotten apples in every barrel. Also, people have different tastes in narrators. I, for example, dislike a BBC accent in sustained doses and like American accents. It's therefore a good idea to listen to a few minutes of any recorded book before putting it into the car. When you're on the road with 250 miles before the next pit stop, you're stuck with what you choose.

We chose David Howarth's *Year of the*

"On the Road Again with Recorded Books"

Like Benchley's essay, Hardison's appears deceptively simple. However, point out to the students that, although his style is informal, Hardison's organization reveals that he is not only a careful craftsman but also an effective persuasive writer. Discussing the "About the Essay" questions should help to reinforce these points. (See page 456.)

Application

See **Journal entry idea** (page 452).

Conquest—about the Norman invasion of England—to take us up to Canada, and Bruce Catton's *Short History of the Civil War* to get us back to Washington. (Don't ask me why we chose those subjects, but we did.)

As it turned out, we couldn't have chosen better. Europe was a complicated place in 1066. There was William over in Normandy, waiting to pounce, Harald of Norway (with an "a"), up in the north, looking for an excuse to go raiding, and Harold (with an "o") in England trying to keep an army together to defend the country against an invasion that never seemed to happen. Meanwhile, Abbot Lanfranc was conspiring with the pope to excommunicate Harold, and Harold's brother, Tostig, was conspiring with Harald.

Marifrancis and I see eye-to-eye on the Norman Conquest. We cheered when the storm dispersed William's first invasion fleet. We fervently hoped the second invasion would be swamped in the Channel by an even bigger storm, and when it wasn't, we hoped the Norman army would get bottled up in its beachhead near Hastings and starve.

When that didn't happen, we rooted lustily for Harold's Saxons, who had just defeated Harald's berserk Vikings at Stamford Bridge. (The word "berserk" was invented by the Vikings to describe the madness that swept over them when they were rattling away with sword and axe.) The Saxons almost made it. They would have had a chance if they had only charged the Normans after delivering the initial repulse. Instead, they held their defensive position and were gradually decimated by Norman archers.

Even after the Norman victory at Hastings, there was hope. Harold was dead but there were other leaders. The Norman army consisted of a few thousand fighting men in a veritable sea of Saxons. Why did the Saxons . . . ?

Suddenly, we had arrived at Stratford, Ontario. In fact, the only way we were able to make our arrival coincide with the end of the book was by driving under 45 for the last 30 miles.

We were not oblivious to the scenery along the way. Some of it was spectacular. The Norman Conquest may have contributed to our enjoyment by relaxing us. We felt none of the fixation about "making time" that can turn two otherwise reasonable people into surly antagonists after a few hours on the road. The trip took perhaps an hour and a half more than it would have without the Norman Conquest, but we reached our destination contented and brimming with energy.

The road back was smoothed by Bruce Catton's masterful retelling of the great events of the Civil War. My wife and I are on different sides in the Civil War. She agonized with Lincoln, while I followed the brilliant but doomed efforts of Jackson and Lee. She almost won for the North before the war had rightly begun by arguing for a vigorous counterattack at First Manassas. I wanted the Confederate sentries at Chancellorsville to be more careful, which would have saved Stonewall Jackson, thereby evening the odds at Gettysburg. . . .

A highway marker announced the diversion of Highway 15's business route through the Gettysburg battlefield.

Ordinarily we would have pushed on to reach Washington before dark. Under the spell of Bruce Catton, we turned off and found ourselves—at the beginning of one of those huge, crimson summer sunsets—standing on Cemetery Hill where the Union soldiers of Hancock's Second Corps watched the great sweep of Pickett's charge moving toward them across the waves of July wheat.

We stood by the stone wall behind which the Confederates paused to regroup before they charged, screaming their wild battle cry. As the Union troops watched the rebel battle flags cut into their lines, they broke in terror.

The Confederate attack split the Union forces—a daring victory seemed close. Then Hancock counterattacked with fresh Union reserves, and history went its way.

We drove past Little Round Top and along the part of Highway 15 that follows the old Emmitsburg Road across the battlefield and back to the main highway. By the time we reached Washington, Lee had surrendered and Lincoln was dead.

I'm not pushing David Howarth's *Norman Conquest* or Bruce Catton's *Civil War,* only saying that recorded books make driving fun again.

I've given my car one of those special washes that uses hot wax, and I've swept up the Mars Bar wrappers.

Next week we are going to Chapel Hill, N.C. We will drive south rather than fly, and will use the time for the unabridged, eight-cassette version of Jane Austen's *Sense and Sensibility.* Look out, Willoughby, because we plan to let Marianne know you are a bounder before she gets serious about you!

With recorded books, it's not where you are going that counts but how long you can take to get there.

About the Essay

1. The opening anecdote illustrates the point Hardison makes in his conclusion. What is that point?
2. What techniques does Hardison use to make his essay seem more like a homespun chat than a formal essay?
3. List at least two of the moods Hardison creates in his essay.
4. List at least one experience you have had that might make a good topic for a personal essay.

About the Author

Before taking a position as professor of English at Georgetown University, O. B. Hardison, Jr. (1928-1990) was for fifteen years director of the Folger Shakespeare Library and, before that, professor of English Renaissance literature and comparative literature at the University of North Carolina. He served as president of the American Shakespeare Association and of the Renaissance Society of America and a member of the executive committee of the Modern Language Association. In scholarship his range was wide. His writings include acclaimed book-length studies of medieval drama, Renaissance rhetoric and poetics, and modern culture, as well as a commentary on Aristotle's *Poetics.* He was general editor of a series of texts in modern European literary criticism and co-editor of the *Princeton Encyclopedia of Poetry and Poetics.*

The preceding article, first appearing as an article in the *Washington Times,* suggests Hardison's range of interests and styles. A distinguished career in scholarship and teaching obviously did not blunt his ability to communicate in lively journalistic fashion to the ordinary reader. His skill as a teacher appears in his ability to create excitement in learning, specifically to bring history and literature to life. It is not hard to see why he was recognized by *Time* magazine as one of the ten best college teachers in America.

About the Essay

1. *"With recorded books, it's not where you are going that counts but how long you can take to get there." In other words, recorded books not only take the "pain" out of traveling but add a great deal of pleasure.*

2. *Hardison uses several techniques: the content of his opening anecdote; his flowing, "chatty" syntax. He also creates a storylike excitement when relating the content of the tapes he and his wife have listened to.*

3. *Answers may vary. One that Hardison creates is that of frustration; he conjures up for us vivid memories of tedious traveling hours. In contrast, he creates a mood of excitement, sharing with us vivid historical tidbits he has learned from tapes he has heard.*

4. *Answers will vary.*

PREPARATION

"A Piece of Chalk"

Overview

Chesterton's essay is excellent for concluding our study in literary analysis. His essay provides ample material for reviewing all of the elements of literature studied thus far.

DISCUSSION

Introduction

Using **Appendix Z: Elements of Literature Review,** review the elements of literature studied thus far. Point out to the students that Chesterton gives us a masterful example of a personal essay and quality literature. All of the elements of literature studied thus far can be found in this essay. Remind students that they have already studied Chesterton this year: he is the author of "The Donkey" (page 94) and "On the Pleasures of No Longer Being Very Young" (pages 102-3).

A Piece of Chalk

G.K. Chesterton

Many of the elements of literature you have studied appear in this masterful essay by G.K. Chesterton. A boyhood experience becomes, during his recollection, emblematic of deep moral truth.

I remember one splendid morning, all blue and silver, in the summer holidays, when I reluctantly tore myself away from the task of doing nothing in particular, and put on a hat of some sort and picked up a walking stick, and put six very bright-colored chalks in my pocket. I then went into the kitchen (which, along with the rest of the house, belonged to a very square and sensible old woman in a Sussex village), and asked the owner and occupant of the kitchen if she had any brown paper. She had a great deal; in fact, she had too much; and she mistook the purpose and the rationale of the existence of brown paper. She seemed to have an idea that if a person wanted brown paper he must be wanting it to tie up parcels; which was the last thing I wanted to do; indeed, it is a thing which I have found to be beyond my mental capacity. Hence she dwelt very much on the varying qualities of toughness and endurance in the material. I explained to her that I only wanted to draw pictures on it, and that I did not want them to endure in the least; and that from my point of view, therefore, it was a question not of tough consistency, but of responsive surface, a thing comparatively irrelevant in a parcel. When she understood that I wanted to draw she offered to overwhelm me with note-paper, apparently supposing that I did my notes and correspondence on old brown paper wrappers from motives of economy.

I then tried to explain the rather delicate logical shade, that I not only liked brown paper, but liked the quality of brownness in paper, just as I liked the quality of brownness in October woods, or in the peat streams of the North. Brown paper represents the primal twilight of the first toil of creation, and with a bright-colored chalk or two you can pick out points of fire in it, sparks of gold, and blood-red, and sea-green, like the first fierce stars that sprang out of divine darkness. All this I said (in an off-hand way) to the old woman; and I put the brown paper in my pocket along with the chalks, and possibly other things. I suppose every one must have reflected how primeval and how poetical are the things that one carries in one's pocket; the pocketknife, for instance, the type of all human tools, the infant of the sword. Once I planned to write a book of poems entirely about the things in my pocket. But I found it would be too long; and the age of the great epics is past.

With my stick and my knife, my chalks and my brown paper, I went out on to the great downs.* I crawled across loose colossal contours that express the best quality of England, because they are at the same time soft and strong. The smoothness of them has the same meaning as the smoothness of great cart horses, or the smoothness of the beech tree; it declares in the teeth of our timid cruel theories that the mighty are merciful. As my eye swept the landscape, the landscape was as kindly as any of its cottages, but for power it was like an earthquake. The villages in the

OBJECTIVES

The students will be able to

- Locate examples of the marks and modes of literature.
- Explain how these elements can be used to clarify difficult concepts and complex truths.

consonance

alliteration

synecdoche

metonymy, alliteration

personification, alliteration

simile

FURTHER HELPS

Additional activities

Look at some other writers, contemporaries of Chesteron, who used the essay to express their personal views. A few are Max Beerbohm (1872-1956), Arnold Bennett (1867-1931), Hilaire Belloc

Analysis

Following your review, have the students find illustrations in Chesterton's essay of each of the marks and modes of literature. Following are several examples:

Imaginative Comparisons

metaphor
"And I stood there in a trance of pleasure, realizing that this Southern England is not only a grand peninsula, and a tradition and a civilization; it is something even more admirable. It is a piece of chalk."

simile
"The landscape was as kindly as any of its cottages, but for power it was like an earthquake."
"the lifting of the whole land was like the lifting of one enormous wave"

personification
"the teeth of our timid cruel theories that the mighty are merciful"

metonymy
"I crawled across loose colossal contours that express the best quality of England, because they are at the same time soft and strong."

synecdoche
"the pocketknife, for instance, the type of all human tools, the infant of the sword."

Sound and Syntax

alliteration
"teeth of our timid cruel theories"
"seas of strange green"
"first fierce stars"
"I crawled across loose colossal contours"

consonance
"primal twilight of the first toil"

assonance
"one enormous wave to wash them all away"

Symbol

Notice that, like Poe in "The Masque of the Red Death," Chesterton uses color symbolically:
"quality of brownness in October woods"
"with a bright-colored chalk or two you can pick points of fire in [brown paper], sparks of gold, and blood-red, and sea-green, like the first fierce stars that sprang out of divine darkness"
"saints in robes of angry crimson and seas of strange green, and all the sacred or monstrous symbols that look so well in bright colors on brown paper"
"the soul [of the cow] was all purple"

Bennett (1867-1931), Hilaire Belloc (1870-1953), and Edmund Gosse (1849-1928). Of course, you do not want to indiscriminately assign reading here; examine a piece before assigning it to a student.

Journal entry idea

Write an essay in which you express your opinion. Use one of the following quotations from this unit as your source or find another. You may agree or disagree with the quotation. Endeavor to support your response with Scripture.

"Now, if there is one thing that I hate to do (and there is, you may be sure), it is to write letters." ("How to Get Things Done")

"Virtue is not the absence of vices or the avoidance of moral danger; virtue is a vivid and separate thing, like pain or a particular smell." ("A Piece of Chalk")

---

immense valley were safe, one could see, for centuries; yet the lifting of the whole land was like the lifting of one enormous wave to wash them all away.

downs: long ridges of rolling hills in southern England

I crossed one swell of living turf after another, looking for a place to sit down and draw. Do not, for heaven's sake, imagine I was going to sketch from Nature. I was going to draw devils and seraphim, and blind old gods that men worshiped before the dawn of right, and saints in robes of angry crimson, and seas of strange green, and all the sacred or monstrous symbols that look so well in bright colors on brown paper. They are much better worth drawing than Nature; also they are much easier to draw. When a cow came slouching by in the field next to me, a mere artist might have drawn it; but I always get wrong in the hind legs of quadrupeds. So I drew the soul of the cow; which I saw there plainly walking before me in the sunlight; and the soul was all purple and silver, and had seven horns and the mystery that belongs to all the beasts. But though I could not with a crayon get the best out of the landscape, it does not follow that the landscape was not getting the best out of me. And this, I think, is the mistake that people make about old poets who lived before Wordsworth, and were supposed not to care very much about Nature because they did not describe it much.

They preferred writing about great men to writing about great hills; but they sat on the great hills to write it. They gave out much less about Nature, but they drank in, perhaps, much more. They painted the white robes of their holy virgins with the blinding snow, at which they stared all day. They blazoned the shields of their paladins* with the purple and gold of many heraldic sunsets. The greenness of a thousand green leaves clustered into the live green figure of Robin Hood. The blueness

of a score of forgotten skies became the blue robes of the Virgin. The inspiration went in like sunbeams and came out like Apollo.*

paladins: champions of chivalry
Apollo: Roman god of the sun and of the arts

But as I sat scrawling these silly figures on the brown paper, it began to dawn on me, to my great disgust, that I had left one chalk, and that a most exquisite and essential chalk, behind. I searched all my pockets, but I could not find any white chalk. Now, those who are acquainted with all the philosophy (nay, religion) which is typified in the art of drawing on brown paper, know that white is positive and essential. I cannot avoid remarking here upon a moral significance. One of the wise and awful truths which this brown-paper art reveals, is this, that white is a color. It is not a mere absence of color; it is a shining and affirmative thing, as fierce as red, as definite as black. When (so to speak) your pencil grows red-hot, it draws roses; when it grows white-hot, it draws stars. And one of the two or three defiant verities of the best religious morality, of real Christianity for example, is exactly this same thing; the chief assertion of religious morality is that white is a color. Virtue is not the absence of vices or the avoidance of moral danger; virtue is a vivid and separate thing, like pain or a particular smell. Mercy does not mean not being cruel or sparing people revenge or punishment; it means a plain and positive thing like the sun, which one has either seen or not seen. Chastity does not mean abstention from sexual wrong; it means something flaming, like Joan of Arc. In a word, God paints many colors; but He never paints so gorgeously, I had almost said gaudily, as when He paints in white. In a sense our age has realized this fact, and expressed it in our sullen costume. For if it were really true that white was a blank and colorless thing, negative and noncommittal, then white would be used

---

"White is a color. It is not a mere absence of color; it is a shining affirmative thing, as fierce as red, as definite as black."
"In a word, God paints many colors."

Notice, too, Chesterton's use of objects as symbols. He states, "I suppose every one must have reflected how primeval and how poetical are the things that one carries in one's pocket." Some objects that he states have meaning beyond their concrete representation are the pocketknife, chalks, and brown paper.

Allusion

"this, I think, is the mistake that people make about old poets who lived before Wordsworth"
"The soul [of the cow] was all purple and silver, and had seven horns and the mystery that belongs to all beasts."

"They blazoned the shields of their paladins with the purple and gold of many heraldic sunsets."
"The greenness of a thousand green leaves clustered into the live green figure of Robin Hood."
"The inspiration went in like sunbeams and came out like Apollo."

Irony

"I remember one splendid morning . . . when I reluctantly tore myself away from the task of doing nothing in particular."
"She seemed to have an idea that if a person wanted brown paper he must be wanting it to tie up parcels; which is the last thing I wanted to do; indeed, it is a thing which I have found to be beyond my mental capacity."
"But though I could not with a crayon get the best out of the landscape, it does not follow

that the landscape was not getting the best out of me."

Sensory Images

"the smoothness of them has the same meaning as the smoothness of great cart horses, or the smoothness of the beech tree"
"a very square and sensible old woman"
"a cow came slouching by in the field"
"the villages in the immense valley were safe, one could see, for centuries"

Continue your analysis using the "About the Essay" questions (page 459).

Application

Chesterton says that he considered writing a "book of poems entirely about the things in my pocket." Have the stuinstead of black and grey for the funeral dress of this pessimistic period. We should see city gentlemen in frock coats of spotless silver linen, with top hats as white as wonderful arum lilies. Which is not the case.

Meanwhile, I could not find my chalk.

I sat on the hill in a sort of despair. There was no town nearer than Chichester at which it was even remotely probable that there would be such a thing as an artist's colorman. And yet, without white, my absurd little pictures would be as pointless as the world would be if there were no good people in it. I stared stupidly round, racking my brain for expedients. Then I suddenly stood up and roared with laughter, again and again, so that the cows stared at me and called a committee. Imagine a man in the Sahara regretting that he had no sand for his hourglass. Imagine a gentleman in mid-ocean wishing that he had brought some salt water with him for his chemical experiments. I was sitting on an immense warehouse of white chalk. The landscape was made entirely out of white chalk. White chalk was piled mere miles until it met the sky. I stooped and broke a piece off the rock I sat on: it did not mark so well as the shop chalks do; but it gave the effect. And I stood there in a trance of pleasure, realizing that this Southern England is not only a grand peninsula, and a tradition and a civilization; it is something even more admirable. It is a piece of chalk.

About the Essay

1. What is the author arguing for when he insists on the importance, and indeed preeminence, of the color white?
2. Against whom, do you think, is his argument directed?
3. What moral truth is Chesterton seeking to convey?
4. Identify and give the significance of one allusion in Chesterton's essay.

dents write an essay or poem about something from their pocket or purse. Encourage them to use as many of the elements of literature as they can without sounding stilted. Remind them that these elements are used not as an end in themselves but to enhance and reinforce meaning. Also encourage them to strive to use the object as a vehicle to express and clarify a specific truth. See **Writing Rubric 11-2: Pocket Ponderings.**

About the Essay

1. *Chesterton explicitly states the reason for his argument by drawing the analogy between "white" and "real Christianity." "White is a color," he says. "It is not a mere absence of color; it is a shining and affirmative thing, as fierce as red, as definite as black." He goes on to say, "the chief assertion of religious morality is that white is a color. Virtue is not the absence of vices or the avoidance of certain moral danger; virtue is a vivid and separate thing, like pain or a particular smell." After drawing his analogy he gives specific examples: "Mercy does not mean not being cruel or sparing people revenge or punishment; it means a plain and positive thing like the sun, which one has either seen or not seen. Chastity does not mean abstention from sexual wrong; it means something flaming, like Joan of Arc." Chesterton makes clear that "morality" "virtue," and "true Christianity" cannot be defined by externals. Christianity's essence is "Spirit" and "Truth." From these essential elements come positive, overt, recognizable characteristics. Chesterton's concept is summarized by Christ in John 7:38: "He that believeth on me, as the scripture hath said, out of his belly shall flow rivers of living water."*

2. *His argument is directed against those who mistakenly believe that good is merely the absence of evil rather than the essence of God.*

3. *A man is not good simply because he does not do evil; he is good because he has clothed himself with the essence of goodness—Christ's goodness. By clothing himself in Christ's righteousness, he is able to become "Christlike" or truly good.*

4. *Answers will vary.*

Index

Page numbers in italics indicate pages containing "About the Author" information.

Illustration and Photograph Credits

The following agencies and individuals have furnished materials to meet the photographic needs of this textbook. We wish to express our gratitude to them for their important contributions.

Brad Carper
Bruce W. Higgs
Corbis
Creation Science Foundation, Ltd.,
    Australia
Digital Stock
Gene Fisher
George R. Collins

Kathy Pflug
Kenneth Frederick
NCAR/NSF
Photodisc
Suzanne R. Altizer
Terry M. Davenport
Theresa K. Scheiderer
Unusual Films

Front Cover
Photodisc

Unit 1
Creation Science Foundation, Ltd.,
Australia x, 2-4; Bruce W. Higgs
1 (left); NCAR/NSF 1(right)

Unit 2
Bruce W. Higgs 24-25, 27;
Kathy Pflug 43

Unit 3
NCAR/NSF 54-55, 57

Unit 4
Terry M. Davenport 88, 93; Suzanne R.
Altizer 89 (left); Brad Carper 89
(right); Photodisc 90-91; George R.
Collins 100

Unit 5
Suzanne R. Altizer 124-25, 129

Unit 6
Brad Carper 146-47, 152; Unusual
Films 182, 183 (left), 184 (both);
Suzanne R. Altizer 183 (right)

Unit 7
Unusual Films 186-87, 189

Unit 8
Digital Stock 224-25, 229

Unit 9
Suzanne R. Altizer 294-96; George R.
Collins 308, 312

Unit 10
Unusual Films 314-15, 319, 321, 327,
332, 341, 345, 347, 352, 367, 369, 374,
376, 384, 396, 401, 404, 419, 423, 427

Unit 11
Unusual Films 434-36, 444 (bottom
right); Theresa K. Scheiderer 442 (top
right); Suzanne R. Altizer 442 (left);
Kenneth Frederick 442 (bottom right);
Corbis 444 (top left)

Illustrators

Kathy Bell
Roger Bruckner
Steve Christopher
Tim Davis

Johanna Ehnis
Tom Halverson
Holly Hannon
Jim McGinnis

Kathy Pflug
Dana Thompson
Stephanie True
Cheryl Weikel

OBJECTIONABLE ELEMENTS

It is impossible to put together a large collection of literary materials without including subjects or situations that some Christians may find objectionable. BJU Press wants you to understand our position toward such issues—issues that we do not take lightly, issues about which we seek to have the mind of Christ based on Scriptural revelation. The following section from *Christian Education: Its Mandate and Mission* (BJU Press, 1992) gives our perspective and the philosophy that guides us when deciding on what literature selections to include. (You may read the full statement, "A Biblical Approach to Objectionable Elements," under White Papers at www.bjup.com.)

The basis of a truly Biblical position concerning censorable elements is the following distinction. If a work of literature or other element of the curriculum treats evil in the same way that it is treated in the Scriptures, we regard it as not only acceptable but also desirable reading, listening, or viewing for someone of sufficient maturity as to benefit from comparable portions of the Scriptures (with the qualification that visual or auditory effects are more potent than those of reading). If it does not treat evil in the way evil is handled in the Scriptures, its content is not good. Evil in the Bible appears dangerous and repulsive. Reflections of evil appear in the Bible in the form of negative examples so as to create a defense against what they represent or to give hope to the fallen for forgiveness and recovery from sin.

We may draw three criteria from the Scriptures for judging literary and other works with respect to their content.

1. Is the representation of evil purposeful or is it present for its own sake? This is the criterion of **gratuitousness.** We know that "all scripture is given by inspiration of God, and is profitable for doctrine, for reproof, for correction, for instruction in righteousness: That the man of God may be perfect, throughly furnished unto all good works" (II Tim. 3:16-17). Nothing in the Scriptures is superfluous or irrelevant to this high spiritual purpose.

2. Is the representation of evil, if purposeful, present in an acceptable degree? Or is it more conspicuous or vivid than the purpose warrants? This is the criterion of **explicitness.** No one with a high view of Scripture would charge it with inappropriateness or excessiveness in its representation of evil. The presentation of evil in the Bible is realistic enough to convince us of its threat as a temptation but not so realistic as to become for us a temptation. Some sins are referred to but not enacted in the text.

3. Is evil presented from a condemning perspective? Is it made to appear both dangerous and repulsive? What is the attitude of the work toward it? This is the criterion of **moral tone.** "Woe unto them that call evil good, and good evil," says the Lord through the prophet Isaiah (Isa. 5:20). A good work of literature does not glorify human weakness or encourage tolerance of sin. It allows evil to appear in a controlled way in order to develop in the reader or hearer a resistance against it. In literature, "vice," wrote Samuel Johnson, "must always disgust." Its purpose is to initiate the reader through "mock encounters" with evil so that evil cannot later deceive him—so that he will be better able to maintain a pure life in a fallen world.

These three criteria are complementary. None is alone sufficient to justify the censorable in a work of literature or another element of the curriculum. Together they work powerfully, because they work Biblically, to preserve moral purity while providing for a developing moral understanding and judgment. (pp. 55-56)

Appendix A: Suggested Teaching Schedule

Note that this schedule covers one semester only. Please revise it as you see fit to make it work for your situation—either a whole year of literature or alternating literature with writing and grammar. Please note also that it is a suggested teaching schedule—do not let it dictate the schedule that works best for your class.

Week	Monday	Tuesday	Wednesday	Thursday	Friday
1	pp. ix-4 Marks of Literature/Imaginative Comparison **Appendix B**	pp. 5-11 Twain **Rubric 1-1**	pp. 12-16 Dickinson/Ruskin **Rubric 1-2** **Appendix C**	pp. 17-23 Whitman/Petrunkevitch **Rubric 1-3** **Appendix D**	Review
2	Test on Unit 1	pp. 26-29 Sound and Syntax/Joyce/Updike **Appendixes E, F, G**	pp. 30-38 Colcord	pp. 38-42 Colcord/Shakespeare **Rubric 2-1**	pp. 43-53 Whitman/Duncan
3	Review **Appendix H**	Test on Unit 2 or Units 1 and 2	pp. 56-59 Thought and Theme/Dickinson	pp. 60-65 Whittier/Shakespeare **Rubric 3-1**	pp. 66-73 Engle/Hardy **Rubric 3-2**
4	pp. 74-80 Roberts	pp. 80-87 Roberts/Cowper/Review **Appendix I**	Test on Unit 3 or Units 1, 2, and 3	pp. 88-93 Modes of Literature/Allusion **Rubric 4-1** **Appendix J**	pp. 94-98 Chesterton/Kipling **Rubric 4-2**
5	pp. 99-101 Poe/Arnold **Rubric 4-3** **Appendix K**	pp. 102-5 Chesterton/Waller **Rubric 4-4**	pp. 105-13 Updike	pp. 113-23 Updike/Review	Test on Unit 4
6	pp. 126-29 Symbol **Appendix L**	pp. 130-36 Hughes/Aesop/Keats/Cowper **Rubric 5-1** **Appendix M**	pp. 136-38 Emerson/Cummings **Rubric 5-2**	pp. 139-44 Poe	p. 145 Browning/Review
7	Test on Unit 5 or Units 4 and 5	pp. 148-52 Irony **Appendix N**	pp. 153-58 Cleghorn/Wheelock/Cary **Rubric 6-1**	pp. 159-63 Lee/Frost/Anonymous/Eastman	pp. 164-67 Kipling **Rubric 6-2**
8	pp. 168-74 Kantor	pp. 174-81 Kantor/Anonymous	Review **Appendix O**	Review	Test on Unit 6 or Units 4, 5, and 6
9	Midterm Week	Midterm Week	Midterm Week	Midterm Week	Midterm Week
10	pp. 182-89 Forms of Literature/Biography **Rubric 7-1** **Appendixes P, Q, R**	pp. 190-98 Thurber/White **Appendix S**	pp. 199-202 Steffens	pp. 203-9 Welty **Rubric 7-2**	pp. 210-13 Whittier/Kipling
11	pp. 214-21 Plutarch **Appendix T**	pp. 222-23 Hayman/Review	Test on Unit 7	pp. 226-29 Fiction **Appendix U**	pp. 230-38 Stevenson
12	pp. 238-47 Stevenson/Tennyson **Rubric 8-1**	pp. 248-56 Doyle	pp. 256-64 Doyle	pp. 265-69 Bradbury	pp. 270-76 Crane
13	pp. 276-82 Crane/Whittier	pp. 283-89 Hardy **Appendix V**	pp. 290-93 de la Mare/Hoey	Review	Test on Unit 8 or Units 7 and 8
14	pp. 296-303 Lyric Poetry/Chávez/Wagoner/Rossetti **Rubric 9-1**	pp. 304-9 Herbert/Magee/Hillyer **Rubric 9-2**	pp. 310-13 Stafford/Frost **Appendix W**	Review	Test on Unit 9 or Units 7, 8, and 9
15	pp. 316-23 Drama/*Romeo and Juliet*	pp. 324-38 Act I, Scenes i-iii	pp. 338-49 Act I, Scenes iv-v	pp. 350-61 Act II, Scenes i-iii	pp. 361-70 Act II, Scenes iv-vi
16	pp. 371-83 Act III, Scenes i-ii	pp. 383-90 Act III, Scenes iii-iv	pp. 391-99 Act III, Scene v	pp. 400-409 Act IV, Scenes i-iii	pp. 409-15 Act IV, Scenes iv-v
17	pp. 416-33 Act V, Scenes i-iii **Rubric 10-1**	Review **Appendix X**	Test on Unit 10	pp. 436-39 Personal Essay/Dubber	pp. 440-49 Keller **Rubric 11-1** **Appendix Y**
18	pp. 450-453 Benchley	pp. 454-56 Hardison	pp. 457-59 Chesterton **Rubric 11-2**	Review **Appendix Z**	Test on Unit 11 or Units 10 and 11

Appendix A

Appendix B: IMAGINATIVE COMPARISON WORKSHEET

PART ONE: Define the following types of imaginative comparison.

1. metaphor _____

   _____

2. metonymy _____

3. personification _____

4. simile _____

   _____

5. synecdoche _____

PART TWO: Identify metaphors, similes, metonymies, synecdoches, and personifications in the examples below. More than one answer may be acceptable for several.

6. Bright April shakes out her rain-drenched hair. (Sara Teasdale) _____

7. The fog comes / on little cat feet. (Carl Sandburg) _____ _____

8. All the world's a stage. (William Shakespeare) _____

9. The Assyrian came down like a wolf on the fold. (George Gordon, Lord Byron) _____

10. The White House has decided . . . _____

11. In the sweat of thy face shalt thou eat bread, till thou return unto the ground. (Genesis 3:19)

    _____

12. All flesh is grass, and the goodliness thereof is as the flower of the field. (Isaiah 40:6)

    _____

13. There is death in the pot. (II Kings 4:40) _____

14. Give us this day our daily bread. (Matthew 6:11) _____

15. All hands on deck. _____

16. Time, the subtle thief of youth. (John Milton) _____

PART THREE: Look up the following verses and tell what kind or kinds of imaginative comparison are used in each.

17. John 12:19 _____

18. Psalm 114:3 _____

19. Matthew 23:37 _____

20. Isaiah 59:1 _____

A Hymn to God the Father
John Donne

Wilt Thou forgive that sin where I begun,
    Which is my sin, though it were done before?
Wilt Thou forgive those sins through which I run,
    And do run still, though still I do deplore?
      When Thou hast done, Thou hast not done,
        For I have more.

Wilt Thou forgive that sin by which I've won
    Others to sin? and made my sin their door?
Wilt Thou forgive that sin which I did shun
    A year or two, but wallowed in a score?
      When Thou hast done, Thou hast not done,
        For I have more.

I have a sin of fear, that when I've spun
    My last thread, I shall perish on the shore;
Swear by Thyself, that at my death Thy Son
    Shall shine as He shines now, and heretofore;
      And, having done that, Thou hast done,
        I fear no more.

Use after "A Bird Came Down the Walk," pages 12-13.

Appendix D: BIBLE CHARACTER SKETCH

Whitman's "A Noiseless Patient Spider" illustrates the power of an effective metaphor. Unlike Whitman, however, Christians must recognize the authority of God's written revelation, the Bible.

Choose one of the Bible people listed below and use Scripture (and possibly a commentary and/or a concordance) to research him. Then answer the questions about the man you have chosen. Use the back of this sheet if necessary.

Moses	Elijah	Ahab	Saul
Solomon	Asaph	Pilate	

1. What was his view of man? _____
_____
_____

2. What was his view of God?_____
_____
_____

3. Give at least one crisis or dilemma he faced. _____
_____
_____
_____

4. How did he view his dilemma? What actions, if any, did he take? What were the immediate consequences of his actions? Were there any long-term consequences?
_____
_____
_____

5. What does the study of this man reveal to you about man's control of his circumstances?
_____
_____

6. List at least one other lesson you learned from your study. ___
_____
_____
_____
_____

Name_____

Appendix E: Psalm 1 Scansion

Read Psalm 1. Then answer the questions below.

Blessed is the man that walketh not in the counsel of the ungodly,

Nor standeth in the way of sinners,

Nor sitteth in the seat of the scornful.

But his delight is in the law of the Lord;

And in his law doth he meditate day and night.   5

And he shall be like a tree planted by the rivers of water,

That bringeth forth his fruit in his season;

His leaf also shall not wither;

And whatsoever he doeth shall prosper.

The ungodly are not so: 10

But are like the chaff which the wind driveth away.

Therefore the ungodly shall not stand in the judgment,

Nor sinners in the congregation of the righteous.

For the Lord knoweth the way of the righteous:

But the way of the ungodly shall perish.   15

1. Locate and give examples of the following:

    A. alliteration_____

    B. consonance (hint: see lines 1-3 and/or lines 8 and 9) _____

    _____

    C. assonance (hint: see lines 6-8) _____

    D. synecdoche _____

    _____

    E. metonymy _____

    _____

    F. simile _____

    _____

    G. metaphor _____

2. Read the psalm again carefully. Note that it divides naturally into two sections.

    What are those two sections? _____

    _____

3. Give one other example of structural parallelism in the psalm. _____

    _____

Appendix E: Psalm 1 Scansion—cont.

4. Use the following lines for scansion—that is, mark stressed and unstressed syllables to show the metrical pattern.

Blessed is the man that walketh not in the counsel of the ungodly. . . .

The ungodly are not so.

5. How does the rhythm of each line support the psalmist's meaning?

_____

_____

_____

_____

_____

_____

Use after introduction to Unit 2, Sound and Syntax, pages 26-27.

Appendix E

Appendix F: The King James Version—A Metrical Study

Types of Metrical Feet	*Terms for Feet Per Line*	
iambic (◡ /)	monometer (one)	pentameter (five)
trochaic (/ ◡)	dimeter (two)	hexameter (six)
anapestic (◡ ◡ /)	trimeter (three)	heptameter (seven)
dactylic (/ ◡ ◡)	tetrameter (four)	octameter (eight)
spondaic (/ /)		

Identify the meter for the following verses by marking the syllables and naming the type of feet and number of feet per line using the terms above.

_____ 1. How art thou fallen from heaven, O Lucifer . . . ! (Isa. 14:12)

_____ 2. Blessed are they which do hunger and thirst after righteousness. (Matt. 5:6)

_____ 3. For all have sinned . . . (Rom. 3:23)

_____ 4. . . . and come short of the glory of God. (Rom. 3:23)

_____ 5. Husbands, love your wives, and be not bitter . . . (Col. 3:19)

Analyze the rhythmical parallelism in the following examples by marking the metrical feet as in the example below. Note that these verses use more than one type of foot per line. Rhythmical reinforcement of meaning is one of the glories of the King James Version.

$$◡ ◡ / ◡ ◡ ◡ / ◡ ◡ ◡ / ◡ ◡ ◡ / ◡$$
I am Alpha and Omega, the beginning and the ending. (Rev. 1:8)

6. In my Father's house are many mansions: if it were not so, I would have told you. (John 14:2)

7. My doctrine shall drop as the rain, my speech shall distil as the dew. (Deut. 32:2)

8. The harvest is past, the summer is ended, and we are not saved. (Jer. 8:20)

9. From the blood of the slain, from the fat of the mighty, the bow of Jonathan turned not back, and

   the sword of Saul returned not empty. (II Sam. 1:22)

10. For, lo, the winter is past, the rain is over and gone; the flowers appear on the earth; the time of the

   singing of birds is come, and the voice of the turtle is heard in our land. (Song of Sol. 2:11-12)

Appendix G: Sound and Syntax—Scripture and the Sea

Like Joyce and Updike, the writers of Scripture often make reference to the sea. This is especially noticeable in the poetic books, for the Biblical poets understood that "They that go down to the sea in ships, that do business in great waters; these see the works of the Lord, and his wonders in the deep" (Ps. 107:23-24).

Choose the letter that identifies the sounds and images of the sea that the Biblical poets (or their translators) used in the following passages. Be prepared to discuss how these poetic devices reinforce and intensify meaning and what the references tell us about God, nature, and man.

_____ 1. God "divideth the sea with his power, and by his understanding he smiteth through the proud." (Job 26:12)

     A. onomatopoeia   B. simile   C. alliteration   D. assonance

_____ 2. "Hast thou entered into the springs of the sea? or hast thou walked in the search of the depth?" (Job 38:16)

     A. onomatopoeia   B. simile   C. alliteration   D. assonance

_____ 3. God "maketh the deep to boil like a pot: he maketh the sea like a pot of ointment." (Job 41:31)

     A. onomatopoeia   B. simile   C. alliteration   D. personification

_____ 4. "When Israel went out of Egypt, the house of Jacob from a people of strange language; Judah was his sanctuary, and Israel his dominion. The sea saw it, and fled: Jordan was driven back. What ailed thee, O thou sea, that thou fleddest? thou Jordan, that thou wast driven back?" (Ps. 114:1-3, 5)

     A. simile   B. metaphor   C. alliteration   D. personification

_____ 5. "But the wicked are like the troubled sea, when it cannot rest, whose waters cast up mire and dirt." (Isa. 57:20)

     A. onomatopoeia   B. simile   C. metaphor   D. alliteration

_____ 6. The Babylonians "shall lay hold on bow and spear; they are cruel, and have no mercy; their voice roareth like the sea; and they ride upon horses, set in array as men for war against thee, O daughter of Zion." (Jer. 6:23)

     A. simile, onomatopoeia   B. personification, consonance

     C. metaphor, alliteration   D. metaphor, personification

_____ 7. "As the host of heaven cannot be numbered, neither the sand of the sea measured: so will I multiply the seed of David my servant, and the Levites that minister unto me." (Jer. 33:22)

     A. onomatopoeia   B. assonance   C. alliteration   D. simile

Appendix H: UNITS 1 AND 2 REVIEW CROSSWORD

Across

5. poetry that uses neither meter nor rhyme (two words)

6. an expression in which a part stands for the whole

7. the repetition of initial consonant sounds in accented syllables

8. the repetition of terminal consonant sounds in accented syllables

9. accented syllables in poetic rhythm occurring at fairly equal intervals throughout a poem

12. sentence structure

13. type of metaphor that uses *like* or *as*

Down

1. units of meter in a poem

2. an imaginative comparison directly comparing two unlike things

3. the repetition of vowel sounds in accented syllables

4. giving human characteristics to objects, ideas, abstractions, or animals

10. words that show a similarity of sound from the vowel of the last accented syllable onward, with dissimilarity in the preceding consonants

11. an expression in which a related thing stands for the thing itself

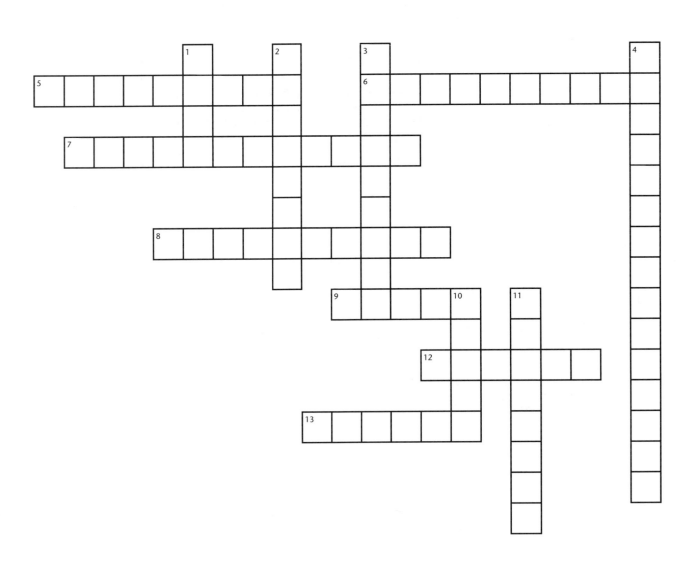

Use after "The Fruits of Toil," pages 44-53.

Appendix I: Unit 3 Review

PART ONE: Answer the following multiple-choice questions about concepts and works covered in Unit 3, Thought and Theme.

_____ 1. The main point of any work, the primary idea that the author is trying to convey, is the work's
   A. metaphor.
   B. allusion.
   C. theme.
   D. persuasive element.

_____ 2. What two types of imagery are primarily used in "It Sifts from Leaden Sieves"?
   A. cosmetics, seamstress
   B. flowers, birds
   C. snow, sun
   D. nature, man

_____ 3. What type of organization is used in "Snow-Bound"?
   A. spatial
   B. chronological (time)
   C. deductive
   D. inductive

_____ 4. Which of the following do "Snow-Bound" and "Winter" have in common?
   A. Both were written by Shakespeare.
   B. Both include the theme of the pleasures of indoor life during the winter.
   C. Both use only spatial organization.
   D. Both cover the events of two days.

_____ 5. Which of the following phrases is used to organize the essay "An Old-Fashioned Iowa Christmas"?
   A. "I remember the days when . . ."
   B. "A barn with the cattle and horses is the place to begin Christmas."
   C. "The past was better than today because . . ."
   D. "There are no such . . . any more."

_____ 6. "Some flakes have lost their way, and grope back upward." This line from "Snow in the Suburbs" illustrates
   A. personification.
   B. alliteration.
   C. consonance.
   D. the poem's theme.

_____ 7. What is the theme of "The Return of the Rangers"?
   A. Winter is the most beautiful time of year.
   B. There are times when man must muster all of his resources if he is to overcome the austerity of the natural world.
   C. All people should praise the Lord for His constant goodness and protection.
   D. The most powerful force in the world is love.

_____ 8. What kind of imagery is *not* used in "I Will Praise the Lord at All Times"?
   A. seasonal
   B. light
   C. Christian
   D. cosmetics

Use after "I Will Praise the Lord at All Times," pages 86-87.

Appendix I

Appendix I: Unit 3 Review—cont.

PART TWO: Match each author with his or her work.

_____ 9. "It Sifts from Leaden Sieves"

_____ 10. "Snow-Bound"

_____ 11. "Winter"

_____ 12. "An Old-Fashioned Iowa Christmas"

_____ 13. "Snow in the Suburbs"

_____ 14. "The Return of the Rangers"

_____ 15. "I Will Praise the Lord at All Times"

A. William Cowper

B. Emily Dickinson

C. Paul Engle

D. Thomas Hardy

E. Kenneth Roberts

F. William Shakespeare

G. John Greenleaf Whittier

PART THREE: Match each statement, quotation, or clue with the work to which it pertains. Each answer will be used only once.

A. "It Sifts from Leaden Sieves"

B. "Snow-Bound"

C. "Winter"

D. "An Old-Fashioned Iowa Christmas"

E. "Snow in the Suburbs"

F. "The Return of the Rangers"

G. "I Will Praise the Lord at All Times"

_____ 16. Emphasizes the precedence of work and duty over rest and pleasure.

_____ 17. "I'm going back to Ammonoosuc myself."

_____ 18. "Winter has a joy for me, / While the Saviour's charms I read"

_____ 19. Snow beautifies the rough landscape the way makeup beautifies a woman.

_____ 20. "The steps are a blanched slope, / Up which, with feeble hope, / A black cat comes, wide-eyed and thin; / And we take him in."

_____ 21. "To eat in the same room where food is cooked—that is the way to thank the Lord for His abundance."

_____ 22. This short poem, taken from a play, uses outdoor/indoor imagery to emphasize its theme.

Use after "I Will Praise the Lord at All Times," pages 86-87.

Appendix J: ALLUSIONS TO THE BARD

The following quotations from Shakespeare have become commonly used allusions in both written and verbal communication. Write what people mean when they use each phrase; then be prepared to give a sentence using each phrase in an appropriate context.

1. It was Greek to me. *(Julius Caesar)* _____

   _____

2. an itching palm *(Julius Caesar)* _____

   _____

3. the green-eyed monster *(Othello)* _____

   _____

4. merry as the day is long *(Much Ado About Nothing)* _____

   _____

5. sink or swim *(Henry IV)* _____

   _____

6. He has eaten me out of house and home. *(Henry IV)* _____

   _____

7. plain as the nose on one's face (This phrase is used in *The Two Gentlemen of Verona,*

   but it first appeared in *Gargantua and Pantagruel* by Rabelais.) _____

   _____

8. wear my heart on my sleeve *(Othello)* _____

   _____

9. in a pickle *(The Tempest)* _____

   _____

10. the short and the long of it *(The Merry Wives of Windsor)* _____

    _____

GROWING OLD
Matthew Arnold

What is it to grow old?
Is it to lose the glory of the form,
The luster of the eye?
Is it for beauty to forgo her wreath?
—Yes, but not this alone.

Is it to feel our strength—
Not our bloom only, but our strength—decay?
Is it to feel each limb
Grow stiffer, every function less exact,
Each nerve more loosely strung?

Yes, this, and more; but not
Ah, 'tis not what in youth we dreamed 'twould be!
'Tis not to have our life
Mellowed and softened as with sunset-glow,
A golden day's decline.

'Tis not to see the world
As from a height, with rapt prophetic eyes,
And heart profoundly stirred;
And weep, and feel the fullness of the past,
The years that are no more.

It is to spend long days
And not once feel that we were ever young;
It is to add, immured
In the hot prison of the present, month
To month with weary pain.

It is to suffer this,
And feel but half, and feebly, what we feel.
Deep in our hidden heart
Festers the dull remembrance of a change,
But no emotion—none.

It is—last stage of all—
When we are frozen up within, and quite
The phantom of ourselves,
To hear the world applaud the hollow ghost
Which blamed the living man.

Use after "The Progress of Poesy," pages 100-101.

Appendix L: SYMBOLISM DEFINED AND ILLUSTRATED

Following your reading of the introduction to Unit 5, Symbol, fill in Part One below in order to see how the terms in the essay fit together. Fill in Part Two as you work through the unit.

PART ONE: Match the following terms to their definitions.

_____ 1. allegory

_____ 2. analogy

_____ 3. fable

_____ 4. metaphor

_____ 5. parable

_____ 6. sign

_____ 7. symbol

_____ 8. symbolic narrative

A. story in which nearly every person and/or item functions on two different levels; an extended metaphor

B. non-allegorical, often true story that includes symbolic elements

C. literary element that stands for something other than (not in addition to) itself

D. basic term for any type of imaginative comparison; in a strict sense, a direct comparison of two basically unlike things

E. an extended comparison, usually a simile, used to explain or persuade

F. literary element that stands for itself and something in addition to itself

G. story in which the details support the meaning collectively; includes a stated moral

H. an allegorical story with two or more strictly correlated levels of meaning

PART TWO: Identify specific examples of symbol from each selection in this unit.

9. "Epigram": Discuss the meaning of the following symbols in the poem.

    A. To what portion of the Bible is Hughes alluding in his first reference to dust?

    _____

    B. To what portion of the Bible is Hughes alluding in his first reference to rainbows?

    _____

    C. What does dust symbolize in line 2? _____

    D. What does the rainbow symbolize in line 2? _____

10. "The Ant and the Grasshopper" may be considered both an _____ and a _____.

    A. The ant represents a _____.

    B. The grasshopper represents an _____.

    C. The seasons represent the _____.

    D. What is the fable's stated moral? _____

11. What does each of the following items symbolize in "The Grasshopper and the Cricket"?

    A. the grasshopper and the cricket _____

    B. the grasshopper's song in summer _____

    C. the cricket's song in winter _____

Appendix L: SYMBOLISM DEFINED AND ILLUSTRATED— cont.

12. "The Nightingale and the Glowworm": What two aspects of poetry are symbolized in this poem?

   A. the nightingale's song _____

   B. the glowworm's light _____

   C. the night _____

13. What allegorical elements are presented in Emerson's "Fable"?

   A. the mountain _____

   B. the squirrel _____

   C. to "crack a nut" _____

   D. Since this is a fable, what is its stated moral? _____

14. "maggie and milly and molly and may"

   A. In this fable/allegory, what kind of person does each girl represent?

   (1.) maggie _____

   (2.) milly _____

   (3.) molly _____

   (4.) may _____

   B. What is the poem's stated moral? _____

15. "The Masque of the Red Death" is an allegory. Explain what each of the following represents.

   A. the abbey _____

   B. the rooms _____

   C. the clock _____

   D. the masqueraders' revelry _____

   _____

   E. the masked figure dressed like death _____

16. What is the symbolism of the star in "My Star"? In other words, what in

   addition to itself does it represent? _____

   _____

Name_____

Appendix M: "THE GRASSHOPPER AND THE CRICKET"— STRUCTURAL PARALLELS

Fill in the chart below to emphasize and clarify the parallelism evident in the poem's structure. Read the lines indicated and then summarize their meaning in the appropriate boxes.

Grasshopper	*Cricket*
Line 1:	Line 9:
Lines 2-8:	Lines 10-12:
Lines 13-14:	

Going Beyond:

How is this parallelism appropriate when considering the symbolic meaning of the poem?

_____

_____

_____

_____

_____

Appendix N: Types of Irony

As you read pages 148-52, the introduction to Unit 6 (Irony), fill in the outline below with a definition of each term.

Irony in a general sense may be defined as _____

_____

I. Types of irony based on incongruity

  A. Paradox _____

    1. Of statement _____

    _____

    2. Of situation _____

    _____

      a. Simple irony of situation _____

      _____

      b. Dramatic irony _____

      _____

  B. Pretense _____

    _____

    1. Simple verbal irony _____

    _____

    2. Sarcasm _____

    3. Hyperbole _____

    4. Understatement _____

    _____

II. Types of irony based on ambiguity _____

    _____

  A. Foreshadowing _____

    _____

  B. Pun _____

    _____

  C. Satire _____

    _____

Appendix O: UNITS 4, 5, 6 REVIEW

PART ONE: Match each title from Unit 4, Allusion, with an allusion contained in that work.

_____ 1. "The Donkey"

_____ 2. "Cupid's Arrows"

_____ 3. "Eldorado"

_____ 4. "The Progress of Poesy"

_____ 5. "On the Pleasures of No Longer Being Very Young"

_____ 6. "The Soul's Dark Cottage"

_____ 7. "Pigeon Feathers"

A. II Corinthians 5:1-4 (our body as an earthly tabernacle) and Deuteronomy 34:1-4 (Moses' viewing of the Promised Land from Mt. Pisgah)

B. Moses' striking of the rock

C. Palm Sunday

D. "the Judgment of Paris turned upside down"

E. *The Outline of History* by H. G. Wells

F. "the valley of the shadow" of death

G. Wolsey, Shakespeare, Napoleon, Charles V

PART TWO: Match each symbol below with the title from Unit 5, Symbol, from which it comes. Be prepared to discuss what each item in the first column symbolizes.

_____ 8. "a gigantic clock of ebony"

_____ 9. dust and rainbows

_____ 10. an insect that stores food for winter and one that does not

_____ 11. celestial body that "dartles . . . red and . . . blue"

_____ 12. a mountain and a squirrel

_____ 13. "a shell that sang," "a stranded star," and "a smooth round stone"

_____ 14. two creatures that "beautify and cheer the night"

_____ 15. an insect that sings in the summer and one that sings in the winter

A. "Epigram"

B. "Fable"

C. "maggie and milly and molly and may"

D. "My Star"

E. "The Ant and the Grasshopper"

F. "The Grasshopper and the Cricket"

G. "The Masque of the Red Death"

H. "The Nightingale and the Glowworm"

Use after "For If His Majesty, Our Sovereign Lord," pages 180-81.

Appendix O

Appendix O: Units 4, 5, 6 Review—cont.

PART THREE: Name the work from which each quotation comes. Then match each quotation from stories in Unit 6, Irony, with the type of irony it illustrates. Answers may be used once, more than once, or not at all. (You may find Appendix N: Types of Irony helpful.)

A. paradox	F. hyperbole
B. irony of situation	G. understatement
C. dramatic irony	H. foreshadowing
D. verbal irony	I. pun
E. sarcasm	J. satire

_____ 16. "highly / Intelligent beings must have been living there."

_____

_____ 17. "No one can know how glad I am to find / On any sheet the least display of mind."

_____

_____ 18. "Her tongue hath worn her teeth away."

_____

_____ 19. "The Fate that looks after the Indian Empire ordained that Wonder should blunder and drop the final 'e,' . . . and that the note . . . should be given to Mellish with the Fumigatory."

_____

_____ 20. "But at the coming of the King of Heaven / All's set at six and seven."

_____

_____ 21. "We were alone, out there in the soft spring sunshine. There was no one to disturb us. We dug silently, carefully." (Hint: These are the story's opening lines.)

_____

_____ 22. "He . . . bent one of [the wheels] straight."

_____

_____ 23. "The working children can look out / And see the men at play."

_____

_____ 24. "The people peering, peering there, / . . . wander also to and fro, / And know not why or where they go."

_____

_____ 25. "If I can get $1,000 for not raising 50 hogs, then will I get $2,000 for not raising 100

hogs?" _____

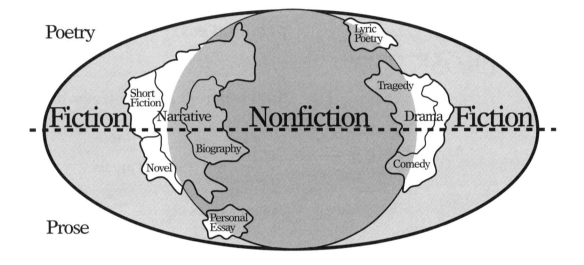

Use with introduction to Part III, The Forms of Literature, pages 182-85.

Appendix P

A Key to Literary Types

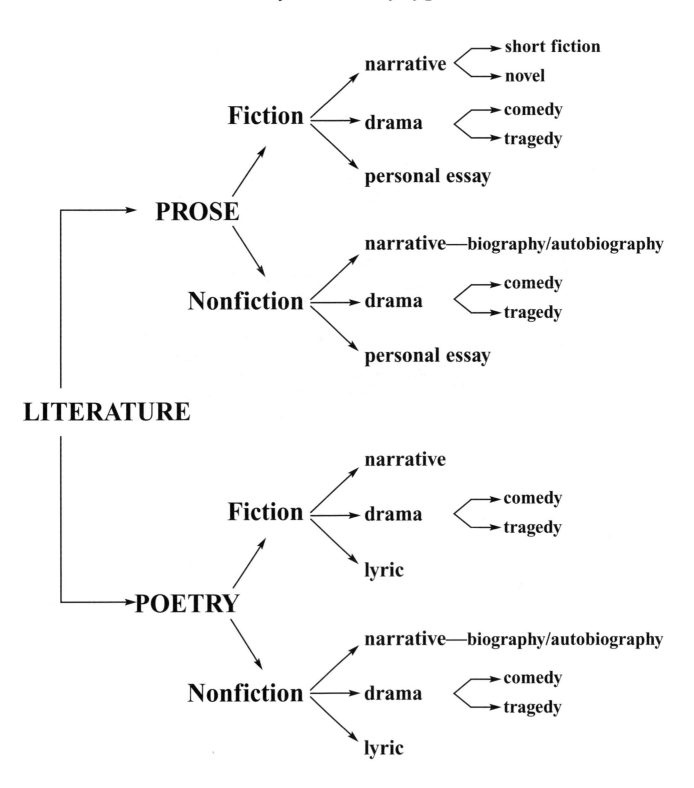

Use with introduction to Part III, The Forms of Literature, pages 182-85.

Appendix R: UNIT 7 INTRODUCTION WORKSHEET

PART ONE: Match each term from the introduction with its definition.

_____ 1. anecdote

_____ 2. autobiography

_____ 3. biography

_____ 4. diary

_____ 5. journal

_____ 6. memoirs

_____ 7. personal anecdote

A. general term for the history of the life of a person

B. the subject is the writer himself; literally means "self-biography"

C. type of autobiography that focuses on events and personalities of the author's public rather than private life

D. generally includes the intimate daily record of happenings and impressions of an individual, written to be read by him alone

E. daily records of happenings and impressions of an individual, written to be read by him alone; usually kept for a specific professional purpose

F. a narrated memorable incident from the life of an important person; basic unit of biography

G. an incident recollected by the author himself

PART TWO: Read each excerpt below. Choose the answer that describes it best.

_____ 8. "I remember the first time I had dinner with the president."

    A. biography   B. memoirs   C. alliteration   D. metonymy

_____ 9. "One incident from Edison's childhood is particularly enlightening."

    A. diary   B. autobiography   C. anecdote   D. synecdoche

_____ 10. "I was born in 1988 in the town of Millersburg, Ohio."

    A. journal   B. autobiography   C. diary   D. alliteration

_____ 11. "Today I saw a small child riding a bike for the first time. I must remember this incident clearly—perhaps I can use it in an essay on children."

    A. memoirs   B. personal anecdote   C. biography   D. journal

_____ 12. "One particularly interesting incident occurred when I first entered a college classroom as a professor."

    A. personal anecdote   B. diary   C. allusion   D. biography

_____ 13. "The composer was born in New York City in 1911."

    A. autobiography   B. personal anecdote   C. biography   D. journal

_____ 14. "I saw _him_ again today—but he has no idea I exist!"

    A. journal   B. personal anecdote   C. autobiography   D. diary

Appendix S: Tradition and the Bible

"A Slight Sound at Evening" by E. B. White discusses family traditions. What does the Bible teach about tradition? Look up each of the verses listed below and write what it teaches about tradition or traditions.

1. Matthew 15:1-6; Mark 7:3, 5, 8, 9, 13—

   _____

   _____

2. Galatians 1:13-14—

   _____

   _____

3. Colossians 2:8—

   _____

   _____

4. II Thessalonians 2:15—

   _____

   _____

5. II Thessalonians 3:6—

   _____

   _____

6. I Peter 1:18-19—

   _____

   _____

7. Summarize what these passages teach about human traditions.

   _____

   _____

Use after "A Slight Sound at Evening," pages 194-98.

Appendix T: Caesar's Character

Make two lists to contrast Julius Caesar's character strengths and weaknesses. Be prepared to discuss the successes and failures that resulted with the character traits that fostered them.

STRENGTHS	WEAKNESSES

Name_____

Appendix U: Short Fiction Crossword

After reading the Short Fiction Introduction, pages 226-29, fill in the crossword puzzle below.

Across

2. characters who change, maturing in self-control, social feelings, or understanding of life
5. an imagined story
8. name for an incident in prose fiction, especially if the story contains more than one
9. the time and place—when and where the story takes place
10. an incident in a biography
14. an essential part of plot; term for the central character's struggle with forces that may destroy him
16. the emotion pervading a story
17. the main character's opponent

Down

1. characters with little individuality
3. connected incidents in a work
4. denying the possibility of unhappiness
6. the basic unit of all narrative
7. chief or main character; literally, "first actor"
11. type of conflict in which the opponent of the central character is a person, situation, or natural force
12. type of conflict in which the central character struggles with a problem inside himself
13. earlier events in a story that have been inserted parenthetically into later events
14. denying the possibility of happiness and goodness
15. characters who are presented in detail as individuals, usually with some inward complexity
18. the attitude of a work toward its subject
19. characters who remain the same during the course of a story

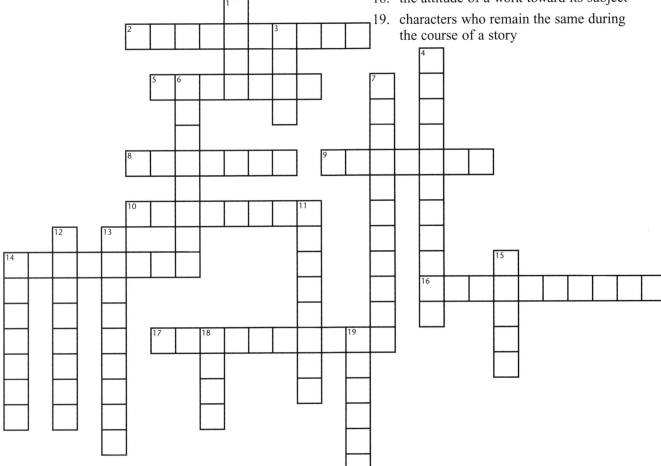

Use after introduction to Unit 8, "Short Fiction," pages 226-29.

Appendix V: "Tony Kytes, the Arch-Deceiver" Analysis

In "Tony Kytes, the Arch-Deceiver," Thomas Hardy is trying to teach a valuable lesson in an enjoyable way. Before we can discern this lesson, however, we must look at the story's conflict, characters, and plot.

1. *Conflict:* Identify the story's central conflict.

   _____

2. *Characters:* Describe each of the following characters in one or two words.

   Tony Kytes _____

   Unity Sallet _____

   Milly Richards _____

   Hannah Jolliver _____

   Mr. Kytes (Tony's father) _____

3. *Plot:* The action in the story can be organized around the three female characters. Plot the action of the story (noting the inciting moment, the rising action, the climax, and the resolution).

   _____

   _____

   _____

   _____

   _____

   _____

   _____

   _____

4. State the theme of the story in your own words. _____

   _____

   _____

   _____

5. What is Hardy teaching by this theme? _____

   _____

   _____

   _____

Appendix W: "Traveling Through the Dark" Analysis

1. What is the setting of the poem? _____

2. Describe the situation of the poem. _____

   _____

   _____

   _____

   _____

3. When was the doe killed? _____

4. What might have happened if the car had swerved? _____

5. Was there more than one person on the scene? Support your answer with a line from the poem.

   _____

   _____

   _____

   _____

6. The poem uses several sensory images. Which is your favorite for each of the following?
   a. sight _____
   b. sound _____
   c. touch _____

7. Do you find the speaker's decision in the last line disturbing? What other decision might he have made?

   _____

   _____

   _____

   _____

   _____

   _____

   _____

Use after "Traveling Through the Dark," page 310.

Appendix X: *Romeo and Juliet* Review

Fill in answers to the questions below according to your teacher's instructions, either during or after your reading of the play.

1. What is the time span of the action of the plot? (I.i–V.iii) _____

2. Make a log of the time setting of each scene (day of week and approximate time of day).

ACT, SCENE	DAY OF WEEK, TIME OF DAY
Act I, Scene i	
Act I, Scene ii	
Act I, Scene iii	
Act I, Scene iv	
Act I, Scene v	
Act II, Scene i	
Act II, Scene ii	
Act II, Scene iii	
Act II, Scene iv	
Act II, Scene v	
Act II, Scene vi	
Act III, Scene i	
Act III, Scene ii	
Act III, Scene iii	
Act III, Scene iv	
Act III, Scene v	
Act IV, Scene i	
Act IV, Scene ii	
Act IV, Scene iii	
Act IV, Scene iv	
Act IV, Scene v	
Act V, Scene i	
Act V, Scene ii	
Act V, Scene iii	

3. Why does Shakespeare make such a careful accounting of time in this play? _____

_____

4. Many critics point out that this play relies heavily on coincidence. List several prominent

coincidences that occur within the play._____

_____

Appendix X: *ROMEO AND JULIET* REVIEW—cont.

_____

_____

_____

_____

_____

_____

_____

_____

_____

_____

_____

_____

5. Do these coincidences make *Romeo and Juliet* a fatalistic play? _____

_____

_____

_____

6. Why does Shakespeare use comedy in the last scene (Scene v) of Act IV following the

Capulet household's discovery of Juliet's "death"? _____

_____

_____

7. Shakespeare incorporates the "generation gap" theme in this play. Which older characters

fail in their attempts to communicate with younger characters? Why? _____

_____

_____

_____

8. Which older character is particularly skilled in his communication with the protagonists? _____

_____

© 2001 BJU Press. Limited license to copy granted on copyright page.

Use during or after *Romeo and Juliet,* pages 320-433.

Appendix X: ROMEO AND JULIET REVIEW—cont.

9. Capulet makes several mistakes in his dealings with the young people in the play.

   Discuss his relationship to Tybalt and to Juliet in this regard. _____

   _____

   _____

   _____

   _____

10. What role does the Capulet-Montague feud play in the final outcome of the plot? Does Shakespeare introduce the feud in the play's first scene as active and virulent or as waning? How did it begin? Which characters, old or young, are willing to see it resolved?

    _____

    _____

    _____

    _____

11. In what ways does Mercutio's Queen Mab speech function in the context in which it

    appears in the play? (See Act I, Scene iv.) _____

    _____

    _____

    _____

    _____

Appendix Y: How Observant Are You?

1. List at least three interesting things you saw on your way to school this morning.

   _____

   _____

   _____

2. What color eyes does each member of your family have? _____

   _____

   _____

3. What color are your best friend's eyes? _____

4. What color was each family member wearing when you last saw him or her? _____

   _____

   _____

5. Without looking, name at least three titles from the books on the classroom bookshelf.

   _____

   _____

   _____

6. Describe what is on the class bulletin board. _____

   _____

7. Name at least three things on the teacher's desk. _____

   _____

   _____

Use before reading "Three Days to See," pages 440-48.

Appendix Z: Elements of Literature Review

Match the following quotations from "A Piece of Chalk" to the literary element they exemplify. Each answer will be used only once.

A. alliteration   F. metaphor

B. allusion   G. metonymy

C. assonance   H. paradox

D. consonance   I. personification

E. irony   J. simile

                    K. synecdoche

_____ 1. "primal twilight of the first toil"

_____ 2. "the pocketknife, . . . the type of all human tools, the infant of the sword"

_____ 3. "loose colossal contours that express the best quality of England"

_____ 4. "the teeth of our timid cruel theories"

_____ 5. "the landscape was . . . like an earthquake"

_____ 6. "old poets who lived before Wordsworth"

_____ 7. "first fierce stars"

_____ 8. "Southern England is . . . a tradition."

_____ 9. "seas of strange green"

_____ 10. "they are at the same time soft and strong"

_____ 11. "I could not find my chalk. . . . Then I suddenly stood up and roared with laughter. . . . I was sitting on an immense warehouse of white chalk."

Appendix B: Imaginative Comparison Worksheet

PART ONE: Define the following types of imaginative comparison.

1. metaphor _____*general term for any imaginative comparison comparing two things that are basically unlike*_____

2. metonymy _____*an expression in which a related thing stands for the thing itself*_____

3. personification _____*giving human characteristics to objects, ideas, abstractions, or animals*_____

4. simile _____*type of metaphor that uses **like, as, as if,** or some similar expression to compare two basically unlike things*_____

5. synecdoche _____*an expression in which a part stands for the whole*_____

PART TWO: Identify metaphors, similes, metonymies, synecdoches, and personifications in the examples below. More than one answer may be acceptable for several.

6. Bright April shakes out her rain-drenched hair. (Sara Teasdale) _____*personification*_____

7. The fog comes / on little cat feet. (Carl Sandburg) _____*metaphor*_____

8. All the world's a stage. (William Shakespeare) _____*metaphor*_____

9. The Assyrian came down like a wolf on the fold. (George Gordon, Lord Byron) _____*simile*_____

10. The White House has decided . . . _____*metonymy: White House/president*_____

11. In the sweat of thy face shalt thou eat bread, till thou return unto the ground. (Genesis 3:19)
    _____*metonymy: sweat/hard labor, ground/grave*_____

12. All flesh is grass, and the goodliness thereof is as the flower of the field. (Isaiah 40:6)
    _____*metaphor: flesh/grass; simile: goodliness/as the flower*_____

13. There is death in the pot. (II Kings 4:40) _____*metonymy: death/poison*_____

14. Give us this day our daily bread. (Matthew 6:11) _____*synecdoche: bread/food*_____

15. All hands on deck. _____*synecdoche: hands/sailors*_____

16. Time, the subtle thief of youth. (John Milton) _____*personification*_____

PART THREE: Look up the following verses and tell what kind or kinds of imaginative comparison are used in each.

17. John 12:19 _____*metonomy, world/majority of men*_____

18. Psalm 114:3 _____*personification*_____

19. Matthew 23:37 _____*personification, simile*_____

20. Isaiah 59:1 _____*synecdoche, Lord's hand/God's power, Lord's ear/not only God's omniscience but also His willingness to hear*_____

Appendix D: BIBLE CHARACTER SKETCH

Whitman's "A Noiseless Patient Spider" illustrates the power of an effective metaphor. Unlike Whitman, however, Christians must recognize the authority of God's written revelation, the Bible.

Choose one of the Bible people listed below and use Scripture (and possibly a commentary and/or a concordance) to research him. Then answer the questions about the man you have chosen. Use the back of this sheet if necessary.

Moses	Elijah	Ahab	Saul
Solomon	Asaph	Pilate	

Answers will vary.

1. What was his view of man? _____

   _____

   _____

2. What was his view of God? _____

   _____

   _____

3. Give at least one crisis or dilemma he faced. _____

   _____

   _____

   _____

4. How did he view his dilemma? What actions, if any, did he take? What were the immediate consequences of his actions? Were there any long-term consequences?

   _____

   _____

   _____

5. What does the study of this man reveal to you about man's control of his circumstances?

   _____

   _____

6. List at least one other lesson you learned from your study. ____

   _____

   _____

   _____

   _____

Appendix E: Psalm 1 Scansion

Read Psalm 1. Then answer the questions below.

Blessed is the man that walketh not in the counsel of the ungodly,

Nor standeth in the way of sinners,

Nor sitteth in the seat of the scornful.

But his delight is in the law of the Lord;

And in his law doth he meditate day and night.   5

And he shall be like a tree planted by the rivers of water,

That bringeth forth his fruit in his season;

His leaf also shall not wither;

And whatsoever he doeth shall prosper.

The ungodly are not so: 10

But are like the chaff which the wind driveth away.

Therefore the ungodly shall not stand in the judgment,

Nor sinners in the congregation of the righteous.

For the Lord knoweth the way of the righteous:

But the way of the ungodly shall perish.   15

1. Locate and give examples of the following:

   A. alliteration ___*standeth/sinners/sitteth/scornful, lines 2-3*___

   B. consonance (hint: see lines 1-3 and/or lines 8 and 9) ___*walketh/standeth/sitteth, lines 1-3;*___
   ___*wither/whatsoever/prosper, lines 8 and 9*___

   C. assonance (hint: see lines 6-8) ___*he/tree/season/leaf*___

   D. synecdoche ___*his delight is in the law of the Lord,   law of the Lord = Word and ways of the Lord*___
   ___*(Answers may vary.)*___

   E. metonymy ___*Nor sitteth in the seat of the scornful,   seat of the scornful = lifestyle, philosophy of the*___
   ___*scornful (Answers may vary.)*___

   F. simile ___*And he shall be like a tree planted by the rivers of water, / That bringeth forth his fruit in his*___
   ___*season, lines 6-7; But are like the chaff which the wind driveth away,   line 11*___

   G. metaphor ___*His leaf also shall not wither,   line 8*___

2. Read the psalm again carefully. Note that it divides naturally into two sections.

   What are those two sections? _____

   ___*lines 1-9, the way of the godly; lines 10-15, the way of the ungodly*___

3. Give one other example of structural parallelism in the psalm. _____

   ___*lines 2 and 3; lines 12 and 13; lines 14 and 15 (Answers may vary.)*___

Appendix E: Psalm 1 Scansion—cont.

4. Use the following lines for scansion—that is, mark stressed and unstressed syllables to show the metrical pattern.

/ ⌣ ⌣ ⌣ / ⌣ / ⌣ / ⌣ ⌣ / ⌣ ⌣ ⌣ ⌣ / ⌣
Blessèd is the man that walketh not in the counsel of the ungodly. . . .

⌣ ⌣ / ⌣ ⌣ / /
The ungodly are not so.

5. How does the rhythm of each line support the psalmist's meaning?

Line one, a description of the godly man, uses iambic, anapestic, and dactylic feet to produce a flowing

rhythm. Line ten, a description of the ungodly man, is the briefest line in the psalm; its "choppy" effect is

reinforced by the inclusion of a spondaic foot ("not so").

Use after introduction to Unit 2, Sound and Syntax, pages 26-27.

Answer Key—Appendix E

Appendix F: The King James Version—A Metrical Study

Types of Metrical Feet	Terms for Feet Per Line	
iambic (˘ /)	monometer (one)	pentameter (five)
trochaic (/ ˘)	dimeter (two)	hexameter (six)
anapestic (˘ ˘ /)	trimeter (three)	heptameter (seven)
dactylic (/ ˘ ˘)	tetrameter (four)	octameter (eight)
spondaic (/ /)		

Identify the meter for the following verses by marking the syllables and naming the type of feet and number of feet per line using the terms above.

<u>dactylic tetrameter</u>
1. How art thou fallen from heaven, O Lucifer . . . ! (Isa. 14:12)

<u>dactylic pentameter</u>
2. Blessed are they which do hunger and thirst after righteousness. (Matt. 5:6)

<u>iambic dimeter</u>
3. For all have sinned . . . (Rom. 3:23)

<u>anapestic trimeter</u>
4. . . . and come short of the glory of God. (Rom. 3:23)

<u>trochaic pentameter</u>
5. Husbands, love your wives, and be not bitter . . . (Col. 3:19)

Analyze the rhythmical parallelism in the following examples by marking the metrical feet as in the example below. Note that these verses use more than one type of foot per line. Rhythmical reinforcement of meaning is one of the glories of the King James Version.

I am Alpha and Omega, the beginning and the ending. (Rev. 1:8)

6. In my Father's house are many mansions: if it were not so, I would have told you. (John 14:2)

7. My doctrine shall drop as the rain, my speech shall distil as the dew. (Deut. 32:2)

8. The harvest is past, the summer is ended, and we are not saved. (Jer. 8:20)

9. From the blood of the slain, from the fat of the mighty, the bow of Jonathan turned not back, and

the sword of Saul returned not empty. (II Sam. 1:22)

10. For, lo, the winter is past, the rain is over and gone; the flowers appear on the earth; the time of the

singing of birds is come, and the voice of the turtle is heard in our land. (Song of Sol. 2:11-12)

Appendix G: Sound and Syntax—Scripture and the Sea

Like Joyce and Updike, the writers of Scripture often make reference to the sea. This is especially noticeable in the poetic books, for the Biblical poets understood that "They that go down to the sea in ships, that do business in great waters; these see the works of the Lord, and his wonders in the deep" (Ps. 107:23-24).

Choose the letter that identifies the sounds and images of the sea that the Biblical poets (or their translators) used in the following passages. Be prepared to discuss how these poetic devices reinforce and intensify meaning and what the references tell us about God, nature, and man.

___A___ 1. God "divideth the sea with his power, and by his understanding he smiteth through the proud." (Job 26:12) *("smiteth")*

      A. onomatopoeia   B. simile   C. alliteration   D. assonance

___C___ 2. "Hast thou entered into the springs of the sea? or hast thou walked in the search of the depth?" (Job 38:16) *("springs . . . sea . . . search")*

      A. onomatopoeia   B. simile   C. alliteration   D. assonance

___B___ 3. God "maketh the deep to boil like a pot: he maketh the sea like a pot of ointment." (Job 41:31) *("like a pot . . . like a pot of ointment")*

      A. onomatopoeia   B. simile   C. alliteration   D. personification

___D___ 4. "When Israel went out of Egypt, the house of Jacob from a people of strange language; Judah was his sanctuary, and Israel his dominion. The sea saw it, and fled: Jordan was driven back. What ailed thee, O thou sea, that thou fleddest? thou Jordan, that thou wast driven back?" (Ps. 114:1-3, 5) *("sea saw it, and fled")*

      A. simile   B. metaphor   C. alliteration   D. personification

___B___ 5. "But the wicked are like the troubled sea, when it cannot rest, whose waters cast up mire and dirt." (Isa. 57:20) *("like the troubled sea")*

      A. onomatopoeia   B. simile   C. metaphor   D. alliteration

___A___ 6. The Babylonians "shall lay hold on bow and spear; they are cruel, and have no mercy; their voice roareth like the sea; and they ride upon horses, set in array as men for war against thee, O daughter of Zion." (Jer. 6:23) *("like the sea . . . as men for war," "roareth")*

      A. simile, onomatopoeia   B. personification, consonance

      C. metaphor, alliteration   D. metaphor, personification

___D___ 7. "As the host of heaven cannot be numbered, neither the sand of the sea measured: so will I multiply the seed of David my servant, and the Levites that minister unto me." (Jer. 33:22) *("As the host of heaven cannot be numbered")*

      A. onomatopoeia   B. assonance   C. alliteration   D. simile

Appendix H: Units 1 and 2 Review Crossword

Across

5. poetry that uses neither meter nor rhyme (two words)

6. an expression in which a part stands for the whole

7. the repetition of initial consonant sounds in accented syllables

8. the repetition of terminal consonant sounds in accented syllables

9. accented syllables in poetic rhythm occurring at fairly equal intervals throughout a poem

12. sentence structure

13. type of metaphor that uses *like* or *as*

Down

1. units of meter in a poem

2. an imaginative comparison directly comparing two unlike things

3. the repetition of vowel sounds in accented syllables

4. giving human characteristics to objects, ideas, abstractions, or animals

10. words that show a similarity of sound from the vowel of the last accented syllable onward, with dissimilarity in the preceding consonants

11. an expression in which a related thing stands for the thing itself

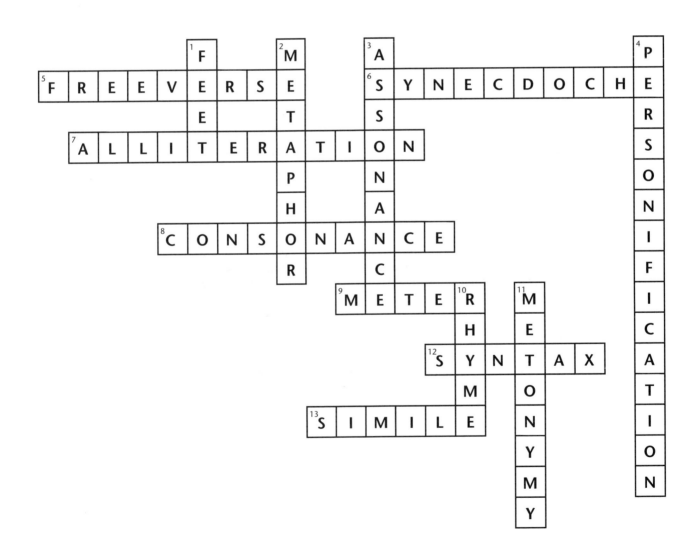

Use after "The Fruits of Toil," pages 44-53.

Appendix I: Unit 3 Review

PART ONE: Answer the following multiple-choice questions about concepts and works covered in Unit 3, Thought and Theme.

_C_ 1. The main point of any work, the primary idea that the author is trying to convey, is the work's
  A. metaphor.
  B. allusion.
  C. theme.
  D. persuasive element.

_A_ 2. What two types of imagery are primarily used in "It Sifts from Leaden Sieves"?
  A. cosmetics, seamstress
  B. flowers, birds
  C. snow, sun
  D. nature, man

_B_ 3. What type of organization is used in "Snow-Bound"?
  A. spatial
  B. chronological (time)
  C. deductive
  D. inductive

_B_ 4. Which of the following do "Snow-Bound" and "Winter" have in common?
  A. Both were written by Shakespeare.
  B. Both include the theme of the pleasures of indoor life during the winter.
  C. Both use only spatial organization.
  D. Both cover the events of two days.

_D_ 5. Which of the following phrases is used to organize the essay "An Old-Fashioned Iowa Christmas"?
  A. "I remember the days when . . ."
  B. "A barn with the cattle and horses is the place to begin Christmas."
  C. "The past was better than today because . . ."
  D. "There are no such . . . any more."

_A_ 6. "Some flakes have lost their way, and grope back upward." This line from "Snow in the Suburbs" illustrates
  A. personification.
  B. alliteration.
  C. consonance.
  D. the poem's theme.

_B_ 7. What is the theme of "The Return of the Rangers"?
  A. Winter is the most beautiful time of year.
  B. There are times when man must muster all of his resources if he is to overcome the austerity of the natural world.
  C. All people should praise the Lord for His constant goodness and protection.
  D. The most powerful force in the world is love.

_D_ 8. What kind of imagery is _not_ used in "I Will Praise the Lord at All Times"?
  A. seasonal
  B. light
  C. Christian
  D. cosmetics

Use after "I Will Praise the Lord at All Times," pages 86-87.

Answer Key—Appendix I

Appendix I: UNIT 3 REVIEW—cont.

PART TWO: Match each author with his or her work.

_B_ 9. "It Sifts from Leaden Sieves"   A. William Cowper

_G_ 10. "Snow-Bound"   B. Emily Dickinson

_F_ 11. "Winter"   C. Paul Engle

_C_ 12. "An Old-Fashioned Iowa Christmas"   D. Thomas Hardy

_D_ 13. "Snow in the Suburbs"   E. Kenneth Roberts

_E_ 14. "The Return of the Rangers"   F. William Shakespeare

_A_ 15. "I Will Praise the Lord at All Times" G. John Greenleaf Whittier

PART THREE: Match each statement, quotation, or clue with the work to which it pertains. Each answer will be used only once.

A. "It Sifts from Leaden Sieves"   E. "Snow in the Suburbs"

B. "Snow-Bound"   F. "The Return of the Rangers"

C. "Winter"   G. "I Will Praise the Lord at All Times"

D. "An Old-Fashioned Iowa Christmas"

_B_ 16. Emphasizes the precedence of work and duty over rest and pleasure.

_F_ 17. "I'm going back to Ammonoosuc myself."

_G_ 18. "Winter has a joy for me, / While the Saviour's charms I read"

_A_ 19. Snow beautifies the rough landscape the way makeup beautifies a woman.

_E_ 20. "The steps are a blanched slope, / Up which, with feeble hope, / A black cat comes, wide-eyed and thin; / And we take him in."

_D_ 21. "To eat in the same room where food is cooked—that is the way to thank the Lord for His abundance."

_C_ 22. This short poem, taken from a play, uses outdoor/indoor imagery to emphasize its theme.

Appendix J: ALLUSIONS TO THE BARD

The following quotations from Shakespeare have become commonly used allusions in both written and verbal communication. Write what people mean when they use each phrase; then be prepared to give a sentence using each phrase in an appropriate context.

1. It was Greek to me. *(Julius Caesar)* __I didn't understand it at all.__

2. an itching palm *(Julius Caesar)* __greediness__

3. the green-eyed monster *(Othello)* __jealousy__

4. merry as the day is long *(Much Ado About Nothing)* __happy all the time__

5. sink or swim *(Henry IV)* __fail or succeed at an endeavor__

6. He has eaten me out of house and home. *(Henry IV)* _____
   __He has eaten everything I have; he has taken advantage of my hospitality.__

7. plain as the nose on one's face (This phrase is used in *The Two Gentlemen of Verona,* but it first appeared in *Gargantua and Pantagruel* by Rabelais.) __obvious__

8. wear my heart on my sleeve *(Othello)* __be easily offended__

9. in a pickle *(The Tempest)* __in trouble__

10. the short and the long of it *(The Merry Wives of Windsor)* __the whole story__

Appendix L: Symbolism Defined and Illustrated

Following your reading of the introduction to Unit 5, Symbol, fill in Part One below in order to see how the terms in the essay fit together. Fill in Part Two as you work through the unit.

PART ONE: Match the following terms to their definitions.

__A__	1. allegory	A. story in which nearly every person and/or item functions on two different levels; an extended metaphor
__E__	2. analogy	B. non-allegorical, often true story that includes symbolic elements
__G__	3. fable	C. literary element that stands for something other than (not in addition to) itself
__D__	4. metaphor	
__H__	5. parable	D. basic term for any type of imaginative comparison; in a strict sense, a direct comparison of two basically unlike things
__C__	6. sign	E. an extended comparison, usually a simile, used to explain or persuade
__F__	7. symbol	
__B__	8. symbolic narrative	F. literary element that stands for itself and something in addition to itself

G. story in which the details support the meaning collectively; includes a stated moral

H. an allegorical story with two or more strictly correlated levels of meaning

PART TWO: Identify specific examples of symbol from each selection in this unit.

9. "Epigram": Discuss the meaning of the following symbols in the poem.

    A. To what portion of the Bible is Hughes alluding in his first reference to dust?

    Man was formed from the dust of the ground (Gen. 2:7).

    B. To what portion of the Bible is Hughes alluding in his first reference to rainbows?

    God's covenant with man (Gen. 9:9-17)

    C. What does dust symbolize in line 2? *the tedious, troublesome parts of life*

    D. What does the rainbow symbolize in line 2? *the hopeful, joyous parts of life*

10. "The Ant and the Grasshopper" may be considered both an *allegory* and a *fable*.

    A. The ant represents a *thrifty person*.

    B. The grasshopper represents an *unthrifty person*.

    C. The seasons represent the *stages of life and/or times of prosperity/adversity*.

    D. What is the fable's stated moral? *"It is thrifty to prepare today for the wants of tomorrow."*

11. What does each of the following items symbolize in "The Grasshopper and the Cricket"?

    A. the grasshopper and the cricket *poets*

    B. the grasshopper's song in summer *poetry of youth*

    C. the cricket's song in winter *poetry of age*

Appendix L: Symbolism Defined and Illustrated— cont.

12. "The Nightingale and the Glowworm": What two aspects of poetry are symbolized in this poem?

    A. the nightingale's song __the aesthetic, the beautiful; "feeling"__

    B. the glowworm's light __reason, didacticism (teaching), oration__

    C. the night __mortal life__

13. What allegorical elements are presented in Emerson's "Fable"?

    A. the mountain __public opinion (massive, inert)__

    B. the squirrel __Emerson or any philosopher__

    C. to "crack a nut" __to solve difficult philosophical problems__

    D. Since this is a fable, what is its stated moral? __"Talents differ."__

14. "maggie and milly and molly and may"

    A. In this fable/allegory, what kind of person does each girl represent?

    (1.) maggie __those with poetic natures__

    (2.) milly __those who are tenderhearted toward living things__

    (3.) molly __those who focus on the threatening and ugly aspects of life__

    (4.) may __those who are sentimental__

    B. What is the poem's stated moral? __"It's always ourselves we find in the sea."__

15. "The Masque of the Red Death" is an allegory. Explain what each of the following represents.

    A. the abbey __man's futile attempts to wall out death__

    B. the rooms __stages of life (see page 140 for list)__

    C. the clock __the passing of time__

    D. the masqueraders' revelry __the futile efforts of man to lose his fear of death through self-indulgence__

    E. the masked figure dressed like death __death—specifically, the Red Death__

16. What is the symbolism of the star in "My Star"? In other words, what in addition to itself does it represent? __being captivated by something whose value or existence baffles others__

Appendix M: "THE GRASSHOPPER AND THE CRICKET"— STRUCTURAL PARALLELS

Fill in the chart below to emphasize and clarify the parallelism evident in the poem's structure. Read the lines indicated and then summarize their meaning in the appropriate boxes.

Grasshopper	*Cricket*
Line 1: **The poetry of earth is never dead.**	Line 9: **The poetry of earth is ceasing never.**
Lines 2-8: **grasshopper's voice in the heat of the day (outdoors)**	Lines 10-12: **cricket's voice in winter (indoors)**
Lines 13-14: **Blending the grasshopper and cricket metaphors; the cricket is a reminder of the summer, of the grasshopper's song.**	

Going Beyond:

How is this parallelism appropriate when considering the symbolic meaning of the poem?

The parallelism is appropriate because Keats is praising two kinds of poets: those who, like the

grasshopper, sing in the summer (the good times of life) and also those who, like the cricket,

cheer us during difficult times of life.

Appendix N: Types of Irony

As you read pages 148-52, the introduction to Unit 6 (Irony), fill in the outline below with a definition of each term.

Irony in a general sense may be defined as _a contrast between what is expected and what really happens or exists._

I. Types of irony based on incongruity

  A. Paradox _a seeming contradiction_

    1. Of statement _the joining of two seemingly contradictory statements or images_

    2. Of situation _the joining together of unexpected or contrasting events_

      a. Simple irony of situation _a contrast between what is reasonable to expect and what actually happens_

      b. Dramatic irony _a contrast between what characters in a work know and what the reader or audience knows_

  B. Pretense _the intentional use of irony to emphasize something other than what is being expressed_

    1. Simple verbal irony _language that means something other than what it actually states_

    2. Sarcasm _mock praise_

    3. Hyperbole _overstatement (See teacher's edition marginal note, page 150, for this definition.)_

    4. Understatement _saying less than the intended meaning; saying something by denying its opposite_

II. Types of irony based on ambiguity _intentionally blending or obscuring meaning; uncertain statements that appear to have several possible meanings_

  A. Foreshadowing _prophetic statement; a hint as to what may or may not follow_

  B. Pun _the (usually humorous) use of a word or phrase in order to convey more than one meaning_

  C. Satire _corrective ridicule in literature; usually involves mockery_

Appendix O: Units 4, 5, 6 Review

PART ONE: Match each title from Unit 4, Allusion, with an allusion contained in that work.

_C_ 1. "The Donkey"

_D_ 2. "Cupid's Arrows"

_F_ 3. "Eldorado"

_B_ 4. "The Progress of Poesy"

_G_ 5. "On the Pleasures of No Longer Being Very Young"

_A_ 6. "The Soul's Dark Cottage"

_E_ 7. "Pigeon Feathers"

A. II Corinthians 5:1-4 (our body as an earthly tabernacle) and Deuteronomy 34:1-4 (Moses' viewing of the Promised Land from Mt. Pisgah)

B. Moses' striking of the rock

C. Palm Sunday

D. "the Judgment of Paris turned upside down"

E. _The Outline of History_ by H. G. Wells

F. "the valley of the shadow" of death

G. Wolsey, Shakespeare, Napoleon, Charles V

PART TWO: Match each symbol below with the title from Unit 5, Symbol, from which it comes. Be prepared to discuss what each item in the first column symbolizes.

_G_ 8. "a gigantic clock of ebony"

_A_ 9. dust and rainbows

_E_ 10. an insect that stores food for winter and one that does not

_D_ 11. celestial body that "dartles . . . red and . . . blue"

_B_ 12. a mountain and a squirrel

_C_ 13. "a shell that sang," "a stranded star," and "a smooth round stone"

_H_ 14. two creatures that "beautify and cheer the night"

_F_ 15. an insect that sings in the summer and one that sings in the winter

A. "Epigram"

B. "Fable"

C. "maggie and milly and molly and may"

D. "My Star"

E. "The Ant and the Grasshopper"

F. "The Grasshopper and the Cricket"

G. "The Masque of the Red Death"

H. "The Nightingale and the Glowworm"

     Use after "For If His Majesty, Our Sovereign Lord," pages 180-81.

PART THREE: Name the work from which each quotation comes. Then match each quotation from stories in Unit 6, Irony, with the type of irony it illustrates. Answers may be used once, more than once, or not at all. (You may find Appendix N: Types of Irony helpful.)

A. paradox	F. hyperbole
B. irony of situation	G. understatement
C. dramatic irony	H. foreshadowing
D. verbal irony	I. pun
E. sarcasm	J. satire

D or E 16. "highly / Intelligent beings must have been living there."

"Earth"

G 17. "No one can know how glad I am to find / On any sheet the least display of mind."

"A Considerable Speck (Microscopic)"

F 18. "Her tongue hath worn her teeth away."

"Scylla Toothless"

B or C 19. "The Fate that looks after the Indian Empire ordained that Wonder should blunder and drop the final 'e,' . . . and that the note . . . should be given to Mellish with the Fumigatory."

"A Germ Destroyer"

B 20. "But at the coming of the King of Heaven / All's set at six and seven."

"Yet If His Majesty, Our Sovereign Lord"

H 21. "We were alone, out there in the soft spring sunshine. There was no one to disturb us. We dug silently, carefully." (Hint: These are the story's opening lines.)

"The Grave Grass Quivers"

A 22. "He . . . bent one of [the wheels] straight."

"A Special Occasion"

B 23. "The working children can look out / And see the men at play."

"The Golf Links Lie So Near the Mill"

C 24. "The people peering, peering there, / . . . wander also to and fro, / And know not why or where they go."

"At the Aquarium"

D or J 25. "If I can get $1,000 for not raising 50 hogs, then will I get $2,000 for not raising 100 hogs?" _"Letter from a West Texas Constituent"_

Use after "For If His Majesty, Our Sovereign Lord," pages 180-81.

Answer Key—Appendix O

Appendix R: Unit 7 Introduction Worksheet

PART ONE: Match each term from the introduction with its definition.

F   1. anecdote

B   2. autobiography

A   3. biography

D   4. diary

E   5. journal

C   6. memoirs

G   7. personal anecdote

A. general term for the history of the life of a person

B. the subject is the writer himself; literally means "self-biography"

C. type of autobiography that focuses on events and personalities of the author's public rather than private life

D. generally includes the intimate daily record of happenings and impressions of an individual, written to be read by him alone

E. daily records of happenings and impressions of an individual, written to be read by him alone; usually kept for a specific professional purpose

F. a narrated memorable incident from the life of an important person; basic unit of biography

G. an incident recollected by the author himself

PART TWO: Read each excerpt below. Choose the answer that describes it best.

Note to teacher: The following "excerpts" are fictional.

B   8. "I remember the first time I had dinner with the president."

     A. biography   B. memoirs   C. alliteration   D. metonymy

C   9. "One incident from Edison's childhood is particularly enlightening."

     A. diary   B. autobiography   C. anecdote   D. synecdoche

B   10. "I was born in 1988 in the town of Millersburg, Ohio."

     A. journal   B. autobiography   C. diary   D. alliteration

D   11. "Today I saw a small child riding a bike for the first time. I must remember this incident clearly—perhaps I can use it in an essay on children."

     A. memoirs   B. personal anecdote   C. biography   D. journal

A   12. "One particularly interesting incident occurred when I first entered a college classroom as a professor."

     A. personal anecdote   B. diary   C. allusion   D. biography

C   13. "The composer was born in New York City in 1911."

     A. autobiography   B. personal anecdote   C. biography   D. journal

D   14. "I saw *him* again today—but he has no idea I exist!"

     A. journal   B. personal anecdote   C. autobiography   D. diary

Appendix S: Tradition and the Bible

"A Slight Sound at Evening" by E. B. White discusses family traditions. What does the Bible teach about tradition? Look up each of the verses listed below and write what it teaches about tradition or traditions.

1. Matthew 15:1-6; Mark 7:3, 5, 8, 9, 13—

   The Pharisees were guilty of making "the commandment of God of none effect" by elevating their traditions (the washing of hands) above God's Word.

2. Galatians 1:13-14—

   Before Paul was saved, he was very zealous in preserving Jewish traditions.

3. Colossians 2:8—

   Paul warns the readers to avoid allowing worldly traditions to deceive them.

4. II Thessalonians 2:15—

   Paul urges readers to "hold" godly traditions they have been taught.

5. II Thessalonians 3:6—

   Christians are commanded to "withdraw" from brethren who will not follow after the traditions (teachings) received from Paul.

6. I Peter 1:18-19—

   Christians were redeemed from "vain conversation [empty ways of life] received by tradition" by Christ's blood.

7. Summarize what these passages teach about human traditions.

   Human tradition may have its place, but it must not be elevated above Bible truth and the teachings given to us in Scripture.

Appendix T: Caesar's Character

Make two lists to contrast Julius Caesar's character strengths and weaknesses. Be prepared to discuss the successes and failures that resulted with the character traits that fostered them.

STRENGTHS	WEAKNESSES
his kindness to soldiers	his penchant for luxury
his unwillingness to give in to physical infirmities	his physical infirmities
his determination and persistence	his superstition
his courage	his pride
his penchant for administration	

Note: Answers above are suggestions. Student may note others. Draw your students' attention to the fact that some of the traits might be considered strengths as well as weaknesses. Caesar's kindness in rewarding his soldiers, for example, might have led to his surrounding himself with sycophants and other men of weak character.

Appendix U: Short Fiction Crossword

After reading the Short Fiction Introduction, pages 226-29, fill in the crossword puzzle below.

Across

2. characters who change, maturing in self-control, social feelings, or understanding of life
5. an imagined story
8. name for an incident in prose fiction, especially if the story contains more than one
9. the time and place—when and where the story takes place
10. an incident in a biography
14. an essential part of plot; term for the central character's struggle with forces that may destroy him
16. the emotion pervading a story
17. the main character's opponent

Down

1. characters with little individuality
3. connected incidents in a work
4. denying the possibility of unhappiness
6. the basic unit of all narrative
7. chief or main character; literally, "first actor"
11. type of conflict in which the opponent of the central character is a person, situation, or natural force
12. type of conflict in which the central character struggles with a problem inside himself
13. earlier events in a story that have been inserted parenthetically into later events
14. denying the possibility of happiness and goodness
15. characters who are presented in detail as individuals, usually with some inward complexity
18. the attitude of a work toward its subject
19. characters who remain the same during the course of a story

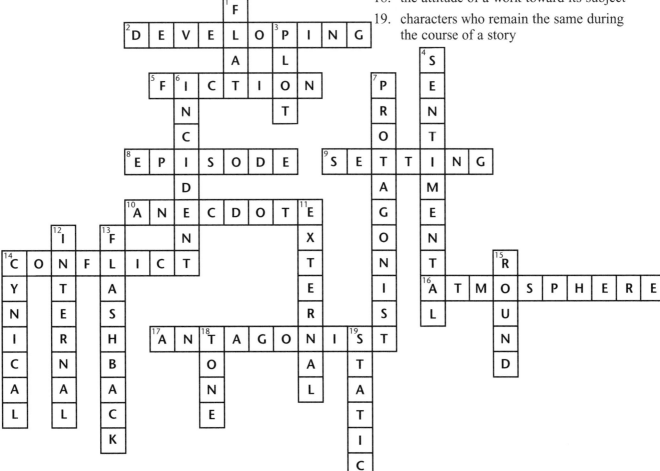

Use after introduction to Unit 8, "Short Fiction," pages 226-29.

Answer Key—Appendix U

Appendix V: "Tony Kytes, the Arch-Deceiver" Analysis

In "Tony Kytes, the Arch-Deceiver," Thomas Hardy is trying to teach a valuable lesson in an enjoyable way. Before we can discern this lesson, however, we must look at the story's conflict, characters, and plot.

1. *Conflict:* Identify the story's central conflict.

   Whom will Tony marry?

2. *Characters:* Describe each of the following characters in one or two words. **Answers will vary.**

   Tony Kytes **immature, deceptive, handsome, indecisive**

   Unity Sallet **"a handsome girl," jealous**

   Milly Richards **Tony's supposed fiancée, pouting, impatient, gullible**

   Hannah Jolliver **abrupt, flattering, pretty, fickle**

   Mr. Kytes (Tony's father) **moral, concerned about his family's reputation, has common sense**

3. *Plot:* The action in the story can be organized around the three female characters. Plot the action of the story (noting the inciting moment, the rising action, the climax, and the resolution).

   Inciting moment: Tony meets Unity, and she asks for a lift home. Rising action: Tony gives Unity a ride; meets Milly and asks Unity to hide; gives Milly a ride, but asks her to hide when he meets Hannah; gives Hannah a ride; sees his father in the field. Climax: Tony's father berates him and tells him to marry whichever girl did not ask to ride with him (Milly); meanwhile, the women discover each other and the horse starts for home, dumping the three girls out. Falling action: Tony says Hannah and he will be married, then Unity and he; finally Milly agrees to marry him.

4. State the theme of the story in your own words. **The story is a humorous look at the trouble we get ourselves into when we are less than honest. (Answers will vary.)**

5. What is Hardy teaching by this theme? **Hardy is taking a critical look at the subject of immature love and the lack of wisdom inherent in entering marriage lightly.**

Appendix W: "TRAVELING THROUGH THE DARK" ANALYSIS

1. What is the setting of the poem? __*night on Wilson River road*__

2. Describe the situation of the poem. __*The speaker finds a dead doe on the side of a narrow road.*__

   __*Concerned for other travelers, he stops to push her body off the edge of the road into a canyon.*__

   __*Before doing so, he realizes that she is pregnant and that her fawn is still alive inside her.*__

   __*He hesitates a moment, then pushes "her over the edge into the river."*__

3. When was the doe killed? __*recently (line 6)*__

4. What might have happened if the car had swerved? __*The speaker might have been killed (line 4).*__

5. Was there more than one person on the scene? Support your answer with a line from the poem.

   __*Answers may vary. Students will probably cite line 16 as proof that others were around. However, the*__

   __*"group" referred to could be the speaker, the dead doe, and the fawn. The meaning is unclear, but this*__

   __*is the most likely reading since nowhere else are any other travelers mentioned.*__

6. The poem uses several sensory images. Which is your favorite for each of the following? *Answers will vary.*
   a. sight __*lines 5 and 6; 13-16*__
   b. sound __*lines 14-16*__
   c. touch __*lines 9-11*__

7. Do you find the speaker's decision in the last line disturbing? What other decision might he have made?

   __*Answers will vary. Some students may argue that he should have done something to save the fawn. Ask*__

   __*them what he should have done—removed the baby surgically? Then what would happen to it? Take the*__

   __*doe to a veterinarian to have the fawn removed? Again, then what? Although his decision is disturbing,*__

   __*it is the only thing to be done in the difficult situation. If opportunity arises, you may want to discuss the*__

   __*difference in the sight of God between the speaker knowingly killing the unborn fawn and those who*__

   __*knowingly kill unborn humans.*__

Appendix X: ROMEO AND JULIET REVIEW

Fill in answers to the questions below according to your teacher's instructions, either during or after your reading of the play.

1. What is the time span of the action of the plot? (I.i–V.iii) _**Sunday morning to early Friday morning**_

2. Make a log of the time setting of each scene (day of week and approximate time of day).

ACT, SCENE	DAY OF WEEK, TIME OF DAY
Act I, Scene i	*Sunday morning*
Act I, Scene ii	*Sunday afternoon*
Act I, Scene iii	*Sunday afternoon*
Act I, Scene iv	*Sunday evening*
Act I, Scene v	*Sunday evening*
Act II, Scene i	*Sunday evening (very late)*
Act II, Scene ii	*Sunday evening (very late)*
Act II, Scene iii	*Monday morning*
Act II, Scene iv	*Monday morning*
Act II, Scene v	*Monday noon*
Act II, Scene vi	*Monday afternoon*
Act III, Scene i	*Monday afternoon*
Act III, Scene ii	*Monday afternoon*
Act III, Scene iii	*Monday afternoon*
Act III, Scene iv	*Monday evening*
Act III, Scene v	*Early Tuesday morning*
Act IV, Scene i	*Tuesday*
Act IV, Scene ii	*Tuesday, near night*
Act IV, Scene iii	*Tuesday evening*
Act IV, Scene iv	*Early Wednesday morning*
Act IV, Scene v	*Early Wednesday morning*
Act V, Scene i	*Thursday*
Act V, Scene ii	*Thursday evening*
Act V, Scene iii	*Late Thursday evening*

3. Why does Shakespeare make such a careful accounting of time in this play? _**It supports the theme**_ _**of impetuosity, which results in haste. Haste is Romeo and Juliet's tragic flaw.**_

4. Many critics point out that this play relies heavily on coincidence. List several prominent coincidences that occur within the play. _**Answers will vary. Act I, Scene ii: The first coincidence of the**_ _**plot occurs at lines 30 and following—a servant sent to invite guests to Capulet's feast cannot read;**_

Appendix X: *ROMEO AND JULIET* REVIEW—cont.

therefore, he stops "the learned" (ironically a group of rowdy young men) for assistance. Act V: Throughout

Act V references to fate and fortune and ironic coincidences are prominent. (In the earlier acts of the play,

however, Shakespeare's emphasis is on Romeo and Juliet's exercise of free will.) Act V, Scene ii: The

most crucial coincidence of the plot occurs in this scene: Friar John's quarantine, which keeps him from

delivering Friar Lawrence's message to Romeo. The ironic significance of Capulet's moving Juliet's

wedding to Paris from Thursday to Wednesday also becomes apparent here, for if Juliet had taken

the potion a day later, the Friar would have had more time to get his message to Romeo. Act V, Scene iii:

Paris's timing in arriving to bestow flowers on Juliet's grave is another large coincidence of the plot.

Notice that Paris is characterized by persistence in love and ignorance of Romeo and Juliet's love.

Ironically it is these very two qualities that lead to Romeo's death as well. (Romeo is persistent in his

love for Juliet; he is ignorant of the fact that she is still alive even though she appears dead.)

5. Do these coincidences make *Romeo and Juliet* a fatalistic play? __*No, characters make choices*__

__*based on their own free will. But circumstances beyond their control do intervene. Thus the play is an*__

__*accurate reflection of life.*__

6. Why does Shakespeare use comedy in the last scene (Scene v) of Act IV following the

Capulet household's discovery of Juliet's "death"? __*He knows that the audience will not grieve twice*__

__*for Juliet, so he makes her family's reactions humorous here. Also, the audience knows she is not*__

__*really dead.*__

7. Shakespeare incorporates the "generation gap" theme in this play. Which older characters

fail in their attempts to communicate with younger characters? Why? __*Capulet and Lady Capulet*__

__*(Act III, Scene v) are unwilling to listen to Juliet; they respond hastily and in unreasonable anger. They*__

__*seem to have little more control over their emotions than do members of the younger generation*__

__*(Romeo, Juliet, Tybalt, Mercutio).*__

8. Which older character is particularly skilled in his communication with the protagonists? _____

__*Friar Lawrence*__

9. Capulet makes several mistakes in his dealings with the young people in the play.

   Discuss his relationship to Tybalt and to Juliet in this regard. ___*In Act I, Scene v, he commands Tybalt*___

   ___*not to fight with the Montagues at the Capulets' party. His manner succeeds only in angering Tybalt further.*___

   ___*As mentioned above (see number 7), he responds with unreasonable anger to Juliet's unwillingness to*___

   ___*marry Paris.*___

10. What role does the Capulet-Montague feud play in the final outcome of the plot? Does Shakespeare introduce the feud in the play's first scene as active and virulent or as waning? How did it begin? Which characters, old or young, are willing to see it resolved?

    ___*The feud serves as an impetus for the action, but the reason for its existence is never given. It is a theme*___

    ___*that is carried throughout the play, recurring even in the Prince's next-to-last speech. For further*___

    ___*discussion, see "About the Play" questions, page 349.*___

11. In what ways does Mercutio's Queen Mab speech function in the context in which it

    appears in the play? (See Act I, Scene iv.) ___*Mercutio's famous lines about the creative power of the*___

    ___*imagination and the shallowness of wish-fulfillment dreams are directly applicable to Romeo, a vain*___

    ___*dreamer at this point in the play. In light of Mercutio's import, we do not take very seriously Romeo's*___

    ___*musings about fatal omens at the end of the scene.*___

Use during or after *Romeo and Juliet*, pages 320-433.

Appendix Y: How Observant Are You?

1. List at least three interesting things you saw on your way to school this morning.

   _____

   _____

   _____

2. What color eyes does each member of your family have? _____

   _____

   _____

3. What color are your best friend's eyes? _____

4. What color was each family member wearing when you last saw him or her? __ _____

   _____

   _____

5. Without looking, name at least three titles from the books on the classroom bookshelf.

   _____

   _____

   _____

6. Describe what is on the class bulletin board. _____

   _____

7. Name at least three things on the teacher's desk. _____ _____

   _____

   _____

Answers will vary. Have fun with the activity and generate good discussion from it, but make the point of the activity clear: sighted people take their vision for granted—in fact, we all take many blessings for granted. You may want to have the classroom bookshelves, your desk, and/or bulletin boards covered before students come to class. (See questions 5-7.)

Appendix Z: Elements of Literature Review

Match the following quotations from "A Piece of Chalk" to the literary element they exemplify. Each answer will be used only once.

A. alliteration

B. allusion

C. assonance

D. consonance

E. irony

F. metaphor

G. metonymy

H. paradox

I. personification

J. simile

K. synecdoche

___D___ 1. "primal twilight of the first toil"

___K___ 2. "the pocketknife, . . . the type of all human tools, the infant of the sword"

___G___ 3. "loose colossal contours that express the best quality of England"

___I___ 4. "the teeth of our timid cruel theories"

___J___ 5. "the landscape was . . . like an earthquake"

___B___ 6. "old poets who lived before Wordsworth"

___A___ 7. "first fierce stars"

___F___ 8. "Southern England is . . . a tradition."

___C___ 9. "seas of strange green"

___H___ 10. "they are at the same time soft and strong"

___E___ 11. "I could not find my chalk. . . . Then I suddenly stood up and roared with laughter.
        . . . I was sitting on an immense warehouse of white chalk."

Writing Rubric 1-1
Personification Paragraph

	MESSAGE
	Personification 3 The writer creatively personifies an animal, object, or idea. 2 The writer adequately personifies an animal, object, or idea. 1 The writer does not personify an animal, object, or idea.
	Paragraph 3 The writer uses proper paragraph form. 2 The writer uses paragraph form with some need for improvement. 1 The writer does not use proper paragraph form.
	Style 3 The writer captures and holds the reader's attention with an exciting style. 2 The writer's style holds the reader's attention. 1 The writer's style does not hold the reader's attention.
_____	**MESSAGE SCORE**

	MECHANICS
	Grammar/Usage 3 Writer displays a command of agreement, pronoun reference, word usage, and complete sentences. 2 Writer demonstrates a basic understanding of agreement, pronoun reference, word usage, and complete sentences. 1 Writer makes errors in agreement, pronoun reference, word usage, or complete sentences.
	Spelling 3 Writer uses and spells words above grade level. 2 Writer spells words on grade level. 1 Writer misspells grade-level words.
	Capitalization/Punctuation 3 Writer demonstrates a command of grade-level capitalization and punctuation. 2 Writer demonstrates an understanding of grade-level capitalization and punctuation. 1 Writer misuses grade-level capitalization or punctuation.
_____ _____	**MECHANICS SCORE** **TOTAL SCORE (Message plus Mechanics)**

A 17-18   B 15-16   C 13-14   D 11-12   F 6-10

Comments . . .

Use after "What Stumped the Bluejays," pages 7-10.

Writing Rubric 1-2
Plotted Poem

EFFORT
9 The poem evidences good creative effort. 8 The poem evidences acceptable effort. 6 The poem evidences poor effort. 0 The poem was not completed.

_____ **EFFORT SCORE**

COMPLETION
9 The poem was completed on time or early. 6 The poem was completed one day late. 3 The poem was completed more than one day late. 0 The poem was not turned in.

_____ **COMPLETION SCORE**

_____ **TOTAL SCORE (Effort plus Completion)**

A 17-18   B 15-16   C 14   D 12   F 0-10

Comments . . .

Use after "A Prompt, Executive Bird," page 13.

Writing Rubric 1-3
Predator-Prey Paragraph

	MESSAGE
	Predator-Prey Relationship 3 The paragraph creatively discusses a predator-prey relationship. 2 The paragraph adequately discusses a predator-prey relationship. 1 The paragraph does not adequately discuss a predator-prey relationship.
	Paragraph 3 The writer limits himself to one example of a predator-prey relationship. 2 The writer uses more than one example of a predator-prey relationship. 1 The writer does not thoroughly cover even one example of a predator-prey relationship.
	Style 3 The style is effective and enjoyable. 2 The style is adequate for the purposes of the essay. 1 The style is not adequate for the purposes of the essay.
_____	**MESSAGE SCORE**

	MECHANICS
	Grammar/Usage 3 Writer displays a command of agreement, pronoun reference, word usage, and complete sentences. 2 Writer demonstrates a basic understanding of agreement, pronoun reference, word usage, and complete sentences. 1 Writer makes errors in agreement, pronoun reference, word usage, or complete sentences.
	Spelling 3 Writer uses and spells words above grade level. 2 Writer spells words on grade level. 1 Writer misspells grade-level words.
	Capitalization/Punctuation 3 Writer demonstrates a command of grade-level capitalization and punctuation. 2 Writer demonstrates an understanding of grade-level capitalization and punctuation. 1 Writer misuses grade-level capitalization or punctuation.
_____ _____	**MECHANICS SCORE** **TOTAL SCORE (Message plus Mechanics)**

A 17-18   B 15-16   C 13-14   D 11-12   F 6-10

Comments . . .

Writing Rubric 2-1
Seven Sentences and a Sketch

MESSAGE
Seven Sentences 3 The writer has composed seven sentences that effectively demonstrate seven types of imaginative comparisons/sound devices. 2 The writer has composed seven sentences but does not demonstrate one or two of the required types of imaginative comparisons/sound devices. 1 The writer has not composed seven sentences or does not demonstrate three or more of the required types of imaginative comparisons/sound devices.
Sketch 3 The writer effectively creates tension throughout the sketch. 2 The writer adequately creates tension throughout the sketch. 1 The writer does not adequately create tension throughout the sketch.
Style 3 The style of the sentences and sketch is fresh and invigorating. 2 The style of the sentences and sketch is appropriate. 1 The style of the sentences and sketch lacks enthusiasm and/or creativity.
_____ **MESSAGE SCORE**

MECHANICS
Grammar/Usage 3 Writer displays a command of agreement, pronoun reference, word usage, and complete sentences. 2 Writer demonstrates a basic understanding of agreement, pronoun reference, word usage, and complete sentences. 1 Writer makes errors in agreement, pronoun reference, word usage, or complete sentences.
Spelling 3 Writer uses and spells words above grade level. 2 Writer spells words on grade level. 1 Writer misspells grade-level words.
Capitalization/Punctuation 3 Writer demonstrates a command of grade-level capitalization and punctuation. 2 Writer demonstrates an understanding of grade-level capitalization and punctuation. 1 Writer misuses grade-level capitalization or punctuation.
_____ **MECHANICS SCORE** _____ **TOTAL SCORE (Message plus Mechanics)**

A 17-18   B 15-16   C 13-14   D 11-12   F 6-10

Comments . . .

Use after "Storm Fury," page 41.

Writing Rubric 3-1
A Faithful Follower

	MESSAGE
	Follower 3 The writer has chosen a person from the Bible and discusses his or her hardships. 2 The writer has chosen a person from the Bible but does not focus on his or her hardships. 1 The writer has not chosen a person from the Bible or has failed to discuss his or her hardships.
	Faithfulness 3 The writer has demonstrated the person's dedication to the Lord in spite of hardships. 2 The writer mentions the person's dedication to the Lord in spite of hardships. 1 The writer does not discuss the person's dedication to the Lord in spite of hardships.
	Style 3 The style is clear and interesting. 2 The style is adequate but not outstanding. 1 The style does not hold the reader's attention.
_____	**MESSAGE SCORE**

	MECHANICS
	Grammar/Usage 3 Writer displays a command of agreement, pronoun reference, word usage, and complete sentences. 2 Writer demonstrates a basic understanding of agreement, pronoun reference, word usage, and complete sentences. 1 Writer makes errors in agreement, pronoun reference, word usage, or complete sentences.
	Spelling 3 Writer uses and spells words above grade level. 2 Writer spells words on grade level. 1 Writer misspells grade-level words.
	Capitalization/Punctuation 3 Writer demonstrates a command of grade-level capitalization and punctuation. 2 Writer demonstrates an understanding of grade-level capitalization and punctuation. 1 Writer misuses grade-level capitalization or punctuation.
_____ _____	**MECHANICS SCORE** **TOTAL SCORE (Message plus Mechanics)**

A 17-18   B 15-16   C 13-14   D 11-12   F 6-10

Comments . . .

Writing Rubric 3-2
A Classic Christmas

	MESSAGE
	Story 3 The writer creatively describes a real-life or fictional Christmas. 2 The writer adequately describes a real-life or fictional Christmas. 1 The writer does not adequately describe a real-life or fictional Christmas.
	Style 3 The style is clear, creative, and engaging. 2 The style is adequate but could be improved. 1 The style is weak and/or needs additional work.
	Purpose 3 The writer gives the reader a sense of nostalgia, of having missed experiencing such a special Christmas. 2 The writer effectively describes a family Christmas. 1 The writer does not effectively describe a family Christmas.
_____	**MESSAGE SCORE**

	MECHANICS
	Grammar/Usage 3 Writer displays a command of agreement, pronoun reference, word usage, and complete sentences. 2 Writer demonstrates a basic understanding of agreement, pronoun reference, word usage, and complete sentences. 1 Writer makes errors in agreement, pronoun reference, word usage, or complete sentences.
	Spelling 3 Writer uses and spells words above grade level. 2 Writer spells words on grade level. 1 Writer misspells grade-level words.
	Capitalization/Punctuation 3 Writer demonstrates a command of grade-level capitalization and punctuation. 2 Writer demonstrates an understanding of grade-level capitalization and punctuation. 1 Writer misuses grade-level capitalization or punctuation.
_____ _____	**MECHANICS SCORE** **TOTAL SCORE (Message plus Mechanics)**

A 17-18	B 15-16	C 13-14	D 11-12	F 6-10

Comments . . .

Use after "An Old-Fashioned Iowa Christmas"
and "Snow in the Suburbs," pages 66-73.

Writing Rubric 4-1
A Persuasive Pitch

	MESSAGE
	Persuasion 3 The advertisement is attractive, appealing, and persuasive. 2 The advertisement is persuasive. 1 The advertisement does not adequately persuade.
	Creativity 3 The approach is highly creative. 2 The approach is creative. 1 The approach lacks creativity.
	Literary elements 3 The advertisement employs symbol, allusion, and/or irony with a clear explanation. 2 The advertisement employs symbol, allusion, and/or irony but without a clear explanation. 1 The advertisement does not include symbol, allusion, or irony, nor does it include an explanation.
_____	**MESSAGE SCORE**

	MECHANICS
	Grammar/Usage 3 Writer displays a command of agreement, pronoun reference, word usage, and complete sentences. 2 Writer demonstrates a basic understanding of agreement, pronoun reference, word usage, and complete sentences. 1 Writer makes errors in agreement, pronoun reference, word usage, or complete sentences.
	Spelling 3 Writer uses and spells words above grade level. 2 Writer spells words on grade level. 1 Writer misspells grade-level words.
	Capitalization/Punctuation 3 Writer demonstrates a command of grade-level capitalization and punctuation. 2 Writer demonstrates an understanding of grade-level capitalization and punctuation. 1 Writer misuses grade-level capitalization or punctuation.
_____ _____	**MECHANICS SCORE** **TOTAL SCORE (Message plus Mechanics)**

A 17-18   B 15-16   C 13-14   D 11-12   F 6-10

To the student: Use the back of this page or another sheet of paper to explain your advertisement's use of symbol, allusion, and/or irony.

Teacher comments . . .

Writing Rubric 4-2
Alluring Allusions

MESSAGE

Allusion

3 The allusion is creatively incorporated into a well-written sketch.
2 The sketch includes a clear allusion.
1 The sketch does not include a clear allusion.

Appropriateness

3 The allusion enhances the main idea of the sketch.
2 The allusion is related to the main idea of the sketch.
1 The allusion is unclear and/or does not support the main idea of the sketch.

Style

3 The style of the sketch is engaging and appealing.
2 The style of the sketch is clear.
1 The style of the sketch is weak.

_____ **MESSAGE SCORE**

MECHANICS

Grammar/Usage

3 Writer displays a command of agreement, pronoun reference, word usage, and complete sentences.
2 Writer demonstrates a basic understanding of agreement, pronoun reference, word usage, and complete sentences.
1 Writer makes errors in agreement, pronoun reference, word usage, or complete sentences.

Spelling

3 Writer uses and spells words above grade level.
2 Writer spells words on grade level.
1 Writer misspells grade-level words.

Capitalization/Punctuation

3 Writer demonstrates a command of grade-level capitalization and punctuation.
2 Writer demonstrates an understanding of grade-level capitalization and punctuation.
1 Writer misuses grade-level capitalization or punctuation.

_____ **MECHANICS SCORE**
_____ **TOTAL SCORE (Message plus Mechanics)**

A 17-18   B 15-16   C 13-14   D 11-12   F 6-10

Comments . . .

Writing Rubric 4-3
Conquistadors—Their Conquests and Character

	MESSAGE
	Theme 3 The essay discusses conquistadors in an interesting manner and makes reference to "Eldorado." 2 The essay discusses conquistadors but does not refer to "Eldorado." 1 The essay does not adequately discuss conquistadors.
	Research 3 Information is clear and accurate, giving evidence of good research. 2 Information is good; research could have been stronger. 1 Information is weak, giving evidence of poor research.
	Style 3 The essay is well written, creative, and appealing in style. 2 The essay is well written. 1 The essay style is weak.
_____	**MESSAGE SCORE**

	MECHANICS
	Grammar/Usage 3 Writer displays a command of agreement, pronoun reference, word usage, and complete sentences. 2 Writer demonstrates a basic understanding of agreement, pronoun reference, word usage, and complete sentences. 1 Writer makes errors in agreement, pronoun reference, word usage, or complete sentences.
	Spelling 3 Writer uses and spells words above grade level. 2 Writer spells words on grade level. 1 Writer misspells grade-level words.
	Capitalization/Punctuation 3 Writer demonstrates a command of grade-level capitalization and punctuation. 2 Writer demonstrates an understanding of grade-level capitalization and punctuation. 1 Writer misuses grade-level capitalization or punctuation.
_____ _____	**MECHANICS SCORE** **TOTAL SCORE (Message plus Mechanics)**

A 17-18   B 15-16   C 13-14   D 11-12   F 6-10

Comments . . .

Use after "Eldorado," page 99.

Writing Rubric 4-4
Poetic Parallels

	MESSAGE
	Structure 3 The poem creatively incorporates a series of contrasting images. 2 The poem includes contrasting images. 1 The poem lacks contrasting images.
	Theme 3 The student's enthusiasm for the topic is evident in the poem. 2 The student's interest in the topic is evident in the poem. 1 The student's interest in the topic is not clear from the poem.
	Style 3 The style is clear, appealing, and creative. 2 The style is clear. 1 The style is weak.
_____	**MESSAGE SCORE**

	MECHANICS
	Grammar/Usage 3 Writer displays a command of agreement, pronoun reference, word usage, and complete sentences. 2 Writer demonstrates a basic understanding of agreement, pronoun reference, word usage, and complete sentences. 1 Writer makes errors in agreement, pronoun reference, word usage, or complete sentences.
	Spelling 3 Writer uses and spells words above grade level. 2 Writer spells words on grade level. 1 Writer misspells grade-level words.
	Capitalization/Punctuation 3 Writer demonstrates a command of grade-level capitalization and punctuation. 2 Writer demonstrates an understanding of grade-level capitalization and punctuation. 1 Writer misuses grade-level capitalization or punctuation.
_____ _____	**MECHANICS SCORE** **TOTAL SCORE (Message plus Mechanics)**

A 17-18   B 15-16   C 13-14   D 11-12   F 6-10

Comments . . .

Writing Rubric 5-1
A Fabulous Fable

	MESSAGE
	Theme 3 The fable's theme is engagingly developed, teaching a clear lesson. 2 The fable's theme is clear. 1 The fable's theme is weak or unclear.
	Moral 3 The fable includes a creative, appropriately stated moral. 2 The fable includes an appropriately stated moral. 1 The fable does not include an appropriately stated moral.
	Style 3 The style is innovative and appropriate. 2 The style is appropriate. 1 The style needs improvement.
_____	**MESSAGE SCORE**

	MECHANICS
	Grammar/Usage 3 Writer displays a command of agreement, pronoun reference, word usage, and complete sentences. 2 Writer demonstrates a basic understanding of agreement, pronoun reference, word usage, and complete sentences. 1 Writer makes errors in agreement, pronoun reference, word usage, or complete sentences.
	Spelling 3 Writer uses and spells words above grade level. 2 Writer spells words on grade level. 1 Writer misspells grade-level words.
	Capitalization/Punctuation 3 Writer demonstrates a command of grade-level capitalization and punctuation. 2 Writer demonstrates an understanding of grade-level capitalization and punctuation. 1 Writer misuses grade-level capitalization or punctuation.
_____ _____	**MECHANICS SCORE** **TOTAL SCORE (Message plus Mechanics)**

A 17-18   B 15-16   C 13-14   D 11-12   F 6-10

Comments . . .

Use after "The Ant and the Grasshopper," page 131.

Writing Rubric 5-2
A Recollection of Recreation

MESSAGE

Topic

3 The poem or paragraph creatively describes an interesting recreational experience.

2 The poem or paragraph describes an interesting recreational experience.

1 The poem or paragraph does not clearly describe an interesting recreational experience.

Connotation

3 The poem or paragraph effectively uses connotative words and phrases to carry forward its meaning.

2 The poem or paragraph uses connotative words and/or phrases effectively.

1 The poem or paragraph does not use connotative words or phrases.

Style

3 The style is clear and pleasing, appropriate for the topic.

2 The style is adequate.

1 The style is not appropriate for the topic.

_____ **MESSAGE SCORE**

MECHANICS

Grammar/Usage

3 Writer displays a command of agreement, pronoun reference, word usage, and complete sentences.

2 Writer demonstrates a basic understanding of agreement, pronoun reference, word usage, and complete sentences.

1 Writer makes errors in agreement, pronoun reference, word usage, or complete sentences.

Spelling

3 Writer uses and spells words above grade level.

2 Writer spells words on grade level.

1 Writer misspells grade-level words.

Capitalization/Punctuation

3 Writer demonstrates a command of grade-level capitalization and punctuation.

2 Writer demonstrates an understanding of grade-level capitalization and punctuation.

1 Writer misuses grade-level capitalization or punctuation.

_____ **MECHANICS SCORE**

_____ **TOTAL SCORE (Message plus Mechanics)**

A 17-18   B 15-16   C 13-14   D 11-12   F 6-10

Comments . . .

Writing Rubric 6-1
An Ironic Incident I

	MESSAGE
	Irony 3 The paragraphs creatively describe an ironic incident from the writer's experience. 2 The paragraphs adequately describe an ironic incident from the writer's experience. 1 The paragraphs do not adequately describe an ironic incident from the writer's experience.
	Theme 3 The theme is clear and worthwhile from a Christian perspective. 2 The theme does not strongly emphasize a Christian perspective. 1 The theme is not written from a Christian perspective.
	Style 3 The style is clear; the paragraphs are well written. 2 The style is appropriate. 1 The style is weak.
_____	**MESSAGE SCORE**

	MECHANICS
	Grammar/Usage 3 Writer displays a command of agreement, pronoun reference, word usage, and complete sentences. 2 Writer demonstrates a basic understanding of agreement, pronoun reference, word usage, and complete sentences. 1 Writer makes errors in agreement, pronoun reference, word usage, or complete sentences.
	Spelling 3 Writer uses and spells words above grade level. 2 Writer spells words on grade level. 1 Writer misspells grade-level words.
	Capitalization/Punctuation 3 Writer demonstrates a command of grade-level capitalization and punctuation. 2 Writer demonstrates an understanding of grade-level capitalization and punctuation. 1 Writer misuses grade-level capitalization or punctuation.
_____ _____	**MECHANICS SCORE** **TOTAL SCORE (Message plus Mechanics)**

A 17-18   B 15-16   C 13-14   D 11-12   F 6-10

Comments . . .

Writing Rubric 6-2
An Ironic Incident II

MESSAGE

Characterization
3 The modern-day John Fennil Wonder thoroughly and accurately mimics his counterpart in "A Germ Destroyer."
2 The modern-day John Fennil Wonder adequately re-creates his counterpart in "A Germ Destroyer."
1 The modern-day John Fennil Wonder does not adequately reflect his counterpart in "A Germ Destroyer."

Irony
3 The incident creatively incorporates irony.
2 The incident includes irony.
1 The incident does not include irony.

Style
3 The style is creative and appealing, incorporating humor.
2 The style is appropriate.
1 The style is weak.

_____ **MESSAGE SCORE**

MECHANICS

Grammar/Usage
3 Writer displays a command of agreement, pronoun reference, word usage, and complete sentences.
2 Writer demonstrates a basic understanding of agreement, pronoun reference, word usage, and complete sentences.
1 Writer makes errors in agreement, pronoun reference, word usage, or complete sentences.

Spelling
3 Writer uses and spells words above grade level.
2 Writer spells words on grade level.
1 Writer misspells grade-level words.

Capitalization/Punctuation
3 Writer demonstrates a command of grade-level capitalization and punctuation.
2 Writer demonstrates an understanding of grade-level capitalization and punctuation.
1 Writer misuses grade-level capitalization or punctuation.

_____ **MECHANICS SCORE**
_____ **TOTAL SCORE (Message plus Mechanics)**

A 17-18   B 15-16   C 13-14   D 11-12   F 6-10

Comments . . .

Use after "A Germ Destroyer," pages 164-67.

Writing Rubric 7-1
An Autobiographical Anecdote

	MESSAGE
	Purpose 3 The anecdote makes a valuable point. 2 The anecdote makes a point. 1 The anecdote does not make a clear point.
	Accuracy 3 The anecdote creatively fulfills the assignment requirements: it covers a memorable incident from the writer's life. 2 The anecdote adequately fulfills the assignment requirements. 1 The anecdote does not fulfill the assignment requirements.
	Style 3 The anecdote is written in a creative and appealing style. 2 The anecdote is written in an appropriate style. 1 The anecdote's style is weak.
_____	**MESSAGE SCORE**

	MECHANICS
	Grammar/Usage 3 Writer displays a command of agreement, pronoun reference, word usage, and complete sentences. 2 Writer demonstrates a basic understanding of agreement, pronoun reference, word usage, and complete sentences. 1 Writer makes errors in agreement, pronoun reference, word usage, or complete sentences.
	Spelling 3 Writer uses and spells words above grade level. 2 Writer spells words on grade level. 1 Writer misspells grade-level words.
	Capitalization/Punctuation 3 Writer demonstrates a command of grade-level capitalization and punctuation. 2 Writer demonstrates an understanding of grade-level capitalization and punctuation. 1 Writer misuses grade-level capitalization or punctuation.
_____ _____	**MECHANICS SCORE** **TOTAL SCORE (Message plus Mechanics)**

A 17-18   B 15-16   C 13-14   D 11-12   F 6-10

Comments . . .

Use after introduction to Unit 7, Biography, pages 188-89.

Rubric 7-1

Writing Rubric 7-2
An Important Influence

MESSAGE

Influence

3 The essay creatively describes someone who was a positive influence on the writer.
2 The essay adequately describes someone who was a positive influence on the writer.
1 The essay does not adequately describe someone who was a positive influence on the writer.

Incident

3 The essay creatively describes an incident that caused the writer to see a new quality in himself.
2 The essay adequately describes an incident that caused the writer to see a new quality in himself.
1 The essay does not adequately describe an incident that caused the writer to see a new quality in himself.

Effects

3 The essay creatively describes how the writer was changed by the incident.
2 The essay adequately describes how the writer was changed by the incident.
1 The essay does not adequately describe how the writer was changed by the incident.

_____ **MESSAGE SCORE**

MECHANICS

Grammar/Usage

3 Writer displays a command of agreement, pronoun reference, word usage, and complete sentences.
2 Writer demonstrates a basic understanding of agreement, pronoun reference, word usage, and complete sentences.
1 Writer makes errors in agreement, pronoun reference, word usage, or complete sentences.

Spelling

3 Writer uses and spells words above grade level.
2 Writer spells words on grade level.
1 Writer misspells grade-level words.

Capitalization/Punctuation

3 Writer demonstrates a command of grade-level capitalization and punctuation.
2 Writer demonstrates an understanding of grade-level capitalization and punctuation.
1 Writer misuses grade-level capitalization or punctuation.

_____ **MECHANICS SCORE**
_____ **TOTAL SCORE (Message plus Mechanics)**

| A 17-18 | B 15-16 | C 13-14 | D 11-12 | F 6-10 |

Comments . . .

 Use after "Listening," pages 203-9.

Name _____

Writing Rubric 8-1
Situation and Circumstance

<table>
<tr><td></td><td colspan="1"><h2>MESSAGE</h2></td></tr>
<tr><td></td><td>

Situation

3 The essay creatively reveals an incident in which an intolerable situation turned out for good—or vice versa.
2 The essay adequately reveals an incident in which an intolerable situation turned out for good—or vice versa.
1 The essay does not adequately reveal an incident in which an intolerable situation turned out for good—or vice versa.

</td></tr>
<tr><td></td><td>

Circumstance

3 The essay emphasizes the dramatic and/or situational irony inherent in the situation.
2 The essay mentions the dramatic and/or situational irony inherent in the situation.
1 The essay does not mention the dramatic and/or situational irony inherent in the situation.

</td></tr>
<tr><td></td><td>

Style

3 The style is creative and appealing.
2 The style is appropriate.
1 The style is not appropriate.

</td></tr>
<tr><td>_____</td><td>

MESSAGE SCORE

</td></tr>
</table>

<table>
<tr><td></td><td colspan="1"><h2>MECHANICS</h2></td></tr>
<tr><td></td><td>

Grammar/Usage

3 Writer displays a command of agreement, pronoun reference, word usage, and complete sentences.
2 Writer demonstrates a basic understanding of agreement, pronoun reference, word usage, and complete sentences.
1 Writer makes errors in agreement, pronoun reference, word usage, or complete sentences.

</td></tr>
<tr><td></td><td>

Spelling

3 Writer uses and spells words above grade level.
2 Writer spells words on grade level.
1 Writer misspells grade-level words.

</td></tr>
<tr><td></td><td>

Capitalization/Punctuation

3 Writer demonstrates a command of grade-level capitalization and punctuation.
2 Writer demonstrates an understanding of grade-level capitalization and punctuation.
1 Writer misuses grade-level capitalization or punctuation.

</td></tr>
<tr><td>_____
_____</td><td>

MECHANICS SCORE
TOTAL SCORE (Message plus Mechanics)

</td></tr>
</table>

A 17-18   B 15-16   C 13-14   D 11-12   F 6-10

Comments . . .

Use after "Lady Clare," pages 245-47.

Writing Rubric 9-1
A Lively Lyric

	MESSAGE
	Topic 3 The poem identifies and describes a creature that evokes mixed emotions on the part of the speaker. 2 The poem identifies and describes a creature. 1 The poem does not adequately identify and describe a creature.
	Lyric 3 The speaker of the poem "thinks aloud" and does not address the reader. 2 The speaker of the poem "thinks aloud" but also addresses the reader. 1 The speaker of the poem addresses the reader rather than "thinking aloud."
	Style 3 The poem is creatively written; its word choice and arrangement on the page emphasize the message. 2 The poem is creatively written. 1 The poem lacks creativity.
_____	**MESSAGE SCORE**

	MECHANICS
	Grammar/Usage 3 Writer displays a command of agreement, pronoun reference, word usage, and complete sentences. 2 Writer demonstrates a basic understanding of agreement, pronoun reference, word usage, and complete sentences. 1 Writer makes errors in agreement, pronoun reference, word usage, or complete sentences.
	Spelling 3 Writer uses and spells words above grade level. 2 Writer spells words on grade level. 1 Writer misspells grade-level words.
	Capitalization/Punctuation 3 Writer demonstrates a command of grade-level capitalization and punctuation. 2 Writer demonstrates an understanding of grade-level capitalization and punctuation. 1 Writer misuses grade-level capitalization or punctuation.
_____ _____	**MECHANICS SCORE** **TOTAL SCORE (Message plus Mechanics)**

A 17-18   B 15-16   C 13-14   D 11-12   F 6-10

Comments . . .

Writing Rubric 9-2
Causes and Consequences

	MESSAGE
	Decision 3 The poem clearly delineates a decision on the part of someone in the poem. 2 The poem includes a decision on the part of someone in the poem. 1 The poem does not include a decision on the part of someone in the poem.
	Causes 3 The poem thoroughly explains the cause(s) of the decision. 2 The poem mentions the cause(s) of the decision. 1 The poem does not mention the cause(s) of the decision.
	Consequences 3 The poem thoroughly explains the consequences of the decision. 2 The poem adequately explains the consequences of the decision. 1 The poem does not adequately explain the consequences of the decision.
_____	**MESSAGE SCORE**

	MECHANICS
	Grammar/Usage 3 Writer displays a command of agreement, pronoun reference, word usage, and complete sentences. 2 Writer demonstrates a basic understanding of agreement, pronoun reference, word usage, and complete sentences. 1 Writer makes errors in agreement, pronoun reference, word usage, or complete sentences.
	Spelling 3 Writer uses and spells words above grade level. 2 Writer spells words on grade level. 1 Writer misspells grade-level words.
	Capitalization/Punctuation 3 Writer demonstrates a command of grade-level capitalization and punctuation. 2 Writer demonstrates an understanding of grade-level capitalization and punctuation. 1 Writer misuses grade-level capitalization or punctuation.
_____ _____	**MECHANICS SCORE** **TOTAL SCORE (Message plus Mechanics)**

A 17-18   B 15-16   C 13-14   D 11-12   F 6-10

Comments . . .

Use after "The Wise Old Apple Tree in Spring," page 308.

Rubric 9-2

Writing Rubric 10-1
Dissecting a Drama

	MESSAGE
	Thesis 3 The thesis statement is clearly stated and is thoroughly discussed in the body of the paper. 2 The thesis statement is clearly stated but is not thoroughly discussed in the body of the paper. 1 The thesis statement is not clearly stated.
	Organization 3 The essay is clearly and logically organized. 2 The essay is adequately organized. 1 The essay's organization is weak.
	Style 3 The style is appealing and creative. 2 The style is adequate. 1 The style is weak.
_____	**MESSAGE SCORE**

	MECHANICS
	Grammar/Usage 3 Writer displays a command of agreement, pronoun reference, word usage, and complete sentences. 2 Writer demonstrates a basic understanding of agreement, pronoun reference, word usage, and complete sentences. 1 Writer makes errors in agreement, pronoun reference, word usage, or complete sentences.
	Spelling 3 Writer uses and spells words above grade level. 2 Writer spells words on grade level. 1 Writer misspells grade-level words.
	Capitalization/Punctuation 3 Writer demonstrates a command of grade-level capitalization and punctuation. 2 Writer demonstrates an understanding of grade-level capitalization and punctuation. 1 Writer misuses grade-level capitalization or punctuation.
_____ _____	**MECHANICS SCORE** **TOTAL SCORE (Message plus Mechanics)**

A 17-18	B 15-16	C 13-14	D 11-12	F 6-10

Comments . . .

Use after *Romeo and Juliet*, pages 320-433

Writing Rubric 11-1
An Enlightening Essay

MESSAGE
Topic 3 The writer's topic is creative and interesting. 2 The writer's topic is appropriate. 1 The writer's topic is weak or inappropriate.
Tone 3 The writer's tone is appropriate for the subject at hand. 2 The writer's tone is inconsistent. 1 The writer's tone is weak or inappropriate.
Christianity 3 The writer thoroughly explains how one would respond to the situation from a Biblical perspective. 2 The writer includes information about how one would respond to the situation from a Biblical perspective. 1 The writer does not take the Biblical perspective on the situation into account.
_____ **MESSAGE SCORE**

MECHANICS
Grammar/Usage 3 Writer displays a command of agreement, pronoun reference, word usage, and complete sentences. 2 Writer demonstrates a basic understanding of agreement, pronoun reference, word usage, and complete sentences. 1 Writer makes errors in agreement, pronoun reference, word usage, or complete sentences.
Spelling 3 Writer uses and spells words above grade level. 2 Writer spells words on grade level. 1 Writer misspells grade-level words.
Capitalization/Punctuation 3 Writer demonstrates a command of grade-level capitalization and punctuation. 2 Writer demonstrates an understanding of grade-level capitalization and punctuation. 1 Writer misuses grade-level capitalization or punctuation.
_____ **MECHANICS SCORE** _____ **TOTAL SCORE (Message plus Mechanics)**

A 17-18	B 15-16	C 13-14	D 11-12	F 6-10

Comments . . .

Use after "Three Days to See," pages 440-48.

Rubric 11-1

Writing Rubric 11-2
Pocket Ponderings

	MESSAGE
	Topic 3 The essay is written about an object that is likely to be found in a pocket or purse. 2 The essay is written about an object that might be found in a pocket or purse. 1 The essay is written about an object that could not be found in a pocket or purse.
	Style 3 The essay creatively and smoothly incorporates elements of literature (simile, metaphor, allusion, etc.). 2 The essay incorporates elements of literature (simile, metaphor, allusion, etc.). 1 The essay does not incorporate elements of literature (simile, metaphor, allusion, etc.).
	Theme 3 The object is used as a vehicle to express and clarify a specific truth. 2 The object is used as a vehicle to express a specific truth. 1 The object is not used as a vehicle to express a specific truth.
_____	**MESSAGE SCORE**

	MECHANICS
	Grammar/Usage 3 Writer displays a command of agreement, pronoun reference, word usage, and complete sentences. 2 Writer demonstrates a basic understanding of agreement, pronoun reference, word usage, and complete sentences. 1 Writer makes errors in agreement, pronoun reference, word usage, or complete sentences.
	Spelling 3 Writer uses and spells words above grade level. 2 Writer spells words on grade level. 1 Writer misspells grade-level words.
	Capitalization/Punctuation 3 Writer demonstrates a command of grade-level capitalization and punctuation. 2 Writer demonstrates an understanding of grade-level capitalization and punctuation. 1 Writer misuses grade-level capitalization or punctuation.
_____ _____	**MECHANICS SCORE** **TOTAL SCORE (Message plus Mechanics)**

A 17-18   B 15-16   C 13-14   D 11-12   F 6-10

Comments . . .